SELF-EVALUATION: *Concepts and Studies*

"To know what we think, to be masters of our meaning, will make a solid foundation for great and weighty thought. It is most easily learned by those whose ideas are meagre and restricted; and far happier they than such as wallow helplessly in a rich mud of conceptions."

C. S. Pierce, 1878

SELF-EVALUATION:
Concepts and Studies

JAMES C. DIGGORY

Department of Psychology
Chatham College
Pittsburgh, Pennsylvania

John Wiley & Sons, Inc.   *New York · London · Sydney*

ACKNOWLEDGMENTS

The following persons and institutions have graciously granted permission for the use of previously published materials. Dr. Thelma G. Alper, Dr. Sylvia Farnham-Diggory, and Dr. Stephen C. Pepper have given me permission to use their materials which are indicated below.

Figures 4.4 through 4.9, and Table 4.4 are from my article (with E. J. Riley and Ruth Blumenfeld) "Estimated Probability of Success for a Fixed Goal," in *The American Journal of Psychology*, 1960, Vol. 73, pp. 41–55; Figures 4.10 through 4.12, and Tables 4.5 and 4.6 are from my article (with Bena Ostroff) "Estimated Probability of Success as a Function of Variability in Performance," in the same Journal, 1962, Vol. 75, pp. 94–101. Dr. Karl M. Dallenbach, owner and chief editor of *The American Journal of Psychology*, granted permission for use of these materials.

The American Psychological Association, and the individual authors, granted permission to use the following materials:

From *The Journal of Abnormal and Social Psychology:*
Dr. Thelma G. Alper, "Predicting the Direction of Selective Recall: Its Relation to Ego-Strength and n-Achievement," 1957, Vol. 55, pp. 149–165 (Table 5.1);
Dr. Sylvia Farnham-Diggory, "Self-Evaluation and Subjective Life Expectancy among Suicidal and Non-Suicidal Psychotic Males," 1964, Vol. 69, pp. 628–634 (Figures 7.12, 7.13, Tables 7.9 through 7.13);
From the following articles of which I was a co-author:
"Motivation of Chronic Schizophrenics by Information about their Abilities in a Group Situation" (with A. Loeb), 1926, Vol. 65, pp. 48–52 (Tables 7.1 through 7.3);
"Level of Aspiration, or Probability of Success?" (with H. C. Morlock, Jr.), 1964, Vol. 69, pp. 282–289 (Figures 4.18 through 4.20, and Table 4.17);

"Values Destroyed by Death" (with Doreen Z. Rothman), 1961, Vol. 63, pp. 205–210 (Figure 8.1);
"The Effects of Personal Liking, Perceived Ability, and Value of Prize on Choice of Partners for a Competition" (with J. W. Whitmyre and D. Cohen), 1961, Vol. 63, pp. 198–200 (Figure 6.14A).

From *The Journal of Experimental Psychology*, my article (with S. J. Klein and M. M. Cohen), "Muscle-Action Potentials and Estimated Probability of Success," 1964, Vol. 68, pp. 449–455 (Figures 5.1 through 5.3).

In the discussions of level of aspiration in Chapter 4, and of status in Chapter 3, I have borrowed heavily from the text of my chapter, "Status, Ability, and Self-Esteem in the Process of Supervision" in G. Fisk (Ed.) *The Frontiers of Management Psychology*, published in 1964 by Harper and Row. The publishers have kindly allowed me these borrowings.

Dr. Wolfgang Köhler, editor of *Psychologische Forschung*, and Springer-Verlag, publishers of the journal, granted permission to reproduce tables from F. Hoppe, "Erfolg und Misserfolg," *Psychologische Forschung*, 1931, 14, pp. 1–62 (Tables 4.1, 4.2, and 4.3).

Dr. Morris S. Viteles, President of the International Association of Applied Psychology, granted permission to use Table 5.3 from my article with D. E. Magaziner, "Self-Evaluation as a Function of Instrumentally Relevant Capacities," in *Bulletin de l'Association Internationale de Psychologie Appliquée*, 1959, Vol. 8, pp. 2–19.

The University of California Press granted permission for the use of Table 2.1 which is taken from their publication (1958) *The Sources of Value* by Dr. Stephen C. Pepper.

PREFACE

This book is an attempt to give a systematic report of progress on the study of self-evaluation which I have been actively pursuing, with the massive help of students and colleagues, since 1957. A summary of our thinking and substantive findings is given in Chapter 9. The outline of the rest of the book is suggested by the titles of the various chapters, and by the subheadings within chapters.

The first three chapters set forth, successively, what I mean by the words "self," "value," and "self-evaluation." In Chapter 1, following a review of writings on "self" and "ego" since Descartes, I state the conclusion that we would clarify our thinking about self if we tried to think about it withtout attaching the definite article. The verbal formula "*the* self" seems almost automatically to call for thinking about an entity, or quasi-entity which has boundaries, and a location. This conceptual automatism seems to crop up even in thinkers who most vigorously deny the intent to reify self. For all its being a non-entity, whatever the word "self" intends must be objective, and I suggest that the lowest objective common denominator of its meaning is the *relation* between the agent and the object of his action in which agent and object are the same organism. The aim of this definition is to scrape away from the word "self" the confusing encrustation of affective connotations which have become attached to it, like barnacles, in the course of centuries. Without an objective definition we could hardly hope to study self by the most powerful investigative methods we have, the methods of experiment.

If we want to concentrate on the specific problem of self-evaluation, we must know what we mean by "value." Chapter 2 is an account of three value theories, those of Christian von Ehrenfels, John Dewey, and Stephen C. Pepper. Their composition covers approximately the last 75 years, but their formal similarity is remarkable and each of them reflects the state of general psychology during the time the value theory was written. In all of these theories, the locus of value is in the structure of human behavior, especially those aspects of it which today we call "motivated" or "purposive." Pepper is the contemporary philosophical writer who most expertly uses the data of experimental psychology on which to build his value theory. The notions about value used in our work lean very heavily on Dr. Pepper's writings. His personal comments on the manuscript of Chapter 2 prevented the appearance of several serious errors there, but he should be completely absolved of all responsibility for defects yet to be discovered in my treatment of value. The chief emphasis throughout the book is on what Pepper calls "conative-achievement" values, whose positive and negative subsets are called, respectively, success and failure. When a person attempts to achieve an objective (goal) his success indicates that the method be used was good. If he fails, however, what then? Was it merely that his method was bad, or is he generally a bad user of any method at all? In either case, he has made a self-evaluation, provided that he cannot assign his success or failure to any influences other than the efficacy of his own actions.

This is the aspect of self-evaluation which is discussed in Chapter 3, and on which all our empirical studies concentrate. Though we recognize that consensus of other people's opinions may affect self-evaluations, as may also the otherwise unsupported opinion of a single "expert," the scope and effectiveness of more objective evaluations of self-as-instrument have not been adequately studied. I have attempted to delineate objective self-evaluation more clearly by contrasting it with evaluations based on the opinions of other people and also by contrasting it with the gratuitous self-assertions and demands for recognition, goods, and services, which are referred to as "pride."

A notable aspect of self-evaluation as it is observed in the midst of life is that individuals are encouraged or discouraged in advance of *de facto* success or failure; they act as though they somehow were accumulating evidence that their *probability* of success was either high or low. Chapter 4 is a technical account of the methods we used to investigate the conditions which affect the level at which probability of success is estimated: rates and accelerations of performance curves, variability in performance from trial to trial, average level of performance, and the distance and clarity of deadlines. Finally we show that there are conditions in which the course of successive estimates of probability of success is very closely paralleled by changes in specific self-evaluations.

We have used the term "probability of success"—symbolized as $P(s)$—to refer to a person's estimate of the likelihood that, with a fixed amount of time or a fixed number of attempts, his performance will equal or exceed some stated level. Thus "success" means simply that the person does a particular thing, but such an accomplishment does not guarantee that he will *feel successful* because his performance exceeds the fixed minimum by an amount that satisfies him. Therefore, estimated $P(s)$ may not always coincide with feelings of success or satisfaction as those terms have been defined since the time of William James. There is, of course, no guarantee that estimated $P(s)$ does not coincide with feelings of success or failure. In fact, most of our experiments included failure conditions, and we have reason to believe that progressive lowering of $P(s)$ estimates is a sign of increasing discouragement. With respect to success, the situation is, at least, equivocal. In two of the experiments reported in Chapter 5, we had occasion to point out that "objective" success might not coincide with an individual's feeling of personal triumph. In one of the experiments we were able to detect this and to alter the conditions so as to demonstrably increase the likelihood of desired coincidence.

Some consequences of changes in self-evaluation are dealt with in Chapter 5. One consequence we studied is functional withdrawal from a hopeless task by decreasing the energy spent on it. This is measured either in terms of actual number of units produced or in terms of the level of electrical activity of the working muscles. Another consequence of expected failure and lowered self-evaluation is quitting the task entirely and either leaving the enterprise or choosing a substitute activity. We have also shown something about the conditions under which changes in the evaluation of a single ability which is tested may spread to changed evaluations of other abilities not directly tested. This has some obvious relevance to more general views about personality structure. We also observed that failure and subsequent lowering of self-evaluation is accompanied by a spontaneous increase in death-imagery in stories the subjects told. The fuller implications of this are dealt with in Chapter 8.

Our few experiments on self-evaluation in social contexts are described in Chapter 6. One of our questions, which we related to the broader problems of "identification," is how a person's estimate of his own probability of success is influenced by his witnessing the success or failure of another individual. Another question is about the fluctuations in self-evaluation and self-confidence that occur in situations that are likely to produce "conforming" behavior. We believe that our results present a strong argument for distinguishing between two different criteria of self-evaluation: that based on objective evaluation of abilities and that based solely on social approval and acceptance. A third problem we touched on was the influence of an individual's objective self-evaluation on the kinds of partners he is likely to choose for cooperative enterprises.

Though we believe, as much of the relevant literature asserts, that understanding self-evaluation is an important component of understanding psychopathology, we have only glanced at psychopathology, as the title of Chapter 7 indicates. Our work is not without substantive outcomes, but we have more of promise than of performance to offer in this area. For example, in stating their successive estimates of probability of success, schizophrenic patients are completely unaffected by the nearness and clarity of deadlines, which have very strong effects on the probability of success estimates made by normal people. This seems to be a highly circumscribed difference between schizophrenics and normals; they did not differ, as far as we could discover, in their responses to any other aspects of goal-oriented behavior. Our single experiment on patients who were diagnosed only as "depressed" showed that the depressed people consistently set far lower estimates of their probability of succeeding than did non-depressed people (some of whom may even have been manic), though both groups worked equally hard on the experimental task.

In Chapter 8, I described our explorations into the connection between general level of self-evaluation and attitudes toward death and the inclination to suicide. The data in Chapter 8 are necessarily a mixture of experimental results and the "soft" data from questionnaires, surveys, and interviews. The experimental data are the findings that situations which produce reductions in self-evaluation also produce sizable increases in *thinking* about death. For the rest, we have relied on questionnaire studies aimed at elucidating more precisely what it is about the prospect of death that is feared. In this perspective the problem of suicide appears as soon as we ask about the conditions under which a person would actively seek his own death or passively accept it.

A reader who wants to go directly to one of the later chapters without reading all the previous pages may do so without serious danger of misunderstanding, provided that he reads Chapter 4 first. The accounts of experiments in Chapters 5, 6, and 7 are likely to be confusing to anyone who does not understand the experimental techniques and the definition of probability of success which are described in the fourth chapter.

Though I assume full responsibility for any defects in this report, the bulk of the credit for getting it done at all goes to my enthusiastic, inspiring, inquisitive, energetic collaborators (students and colleagues): Dr. Ruth Blumenfeld, Dr. Isabelle G. Cetlin, Dr. Robert E. Cetlin, Dr. David Cohen, Dr. Robert A. Cutick, Dr. Stanley S. Fagen, Dr. Sylvia Farnham-Diggory, Mr. Bernard Liberman, Dr. Armin Loeb, Dr. Daniel E. Magaziner, Dr. Henry C. Morlock, Jr., Miss Bena Ostroff, Mr. Eugene J. Riley, Mrs. Bonnie S. Rosen, Dr. Marvin Rosen, Dr. Doreen Z. Rothman, Mr. V. Rudraswamy, Mr. Floyd Shupp, Mr. Robert Tuthill, and Dr. John M. Whitmyre. Their contributions are more specifically described in the text and in footnotes and references. I am also deeply grateful for the devotion and care which Miss Carolyn Dunn, Mrs. Dorothy Lynn, Miss Faye Meisler, and Mrs. Barbara Tabor brought to the typing of the manuscript. Much of the writing was done while I was a Fellow of the Center for the Scientific Study of Suicide in Los Angeles. I am indebted to the Director of the Center, Dr. Edwin S. Shneidman, for inviting me to spend a year there and for providing me with office space, secretarial help, and congenial colleagues. Others to whom we are indebted for opportunities and encouragement to carry on our researches are named and thanked at appropriate places throughout the book. To the children, high school and college students, and adults, more than 2,000 of them, who served as our subjects, we all tender our heartfelt thanks.

Dr. Sylvia Farnham-Diggory is more than a valued colleague and collaborator; she is also my wife, and she provides me with an atmosphere of living which makes all my work a joy.

James C. Diggory

Los Angeles, California
May, 1965

CONTENTS

Chapter 1
"SELF"

The main thesis of this book is that within the narrow confines of a single specialty, psychology, the method of experimental thinking should and can be intruded into a field where it has so far not penetrated very deeply. That is the field of problems relating to the notion of self. The purpose of this chapter is to examine what has been said about self and related topics with a view to deriving a definition suitable for experimental work.

EARLIER VIEWS ON THE SELF

The origins of some current ideas about self are very ancient. Perhaps they were current before writing was common. At any rate they are clearly discernible in the Homeric writings which express the distinction between the physical human body and some non-physical entity or function, variously described and translated to English as "soul," "spirit," or "psyche" (Reeves, 1958). Later developments in philosophy and science in the Greek world produced considerable speculation about the nature of "soul," so that Aristotle was able to refer to several of his contemporaries or predecessors who had written something about it. Aristotle refrained from taking sides on the issue whether the soul is mortal or immortal, corporeal or non-corporeal, but in his discussion of vegetative, animal, and rational souls the notion of soul seems to correspond closely to the modern notion of organic functions. The chief characteristic of the vegetative soul is growth and reproduction, to which in the animal soul are added sensitivity to stimuli and locomotion, and the rational soul adds to these things choice, thought, and evaluation. In other writings Aristotle was not clear about just what he meant by "soul"; perhaps he changed his mind from time to time. That is beside the point. The point is that among the Greek thinkers there was no unanimity of belief about the nature of soul, no more unanimity than there is among present-day thinkers.

With the entry of Christianity into the main stream of European political, social, and intellectual history competing notions about the

1

nature of "soul" lost ground to the official dogma that man is composed of two parts, body and soul, which are distinct in their principles of operation. Body had a lot in common with non-human nature; it could fall, be broken, and decay. Whatever principles applied to the soul, these simple physical tests did not, and soul came to be regarded as the seat of desire, choice, thought, etc., activities which distinguished man from animal and mental from physical. Individual differences in affect or capacity led to the view that each soul was unique, that its properties comprised all that were necessary to define the individual personality, that the soul, and therefore the person, was a tenant of the body from which it would separate when the body died. Huizinga (1924) describes how popular and widespread this view was and some of its consequences in individual and social action.

Though the distinction between soul and body was well-nigh universal during the Middle Ages of Europe, and though philosophers and other learned gentry wrote about it, it hardly constituted a problem for them. Soul and mind were pretty much the same thing and that was that. A few inquiring spirits pointed to certain striking correlations between the physical accidents of brain damage and drunkenness, on the one hand, and disturbances of soul or mind on the other hand, but these observations had little effect on the habits of thought of philosophers or laymen. Whether or not a set of beliefs constitutes a problem depends on what kinds of questions are asked, and nobody with any influence was asking questions about soul and body in those days.

The first real question was posed in 1644 with the publication of René Descartes' *Principles of Philosophy*. Descartes' view on the principles of human knowledge were set forth, in the first part of this book, with the beautiful clarity and directness which characterized most of his writings. So clear and direct is his exposition that it can be paraphrased without fear of serious error. If we want to *"examine into the truth,"* he wrote, *"it is necessary once in one's life to doubt of all things, so far as this is possible"* (Descartes, 1644, italics in original). He argued that we can doubt the evidence of our senses and the demonstrations of mathematics, and urges that we ought to consider as false *anything* which we can successfully doubt. But, "While we thus reject all that of which we can possibly doubt, and feign that it is false, it is easy to suppose that there is no God, nor heaven, nor bodies, and that we possess neither hands, nor feet, nor indeed any body; but we cannot in the same way conceive that we who doubt these things are not; for there is a contradiction in conceiving that what thinks does not at the same time as it thinks, exist. And hence this conclusion *I think, therefore I am,* is the first and most certain of all that occurs to one who philosophizes in an orderly way" (Descartes, 1644, italics in original). Another thing which Descartes did not doubt was that men possess free will which enables them to reject as false what they can doubt and accept as true what they cannot doubt. Thus, free will saves us from error in action, provided we have adequate criteria of truth and falsity. Descartes' criteria for determining the truth applied only to cognitions, not to action. He said that while we are winnowing truth from falsehood by systematic doubt we should not order our lives this way. In practical affairs, he noted, we have to choose our courses of action on the basis of opinions which are merely probable, and choose we must, even though often "we do not perceive the probability of the one more than the other." Happy philosopher, who can have the best of both worlds! Descartes thought that the first indubitable truth—I think, therefore I am—led to the discovery of the nature of mind or soul (that which thinks) and its distinction from body (that which is corporeal). If we can doubt the existence of all bodies, but not doubt that we think, then it follows that mind and body are to be distinguished by their attributed characteristics. *Thought,* without reference to "extension, figure, local motion," is characteristic of mind (or soul) and thus uniquely pertains to "our nature." Conversely, body lacks the property of thought and has, instead, the properties of extension, figure, and local motion.

In *Les Passions de l'Ame* (1650) Descartes assumed that the body is not only subject to physical laws in the mass, but that the motions of its parts and all its activities can be explained solely on hydromechanical principles; that the body of a living thing, whether human or animal, is, to put it briefly, a machine. But the soul, which was joined to all parts of the body, and which had the functions of desire and thought, *interacted* with the body-machine by producing slight perturbations in the position of the pineal gland. The gland was so situated, Descartes thought, that changes in its position altered the direction of flow of the animal spirits from the cavities of the brain into the hollow tubes of the nerves. Different volumes of animal spirits in different nerves produced different kinds of activities in the muscles. Stimulation of peripheral sense organs led to reverse disturbances in the animal spirits which appeared as perturbations imposed on the pineal gland and were thus sensed by the soul. Though this conception is wrong on the fine anatomical details (nerves are not tubes in the sense Descartes meant it) and dead wrong in its physiology, it is nonetheless a tremendous intellectual achievement because it asks a clear question: how can the physical influence the non-physical, and *vice versa*? It is the original formulation of the mind-body problem. Descartes' solution of the problem is, *ex hypothesi*, an impossibility. In fact, the mind-body problem arises only from Descartes' premise of the existence of two entities which differ so radically in their operating principles. But as this premise constitutes the problem, at the same time it invalidates its solution on the basis of *interaction*. Later writers took a variety of ways around the difficulty. Some of them accepted the dualistic premise and proposed other solutions, some got rid of the problem by rejecting the premise in favor of some form of monism, and others busied themselves with other psychological matters for which, they said, any solution of the problem is irrelevant.

Leibniz accepted the dualistic premise, but he clearly saw that a solution of the mind-body problem in terms of interaction was impossible, so he proposed another solution which involved the hypothesis of a third agency—God. According to Leibniz, body and mind are so different in principle that they cannot interact. There are two universes: the mental (or spiritual) and the physical. In the mental universe the discrete entities are called minds, and in the physical universe they are called bodies or things. In neither universe do the different entities interact, neither mind with mind, body with body, or mind with body. The entities are, in Leibniz's word, "monads," i.e., relative to each other they are completely distinct *units*. The impression of interaction or mutual influence is illusory. The monads each follow their own laws of development and in the course of events they seem to interact because certain events are parallel in the various systems. However, the cause of this parallelism lies only in the fact that God has pre-established this harmony.

After Leibniz, the history of the mind-body problem took a different course. Subsequent thinkers generally concentrated on the nature of subjectivity.

Descartes had distinguished mind as knower or *subject* of knowledge from what is known, or the *object* of knowledge. If, in the Cartesian formula, "I think, therefore I am," we emphasize the personal pronoun "I," we come near to a source of the confusion which still troubles many thinkers. If it is simply a defect of language, there is no problem. We might just as well say, as James (1890) did, that we cannot doubt that thinking occurs. But Descartes is a little more definite than that. He concluded that since thinking occurs, "I" exists. But does "I" refer to the whole person or only to a part? Is it a sentient (incorporeal) entity to which messages from sense organs are presented, something like a recording camera film, or the spectator at a play? Is "I" in the Cartesian sentence the same as "self"? From Descartes' own writings we cannot answer these questions, but other writers have attempted to supply answers, and we shall turn to them now. In these writings we shall discover that the basic Cartesian dualism still survives, but the attempt to explain the mutual influence of mind and body is either frankly abandoned or made unnecessary by monistic assumptions of various sorts.

Spinoza is generally credited with having offered another solution to the mind-body problem, besides Leibniz's notion of *pre-established harmony*, and Descartes' impossible notion of *interaction*. Spinoza's solution is generally called a "double aspect theory," because he says, "Mind and body are one and the same thing, conceived first under the attribute of thought, secondly under the attribute of extension." Now this might suggest that philosophers should classify Spinoza as a monist, but they have not generally done so because, taken at large, his complicated metaphysical system leaves doubt as to just what he meant in his proffered solution to the mind-body problem. There is certainly no necessary relation between a man's acceptance of the mind-body problem or his preferred solution to it, on the one hand, and his empirical knowledge on the other. For example, Thomas Browne (1820) could discover no organ of the soul. He found the contents of the skulls of beasts and men to be essentially the same, but he uses this as an argument for the immateriality of the soul: "Thus we are men, and we know not how; there is something in us that can be without us, and will be after us; though it is strange that it hath no history that it was before us, nor cannot tell how it entered in us."

Other thinkers have escaped from the necessity of attempting to solve the mind-body problem by frankly denying its major premise of two distinct types of entities, radically different in principle. They assumed that a single principle can account for all the phenomena of experience, but whether that principle is psychic or physical is still open to choice. Hobbes (1651) clearly preferred physical monism, a position in which Hartley (1749) concurred. Locke (1690) indicated that he knew the issue could be raised, but declared that it was unnecessary to raise it formally, and he proceeded to erect a detailed account of how knowledge arises from sensory impressions made on an originally totally unformed mind. Berkeley, on the other hand, took the empiricist solution of the problem of knowledge literally and derived the conclusion that there is indeed one type of substance, not two, and that the existing one is mental.

Berkeley's argument (Berkeley, 1710) runs somewhat like this.

Since all that I know is derived from sensory experience, I cannot assert the existence of anything but sensory experience or its consequences in memory. I can exercise my will to change the appearances which some "objects" make upon my senses: I can walk around them and note their different aspects of color or contour; I can move farther away from them or closer to them and they appear smaller or larger and with less or more detail; I can close my eyes or stop my ears and the sight or sound disappears until I will them to reappear. Now will, like sensory experience or memory, is a mental phenomenon, so I need assume no other principle than my own mind to account for this much of my experience and its alterations. But there are other alterations of experience which are independent of my will, even contrary to it. Falling leaves, or the movements of other people, I cannot alter merely by wishing that the perceived actions would be otherwise. How do these come about if there is no independent substance opposed to mind? Without any flaw in his logic, Berkeley asserted that there are other minds, separate from his. So alterations of experience which I did not will are due to some other will. This is easy to do in the case of other people who, I assume, can will as I do. But what of objects which have no will, no power of choice? Ah, said Berkeley, *these* alterations, which I did not will, are willed by the universal will—the will of God.

It is a neat system. It has the advantage of parsimony, explaining all the facts without superfluity of underlying principles. There are minds—and nothing else. At least we *can* know nothing else, and *need* know nothing else, to account for all our experiences. With such a theory the mind-body problem evaporates. We need only the knowing, thinking, willing subject, which Descartes had said we could not doubt the existence of.

But Berkeley proved merely that the mind-body problem is a problem only if we accept its premises, and that there is no compulsion to accept them. He showed the logical non-necessity of assuming physical substance in which the qualities of things inhere. Very well, we know only what we know and we know only through the senses, and that is enough. Berkeley's own busy preoccupations with the affairs of the world, with the theory of visual space perception, and with the applications of mathematics to physical problems prove that his views about the underlying substance of the world gave him no special difficulties with the notion of law or causation. However, he did assert or assume the existence of the mind as the knower to which experience is presented. Further, he assumed particular minds, his mind as distinguished from both mine and yours which are similarly distinguished from each other. Thus minds were personal and some-how intimately connected with "self." It then became David Hume's turn to use Berkeley's own form of argument against the notion of substantive mind, to show, in short, that if experience is all we know we have no direct knowledge of the knower.

Hume saw clearly that the notion of substantive mind was only an hypothesis. As an hypothesis it was no more and no less satisfactory than its opposite—a monistic assumption of material substance in the manner of Hobbes. Hume accepted neither and thus involved himself irretrievably in skeptical doubts. His passage on "self" as an object of experience is worth quoting.

There are some philosophers who imagine we are every moment intimately conscious of what we call our SELF; that we feel its existence and its continuance in existence, and are certain, beyond the evidence of a demonstration, both of its perfect identity and simplicity. . . . Unluckily all these positive assertions are contrary to that very experience which is pleaded for them, nor have we any idea of Self, after the manner it is here explained. . . . It must be some one impression that gives rise to every real idea. . . . If any impression gives rise to the idea of Self, that impression must continue invariably the same throughout the whole course of our lives, since self is supposed to exist after that manner. But there is no impression constant and invariable. Pain and pleasure, grief and joy, passions and sensations succeed each other, and never all exist at the same time. . . . For my part, when I enter most intimately into what I call *myself*, I always stumble on some particular perception or other of heat or cold, light or shade, love or hatred, pain or pleasure. I never can catch *myself* without a perception, and never can observe anything but the perception. When my perceptions are removed for any time, as by sound sleep, so long am I insensible of *myself*, and may truly be said not to exist. And were all my perceptions removed by death, and could I neither think, nor feel, nor see, nor love, nor hate after the dissolution of my body, I should be entirely annihilated, nor do I conceive what is farther requisite to make me a perfect non-entity. If anyone, upon serious and unprejudiced reflection, thinks he has a different notion of *himself*, I must confess I can reason no longer with him. All I can allow him is, that he may be in the right as well as I, and that we are essentially different in this particular. He may, perhaps, perceive something simple and continued which he calls *himself*; though I am certain there is no such principle in me.

But setting aside some metaphysicians of this kind, I may venture to affirm of the rest of mankind that they are *nothing but a bundle or collection of different perceptions,* which succeed each other with an inconceivable rapidity, and are in a perpetual flux and movement. Our eyes cannot turn in their sockets without varying our perceptions. Our thought is still more variable than our sight; and all our other senses and faculties contribute to this change; nor is there any single power of the soul which remains unalterably the same, perhaps for one moment. The mind is a kind of theatre where several perceptions successively make their appearance, pass, repass, glide away and mingle in an infinite variety of postures and situations. *There is properly no simplicity in it at one time, nor identity in different;* whatever natural propension we may have to imagine that simplicity and identity. The comparison of the theatre must not mislead us. They are the successive perceptions only, that constitute the mind; nor have we the most distant notion of the place where these scenes are represented, nor of the material of which it is composed (Hume, 1739, chapter on personal identity).

It is well to emphasize that Hume argued against the idea of self only "after the manner it is here explained," i.e., an entity, an object of consciousness, of whose existence and perfect identity and simplicity we are unceasingly aware. He obviously found use for the word "self," for example, in making the distinction between his views and the opinions of others. He clearly inveighed against the notion of a *substantial* self, against Berkeley's notion, when he warned that the image of the mind as a theatre must be limited strictly to the fact of succession and mingling of perceptions. They are not presented *to* anything, at least not to anything we have any idea of, for the mind *is* the succession of impressions, and we haven't the faintest notion of where these perceptions occur or what that place might be made of. Essentially this view of mind and of the supposedly substantial self was adopted later by Wundt (1878), who viewed mind as process, and by Ernst Mach (1886). Hume insisted that we must not seek a unique referent for the word self among the contents of our conscious experience. His argument cut the ground from under the notion of substantial self just as surely as Berkeley argued the baselessness of direct experience of substantial matter.

During the nineteenth century discussions of the notion of self became more detailed and differentiated. A persistent question, which arose in various forms, can be paraphrased as, "What are the phenomena without which we would not be conscious of ourselves in any sense?" James Mill (1829) wrote that a person's *memory* of having performed an action and his *consciousness* of being the same person who performed the action are two ways of stating the same fact. And this kind of fact cannot be reduced to anything more elementary. A fact and the thought of the fact are different things and *memory* consists in relating present ideas to the past. Indeed, if we believe that any present idea results from a previous sensation, "there is the further conviction that this sensation. . . was my own; that it happened to myself." There is a succession of feelings stretching from the farthest reach of memory to present sensations all connected by an "inexplicable tie." And *that tie* distinguishes them from any series imposed by thought, and from the sequences of feelings which happened to other people. Memory of the past, in this sense, is the basis for distinguishing "myself." "Myself is the person who had that series of feelings, and I know nothing of myself, by direct knowledge, except that I had them." And the *bond* which connects the feelings in the series, "which makes me say that they were feelings of a person who was the same person throughout and a different person from those who had any parallel successions of feelings; . . . this bond, to me, constitutes my Ego." Note how Mill, in this passage, deftly reinserted the ghostly remnant of the substantial self-as-knower—not, to be sure, as the directly apprehended object asserted by the metaphysicians whom Hume attacked. Hume had warned Mill off that line and Mill talked of "Self" as the name for the possessor of a certain set of memories of the past, but the "*I*" which "had them" is the truly defining feature of the series, and this "inexplicable tie" has a new name: "Ego." Whatever his shortcomings as a definer, James Mill certainly was cautious about his metaphysics and he clearly implicated memory as an important determiner of whatever awareness of self refers to.

But John Stuart Mill (1865) was more explicit than his father in espousing what Hume had ejected. He wrote that "the *inexplicable tie* . . . which connects the present consciousness with the past one of which it reminds me, is as near as I think we can get to a positive conception of Self. That there is something real in this tie, real as the sensations themselves, and not a mere produce of the laws of thought without any fact corresponding to it, I hold to be indubitable. . . . This original element, . . . to which we cannot give any name but its own peculiar one, without implying some false or ungrounded theory, is the Ego, or Self."

It should be noted, parenthetically, that J. S. Mill came face to face with the answer which James (1890) later gave to the riddle of how we are aware of the continuity of ourselves. Mill considered it and rejected it. "If, therefore, we speak of the mind as a series of feelings we are obliged to complete the statement by calling it a series of feelings which is aware of itself as past and future; and we are reduced to the alternative of believing that the mind, or Ego, is something different from any series of feelings, or possibilities of them, or of accepting the paradox that something which *ex hypothesi* is but a series of feelings, can be aware of itself as a series" (J. S. Mill, 1865).

Hume had written that we can know nothing but succession and mingling of the conscious perceptions, that real connections between them are beyond our ken. The Mills seemed to accept this idea with one hand and reject it with the other. Possibly, in regarding the sequence of conscious events as a *mere* succession, they made an unnecessary difficulty for themselves and had to explain the indubitable fact of awareness of self ultimately by reference to an unknowable joiner (the ego) which "had" the experiences and was aware of their succession.

Up to this point, ideas about self and ego had been developed almost exclusively on the basis of reports of direct conscious experience, usually the experience of the theorist himself. This method of introspection dominated psychology until the functionalist-behaviorist revolution was fomented in America in the second decade of the twentieth century (Watson, 1919). But the opposition to pure introspection as the only method of psychology did not begin with Watson and his followers. One early opponent, also *ganz Amerikanisch*, to use Wundt's phrase, was the philosopher, C. S. Pierce. In one of his numerous articles Pierce (1868) posed a series of "questions concerning certain faculties claimed for man." First, he argued that we cannot determine, merely by examining a given cognition, if it is produced by present stimulation (a sensation or intuitive cognition) or by stimulation sometime in the past (a memory image or mediate cognition). Every cognition includes the object, of which we are conscious, and some action "of the self," an action which produces the object in consciousness. Pierce called the object the *objective* element of the cognition and the mediating action the subjective element, and asked whether we can distinguish among the subjective elements of various cognitions. We cannot thus distinguish, he concluded, because every present cognition is either determined by characteristics of "the not-I" or by previous cognition. And since we have no intuitive power of distinguishing present sensations from memory images, "It appears, therefore, that there is no reason for supposing a power of introspection; and, consequently, the only way of investigating a psychological question is by inference from external facts." Thus, for Pierce, the basic knowledge of ourselves is not based on intuitive, direct apprehension of a self-evident entity, but is the inferred result of commerce with objects and the testimony of other people, plus the learned connections between movements of our bodies and certain events. The evaluative "feelings" good and bad are first predicated of things which are not oneself and later applied to oneself.

By self-consciousness Pierce meant: "Not a mere feeling of subjective conditions of consciousness, but of our personal selves. Pure apperception is the self-assertion of the *ego;* the self-consciousness here meant is the recognition of my *private* self. I know that *I* (not merely *the* I) exists. The question is, how do I know it; by a special intuitive faculty, or is it determined by previous cognition?" Since we have no intuitive power of distinguishing between mediate and intuitive cognitions it is obvious that self-consciousness is intuitive. Then the question remains whether self-consciousness can be explained "by the action of known faculties under conditions known to exist. . . ." Pierce further departed from his introspectionist forerunners in his *method,* which was to study the development of self-consciousness in children.

He asserted that very young children display "powers of thought" before they display any self-consciousness. A very young child is interested in his own body because to him it is the most important thing in the universe. "Only what it touches has any actual and present feelings; only what it faces has any actual color; only what is on its tongue has any actual taste." When a child hears a sound he doesn't think of himself hearing but of the bell sounding. When he wills to move a table, it is doubtless because he thinks the table is fit to be moved, but it is merely arbitrary to assume that he thinks of himself as moving it without the demonstration of intuitive self-consciousness. "The child, . . . , must soon discover by observation that things which are thus fit to be changed are apt actually to undergo this change, after a contact with that peculiarly important body called Willy or Johnny. This consideration makes this body still more important and central, since it establishes a connection between the fitness of a thing to be changed and a tendency in this body to touch it before it is changed."

Beyond this rudimentary concept of his own body-as-cause are two criteria by which, more than by any others, the child can become aware of his own independent status, his personal self. These criteria are *ignorance* and *error.* The concept of ignorance develops from the child's attempts to validate testimony in lieu of facts. He thinks, for example, that a stove (which he hears is hot) is not hot because he is not touching it. His touch confirms the testimony and convinces him of ignorance. Error also involves conflict of testimony with apparent fact. But in this case the facts "are those predicates which *we* know to be emotional, but which *he* distinguishes by their connection with the movements of that central person, himself (that the table wants moving, etc.). These judgments are generally denied by others. Moreover, he has reason to think that others, also, have such judgments which are quite denied by all the rest. Thus, he adds to the conception of appearance as the actualization of fact, the conception of it as something *private* and valid only for one body. In short, *error* appears, and it can be explained only by supposing a *self* which is fallible. Ignorance and error are all that distinguish our private selves from the absolute *ego* of pure apperception. . . . Thus we find that known faculties, acting under conditions known to exist, would give rise to self-consciousness. The only essential defect in this account of the matter is that, while we know that children exercise *as much* understanding as is here supposed, we do not know that they exercise it in precisely this way" (Pierce, 1868, p. 29).

As to normal adults, none of us, Pierce believed, are absolutely individual. Our knowledge of ourselves, and of other things, is based on a dialogue, either with another part of ourselves, or with "society." A person's "thoughts are what he is 'saying to himself,' that is, is saying to that other self that is just coming into life in the flow of time. When one reasons, it is that critical self that one is trying to persuade. . . . The second thing . . . is that the man's circle of society (however widely or narrowly this phrase may be understood) is a sort of loosely compacted person, in some respects of higher rank than the person of an individual organism. It is these two things alone that render it possible for you—but only in the abstract . . . sense— to distinguish between absolute truth and what you do not doubt" (Pierce, 1905, p. 191).

Pierce had emphasized the importance for the development of self-awareness, of a child's recognizing his own body as a cause, of his associating his own movements with changes in the objects around him. A similar view of the origin of self-awareness was elaborated by Wundt (1880), who specifically called attention to the role which kinesthetic sensations from the muscles could play in it. Among the various classes of sensations, those arising from our own body and its movements distinguish themselves by forming a permanent group, because *some* muscles are always tense or active. This permanent mass of feeling which may fluctuate in intensity, *is* "the consciousness of self." Early in our lives it is merely sensational, but gradually, because we can alter experience by our own movements, we develop the notion that this permanent core of sensations is subject to our will. Indeed, we come to recognize that all classes of sensations are, to some extent, dependent on our will and in this sense self-consciousness broadens. But simultaneously it narrows by progressive concentration of our attention on the inner activity of being aware ("apperception" is Wundt's term) and it is this progressive narrowing which produces at last the philosopher's notion of the pure ego. Thus, by reversing the order of events from that imposed by the philosophers, who begin with the pure ego, Wundt thought he had explained what the philosophers were talking about. Like Pierce, Wundt sought to explain self-awareness in terms of "known faculties under conditions known to exist."

Thomas Brown (1820) had already suggested a view something like Wundt's on the origin of self-awareness from experience. Brown was concerned with the problem which worried the Mills so much: the impression of personal sameness in the midst of constantly fluctuating experience. Wundt's solution, in terms of the permanent grouping (association) of the sensations arising from the body, was anticipated by Brown's suggestion that the *nature* of the successive conscious events might give the clue for explaining the impression of sameness in spite of change. Brown also suggested that the impression of sameness may arise with respect to a limited number of aspects of experience which remain relatively permanent while the others are free to change. This sort of notion was developed in detail by Ernst Mach (1886).

Mach stated: "The apparent stability of I consists primarily only in continuity, in slow change . . ." (Mach, 1886, p. 3, footnote). He called attention to the similarity of his view of experience to that of Hume, but his analysis of self-awareness began with a distribution of experiences into three classes. In each class the elements are associated spatially and temporally. In one class (O) are those sets of elements to which we give names and call objects. Class o is our own organic body, which is a one-object sub-set of O. In class P belong will, memory images, etc. Customarily, o and P together stand in opposition, as I, to the world of objects (class O), though sometimes P is I in distinction to o and O. Class O appears almost independent of I, but this independence is only relative. The elements in P can change without corresponding change in O, and conversely. Many changes in P, however, follow changes in O which are mediated by changes in o, and conversely.

Before 1890, then, some philosophers and some psychologists had made a bit of progress toward stating the problems of self-awareness in objective terms. But parallel with this development, other philosophers and psychologists, influenced by Kant, continued to elaborate the notions of the pure ego and the substantive self in ways that had no possible bearing on questions of fact. They stated logical connections between named entities, but suggested no connection with facts or with the mechanisms by which these connections might occur. Edward Caird's (1883) discussion of Hegel is a good example:

The self exists as one self only as it opposes itself, as object, to itself as subject, and immediately denies and transcends that opposition. Only because it is such a concrete unity, which has in itself a resolved contradiction, can the intelligence cope with all the manifoldness and division of the mighty universe, and hope to master its secrets. As the lightning sleeps in the dew-drop, so in the simple and transparent unity of self-consciousness there is held in equilibrium that vital antagonism of opposites which . . . seems to rend the world asunder. The intelligence is able to understand the world, or, in other words, to break down the barrier between itself and things and find itself in them, just because its own existence is implicitly the solution of all the division and conflict of things.

One would suppose, from the way their science was developing, that psychologists would have less and less interest in writing of this *genre*, but such is not the case, as we shall soon see.

The contributions of William James (1890) to our ideas about self can hardly be esteemed too highly. In addition to the fact that he gave the topic broader coverage than any of his predecessors,[1] his writing is a transition-point between older and newer ways of thinking about it. He was militantly objective in his treatment of the problem and flung sharp barbs at earlier notions of it. "Altogether," wrote James, "the Soul is an outbirth of that sort of philosophizing whose great maxim, according to Dr. Hodgson, is: 'Whatever you are totally ignorant of, assert to be the explanation of everything else'" (James, 1890, p. 347). And Kant's transcendentalist theory of the pure ego, based on "the original transcendental synthetic unity of perception"—we can know nothing about it. The pure ego cannot be the object of our self-love because we can love only objects and the pure ego is not an object.

In his attempt to account for the feeling of personal identity through time, which tangled the Mills in their "inexplicable tie" between successive conscious events, James assumed that everything experienced, whether self or not-self, is *objective*. Beyond these is only the fact that they are known, a fact which appears only on subsequent reflection. For ordinarily we have *sciousness* rather than *consciousness*. The sciousness (the passing thought) *is* the "only *verifiable* thinker." The feeling of personal identity is "a conclusion grounded either on

[1] Chapter X, "The Consciousness of Self," is one of the longest chapters in his two-volume *Principles of Psychology*, 1890.

the resemblance in a fundamental respect, or on the continuity before the mind, of the phenomena compared" (James, 1890, p. 334), and such judgments of sameness apply indifferently in the first, second, or third persons. For James, consciousness (not sciousness) was a stream where, in the "specious present," the thoughts which are dying away mingle with and thus come to know the thoughts that are arising. On this basis, James wrote: "My present thought stands . . . in the plenitude of ownership of the train of my past selves, is owner not only *de facto,* but *de jure,* the most real owner there can be, and all without the supposition of any 'inexplicable tie,' but in a perfectly verifiable and phenomenal way" (James, 1890, p. 360).

In his treatment of psychological problems related to self, James is at his best. In the broadest sense, the "empirical self" is everything that a man can call his—the distinction between "me" and "mine," James said, is hard to make, and he spent little time attempting it. The components of the empirical self are classed, in descending order of their implications in self-esteem, as "spiritual Self," "material . . . and social selves," and "bodily Self."

By spiritual self James meant the concrete psychic powers and dispositions. These are what we most truly seem to *be.* "We take a purer self-satisfaction when we think of our ability to argue and discriminate, or our moral sensibility and conscience, or our indomitable will, than when we survey any of our other possessions. Only when these are altered is a man said to be *alienatus a se*" (James, 1890, p. 296). But whether we identify ourselves with each faculty separately or with their interactions as they appear in the stream of consciousness, "*a certain portion of the stream abstracted from the rest*" is identified with self "in an altogether peculiar degree." This is the active principle in consciousness, the center around which all other aspects of it cluster; it is the source of interest, effort, attention, will, and choice. Physiologically, this nuclear self consists in the feelings which stand between thought and execution, the feelings of internal *adjustments* which, in principle, are no different from acts of *execution.* In his own case, James described a "nucleus of cephalic adjustments": slight movements of the eyeballs, glottis, soft palate, and jaw muscles, movements which are overlooked by most people.

James did not attempt to say whether the material selves or the social selves were the more important, merely that both of them were between the bodily self and the spiritual self. A person has as many different social selves as there are groups about whose opinions he cares. Some of these social selves may conflict with one another. The most important of them relates to the person we are in love with.

One's wife and children belong to the social selves only because they are human beings; otherwise they are coordinate with aspects of the material selves: house and lands, yacht, and bank account. Action, with respect to the social and material selves, is initially instinctive, involving the instincts of fear, anger, hunting, acquisition, home-constructing, tool-constructing, amativeness, parental fondness, curiosity, and emulation. Social self-seeking is "carried on directly through our amativeness and friendliness, our desire to please and attract notice and admiration, our emulation and jealousy, our love of glory, influence, and power, and indirectly through whichever of the material self-seeking impulses prove serviceable as means to social ends" (James, 1890, p. 308). Our various acquisitions are more or less intimately ours to the extent that they are "saturated with our labor."

Though the bodily self is placed last in importance "by a tolerably unanimous opinion," this appears to be its status only among adults. It is instinctive to nourish and preserve our bodies and to deck them with clothes and ornaments. Each of us must have a minimum of selfishness in the bodily sense in order to live. "My own body and what ministers to its needs are thus the primitive object, instinctively determined, of my egoistic interests. Other objects may become interesting derivatively through association with any of these things, either as means or as habitual concomitants; and so in a thousand ways the primitive sphere of the egoistic emotions may enlarge and change its boundaries" (James, 1890, p. 324).

Normally, the determinant of the level of a person's self-evaluation (James used "self-feeling" and "self-regard" as synonyms for this) is the position he holds in the world, contingent on his success or failure. Though instinctively we desire to aggrandize all of our various selves, limitations of talent and time make this impossible so each of us has to choose the self "on which to stake his salvation." Having chosen, our level of self-regard can be reduced only by deficiencies (or raised only by achievements) which are relevant to our "pretensions." "With no attempt there can be no failure; with no failure no humiliation. So our self-feeling in this world depends entirely on what we *back* ourselves to be and do. It is determined by the ratio of our actualities to our supposed potentialities; a fraction of which our pretensions are the denominator and the numerator our success: thus,

$$\text{Self-esteem} = \frac{\text{Success}}{\text{Pretensions}}. \ \cdot \ \cdot \ \cdot$$

To give up pretensions is as blessed a relief as to get them gratified; and where disappointment is incessant and the struggle unending, this is what men will always do" (James, 1890, p. 313). As long as his motives are positive, aimed at some achievement, the thought of suicide can hardly occur to a man; but when he is afraid, trying to get *away* from something regardless of what he gets *into,* then there can "unquestionably be genuine thoughts, and genuine acts of suicide, spiritual and social, as well as bodily. Anything, *anything,* at such times, so as to escape and not to be! But such conditions of suicidal frenzy are pathological in their nature and run dead against everything that is regular in the life of the Self in man" (James, 1890, p. 317).

In what capacity is it that I claim and demand a respectful greeting from you instead of this expression of disdain? It is not as being a bare I that I claim it; it is as being an I who has always been treated with respect, who belongs to a certain family and 'set,' who has certain powers, possessions, and public functions, sensibilities, duties, and purposes, and merits and deserts. All this is what your disdain negates and contradicts; this is 'the thing inside of me' whose changed treatment I feel the shame about; this is what was lusty, and now, in consequence of your conduct is collapsed; and this certainly is an empirical objective thing.

. . . Which of my spiritual selves do I really care for? My Soul-substance? My 'transcendental Ego,' or 'Thinker'? my pronoun I? my subjectivity as such? my nucleus of cephalic adjustments? or my more phenomenal and perishable powers, my loves and hates, willingness and sensibilities, and the like? Surely the latter (James, 1890, pp. 322–323).

The Danish psychologist, Harald Höffding (1891) explored the developmental aspects of empirical self-awareness more thoroughly than James. He asked how do we come "to distinguish between our own self and the things outside of us?" (Höffding, 1891, p. 3). Prenatally, it is possible that feelings of discomfort and sensations of movement contrast sufficiently with those of resistance, contact, and taste to form the beginnings of consciousness of an external world, however dim and dreamlike it may be. Separation from the mother at birth provides "a more definite contrast between a subjective and an objective pole" because of the greater contrast between feelings of pleasure and pain, the intermittentness of organic sensations, the greater energy of sensations of movement, and the increased input from the other senses. Furthermore, the child is not passive; from the beginning he grasps at the world by involuntary movements, and thus secures the best knowledge as to the limit between the world and himself. The not-self begins wherever movement meets with resistance, especially if the resistance causes pain. Later, when memory images become numerous and connected, the child can distinguish between the clearer and stronger sensory impressions which arise "immediately, unexpectedly, and often disconnectedly," and the weaker memory images which "are at the disposal of consciousness under all circumstances."

Initially, the boundaries of self and body are the same. The body is explored, and gradually discovered, by all the senses. Special attention is given to the limbs and movement because they can be seen and grasped, they offer resistance, and thus have features in common with not-self. But they participate in willed movement, and so pertain to the subject. These aspects of body-experience, along with the distinction between memory images and the immediate action of the not-self on the sensorium, establish the notion of "self as the subject of thought, feeling, and will" (Höffding, 1891, p. 6), and also lead to the figurative distinction between inner and outer.

The idea of self, or ego, is not derived from immediate perception, but is inferred from the general nature of consciousness: i.e., the general synthetic activity (unity) which all consciousness presupposes. But the unity which is inferred from the facts of memory and synthesis is purely *formal. Individuality* consists in the *real* unity of the specific contents embraced by the formal unity. Indeed, this "embracing" is only a logical expression, for the *formal* unity depends upon the *real* one. Consciousness will lose even its formal unity if the contrasts among the elements become sufficiently great, as they do in mental illness, double consciousness, and hypnotic dissociation.

Among the various classes of conscious elements, Höffding suggested, feelings of pleasure and pain, and will, are more important than sensations and ideas in producing the sense of identity.

The more developed and energetic form of our self comes to the fore in our dominant aims, in our desire and our passion. No true personality is developed without a concentration of the life of feeling and will. A man who has no dominant feeling, but flies from one thing to another in a constant search for novelty, has not time and strength enough to gather himself together or to be himself; to know oneself is to *recognize* oneself and this presupposes constantly recurring elements of consciousness. . . . Thus at the age of puberty quite new feelings, new desires and wishes, make their appearance; the individual feels himself drawn out of himself. He no longer understands himself. This unquiet frame of mind, this bold soaring of the imagination makes him strange to himself. Mental maturity also, especially in deep natures, is attained through a similar fermentation. Different inspirations, ideas and impulses stir chaotically; mental growth often begins, like the formation of the bones, at scattered points. The sporadic character of development is only gradually overcome, and not completely in any individual. But the very fact that the inner division and fermentation and the inner doubt are *felt*, bears witness to a unity which embraces the scattered and contending elements. It is only because one and the same self is active in all opposing elements that their mutual relation comes into consciousness (Höffding, 1891, pp. 139–140).

Since the newborn infant's ideas are not clear enough to contrast self with not-self, it is as meaningless to speak of native egoism as it is to speak of native effrontery when the child knows neither bashfulness nor shame. Initially, pleasure and pain arise exclusively from conditions which abet or hinder the instinct of self-preservation, but when we have developed ideas of the *objects* which incite pleasure or pain, this instinct is manifested as love or abhorrence. "When now the feeling is determined by the idea of what promotes or hinders self-assertion (self-preservation and self-development), it will appear as a *feeling either of power or of powerlessness,* according as we think we have or have not at our disposal sufficient means of self-assertion. Under self-assertion must be included here, not merely the maintenance of physical existence, but also the power of mental clearness and freedom, and of 'making oneself felt' in relation to others (by controlling them, being recognized by them, etc.). That the feeling of power is the active or positive form of the feelings linked with self-assertion, is due to the fact that the idea of the cause of a feeling of pleasure (or of the hindrance to a feeling of pain) can excite pleasure only when we conceive this cause (or this hindrance) to be within our reach. 'All conception of the future,' says Hobbes, 'is conception of power able to produce something. Whoever therefore expecteth pleasure to come, must conceive withal some power in himself by which the same may be attained'" (Höffding, 1891, p. 243). Höffding clearly related the feelings of power or powerlessness to self-evaluation. The tendency, arising from the instinct of self-preservation, to make the individual self the center of existence, persists "so long as no motive arises for the recognition of other centres of pleasure and pain in the world besides self" (Höffding, 1891, p. 244).

Whence comes the motive to feel pleasure or pain in something that is not a means to one's own existence? Höffding's answer is remarkably similar to Allport's (1937) notion of "functional autonomy" of motives: "An idea which has occasioned the birth of another idea, may itself disappear, and this other idea obtain effect immediately and solely. An example often given is the independent value attached to money, although this is only a means of procuring certain commodities. For the miser, the intermediate link, without which the value cannot be established, and by means of which it originally arose, is wholly and completely forgotten. He loves the money for the money's sake, even indeed denies himself entirely the things it can procure. The feeling has been transferred from the end to the means, or rather it has made the means an end" (Höffding, 1891, pp. 244–245). Similarly, other people who originally were loved because they caused pleasure, are now loved for their own sakes, without regard to "the reason why." Association by contiguity predominates in the previous cases, but there are also cases in which association by similarity plays the chief part. People who are similar to us in nature, appearance, circumstances, and interests are not distinguished from ourselves, so we involuntarily put ourselves in their place, suffer and feel with them. Not only the feeling of sympathy, but also envy and ambition arise from this realization of the feelings of others. Sympathy is based on an instinct in man to imitate, to feel and suffer with his like. And furthermore, the individual's pleasure in serving the instinctive process of procreation which extends beyond his own egoism, and the relation of mother and child, make a pure state of nature, an absolute individualism, impossible. One indication that half unconscious instinct precedes the full awareness of the relevant ideas is that sympathy is more strongly aroused in those who give benefits than in those who receive them; the love of parents for children is stronger than the love of children for parents. Love itself emerges at puberty from a previously unconscious instinct. Given the appropriate associations, the above-mentioned instincts can just as well serve as the ground for ill-will as for love and sympathy, and this accounts for the ease with which these two merge into one another. "It is merely a question of shunting the train, already on its journey, so as to send it in another direction" (Höffding, 1891, p. 153).

Among the psychological writers we have so far examined the term "ego" has been applied to some tiny part of "self"—the "nuclear self" (James, 1890), the "formal unity" of consciousness (Höffding, 1891), will and memory images (Mach, 1886), the activity of "apperception" (Wundt, 1880). By comparison with what they meant by "self" in its various extended uses, "ego" had very little importance in their theories of human behavior. But in the work of Sigmund Freud the word "ego" bears most of the emphasis, and "self" almost none. Psychological writing since Freud has paid him the tribute of referring to "ego" almost as often as to "self," so it is necessary to examine Freud's ideas carefully to see whether and to what extent "self" and "ego" differ in more than the labels. I shall attempt to do this without regard to chronological development except in cases where that is absolutely necessary.

It is generally admitted that Freud had little formal training in academic psychology, and little contact with psychologists (Jones, 1953, vol. 1, pp. 365–407). G. T. Fechner, whom Freud quoted several times (especially, Freud, 1921a, pp. 23–24) got many of his psychological notions, including that of sensory thresholds, from J. F. Herbart (e.g., Herbart, 1824–1825). Meynert, whose lectures on psychiatry Freud attended, held essentially Herbartian views of general psychology. Whether Freud himself ever studied Herbartian writings is uncertain, but during his last year at the Gymnasium "a compendium of the Herbartian psychology" (Jones, 1953, vol. 1, p. 374), G. A. Lindner's *Lehrbuch der empirischen Psychologie nach genetischer Methode* (1858) was used there as a textbook. In any event, Freud's debt to Herbart and his followers was a general one and the Freudian psychological views were related to Herbart's as a diver to a springboard, not as a benighted traveler to the bed of Procrustes. In fact, because of his relatively slight contacts with psychological writings, Freud's terminology developed in so specialized a way that communication between psychoanalysts and psychologists requires translation between two quite different vocabularies. Good modern examples of such successful translations by psychologists are to be found in the writings of R. W. White (1959, 1963) and Dollard and Miller (1950).

The kind of *repproachement* between experimental psychology and psychoanalysis which Dollard and Miller attempted was facilitated by the fact that the theories of motivation advocated by Freud and the academic psychologists are closely analogous at many points. White (1959, 1963) lumps such theories together as "need primacy" theories. The Darwinian notion of a common origin of man and the infra-human species stimulated a search not only for anatomical similarities between them but for functional similarities as well. This led to the assumption by many nineteenth century psychologists, James (1890) and Höffding (1891) among them, that the activities of men, like those of their fellow creatures, were largely governed by "instincts," that is, by innately determined tendencies to exhibit more or less complicated behavior patterns in response to certain kinds of stimuli arising from within the body or outside it. In sharing this view, as in so many other ways, Freud was a child of his time (Jones, 1953); his psychological system is incomprehensible without the recognition that one of its basic assumptions was the determination of behavior by instincts (Freud, 1915a, 1920, 1921a, 1921b, 1923, 1926, 1940).

Fundamentally, instincts are all qualitatively alike, but they differ in that irritated states of different bodily tissues (e.g., mouth, anus, genitals) give rise to the stimuli which represent the instincts in consciousness (Freud, 1915a). Freud never abandoned the idea, which he got from Fechner (Fechner, 1873), that stimulation intensities above some threshold are unpleasant and those below that threshold are pleasant (Freud, 1915a, 1920, 1921a, 1923, 1926, 1940). For Freud the problem of the origins of "pleasure" and "unpleasure" was always at the core of the problem of quantifying psychological observations (the "economic" problem, as he called it), but he never could decide how to conceive the pleasure-unpleasure threshold without somehow violating his previously established axioms. At times he spoke of the threshold as referring to some absolute amount of stimulation; at other times it was a threshold of *rates* of decrease or increase in stimulation; at still other times only the *direction* of change served to define it. Phylogenetically, the mechanism of consciousness results from the action of "potentially lethal" energies (stimuli) on the surface of the protoorganism, which Freud described as an "undifferentiated sac" of substance capable of being affected by stimuli (Freud, 1921a). This bombardment "bakes through" a crust on the surface of the sac, a crust which thereafter cannot be modified but which has the properties of protecting the interior against most stimulus energies (like a filter), of receiving stimuli and registering them, and which thus gives rise to consciousness (Freud, 1921a). Freud had long maintained that the functions of perception (registration of stimuli) and consciousness were closely connected in a complex perceptual-conscious system (*Pcpt.-Cs.* was his characteristic abbreviation for it: Freud, 1900, 1921a, 1923). This system lies, anatomically, between what is inside the organism and what is outside; it even corresponds to the localization of the seat of consciousness in the cerebral cortex—on the outside of the brain (Freud, 1921a, 1923). In this position, the sense receptors and the nervous system are bombarded by stimuli both from outside and from inside the organism (Freud, 1895, 1915a, 1921a, 1923). Most *external* stimuli can be gotten away from by appropriate motor adjustments—locomotion to avoid them altogether, or averting or shielding the relevant receptors; but there is no escaping the internal stimuli, which can be reduced only by the method of "satisfaction." Thus the nervous system must be equipped to make such changes in the outer world "as enable it to offer satisfaction to the internal sources of stimulation" (Freud, 1911, 1915a, p. 63). This demands a nervous system more complex than the original filter for outer stimuli so Freud decided that the inner, rather than the outer, stimuli were the forces which led to the evolution of the more complex nervous system.

Now every internally originating stimulus (instinct) requires some activity to quell it, and this forces the organism to develop innately determined or learned methods of dealing with "objects" in the outer world. Some external stimuli, too, might activate memories of unpleasure. So the nervous system has a double problem relative to external stimuli: it must discriminate objects and execute appropriate action toward them, and it must inhibit certain externally aroused excitations lest they stir unpleasant memories (Freud, 1895). The parts of the nervous system that accomplish these functions are called "the ego" (Freud, 1894, 1895, 1900, 1915a, 1921a, 1923, 1926, 1940). In his "Project" for a scientific psychology (1895) Freud outlined a purely neurological scheme in which the ego—coherent set(s) of well-energized (cathected) neurons—accomplished both these functions by attracting to itself the bulk of the stimulus-aroused energy before that energy had a chance to arouse unpleasure. After this lateral drainage of neuronal energy by the "ego" network, the remainder of the energy, unabsorbed by the ego, could arouse only a weak remembered unpleasure or a weak tendency to act inappropriately. Acting inappropriately included undertaking a real action toward a fantasied object instead of a real object. This would inevitably give rise to a net increase in unpleasure through frustration. Thus, early in his career, Freud assigned to the ego an inhibitory function which accomplished the result of avoiding the arousal of unpleasant memories and preventing unrealistic actions (Freud, 1895, pp. 385–389). Though he probably never abandoned the notion that the ego was somehow related to the nervous system (cf. Freud, 1915a, 1921a, 1923, 1926), after the "Project" (1895) he never again attempted to relate its workings to the details of neuronal action. Even two years before he wrote the "Project" he wrote of the ego without any special physiological reference: ". . . the lesion of hysterical paralysis consists of nothing but the inaccessibility of the concept of the organ or function to the associations of the conscious ego . . ." (Freud, 1893, p. 58). This rendering of something remembered inaccessible to the conscious ego is the prototype of repression (Freud, 1894, 1895, 1900, 1920, 1921a, 1923, 1926, 1940), which is accomplished by the ego itself. Though the ego is often unaware of its repressions it frequently offers strong resistance to any attempt to get rid of them (Freud, 1920, 1923, 1926, 1940).

The extent to which any instinctual stimulus makes demands on the organism's supply of energy for actions which lead to stimulus quiescence (gratification or satisfaction) is what Freud calls the "*impetus*" of the instinct. The "*aim*" of all instincts is the quiescence of organic stimuli, achieved through gratification. The "*objects*" of instincts are those things by means of which the "aim" is achieved (Freud, 1915a, pp. 64–68). Dealing with objects so as to achieve quiescence of instinctive stimuli is acting by what Freud called the "pleasure principle" (Freud, 1915a, 1921a, 1920, 1923, 1926, 1940), characteristically to be observed in sucking (oral gratification), retention and release of feces (anal gratification), and manipulation of the genitalia (genital gratification). In man these types of pleasure are all sexual, in Freud's view, because they all involve stimulation of the mucous membranes of bodily orifices, and each of them is more or less prominent in the various sexual perversions. Indeed, the "psychosexual" development which occurs in the normal person between infancy and adulthood involves, in Freud's opinion, a more or less regular sequence of stages (oral, anal, phallic, genital) during each of which the individual is preoccupied by the appropriate organ pleasure. Between the phallic and the genital stages comes the "latency" period so-called because special sexual preoccupation of any kind is more or less absent—a period lasting from about eight years of age to the onset of puberty. During the first three periods, the child can get the appropriate organ pleasure by manipulating his own body; that is, the sexual instincts are *auto-erotic*. Thus, the sexual instincts persist for a relatively long time under the domination of the pleasure principle because the child does not have to seek objects external to himself to obtain gratification.

But he does come to recognize the necessity of objects in connection with the self-preservative instincts (ego instincts as distinct from the sexual ones) because relief of the unpleasure of hunger, cold, wet, thirst, tight clothing, or collisions with objects is never immediate. This delay of gratification contributes to the child's recognition of himself as a separate entity and to his recognition of other objects, and thus strongly forwards the development of the ego. Also, because of delay in gratification and because of painful experiences in attempts to reduce the delay, the young ego learns to operate by the "reality principle," to deliberately delay the gratification of any instinct either until a real object is present or until other circumstances (including the presence of the object) are propitious (Freud, 1895, 1915a, 1920, 1921a, 1923). The first sexual object chosen (in infancy) is the nourishing mother, whose gratification of the self-preservative instinctive demands of hunger produces pleasure which in turn is associated with the stimuli of the sexual instincts. The sexual instincts cannot *choose* objects. Only the ego can do that. So throughout life the sexual instincts are dependent for their objects on the ego's activities. The ego can learn which objects are gratifying and permitted, and which are possibly gratifying but whose use is fraught with danger. So it is with the mother, the first object of the sexual instincts. Freud believed strongly in the universal and genuine desire, by male children, for their mothers as sexual objects. In his first series of lectures to medical students he quoted from Diderot's *Le neveu de Rameau* the following passage which I here translate: "If the little savage were left to himself, so that he retained all his imbecility and united with the paucity of reason of the child in the cradle the violence of passion of the thirty-year-old man, he would wring his father's neck and sleep with his mother" (quoted by Freud, 1920, p. 346). So not only is the mother an object of sexual love to a boy but the father is the chief aspect of reality that seems to stand between the child and his object. Prior to this recognition of the father's antagonism, the child's relation to him is one of affection, of wanting to be like him and to take his place everywhere (Freud, 1921b, pp. 60–61, 1923, 1925), the first developmental stage in identification. An essential aspect of wanting to supplant the father is the desire to possess those qualities in virtue of which the father maintains his position of supremacy with the mother and shuts out the child. But try as he will the child experiences nothing but failure when he attempts to perform his father's functions (e.g., the child finds he cannot make a baby) and thus not only the threat of retaliation by the father, but his own ineptitude as well, bar him from his object.

Now in Freud's terms, a sexual *object* is one for the attainment of which the organism spends energy, an expenditure which will be terminated only when the instinctive stimuli are quelled. And energy continues to be spent on loved objects even when the desire to remain near them or to gain their favor is not that of immediate sexual gratification, but merely the wish to maintain a high probability of such gratification in the future.[2] If, in the course of such energy expenditure, an object becomes unavailable for any reason (e.g., the loved one dies, makes another alliance, or gratuitously refuses to gratify the passion) the person must stop the energy expenditure (cathexis must be withdrawn) and transfer it to some other object.

[2] Freud's terms "investment of objects with libido" and "libidinal cathexis of objects" are equivalent. Both refer to "energy directed by the ego toward the objects of its sexual desires . . ." (Freud, 1920, p. 424). Energy directed by the ego for the gratification of self-preservative instincts he called "interest" (Freud, 1920, p. 424).

Psychologically, this is what takes place in mourning (Freud, 1916–18); but in melancholia the lost object is set up (perhaps as an image) in the ego, in fact becomes identified with the ego. Thus, the self-reproaches of melancholiacs don't apply to themselves as well as they do to the object, which they love, have loved, or should love, and with which they are now identified. Identification in this sense occurs with both the mother and with the father and constitutes the core of the special substructure in the ego which Freud first called the "ego ideal" (1915a) and later the "superego" (1923). Identification by incorporation into the ego involves both the good and bad aspects of the incorporated objects; that is, of objects which are both loved and hated (the conflict of ambivalence). Thus, the tendency to behave destructively toward the object because of its being hated (that is, the sadistic tendency) is now evidenced in the identifier's behavior toward himself. This self-directed sadism, thought Freud, uniquely solved the problem of suicide (1916–18) or any other patently self-destructive behavior (1928a).

Here is the importance of the ego in Freud's theory of psychology. It is the representative of the instincts of self-preservation (1915a, et seq.), though later (1923, et seq.) *all* instincts were relegated to "the id" and perception was the only innate capacity which remained to the ego. In contrast to the unorganized and impulsive id, the organized and coherent ego represents all that is sane and rational in mental life (1923, 1926). The ego perceives and thinks, and distinguishes between imagined and real objects. It includes consciousness, though "heaven knows how important a part" of it is unconscious (1923, p. 17). By motor activity, by repression, and by censorship on dreams the ego determines what shall be allowed to enter consciousness. It chooses objects and occasions for the gratification of the sexual instincts (1895, 1915a, et seq.). It permits and inhibits motor activity and coordinates all its own processes. A special subsystem of the ego becomes differentiated as a result of the ego's identifications (1915a, et seq.). This latter part, the "ego ideal" (1915a), later the "superego" (1923), is the repository of the various standards inculcated by parents, educators, religious leaders, and other authority figures—that is, by "society" (1923). Though the ego often cannot live up to these standards it judges itself by them, so the ego ideal is the basis for self-evaluation, self-criticism, conscience, and the feeling of guilt (Freud, 1915a, 1921b, 1923, 1926, 1940). Furthermore, the aim of psychoanalysis is to strengthen the ego, especially in its capacity to limit action in the service of instinctual gratification to appropriate objects and occasions (Freud, 1920, 1940). The process of analysis is impossible without the cooperation of the ego and a minimal condition for this cooperation is that the ego have some objects and interests outside itself. Schizophrenics have no such objects and interests and therefore cannot be treated by psychoanalysis (Freud, 1920).

For all these considerations, adduced by Freud himself, I maintain that psychoanalysis was first and always an "ego psychology"; that "ego," in the Freudian language, refers to the same nest of problems which were subsumed under "self" by Pierce, James, Wundt, Mach, and Höffding;[3] that Freud admired and desired the sway of rational conscious control in human behavior, but his pathological material allowed him to see, more clearly than the others, that irrational unconscious determiners of behavior had to be reckoned with too. Neurosis arises, he said, from the fact that actions required to gratify sexual instincts often conflict with the sanctions imposed by local custom, the physical characteristics of the situation, or the self-respect of the ego (the "ego ideal"). In fact, he observed that (local custom and the physical situation permitting) the self-respect of the ego is the only thing that makes some men turn in disgust from actions which others readily undertake.

Because of its origin, the ego is first and foremost a "body ego" (1921a) and perhaps it was with this notion in mind that Freud first introduced his own use of the term "narcissism"—treating one's own body in the same way as one would treat the body of a sexual object. Freud's studies of adult neurotics suggested to him that "auto-erotism" during childhood, and the beliefs of children and primitive peoples in the "omnipotence" of their own wishes and thoughts (cf. Freud, 1913) would support the hypothesis of a "primary and normal" narcissism (Freud, 1914). Subsequently (1915a, p. 74, 1920, 1921b) this was no tentative hypothesis, but a firmly established part of his thinking: "For a child loves himself first and only later learns to love others and to sacrifice something of his own ego to them. Even the people whom he seems to love from the outset are loved in the first instance because he needs them and cannot do without them—again therefore, from motives of egoism: it is a literal fact that the child learns how to love through his own egoism" (1920, p. 214). And, in children,

---

[3] Freud recognized, as did James (1890) and Höffding (1891) before him, that the aggressively self-interested behavior guaranteed by the self-preservative instincts was tempered not only by experience (the "reality principle") but also by the individual's dual relation to the processes of life. On the one hand, in the sexual act, the individual acts for himself and derives his private pleasure; but on the other hand, he acts in the interest of the species, as an "appendage" of the "(possibly) immortal" (1914, p. 36), "quasi-immortal" (1915a, p. 68), "virtually immortal" (1920, p. 421), "immortal" (1921a, pp. 81–82) germ plasm. Freud was referring here to Weismann's distinction between somatic and germinal substances (e.g., Weismann, 1889, 1892).

the development of group feeling grows out of original jealousy which the ego represses as soon as it learns that it cannot be jealous without self-damage. Jealousy is replaced by demands for fairness and equal treatment for all members of the group: If I can't be the first, no one alse can (Freud, 1921b). But there is a *secondary* form of narcissism in which energy, previously directed to getting gratification from objects external to the organism, is turned (introverted) to the attempt to obtain gratification from the agent himself ("libidinal cathexis of the ego"). Parents reinforce both primary and secondary narcissism in their offspring by giving the child to understand that he is worthy to have better things than they had, to escape the harsh realities of life, death, frustrations, illness, or restrictions on his own will; "parental love . . . is nothing but parental narcissism born again . . ." (Freud, 1915a, p. 49). But parents also combine with the rest of society to define standards for the child's behavior and to impose punishments and other sanctions to see that he lives up to those standards. The standards, which can hardly be met perfectly, are nevertheless incorporated into the ego in the role of "ego ideal" or "superego." By the time the ego ideal is well developed the ego itself, because of its many inevitable failures and blunders, is no longer worthy of the self-love lavished upon it during the happy days in childhood when primary narcissism ruled. But the love withdrawn from the ego is transferred to the ego ideal and from then on the ego itself is measured and its worth determined by the amount of its departure from that ideal.[4] I shall postpone a fuller discussion of Freud's views on self-evaluation to chapter 3 and conclude the present discussion with his views on the ego's weakness.

What I will call the "weak-ego" period in Freud's published writings lasted from *"Beyond the Pleasure Principle"* (1921a) through *"The Ego and the Id"* (1923).

In 1921 Freud derived, from Fechner's (1873) notion that pleasure and pain arise, respectively, from equilibrium and disequilibrium of sensation intensities, and from his own notion of the "conservatism" of all instincts, the view that *"the aim of all life is death"* (1921a, p. 71). The instincts are conservative in the sense that they continually push the organism toward pleasure—the total elimination of all sensation (the "Nirvana principle"). There could be no purer pleasure than a return to the insensate, non-organic conditions from which life had

---

[4] This notion of self-evaluation has been adopted intact by some contemporary students of "the self-concept" who attempt to measure self-evaluation, e.g., Brownfain (1952); Bills, Vance, and McLean (1951); Calvin and Holtzman (1953); Cowen, Heilizer, and Axelrod (1955). Wylie (1961), Tables 1 and 2, gives a description of these and similar "instruments."

emerged. The evolution of more complex organisms, with correspond-ingly complex instincts, produced only species in which *natural*, in-stinctive death is achieved by relatively complex processes, processes which we mistakenly regard as the phenomena of life. "Seen in this light, the theoretical importance of the instincts of self-preservation, self-assertion and of mastery greatly diminishes. They are component instincts whose function it is to assure that the organism shall follow its own path to death, and to ward off any possible ways of returning to inorganic existence than those which are immanent to the organism itself" (Freud, 1921a, pp. 71–72). The instincts formerly called self-preservative (ego instincts) he then regarded as exercising "pressure towards death" and the sexual instincts favored the prolongation of life. Weismann (e.g., 1889, 1892) had said that the germ plasm passed in an unbroken succession from generation to generation and there-fore was immortal, in a sense, while its appendages, the bodies of indi-vidual organisms, were mortal. So Freud took the position that Weis-mann attributed death only to multicellular forms, and then inquired whether death is a characteristic of all species, including unicellular ones, and "immortality" only a lately developed accident of sexual re-production; or was it the other way around. Do the protista die? Freud examined the available evidence and decided there was no clear answer. So from the fact that there was no evidence *against* the idea of a death instinct, and the allegation that "primitive peoples" don't believe in natural death, Freud concluded that there is room for his hypothesis after all, though near the end of the book he wrote, ". . . I am not convinced myself. . . . Or, more precisely, . . . I do not know how far I believe . . ." (Freud, 1921a, pp. 102–103). Given the hypothesis of a death instinct, Freud tried to find a positive repre-sentative for it among the ego instincts. The initial reactions of the perceptual-conscious mechanism (the original core of the ego) to stimuli from the external world is either to register and discriminate among them or to be indifferent to them (filter them out, ignore them). But indifference, to Freud, is one form of hate, and hateful or destruc-tive tendencies are to be noted in the more fully developed ego, so perhaps sadism is the positive representative he sought. In 1923, at the beginning of the publication in which he finally applied the name "id"[5] to the part of the mental "apparatus" which corresponds to the sexual instincts, Freud announced that the book was a continuation of

---

[5] From the German *Es* = it. Freud said he got the idea for using the word in this sense from Georg Groddeck (cf. Groddeck, 1923), who "never tired of pointing out that the conduct throughout life of what we call our ego is essentially passive, and that, as he expresses it, we are 'lived' by unknown and uncontrollable forces. . . . Groddeck himself no doubt followed the example of Nietzsche, who

his thoughts on the death instinct. It is certainly the nadir of the ego's importance in Freud's writing. Freud wrote: "We shall now look upon the mind of an individual as an unknown and unconscious id, upon whose surface rests the ego, developed from its nucleus the Pcpt-system. . . . the ego does not envelop the whole of the id, but only does so to the extent to which the system Pcpt forms its surface, more or less as the germinal layer rests upon the ovum. The ego is not sharply separated from the id; its lower portion merges into it" (Freud, 1923, p. 23). Freud did not revise the list of ego functions noted in his previous writings, but he dropped all reference to ego instincts, and emphasized the weakness of the ego: ". . . in its relation to the id it is like a man on horseback, who has to hold in check the superior strength of the horse; with this difference, that the rider seeks to do so with his own strength while the ego uses borrowed forces . . . ; in the matter of action the ego's position is like that of a constitutional monarch, without whose sanction no law can be passed but who hesitates long before imposing a veto on any measure put forward by Parliament" (Freud, 1923, pp. 81–82). This is as far as Freud went, in 1923, toward admitting any strength in the ego. Stripped of its instinctive self-preservative powers, it functions as best it can with borrowed forces, and though Freud invited his readers to see the ego "in its strength and in its weaknesses" (1923, p. 81), it is the weaknesses that were most apparent. "From the other point of view . . . we see this same ego as a poor creature owing service to three masters and consequently menaced by three several dangers; from the external world, from the libido of the id, and from the severity of the superego" (Freud, 1923, pp. 82–83).

But this emphasis on the weakness of the ego was only temporary, as shown by Freud's later explicit wish to de-emphasize it (1926, pp. 24–25). Indeed he came close to recognizing the overriding importance of organic unity; the ego is part of the id—the organized part (1926). The id represents all behavioral apparatus that is given at birth and the ego has developed from "what was originally a cortical layer, provided with organs for receiving stimuli and with apparatus for protection against excessive stimulation . . ." as a "special organization . . . which acts as an intermediary between the id and the external world" (1940, p. 14).[6] The relation of superego to ego is

---

habitually used this grammatical term for whatever in our nature is impersonal and, so to speak, subject to natural law" (Freud, 1923, p. 23 and footnote).

[6] In his accounts of development Freud did not distinguish clearly between the phylogenetic and ontogenetic aspects, though it was clear that he recognized the necessity for the distinction (e.g., Freud, 1914, 1915a, 1921a, 1921b, 1923).

analogous to the relation of ego to id: the superego is a part of the ego, developed from the child's experiences with the demands of social reality, most importantly those represented by the parents though by no means limited to parental influence (1940, pp. 14–17). The pitiful weakness which Freud had attributed to the ego (1923) he later expressly restricted to the *neurotic* ego (1940, pp. 76–77). In the normal person the ego's functioning so smoothly integrates the actions required by instinctive stimuli (id) with societal prescriptions and prohibitions (superego) and the requirements of physical reality that it is almost impossible to distinguish ego from id and superego, both of which are said to be "ego-syntonic" in such a case.

Much of Freud's published writing through the year 1906 (Breuer and Freud, 1895; Freud, 1904, 1905a, 1905b, 1906) was summarized by Hirt (1909),[7] including Freud's admission that he had overemphasized the frequency of real childhood and adolescent sexual experience, and overlooked the fantasy life of the child, especially the adolescent, and his present assumption that these, together with personal sexual arousability, determine whether one will attempt to "fend off" or "repress" recognition of an experience unbearable to his ego—a condition Freud earlier assumed to be the cause of splitting of consciousness in hysteria. Freud now assumes sexual repression as a physiological process in distinction from the formerly assumed, purely psychological, "fending off" (or defense). Hysteric symptoms, in any event, are symbols of sexual ideas.

In this period (1893–1906) Hirt noted that Freud had dropped hypnosis as a method of therapy and began to use free conversational discussion of the patient's ideas, a method which included not only the impressions of the patient, but also his dream experiences, his unintentional (planless) actions, disturbances of expression, understanding, etc., all of which are utilized in the "art of interpretation." All of these, Hirt asserted, display the tendency of our psyche to rework its view of the world as it expresses our wishes and strivings.

Hirt also noted that Bleuler (1906) and Ricklin (1906) were then seeking to apply, to other types of psychopathology, the ideas which Freud had applied to the neuroses. In delirium, in the so-called flight into psychosis in wish dreams, in poetic forming and reforming of painful experience and abreacting the pain in poetic expression, and in the overvaluing of traits lacking in one's own nature there lies an unconscious symbolism expressed in wishes and anxieties, hence a symbolic thought and a symbolic language, shared by many men of

---

[7] In the two articles considered here Hirt (1909, 1910) reviewed only *German* psychiatric literature.

quite varied types. The entire memory contents of patients and normals is organized around one or a few ideas strongly charged with affect, the nuclei of "complexes." The past admits of no change and remains, in spite of all attempts, a part of our ego (Ich). And Jung too, Hirt observed, was also insisting that all psychogenic neuroses contain a complex. However, neurotic complexes are differentiated from normal complexes in that the former are set up with inordinately strong feeling tone and thus possess so much organizing power that they bring the entire individual under their sway. But Jung believed that this formulation was insufficient because individual *disposition* is excluded from consideration.

In his other review article Hirt (1910) wrote, "The description of any sort of psychic process always leads necessarily to the most general of psychological ideas, the ego, and to the question of the relation of this ego to the conscious experiences" (Hirt, 1910, p. 139). Understanding the idea of the ego, Hirt believed, requires clear understanding of the mind-body relation and the latter can be essayed by studying cases of hypochondria which (according to Hirt) have in common a disturbed perception of one's own body, apparently without any physical bases. Some authors equated "body perception" with "body sensations" and maintained that from disturbances of body sensations, all the symptoms of hypochondria could be deduced. The organic basis of this disturbance was explained as hyperesthesia of brain centers or of peripheral sensory nerves, or to vaguely described pathological processes in the brain or in the peripheral nerves. Some writers took the position of Wundt (1880), Mach (1886), and James (1890) that self-awareness, in its narrowest sense, *is* the awareness of stimuli from the body itself. Others regarded body sensations as part of "not-I." However they described the locus of these disturbances, and however directly or indirectly they related them to what they called "self," these authors also differed about the conditions which produced them. Some claimed that the disturbances were "primary," that is, given by innate disposition; others maintained that the disturbances arose somehow after birth, from experience or from some other environmental influence. Mendel (1889) had stated that the severest form of hypochondria involves pathology in the realm of the higher sense organs so that visual, auditory, and tactual objects all appear different than previously. Hirt wrote that this "alienation of the perceptual world" leads easily to the phenomena of depersonalization, in which pathologies of feeling, thinking, and willing are evident. According to Hirt, the customary view is that we often have purely subjective experiences (pure ego experiences) without precise localization and referring only to the orientation of the ego to what goes on in it. When it relates to objects, the ego is in some sense always active and willing. These will processes make up a great part of what Wernicke (1894–1900) called psychic feelings, though they are in turn determined by simple pleasure and displeasure (Wernicke's organic feelings). Thus, Wernicke's distinction between pleasure-displeasure and psychic feelings is meaningless because it would be difficult to say in any case whether a psychic process was more influenced by one or the other.

Hirt attacked Wernicke's view that the belief in a possibly willful change in the direction of attention is a delusion, like the delusion of self-consciousness. Hirt said that Wernicke would have to show not only that organic sensations can disturb attention, but that they were responsible for its initial direction, a particularly difficult job in connection with modification of instincts (especially the activity instincts), the relation of inner to outer work, and the initiation of action in general. How can one explain, in Wernicke's terms, that the child's discovery that he himself can make sounds, plus his pleasure in the babbling, leads to his striving for *speech?*

Thus, according to Hirt, ego, which is the bearer of all conscious facts, and the *reality* which creates associations of experiences, reveals itself especially in attention and will. Hirt stated that Maine de Biran's philosophical theory (Maine de Biran, 1812) is closely related to depersonalization. In his own experience, Maine de Biran had said, as the feeling of activity gradually declined he could recognize the basic fact that we immediately experience in will our own active ego (*moi*) and the opposition of the world (*non-moi*). Next, not-ego becomes his own body, an indication of how unclear we have been so far on the relation of ego to body. Maine de Biran was so convinced that self-awareness depended on will that he substituted, for the Cartesian *Cogito ergo sum*, the notion *Volo ergo sum*.

Hirt used lengthy quotations from case histories, published by himself and others, as the basis for arguing his own view that "feelings" of pleasure-unpleasure, whether arising spontaneously in the central nervous system or induced by external stimuli, are the basis for recognizing ego and distinguishing it from non-ego. "It is uniquely and alone the feelings which differentiate ego and non-ego: in them we have our ego set against its conscious contents and opposing objects. All patients with the symptoms of depersonalization and alienation of the perceptual world have little lively feeling. . . . The thoughts they had were not their thoughts, what they said was said as if half consciously, they did everything mechanically, like an automaton, indeed they doubted if they really existed" (Hirt, 1910, p. 155). It is not the sensations from the body, but the power and spontaneity of the ego with respect to its contents, which makes these contents *my* contents. Body sensations serve only to indicate that the ego is customarily *active*. ". . . If the reality of the ego, depends on the belonging of the organ sensations to *my* feeling, *my* reality, then [in the cases mentioned] the body sensations have become, so to speak, leaderless. There are no longer contents which I formerly knew as my contents, they are strange, unusual, uncanny contents" (Hirt, 1910, p. 157). Hirt denied that consciousness of ego is at its height in activity feelings, because disturbance of feelings of activity is not known to be the cause of depersonalization. The assumption that depersonalization results from a general disturbance of sensitivity is, in Hirt's opinion, only a logical deduction without evidence.

In the extensive bibliography of C. G. Jung two essays (Jung, 1943, 1945) most conveniently summarize his differences from Freud and from his one-time co-disciple, Adler, in his conception of the underlying cause of psychological illness, in his stronger emphasis on the "racial unconscious," and (most radically) in his conceptions of self and ego and the relations between these concepts. On the premise that human behavior is determined by unconscious forces Jung agreed with Freud and Adler. In fact, Jung regarded dream analysis, the method by which all analytic treatments mostly proceed, as Freud's greatest discovery. But Freud terminated the exploration of the unconscious as soon as he judged that the patient's ego could confront, without further difficulty, the pathogenic repressed contents and the instinctual urges and either acquiesce in them or reject them once and for all. By exploring the unconscious beyond this point Jung became convinced that the unconscious has two kinds of contents—personal and impersonal. The *personal* unconscious includes the neural representatives of all the experiences the individual has had in his lifetime: repressed material that was once conscious, memory processes that have fallen below the threshold of consciousness, the results of subliminal sense impressions, and also the possibilities of unique experiences given by unique brain structure. Since, from the analyst's point of view, the personal unconscious has its limit at the earliest impressions which occurred in the life of the individual, it might be expected that the contents of the unconscious are as finite as individual life is.

But there is more. There is the impersonal unconscious which usually begins to reveal itself in later stages of analysis after the bulk of the patient's personal unconscious has been dealt with. Then, in the transference relation, the patient attributes to the analyst properties which in healthy conscious reasoning he would not attribute to any mere human: godlike qualities, including those of father and mother "images," heroes, and saviors. Jung said that these attributions are "projections" from a layer of the unconscious which lies deeper than the personal. Because the images and feelings thus "projected" are like the contents of myths which differ greatly in the times and places of their origins, Jung decided that they are produced by physical and functional similarities of the nervous system which all men share. So the impersonal unconscious is also called "transpersonal" or "collective."

The collective unconscious is inherited, not as common ideas or images, but as the common structural possibility of having such ideas or images. This possibility may be the deposit "of the commonly repeated experiences of humanity, . . . a kind of readiness to produce over and over again the same or similar mythical ideas"; such processes may even exist in animals (Jung, 1943, pp. 79–80). "The universal similarity of the brain yields the universal possibility of a similar mental functioning. This functioning is the collective psyche. In so far as differentiations exist that correspond to race, tribe, or even family, there exists also a collective psyche limited to race, tribe, or family over and above the 'universal' collective psyche" (Jung, 1943, p. 157). The images produced by the collective psyche are called the "archetypes" or "dominants" of the collective unconscious. A long list of these archetypes could be compiled from Jung's writings, a list that would include gods, demons, demigods, evil spirits, heroes, personifications of natural forces like *energy* and *aether,* and common human social relations and other "situations." The collective unconscious conditions the operation of individual consciousness, as every truly great human discovery indicates.[8]

For our present purposes it will be necessary to consider only three of Jung's specific archetypes: the shadow, the persona, and the mana-personality. The shadow represents the universal abstraction of evil, especially the intended or accidental evil which appears in the outcomes of an individual's acts. *Persona* and *mana-personality* represent the distillate of mankind's experience with individuality, personality, ownership, and privilege. In them the collective psyche defines what we mean by socially prescribed roles, but they are only the masquerade of individuality, not the genuine article. *Persona* originally meant the mask worn by an actor to signify his role. As such, it is

---

[8] Jung (1943, p. 79) discussed Robert Mayer's enunciation of the principle of the conservation of energy as an example of this.

an appropriate name for this archetype which "tries to make others and oneself believe that one is individual, whereas one is simply playing a part in which the collective psyche speaks" (Jung, 1945, p. 167). The mana-personality appears to be included within the persona, but distinguished from it by the fact that "historically, the mana-personality is always in possession of the secret name, or of some esoteric knowledge, or has the prerogative of a special way of acting . . ." (Jung, 1945, p. 247). Persona, therefore, can apply to any prescribed social roles, but the mana-personality relates to specially powerful roles.

What Jung called the psyche embraces not only the personal and collective unconscious, but the conscious ego as well. Both the ego and the unconscious parts of the psyche are usually active independently of each other. Sometimes they come into conflict but their usual relation is mutual compensation. Thus, in the inescapable interplay between the ego and the unconscious, the *whole psyche* is a self-regulating system (Jung, 1943, p. 71). *Essential man* is defined by the existence of both his conscious ego and the unconscious parts of his psyche and the process of psychological development during the lifetime of the organic individual *is* the conscious ego's coming to terms with the unconscious. The organism is endowed by nature with the capacity, "the transcendent function," for achieving this accord between ego and unconscious. The aim of this process is the emergence of genuine individuals, so Jung called it the "individuation process" (Jung, 1943, p. 121). "A special position must be accorded to those archetypes which stand for the goal of the developmental process. . . . The transcendent function does not proceed without aim and purpose, but leads to the revelation of the essential man. It is in the first place a purely natural process, which may in some cases pursue its course without the knowledge or assistance of the individual, and can sometimes forcibly accomplish itself in the face of opposition. The meaning and purpose of the process is the realization, in all its aspects, of the personality originally hidden away in the embryonic germ plasm; the production and unfolding of the original, potential wholeness. The symbols used by the unconscious to this end are the same as those which mankind has always used to express wholeness, completeness, and perfection: symbols, as a rule, of the quaternity and the circle" (Jung, 1943, pp. 120–121).

Thus, the process of individuation, by the ego's coming to terms with the unconscious is an "ineluctable" psychological necessity, but it is often a dangerous and laborious process. The initial requirement is that the ego confront the symbols of the unconscious of which it becomes aware and clearly understand that they are not part of itself, that they are non-ego. The process of psychological analysis is the chief way of accomplishing this, if it doesn't occur spontaneously. The benefits of the process are obvious, but the dangers are many and grave. Probing the unconscious is like trying to dig a well with the risk of opening up a volcano (Jung, 1943, p. 124). Latent neuroses and psychoses may become operative in spite of the efforts of psychiatrist and patient, or the unconscious may drive the patient into injurious or fatal "accidents", or the analyst may be clumsy and dogmatic in interpreting things to the patient and thus wreck a case that need not have turned out badly. Above all, there is the danger that the ego will not recognize its own distinctness from the archetypes of the unconscious, but will identify with them. The chief cause of people's resistance to exploring their own unconscious is fear of what they will discover there—particularly fear of the "shadow" archetype (Jung, 1943, 1945, 1957).

If the ego identifies itself with the archetypes of the collective unconscious the result is "inflation" of the ego, overvaluing it to the point of megalomania. In behavior this has either the effect of producing a full-bloom episode of schizophrenia (Jung, 1945, p. 156), or of increasing the individual's demands on other people and making him at least a bully or petty domestic tyrant or, at worst, the monocratic dictator of a totalitarian state (Jung, 1957, pp. 10–15).

Jung was passionate in his demands for the development of genuine individuality; the plea and the arguments for it are constantly repeated, especially in his later writings (e.g., Jung, 1957). But individuality is not ego consciousness; it is rather the goal of the individuation process. This ideal union of conscious and unconscious influences in human behavior is itself represented by an archetype—the self. This self has as much to do with the ego as the sun with the earth; it is not what we are at any moment, but the never completely realizable possibility of what we *could become* if our individual organic destiny were fully realized. Human happiness and all human achievements depend on the existence of genuine individuals. "Consciousness is a precondition of being" and the individual is the irreducible unit of consciousness (Jung, 1957, pp. 59–60). "All the highest achievements of virtue, as well as the blackest villainies, are individual" (Jung, 1945, p. 162). And it is toward this individuation, this "undiscovered self" (Jung, 1957) that our vital processes move. "Yet it would be wrong . . . to suppose that . . . the unconscious is working to a deliberate and concerted plan and is striving to realize certain definite ends. I have found nothing to support this assumption. The driving force, so far as it is possible for us to grasp it, seems to be in essence only an urge toward self-realization" (Jung, 1945, pp. 193–194). With this statement Jung placed himself clearly in the tradition with other psychological writers (e.g., Allport, 1955, Maslow, 1950, and Goldstein, 1939).

The early twentieth century was, for psychology, a period of hectic system-building. The adherents of the various "schools" were distinguished by their ardent advocacy of unique positions on a variety of issues: *Gestalt* psychologists opposed the metaphysics and epistemology of the *structuralists;* structuralists objected to the aims of psychology proposed by the *functionalists;* and the *behaviorists* opposed all others on questions of method and subject matter. Another group, with otherwise heterogeneous opinions, found common cause in attempting to establish what was called "personalistic psychology" or a "psychology of selves." Mary Whiton Calkins was a fervent spokesman for this group, and her writings (e.g., Calkins, 1912, 1916, 1919, 1927) showed that she had decided views of her own about what she meant by "the self," though it is hard to tell exactly what they were. She said that self-consciousness is persistent (1912) and that subjects who denied its persistence, as some of Titchener's introspectors did (Titchener, 1911), had misunderstood what they were being asked about and so had confused self-consciousness with some particular aspect, phase, or stage of it. At other places she sounded like J. S. Mill: "If consciousness as content exists and content can only exist as content of a subject or I, then the experiencing self must exist by the same right as the experienced content" (Calkins, 1912, p. 28). She approved the view of Oesterreich (1910) that "I" is directly experienced as a feeling, willing, perceiving, or thinking "I." And she cited reports to show that self was apprehended by introspection: that Ss were often able to distinguish between "objective" and "subjective" on the grounds that the "objective" is forced upon them, independently of their will (Berliner, 1914); that recognition was characterized by a "feeling of familiarity" defined as "connected with the very feeling of our 'self' and . . . enveloped by" it (Katzaroff, 1911); that choice between two arithmetic operations involved a "consciousness of activity" (verbal images and affective experience) which was distinct from feelings of muscular activity and thus stood as evidence for the intervention of the self (Michotte and Prüm, 1911); that introspective reports could be classified into four stages of volition (the most important being consciousness of end or purpose) *and* the ubiquitous experience of self (Ach, 1910). She found that other introspective protocols (Amen, 1926; Martin, 1922) were full of self-references, and noted that other psychologists asserted that the self can be found in experimental introspection (Aveling, 1926; Spearman, 1923). But in none of these references did Calkins tell us how the self *appears* in consciousness. Perhaps a clue lies in what she said consciousness of self is *not*.

First, though self is an object of consciousness, it is not like any other object. In fact it is unjustifiable to apply subject-object categories to an experience which is fundamental to these categories (Calkins, 1912). Nor can the "I" be the total content of consciousness, for if it were then there would be no distinction between "I" and "not-I" (Calkins, 1912). But though consciousness of self is persistent, *not* intermittent, "constancy of the experience of self makes for inattention to it" (Calkins, 1915, 1916)! And if we are preoccupied with conscious *contents*, as most introspectors were, our consciousness of self will be less prominent (Calkins, 1916); and if we are looking for a mental *element* which represents self, as Wheeler was (Wheeler, 1920, 1922) then we will miss the conscious evidence of self-activity altogether (Calkins, 1927). And she insisted very strongly that her conception of self-consciousness did not include its unanalyzability (Calkins, 1927). This list of assertions about self-consciousness doesn't help us much either. Perhaps we can learn more from Calkins' broader assertions about "psychology as a science of selves."

Apparently the basic tenet of "personalistic" or "self" psychology is that all experience is that of some *person*, that ideas and percepts are not found unconnected with some *subject*. Laird (1920), William McDougall (1923), and Stern (1917, 1918–1919) espoused this view, but Calkins (1927) preferred Stern's formulation to McDougall's which was otherwise too "atomistic." She also approved Pfonder's (1904) view which she paraphrased: "I, or subject . . . stands in a relation to experienced or imagined objects which is comparable to the relation of center to periphery" (Calkins, 1916, p. 25); and Meumann's (1913) statement that "our whole soul life is analyzable into a sum of intellectual processes . . . which, however, possess a distinctive character through their immediate relation to the I." The experience or existence of self is "a basal fact of experience" as R. MacDougall (1916) had written, and as Calkins everywhere maintained. By 1916 she was noting implicit or explicit references to what she called self in the writings of social psychologists, behaviorists, and test constructors. In social psychology Calkins noted the opinions that: the aim of psychology should be "to comprehend man as a personality" (Griese, 1914); the key to primitive beliefs and customs is *participation*, which defines the unity between man and what is external to him (Levy-Bruhl, 1912); social psychology is interested in the nature of individuals rather than in groups (Ellwood, 1912, 1917); and Bentley's (1916) regard for the individual as the "unit in social interaction." The behaviorists, in attacking the structuralists, had become allies of the self-psychologists; and Calkins constructed an analogy to show how close behaviorism and self psychology really were. In behaviorism, the *body* corresponds logically to what the personalists called *self;* and either the behaving body or the active self are preferable constructs to the empty "mental states" of the structuralists (Calkins, 1919, 1927; also, cf. Mursell, 1922). Calkins also concluded, from writings on intelligence testing (Dodge, 1918; Lough, 1916; Terman, 1918), that the testing movement had assumed the "language of self psychology . . . the unity of the intelligence test has come to be the conscious self" (Calkins, 1919, pp. 114–115).

Though she never did make a clear statement of what she meant by self or what we are supposed to be *conscious of* in self-consciousness, Calkins seemed to be impressed by some connection between self and particular classes of experiences, especially emotions and sentiments; the *processes* of perception, thinking, willing, imagining, liking, and disliking. She seemed to be concentrating on *activity* as a characteristic of whatever she meant by "self." She wrote (Calkins, 1923) that "certain experiences—recognition, emotional sympathy, and pride, for example—are obviously indescribable without specific reference to the consciousness of selves—one's own self and one's fellows."

It may be that we can learn something from this sketch of the early personalists. They were perhaps talking about interesting and important problems, but they were so addicted to an old and inadequate method (introspection), so mistrustful of the new method (behaviorism), so forgetful of what they should have learned about self from James and the British empiricists, that they could not formulate their problems in a way that would convince any scientist that they were worth working on. Good will is not a sufficient tool for solving problems; we must find a *way* or make one. Perhaps the early personalists were cheated by history in that no methods or concepts relevant to their problems lay ready at hand, but I doubt it. I think that their difficulty was emotional. The importance of the problems, as they saw it, got translated into a need for urgency in dealing with them, so they tried to prove too much on purely deductive grounds, and they tried to gain adherents by arguments that were more specious than substantial. And I believe that their spirit of urgency is not dead, that it lives still among contemporary psychologists who write about self. It is certainly true that self, as an object of research interest among psychologists, went into limbo for a long time after the personalist episode. Some (e.g., Allport, 1943) have laid the blame for this at the behaviorists' door, but I think that is unfair. Since 1940, writing about self has steadily increased in annual volume and very little of this newer literature describes *experiments,* and *virtually none of it contains references to general experimental psychology.* In fact some of the self literature, even the most recent, states categorically that "the self," as these writers define it, would only be violated by experimentation (e.g., Moustakas, 1956) or that "the objective approach" will not get at it (e.g., Wylie, 1961). We now turn to an examination of the body of writing about self during the last thirty years.

By the end of the first quarter of the twentieth century all the major questions relating to "self" and "ego" had been raised and, for about the next twenty years, writing on these questions ran to reviews or syntheses of what had already been written. So many specialists had spoken of the problem from their special viewpoints that some confessed uncertainty about whether the problem belonged to psychology or to biology or sociology (Blondel, 1924). Granting that "self" belongs to any of them, even in part, Blondel traced the difficulties in studying it to inadequacies of existing methods. Even so, the domain of the objective self, the "me," is definable and reducible to law, largely, it seems, on James' terms. And "I" as observer, knower, and selector of awareness and action, is "given to us" in its entirety in the never-ceasing present in which our "conscious contents" are born, and grow, and die. But "I" is not, as some had said, merely the sum of all past experiences; it is only so when the future is closed to us. "I" is not only what it is and has been, but what it shall be; the future is of great interest to us (Blondel, 1924). It is to "I" rather than "me" that we apply feelings of unity, identity, specificity; and of value too, for "we enclose ourselves in an aura of positive or negative partiality" (Blondel, 1924). "I" was still, to Blondel, the *"quaestio vexata"* of psychology, because he did not follow the implications of James' (1890) suggestion that the present thought is itself the only *verifiable* knower. Objectivity was not yet full-blown.

Another writer with a strong Jamesian bias was DeWitt Parker (1917). At least his answer to the question of how the subject can be its own object reminds us of James: at any moment the self is a complex set of acts of which one act is in the process of discovering the rest. One act of discovery is itself discovered, but this leads not to an infinite regress but to the *concept* of acts of discovery (Parker,

1917, ch. 1). So consciousness of *self* is consciousness of the interconnectedness of the *activities*, but we also have consciousness of *contents*. The unity of the *mind* is given by the contact of the mutually interacting *activities* (i.e., the *self*) with *contents;* so mind and self are not co-extensive. Personal identity, the *sequential* unity of the mind is not absolute; identity can be more or less as the number of identical elements in an object change. The self, as an object, persists but it also changes as the Mills, Wundt, Mach, and James had noted. Parker relied, as Mach had, on our awareness of simultaneous sets of fast- and slow-changing variables to account for this appearance, but he gave particular emphasis to experiences of activities: thinking (identity of concepts), volition (identity of purposes), and desire (identity of activity-goal relations).

Consistently with his view that self-awareness depends especially on awareness of activity, Parker emphasized the connection of activity with tools, especially that utterly unique tool, the body, not made by the "user," impossible for "another" to use, and whose existence conditions the existence of the "user" itself. To lay aside our detachable tools, hoes, pens, paintbrushes, musical instruments, books, is to lay aside *parts* of ourselves; and when the body is laid aside, *all* of self goes with it (Parker, 1917, p. 76).

If self is uniquely revealed in activity, then Parker was a self-realizationist: "Every interest, every plan, unless opposed, must work itself out . . . in the special fashion required by its character . . . These all require certain determinate acts in order to fulfillment. . . . Interest . . . desire . . . , wish and will are for something which is to grow out of a definite situation in the present existing world" (Parker, 1917, pp. 135–136). To describe a purpose is to foretell some long or short future sequence of acts necessarily related to it, a sequence which can be interrupted only by the intervention of a desire relating to another purpose (Parker, 1917, p. 141). Desire, without intent and action, is nothing real—only a dream.

The relations between an individual and other people or things are defined by the effects of their actions on each other; and the relative immediacy or indirectness of the means required to produce these effects defines the distance (and the time) between the agents. "When we are far from each other . . . we require more indirect methods of communication and interaction, more agents and emissaries, and so a longer time. . . . To be in the spatial neighborhood of his action, is to need, in order to influence him, the cooperation of a smaller part of the whole environment" (Parker, 1917, pp. 165–166).

The relations of the individual to his fellow men had hitherto been considered on the assumption that individuals, existing prior to the relation, somehow met and entered into the relation. Hobbes' theory of the social contract and utilitarian theories of social organization made this assumption. By 1920, as reflected especially in the writings of James, Höffding, and Freud, a new view had emerged which emphasized the necessarily prolonged dependence of the infant human on adults and the consequently rich opportunities for him to learn socially approved standards of conduct from them. This, together with the assumption by these and other writers of a variety of social instincts, profoundly influenced the development of social psychology (e.g., McDougall, 1908; Thorndike, 1920) and the inclusion of psychologists' ideas in the writings of sociologists (e.g., Cooley, 1899, 1911, 1922).

It was clearly Cooley's theory that individuals are prior to society; that the character of society is determined more by the demands of individuals than the other way around; and that, as Thorndike (1920) put it, ideals and values come from some aspect of man's original nature, an aspect which is modified by social pressure. According to Cooley (1899) personal competition operates to assign each individual his role in the social system—a function for which we have no other criteria of selection. This mode of selection, Cooley thought, is good for those who are natively endowed with sufficient capacity to meet the competition; but it is unduly hard on "the weak, the misplaced and the unprepared, among whom are many who in circumstances more fortunate would make an honorable and important part in the general life" (Cooley, 1899, p. 91). Success requires two capacities: the ability to distinguish oneself from other men by performing individual functions (intelligence); and the ability to relate one's special capacities to the present social situation (sympathy). Intelligence and sympathy are also requisite to a sense of justice; so there is a high, though not perfect, correlation between success and morality.

Later, when he had read more psychology and had more to read, Cooley modified his view by a heavier emphasis on society. "Self and society are twin-born . . . and the notion of a separate and independent ego is an illusion" (Cooley, 1911, p. 5). This is a *logical* argument based on the premise, which we have traced at least as far back as Pierce (1868), that self-awareness *rises* with the distinction between agent and object. But the twinning of self and society can also be based on the observation that individual acts and social pressures mutually modify each other and, in general, there are no grounds to assert that the influence in one direction is stronger than in the other (Cooley, 1922, pp. 30–38); "identification" with others (in James' sense of the "social self") blurs the boundary between self and other. This is a change in emphasis only: a human being "*is* an individual, a specialized, contending bit of psychical force" (Cooley, 1922, p. 66), born with strong needs for self-expression (1911), and self-assertion (1922), needs which are modified by social conditions only to the extent that the latter include limitations of number and kinds of opportunities for individual action (1911, 1922).

Self-feeling is instinctive and, as such, "was doubtless connected in evolution with its important function in stimulating and unifying the special activities of individuals. It appears to be associated with ideas of the exercise of power, of being a cause, ideas that emphasize the antithesis between the mind and the rest of the world. The first definite thoughts that a child associates with self-feeling are probably those of his earliest endeavors to control visible objects—his limbs, his playthings, his bottle, and the like. Then he attempts to control the actions of the persons about him, and so his circle of power and of self-feeling widens without interruption to the most complex objects of mature ambition. Although he does not say 'I' or 'my' during the first year or two, yet he expresses so clearly by his actions the feeling that adults associate with these words that we cannot deny him a feeling of self even in the first weeks" (Cooley, 1922, pp. 177–178). Though other people may at times react to limit our self-expression, they are also its indispensable audience and the presence of others may be the occasion of its more ebullient outbursts, or we may be saddened by their absence when we have something to show off. Genuine love of others and a healthy self-love cannot exist apart, for love is an action and the healthy self is nothing if not an agent. But love returned also strengthens the self-love, so the question of which *causes* which is moot.[9]

Thus Cooley shifted the emphasis in the individual-society relation by insisting that the adult individual needs society, just as Höffding (1891) has emphasized that society needs the individual. A further apparent shift of this emphasis was to come, in Mead's argument that mind and self both *arise from* social conditions.

Mead was an heir of the two intellectual traditions in America which has jointly produced Watsonian behaviorism: *pragmatism* in philosophy (Pierce, James, and Dewey) and *functionalism* in psychology (Angell, Carr, Dewey, and Woodworth). Mead called himself a "social behaviorist" and his plan for psychology was to expand its

[9] This is reminiscent of Freud's view (e.g., 1916–18, 1921b). Cooley did not refer to Freud's writings in any of the works cited above (Cooley, 1899, 1911, 1922).

domain into the objective study of purposive action and to retain whatever had been gained from the introspective study of consciousness. His views on self were essentially complete in his paper on "The Genesis of the Self and Social Control" (Mead, 1925), but they were more elaborately worked out later in the lectures which were published after his death.[10]

Mead's analysis of consciousness agrees in many points with Jamesian empiricism, especially the conception of the "present." The present, in Mead's view (Mead, 1932, 1934, 1936, 1938), appears in consciousness as *passage,* namely, the becoming and disappearing of real events. Real events, which occur only in such a present, are not themselves parts of passage. But each event arises only under necessary conditions (i.e., the event has a history), so the past is implied in the present; and each event is itself part of the conditions for a rising event, so the future too is implied in the present. The notion of time arises through the ordered passage of unique events. Past and future have no genuine reality; they are concepts or ideas generated by the activities of memory and forecast. As ideas, past and future belong uniquely to mind, to organisms—those emergent events whose nature it is to maintain themselves by interaction with environments which they create as a result of selective reception and action. Mind is the "larger environment" in which organisms transcend the present. The duration of a present, or passage, is that of "its undertakings—of what we are doing. The pasts and futures belonging to such activity belong to the present. . . . The undertakings belong . . . within larger activities, so that we seldom have the sense of a set of isolated presents" (Mead, 1932, p. 88).

The central problem of mind is that of consciousness; i.e., the reflective intelligence of the adult human who, unlike children and other animals, "presents to himself what is going to happen" (Mead, 1934, p. 119). Only in this sense of reflexively presenting something to himself can a person be said to be genuinely *cons*cious (Mead, 1932, 1934, 1936, 1938). Mere sensory awareness is not knowledge. "Knowledge is a process in conduct that so organizes the field of action that delayed and inhibitive responses may take place. The test

[10] Mead's writing was voluminous and his thought was subtle and complex. I have no space here to do more than extract the essence of his views about self. Even so limited an exercise will inevitably show how widely this topic ramified in his thinking. As far as I can discover, Mead published no books in his lifetime though he published enough articles in learned journals to fill several thick volumes. The *books* which bear his name (Mead, 1932, 1934, 1936, 1938) were all published posthumously from lecture notes collected by his students and colleagues.

of the success of the process of knowledge . . . is found in the discovery or construction of such objects as will mediate our conflicting and checked activities and allow conduct to proceed" (Mead, 1932, p. 68). Mead was obviously referring to James' (1890) distinction between "sciousness" and "*consciousness*," and he might well have quoted James' happy formulation, but he did not. As Mead defined the terms, mind and self are the same thing, at least they have the same origin and are never separated. Consciousness requires two interacting systems, be they physical or biological, and any interaction between two systems is an instance of *sociality* (Mead, 1932). Thus Mead's emphasis on *human* society is, on his own premises, a matter of choice. The not-self, which is distinguished from self and so causes self to be recognized, can be *anything at all* which resists our purposive actions and so causes us to behave reflectively (i.e., *cons*ciously) in the attempt to find or construct objects which will facilitate the continuance and consummations of our purposive acts (Mead, 1934; 1938, p. 150). In purposive activity, *cooperation* refers as much to successful commerce with inanimate objects (tools and materials) as to successful interaction with other humans (Mead, 1938, p. 150). When purposive acts are thwarted, the self is identified first with the defeated element of the act and then with the whole act minus the defeated element. Thus it seeks to reorganize itself and so becomes aware of (constructs or discovers) objects that would otherwise not have existed for it (Mead, 1938).

Thus, mind is a property of organisms. Moreover, its uniquely human reflexive mode requires communication between at least two organisms which are capable of substituting functionally for each other. The most primitive form of communication is the gesture which, according to Darwin (1872), expressed emotion—a function to which Wundt (1900, vol. 1, ch. 2) added the expression of intent; at least, Mead said, an observer can read intent into an animal's gesture without attributing consciousness to the animal (Mead, 1934, part 2). Some gestures, such as facial expressions, can be observed by a witness, but not by the producer himself. But a vocal gesture is available equally to witness and producer, and thus it can evoke the same response from both. When this happens the vocal gesture is a "significant symbol . . . and involves a reference to the self of the individual making it" (Mead, 1934, p. 46). With the appearance of significant symbols, gestures become *language* and instantaneously, simultaneously, mind, meaning, and self-consciousness also appear. It is indifferent, on these grounds, whether meaning is communicated between two individuals or between one individual and himself. If an individual, by a vocal gesture, can evoke the same response in himself as in another then he can put himself in place of the other, can take "the attitude of others toward himself" (Mead, 1934, p. 90). And when he has combined many instances of the attitudes of others toward himself into the concept of the "generalized other," then the "universality and impersonality" of thought are guaranteed (Mead, 1934, p. 90); an individual can see another demand rights and so come to demand them for himself (Mead, 1936); and, even in the absence of a real interlocutor, conversations between the "I" and the "me" can take place—so the problem of how an individual can be an object to himself has been solved (Mead, 1934, 1936, 1938).

After deriving mind (self) from the social nexus Mead turned to consider self-assertion, self-evaluation, and social status. The fullest expression of self includes both its aspects of "I" and of "me." Whether the emphasis is on one or the other of these aspects depends on the situation. In questions of membership in a community, the possession of status and its attendant privileges and obligations, the emphasis is on the responses of the others to the self as object, so "me" is to the fore. But when a person asserts himself against a situation or when he attempts to distinguish himself from others by doing things which he can do better than others, when he attempts to "realize" himself in terms of his unique capacities by asserting his superiority *as the means* of preserving the self—then "I" is emphasized. Though an ordered society is essential to our existence, social organization must allow for individual expression lest we be "thrown back on the sort of structure found in the mob, in which everybody is free to express himself against some hated object of the group" (Mead, 1934, p. 221). Mead asserted that the development from primitive to civilized society depended upon progressively increased opportunities for individual self-expression (Mead, 1934, 1936).

Clearly Mead did not demonstrate that mind and self-awareness arise from communication between two organisms. His assertion that they did so originate is only an hypothesis, and possibly not even a testable one. His restriction of mind to limits almost as narrow as those imposed on it by the introspectionists was a retrograde step for a self-professed behaviorist. His emphasis on behavior was but a timid advance in the direction of objectivity—and there were bolder spirits abroad. But timid or not, his insistence on objectivity led him to emphasize that whatever we mean by "self" belongs to the reflexive mode, that "self" refers to situations where the agent is the object of his own activity. No previous writer had said this so clearly as Mead, and it is his pointing to this fact (rather than his attempt to explain it) for which he ought to be remembered. In his discussion of the relation of the fully developed adult to human society Mead obviously came full circle back to Höffding's (1891) emphasis on society's need of the individual; and in asserting his conception of the practical relations between individual and society Mead was obviously not enabled, by his hypothesis of the social origin of the self, to offer any new suggestions for fruitful research on these problems.

Pragmatism and behaviorism had affected Mead, as we have just seen. They also affected Bertrand Russell who published his lectures on the *Analysis of Mind* (1933) a year before the appearance of Mead's *Mind, Self, and Society* (1934). Russell analyzed the "act psychology" of Brentano (1874), according to which thinking has three components: (1) the *act* of thought which is the same whatever you are thinking about, (2) the *content* which differentiates one occasion of thinking from others, and (3) the object which the content represents. Russell thought the distinction between act and content was unnecessary because the content *is* the thought. Apart from content, nothing appears in consciousness (cf. Wundt, 1878; James, 1890; Mead, 1934). Thus, the "'act' is the ghost of the subject, or what was once the full-blooded soul. It is supposed that thoughts cannot just come and go, but need a person to think them. Now, of course, it is true that thoughts can be collected into bundles, so that one bundle is my thoughts, another is your thoughts, and a third is the thoughts of Mr. Jones. But I think the person is not an ingredient in the single thought: he is rather constituted by relations of the thoughts to each other and to the body" (Russell, 1933, pp. 17–18). And so he wrote that, "James is right in rejecting consciousness as an entity" (Russell, 1933, p. 25).

"Images," that is, memories or invented experiences, in Russell's definition, change according to psychological laws, for example, the laws of association. But events which are outside of any experience, if there are any such events, change according to physical laws, for example, the law of gravitation. The objects studied by physics and by psychology are thus differentiated and defined by the laws which apply to them. But sensations are subject to both physical and psychological laws and so occupy "neutral" ground between the two sciences. In our awareness there is nothing which is not composed of images and sensations, and though these differ in the causal laws which apply to them, they are not intrinsically different. Russell maintained that there is an important kernel of truth in the behaviorist rejection of introspection because the things we can discover by introspection don't differ in any fundamental way from those we can discover by external observation. Introspection may give us much richer immediate awareness of certain mental or physical events than we can get from external observation, perhaps even of observations which theoretically cannot be shared with another. But observation is the superior method when we intend to gain a scientific understanding of the phenomena in question. "Consciousness is a complex and far from universal characteristic of mind" (Russell, 1933, p. 308): it may be a *spectator* at any stage of purposive activity, but it is not *necessary* at any stage.[11] One aspect of the causal laws of behavior is *"mnemic causation"*—that is, the results of past experience: memories, skills, habits, knowledge.[12] Another aspect of psychological causation is *subjectivety* and Russell was at great pains to show just how far subjectivity can be dealt with objectively.

Russell's discussion of subjectivity depends largely on visual experience of objects but, *mutatis mutandis*, the argument holds for any sense modality. Any observation of a light-emitting or reflecting object involves two "places": the "active place" where the object is, and the "passive place" where the percipient (brain, photographic plate, or selenium cell) is. If several different people look at a table, each of them collects a different set of appearances, and according to Russell the table *is* "the set of all those particulars which would naturally be called 'aspects' of the table from different points of view" (Russell, 1933, p. 98). At each passive (percipient) place the particulars are collected together by their similarity and by their relations according to "the laws of perspective and of reflection and diffraction of light" (Russell, 1933, p. 99). By noting the sets of particulars at several passive places and the laws of perspective and of the transmission and reflection of light we can define and identify a physical object and its active place. The collection of all the appearances of different objects at the same passive place defines a "perspective," and if the passive place is a human brain, then the perspective is basic to defining what we mean by one mind. The set of perspectives at the same passive place at different times constitute the *biography* of the place. And the sequence of sets of particulars assigned to a given active place define the *history* of an object. And all these things apply

[11] I use the term "purposive activity" as equivalent to Russell's term "behavior cycle." His description of "behavior cycles" shows clearly that the substitution is legitimate (cf. Russell, 1933, Chapters 2 and 3); it is exactly what others have called "purposive behavior" (Tolman, 1932; Murray, 1938; Morgan, 1943; E. S. Russell, 1945; Pepper, 1958).

[12] Russell got the term "mnemic" in its present application from R. Semon (1904, 1909).

just as well if the passive place is occupied by a brain or by a reel of film in an automatic camera. So Russell concluded: "Physics and psychology are not distinguished by their material. Mind and matter alike are logical constructions. The particulars out of which they are constructed, or from which they are inferred, have various relations, some of which are studied by physics, others by psychology. Broadly speaking, physics groups particulars by their active places, psychology by their passive places" (Russell, 1933, p. 307). Whether or not Russell is correct in all details is of small import. It is important that his argument shows the possibility of dealing with subjectivity in an objective way. It is a powerful argument against those who maintain, as a principle, that objective methods are of no use in studying self.

A cardinal tenet of the behaviorist revolutionaries was that psychologists should pay attention only to strictly observable and manipulable features of organisms and their environments: stimuli and responses; and forget all such "mentalistic" notions as self, purpose, desire, hope, expectation, and sensation, everything that the introspectionists had ever connected with "consciousness." But the intent of the original revolutionary purists was soon overthrown by the ingenuity with which other ardent behaviorists redefined most of the proscribed words in objective terms. Tolman (1932) introduced objective definitions of purpose, thinking, expectancy, and hypotheses, in a book whose title was designed to torment the orthodox behaviorists and which was dedicated to *Mus Norvegicus albinus*—the albino Norway rat! And Hull spoke of intelligence, purpose, symbolic processes (Hull, 1930), and insight (Hull, 1937). When Bertrand Russell got around to analyzing mind (Russell, 1933) he had occasion to remark how "frighteningly successful" the American behaviorists had been in defining old psychological concepts in objective terms.

At the same time that the behaviorist revolt erupted in America, there occurred in Europe the revolt of *Gestalttheorie*. The *Gestalt* theorists were concerned with the "mentalistic" problem of perception. The were determined to extinguish forever the long-held associationist doctrine that perceptions of complex objects are built up by the agglutination of simpler sensory elements. Their problem of *configuration* in a variety of sensory modes had been considered much earlier by Mach (1886) who decided that in some cases *form* is directly apprehended. It was then not so much their problem as it was their new epistemology that distinguished the Gestalt psychologists (Petermann, 1932).

The Gestalt psychologists maintained that the fundamental distinction between figure and ground is given immediately in experi-

ence. Compared with ground, figure has contour and greater differentiation of detail. Objects are segregated from their backgrounds by
the good continuation of their contours, the similarity and connected-
ness of their parts, and by the predictable movement of all of their
parts when any one of them moves ("common fate"). Figure and
ground are segregated in the external world, in the retinal process, and
in the central cortex by *forces* which correspond to the descriptive principles of figure-ground separation. Since a change in any part of an
object produces a change, or a tendency to change, in all other parts,
objects are called *Gestalten*.[13] But the visual appearance of objects
depends on the nature of their backgrounds; and that of backgrounds
on the objects they contain. So the visual field at any moment is itself
a kind of *Gestalt*, a *whole* which can be altered by change in any
one of its parts./The wholes, or *Gestalten*, are not fixed and rigid
entities like the Platonic ideals; they change. But because they change
in accordance with certain dynamic laws adduced by the Gestalt psychologists, they are even in change still Gestalten.

When they expanded their domain from perception to personality
theory, motivation, and social psychology, the Gestalt psychologists
supplemented their original principles with a theory of needs or motives. And they extended their notion of a perceptual field, by analogy,
to a behavioral field. This expansion was attempted by Koffka (1935),
and his conceptions of motivation and of the behavioral field are
largely borrowed from the writings of Kurt Lewin and his students
(Lewin et al., 1926–1937).[14] Koffka introduced the ego (1935, pp. 319
ff.) as quite literally the *center* of the space-coordinate system of the

[13] *Gestalt* is a common German noun which has been translated as configuration, figure, form pattern, or shape. The connotations of these words do not
suggest the special technical implications of the *Gestalttheorie* so psychologists
have learned to understand Gestalt, without translation, as shorthand for the
theory or for types of objects defined by the theory.

[14] Lewin, trained by the Gestalt psychologists, at the time of Koffka's (1935)
publication had been for several years a member of the staff of the *Psychologisches Institut* at the University of Berlin. So Koffka was familiar with the bril-
liant series of papers edited by Lewin under the general title "Untersuchungen
zur Handlungs—und Affekt—Psychologie" and published at irregular intervals
from 1926 to 1937. Some writers have regarded Lewin as a Gestalt psychologist,
but there are strong, though subtle, reasons for deciding that he was not a
Gestaltist—at least not an orthodox one. Lewin was distinguished from the orthodox Gestaltists by his more detailed and stronger emphasis on the person-environ-
ment combination as the basic determinant of action; by his merely tangential
acceptance of the fact of perception without narrowly considering its detailed
processes; and by his total lack of concern with "isomorphism," the main article
of faith in the orthodox *Gestalt* creed (cf. Petermann, 1932).

behavioral field since ego always lies *between* before and behind, right and left, above and below. Our primary awareness of ego is of *I doing, I thinking,* or *I seeing;* and the body or some part of it are always intimately related to the ego. The ego is like any other object in the behavioral environment in that it is bounded, segregated from the environment, and articulated within itself. The parts of the body, for example the hands, are seen as connected by the visual principles of similarity, good continuation, and common fate. But vision functions mainly to make us aware of the segregation and articulation of objects which are *not* ego so, both initially and throughout life, the basic sensory sources of ego-referred experiences are the interoceptors and the proprioceptors. Though ego and body are intimately related, they are not identical. In ways that the body boundaries cannot, the boundaries of the ego may expand and contract anywhere between the limits of withdrawal and ecstasy. Yet through all these changes the ego is segregated from the behavioral environment, so in the very fact of its changing boundaries the ego determines what is non-ego and thus the ego and the behavioral environment interact to define each other.

True to his Lewinian sources, Koffka wrote that the ego is organized into layers. Within each layer are subdivisions corresponding to various organized intentional acts. In the layers near the surface the acts represented are those which momentary environmental exigencies demand of the organism, acts corresponding to "quasi-needs" (Koffka, 1935; Lewin, 1926, 1935). The core of the ego is the *self* which represents acts corresponding to *genuine* needs. With respect to their influence on behavior the various quasi-needs and genuine needs are not fixed in any rigid hierarchy. Their relative influence shifts with the demands of the situation. But in a relatively stable environment a person usually operates in response to a genuine need; that is, he is trying to do something which is uniquely his own, something that belongs to the *self*.

By the time Koffka (1935) wrote his systematic treatise the American behaviorists had settled on a more or less well defined list of innately prepotent drives or needs: hunger, thirst, sex, elimination, sleep, and thermoregulation. The stimulus-response theories of behavior (S-R theories) used the process of learning to derive complex human purposive activity, such as seeking for prestige, power, affiliation, and intellectual creativity, from the small number of organic needs. With the success of their campaign against the associationist theory, and with their influence everywhere on the increase, the Gestalt psychologists opened a second front against the behaviorists,

specifically on the issue of the nature of human motivation. Their battle cry was "wholeness." We must consider the *whole* person, the
whole organism, the *whole* situation. This appeal was reiterated (and
still is) by many writers on the fringes of psychology in the manner
of a slogan—without specification of what data we should collect in
order to describe the whole person in the whole situation and test
assertions about either of them. Among the Gestaltists themselves
motivational theory took the character of a special form of reduction-
ism—we can be sure we are considering the whole man if we examine
the one motive that really makes him go. All the particulate "so-called
drives" are either tangential responses to the momentary demands of
the environment or else they are characteristic of a "sick organism"
whose activities are reduced to the mere holding operation of self-
preservation (Goldstein, 1939). According to Goldstein, ". . . we have
to assume only one drive, the drive of self-actualization . . ." (1939,
p. 17, italics in original). The various actions which become outstanding or central in the organism's behavior under different conditions
give the impression of independently existing drives, but they are
really only actions which occur in accordance with the various capacities belonging to the nature of the organism, and these capacities are
being used instrumentally for the single aim of self-actualization
(Goldstein, 1939). Views recognizably similar to this were advanced
by Allport (1943, 1946, 1955). Fromm (1941, 1955), Frondizi (1953),
Maslow (1950), Rogers (1955), and Snygg and Combs (1949).

The "self psychologists" had not died. They had only become
mute; and the developments in Gestalt psychology gave them their
voice again. Some of them declared that Gestalt psychology, by presenting a system where behavior depends on both self and environment, had solved all the problems preliminary to a self psychology.
The self develops its potentialities by assimilation from its environment, so ". . . the larger whole converges into a self . . . a seat of
consciousness and a channel of self-expression of the cosmos" (Josey,
1935, p. 53). Lundholm, who drew his inspiration from sources other
than the Gestaltists, nevertheless makes the same point as Koffka did
about the variability of the boundaries of the self (Lundholm, 1940):
his references are to Mach (1886) and to anecdotes from his own
experience. Lundholm also espoused Sherrington's (1941) dualistic division of nature into energy systems and finite minds. The latter are
the observers to which experience is presented and there is no place
for them, alas, in Köhler's (1938) system (Lundholm, 1946). Lundholm agreed with Sherrington (1941) and McDougall (1923, 1933)
that we get our impressions of self most prominently from acts of

striving (Lundholm, 1940), a proposition that accords with Koffka's (1935) notion that the ego is revealed in awareness as *I* acting, and which was concurred in by Allport (1937, 1955), Frondizi (1953), and Litwinski (1951). Lundholm and Sherrington were at fault, I think, to the extent that they urged a substantive dualism of mental and non-mental events in the universe. Previous sections of this chapter have shown that dualism of this kind is irrelevant to scientific knowledge and if it was for Köhler's taking essentially this position that Lundholm criticized him, he might well have criticized Pierce, James, Höffding, Mead, Freud, and a host of others. It is significant that critics of this kind have advanced no programs of research which have added to our knowledge, though most of those who have ignored the "problem" of metaphysical dualism have produced vast quantities of important data. Most of the latter have asserted that we are indeed aware of ourselves, though this awareness involves no mysterious "immediacy," but comes from the same sources as our knowledge of things not ourselves (e.g., Koffka, 1935; Köhler, 1938; Murphy, Murphy, and Newcomb, 1937; Murphy, 1947; Singer, 1924).

Self-knowledge may arise from the same sources as does our knowledge of other things, but the chief *occasions* for self-knowledge are situations in which we are engaged in some kind of striving; that is, in attempts to achieve goals. The "self psychologists" had always emphasized this aspect of self-awareness, and no later psychologist emphasized it more than Murray (1938), Allport (1937), and Murphy (1947), the three leading constructors, among academic psychologists, of modern "personality theories." For all of them, and for many other personality theorists as well, the complex motivated behavior of the normal human adult was a central problem, perhaps *the* central problem, in their systematic thinking. Allport's thinking about this aspect of motivation has important links with the history of general motivation theory in this century, so we will pay some special attention to it here.

Allport's description of personality (Allport, 1937) depended heavily on "traits" which he described as systems of motives. He assumed that purposive behavior was to a large extent determined by innately given tendencies, which humans shared with other animals, to respond adaptively to certain organic disturbances arising from deficits or other "imbalances" within the organism. Thus, he accepted the general list of organic needs or "viscerogenic" drives (White, 1959) advanced by the behaviorists. But, Allport noted, though these drives might account for behavior in infants and children, they could hardly account for typical adult behavior. The directed behavior of children is mostly reactive, responsive to deficits of what the environment has not provided or to noxious stimuli from the environment, and it thus has an episodic, opportunistic character which is less noticeable in adults. From infancy to maturity, said Allport, motivational systems change in the direction of definiteness and consistency. The mature personality has ". . . sophisticated and stable interests . . . and a predictable style of conduct" (Allport, 1937). Adult motives are "infinitely varied, self-sustaining, contemporary systems" (Allport, 1937). The S-R theorists attempt to explain these facts by appeal to secondary reinforcement or to some other principle according to which the energy for all activities derives from the narrowly biological directive mechanisms of nourishment, thermoregulation, and reproduction. Allport admitted the *historical* coupling of these biological drives with typically adult motives, but he denied that the coupling lasted forever. There is a *détente*, after which the adult motives operate on their own power: they have become, in Allport's famous phrase, "functionally autonomous." We have seen that Höffding (1891) had similar notions, and Woodworth (1918) had asserted that habitual or learned activities, which serve originally as the instrumental mechanisms for stilling the native organic drives, may later be exercised for no discoverable reason except the pleasure in performing the actions themselves; that is, "mechanisms may become drives" (Woodworth, 1918). Tolman apparently had something like this in mind when he wrote that ". . . acquired specifications of ultimate goals or . . . acquired adherences to specific types of means-objects, . . . often set up in their own right . . ." (Tolman, 1932). But it is Allport's label, "functional autonomy," which has served to characterize this problem for contemporary psychologists.

The problem which Allport and the others tried to solve by appeals to the notion of "functional autonomy" is a curiously difficult one, probably because of the way it was stated. The fact is that no one has advanced a genuinely satisfactory description of the means by which mature adult motives can become functionally autonomous of their viscerogenic origins. Seward (1963) argued that the problem of functional autonomy is not a genuine problem after all, that the complex motives of the human adult can be explained by adding to the list of natively given motives a small set of equally unlearned "exogenous motives" for motor activity and sensory stimulation. The idea of such motives is not exactly new. Woodworth (1918) had suggested innately autonomous activity motivation; Warden (1931) and his colleagues had described an "exploratory drive" in the albino rat; and Murphy (1947) had argued for the possible existence, and the conceptual usefulness, of unlearned motives to explore and to manipulate. What was new at the time of Seward's writing (1963) was the *evidence* that motives of curiosity, exploration, gratuitous sensory gratification, manipulation, and general activity operate independently of their instrumentality in satisfying viscerogenic needs; that such motives, in the absence of aroused viscerogenic needs, can support learning which is at least as highly resistant to extinction as that based on hunger or thirst drives (cf. Harlow, 1953; Harlow, Harlow, and Meyer, 1950; Schiller, 1957; Berlyne, 1950, 1955, 1957, 1958). With the new set of native drives added to the previous list, Seward derived all the types of motivation which Allport said were characteristic of the human adult, and so he concluded that the notion of "functional autonomy," in Allport's sense, is superfluous.

What Seward called the "new look" in motivation has been used by various generalists inside of psychology (White, 1959, 1963; McCall, 1963) and outside of psychology (Barnett, 1963). Barnett (1963) referred to it in his general discussion of the changing conception of "instinct" in the biological sciences. McCall (1963) used it as a basis for a new "self-psychological" taxonomy of human motives. White (1959) argued that the experimental data on the new motives was paralleled in many important respects by the increasing interest in "ego psychology" among psychoanalysts. In the same paper White argued that motives for self-gratification and dealing effectively with the environment could be subsumed under "effectance" motivation which aims at achieving "competence." In a later writing (White, 1963) he used the concepts of "effectance" and "competence" in a thoroughgoing attack on the orthodox Freudian views of motivational development, and as the basis for proposing a new way to attack the problems which currently preoccupy the psychoanalytic "ego psychologists."

McDougall's (1920) objection to Woodworth's (1918) formulation of the notion of functional autonomy, that habits and skills do not seem to acquire additional driving power as they improve, led Allport to modify Woodworth's formulation in the direction of the self-actualizing position: perfect talents and automatized habits do not have as much driving power as habits-in-the-making; becoming is more energetic than being (Allport, 1937, 1955). In any case, Allport repeatedly insisted that he was trying to account for the uniqueness of the motivations of individuals and since individualized motives do not develop apart from experience it is better to link their development to learning (Allport, 1940) than to an instinct theory, even so subtle an instinct theory as McDougall's, as Bertocci (1940) urged.

In learning, or any other motivated behavior, the rewards and punishments required by the "law of effect" are not the prime conditions for learning. It is not a question of satisfying *this* or that drive—the *ego* must be satisfied. "Ego involvement is . . . a condition of total participation of the self—as knower, as organizer, as observer, as status seeker, and as socialized being" (Allport, 1943). Honesty is not specific to opportunities to be honest, but to the aroused motives of the individual (Allport, 1937, 1943); in ego-involved conditions confidence in ones' own performance is rated higher than otherwise; opinions about which one has intense feeling are strongly held; statements about one's self or one's beliefs are designed to avoid losing the favorable opinion of others; and things are better learned and remembered if they are consistent with the system of beliefs to which the individual is committed (Allport, 1943). This outline of Allport's views is matched very closely in Lecky's theory of "self-consistency" (Lecky, 1945).

The fact that the new self psychologists (e.g., Allport) were able to argue substantive matters of learning theory and motivation with the heirs of the behaviorists made the latter pay attention, and finally to agree that there might be something to the idea of self after all. Hilgard (1949) reviewed the history of writing about the "defense mechanisms" from Freud (1900) to Symonds (1949) and concluded that the "mechanisms" of defence against anxiety, and of self-deception in the interest of bolstering self-esteem, demand the use of the notion of self. He rejected the idea of returning to the introspection method to study self and proposed a broader view of what he called the "inferred self," a concept in terms of which we might comprehend continuity, permanence, or persistence of patterns or motives and attitudes throughout a person's life history; the important human motives being "interpersonal both in origin and expression" (Hilgard, 1949). Sarbin's "epistemogenic theory" starts with the assumption that "behavior is organized around cognitive structures" which result from an organism's responses to present objects or memories of objects, including one's own body and one's beliefs and statuses. The Gestalt influence is evident in Sarbin's assertion that cognitive structures contain substructures ("empirical selves") whose properties are determined by "the total interbehavioral field of which the substructures are a part" (Sarbin, 1952). "The self" as a cognitive structure develops in the "direction from low-order inferences about simple perceptions to higher-order inferences about complex cognitions," these changes being produced by organic maturation and by learning. But both maturation and learning are limited in their effects by the properties of the cognitive structures at any moment: previous overlearning may have resulted in "resistance to dedifferentiation," so that a given structure cannot be made to coalesce with others to form larger wholes; and the structures may differ in breadth, i.e., their ability to accommodate few or many dissimilar perceptions. Sarbin described a developmental sequence of five stages beginning, at the earliest, with the "somatic self," and progressing through the "receptor-effector self," "the primitive construed self," "the introjecting-extrojecting self," to "the social self"—the recognition of roles. In later stages of development the various empirical selves are "semi-independent substructures which later become overlaid with substructures of the social self—the roles," and the processes of development can lead to fixation or to shifting emphasis on some one of the empirical selves rather than the others. Hebb (1950) emphasized that the so-called higher processes need no longer be rejected by behaviorists and that, until it includes the "esoteric" problem of the self, experimental psychology will continue to be inadequate in clinical matters and in dealing with the general problem of thinking. Hebb believed that evidence is accumulating to show that there is a mental construct or set of mediating processes arising out of experience, in part consisting of the so-called body image, in part what seems to be a pure fantasy of an immaterial self which in certain circumstances separates itself from the body. This is a *real* fantasy which affects behavior. By way of illustration Hebb referred to the break-off phenomenon experienced by aircraft pilots at high altitudes (Clark and Graybiel, 1957) which involves self-awareness and the subject's construct of personal identity; the disturbances of the body image sometimes observed during extreme sensory deprivation (e.g., Bexton, Heron, and Scott, 1954); and the phantom limb phenomena reviewed by Simmel (1956).

The terminological confusion still persists. Earlier writers had spoken of ego as the subjective knower and of self as object when the knower or agent reflects about his knowing or acting. Koffka did not make that distinction, but he distinguished the self as the core of the ego, less extensive than the ego and involving more important motives. Allport (1943) specifically used self and ego as equivalent terms. Chein argued that self and ego are not identical because we are directly aware of the self but not of ego functions, "such as repression or self-actualization" (Chein, 1944). Chein adopted Brentano's old distinction between the *object* of awareness and the *content* of awareness. An important *object* in self-awareness is the body, but the *content* of awareness is the self, and as such, the two are "phenomena of different orders" (Chein, 1944, p. 307). The ego, according to Chein, is essentially a structure of motives of self-interest (e.g., dependency, self-preservation, and prestige). In this sense, the self is central and, "from an item, in a universe of observable items, it becomes a supreme value and the core of an evaluative system" (Chein, 1944, p. 311). According to Chein, there are motives which are not polarized on the self, so the total personality is larger than and includes the ego structure. But, according to Bertocci (1945), the "psychological self" is equated with what Allport called "personality" and ego is a sub-part of it. If, as Allport said (Allport, 1943), the ego develops and changes then we need, said Bertocci, a psychological agent which persists throughout ego changes, something which can be said to *have* an ego or a personality or an experience. This is the psychological self, and though it too changes, Bertocci is not at all clear on how it accounts for persistence and serves as the relatively immutable possessor or subject of experience. The psychological self can be defined by only two functions, knowing and wanting. The activities of the ego in directed behavior must be evaluated but they cannot evaluate themselves; the psychological self evaluates them. "Generally speaking, . . . the ego will be the core or cluster of values . . . with which the self identifies its 'security' or success at the time. When the ego is involved, the self's value citadel is in question, its investment in life is at stake. That is why what is relevant in the ego produces tensions in the self; for the conflict with or threat to the ego is really conflict with or threat to the self's prized achievement (ego)" (Bertocci, 1945, p. 96). Hallowell (1959) synthesized all these notions from the viewpoint of anthropology. Self, he said, is a phenomenal datum, but ego is a construct. The ego construct refers to a set of functions connected with the use of attention, perception, thinking, and judgment in determining adjustment to the outer world in the interest of inner needs, choice, decision, delay, or postponement of action. Ego functions involve tool-making and tool-using in man, and as such, the rudiments of these functions can be studied in lower organisms and in human infants. Culture, the uniquely human characteristic, requires language for its transmission, but culture can only arise in groups that are large enough and differentiated enough with respect to roles to be able to function as a *moral* order. And a moral order requires, in turn, the capacity for self-objectification, self-evaluation of one's conduct.

In spite of all the differences of opinion about the meaning of "self" and "ego" it is noteworthy that many writers have emphasized in one way or another that what they mean by either of these terms is somehow intimately connected with motivated, or directed, or purposive behavior. This was certainly true of James (1890), Höffding (1891), Freud (1940), Allport (1943), Chein (1944); and it was also true of Litwinski (1951) who spoke of "the self that is flattered, that glorifies itself openly and frankly, that is proud of its acquisitions or achievements and that consequently likes itself" (Litwinski, 1951, p. 247); and of Frondizi who said, "The self is revealed in its action. . . . Its *esse* is equivalent to its *facere*" (Frondizi, 1953, p. 147). As we have seen, many writers went further and reduced all normal human motivation to the single drive of self-actualization. Among the latter, Rogers and Fromm emphasize what can go wrong when the environment frustrates the self-actualizing motive. According to Rogers (1955) psychotherapy consists in providing a disturbed person with a social atmosphere in which he can express, and come to accept, all of his feelings and impulses. In such an environment the self will spontaneously grow toward increasing health and strength, more zestful activity, and better relations with other people. Fromm was less sanguine. Man's psychological health depends on complete freedom to realize his abilities in action, but this freedom is conditional. "Unless he belongs somewhere, unless his life has some meaning and direction, he would feel like a particle of dust and be overcome by his individual insignificance. He would not be able to relate himself to any system which would give meaning and direction to his life, he would be filled with doubt, and this doubt eventually would paralyze his ability to act—that is, to live" (Fromm, 1941, p. 22). In this situation a man has two alternatives. Either he can relate to the world in "the spontaneity of love and productive work," (Fromm, 1941, p. 23), or else he can choose to submit to authoritarianism, lapse into destructiveness, or into automaton conformity. One of the latter three alternatives is the fate of all too many individuals because contemporary society is sick. Though it has freed men *from* restrictions of caste, religion, ignorance, and penury, society has not freed them *to* engage in the fullest possible realization of their own capacities. If the overt demands of authority do not make for indiviual restrictions, then the anonymous authority of public opinion and the market will do so. Contemporary character structure is characterized by *alienation* because society is too big for human compass. "We live in figures and abstractions; since nothing is concrete, nothing is real" (Fromm, 1955, p. 120).

If we attempt to assess how far these various currents and crosscurrents of opinion about self have taken us toward scientific knowledge, we must conclude that they have not taken us very far at all.

The most productive group of researchers have been those who deal with the "phenomenological" notion which they call the "self-concept." This term was introduced in its most widespread usage by Victor Raimy (1943) but it received its greatest currency at the hands of Snygg and Combs (1949). Snygg and Combs said that since they wanted to develop a method for predicting the behavior of individuals in specific situations they would have to abandon the objective methods of general psychology because these methods lead only to "normative" predictions on the basis of persistence forecasting without specifying causal relations. In developing their method they assumed that all behavior is dependent on the actor's personal frame of reference, i.e., his phenomenal field, which is the universe as it appears to him at any moment. The phenomenal field is the cause of behavior. Given a description of behavior the phenomenal field can be inferred, and given a description of the phenomenal field behavior can be predicted. The phenomenal field changes with changing needs and activities related to needs, the nature of the change depending on the condition of the field at any moment. In this sense, the field is self-regulating. Throughout its changes the phenomenal field is always organized on the analogy that figure is to ground as the focus of the field is to the field's margin. The phenomenal self is a special segregated part of the phenomenal field: ". . . *all those parts of the phenomenal field which the individual experiences as part or characteristic of himself*" (Snygg and Combs, 1949, p. 58, italics in original). The fundamental aim of all behavior is the preservation and enhancement of the phenomenal self, which is the individual's only frame of reference, his only reality. A further subdivision of the phenomenal self is the self-concept, which "*includes those parts of the phenomenal field which the individual has differentiated as definite and fairly stable characteristics of himself*" (Snygg and Combs, 1949, p. 112, italics in original).

Since all behavior is a function of an individual's phenomenal field, and the understanding of individuals is prerequisite to the study of groups, it follows that diagnosis and research are the same thing. For diagnosis, we need the objective facts and the phenomenological facts. Since it is impossible to get all the facts, we must select those that are most relevant for the purpose at hand. Objective facts are not all relevant—only those which the individual has differentiated and which have meaning for him in terms of his present needs, which is to say, the only relevant facts are phenomenal ones. The best way to get at these is to ask the subject. The phenomenal facts, S's view of the situation, are: meanings of certain external events, definition of phenomenal self and self-concept, goals differentiated by the individual to satisfy his needs, and the techniques he uses in attempting to reach his goals. Taking the subject's word for these involves difficulties; but these can be overcome if we "supplement" S's statement by special techniques: informal conversations about self, use of autobiography, use of tests and questionnaires, inferences from inferred behavior (needs ↔ behavior), use of controlled observations, controlled behavior situations, expressive movement, conversations about others, projective tests, play diagnosis, and case histories. Phenomenological conclusions are accurate if they are accompanied by feelings of subjective certainty, if they conform with other known facts, survive mental manipulations, have predictive power, achieve social agreement (especially with the opinions of experts), and display internal consistency.

In 1961 Ruth Wylie published a critical review of the research literature on the "self-concept," a literature to which she herself has contributed. The review included over four hundred titles and Wylie's critical acumen has performed a momentous service in revealing the utter bankruptcy of it all. Phenomenologists are those who "stress . . . the role of the conscious self-concept in determining a person's behavior" (Wylie, 1961). "It is implicitly or explicitly assumed by all theorists that the self-concept is not entirely 'realistic,' and that lack of 'realism' may have psychodynamic significance and important behavioral consequences" (Wylie, 1961, p. 5). Wylie distinguished between phenomenal aspects of the self-concept, which are somewhere on a continuum of conscious clarity; and non-phenomenal aspects of which the individual is, or is supposed to be, unconscious; and she stated that the question about how consistently and purely phenomenological any theorist can be has not been faced squarely by any of the system builders. Moreover, "As yet there is no systematic plan in phenomenological personality theories for establishing fruitful behavior categories" (Wylie, 1961, p. 11)—they have not even decided what they want to study! Wylie concluded, after analyzing the various studies in terms of validity and reliability of measuring instruments, and the adequacy of research designs for guarding against artifacts, that there is precious little of value in all this work: the total of substantive findings is very small relative to the amount of effort expended. This, she thought, is due in part to "scientific shortcomings of all these personality theories which emphasize constructs concerning the self." These constructs "have been stretched to cover so many inferred cognitive and motivational processes that their utility for analytic and predictive purposes has been greatly diminished" (Wylie, 1961, p. 317). Thus, we have the choice of either abandoning these constructs and hypotheses as scientifically sterile, or improving them, by attending to the *more molecular constructs.* Self-actualization, self-differentiation, and self-consistency have not led to enlightening research, but self-acceptance or self-esteem, *especially when they refer to specific attributes,* seem to have "yielded more manageable and fruitful research problems" (Wylie, 1961, p. 318). And at last Wylie wrote: "If . . . self theorists were to seek connections with general behavior theories, the 'tough-minded' approach could be helpful in making the needed reformulations in hypotheses involving the self" (Wylie, 1961, p. 321).

Are the theories and the overblown axiom systems scientifically sterile? Let us abandon them. Are the concepts stretched to cover so much that they point to no distinctions at all? Let us reduce their coverage. In the remainder of this chapter, I intend to set forth a statement which will both abandon theory and restrict the usage of the word self. I think we should start by abandoning the definite article. We will not ask what is "the self" but what do we mean by the word "self." The aim is to try to describe something objective to which the word "self" can apply, something about which we can ask questions of fact. If we answer a sufficient number of questions of fact we may begin to see the outlines of a theory of self. At any rate this seems to be the one strategy which has not been tried. All the extant theories of self are sterile from the point of view of scientific knowledge.

SELF AS AN OBJECT: A PROPOSAL

The essence of an object is its publicity, its openness to observation. The observation need not actually occur, as long as it is possible *in principle.* The brain of a human being is not often observed; its status as an object derives from the confirmable expectation that, under certain conditions, we *could* observe it. The *ease* of observing anything has nothing to do with its objective status. In English, when we use a noun or group of words with the functions of a noun, we usually intend to convey that it is the name or label for an object. The most fruitful question we can ask about a word when the nature or existence of its supposed referent is doubtful is this: "What is it that I can observe which makes it necessary (or convenient) to use this separate label, this word, or its equivalent symbols?" Take the word "mind" and ask that question. If you begin your answer with a list of conscious events or processes which you can experience, than you are heading into one of the most densely populated blind alleys in history. I cannot observe your consciousness as you experience it, nor can you observe mine. If you say that you infer my consciousness from observing that we are superficially similar and that we must therefore be alike throughout, you are simply attempting an inference from a single instance which, logically, is very bad form. The pitfalls of such a procedure are obvious. The only things you and I can observe about each other are the actions we perform and the conditions under which they occur—that is, we can observe *behavior,* and *only* behavior. Furthermore, we can make experiments on behavior. The fact that it may be very difficult to do this is irrelevant; what matters is that it is possible *in principle.*

The late Edgar A. Singer, Jr., in his book *"Mind as Behavior"* (Singer, 1924) wrote, "Mind is not something inferred from behavior, it *is* behavior." We can learn about mind or minds by observing the behavior of organisms, not casually or informally, but by the most rigorous rules of experimentation. A scientific observer, Singer said, can know a person better than that person knows himself. And many have had the experience of recognizing that another person knew them better, in some respects, than they knew themselves. How can one best know oneself? By the same means that he can best know others. Singer wrote, "The self is of such a nature that it can very well be its own other." Thus, he noted, the principles of observation in psychology are the same for every observer, and it is only an accident if the observer and the observed are the same organism.

In the following paragraphs I intend to set forth a description of what I believe we can take the word "self" to mean in its minimal sense. The use of abstract symbols is only for brevity of expression; it should not imply that an axiomatization, in the manner of formal logic, is intended here. Nor do these remarks constitute a *definition* of self. The formulation of definitions should be put off until we have enough data to appreciate the structure of the relevant phenomena. The argument is intended to suggest that a type of reflexive relation is basic to a definition of self. But whether self *is* a reflexive relation or is some *function of* a reflexive relation cannot be decided now. It does seem clear, however, that the meaning of "self" is not to be found in the notion of *formal identity* as that notion is defined in logic and mathematics. The discussion contains enough detail to suggest that if we accept such a reduced view of the basic meaning of "self," then we are not thereby necessarily condemned to ignoring important aspects of behavior which are generally accepted as related to "self."

Now any organism, X, can observe another organism, Y; and X can perform many other operations with Y as object, operations such as judging, measuring, classifying, striking, feeding, loving, hating, remembering, or longing for the presence of. If we designate any operation by the symbol "*o*" then all the cases where X is the agent and Y is the object of X's activities can be compactly summarized by the symbol $(X \ldots o \ldots Y)$. If we agree that it is only an accident that the observing agent and the object of the observation are one and the same organism, then we can represent that situation by the formula $(X \ldots o \ldots X)$. Situations of the form $(X \ldots o \ldots Y)$ and $(X \ldots o \ldots X)$ are both open to inspection by a third observer, Z; so if the former designates operations of one organism on another and the latter is the referent for "self," then self is just as objective as anything else. Furthermore, self is not an *entity* in this view; it is a *relation* of the form $(X \ldots o \ldots X)$, or perhaps self is some not yet determined aspect or property of that relation.

Not all operations (*o*) will fit both the self and non-self relations. Such operations as "jumping on from above," "increasing the distance between," or "clasping the two right hands" are simply impossible in $(X \ldots o \ldots X)$ for all their commonness in $(X \ldots o \ldots Y)$, so the possible domain of "*o*" is different in the two situations. If it should turn out, as seems likely, that every "*o*" possible in $(X \ldots o \ldots X)$ is also possible in $(X \ldots o \ldots Y)$ then the domain of $(X \ldots o \ldots X)$ is smaller than that of $(X \ldots o \ldots Y)$.

There are several classes of self-report, distinguished by their common linguistic forms, whose ability to fit the $(X \ldots o \ldots X)$ paradigm should be explored:

1. *Authorship*, as when someone says "I did that," fits the formula if "*o*" is made to stand for "reports that . . . was done by."

2. *Ownership*, represented verbally by "That is mine," fits the formula if "*o*" is made to stand for "states that an object bears the relation of property to." Though this ultimately requires a suitable definition of the word property, that definition will not be attempted here. It is enough to note that in practical affairs there is sufficient agreement about property to permit cooperation between individual persons or groups.

3. *Role identity*, as when a person says "I am a teacher," fits the formula by letting "*o*" stand for "reports that a member of the class teacher is."

4. *Reputation*, as when a person says "I heard John say that I am a liar," requires that another person's action be taken into the formula. Thus: $(X \ldots o \ldots Y \ldots o \ldots X)$. Formally, this comes down to the same thing as $(X \ldots o \ldots X)$ and it was in anticipation of such cases that the ellipses were introduced. It

does not matter how many organisms or operations intervene between the initial and terminal Xs, as long as one of the "os" stands for an operation by X. Thus, in the example of reputation, $(o \ldots Y \ldots o)$ is a condensation of the complex statement "reports that Y attributed membership in the class 'liar' to."

5. *Being the object of another's action,* as in the statement "Peter punched me," requires a format similar to that for reputation, and $(o \ldots Y \ldots o)$ stands for "reports that Y punched."

6. *Body identity* gives a bit of difficulty to the formula if we are to avoid linguistic habits of expression that suggest hypostatization of self as an entity. The expression, "That is my hand," and other locutions for "o" such as asserting that the hand can "be controlled by," "the hand belongs to," or is "part of," or "pertains to" or is "connected to" all suggest hypostatization. Perhaps a way out appears only by reversion to the view of Hume (1793) and Mach (1886) that the elements of experience constitute the "I," not the other way around. Mach argued that there is a certain complex of experiences that go together and come to be recognized as the body. This set of experiences can be regarded as a "class" in the usual sense applied when discussing concepts. Thus, the representation of body identity in our formula is possible without hypostatization if "o" is made to stand for "reports that a body member is a member of the class."

There is no ideally perfect criteria for knowledge, attribution, or credibility when they appear as "o" in $(X \ldots o \ldots X)$. But the common human criteria will do: in principle, the o in $(X \ldots o \ldots X)$ is just as adequate as it is in $(X \ldots o \ldots Y)$ or $(Y, Z, W, \ldots o \ldots X)$. In principle, our objective knowledge of ourselves is just as good as, certainly no better than, our knowledge of anything else. And in principle, another observer, Y, can know $(X \ldots o \ldots X)$ as well as he knows anything else. Either in $(X \ldots o \ldots X)$ or in $[Y \ o \ (X \ldots o \ldots X)]$, the os, when they stand for knowledge, are all equally valid. The argument is not that we have perfect knowledge, but that if we can know anything at all, we can know the objective referent for self and we can find out the functions that are peculiar to it.

The formal statements of role identity and body awareness appeal to class membership. The classes are different. The classes in role identity contain elements which share only a common function. They *must* each necessarily have different space and time coordinates to an extent defined by the limits of the race. Caesar belongs as much to the class "husband" as any married man now living. With parts of the intact body, it is otherwise. They cannot differ more in their space coordinates than the fullest extent of their reach from a fixed center, nor can they differ very much in time of arrival at a given point. In terms of *Gestalttheorie* they share (with relatively slight deviations) a common fate. Furthermore, within the class of body parts, each part is unique. For each body there is only *one* left hand, *one* right eye, *one* skull, etc. For many purposes, "the hand" may designate the class of human hands, but when X takes his friend by "the hand," the hands (the taker and the taken) referred to are unique; one is reportable by X as a member of the class X, and the other by Y as a member of the class Y. The class does the defining of its absolutely unique members, which is not so in other cases, where common features of the members define the class.

It would be appropriate to close this discussion by suggesting some fruitful lines of study. The way of defining the objective referent for the word self which has been outlined is not totally new or original with this author. It is basic to the operation, quite common in recent psychology, of asking a subject to indicate, for each of a large number of statements about behavior, the extent to which each describes (a) the "average" person, (b) the subject as he actually operates, and (c) the subject as he wishes he would operate. Clearly the latter two of these are ($X \ldots o \ldots X$) situations where the operation is "endorsing descriptions of." But this method is not often applied experimentally; that is, where the investigator controls and manipulates the conditions under which the subject performs his operations. One way to study self objectively would be to isolate a well defined bit of behavior which can be subjected to some operation such as "describing," "explaining," or "evaluating," and compare for each subject (X) the descriptions, explanations, or evaluations for that behavior, operations which we will get him to perform both in ($X \ldots o \ldots Y$) and in ($X \ldots o \ldots X$) with everything but that difference held constant. For example, suppose X estimates the likelihood that Y will succeed in achieving a certain goal by his own effort; how will that estimate compare with the one he gives when he himself tries to achieve the same goal? Under what conditions can we make the difference large or small?

Another experimental strategy would be to study the relative values X places on objects he acquires as gifts from Y and those he gains by his own efforts. In another class of experiments we could observe how much energy X will spend at a task when Y is to reap the benefits, as compared with X's getting the payoff. This can be extended to a study of the conditions under which X will choose to cooperate with Y rather than choosing to work alone. We can also study the conditions under which X's behavior conforms to that of Y.

Work on these problems has already been done, but there is not enough of it; and few of those who write most prolifically about "self" ever refer to it. They are too committed to the dogma of the unanalyzable, "global" self to bother with questions of fact. The data reported in this book relate to self-evaluation and in the next two chapters I have attempted to make clear what the terms "value" and "self-evaluation" mean in our research.

Chapter 2
VALUING

It is necessary to survey the domain of phenomena to which "value," "valuing," "evaluation," and related terms apply before we can talk sensibly about self-evaluation. It was not necessary to make this chapter as long as the one on "self" and "ego" because there is already a clear tradition which links value and the process of valuation to the fundamental facts and modes of thought current in general psychology. This tradition, including the conflicts within it, can be seen in the writings of Christian von Ehrenfels, John Dewey, and Stephen C. Pepper.

Ehrenfels was a member of the Austrian group of philosopher-psychologists who were active in the fifty years, 1875–1925.[1] The present account of his value theory is based upon the analysis by Howard O. Eaton (Eaton, 1930). By contrast with Meinong, another of the Austrian value philosophers, Ehrenfels was a subjectivist or introspectionist interested in descriptive or genetic psychology. Though he occasionally relied on Brentano's "inner perception" to support the more precarious parts of his theory, Ehrenfels went beyond Brentano's psychology because he was interested not merely in descriptive psychology but in its dynamic genetic aspects. He sought casual explanations for purposive (goal-oriented) behavior, choice of goals and means, "willing," and "striving." Though his writings sometimes have a modern behavioristic flavor we cannot understand him if we forget that, like all introspectionists, he took the domain of psychology to be the phenomena of consciousness. Thus, "ideas" are the fundamental terms of his argument. His first published work (Ehrenfels, 1887) was a study of the nature of desire in which he attempted to provide the psychological basis for the value-utility theory of the Austrian economists Menger and von Weiser. This theory was an elaborate hedonic calculus derived from premises of Bernoulli and Bentham.

[1] For an account of Ehrenfels' relation to the work of Franz Brentano and Oswald Külpe, see E. G. Boring (1950).

Ehrenfels' major premise about values is that they are the products, not the causes, of desires. Desire, in turn, is based on feelings which are either pleasant or unpleasant in various degrees. But the feelings alone do not constitute desire:

1. The origin as well as the strength of the desire will be conditioned solely by the state of feeling which the individual experiences upon the realization of the existence or the non-existence of the to-be-desired object. The influence of the faculty of thought upon the desire is restricted to the calling up of the idea of the desirable object, as well as to the suggesting of the means whereby it may be attained, and the judgment that these means will lead to the object.

2. This conclusion contains no tautology, inasmuch as the inner core of desire is not to be found in the feeling, but rather a desire lies in the realm of the possible, which exhibits no characteristic in common with the simple feeling of pleasure and displeasure. And just as little is the feeling a product of the desire (Ehrenfels, 1897, vol. 1, p. 23, cited by Eaton, 1930, p. 120).

"What we call desire is nothing else than the idea—which supplies the basis of a relative enhancement of happiness—of the inclusion or exclusion of some object in or out of the causal nexus surrounding the momentary, concrete ego idea" (Ehrenfels, 1897, pp. 248 ff., cited by Eaton, 1930, p. 173, italicized by Eaton). Desire, then, refers only to those ideas of objects which are associated with a relative increase in happiness and which are judged as real objects in that they are in the causal nexus of the ego; i.e., they can be influenced by our actions or they have an influence upon our actions.

Desires persist because of the influences which account for the persistence of any ideas in consciousness. All initial stimulus impressions leave residues in the mind, residues which association theorists have usually referred to as "traces," and which Ehrenfels called "unconscious dispositions" for the recurrence of ideas. All memory dispositions weaken with the passage of time, but those which were initiated by more vivid and intense sensory impressions persist longer than others. Furthermore, if two ideas are similar or have occurred simultaneously, the stronger of the two may facilitate the recall of the weaker. The occurrence of any idea in consciousness, by whatever influence, increases the probability that it will acquire additional associations, and hence the likelihood of its subsequent recall is increased. The habitual or customary recurrence of ideas reduces the fidelity with which they reproduce details of the original impression, and fatigue also modifies them in the sense that constant repetition may make a word lose its meaning. Emotion, especially relatively pleasant emotion accompanying an idea, strengthens it. "If one compare now the course of an idea, in so far as it is accompanied by an emotion, with the course of an idea which plays its role without the supplementation of an emotion, one will notice that the latter may be explained with little deviation from the laws of habit and fatigue, whereas in the former case where feelings are also cooperating it is clear that a new power has come into play. And in fact it can be observed here that the more pleasant imaginations or as the case may be the less unpleasant imaginations always last longer than one would expect them to do from the viewpoint of habit and fatigue—that the more pleasant ideas exercise, as it were, an attraction on our consciousness—or our consciousness an attraction on them, by grace of which they persist longer and more vividly *without any inner act of will to this end* than under otherwise comparable circumstances the indifferent or indeed the unpleasant" (Ehrenfels, 1887, pp. 578 ff., cited by Eaton, 1930, p. 141). Later Ehrenfels (1897) carefully spelled out that the duration of ideas in consciousness depends on nothing *absolute* in the quality of the feeling or on the tendency of pleasant feelings to increase. It depends rather on the *relative* pleasantness or unpleasantness of ideas competing for inclusion in consciousness. In any pair of such competing ideas, the more pleasant or the less unpleasant of the two will endure the longer because it benefits from the natural affinity between consciousness and the more pleasant feelings. While it is conscious the idea is likely to be further reinforced by additional associations, especially by judgments of its reality and of the availability and adequacy of means for attaining it, if it is an object. But all ideas, however reinforced, sooner or later succumb to fatigue, "which finally brings about the dissipation of even the most blissful fantasies" (Ehrenfels, 1897, p. 191, cited by Eaton, 1930, p. 142).

The affinity between consciousness and relatively pleasant ideas, as already explained, is not a matter of conscious volition according to Ehrenfels. He reinforced this point with a physiological speculation very similar to the one Freud borrowed from Fechner.[2] Furthermore, the influence of the judgment in reinforcing real ideas at the expense of unreal and imaginary ones is not necessarily a matter of internal striving or willing. Striving or willing occurs in this connection only when action with respect to an object idea is contrary to the judgment. If a desire object remains long enough in consciousness and with sufficient intensity of relative increase in happiness, then it will inevitably

[2] Cf. Chapter 1, p. 22.

and automatically lead to some sort of overt action. General restless activity *caused in this way* Ehrenfels called "striving," and when the individual judges that his own striving is the *only* remaining prerequisite for his affecting the object or being affected by it, then the striving is called "will." In fact Ehrenfels designated as "striving" all cases of idea-induced action in which the person's judgment about the requisiteness of his own striving had a probability of being correct which was less than .50. If the probability was greater than .50, the action was called "will."

Ehrenfels' definition of psychological reality of an object in terms of its inclusion in or exclusion from the causal nexus of the ego was consistent with his recognition of the principle that desire for means is *ipso facto* a desire for the object to be attained by those means. The converse is not necessarily true: according to Ehrenfels it is always possible to desire an object without desiring the means to get it. But usually the two kinds of desires go together. Indeed Dewey was later to argue (Dewey, 1939) that they necessarily go together for any end desired without its means is no real end at all, but a dream or fantasm. According to Ehrenfels value is ". . . that relation, falsely objectified by speech, of a thing or object O to the desire disposition of a subject S, as a result of which the O would be desired by S insofar as and as soon as the S does not now possess or might lose the conviction of the existence of O" (Ehrenfels, 1896, p. 103, cited by Eaton, 1930, p. 197). "We ascribe value to those things which we either actually desire, or would desire in fact if we were not convinced of their existence. *The value of a thing is its desirability. . . .* Also the magnitude of the value is the desirability, that is, it is proportional to the strength of the actual desire with respect to it; the stronger we desire an object or would desire it, the higher the value which it possesses for us" (Ehrenfels, 1897, p. 53, cited by Eaton, 1930, p. 183).

What is the ultimate aim of desire? Ehrenfels rejected the notion of absolute egoism, that every desire is ultimately directed at one's own pleasure or the elimination of one's displeasure. He also rejected the view that anything the idea of which awakens actual pleasure is desired, and that avoided the idea of which would awaken displeasure. Basically his argument for rejecting these notions is that they rely too heavily on judgment of what would increase or decrease our pleasure. Logically, this will not do for our judgments are often wrong in this respect and the intensity and persistence of striving or willing are independent of the correctness or error of our judgment. Furthermore, introspection does not always reveal that we are consciously considering our own happiness or unhappiness when we make up our minds, especially in routine daily matters. The ultimate aim of desire is to set in motion the processes by which we achieve the specific objects of desire. "David Hume . . . opposed the egoistic standpoint in basing his position on the true state of affairs. And indeed it is not only the ethically commendable desires, to which Hume grants the possibility of being based on other than one's own happiness, but also he brings to attention that even a desire like that for eating or drinking, for fame, power, or revenge, can be based directly on these objects, without it being necessary to imagine one's own pleasure" (Ehrenfels, 1887, p. 623, cited by Eaton, 1930, p. 124).[3]

In Ehrenfels' classification of values we need to concern ourselves closely only with his distinction between objects which are desired for their own sake (immediate or intrinsic values) and objects which are desired because of the judgment that they will be useful as means (hence, mediate or extrinsic values) for getting some intrinsic value.[4]

[3] Eaton apparently did not believe that the Ehrenfels-Hume attack on absolute egoism was adequate. He wrote in comment on the above citation from Ehrenfels: "There is, nevertheless, here a certain misunderstanding of Hume's famous argument. With Hume it was not a question as to whether one might have strictly non-egocentric desires without having egocentric desires *at all;* for him it was simply a question of priority. In the first place he has shown, in the passage already quoted, that even in the relatively egocentric cases these egocentric desires *must* be preceded by the non-egocentric propensities implanted in us by Nature. And he goes on immediately to suggest that similarly it might be that among these innate propensities one might occasionally find a strictly non-egoistic desire for the good of another" (Eaton, 1930, pp. 124–125). Eaton himself may have missed the point. The argument is over the basic determiners and origins of human directed behavior, not over the objective existence of egocentric aims, which neither Hume nor Ehrenfels denied. Both of them argued as well as anyone ever has that egocentric considerations are an inadequate source, logically, of human directed behavior. The egocentricity of any beneficient or maleficient act cannot be decided by arguing about undiscoverable origins; but it is self-evident in the discovery of whether the agent or another benefited from or was harmed by, the act. The possibility of discovering who benefits, or who is intended to benefit, by any action is the sole justification for retaining the word "egocentric" in the language.

[4] Ehrenfels also distinguished *individual* values from the *social* values common to a class or group. Under individual values he further distinguished *normal* value (the value of a particular object for the normal person), and *normative* values assigned to given objects by adequately informed persons to control the behavior of others (e.g., building codes, aircraft safety factors, physicians' prescriptions). Further there are the *imperative* values enforced by special social sanctions (jural, customary, moral, ethical); these are often desiderata rather than actual values. The possibility of errors in judgment give the distinction between *real* and *imaginary* values.

The relations between desires for intrinsic values and for extrinsic values are interesting. No matter how strong the initial desire for an intrinsic value, the desire will speedily fade in the competition with other ideas or stimuli in the immediate environment unless it is reinforced. Ehrenfels' illustration indicates that this reinforcement is most likely to occur if it is possible to make the judgment that the relevant extrinsic values (means) are available. A student in his room sits at his table with the intention of studying. He considers how pleasant it would be to take the day off and go for a hike and a picnic lunch in the mountains. He alternately returns to studying and to considering the outing. Suddenly he glances at the clock and sees that he has just enough time to catch the train to the foot of the mountain trail, and this recognition of the availability of the means decides him on the instant to undertake the outing. Thus one kind of conflict between motives is resolved because the idea of one intrinsic value was strengthened, relative to the other, by the sudden judgment that the means for attaining it were at hand.

However, in another passage Ehrenfels returned to the same hypothetical student to argue that the possibility of conflict of motives remains even though there is no longer vacillation between two courses of action toward different intrinsic values. Generally, among the requisite means there may be some actions which in themselves tend to a relative net decrease or increase of the happiness associated with the whole project. Specifically, if the student cares at all about his supply of money, his happiness at the prospect of the outing may be diminished on consideration that he will have to buy a ticket for the train. Similarly, the idea of not studying might lead to the judgment that the student would be inadequately prepared for his next classes. In any case, the conflicts are possibly multifaceted and action toward one object or another will ensue only if the idea of that object and the associated relevant judgment about means combine to produce a greater relative enhancement of happiness than any other available combination of ideas. It is also clear from this illustration that values which are classed as intrinsic in one context may be extrinsic in another. Ehrenfels' rejection of the notion of a special value essence clearly shows that he did not regard "intrinsic" values as ultimate or absolute except in the sense that such values are objects which we desire because of the dispositions implanted in us by Nature. Desires of this kind arise without the judgment that the object would be *useful* for something. When that judgment occurs the value to which it refers is an "extrinsic" one.

Ehrenfels had shown the ubiquity of the valuation process in behavior and he regarded the process not as mysterious and hidden but just as open to inspection as any other behavioral process. Though his method depended heavily on introspection, the formal structure of his theory is easily translated into more objective terms and we cannot be led far astray from an experimental treatment of the problem if we look where he pointed for our data about values and the process of evaluation. If the distinction between intrinsic and extrinsic values is not a fundamental flaw in Ehrenfels' theory, it is at least a possible source of confusion. In a previous paragraph I have outlined an interpretation of this point which reduces the importance of the distinction. However, Eaton seemed to think the point was rather more significant. Eaton set forth at length his own view that Ehrenfels "thought about values essentially from their extrinsic aspect" while Meinong, "who was primarily interested in abstract analysis, in the theory of knowledge, in axiology, . . . found a definition which fits most closely the intrinsic values" (Eaton, 1930, p. 203). And, having searched the writings of both Ehrenfels and Meinong for a definition of value, Eaton wrote that, "We must conclude our attempt to find a definition of value with the confession that there is no such definition, or rather that there must be at least two such definitions, depending upon whether one has reference to extrinsic or intrinsic values" (Eaton 1930, p. 203). Eaton stated it as his own view that, "In the interrelation of intrinsic and extrinsic values lies the paradox of valuation, or more properly the paradox of motivation. Should one choose the extrinsic or intrinsic values? Without the former the latter seldom can exist; without the latter, the former are valueless" (Eaton, 1930, p. 205). As we shall shortly see, later value theorists have been able to get along very well without the distinction between extrinsic and intrinsic values, as Ehrenfels himself might have done had he followed his premises to their logical conclusions.

As Dewey described it, the range of views on the subject of value ran "from the belief, at one extreme, that so-called 'values' are but emotional epithets or mere ejaculations, to the belief, at the other extreme, that a priori necessary standardized, rational values are the principles upon which art, science, and morals depend for their validity" (Dewey, 1939, p. 1). Ehrenfels' position was between these extremes. If we accept Dewey's characterization, then in the continuum of opinion about values the extreme positions are narrow and exclusive and limit the domain of value phenomena to a very small compass. At the "epithet" end the phenomena are trivial, and at the "a priori necessary" end they are undemonstrable. Dewey agreed pretty much with Ehrenfels on the broad domain of value phenomena and on their locus in purposive activity. "All conduct that is not simply either blindly impulsive or mechanically routine seems to involve valuations" (Dewey, 1939, p. 3). Dewey differed sharply from Ehrenfels on the use of the introspective method. In his discussion of the view that value expressions are expressions of feelings Dewey expanded on "the ambiguity of 'expression' and the irrelevance of 'feeling'" (Dewey, 1939, p. 12). "The serious problem . . . is why the word 'feelings' is introduced in the theoretical account since it is unnecessary in the report of what actually happens. There is but one reasonable answer. The word is brought in from an alleged psychological theory which is couched in mentalistic terms, or in terms of alleged states of an inner consciousness . . . Even if there be such states, they are by description wholly private, accessible only to private introspection. . . . the important part of the account given is the use of 'value expressions' to influence the conduct of others by evoking certain responses from them" (Dewey, 1939, p. 10). He also departed from Ehrenfels' analysis of means-end relations. Dewey maintained that means are valued in terms of their relevance to ends and ends themselves are valued in terms of the demands they make upon means or in terms of the ulterior or collateral consequences of realizing them. Thus it is bootless to denominate ends as "intrinsic," or "immediate," or "absolute" values, and to talk about means as "extrinsic," or "mediate," or "derived" values and to imply, as is usually done, that the latter are less important than the former.

Dewey insisted that verbal expressions or assertions that something is valued can mean anything or nothing unless the "existential contexts" in which they occur are specified. By "existential context" he meant to include states of organisms, states of their environments, and the relation of organism to environment. Of course the inner conscious states of organisms are irrelevant in describing existential situations: Dewey was no phenomenologist. The evidence that an individual prizes, cares for, desires, or has interest in something is the effort he spends or the pains he takes to bring it into existence or to prevent its going out of existence, *not* what he *says* about the preciousness of the object. Put another way, the origin of the meaning of these value terms is not in inferences from the observer's conscious desire to the supposed desire of another. Their meaning arose and persists because of observations that action does or does not take place to produce certain effects.

All valuations occur in existential situations which involve the relation of means to ends, and valuation is primarily in terms of serviceability of materials and processes for achieving the "end-in-view."

Unless the agent values the means, he cannot truly value the alleged end. The difference between immature impulsive action and mature reflective action lies just here. The shift from impulsive to reflective behavior which occurs in the lifetime of most individuals, and which Dewey believed had occurred in the history of the human race as well, consists in the increased attention to details of materials and processes to see whether they will increase the likelihood of attaining ends-in-view. We may estimate the adequacy of desires and the wisdom or silliness of actions by concrete observations of the care taken over the means. "Action may take place with or without an end-in-view. In the latter case, there is overt action with no intermediate valuation. . . . In case an end-in-view exists and is valued . . . the (motor) activity engaged in is, tautologically, mediated by the anticipation of the consequences . . . things can be anticipated or foreseen *as ends* or outcomes only in terms of the conditions by which they are brought into existence. It is simply impossible to have an end-in-view or to anticipate the consequences of any proposed line of action save upon the basis or some, however slight, consideration of the means by which it can be brought into existence. . . . the contents of dreams and air castles are *not* ends-in-view, and what makes them fantasies is precisely the fact that they are *not* formed in terms of actual conditions serving as means of their actualization" (Dewey, 1939, pp. 34–35, italics in original). The notion that there are such things as ends which are valued apart from the means for getting them must have come, Dewey thought, from the mentalistic premise that reduces affective motor activities to feelings. He hoped to make it clear that ends cannot be valued in a vacuum, but that they are valued *as ends* and in this sense their value is mediated.

In one sense, the relation of means to ends is that of an endless temporal continuum in which the end of one causal sequence becomes, and is evaluated as, part of the causation of further ends. The maxim that the end justifies the means, "under the guise of saying that ends, in the sense of actual consequences provide the warrant for means employed—a correct position—actually says that some fragment of these actual consequences—a fragment arbitrarily selected because the heart has been set upon it—authorizes the use of means to obtain *it*, without the need of foreseeing and weighing other ends as consequences of the means used. It thus discloses in a striking manner the fallacy involved in the position that ends have value independent of appraisal of means involved and independent of their own further causal efficacy" (Dewey, 1939, pp. 42–43).

To this view of the means-end continuum a traditional objection in value theory would be that it provides no stopping point, that it leads to an infinite regress. Dewey's response to this objection lies in the definition of a *problem*, a specific difficulty which will be ended with the achievement of a particular state of affairs. This view is applicable to all practical attempts and to all theoretical inquiry as well. In any case the proposed solution, conclusion, or outcome is evaluated in terms of its ability to solve the problem. From many problem situations there develops a general conception of conditions to be satisfied in typical cases, and these general conceptions—health is one of them—are not therefore a priori necessary goods.

Dewey's summary characterization of the nature and function of "ends-in-view" is that, "The *end-in-view* is that particular activity which operates as a co-ordinating factor of all other subactivities involved. . . . The *form* of an attained end or consequence is always . . . that of adequate co-ordination. . . . It has the qualities and properties appropriate to its being the consummatory resolution of a previous state of activity in which there was a peculiar need, desire, and end-in-view. . . . Instead of there being anything strange or paradoxical in the existence of situations in which means are constituents of the very end-objects they have helped to bring into existence, such situations occur whenever behavior succeeds in intelligent projection of ends-in-view that direct activity to resolution of the antecedent trouble" (Dewey, 1939, pp. 48–49). This notion of an attained end as the consummation of an activity sequence is an important ingredient in modern objective definitions of directed behavior, and it is an important bridge between Dewey's thinking and the central value concept developed by Stephen Pepper, that of a *selective system*.

Pepper described his book, *The sources of value*, as a sketch presenting a comprehensive hypothesis of the many lines of "relationship among the facts bearing on human decisions" (Pepper, 1958, p. 1). These facts range from "fugitive impulse . . . to the effects of natural selection in organic evolution . . ." (Pepper, 1958, p. 1). The formal paradigm of Pepper's value theory comes from experimental psychological data on purposive behavior and learning. This analysis depends heavily on the work of E. C. Tolman (1932, 1942) and included the phenomena considered by Ehrenfels and Dewey. Pepper analyzed two classes of purposive activity: appetitive purposes, which seek a positive reward; and aversive purposes, which avoid a harm.

Following Tolman (1932) and R. B. Perry (1926), along lines that are by now pretty much traditional in psychology, Pepper decomposed objectively describable purposes into the hypothetical components "drive" and "anticipatory set." "The mobilization of energy to a final aim and the pattern of activities directly connected with this mobilization of energy is what we mean by a drive" (Pepper, 1958, p. 48). Drives are cognitively blind, so goal choice or direction *per se* is not one of their defining characteristics. Drive is the mobilized energy upon which the actions of a purposive sequence depend. For example, the thirst, hunger, or sex drives may be identified by (*a*) the history of the organism's deprivations immediately prior to the occurrence of the observed behavior, or (*b*) a detailed description of its physiological state, or (*c*) a description of the specific conditions under which the activity in question is spontaneously terminated. But, according to Pepper's definition, drive is characteristic of all adaptive activities of organisms, including behavior like the reproductive cycle of the solitary wasp which is a rigid sequence of reflexes each of which serves as the stimulus for its successor. The directedness of the wasp's behavior is given by its "wiring diagram" and the occurrence of the relatively simple set of internal and external stimuli which activate the circuit. On the other hand, much of the directed behavior of mammals, including man, must be learned (it is *docile* in Tolman's terms) and to that extent it is modifiable for achieving ends under a variety of conditions. Pepper likened the more variable activities of mammals to a broken-down chain reflex in which the instinctive connections between successive acts have fallen out and the sequence of acts leading to the terminating conditions must be reconstituted by the process of learning which connects the acts, not by innately given ties, but by a series of "anticipatory sets." Pepper said that an anticipatory set provides the goal of an action just as a drive energizes action. But events may prove that an anticipatory set was wrong in that either the action prescribed did not in fact lead to the goal or the goal proved not to be satisfying after all. Whenever a directed activity includes or depends upon anticipatory sets that may be in error, Pepper called the act purposive.

All purposive acts thus have *structure* in that they consist, typically, of a series of acts each of which leads to a sub-goal or means for performing the next act. All the acts are energized by the aroused drive which began the sequence and to each successive act there corresponds its peculiar anticipatory set. This is a post facto, historical description. As the agent proceeds through the sequence of acts it changes its relation to the physical environment and may come upon unexpected conditions (difficulties) which demand the invention or discovery of anticipatory sets leading to acts which will circumvent the difficulties. Pepper cited the instance of a geologist exploring arid territory. He becomes thirsty and discovers that his canteen is empty. So he needs water and he institutes a search plan. Part one of the plan may be derived from the belief that he is most likely to see water or the evidence of its presence if he views the surrounding country from the highest available vantage point. His first act, then, is to get such a vantage point and this will involve climbing. While he is climbing he may have to decide between relatively safe easy paths and relatively dangerous difficult ones. His actual modes of physical exertion will depend on the types of paths available. Taking an apparently easy path to the top may bring him to the foot of a cliff too steep to climb, so he must retrace his steps and explore other paths. The anticipatory set for the "easy" path was in error. Having gained the top the geologist must discover by visual inspection the most likely evidence for the presence of water. If he discovers a patch of greenery and goes to it he may find no surface water but he might decide that sufficient water will collect if he digs a hole. Thus, his behavior involves the successive testing of various expectations about the presence of water and how to discover it, and, ideally, the behavior also includes non-repetition (discarding) of those acts whose anticipatory sets proved wrong. If the geologist finds water he will probably remember its location so that if he becomes thirsty in the same territory on a later occasion he will perform the sequence of acts that will bring him most quickly to the water—*not* the sequence that led him to find it in the first place. In either case, having drunk and filled his canteen, he will stop looking for water and will get on with his other business.

In terms of the above illustration, the geologist's quest for water and his drinking were based on present thirst discomfort. If we agree with Pepper in assigning his initial drinking to a deprivation-induced drive, then we must also agree that the drive aroused on that particular occasion was quieted by the drinking. The subsequent filling of the canteen was not based on a currently aroused thirst drive, but on the anticipated recurrence of its arousal. Pepper insisted that the terminus of any purpose is the consummatory act, the act which satisfies all the conditions necessary for the quiescence of the drive and which he calls the "consummatory pattern" of appetitions and the "riddance pattern" of aversions. In the structures of appetites and aversions, then, value is evident. Those implements and activities are valued which prove to be instrumental to the performance of the consummatory or riddance activities. Furthermore they are valued only while the relevant activities, including the terminal ones, are energized by a drive. There is no valuing of them before a drive is aroused and the valuation ceases once the drive has been quieted. Each rearousal of a drive is the occasion for a new act of valuing. Thus value is contingent for Pepper, as it was for Ehrenfels and Dewey, on the motivational state of a purposefully active organism. In the structures of purposes there is selection for and against certain actions. Those selected *for* are valued in the positive sense; those selected *against* are negatively valued. But Pepper's insistence on an aroused drive as the occasion of valuing involves an inconsistency. Did the geologist really not value water if he was not thirsty? The inconsistency can be dissipated by understanding the formal status of "drive" in the psychological theory which Pepper expounded.

It is important to distinguish, in Pepper's analysis, between what is objectively observable and what is hypothetical and speculative. There can be no real objection to using the word "drive" as a label for the persistent expenditure of energy in acts which lead ultimately to the removal of a deficit and to the termination of the activity in question. Drive is especially admissible if the deficit states and the associated activity can be independently defined and described as they can in the so-called thirst and hunger "drives." But such independent definition is not possible over the whole range of purposive phenomena. Perhaps it is legitimate to speak of a sex "drive," though certainly no clear-cut deficits are involved, because it appears possible to describe the physiological state of the sexually aroused organism independently of its behavior and of the conditions which terminate the arousal. And the same might be said for thermoregulatory "drives." But with sleep and wakefulness we are in possession of fewer objective facts which define the relevant physiological state independently of the observed behavior. And when we get to such objectively purposeful acts as the geologist's trying to get his canteen full even though he is not at the moment thirsty we almost certainly cannot describe a unique concomitant or antecedent physiological state which might be the "drive" energizing the sequence of acts. Nonetheless, we can and do correctly judge that the sequence of acts was purposive, aimed at filling the canteen. By purpose we mean only that the behavior was aimed and that it persisted, modified occasionally to meet changed conditions, until a particular relation between the organism and its environment emerged, a relation whose persistence was associated with the spontaneous ending and non-recurrence of the previous behavior. The observation of such persistent, modifiable, self-terminating behavior is by itself necessary *and sufficient* to justify our use of the word "purpose" and to supply its meaning. Such observations do not explain the behavior. "Drive," as Pepper and many contemporary psychologists have used the term, is offered as an explanatory hypothesis.

As a hypothesis, the notion of "drive" must stand the tests usually imposed on all hypotheses. How many classes of observations does it cover? How adequately does it cover them? What non-obvious facts and experiments does the hypothesis suggest? As indicated above, there are some pretty hard facts to which the notion of drive can be applied. But the word drive is merely a convenient label, not in itself a description or explanation of those facts. We are merely labeling our ignorance if we extend the meaning of "drive" to cover part of the causation of such acts as supplying expendable materials in advance of our immediate need to use them, seeking to affiliate with groups, seeking to exculpate ourselves for foolish or harmful acts, seeking to acquire social power, status, or prestige. It is unmistakable that all these are among the purposes of men; they are identifiable as purposes in terms of the objectively describable terminating conditions of persistent, modifiable behavior sequences. When we say that a person's acts are energized by "drives" for status, avoidance of blame, affiliation, or power we harm our science by pretending that we know something about the detailed causes of these behaviors and by pointing away from the phenomena to a possibly empty supposition.

I submit, nevertheless, that Pepper's *formal* embedding of values in the structures of appetitive and aversive purposes is not vitiated by his use of the "drive" concept. We can substitute any motivational or energic hypothesis we like in place of "drive" without invalidating his description of the objective observable characteristics of acts which we call purposive. We could go so far in confessing our ignorance as to say that from time to time all men and animals persist in spending energy faster than their basal rates; that though the details of the conditions which initiate and sustain this activity are often obscure, the conditions under which it terminates are relatively easy to describe; that the latter description provides the name for the "motive" or "drive" in question without prejudice as to the nature of the antecedent conditions which might be its cause. Ultimately we must learn about the causes, but we probably will not do so until we have loosened the hold which the conventional concept of "drive" has on our thinking. There is already plenty of evidence that the mechanisms which determine our behavior are quite heterogeneous. We should devote our energies to ferreting them out, or wait patiently until someone ferrets them out for us, rather than homogenize them all under the obscuring blanket of "drive." It is clear, though not obvious from our current language habits, that taking such an attitude will not decrease scientific preoccupation with problems of motivation. Studies of goal choice, frustration, and conflict have never depended substantively on adequate definitions of "drive" though such definitions may have been essayed in their preambles. To make such studies it is sufficient to know what we mean, in objective terms, by direction and purpose.

We return to Pepper's value theory at the point of the observation that selection is inherent in the process of purposive acts because in mammalian behavior some of the attempts to achieve the conditions of quiescence are unsuccessful. Until the quiescence conditions, consummatory or riddance patterns, are realized the activity persists as a sequence of subactivities. In retrospect an observer can indicate that a subset of these activities formed an instrumental chain leading to the execution of the consummatory or riddance act. In typical animal learning experiments, successive sequences leading to the same terminating conditions show an increase in the proportion of instrumental activities and a corresponding decline in non-instrumental or unsuccessful activities. In this sense the useful activities are selected *for* and the useless ones selected *against*. The criterion of selection is the "natural norm" that the behavior persists, with appropriate modifications, until the quiescence conditions occur; they cannot occur without a sequence of instrumentally useful acts, regardless of the number of useless acts that were performed on the way. The successful acts have positive value as instruments; the unsuccessful ones have negative value as frustrators. The natural norm of selection in purposive acts is thus in favor of whatever furthers the end of the purpose and against whatever hinders the end. Pepper's maxim for the empirical study of value is: "Follow the *dynamics* of selective action. In traditional terms this means: Watch for the *sanctions*" (Pepper, 1958, p. 3, italics in original). Following this maxim Pepper conceived of purposive acts as "selective systems," and, having identified one selective system, he proceeded to identify others. This concept of selective system he regarded, I think rightly, as a major contribution to thinking about value. Though the notion of a selective system was first explicated in terms of the purposive acts of individual organisms and though the energy of individual organisms is the ultimate source of energy for all valuings, individual values are not always and necessarily predominant in acts of valuing. The place of social and cultural values in Pepper's view will be made clear shortly.

Though purposive acts are intimately connected with consummatory and riddance patterns, as selective systems they are distinct.

Narrowly considered, consummatory and riddance patterns select relative pleasantness rather than unpleasantness; that is, they select among the generically affective values. Relative pleasantness may be merely incidental to the broader biological functions of the act, as the pleasure of a full belly is incidental to the nutritional function of the food; or relative pleasantness may be the only discoverable value selected, as for example in what Pepper called "gratuitous satisfactions" and what others have called unconditioned sensory gratification (cf. Seward, 1963, for a review of relevant literature). Thus Pepper limited the domain of hedonism in determining behavior. Here are included all values which are in the purest sense "esthetic." The criterion by which the subacts in a purposive act are chosen is their success or lack of it in producing the conditions for terminating the act. Though a feeling of pleasure, or more precisely of "triumph" may accompany success as unpleasure or "chagrin" may accompany failure, it is not these feelings but the success or non-success of the subactions which determine whether or not they are chosen. Generically, Pepper included success and failure under "conative-achievement" values. Thus he avoided the issue whether all purposive activity is fundamentally motivated by considerations of pleasure or unpleasure. Empirically, so many of even our most ardent strivings continue in spite of painful stress and opposition that we cannot defend the view that they are aimed at anything other than the concrete achievements which terminate them. The assumption that they are all aimed at pleasure is as gratuitous as the assumption that each is energized by some specific "drive."

Thus far the consummatory and riddance patterns and the purposive structures have been considered out of context in the way an experimenter might study them in a laboratory. In the general course of human affairs, individuals interact with concrete environments, with other individuals who also have purposes, with prescriptions and prohibitions for behavior, and with institutions which force specific prescriptions and prohibitions upon particular individuals; finally, the whole interacting tangle of opposed and crossed purposes is subject to the overriding criterion of species survival. Pepper analyzed several other selective systems out of this melange: the "personal situation" (the Lewinian "life space"), personality structure, the social situation, the cultural pattern, and natural selection. Each of these corresponds to a particular type of value selected in accordance with its peculiar natural norm, and each may assert its selective function over that of the others—in Pepper's terms, each may "legislate over" the others—under certain conditions.

Pepper said that in the "life space" as Lewin (1936) described it, there is inherent the possibility of conflict over which goals[5] to pursue and, given a single goal, there may be conflict about means for getting it. The problem in either case is to choose which of several purposive sequences to activate. The reality of the life space includes the hard incorrigible facts which, depending on the motor and sensory discrimination capacities of the organism, may be goal objects or implements (valences), pitfalls or pathways, gateways or barriers. The available discriminated possibilities for action impose a selection in terms of what it is prudent to do, under the circumstances, to maximize the positive value. Actions are imprudent to the extent to which they either fail to maximize positive value or actually decrease it. The energy involved here is the same as that which produces individual purposive acts. Only a new criterion of selection has been imposed, the criterion of conformity to reality which, if the organism has learned properly, modifies its purposes and thus "legislates over" them.

The facts of affective, conative-achievement, and prudential values, and the selective systems which produce them, do not exhaust the regularities observed in individual behavior. Any two individuals are likely to display characteristically different patterns of purposive activity, patterns which will differ consistently, even in objectively similar environments, over long or short spans of time. Observations of this kind lie at the root of what is called "personality theory." Personality structure is Pepper's fourth selective system. With caution to the reader to remember what was said above about the concept of "drive," Pepper's own words are best to show his meaning. Personality or character, he said, are names commonly given to a man's system of attitudes—"the repertory of instinctive and acquired drives and their interrelationships which make up the personality structure"

[5] Pepper said that the conflict is between "drives." I have already discussed the reasons for describing purposes in terms of their demonstrable terminating conditions (goals) rather than in terms of the vague hypothesis of "drive." Pepper's account of conflict resolution is basically the one advanced by Ehrenfels (1897) and most recently elaborated by Tomkins (1962): that the strength of a drive, relative to other drives, is amplified by the addition or "injection" of emotion. Conflict among "drives" is resolved when one of them is thus amplified. From Tolman's (1942) list of "instinctive drives" Pepper extracted "fright, aggression, and initiative" and classed them as "injectives." He used the notion of injective-amplified drives in his proposed solution of the Höffding, Woodworth, Allport problem of "functional autonomy." In my review of Pepper's book (Diggory, 1962) I wrote that his solution to this problem was among the best so far offered. Seward (1963) has since convinced me that the "problem" exists only if we continue to make unnecessary assumptions about the number and types of unconditioned mammalian motives (see Chapter 1, pp. 55–56, above).

(Pepper, 1958, p. 455). "A man's personality structure faces two ways. In one direction, it determines the drives that are released in a given situation. It determines what at any given time interests a man, and so forms the pattern of his drives in life-space. . . . But, in the other direction, a personality structure makes its own demands upon its own internal organization. It develops a selective system for its own internal equilibrium. The result, when successful, is commonly called the *integrated personality*. This process of selection may then be aptly called an *integrative process*. Its distinctive trait is that it operates not on acts but on dispositions to act—that is, on drives and their interrelationships. The dynamics of the process are the drives themselves . . . " (Pepper, 1958, pp. 455–456). The selective system for the pattern of drives released in a life space is called the *distributive action* of personality. The distributive and integrative functions together comprise the selective system called personality structure. The values selected are, generically, called character and are positive or negative as they are integrative or unintegrative.

Though integration is the aim of an unhindered person, this process is not literally purposive, for it is a directional tendency which is neither an appetitive or aversive structure, but it is just as innate to the organism as either of these. It goes on all the time whether the person knows it or not, but if he is aware of it, he can deliberately assist it. This is what the self-realizationists mean by being in harmony with nature. The process of personality growth results in a series of structures of increasing newness laid down over older ones, thus leading to the metaphor of stratification.[6] Personality integration must steer between the Scylla of unadaptive narrow specialization and the Charybdis of unadaptive breadth of interests. "The most highly integrated personality . . . would be the ideal for a member of an instinct-structured society like that of ants or bees, but not for a member of a docility-structured society like the human. . . . The ideally integrated human personality would be devoid of repressions and so also of an irrational conscience; consequently he would be free to adjust through his untrammeled docility to any type of physical environment. . . . So the modern self realizationist slogan should be: not fit yourself to nature, but fit yourself for many natures or even fit yourself to make nature fit you" (Pepper, 1958, pp. 512–513).

When the purposes of two or more individuals interact either in cooperation or in opposition, there exists the selective system which Pepper called the "social situation." According to Pepper, the temporal boundaries of a social situation are those of the problem whose solu-

---

[6] Pepper's account of personality development leans heavily on the neo-psychoanalytic outline provided by Erikson (1953).

tion demands, or is demanded by, the individual purposes of the persons involved. Social situations end when their constituting problems are solved. Social situations are bounded laterally by the number of persons involved in the problem. Strictly speaking, Pepper's notion of a social situation as a selective system covers only those problems which can be solved, with maximum total satisfaction of the interacting persons, without alteration of the cultural pattern. Most "small group" problems are of this type, intramural problems of families, schools, businesses, committees, or groups of friends. The natural norm of mutual enhancement of value by which trial acts are selected in social situations leads to the successive rejection of "uncongenial" solutions until a "congenial" solution is discovered.

When the problem which generates a social situation can be solved only by change in the cultural pattern (e.g., slum clearance or other community "improvements") or when such change is required by considerations of biological survival (as in war or the threat of natural disaster), then the cultural pattern as a selective system operates and legislates over the congeniality norm of social situations. "For in a social situation a cultural pattern performs the same sifting functions respecting the persons it precipitates into a situation that a personality does in a personal situation (e.g., functions of persons involved in a trial at law). But the cultural pattern also serves another function which is selection according to the principle of survival value. Human survival in biological competition depends upon man's social solidarity" (Pepper, 1958, p. 557). The relevant selective element of cultural patterns is cultural conformity; that of natural selection is adaptiveness which determines survival. "Because of the legislative priority of a cultural pattern as a natural norm over the natural norm of purposive values in periods of emergency or extensive suffering, the cultural values are often referred to as the deeper values" and thus individualistic theories are often regarded as superficial. But, "In the end we must give each its full due—the aim of individual satisfaction and that of social survival" (quotations from Pepper, 1958, p. 570).

Survival in the evolutionary sense functions as a selective system though not in the same way as selective systems in purposive structures. Natural selection does not operate primarily through tooth and claw struggle, but rather through all the forces, sometimes subtle ones, that determine reproduction. Adaptation refers to the fitness of an organic form for its particular environment. If it is too highly specialized, it will not survive radical environmental changes. Adaptability is the unique evolutionary acquisition of man and refers to the ability to learn how to use new environments in such a way as to survive and reproduce in them, and to transmit this information (an acquired characteristic) to successive generations (culture). Cultural evolution is significant for human survival because man (perhaps uniquely among other species) can determine the degree of probability of his own survival by virtue of the cultural arrangements he invents. Thus, in man, biological survival is linked to cultural sanctions, and survival value legislates over all other value ranges when questions of survival are at issue.

The relation of values to selective systems (the pivotal concept in value theory) is summarized by Pepper in Table 2.1.

There are two basic dynamic agencies operating in the whole value field: the purposes of individual organisms and the reproductive process of interbreeding populations. Each selective system except the first and the seventh of the table is energized in some degree on some occasion by both dynamic agencies. Depending upon the situation, each of the selective systems legislates over all the others, except that the affective system never legislates over the survival system. There are as many different kinds of value as there are selective systems, and the empirical field of values is the set of selective systems integrated by the lines of legislative priority among them. Man's (individual) happiness and his survival (as a species) depend upon his evolving a truly docile society which avoids the extremes of individualistic democracy where "happiness" is the dominant motive, and authoritarianism, with survival as the dominant motive, but which tailors its institutions to function in accordance with the social needs of the members.

It is clear from the preceding development that the objective study of value must start with the facts of purposive behavior. Value must always be defined in terms of some goal or objective of an individual organism, however that goal is instituted or chosen. Values are assigned to objects in terms of their usefulness in achieving these ends or goals. This is a utilitarian theory of value. Whether it is also a materialistic one is decided by the nature of the goals, and these can range from building a house to controlling one's temper, or cultivating religious experiences.

This theory of valuation can be validated by experiment and observation on behavior. This is the best test to make of it, because the reason we need the word value in the first place is to refer to certain aspects of behavior. These behaviors lie in three broad categories which shade imperceptibly into one another, thus giving us the idea of a scale of value: (1) actions which seek to preserve objects or materials or to continue or increase their supply (the indication of

TABLE 2.1
Summary of Selective Systems and Their Corresponding Values

Selected Values	Selective System	Names for Positive and Negative Values
1. Affective	Consummatory field and riddance pattern	Pleasant versus Unpleasant
2. Conative-Achievement	Structures of appetitive or aversive purposive acts	Successful versus Unsuccessful
3. Prudential	Personal situation (Lewinian life-space)	Prudent versus Imprudent
4. Character	Personality structure	Integrative versus Unintegrative
5. Social	Social situation	Congenial versus Uncongenial
6. Cultural	Cultural pattern	Conforming versus Nonconforming
7. Survival	Natural selection	Adaptive versus Unadaptive

(After Pepper, 1958, Table 8, p. 673)

89

positive value); (2) actions which are indifferent to or irrelevant to the continued existence or supply of an object or material (the indication of indifference or zero value); (3) actions which aim at the destruction or removal of an object or material (the indication of negative value). The notion of value implied here is consistent with the following propositions.

The value of anything is a function of the purposes of the user. Most simple hand tools illustrate this point well. A hammer can be used as a nail driver, nail puller, ice crusher, metal shaper, nutcracker, paper weight, or plumb bob. If we never need to do any of the things a hammer can do, it has no value for us. Now, let us consider people. A football coach brings a premium price at any Big Ten university, but there are colleges in this country to which you couldn't *give* a football coach, just as there are businesses which have no use for machinists or physicists.

The value of an object is to some extent independent of its immediate usefulness. We may value a thing simply because we *expect* to use it sometime in the future, not because we need to use it now. This is most obvious in the case of food, which is generally supplied in advance of immediate demand, but it also holds for tools and equipment of various kinds and for people with special skills as well. The value of an object goes from positive to zero or negative only when we permanently abandon the expectation that it will be used again.

Other things being equal, *the greater the number of goals to which an object is relevant, the greater its value and the longer its value will be maintained.* This is precisely the source of the value of money in our society—it can be traded for so many things. It is also the basis for the undisputably supreme value of individual human beings, particularly young human beings. They are multi-purpose machines, self-starting, and insatiable in their curiosity, always coming up with something new to amaze and dismay their jaded, know-it-all elders. There is no telling what they might do or what they might become if they are given adequate opportunity to transform their talents to skills and to use them effectively. The greater the number of skills and amount of information a man has the more likely he is to be useful, and hence, valuable, to himself and to others.

It would be possible at this point to state the general view of self-evaluation on which the research presented in this book is based. But to do so would leave open the question of how our view relates to the views of others who have thought about the problem. Therefore our view is presented after we have surveyed a great many other opinions on the subject.

Chapter 3
SELF-EVALUATION

Chapter 1 ended with the assertion that the word "self" is not the label for some unique class of *entities,* but for the *relation* in which an agent and the object of his act are the same organism, a relation which we symbolized as $(X \ldots o \ldots X)$. If the action designated by the o is a sensory inspection or a more complex (conceptual) cognition then we will call it an act of self-knowledge. There is no reason to assume that, in general, the actions possible in $(X \ldots o \ldots X)$ are qualitatively different from those which are possible in $(X \ldots o \ldots Y)$. In other words, the sources of knowledge of ourselves are the same as the sources of our knowledge about anything. We demonstrated, by trivial and obvious examples, that the only difference between the sets of actions possible in $(X \ldots o \ldots X)$ and $(X \ldots o \ldots Y)$ is that the domain of the former is the smaller of the two; that is, there are fewer actions possible in the self relation than in the other relation. If anyone finds this situation paradoxical we can only suspect that he harbors a belief in the possibility of an immediate direct awareness of something he calls "self," and it is precisely this assumption that we are anxious to avoid. If someone asserts that he knows himself in this direct and immediate way, we cannot deny it. Instead we assume the burden of showing him that by objective means we can acquire, and give him, a fuller self-knowledge than he could otherwise obtain. Whatever about self is by definition private is no affair of science.

In this chapter we want to consider especially those situations in which self-related actions are specifically those of evaluation. Whether the act is complex or simple, whether its implications and effects are limited and brief or broad and persisting, if it is an act (o) of *valuing* in the context $(X \ldots o \ldots X)$ it is self-evaluation. If the act of valuing occurs in the context $(X \ldots o \ldots Y)$ it is an evaluation of whatever Y stands for; it is not a self-evaluation. We will want to know two things: how to recognize an act of evaluation, whether of self or not; and what, specifically, is valued. The general views about valuing which were reviewed in Chapter 2 will assist in meeting these requirements. Ehrenfels, Dewey, and Pepper, regardless of their differences in method and emphasis, agreed that behavior has objectively describable features which suffice to define the word "purpose." Perhaps we might use the words "directed" or "motivated" if these make the matter clearer. The point is that we can recognize behavior as purposive and tell what it is aimed at even though the behaving organism is unable or unwilling to tell us what he is trying to accomplish. Furthermore, it is characteristic of purposive behavior that only some of the acts involved in it are instrumental in moving the agent closer to his goal; the rest are mistakes. If the same or similar purposive sequence of acts is carried out several times in succession the sequence itself may improve in its character as an instrument for getting to the goal, either because some of the mistaken acts are modified or because other acts substituted for them. This is what Pepper meant by saying that certain acts are selected *for* and others are selected *against.* The criterion of selection is, as Pepper said, whatever promotes success in achieving the conditions for terminating the purposive behavior. Therefore, in this view, the central value terms "good" and "bad" have no meaning in the abstract or absolute sense. To be consistent with the foregoing notions we should always ask: "good or bad *for what*"; or assert that something is good or bad for such-and-such a purpose.

POWER AND POWERLESSNESS

Therefore we will begin our attack on the numerous and complex problems of self-evaluation by considering the simplest, most clearly defined situations in which a person might evaluate himself. I repeat, though by now it is probably unnecessary, that when we say a person evaluates himself we do not mean that he is evaluating some global entity which could be called his "whole self," though such evaluations probably do occur. We will most often refer instead to his evaluation of some limited aspect of his own activity: his evaluation of himself as a chessplayer, a marbles player, a singer, a batter, a weight lifter, a solver of crossword puzzles, a lover, a driver, a writer, a wine taster, a theoretician, a mountain climber, or a mechanic. To say that an individual is "good" at any of these things (even if he says it of himself) is to imply that he has certain hypothetical innately determined receptor and motor capacities and has acquired certain skills and knowledge of techniques and materials, and that in his activity he coordinates all these so as to produce some specific kind of change in his physical or social environment. In common parlance we say that he has demonstrated the ability to achieve a particular goal.

Psychologists have spent a great many man-years studying what they call "abilities" and compiling a large literature on the subject. Much of that effort has gone into identifying classes of abilities, called motor, perceptual, or cognitive, for example. An equally large effort has gone into the attempt to identify individuals who "have ability" and to devise "tests" for selecting those individuals from among those who have "less ability" or "no ability." Now if we strip away all the fancy names used to describe the tests and pay attention only to how they were constructed, how they operate, and what they are expected to do, it immediately becomes clear that what is usually referred to as an "ability" is no more than an hypothesis about an individual. The hypothesis may be of the form of expecting that what a man has done once he can do again, or the expectation may be that if we have seen a person do a number of different things then he can do other things which he has not yet actually attempted. This is the logic behind tests of "general intellectual ability" or "intelligence." A person who takes an intelligence test successfully solves a greater or smaller number of a set of problems. The person who constructed the test, or the one who gives the test, knows that people who previously solved a high proportion of the test problems then went on to solve other problems, including perhaps the problem of completing a standard course of study leading to an academic degree or the problem of performing some specific job or duty. Knowing this, the tester then says that his latest client has (or has not) the ability to solve such additional problems, but this statement is an inference. The fact of the matter is that the persons who took the test, including the latest client, have demonstrated their abilities only to the extent of what they have actually accomplished. This is not intended to cast any more doubt on psychological testing than others have already done. It is only to make the theoretical position clear. What we call an ability is an hypothesis inferred from the observed empirical correlations among certain successfully completed purposive acts. The names we give to abilities are derived either from the processes involved (motor, perceptual) or from the effects produced (problem-solving, learning). All this is said because I want to use "abilities" more loosely and broadly than the present psychologists' lists and compendia will permit. I want to know whether, objectively or in his own opinion, a particular individual confronting a concrete existing situation can solve the problem which that situation presents. If he solves the problem I shall say he demonstrated the requisite ability. If I change the conditions ever so slightly and he does not solve the problem I shall only say that he has not demonstrated the ability to do *that*. He may do it after several additional attempts. But then the description of his ability should include what he accomplished *and* the process he used, including the number of trials.

If, as our value theory asserts, things are valued as a function of their instrumentality in relation to our purposes, and, as our view of "self" has it, the sources of our knowledge and valuation of ourselves are the same in principle as our sources of knowledge and valuation of objects not ourselves, then it follows that we value ourselves because of the part we play in accomplishing our goals. That is, what we value about ourselves is primarily our abilities, of which our achievements and accomplishments bear witness. In the following paragraphs I shall attempt to show that this view was substantially agreed with by a large number of people who have written about self. This may not be obvious to the casual reader because, as we have already seen, the terminology used in dealing with self and self-evaluation is not standardized. Furthermore, the issues are likely to be obscured by the persistence of some writers in shifting the theoretical psychological emphasis away from descriptions of concrete behavior to "feelings." This occurs even among contemporary writers. It is the vestige of the once prevalent view, from which our science is gradually freeing itself, that the subject matter of psychology is consciousness, that introspection is its method, and that Wundt and Titchner were its prophets. Some form of this view is still to be found among psychologists and nowhere more prevalently than among those who write about self. Consequently, among the writings we are about to survey we will find a kind of obbligato dialogue between the proponents and opponents of introspection. But at the same time there is a fundamentally recurring theme, common to all of them, that the locus of our self-evaluations lies in our purposive actions.

The earliest written records of European civilizations indicate that individuals were concerned with their self-evaluations and with the evaluations which other men made of them and of themselves. The English language is very rich in terms which are used equivalently for the various levels of the continuum of self-evaluation, a continuum which we might say extends from pride to humility, though other terms might fit the extremes as well or better. None of the value terms is in itself unambiguous. We must always look to its context to see what its author meant by it. "Pride" furnishes a good example.

In one sense, "pride in an achievement," it refers to an objectively based favorable self-evaluation, but it may also refer to a groundless gratuitous self-arrogation and disdain for all that is not self. In the latter sense pride has been castigated by moralists of all ages. We shall refer to these two different kinds of pride in more detail later in this chapter.

In the writings of many of the "literary psychologists" of the eighteenth century, "pride" referred to "self-esteem, or the craving to think well of oneself, in its many degrees and forms, especially its emulative form; and the desire for, and pleasure in, the esteem, admiration or applause of others, especially the craving for 'distinction,' the *fureur de se distinguer*" (Lovejoy, 1921). In this sense it was regarded as the chief motive of human behavior. It was also the source of social control, for by giving or withholding their approbation men could channel each other's behavior. As Locke put it, "He who imagines commendation and disgrace not to be strong motives to men, to accommodate themselves to the opinions and rules of those with whom they converse, seems little skilled in the nature or history of mankind: the greatest part whereof he shall find to govern themselves chiefly, if not solely, by this law of fashion; and so they do that which keeps them in reputation with their company, little regard the laws of God, or the magistrate" (Locke, 1812, vol. 1, pp. 376–377). Lovejoy's concern with the history of ideas about "pride" in the seventeenth and eighteenth centuries (Lovejoy, 1921, 1961) led him to sketch a general theory of value, a theory which is essentially identical with that of Ehrenfels. He spoke of these "varieties or degrees" of a general desire which he called "approbativeness": (*1*) the wish merely to be an object of others' attention and interest; (*2*) the desire to be the object of others' "sympathy, friendliness, affection, love," which are not necessarily evaluations, but which may be conditioned by evaluations; (*3*) the desire that others should evaluate oneself highly (Lovejoy, 1961, p. 85). When an individual wants to evaluate himself highly his desire is called "self-approbativeness." The desire for a favorable self-evaluation is one of the two desires inherent in the motivation of purposive acts: the desire for the valued *end* of the act ("terminal value") and the desire to *be* something in the act ("adjectival value") (Lovejoy, 1950, 1961). The latter desire, the desire for adjectives, is the one involved in self-evaluation. In addition to these, Lovejoy distinguished a desire for superiority or the feeling of superiority. He called this "emulativeness" and thought that this motive could be satisfied in most men' by the recognition that though some others are better than they, some are also worse (Lovejoy, 1961, p. 112).

Pierce's view of the roots of self-evaluation is consistent with his rejection of the idea of a special faculty of introspection and his assertion that the only way to answer psychological questions is to study objective behavioral events. A young child automatically and necessarily values his own body because it is instrumental to his experiences and to the changes he makes in his surroundings. "Only what it touches has any actual and present feeling; only what it faces has any actual color; only what is on its tongue has any actual taste. . . . When he wills to move a table, it is doubtless that he thinks of the table as fit to be moved, but whether he thinks of himself as desiring to move it is an arbitrary and baseless supposition without the former proof of an intuitive self-consciousness.[1] The child . . . must soon discover by observation that things which are thus fit to be changed are apt actually to undergo this change, after a contact with that peculiarly important body called Willy or Johnny. This consideration makes this body still more important and central, since it establishes a connection between the fitness of a thing to be changed and a tendency in this body to touch it before it is changed" (Pierce, 1868, pp. 27–28). As the child ages, his comparisons of his own acts with the testimony of others convinces him of error and fallibility and these result in self-reproach. He successively reduces the occasions for self-reproach by preparing his subsequent acts so that they "approximate indefinitely toward the perfection of that fixed character, which would be marked by entire absence of self-reproach" (Pierce, 1905, p. 190).

Bain (1880) wrote that "from the primary motives of our being" we desire money, love, and admiration. We learn that others get these things as rewards for certain kinds of effort, and the amount of the reward is proportional to the effort expended. So since we desire to possess the rewards we also desire to possess the means. Then, when we exert ourselves to get our share of good things we are likely to be reminded (by association) of others and the values we assign to them because of their skills and efforts. Furthermore, we are like the others and so, just as we decide which of two others is worthier, we evaluate ourselves in comparison with others by the same criteria. However, because of the bias of our desires we are likely to apply the standards more favorably to ourselves than to others in objectively similar circumstances.

Speculation about the "springs of action" and the "primary motives of our being" became focused, through the Darwinian influence,

---

[1] Pierce's (1868) argument against the existence, or at least the utility, of intuitive self-consciousness is referred to in Chapter 1, pp. 10–12.

on the idea that basically all our actions are instinctively determined, and that our very existence depends on the successful completion of instinctive acts of self-preservation. In the course of life the objects which minister to the body and its needs come to be associated with the body, and in this way the primitive egoistic strivings expand their boundaries. James, Höffding, and Freud all accepted these premises, and each in his way had something to say about self-evaluation.

In James' view (James, 1890) various objects and activities become associated with our bodies during the course of our instinctively determined behaviors, and thus we come to define possessions, family, friends, reputation, abilities, and knowledge which are uniquely *ours.* Any of these acquisitions elevates our positive self-feelings, but most especially those which are "saturated with our own labor." In fact, we most truly seem to *be* our "psychic powers," our abilities and capacities, knowledge and skills, in the use of which we encounter success or failure and consequent changes in the level of our "self-feeling." For although, as James pointed out, our self-feelings may maintain a relatively constant level "independent of the objective reasons we may have for satisfaction or discontent," or "the barometer of our self-esteem and confidence" may vary with "causes that seem to be visceral and organic rather than rational," nevertheless, "the normal provocative of self-feeling is one's actual success or failure and the good or bad position one holds in the world" (James, 1890, pp. 306–307, italics in original). But though all selves may be logically possible it is physically impossible to be and do everything, so one must choose a "self" on which to

stake his salvation . . . I, who for the time have staked my all on being a psychologist, am mortified if others know much more psychology than I. But I am contented to wallow in the grossest ignorance of Greek. My deficiencies there give me no sense of personal humiliation at all. Had I 'pretensions' to be a linguist, it would have been just the reverse. So we have the paradox of a man shamed to death because he is only the second pugilist or the second oarsman in the world. That he is able to beat the whole population of the globe minus one is nothing; he has 'pitted' himself to beat that one; and as long as he doesn't do that nothing else counts. He is to his own regard as if he were not, indeed he *is* not.

Yonder puny fellow, however, whom everyone can beat, suffers no chagrin about it, for he has long ago abandoned the attempt to 'carry that line,' as the merchants say, of self at all. With no attempt there can be no failure; with no failure no humiliation. So our self-feeling in this world depends entirely on what we *back* ourselves to be and do. It is determined by the ratio of our actualities to our supposed potentialities;

a fraction of which our pretensions are the denominator and the numerator our success: thus,

$$\text{Self-esteem} = \frac{\text{Success}}{\text{Pretensions}}. \quad . \quad . \quad .$$

To give up pretensions is as blessed a relief as to get them gratified; and where disappointment is incessant and the struggle unending, this is what men will always do (James, 1890, pp. 310–312).

According to Höffding, the mental life of a newborn infant does not involve "ideas" of objects and their relations. It consists chiefly of feelings of pleasure and pain which are occasioned by events that abet or hinder the instincts of self-preservation. As the child matures it develops ideas of the objects which incite pleasure or pain, and the instinct of self-preservation is manifested as love or abhorrence for these objects.

When now the feeling is determined by the idea of what promotes or hinders self-assertion (self-preservation and self-development), it will appear as a *feeling either of power or of powerlessness,* according as we think we have or have not at our disposal sufficient means of self-assertion. Under self-assertion must be included here, not merely the maintenance of physical existence, but also the power of mental clearness and freedom, and of 'making oneself felt' in relation to others (by controlling them, being recognized by them, etc.). That the feeling of power is the active or positive form of the feelings linked with self-assertion, is due to the fact that the idea of the cause of a feeling of pleasure (or of the hindrance to a feeling of pain) can excite pleasure only when we conceive this cause (or this hindrance) to be within our reach. "All conception of the future," says Hobbes, "is conception of power able to produce something. Whoever therefore expecteth pleasure to come, must conceive withal some power in himself by which the same may be attained." . . . The feeling of powerlessness appears in humility, in repentance, or in self-contempt, which have their rise in the failure to obtain the control over the conditions of life which is recognized as desirable" (Höffding, 1891, pp. 243–244, italics in original).

The motive to cherish people or objects besides ourselves arises in many ways. First we associate some people or objects affectionately with our own self-assertion because they are its instruments. Later we may forget the instrumental connection between the feeling of love and its objects and love the objects for their own sakes, without regard to "the reason why." Furthermore, the instinct of sympathy makes humans feel and suffer with those who are similar to them.

Love is also based on the sexual instinct in which the individual can take pleasure from his part in a process which extends beyond his own egoism. Again, the relation between mother and child makes a pure state of nature, an absolute individualism, impossible. Consequently one cannot draw a fundamental distinction between the desires and interests of the individual and those of the race.

Freud echoed this final conclusion of Höffding's in almost identical words. It is consistent with the fact that the sexual instincts and parent-child relations were at the very core of his theory. Self-love and self-evaluation were the same thing to him. Even in young children Freud thought he detected an instinctive tendency to treat one's "own body in the same way as otherwise the body of a sexual object is treated," a tendency which he called "primary narcissism" (Freud, 1914). Because the sexual instincts are initially gratified auto-erotically they cannot be distinguished from the self-preservative, self-assertive "ego instincts" until the individual has a love object outside himself (Freud, 1914). The person, usually the mother, who supplies the demands of the ego instincts becomes thereby the first definite object of the sexual instincts. Thus the choice of the initial sexual object is dependent (*anaclitic*) on the conditions under which the self-preservative instincts are gratified (Freud, 1914, 1920, 1921b) and "it is a literal fact that the child learns how to love through his own egoism" (Freud, 1920, p. 214). The self-loving tendencies of primary narcissism are reinforced in "His Majesty the Baby" by the parents' attitudes that the child shall have a better lot than theirs, not be subject to the harsh realities of life, to death, frustrations, illness, or restrictions on his will. This is "nothing but parental narcissism born again" (Freud, 1914, p. 49).

When the individual has developed psychologically to the point where his own ego can be an object, more or less of the energy of the sexual instincts can be withdrawn from objects and directed onto the ego. This is secondary narcissism. The combination of the tendencies of primary and secondary narcissism makes the ego the principal love object. The process of secondary narcissism is best noted in people who are organically ill: "the sick man withdraws his libidinal cathexes back upon his own ego, and sends them forth again when he recovers" (Freud, 1914, p. 39); and in hypochondriacs and schizophrenics (Freud, 1914, 1920), but the process occurs to some degree in all of us, and so we love ourselves. However, the increasing impact of reality on the normally maturing individual reduces his self-love. "Loss of love and failure leave behind them a permanent injury to self-regard in the form of a narcissistic scar, which . . . contributes more than anything to the 'sense of inferiority' which is so common in neurotics. The child's sexual researches, on which limits are imposed by his physical development, lead to no satisfactory conclusion; hence such late complaints as 'I can't accomplish anything; I can't succeed in anything' . . . The lessening amount of affection he receives, the increasing demands of education, hard words and an occasional punishment—these show him at last the full extent to which he has been scorned" (Freud, 1921a, pp. 42–43). Thus reality shows each of us that his childish megalomania was unjustified, and in the normal adult various impulses, goals, and experiences are controlled and some of them eliminated, chiefly by the process of repression. But reality, in the form of parental criticism reinforced "by those who trained and taught the child and by all the other persons of his environment—an indefinite host, too numerous to reckon (fellow men, public opinion)" (Freud, 1914, p. 53), beyond merely reducing self-regard, also implants in the individual as an "*ego ideal*" the very standards and precepts in terms of which he has fallen short. This ego ideal "deems itself" perfect and it becomes the object of the love which the ego, because of its demonstrable failures, is not worthy to receive.

What, precisely, are these failures? Freud was never completely explicit on that point. We must synthesize his view by sampling from his desultory writings on the subject, writings which extend over a broad span of time. It must be clear so far that the self-love of the normal adult is not unconditional. One's level of self-regard—his ability to love himself—depends on his achievements. "Everything we possess or achieve, every remnant of the primitive feeling of omnipotence that experience has corroborated, helps to exalt the self-regard" (Freud, 1914, p. 55). These are achievements in the exercise of ego functions, functions which in Freud's clearest summary (Freud, 1926, pp. 12–14) can be seen as more or less complex sequences of purposive motor acts: sexual, eating, locomotion, and occupational activities. Similarly, in his latest discussion of the nature of anxiety Freud (1926) rejected his earlier view that anxiety is like a conversion symptom in that it is the conscious representative of the unpleasure of repressed but still forceful instinctive impulses. The later view is that the *feeling* of anxiety is itself an ego function, a signal emitted by the ego in the presence of danger cues for the purpose of mobilizing all available psychic energy for effective counteraction. The occasions which arouse this feeling differ typically with the individual's stage of development: at birth, separation from the mother, increased stimulation, and prolonged anoxia; in childhood, real or threatened loss of love; in the Oedipal period, threat of castration. What of the adult—what occasions his anxiety? The feeling of anxiety is the same whatever the occasion, and the occasion in adults is a situation of danger. "What is the kernel, what is the true significance, of the danger situation? Evidently it is the estimation of our strength in comparison with its magnitude, the admission of our helplessness in the face of it—of material helplessness in the case of a true danger, of psychic helplessness in that of instinctual danger. Our judgment in this regard will be guided by actual experience; whether one is mistaken in one's evaluation makes no difference to the result. Let us call our experience in a situation of helplessness of this kind a *traumatic* situation; we then have a sufficient basis for distinguishing the *traumatic* from the *danger* situation" (Freud, 1926, pp. 113–114). In the course of development, traumatic situations come to be foreseen, and a danger situation is one in which trauma is *anticipated.* The distinction between inner (instinctual) and outer dangers is unimportant, for instinctive impulses are dangerous only when they lead to actions which are likely to incur collisions with physical objects, or social disapproval, or punishment. Therefore, all dangers are external. "The danger situation is the recognized, remembered and anticipated situation of helplessness. Anxiety is the original reaction to helplessness in the traumatic situation, which is later reproduced as a call for help in the danger situation" (Freud, 1926, pp. 114–115).

The various points about the bases and conditions of self-evaluation which our review has so far uncovered have been repeated, with various shifts of emphasis and changes in definition, by more recent writers. It may be that self-awareness never exists apart from self-evaluation (Hallowell, 1959) either as a merely empirical connection, a fundamental principle of nature, a logical artifact of unanalyzed premises, or because, as Festinger (1954) said, there is a fundamental "drive" to evaluate ourselves. When we evaluate our purposive acts in terms of their success or failure, and the abilities revealed in purposive acts in terms of their power, there may be a universal "upward push" with respect to abilities (Festinger, 1954) which biases our evaluations toward the favorable end of the scale in spite of possible evidence that they ought to be lower (Allport, 1943; Hallowell, 1959; Hilgard, 1949; Rogers et al., 1949; Wylie, 1961). Whatever their emphasis, however they define their terms, it is clear that modern writers embed their discussions of self-evaluation in the context of purposive action. It is the same whether the appeal is to a single motive of "self-actualization" (Goldstein, 1939), to satisfy "the ego" (Allport, 1943), or to a variety of motives (Chein, 1944; Litwinski, 1951;

McCall, 1963; Woodworth, 1958). Even writers (e.g., Bertocci, 1945; Chein, 1944) who revive the useless old metaphysical-epistemological distinction between entities which know and entities which are known—even they speak of self-evaluation in the context of motives. Chein (1944) regarded "value" and "significance" as equivalent terms. Though all motives necessarily involve action on the environment, there is an organized subset of them which are peculiarly self-referent (e.g., dependency, self-preservation, prestige), and this subset *is* the ego. "Finally, it should be noted that, by virtue of the central role it plays in the ego structure, the significance of the self becomes enormously enhanced. From the center of the person's awareness, it becomes the center of his existence. From an item, in a universe of observable items, it becomes a supreme value and the core of an evaluative system" (Chein, 1944, p. 311). According to Bertocci (1945) the self both knows and is known, the ego is only known. The self also wants, and the self is the "referent for *I*, or *he, my*, or *his* to whom egos, personalities, or experiences are attributed" (Bertocci, 1945). "The ego . . . is the variable region of the personality which the self evaluates. . . . Such expressions as 'My ego is hurt' or 'My ego won't stand that,' suggest that the ego is a knower and a fighter, but they really mean: 'I (the self) don't like, and disagree with, the evaluation you are putting on my activities, and what is more, I'll fight to prevent your doing that again'" (Bertocci, 1945).

SOCIAL COMPARISONS

All of the writers whose views we have so far discussed have emphasized sufficiently that the purposive activities of individuals are often interactions with the purposes of other individuals; that is, that purposive action often takes place in a social context and is subject to evaluation in terms of the standards generated by group consensus. The study of group processes and their influence on the behavior of the individuals who constitute the groups requires different techniques than those used for studying the behavior of isolated individuals. The development of these techniques and of the systematized knowledge resulting from their use has led to the increasingly clear distinction of sociology and social psychology as separate disciplines. The increasing professionalization of these disciplines has been marked inevitably by their members' adopting certain common opinions, attitudes, or world views. One of these is that self-evaluations are made exclusively in terms of social criteria or by comparisons with others, or that the self-evaluations which are so made are the only ones worth considering. This view admits either or both of two kinds of social criteria for self-evaluation: affective acceptance or rejection of individuals by groups, which allegedly produces in the individual a feeling that he is in some degree worthy or unworthy, regardless of the objective value of his powers and achievements;[2] the comparison by the individual of his own powers and achievements with those of others. This body of opinion not only presumes more than is covered by the available facts, it also is contradicted by some of the facts. Moreover, such views are not consistent with the opinions of the influential theoreticians of self in society, the views, for example of Cooley, Mead, and Festinger.

Cooley maintained that each of us *is* an individual, "a contending bit of psychical force," born with the need to assert ourselves and with an "instinctive self-feeling . . . associated chiefly with ideas of the exercise of power, of being a cause, ideas that emphasize the antithesis between the mind and the rest of the world" (Cooley, 1922, p. 177). Such individualistic purposive striving has always characterized human beings; only the things they strive for change from time to time in accordance with the opportunities available in the social process, and sometimes men make themselves unnecessarily miserable by accepting a currently prevalent social norm (e.g., pecuniary success) rather than the norms of the "instinct of workmanship" (Cooley, 1911, p. 304). "The main need of men is life, self-expression, not luxury, and if self-expression can be made general material inequalities will excite but little resentment" (Cooley, 1911, p. 304). Indeed, society is at fault whenever its conditions restrict the self-expression of indivduals, especially that of the "finer spirits." Though the approval and disapproval of our fellow men are very powerful determiners of our self-esteem, they are not its sole and necessary determiners. Every productive mind, whether productive merely of psychological self-development or of works of art, letters, politics, religion, or science, must have intense self-feeling, but the self-feeling of such people is not particularly sensitive to praise or deprecation. They are not preoccupied with the impressions they are making because their selves are too usefully occupied elsewhere. In fact, "persons of great ambitions, or of peculiar aims of any sort lie open to disorders of self-feeling, because they necessarily build up in their mind the self-image that no ordinary social environment can understand or corroborate, and which must be maintained by hardening themselves against

---

[2] The affective acceptance may depend upon the value of the individual's abilities (cf. the previous remarks on Lovejoy, 1961, p. 95), but self-evaluation is contingent solely on the degree of acceptance which is accorded the individual for whatever reason, according to the view explained here.

immediate influences, enduring or repressing the pains of present depreciation, and cultivating in imagination the approval of some higher tribune" (Cooley, 1922, p. 258). Thus, standards for self-evaluation may be matters of individual choice. Cooley saw unique purposive individuals clearly. He saw that they are related *to* society or that society is *composed of* them. He sought a clearer formulation of the problems which Pepper (1958) assigned to the selective systems of individual purposive acts, personal situations, personality structures, social situations, and cultural patterns, and the conditions under which the norms of any of these systems "legislates over" the others.

Mead's case is even more instructive for he insisted, as Cooley did not, that our very idea and feeling of self is a product of social interaction, but self-evaluation depends on our abilities and capacities as they are realized in the performance of definite functions. Self-evaluation may to some extent be determined by the superiority of the group of which one is a member, but "genuine superiority . . . rests on the performance of definite functions. . . . We change things by the capacities which we have that other people do not have. . . . The superiority is not the end in view. It is a means for the preservation of the self. We have to distinguish ourselves from other people and this is accomplished by doing something which other people cannot do, or cannot do as well" (Mead, 1934, p. 208). An ordered society is a condition of our existence, but no society is good unless it provides opportunity for genuine individuality of purposive activity. That is a value of great moment. How much of such value any of us has realized is gauged, in Mead's view, by comparison with others on the basis of objective standards of achievement, not on the basis of gratuitous affective acceptance or rejection.

Perhaps the most systematic theory of "social comparison processes" is that of Festinger (1954). Certainly it has been the most influential one in recent years. It is a long and elaborate series of hypotheses, corollaries, and derivations. I shall not attempt a complete analysis of it here because I want only to emphasize those features of it which are directly relevant to our present discussion, features which I believe are misunderstood by some of Festinger's admirers. Various other points of the theory are discussed in Chapters 5 and 6. To begin with, Festinger paid tribute to the fact that self-evaluations occur by the formal assertion (hypothesis 1) that "there exists, in the human organism, a drive to evaluate his opinions and his abilities" (Festinger, 1954). Festinger's distinction between opinions and abilities is never made completely explicit; the reader has to gather most of it from what he says about the different effects which group processes have on opinions and abilities. I will essay a brief descriptive distinction here, one which I hope will do no injustice to Festinger's theory. Opinions are the contents of verbal declarations about supposed causes, effects, or courses of action. Opinions can be stated in the absence of any relevant facts, or even in the absence of the possibility of getting such facts. In the latter case, the opinion is not corrigible, except that social pressures can make a person change his statement for reasons that are irrelevant to its content. In such a case, to ask whether the opinion "change" is "genuine" is to plumb the depths of metaphysical obscurity. However, my opinion that I can repair a leaky water pipe by myself is quickly corrigible upon exposure to the relevant facts. No amount of social pressure can prevent me from sending for a plumber. As a result, I have evaluated an opinion and an ability at the same time, for an ability is always revealed and evaluated by the results of a genuine attempt to do something. This is not quite the same as what Festinger meant by cases which are a mixture of opinion and ability evaluation. He referred to cases where an individual has to estimate the number of beans in a jar with no opportunity to count them or to infer their number by computing volumes. Such "abilities" are artificially limited to expressions of "opinion" which may be demonstrably biased by various kinds of social pressure. Festinger was fully aware of these distinctions but he discussed them offhandedly and proceeded at once to state his second hypothesis: "To the extent that objective, non-social means are not available, people evaluate their opinions or abilities by comparison respectively with the opinions or abilities of others" (Festinger, 1954). We want to know both the *adequacy* (or power) of an ability and the *accuracy* with which that power is assessed. Festinger seems to have insisted, without qualification, that the *accuracy* of the assessment depends on how one compares with other persons. I object to this lack of qualification; it is a poor basis on which to build a theory because it overlooks the relevance of describing exactly what the individual is trying to do. If that involves demonstrating his superiority to other people, then of course the social comparison is relevant, but surely not all of our ability evaluations are of that nature. We have to know something about the conditions under which social and nonsocial criteria are likely to be used; we must know the relative extent of each in our everyday life, and theories of this type will not guide us to ask the proper questions.

Though practically all of Festinger's propositions are couched in terms that apply equally to opinions or abilities, he modified many of them either because he already had plenty of evidence to support what he was saying about opinions and little or none about abilities; or because available data or common observation reveals that opinions and abilities must and do respond differently to social pressures. The effective group pressures operate to promote uniformity of opinion, but the facts that we always seek to achieve more and more with our abilities (hypothesis 4), and that mere social pressure or the desire to conform to it can only make a person *wish* he had more or less ability without altering his real powers (hypothesis 5), makes these pressures toward uniformity operate so as to segregate and classify people on the basis of ability. If we differ on opinions we can reduce the difference either by changing ourselves or by influencing others to change, but if we differ in ability, we can achieve uniformity only by choosing to associate with those who differ minimally from us, or by seeking to improve our abilities by practice and study. Thus, Festinger admitted that actions, caused by discrepancies which relate to abilities, are not generally *social* in nature but are directed "against the environment which restrains movement." In this connection he mentioned practice, but surely a person who tries to improve his technique on the violin is trying to change himself, not the instrument. These views, insofar as they relate to opinions, have been substantiated by research in a very convincing manner. We are still waiting for an equally impressive body of data on the evaluation of abilities. Festinger himself had to conclude that "the power of the group to influence its members is relatively unimportant with regard to abilities. The social process itself, no matter how much power the group has, cannot achieve movement toward uniformity on abilities. The power of the group successfully to influence its members will be effective only insofar as changing members' values concerning a given ability and increasing motivations can be effective. With respect to values and motivations concerning the ability the situation is identical with the social process that goes on concerning opinions" (Festinger, 1954, p. 135). Now this says no more than what we have already recognized: that the selective norms of a social situation may determine whether or not a certain ability is used, whether it is good for whatever has to be done in that context. This verges on telling us again that social conditions can determine the range of our opportunities to achieve, the content of the goals we seek. No doubt social comparisons also occur with respect to abilities, but these propositions do not add up to a demonstration that self-evaluation is determined always and solely by social criteria. It is a question of fact whether, and under what conditions, social or non-social standards for self-evaluation of abilities is the more important. In our present almost complete lack of facts there is room for investigators with both interests, but there is no room for pure dogmatism.

SELF-EVALUATIONS, GLOBAL AND PARTICULATE

There are many today who share the opinion that we must understand the causes and consequences of different levels of self-evaluation, especially extremely high and extremely low ones, before we can solve the nagging practical problems of individual adjustment and social relations. Snygg and Combs (1949), the popularizers of the current quasi-technical "phenomenal self-concept," justified their "phenomenological" theory of behavior causation partly on the ground that the tenets of that theory could be learned easily by workers in various fields of applied psychology. In their view, self-evaluation is high or low as the individual's history shows him to be "adequate" or "inadequate" in gratifying his individual needs. Though they agreed that the individual's history includes his success or failure in meeting social norms of conduct, their discussion of self-evaluation and social evaluation very circumspectly avoided the question of causal relations between them. They described the relations as mere empirical contingencies in which independent and dependent variables cannot be distinguished: (*1*) when self-evaluation and social evaluation are equal, the subject will be realistic and his goals and behavior will be consistent with the culture and with his own possibilities; (*2*) when self-evaluation is lower than social evaluation the person will have strong interests, will be gratified by the results of his own behavior, and will be encouraged by social reactions to continue his efforts, will be modest and unassuming until self-evaluation and social evaluation achieve the parity of case *1*; (*3*) when self-evaluation is above social evaluation the behavior of others is threatening to the "organization of . . . phenomenal self," so the individual becomes defensive and sets high goals to prove that his self-evaluation is justified (Snygg and Combs, 1949).

Modern views on self-evaluation have been influenced by psychiatric writings on depression and megalomania, especially—but not exclusively—the writings of Freud. Freud (1918–19), writing of the self-deprecations of melancholics, said that "whoever holds, or expresses to others, such a low opinion of himself is ill whether he is speaking truthfully or being unfair to himself." He also stated his opinion that schizophrenics suffer from extreme megalomania (Freud, 1914, 1920). Freud made the most comprehensive attempt to explain extreme depressions of self-esteem, but he joined all the others when he threw up his hands at the mystery of megalomania. In part, it is the persistent bafflement of all attempts to explain excessively high self-evaluations that has led the "self-realizationists" (e.g., Angyal, 1941; Goldstein, 1939; Rogers, 1955; McCall, 1963) to posit an unconditional motive for self-assertion or self-aggrandizement. The problem of "pathological" extremes of self-estimation has fascinated and baffled psychiatrists in Germany (cf. Hirt, 1909) and in France (cf. Blondel, 1924) since the latter half of the nineteenth century. Melancholics believe their delusions in the face of all contrary evidence and can try to kill themselves at any moment—that is all we know (Hirt, 1909); or the concept of "mine" can expand to include the entire universe and more, or it can contract to the extent that we deny possession even of ourselves (Blondel, 1924). Hilgard (1949) reviewed the history of our current lists of "defense mechanisms," which include defenses against anxiety and against influences which might reduce self-esteem. They defend self-esteem chiefly by self-deception. "To feel guilty is to conceive of the self as an agent capable of good or bad choices. It thus appears that at the point that anxiety becomes infused with guilt feelings, self-reference enters. If we are to understand a person's defenses against guilt feelings, we must know something about his image of himself" (Hilgard, 1949). In Hilgard's view, psychologists need no other justification for their interest in "self."

It is a premise of Rogers' client-centered therapy that in an atmosphere of acceptance and encouragement (provided by the therapist) the client will spontaneously develop, change, or grow in the direction of psychological health, adaptive behavior, and generally approved relations with other people (Rogers, 1955). Rogers (1949) and some of his colleagues attempted to explain what they mean by "successful therapy" (Raskin, 1949), that in the course of it the client's verbal "defensive" statements decrease in number (Haigh, 1949), his acceptance of and respect for himself and others increase (Sheerer, 1949), that we cannot tell whether acceptance of self causes acceptance of others or the reverse (Stock, 1949), that the course of the changes is regular and sequential (Seeman, 1949), but not all clients are successful in this sense (Hoffman, 1949).

Wylie (1961) concluded that there is some evidence, not free from possible artifacts, that children's self-concepts and their self-evaluations are similar to what they believe their parents, especially their like-sexed parents, think of them, and that maladjusted children believe that their two parents hold disparate views about them. The relation between self-evaluation and social status is not clear; leaders of clearly defined groups may have on the average a higher opinion of themselves than their followers but there is at best contradictory evidence on the relation between self-evaluation and the attributed social rank of the group or class to which one belongs. There are small and usually insignificant correlations between level of self-evaluation and resistance to persuasion.

"It is generally conceded theoretically that a low degree of phenomenal self-regard should be indicative of, or an aspect of, or perhaps even a cause of, 'maladjustment'" (Wylie, 1961, p. 203). But the reverse of this proposition is less clear because high phenomenal self-regard may indicate either good adjustment, denial of difficulties and of self-rejection, or merely conventional responding.

After reviewing several papers on this problem in which the expected positive correlations between phenomenal self-regard and level of adjustment were reported, Wylie decided that most of the evidence is contaminated because the subjects responded in terms of social desirability, and, when persons with various degrees of pathology were compared, there was considerable overlap between the groups in level of self-regard. Furthermore, when adjustment was *inferred* from popularity in groups or number of visits to the infirmary then the association between adjustment and level of phenomenal self-regard was tenuous and insignificant (Wylie, 1961).

In 21 studies the evidence suggests that self-acceptance and acceptance of others covary positively, but most of the results, in Wylie's opinion, could have arisen from "response sets" or other artifacts. Furthermore there were some negative findings and, most important from Wylie's point of view, all the studies were of the R-R type so no conclusions can be drawn about causes.

After reviewing a number of studies in which success and failure were experimentally manipulated Wylie wrote: "It seems that Ss will, under certain conditions, change their self-evaluations after experimentally induced success or failure. These changes are most likely to involve self-ratings on the experimental task itself, or on the characteristic which has been evaluated, and are least likely to involve reports on global self-regard. The latter seems to be affected little if any by a single experimental failure or evaluation. There is some evidence that changes in self-rating upward after success are more frequent than are changes downward after failure" (Wylie, 1961). This lack of change in ratings of global self-regard Wylie thought was congruent with self-concept theory because covert evaluation may change even if overt does not, defensive behaviors may substitute for or prevent changes in global self-regard, or other characteristics of S may be important determiners of his behavior after success or failure.

PRIDE

History and legend have recorded the widespread, if not universal tendency of human and superhuman individuals to think better of themselves than the facts will justify, to dare beyond the limits of their powers, to claim more than they have earned of material and social rewards. As Lovejoy (1961) noted, there is no way of telling what actions the desire for self-approbation may lead to. Payne (1960) has detailed its varieties, chiefly from literary sources. The inevitability of *hubris* and its ineluctable consequences in death, destruction, and misery were recurrent themes in the poetry of Homer, Pindar, Aeschylus, and Sophocles. Whether it was called "pride" or "*hubris*" this gratuitous self-aggrandizement has both attracted and terrified men. It has been condemned by theological and secular moralists for thousands of years, even by those who thought it was based on a necessary, desirable, and potentially good aspect of human nature. Plato wrote that, "Of all the faults of the soul the gravest is the one inborn in most men, . . . and this fault is conveyed in the maxim that 'everyone is naturally his own friend,' and that it is only right and proper that it should be so. Yet in truth this same violent attachment to self is the constant source of all manner of misdeeds . . ." (Plato, *Laws*, v, 731, D, cited by Payne, 1960, p. 31). And in the seventeenth and eighteenth centuries, "The specific counts in the indictment of 'pride,' in terms of its concrete effects, were numerous and formidable. Emulative pride—and pride always, it was assumed, tends to be emulative—was declared, by one or another of those who inveighed against it, to be solely or chiefly responsible for the following evils with which human life is afflicted: 1. A multitude of desires for objects which are not needful for man's happiness, which, indeed, he would be far happier and better without. 2. Science and philosophy. 3. Unnatural excess of morality. 4. Inequality of various kinds, especially economic inequality. 5. The demand for equality. 6. Most of the rivalries, jealousies, and conflicts between individuals and between classes within a society. 7. International wars. 8. The pursuit of insubstantial, purely imaginary values. 9. Insincerities and affectations which vitiate the integrity and the social intercourse of men. 10. What may be called hedonic parasitism, i.e., the obliteration of the very personality of the individual" (Lovejoy, 1961, p. 219).

Few men have dealt with pride temperately, whether they were its devotees and prisoners or its haters and avoiders. It is a mark of pride that however it is approached the terms are always absolute, black or white. There is no middle ground. This may be the chief source of our persistent difficulties with it. When yielded to completely, as it usually is, it produces the exalted ravings of the mystics, Saint John of the Cross, Meister Eckhardt, or Pascal, claiming all things, visible and invisible, for themselves because of their identification with the Most High. Some have said that pride leads to withdrawal, despair, or madness (Payne, 1960). It has produced the "honorable frauds, generous cruelties, glorious crimes," the *terribiltá* of Renaissance Italy celebrated by Machiavelli; and the German fascination with Götterdämmerung, the inevitable consequence of pride, "the great glory lying dead" (Payne, 1960). To Anthony and Augustine and many another Church Father, pride was a sin, perhaps the root of all sin, and as such it must be rooted out absolutely, not merely modified. It had come, in the course of church history, to be recognized as the spiritual hallmark of Satan and his followers (Murray, 1963). Pride is a movement of "the will" so the will must be extinguished, but this has merit only if the extinction itself is an act of will. So there is no way out. The will battens on the very act of subduing itself and the occasion for pride remains—a hopeless situation indeed. Some tried to take a moderate position. Jerome decided that pride was all right if it were pride in God, "*sancta superbia*," but the difficulty remained of distinguishing, even in oneself, between holy pride and its malignant or Satanic form.

The word "pride" by itself is ambiguous. We may speak of "pride" in our abilities and achievements and mean no more by it than the fact that we evaluate ourselves favorably as purposive agents. This kind of pride is based on evidence and, if we limit its degree to what the evidence will support, it is good. In fact, it is indispensible. We must be able to evaluate our powers with fair accuracy if we are to use them adequately. Unless we evaluate ourselves *favorably* as instruments we would attempt nothing and therefore we would achieve nothing. Without this kind of realistic self-evaluation, this pride based on evidence, man's genuine achievements to date might well not have been realized. However, the other kind of pride, that which desires and dares without limit or justification, is equally real; it is no chimaera. It is just as real as mass extermination, gang "rumbles," race riots, murder "for kicks," status-grabbing, and the justification of our acts and wishes by their alleged congruence with the revealed designs of a "higher power." In these terms we can only describe what we mean by "pride"; we cannot explain it. As Murray (1963) said, we have no theory of it. However, we may be able to work toward such a theory, beginning with our ability to distinguish the two kinds of "pride."

We may take it at the outset that "gratuitous" pride is always emulative. It involves social comparisons, and its pressure is always in the direction of commanding more than anyone else of goods, services, honors, and attention. There is a name in our society for the condition of being able to command such things; it is "status," specifically "high status." The higher the status one has, the more of the available desiderata he can command. Ideally, status may be conferred on individuals as a reward for real achievement in the production of some social good. Such *earned* status, rationally graded according to the individual's real social utility, is then also the badge and symbol of his value as an agent, but, in actual practice, status can be gained by other means. It may be *donated* by accident of birth, or it may be *usurped* by the exercise of what I have elsewhere called mere status-getting abilities (Diggory, 1964); that is, by flattery, sycophancy, or other manipulations of the social machinery solely for one's own benefit. "Everybody knows" that it is often difficult to decide which of two possessors of identical badges and titles has fairly earned his and which has them by donation or by usurpation. If we desire only the symbols of status and the powers and privileges which they confer, then all means for getting the symbols are equally good. The only way to tell whether or not status has been fairly earned is to watch its possessor trying to perform the functions which his status implies. Opportunities to do this are rare and the observer may lack the knowledge or the time required for the process, so we accept the evidence of status to mean that its possessor has the ability to do certain things which in fact he may not be able to do at all. The correspondence between status and ability is further blurred by unwarranted generalization, in line with the myth of the "omnicompetent citizen," from real abilities by which the status may have been earned to abilities which the individual has not demonstrated. Thus we seek the counsel of popular actors about social problems, of retired military officers about international relations, of physicians about scientific research—the list is too long to recite.

Since high status carries with it all the recognition, acceptance, and power over goods and services which our emulative tendencies demand, people are likely to value themselves in accord with their status level. I suggest that the common denominator of gratuitous "pride" in our society is that self-evaluations are often made in terms of donated or usurped status. If status is their only criterion, then self-evaluations are peculiarly vulnerable. Depending, as they do, solely on the willingness of other people to acquiesce in our possession of status, they must necessarily decline if recognition or acceptance are withdrawn. This withdrawal is likely to occur whenever the possessor of unearned status has to use the abilities which are properly relevant to his position. Therefore it is the possession of status which must be constantly checked and reinforced by our attention to the impression we are making, by seeing how far our demands will be met no matter how unreasonable they are. There is no logical upper limit to such demands. Limits are imposed solely by the extent to which people of lower status will act in accord with our wishes. Furthermore, if the actions of other people seem to imply that our status is taken lightly or that they think it is lower than we deem it, such actions will be viewed as of great moment and counteracted accordingly. This counteraction may involve isolation and punishment of the offending person, or a program of rehabilitating his opinions until his opinion of us agrees with the one we have of ourselves. We might seek to make him guilty by threatening suicide, or by publicizing his rudeness, unfairness, or heartlessness. If none of these techniques succeed with anybody, then self-esteem is at an end; the individual is worthless by criteria of his own choosing, and he may genuinely seek to destroy himself and to take others with him in the debacle. I think this sketch fairly covers Murray's four components of "absolute malignant pride" (Murray, 1963, pp. 47–48). I want only to emphasize, more strongly than Murray did, that this kind of pride need not begin with any mysterious hypothetical "narcissism" but only with the desire to take what appears to be the easy road toward the enjoyment of real goods and benefits (or to hold onto what was initially a free gift). Gratuitous pride is "absolute" only in the sense that it is not founded in real achievements. The goods it seeks are not "saturated with our labor," as James put it, so our possession of them is no evidence of our possession of the concrete abilities which, to quote James again, "we most truly seem to *be*." This kind of demanding pride has a wide range of effects from a few individuals in a face-to-face group to the whole world. If it involves a demand for superiority (or at least non-inferiority), this demand can be met by derogating others so as to increase the status gap if it favors us or to decrease it if it favors them. The latter technique can be best illustrated in Basque pride.

"The Basque thinks that the mere fact of having been born and of being a human individual gives him all the value that it is possible for one to have in this world. Being bright or stupid, learned or ignorant, handsome or ugly, inventive or obtuse are differences of slight importance, almost unworthy of attention compared with what it means to be a living human being. . . .

"This attitude, though it has a certain rugged greatness . . . is satanic. . . . The Basque cannot admit that another might be superior to himself. Strictly speaking, within his hermetic solipsistic world . . . he is superior and even unique. This renders any individual hierarchy impossible, and since he cannot avoid the consequences of some social intercourse, minimal in the Basque, he rancorously accepts as the lesser evil 'i Todos iguales!' ('All are equal!'), a terrible, negative, destructive phrase . . ." (Ortega y Gasset, 1961, pp. 115–116).

Gratuitous pride is destructive in its tendencies simply because it rejects the fruits of the cultivation of talent. "Einstein's theory of relativity was judged by many Spanish scientists not as an error—they hadn't taken the time to study it—but as an affront" (Ortega y Gasset, 1961, p. 115). The present writer was a witness to a discussion between an intelligent, moderately educated, socially conscious, strongly opinionated woman and a college professor. The woman stated her case clearly and enthusiastically and illuminated it more with emotion than with reason. The professor gently but firmly led her along the main stem of the argument, pruning off the irrelevancies she wanted to pursue and demolishing her citadel bit by bit. It was a virtuoso performance. It was instructive as to substance and also as an example of the art of discourse. However, when the lady saw that she was going to "lose" the argument, she broke in and ended it by saying, "You know, you're being unfair to me—by using your education against me!" The whole episode made no impression on her at all, except to stop any further discussion with that professor. She is the worse for it today, but she is probably still proud.

This long discussion of gratuitous pride has been introduced for its contrast effect, not as prolegomena to a theory of pride. We are as much in the dark as ever about the origins of pride. We have accepted it as a fact in human life and we have suggested concrete conditions in terms of goals and means which will reasonably produce proud behavior in anyone who chooses those goals and means, but why such choices are made we do not know. There is no general explanation for the variety of contents of human purposes, but a great deal is to be gained by accepting the fact of human purposive acts in which the process of evaluation constantly occurs. The typical situation we have chosen for our study of self-evaluation is one in which individuals are evaluating their own capacities for doing certain clearly defined things, whether these evaluations are made in a social context or not.

Chapter 4
PROBABILITY OF SUCCESS

The assumption that individuals can and do evaluate themselves as instruments for achieving goals raises the question of what evidence they use for their evaluations. Generally, people are not equally good instruments in all humanly possible performances. They may differ either in the number of things they can achieve, in their speed of achievement, or in the number of different means (capacities) they can bring to bear in a single attempt at achievement. Most abilities are not, in actual use, the unconditioned flowering of innately determined propensities for carrying out certain purposes. Achievement in most fields of endeavor requires long and arduous work. Talent or raw ability must be turned into skill, and skill is usually, if not always, a mixture of several things that are learned: about materials and implements; manipulative skill; and the ends which materials, implements, and skills can be used to accomplish.

In Chapters 2 and 3 we urged that the process of evaluation appears in situations where organisms use their cognitive and manipulative capacities to effect changes in their relations to their environments. In this view the process of evaluation is quite a common one, not incessant, certainly, but recurring with great frequency in the daily activities of most individuals. If an individual assumes a certain function, or has it thrust upon him, there is always the presumption that he can *do* it; that is, that he can meet certain criteria of performance. If he meets the criteria he is good *for that;* if he doesn't meet the criteria he is not good *for that.* In the case of *self-evaluation* the agent decides without the intervention of another opinion whether or not he can accomplish the task at hand. If he is informed of his adequacy or inadequacy by another person, his own evaluation may agree or disagree, but in either case he is evaluated and included in, or excluded from, the set of those who can accomplish the task in question. If he is trying to achieve a position on the varsity baseball team, for example, he will either get the position or he will be "cut" from the squad. If he cuts himself we have to ask whether he did it because he thought he wasn't good enough, or had changed his

115

momentary system of valuings and retired from the pursuit of baseball to devote his time and energies to something more important.

If the process of valuation is embedded in the process of purposive activity, we must try to discover in purposive activity the specific kinds of information which a person might use to evaluate himself. We can well begin our search in the work of Ferdinand Hoppe (1931), one of that remarkable group of students who worked under Kurt Lewin at the University of Berlin and whose names are attached to the various papers in the series edited by Lewin under the general title "Untersuchungen zur Handlungs-und Affekt-Psychologie."[1] Hoppe's starting point was the work of Anitra Karsten (1928) on "psychic satiation." Karsten had shown that with continued repetition of a monotonous task, the activity became increasingly distasteful to the subjects (Ss) who, by words and actions, indicated clearly that they wanted to get out of the situation. They complained of muscular fatigue—writers' cramp and pains in the back and legs—and showed considerable fluctuation in the rate and quality of their work. Karsten showed that genuine muscular fatigue was involved little, if at all. As she paid each S at the end of the experiment she required him to make exactly those writing or stooping actions which a moment ago had caused him so much anguish and which seemed so hateful to him. She changed the *purpose* for which the actions were carried out—writing one's name was now signing a receipt for his fee, and stooping was to pick up the mark notes which had "accidentally" fallen to the floor. In both cases the action was prompt, smooth, and efficient, and accompanied by no complaints or evidence of muscular impairment. If fatigue were significantly involved, the discomfort and distaste attending the actions would not have dissipated so rapidly. Recovery from *fatigue* requires fairly prolonged *rest* of the involved muscles, but here we see that recovery from *satiation* (the mere fact of "being fed up" with a task) requires only a change in the *aim of the action.*

Karsten's tasks were so simple that there was never any question but that the Ss would be successful by *objective criteria.* Hoppe (1931) used Karsten's results as the basis for attacking the notion that, with repetition, success becomes associated with pleasure and failure with displeasure. Even a successfully accomplished task, repeated often enough, becomes more and more unpleasant. Thus psychic satiation produces a disinclination to repetition even when the task is successfully completed. Therefore we must distinguish between satiation and satisfaction. A person can be satisfied by a task and

[1] The twenty papers in this series appeared at irregular intervals from 1926 to 1937 in *Psychologische Forschung.*

still have a tendency to repeat it, or he can be sated by it without satisfaction, or he can be both sated and satisfied. A satiated S will do *almost anything* but continue the activity in question; a satisfied S may continue the same manipulations, but with a different purpose.

In one of Hoppe's preliminary experiments one group of Ss had to carry certain tasks to *satisfaction,* and another group had to carry the same tasks to *satiation.* One task required S to hang 16 rings on the hooks of a moving belt, and the Ss all gave evidence of great satisfaction when they had hung the 16 rings; they praised themselves and told the experimenter (E) the good news. The E then said the experiment was over, excused himself, and left S alone in the room—but he secretly watched S through a concealed peep-hole. After satisfaction, all ten Ss spontaneously resumed work at the same task, but, in the satiated group, who had been kept at the task past the point of satisfaction until they spontaneously stopped working at it, only three of the ten subjects repeated the task or showed any interest in it at all. Introspective reports and observations of the Ss showed that those who resumed the tasks did not regard their action as mere repetition, but saw it as serving a different goal. Mostly they attempted to do it more easily and quickly, as was most noticeable when S had been only incompletely satisfied with his original performance.[2]

If one assumes a residual tension remaining in spite of the satisfaction, one must assume that it will tend to reproduce the same action and goal as before. This assumption is not justified, said Hoppe, and he gave as an example the experience of one of his subjects. At first she thought that throwing all 16 rings over the moving pegs was impossible and had no idea how many she would be able to get on. On the first trial she got four on. On subsequent trials she made six and then ten. Then she reverted to six and regarded this performance as a failure though she had previously regarded it as a success. Thus, her feeling of success and failure was determined by the relation of her performance to her level of aspiration (*Anspruchsniveau*). The quality of performance regarded by the Ss as success or failure was quite variable. Even for the same person, as the previous illustration shows, success and failure are not bound to a single fixed performance. The relation of the action to a striven-for goal is the important determinant. The S begins to work with certain aspirations and expectations which can be modified in the course of the work. These expectations,

---

[2] Hoppe did not use quantitative measures of his dependent variables. His statements recorded his impressions and interpretations of what his Ss said and did.

goal settings, or aspirations, for some future attempt, be they changed
with each attempt, now uncertain, now precise, Hoppe called the S's
level of aspiration (LA).

When Hoppe attempted to study the conditions which produce
changes in LA, he used nine tasks of the most diverse possible kinds.
One set he called *record actions*, in which S had to achieve or exceed
some quantitative standard, and the other type he called *thinking
tasks*. Each S was told, "You will be given different tasks which you
must perform. You are not in any way bound by the experiment to
the accomplishment of these tasks but it will satisfy me if you quite
freely and naturally attempt to do them. When you don't want to
work at a task any more and want to try another, say so freely." The
situation was quite free and the Ss chatted with E about what they
were trying to do at each moment. Hoppe made inferences about their
LAs from what they said and did.

The Ss had no previous contact with the tasks, therefore no idea
of their difficulty relative to their own abilities, and therefore no certain LA at the outset. They began by testing the tasks to see whether
they were "possible" or not. When they began setting goals they set
modest ones which they thought they could reach: the initial LAs
were the lowest ones which might assure a feeling of success. Table
4.1 summarizes Hoppe's observations on 165 LAs from different Ss
working on different tasks, several LAs per S.

TABLE 4.1
*Changes in LA, and other actions, as a function of success and
failure*

Following	Change in LA			Realization of Past Success	Stop Work on Task
	Up	Down	Same		
Success	32	0	3	0	11
Failure	0	27	12	1	15

Numbers are percentages of 165 observations.
(After Hoppe, 1931, p. 18.)

These are the data which led to Hoppe's conclusion that LA generally
is raised after success and lowered after failure. Ss might change their
LAs not only by shifting along the same continuum (e.g., attempting
to produce the same amount and quality of output in longer or shorter
time) but also by changing from the continuum of speed to that of

amount, disregarding time altogether; or from amount to quality of output or performance. After success Ss sometimes invented new criteria of performance in terms of which they actually made the tasks more difficult than E had intended. Also, during a series of successes, S might raise his LA until he realized that he had reached a limit in terms of the nature of the task or in terms of his own ability.

After failure S would sometimes ask E whether what he had done so far was correct. Then he might ask E for help. But if help was offered, it was frequently rejected with the remark, "I'll do it myself." After a series of failures, S's activity often became a mere hopeless fumbling with no clear sense of direction toward the original aim. Sometimes real anger appeared, and Hoppe noted that Dembo (1931) had already briefly set forth characteristics of LA in her paper on anger. Sometimes if the S quit a task completely after a series of failures, he would "realize a past success" by observing that on some previous trial he had at least done so-and-so (cf. Tables 4.1 and 4.2). Hoppe gathered the impression that not all successes and failures were of equal weight to the Ss. Table 4.2 gives his classification of degrees of success and failure and Ss' reactions.

Hoppe noted that a single success has to be evaluated by S to see whether it can be regarded as attributable to himself or merely accidental. Single failures have not, as a rule, any influence in producing changes in LA. Mostly, Ss found excuses for single failures.

The LA and the task goal are related but not identical. In many life situations the goal of an action is imposed on a person either

TABLE 4.2
Number of observations of changes in LA, and other actions as a function of degree of success or failure

Following	Change in LA			Stop Work on Task	Realizing Earlier Success
	Up	Down	None		
Complete Success	44	—	3	10	—
Partial Success	7	—	2	—	—
Single Success	1	—	—	8	—
Complete Failure	—	45	8	23	2
Single Failure	—	—	11	1	—

(Total, 165 observations in all)
The unit of observation is the individual LA, not individual Ss. (After Hoppe, 1931, p. 20.)

by command or suggestion, or by the nature of the situation (*"von der Sache her"*). Thus the task goal can have a certain objective character even if S does not adopt the notion that this goal relates to his own LA. This point of Hoppe's has not been elaborated at all in subsequent work on LA. The disjunction between an objectively given goal and a momentary LA may be seen in the "drive-related" (*triebhaft*) activities of young children. Also, "purely objective" sets may occur for certain tasks and, even if an LA is present, the goal of the *task as such* is different from the LA which momentarily fluctuates with the success and failure the person experiences.

Though each task has a characteristic difficulty level, this is not a fixed quantity. It can fluctuate over the *natural range of play* (*Spielraum*) of the task, which in turn varies from task to task. The natural maximum of the range of a task is given by complete accomplishment; its natural minimum is the least that can be accomplished without changing the essential nature of the task. By these criteria some tasks are "all or none"; their maxima and minima coincide. In other tasks there may be only a small separation between maximum and minimum. In a third category the separation between the natural maxima and minima is large. Finally there are tasks in which maxima and minima do not occur at all. Hoppe classified his tasks into those in which the difference between maximum and minimum was small and those in which it was large. Then he tabulated frequency of changes in LA in both types of tasks as a function of success and failure (Table 4.3).

In attempting to explain his findings, Hoppe adhered to the Lewinian assumption that the "quasi-need" to complete a task is eliminated by a successful performance. On this assumption alone the tendency to continue with an activity after success and to abandon it after failure cannot be explained. On the contrary, success should lead to quitting and failure to continued striving. But continuation after success and quitting after failure can both be explained on the assumption that success increases the valence (attractiveness) of the instrumental activity and failure lowers its valence. However, this assumption cannot account for raising LA after success or for quitting after success. If S's aim were merely to achieve pleasure by continuing an attractive activity and adding to his string of successes, the proper prediction would be no increase in his LA at all, and there is no basis for predicting quitting unless performance deteriorates to the point where failures occur.

Changes in LA during a specific task can be understood by assuming that each momentary LA corresponds not only to its unique quasi-need but also to a more comprehensive tension system characterized by the ideal goal. Thus, the actions relating to successive LAs have the sense of being stepwise approaches toward an ulterior goal. As one of Hoppe's Ss put it, "There is a whole hierarchy of goals, of which the chief—'to carry out the task in the given conditions'—does not quite come into question, though it is always present." This general goal Hoppe called the *ideal goal* to distinguish it from the *real goal* which is expressed by the momentary LA. The ideal goal is usually the natural maximum of the task, and thus remains constant. But LA typically fluctuates and so the separation between the real and ideal goals changes during the course of activity as a function of success and failure. Furthermore, success and failure affect the "reality" of the ideal goal, which gains in reality as performance approaches it, and vice versa. Only when the ideal goal is real can it determine behavior, and it is most real when it coincides with LA.

More broadly considered, changes in LA point to the person's consciousness of self, to his self-level (*Ich-niveau*), which he tends to raise *as high as possible*. A series of facts makes it clear that the

TABLE 4.3

Frequency of changes in LA as a function of success and failure, and of size of difference between task maxima and minima

	Difference (Max. − Min.)	
	Small	Large
After Success		
Raise	0	21
Same	1	4
Lower	—	—
Quit	2	9
Early Success	—	—
After Failure		
Raise	—	—
Same	4	7
Lower	18	14
Quit	8	5
Early Failure	2	—

The unit is the individual LA, not the individual *S*.
(After Hoppe, 1931, p. 27.)

displacement of LA depends not so much on the characteristics of different tasks, but on the *set* (*Einstellung*) and *character* of the S: (*a*) holding task constant, there is variation in the initial LA over a group of Ss; (b) the general behavior of the S shows that success and failure have an "immediate reference" to the central "I" of the S, e.g., they change his relations with E; (*c*) the experience of success or failure is regarded by S as an expression of his own value. Thus S often seeks to separate himself from responsibility for failures, or to regard outstanding successes as merely luck, or to regard successful performances as "humanly impossible;" (*d*) success and failure are often referred to the evaluation of S as a *social being;* there is greater anxiety when E is present than when he is absent. The tendency to maintain the highest possible self-level implies a continuing pressure to raise LA. This pressure also explains why Ss sometimes set goals which transcend the natural maxima of their tasks; "a relation which is explained neither from a fixation of pleasure on the activity, nor as the after effect of the original quasi-need" (Hoppe, 1931, p. 36). This pressure for the *highest possible* self-level also induces conflict between the desire to lower LA so as to avoid failure and the desire to raise it to assure success at the highest possible level.

Shortly after Hoppe's pioneer work, American psychologists began to study LA. They reported that changes in LA depended less on the characteristics of tasks than on the set and character of individual Ss (Frank, 1935a), and so they urged the use of LA procedures in the study of "personality" (Frank, 1938; Rotter, 1942). The effect of performance in one task on LA in a subsequent task was less dependent on the similarity of the two tasks than on the characteristics of the Ss (Frank, 1935b), although children who generally succeeded in school set characteristically different LAs than did those who failed (Sears, 1941; Jucknat, 1937). The *average* LAs of successful and failing children were not different, but the forms of the LA distributions were. In the successful group the distribution had a single mode with a mean close to and slightly above the level of actual performance, but in the failure group the distribution was *bimodal,* with some of the Ss setting LAs consistently far higher than their actual performances and others setting LAs consistently far below their performance levels. According to criteria suggested by Lewin and formalized by Irwin (1944), the LAs of the successful children were "realistic," and those of the unsuccessful children were "unrealistic." The realism of S's stated LAs depends on the form of the question he answers: realistic if he attempts to *predict* his next score or to state his actual goal for the next trial; unrealistic if he announces what he regards as his best (or worst) possible score, the score he hopes (or fears) to get, or the score which would completely satisfy him (Preston and Bayton, 1941; Irwin and Mintzer, 1942; Diggory, 1949). Changes in LA also depend on the prestige and presumed ability of the reference group with whose norms S's performance is compared (Chapman and Volkmann, 1939; Preston and Bayton, 1941; Festinger, 1942b, 1954).

Since 1944, when the LA literature was reviewed and summarized by Lewin and his colleagues (Lewin, Dembo, Festinger, and Sears, 1944), no essentially new notions have been introduced. The only noteworthy use of the ideas on a large scale has been in connection with the analysis of the "achievement motive" (n-Ach) (McClelland, Atkinson, Clark, and Lowell, 1953). Lewin et al. (1944) presented an elaborate "resultant vector" theory of choice of LA (or goal), a theory that had been worked out by Escalona (1940) and Festinger (1942a) in accordance with Hoppe's suggestion that a person chooses his LA so as to resolve the conflict between setting it low enough to avoid failure and high enough to assure the maximum possible success. Atkinson's (1957) model has many points in common with the earlier theory. Both assume a motivated S who finds that the available goals or incentives are not equally attractive. Both assume that S estimates his probability of success, $P(s)$, vis-à-vis any goal (LA) and chooses the one whose attractiveness multiplied by its estimated $P(s)$ gives a product that is maximal in the available set of alternatives. Both theories also assume that failure is aversive (valence or incentive value is negative), and goals in which the product of the aversiveness of the goal and the probability of incurring the aversive state is maximal are avoided.

These theories part company on the interesting question of whether goals which are highly attractive are also very difficult to achieve, and conversely. The Lewinian formulation admits this as a question of fact because it *assumes* no automatic correlation between valence and difficulty of achievement. Doubtless the Lewinians would agree that a case for such a correlation could be made empirically, but they would also agree that important exceptions might occur which would make the correlation less than perfect. Thus the Lewinian theory has the virtue of flexibility in that it does not specifically prohibit the design of experiments which attempt to vary (or measure) goal attractiveness and $P(s)$ independently. On the other hand, Atkinson quite consciously leaves no room for questions of fact on this issue. His theory asserts that if, for example, the incentive value (I) (Lewinians read "valence") of a goal has the hypothetical maximum value of 1.00, then the probability of success $P(s)$ for that goal is zero, and if $I = .90$, $P(s) = .10$; $I = .10$, $P(s) = .90$. Thus a perfect negative correlation between goal attractiveness and $P(s)$ is *built into* the theory. Another point of difference is that Atkinson distinguished two kinds of situations in which a person might be motivated to work at a particular task: first, if only one task is available then S can choose only how hard to work at it (a "constrained" situation); and second, the situation where S is confronted by several tasks and must choose among them (a "free" situation).

From the above discussion of LA there appears the high probability of its being raised after success and lowered after failure; that aspirations are not set at all for completely unfamiliar tasks; that success or failure may be interpreted, at least by some Ss, as reflecting on their own value; that LA can change both within the continuum defined by a single criterion such as speed of performance, or it can change by shifting from one criterion to another, for example from speed to quality, or from method to product; that spontaneous cessation of work on a task can occur (a) in monotonously repetitive easy tasks where LA can hardly be defined at all, (b) in tasks where S has achieved and raised his LA to the natural limit of the task so no further advances in LA are possible, or (c) in tasks where S has set an LA but achieved it only rarely if at all so that it appears that advances in LA are impossible because of limitations on S's ability; that social factors are important in determining S's response to his success or failure; that successes and failures apparently differ somehow in intensity, a difference which appears correlated with S's subsequent LAs; and that any individual LA is a momentary (real) goal, not necessarily the ultimate goal of the performance which S undertakes.

The quantitative methods later introduced into the study of LA, however crude they were, have definite advantages over the impressionistic observational methods which Hoppe used. Generally this quantification has been achieved by defining a numerical performance scale for S in terms of amount of product per unit time or amount of time per unit product. When S performs the task his performance is timed or his product measured and either his real score or a falsified score is reported to him. For the next trial, and for every subsequent trial, S is asked to state his LA in units of the same scale on which his performance is being measured. Readers unfamiliar with this technique are referred to the review by Lewin, Dembo, Festinger, and Sears (1944) and to the experiments described later in this chapter. This quantification made possible the demonstration that LA was sensitive to instructions, and to the elaboration of the notion that LA series differed, by fairly precise criteria, in their degree of "realism;" it also made possible the studies of the conditions under which experience on one task affected the LA in a subsequent task, and of the effect on LA of comparing S's performance with various reference groups. These results constitute the main contribution to our knowledge of LA since Hoppe. However, quantification has also had a narrowing effect.

First, there are no experiments known to this author which attempted to study the conditions under which S changes his LA by shifting from one criterion to another, a topic of great importance for our final understanding of what "mastery" means. We should be long past the point where it is sufficient merely to register whether or not we agree with Woodworth (1958) that organisms, especially man, strive to master their environments, or our agreement with White (1959) that "competence" is a fundamental human motive. Though perhaps we cannot yet decide the extent to which such motivation is primary, or conditioned somehow by learning or other contacts with the environment, we can certainly observe the ubiquitous occurrences of the phenomena that Woodworth and White are talking about and we can begin to unravel some of their details. It is likely that an experiemntal unraveling of the details will help us decide what kinds of phenomena these are and to give them at least a tentative place in a theory of behavior. If a person freely chooses his own goals, his behavior is based on certain contingencies which he confronts in the course of his action. If he chooses an activity which he never attempted before, his first attempts will be purely exploratory. He will test his skill, the materials, the time requirements, and the tools and equipment. He will discover minor problems and solve them if he can. He is likely to make only a minimal commitment to the task. The question of success or failure does not arise because his goal, if he has one, is merely to see whether or not the thing is possible at all. Once this exploration ends and he begins a more or less systematic attempt to produce something, he very likely will set implicit or explicit LAs for his successive attempts; then he can define success or failure. He seldom needs anyone to tell him when he succeeds or fails because he sets his own standards of performance. At first these standards are likely to be modest, relatively easy to achieve, but he moves always toward standards more difficult to achieve. The standards he uses are quite varied and may change from one attempt to the next. Now he tries to produce a result as good as the last one, but quicker. Next, he may disregard time altogether and try to improve the product. Later he may concentrate on the smoothness of the process and attempt to swing elegantly through a well-ordered and efficient routine. He may discover and invent new processes, or adapt new materials or new methods of work. To the casual uninterested observer this may all seem repetitive and dull, but the operator, the worker, may be intensely interested because he never has exactly the same goal on two successive trials. He is in charge of the goals and their general trend is upward, always ahead of his actual performance, always aimed at doing something better. By this process of gently spurring himself to successively higher achievements, he approaches mastery of himself and his environment. He is making himself a better man. Things like this happen occasionally to most of us. Sometimes they happen without warning or without previous intent on our part, and we discover only retrospectively that we have spent time improving ourselves and our work, completely oblivious of our surroundings or of the passage of time, trapped in the pathway to mastery. So much we can compose from the materials of our common observation and from the LA literature.

Another important point on which there is no systematic information in the LA literature is Hoppe's observation that the series of LAs adopted by S in the course of several trials of a particular task may be S's attempt to approach an ultimate goal stepwise. Third, neither Hoppe nor any other student of LA thought to consider how important, in determining our estimate of the likelihood that we will achieve an ultimate goal, is the amount of time or number of opportunities we have to reach it, but time, or more precisely limitation of time, puts the term to all our strivings. None of us has infinite time to accomplish anything, and it is a rare society indeed that can afford all of its constituent individuals very large amounts of time to accomplish even the most mundane tasks. We all face deadlines, whether they are long or short or whether they are imposed by other people, natural circumstances, or by ourselves is no matter; they are there.

Suppose that a person is trying to achieve a goal of performance which is set by other people or by circumstances. It is not necessary to suppose that this is his ultimate goal. It may be a sub-goal, a way station on the route to what he is "really after." For example, if he wants to become a lawyer or physician or mathematician or theologian he must demonstrate, *in advance of* his admission to any of these groups, that he can meet the minimum performance criteria which are established by the group as the precondition of admission. Furthermore, in most such cases no one is expected to achieve the criterion performance instantaneously or in a single short-term attempt.

We don't expect anyone to become adept at bridge or chess or base-ball or conversation or thinking or painting or housecleaning in a single attempt.[3] We allow time (in fact, a number of attempts) for the individual gradually to approach, and hopefully to surpass, the minimum standard of mastery, but we do not, we *cannot*, allow unlimited time. The deadline is always there. We do not have unlimited time to give, for death puts a term to all our strivings. Furthermore in even the most commonplace life there are many goals to be achieved and therefore, as Murray (1938) has emphasized, some kind of scheduling must take place. If X *must* be done before Y can be attempted, then the urgency of getting Y done at all puts a term on behavior related to X. The intricate interlocking of our many purposes suggests that the notion of time can be discovered in the phenomena of purposive behavior without regard to sidereal time, clock time, or any other temporal conception.

The mere fact of improvement in performance, or even the experience of an uninterrupted series of "successes" by the criterion of achieving a series of constantly increasing LAs, does not guarantee success with respect to the ultimate goal. Indeed people often act as though they expected success or failure *in advance* of the hard evidence, and that they react to this expectation as though it were a certainty. Many a person quits, in advance of the final proof of his failure, under circumstances that lead us to believe that the only basis for his quitting is the *expectation* that he *will* fail. His performance may have improved steadily, and may now be not far from the minimum standard demanded of him, but he quits. Another man, in apparently identical or similar circumstances, continues to work diligently toward the goal. Why does one quit and the other continue, supposing that at the beginning of their efforts each found the goal equally inviting and that they are not competing in a one-person zero-sum game? A plausible answer is that the two made different estimates of $P(s)$. The one who quits estimates his $P(s)$ too low to justify further attempts; the other estimates his $P(s)$ high enough to encourage himself to go on working. What data do they have or what *could* they have on which to base their different expectations? Obviously, if the average level of a person's performance is close to the goal level, he should estimate his $P(s)$ higher than if there is a large difference between his performance and the goal. Possibly also the rate of improvement in performance, or the change in rate over a series

[3] Judging from current practices, people often *do* think that a person injected into husband-wife or parent-child relations can automatically perform the tasks thus laid on him. However, that is another story.

of past performances, influences the estimation of $P(s)$. Specifically, if performance is improving (though still below the level of the goal), the higher the rate the higher should the $P(s)$ estimate be. Or, if the rate of improvement is increasing, $P(s)$ should be high and perhaps also increasing; and conversely if the rate of improvement is decreasing. Where does the deadline come in? As we shall see, there is some reason to suppose that the effect of level of performance and its rate of improvement and changes in the rate have only contingent effects on the way $P(s)$ is estimated. Their effects depend on how near the deadline is. For equal rates of improvement, from an arbitrary fixed distance below the goal, $P(s)$ will be higher the further away the deadline is.

METHODS AND PROCEDURES

Independent Variables

Performance Curves. The experiments reported here have several common points of technique which will be explained first. The general idea is to set up in the laboratory a miniature scale model of the kinds of goal-striving situations just discussed. In this situation S should be presented continuously with complete information about (a) the fixed performance goal he is expected to try to achieve, (b) the number of attempts he will be allowed to have, and (c) his performance at every trial. He should be able to see his complete performance curve, up to any given time, in relation to the fixed goal and the deadline. The simple apparatus shown in Fig. 4.1 provides such a record. The board is a piece of perforated tempered masonite (known also as "pegboard") $\frac{1}{8}$ inch thick with holes $\frac{1}{2}$ inch apart, center to center. The edges of the holes are subject to pressure and abrasion in repeated use, and these effects are best resisted by the *tempered* material. The frame should be at least $1\frac{1}{2}$ inches wide on the front face and at least $\frac{3}{4}$ inch thick. On the front face of the frame, flush with the inner edge, are mounted long channels formed of heavy-gauge aluminum (about $\frac{1}{16}$ inch thick) and extending the length of the frame on three sides. These channels are attached to the frame with small flat-headed screws which are countersunk flush with the bottom of the channel to allow cardboard strips with appropriate numbers on them to be slid in and out. Placing channels for the number strips on three sides of the frame permits the board to be used with its long axis either horizontal or vertical. The dimensions of the usable area of the board should be generous, but they may be varied to allow for portability or ease of storage. In our main laboratory we have a board, mounted on the wall, with usable surface 7 feet 11 inches long and 3 feet 11 inches high. The board shown in Fig. 4.1 is semi-portable with usable dimensions 3 feet 11 inches long and 27 inches high. We have made and used models as small as 24 inches by 30 inches and this is approximately the lower limit of usefulness unless one uses perforated material with smaller holes closer together. The reason for this is that the size of the board sets the limit on both number of trials and the range of the performance measure for which it can be used.

The performance goal which S is supposed to try to achieve is indicated by the horizontal white stripe at level 40, and the end of the trial series (the deadline) is indicated by the vertical white stripe. In the board pictures the stripes are of white plastic "gemp," available in most places where hobby supplies are sold, but thick white cotton twine serves just as well. Both these markers should be easily movable, and they should permit rapid extension of their *length*. In some of our experiments we had to change them rapidly between two adjacent trials. A convenient way to attach them to the board is to tie them

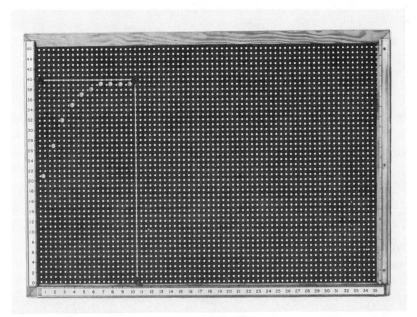

Fig. 4.1   Photograph of performance display panel. See text for detailed description.

around ordinary tapered golf tees which are pushed tightly into the appropriate holes in the panel.

In most of our experiments we controlled the information which S got about his performance. Such control eliminates the messy routine of dealing with differences between LA and related performances (called D scores, for "discrepancy scores" in the LA literature), and the need to control for inter-subject variability in performance when trying to demonstrate that a certain phenomenon is a function of performance. Furthermore, control of the form of the performance curve permits us to examine in detail the effects on $P(s)$ and LA of level, rate, acceleration, and other aspects of the performance curve in a fairly precise manner whenever we want to. Our method of control required that S's task should consist of discrete units of output that could easily be counted either by S or by E. Furthermore we wanted tasks to which, by instructions, we could attach some psychological significance; the task must appear to S to be a plausible measure of what we said it was measuring. Card sorting is a task which meets both these criteria and we used it in several of our experiments on the basic properties of $P(s)$, though as occasion demanded we used a variety of other tasks as well, which will be explained at appropriate places in this and the following chapters.

In the card-sorting task, the typical method of controling the performance curve was this. First we told S what we wanted him to believe about the purpose of the experiment. Then we described the task and its relation to the alleged purpose. Usually we told him that he was to try to improve his card-sorting performance to the point where he could sort 40 cards correctly into the ten suits (see Fig. 4.2) at least once in ten trials. Each trial was to last for 25 seconds. The experimenter had a stopwatch which he turned on when he said "Go" at the start of each trial and which he stopped when he said "Stop" at the end of the trial. However, E, instead of looking at the watch, was watching S, counting the cards as they were sorted, and E said "Stop" when S had correctly sorted out a *predetermined* number of cards for each trial. Then E collected the cards, ostentatiously discarded errors, counted the correct ones, and told S his "score" for that trial. Also, E stuck a golf tee into the appropriate hole in the masonite "graph" to show S the score. When several trials' scores had been thus displayed, the performance curve began to take form. Fig. 4.1 shows one of the performance curves thus generated after S had completed the allotted ten trials. In our various experiments we used many different performance curves, as explained below. In some experiments the characteristics of the performance curve

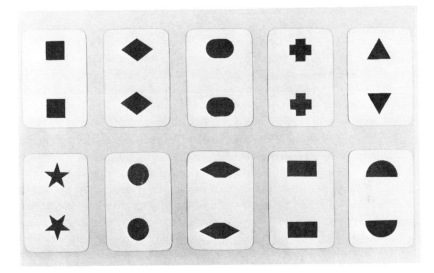

Fig. 4.2   Typical display presented to Ss in card-sorting tasks.

reported to S were the only independent variables, but we often combined them with other independent variables, notably those of "motivation" and clarity and distance of the deadline, both of which will now be explained.

Motivation

In our usage, the variable of motivation refers to S's supposed intensity of desire to achieve the required standard of performance in our experimental tasks, not because the performance is especially important in itself but because it is instrumental to some reward or benefit which is contingent on the performance. Thus, in one experiment with children, the Ss were told in effect, "If you can make a score of 40 on at least one trial out of the ten then you can have this toy." The toys had been previously examined by the children and there was little doubt that they universally preferred the expensive, intricate, large toys (suitably varied; for example, compressed-air powered missiles—"soars 150 feet 150!"—for boys; and elegant, near life-size dolls for girls) to small, uncomplicated, cheap toys (also selected appropriately for the sex of the Ss). Since *objectively* the toys were quite different in play value as well as cost and impressiveness in size, and the children's *reactions* were correspondingly different, we assumed that a child would be more "motivated" if he were offered one of the grand toys for a good performance than if he were offered a less impressive toy or none at all. In other experiments the motivation variable was introduced by offering half the Ss a sum of money for a good performance while no prize at all was mentioned to the others. By thus "sweetening the pot," we could select Ss from a wide variety of groups and assign them randomly to planned experimental conditions.

It is clear that such manipulations cannot approach the limits of intensity of desire especially for college students who, as young adults, are already involved in the long-range serious purposes of life, or at least are interested in larger sums of money and more elaborate benefits than we could offer. Therefore, for college students we developed another tactic. This involved trading on our position as psychologists, and on the widespread knowledge that psychologists develop and use "tests" to discover whether people are qualified for admission to various statuses or functions. We represented ourselves as carrying out such testing and selection functions. The various activities for which we allegedly served as "gate-keepers" were: (a) admission to a special program which provided free training in the physical sciences to qualified and interested individuals; (b) admission to a special "Career Liaison Group," designed to give college students the opportunity to integrate their academic programs with specific professional and administrative roles in business and industry; (c) admission of S to a special experimental program on the learning of complex strategies from which the individual could derive the benefit of expert training in the basic principles underlying games like chess and Go; (d) admission to either the administrative or the scientific hierarchy of a "National Space Science Program." The usual procedure was to give a detailed explanation of one of these prospective goals to students, either singly or in classroom groups, and then to schedule private interviews with those who volunteered. Sometimes the interview began with a detailed explanation of what would be required of the person if he were admitted to the "program." This permitted a fuller evaluation of S's interest and those who admitted only superficial interest or who flatly refused to have anything more to do with it were dismissed with our expression of complete understanding and respect for their decision, but with no further explanations. When procedures like these were in operation, the word *experiment* was *never* used, and the word *test* was always substituted for, or combined with, the word *task*. We tried by every means to convince our prospective Ss that we were intent on serious business and to elicit, at least until we had the data we wanted, their most complete commitment to the attempt to qualify for the program in which they had expressed an interest. Our experimental tasks became the qualifying tests. We believe that, by thus using as Ss people who volunteered to try and qualify for a particular activity, we greatly limited the variability of interest in our experimental groups. We are under no illusions, and neither should the reader be, that we have produced groups with perfectly homogeneous motivation. We undoubtedly used Ss who had private reservations about the intensity of their commitment and whose real motive was to satisfy their curiosity about the activities of psychologists. They might have planned, without telling us, to make their full commitment only after they discovered how well they did on the qualifying tests. However, to the extent that they believed our speeches, our subjects were homogeneous (relative to randomly selected people) in that they knew what they were there for, and that they had gotten themselves into the situation because of their interest in the advertised program.

Caveat: Credibility of the Experiments and Care of Ss

Did the Ss believe us? Did they doubt our elaborate ruses to control the information about their performance or to manipulate their motivation? For the most part they did believe us, or there is no reason to doubt their belief. It is easy to discard the data of a subject who unerringly puts his finger on the very heart of the ruse, who says, for example, "You're not keeping the right time." It is also easy to discard those who simply go routinely through a procedure and then announce at the end that they have no faith whatsoever in the validity of psychological tests, that they wanted to see "what was up," and had been putting us through our paces when we thought it was the other way around. Of the 2,232 Ss originally recruited, only 31 were rejected for these reasons.

There is another kind of apparent disbelief which is liable to worry the neophyte experimenter; namely, the case in which the subject voices a suspicion that all is not well. Alert and interested Ss, particularly intelligent ones, are curious about every aspect of their surroundings, especially when they are being "tested." Many times what appears to be suspicion is really only their lack of understanding of some irrelevant event or of some aspect of the procedure. Such apparent suspicions can be tested and often allayed if E can produce a plausible explanation of something S asks about. If the question is asked by a large number of Ss, E can revise his introductory instructions so that the question is answered before it is raised by subsequent Ss. This we were able to do in several cases when we found the Ss puzzled about the plausibility of the connection between our actual test procedures and the kind of abilities we said we were testing. In most cases it was evident that Ss accepted these explanations and it was also easy to recognize when they did not accept them. In the latter case the S was excused with a full explanation if he had literally caught us "red-handed;" if it were more expedient, he was continued in the procedure but his data were excluded from the analysis. Some Ss wondered aloud that the time for one trial didn't seem the same as the time for the previous trial. We handled this by saying that short time intervals are not accurately judged or experienced especially when a person is hard at work on an interesting task. This bit of otherwise accurate information usually stopped any further questioning.

Other evidence of the credibility of our stage settings in Ss' eyes is that many Ss were visibily disturbed by the evidence that they had failed or were about to do so. This was most often noticed in conditions where the outcome was of an important or serious nature. When these Ss were told, and had it proved to them, that the whole procedure was a sham and that we actually knew no more about their abilities after the experiment than we did when we started, their relief was often strongly evident. On the other hand, those Ss who had been allowed to "succeed" were disappointed when we told them that their performance did not lead to the promised rewards.

The importance of post-experimental care of Ss in experiments of this kind cannot be emphasized too strongly. To the extent that we raise S's motivation anywhere near to the desired intensity, and tap his attitude toward abilities that are genuinely important to him, there is always the danger of permanently damaging his self-confidence. This poses a dilemma. Ideally, no S should ever leave the laboratory, after such an experience as we have described, without a full explanation of what happened, exactly what deceptions were employed, and why the whole thing was done. However, if the Ss are recruited from a group in which person-to-person communication is as easy as it is in a school, or a university, or a ward in a mental hospital, E may find all but his first two or three Ss "spoiled" by the information they get from their mates who have already been through the procedure and heard the explanation. With groups of children and with mental patients this risk is too high even if E swears each S to secrecy. Youngsters and psychotics, even if they have no malevolent intentions, are too irresponsible to be trusted. There is no way to pass cleanly between the horns of this dilemma. Our solution was to withhold all explanations from children until the experiment was finished and then to explain to all of them at once just what had happened. When prizes had been awarded on obviously spurious grounds then consolation prizes were given to each child or the entire group was rewarded with a party. We were always prepared to take immediate and radical action if it appeared that a child was deeply disturbed over the results of his participation in the experiment, but we never had to do so. In the case of psychotic patients, on the other hand, we always told them that they were in an experiment, and the motivational pressures were always kept pretty low and dealt with immediate and relatively trivial objectives. This relatively low-pressure feature also characterized our experiments with children. At best our procedures with children and psychotics elicited the amount of intense momentary interest one would normally arouse in an absorbing and moderately difficult game. We never attempted to explain the methods or purposes of our experiments to psychotic Ss.

With students in high school and college, we proceeded differently. Not only did we credit them with the capacity to be aroused by the strongest motivational pressures we could produce, we also frankly relied on their responsibility. None of these Ss ever left the experimental setting without a full explanation of our purposes and procedures. This explanation, which began when the last bit of data was recorded, aimed to make it clear that S had not been subjected to a *real evaluation*. This was facilitated by the fact that we could *prove* in most cases that what we were *now* saying was true. We displayed our neatly drawn tables of the design of the experiment, the typed or mimeographed lists of false scores which had been reported to S, revealed any hidden apparatus we had, told him about the results of previous experiments, and if possible showed him the data previously collected in the present one. We told him about the random process of assignment to experimental conditions and the role played by "blind chance" in what had happened to him. If S appeared exceedingly angry or otherwise disturbed we sought catharsis: an oft-used gambit was, "I wouldn't blame you much if you punched me." By the time these Ss left the laboratory their mood was at least that of polite interest; more often it was quite profound. Some of the Ss kept us for as much as an hour after the experiment was over, talking about self-evaluation as an interesting intellectual problem. Some sought us out later for additional discussion and many asked for references to published work in this field, including descriptions of our own experiments.

We made no systematic attempt to follow up our Ss, but the writer has met several of them in classes or at social functions two or three years after their participation in the experiments. Several of them spontaneously referred with amusement to their service as Ss and evinced great interest in later developments. Our relations were cordial; the former Ss, to the extent that we know about them, are co-conspirators, sharers of a secret.

After we had made a clean breast of our deceptions the Ss hardly needed to be told how greatly we depended on their keeping the secret, and by and large they kept it very well. We have had exasperated queries from students who knew someone who had been in one of our experiments, but who steadfastly refused to give any information, and referred the curious to us instead. One prospective S appeared for his appointment and told E that he had been "spoiled" by overhearing a conversation between two former Ss who didn't know anyone else was around. We have no evidence, then, that an experimenter runs a serious risk of contaminating his subject pool by taking his Ss completely into his confidence as we have described. A full elaboration of this technology would require detailed study of the conditions under which people keep secrets, but that is not what this book is about. We have only the suspicion that in such a situation E should be willing to submit to detailed probing by S after the experiment until S is convinced that E has nothing further to hide. A relation of mutual *confidence* is probably a precondition for one that is genuinely *confidential*.

Deadlines

In manipulating the clarity and nearness of the deadline we generally scheduled each S for an hour, though the procedure would take at most 25 minutes. Thus, we could leave the deadline marker off the masonite graph at the beginning and tell S that we could not be sure how many trials we would have time for, but that there would surely be time for at least ten, or any other convenient number. Then E promised that at the end of the tenth trial (if ten were the minimum promised) he would consult his watch and inform S of how many additional trials there would be. When that was done, E announced some predetermined number of additional trials and quickly put the deadline marker in place and extended the performance marker to cover the entire span of trials. This produced a series of early trials, of any length we wanted, in which the deadline was not clearly defined at all, and also allowed us to manipulate the distance of the deadline from the time it was first made clear.

Dependent Variables

The tale of how the dependent variables were measured is soon told. They were (*a*) Ss' estimates of *P*(*s*); (*b*) Ss' stated LAs; (*c*) Ss' evaluations of their own abilities (self-evaluations); and (*d*) Ss' real performances, as distinct from the false performance reports he was given.

P(*s*). Estimates of *P*(*s*) were obtained by the use of linear rating scales like the ones shown in Appendix A. Before each trial, including the first, S filled in trial number and score (trial "0" and score "X" for his preliminary estimate before the first trial) and then made a single mark on the scale to answer the question. For each estimate S used a clean slip of paper and he placed each marked slip face down on a pile to reduce the likelihood that his next response would be contaminated by previous ones. In the "high motivation" (Hi Mot) conditions, the question which accompanied the scale always referred to a test. For low motivation conditions (Lo Mot) the question merely asked S about his chances of sorting at least 40 cards correctly on at least one of the remaining trials. Thus, *P*(*s*) is intended to be S's estimate of the likelihood that he will reach the goal sometime within the remaining trials. It does not refer to the likelihood that he will make it on any particular trial, nor to the likelihood that he will achieve some private LA (goal) on the *next* trial.

For work with children, Sylvia Farnham-Diggory modified the *P*(*s*) estimation procedure in the following way. On an area of the masonite graph which was not to be used for the display of performance data, a heavy cord was stretched between two golf tees which were about 28 holes (14 inches) apart. On the cord was strung a large red wooden bead. Above the cord was a row of ten golf tees equally spaced. After the task had been explained to the S in a general way, E filled in th first three trials of a sample performance curve on the graph. These, E said, were scores made by another boy (or girl) when he (she) began the task. The golf tees were spoken of as a line of marching soldiers and S was asked to state how sure he was that the remaining 7 "soldiers" had "marched across." S was to push the bead to the extreme right-hand end of the cord, the end which was marked by a label "March Across" (see Fig. 4.3). S moved the bead to the other end near the "Bump" label when he was very sure the "soldiers" would not march across. Then E required S to explain what various intermediate positions of the bead meant. When it was clear that S understood how to register his estimates by this method, he was asked to estimate, before the first trial, how sure he

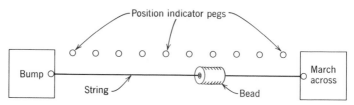

Fig. 4.3 Diagram of string-and-bead indicator used to obtain $P(s)$ estimates from children.

was that he could make his "soldiers" march across the goal line before they bumped into the deadline. On each trial S's score was recorded on the graph in the manner described above and E moved the bead back to the extreme left-hand end of the cord and said: "Look how your soldiers are marching. Show me, with the bead, how sure you are *now* that your soldiers will march across the goal line before they bump into the deadline."

None of the children in our experiments had any difficulty in understanding these instructions. Often they stated their reasons for placing the bead. For example, an eight-year-old boy placed the bead one graduation below the "March Across" label and said: "This means I'm absolutely one hundred per cent all the way sure of making it. Almost." Many of the children, at some time during their series of trials, spontaneously traced the projected path of the pegs, and compared the distance of the goal with the distance from the deadline, thus showing their comprehension of the displayed information. The E recorded the children's $P(s)$ estimates on a ten-point scale by noting the number of the reference peg which was nearest to where the child set the bead (cf. Fig. 4.3).

Whenever Ss, whether children or adults, were allowed to have successful performances they were asked to estimate the likelihood that they could do at least that well *again*. This makes the $P(s)$ estimates during success experiences incomparable with those from failure experiences and we have always been careful to distinguish in our analyses the $P(s)$ ratings from the success and failure trials. Since most of the curves we used were monotonically rising ones, it was natural to put any success trials at the end of the series so that, even under success conditions, we lost very few trials from the analysis.

LA. For LA we always took S's answer to the question, "What score are you going to try to make on the next trial?" College and high school student Ss typically wrote this down in a space provided on a modified $P(s)$ rating slip. Children and mental patients typically gave an oral answer which was written down by E. It is important to emphasize that in asking the LA question in the indicated form we are getting as close as we can to asking for *S*'s *goal* for the next trial and *not* his *prediction* of the actual outcome ("What score do you *expect* to make . . . ?") nor his best imaginable performance ("What score do you *hope* to make assuming the best imaginable circumstances . . . ?").

Self-evaluations. For the most part our measures of self-evaluation have been strictly limited to *S*'s estimate of how good he thinks one of his specific abilities is. These ratings were obtained mostly by the use of linear rating scales, but the specific questions asked have not been as standardized as have those for $P(s)$ and LA. Sometimes we asked *S* to consider all the opportunities he has had to use an ability and to estimate the percentage of those occasions in which he has used is successfully. In other experiments we have used a linear rating scale with five equally spaced marks corresponding to the adjectives and numbers as follows: "Completely inadequate" (0), "Inadequate" (1), "So-so" (2), "Adequate" (3), and "Completely adequate" (4). On other scales, the equally spaced points corresponded to adjectives ranging from "Poor" to "Superior." In all cases *S*s were asked to mark the scale *at any point* they chose; they were not limited to choosing one of the graduation marks. We also occasionally used overall self-evaluation or "global" rating scales. In the following discussion it will be made clear in connection with each experiment just what measure of self-evaluation was used.

Real Performance. The measurement of *S*'s real performance, without his being aware that it was being measured, was first undertaken by Henry Morlock. Morlock hid a kymograph in a closet adjacent to the laboratory room. The kymograph could be started and stopped by *E*'s manipulation of a silent switch hidden just under the edge of the table at which he and *S* were sitting. When power was supplied to the kymograph, it also started an automatic timer which caused a stylus to mark one-second "blips" on the wax paper record. By means of another switch, *E* could cause a second stylus to record the beginning and end of any period he chose and the total length of this interval could be read, against the automatic time record, to the nearest tenth of a second. Then in a card-sorting task some convenient number of cards was chosen, a number which had to be sorted at least once by all the *S*s in the experiment. Typically, this was the minimum number required of all *S*s. All *E* had to do then was to record on the kymograph the beginning of each trial and the point in time at which *S* had sorted the standard number of cards, regardless of how many more cards the schedule permitted him to sort. This method has disadvantages in that it is not readily portable; and in schools and hospitals one cannot guarantee that power outlets will be conveniently located, or that administrators will permit holes to be drilled in the furniture for mounting hidden switches, or holes to be punched through walls to allow switch leads to pass from the kymograph closet to the laboratory room. Furthermore, kymographs break down and data are lost because, without further instrumentation, E cannot easily have a trouble signal; even if he had it he could not respond to it in the middle of an experimental session without arousing Ss' suspicions in one way or another. Having learned these disadvantages from practical experience, we devised a simpler method of measuring actual performance. This method, first used by Armin Loeb, requires only that E record (secretly) the actual elapsed time for each trial. Since we already have a record of the number of cards correctly sorted by S for each trial, we simply compute seconds-per-card as our index of performance, instead of recording, as with Morlock's method, the total number of seconds to sort a standard number of cards. Within any experiment all trials are comparable on either of these measures, and the two measures can be made comparable, where necessary, by converting the Morlock index to the Loeb index.

EXPERIMENTS ON P(S)

The Effects of the Performance Curve

Our first experiment was carried out by Eugene J. Riley simply to determine whether $P(s)$ estimates were in any way sensitive to variations in the type of performance curve reported to S. The design and results of the experiment are shown in Fig. 4.4. The eight small graphs in the figure correspond to the experimental conditions which were defined by the performance curves indicated by the dashed lines. There were four types of curves: (1) constant increment of two units per trial, (2) constant increment of one unit per trial, (3) negatively accelerating, and (4) positively accelerating. Each of these types began at a different level: the "High Start" at 21 cards sorted on the first trial and the "Low Start" at 11 cards sorted on the first trial. The Ss were 32 male college students recruited from an undergraduate psychology course in response to an announcement which was intended to make S expect that the experimental task was actually a screening test for an important career opportunity in the physical sciences (see Appendix B). This appeal corresponds to a condition of "high motivation" as explained earlier. Four Ss were randomly assigned to each of the eight experimental conditions. When

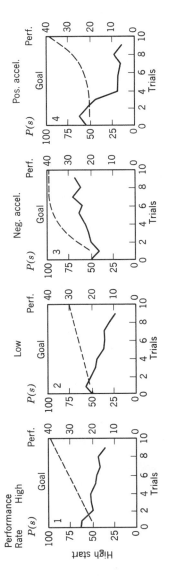

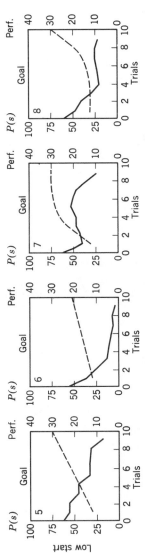

Fig. 4.4 Estimated $P(s)$ by trials as a function of level, slope, and shape of performance curves reported to Ss. Solid black lines are $P(s)$ trends. Dashed lines show reported performance curves. Each data point is the mean of four Ss. (After Diggory, Riley, and Blumenfeld, 1960.)

each S appeared for his "testing" appointment, he immediately signed a form authorizing that his name be included in the "list" referred to in the above announcement. It was explained that this form would later be countersigned by E, the test administrator, "if S passed the test." The E read the following instructions:

> The basic task (in this test) is to sort cards according to a pattern I will set up. Each card has a pattern on its face and there are 10 different patterns. You will be given a well-shuffled pack of 70 cards which you must hold face down in one hand. When I say go, take the top card of the pack, turn it over, and place it on top of the card on the table which has the same pattern on it. Do the same with the next card, and so on, until I say stop. (To pass the test) you must correctly sort at least 40 cards in 25 seconds.
>
> This (test) task may seem very simple, but actually several basic processes must be well coordinated to do a good job: memory for the forms and their locations, rapid perception of the forms as they appear, and manual dexterity in handling and placing the cards.
>
> Notice that on the board there is a string stretched at level 40 to indicate the score (the passing score) you are to try for. There is another string here [point] just after 10, to remind you that you will have 10 trials [used only for clear deadline conditions; see earlier]. I will show you your score after each trial by putting a peg in one of these holes.
>
> I will count only cards that are correctly placed, so if you sort 35 cards, but two are wrongly placed, your score is 33. Do you have any questions? I am going to ask you a question.

The question E asked was the question on the $P(s)$ rating form. The question was repeated and S filled out a new form before each subsequent trial.

As Fig. 4.4 clearly shows, the form of the trend in $P(s)$ is affected by the nature of the performance curve reported to S. In conditions 1, 2, 5, and 6, where the performance curve had a constant rate of improvement, we have a clear indication of the effect of rate and level on the $P(s)$ trends. First, there were no significant differences among conditions in initial $P(s)$ estimates (trial 0). This has been so generally true in our experiments that it will be taken for granted in all subsequent discussions, except where the initial differences were significant.[4] Table 4.4 summarizes the slopes of the $P(s)$ curves as

---

[4] Initial levels of all dependent variables in factorial designs were tested by analysis of variance. Differences between the slopes and the overall means of trend data were tested by Alexander's (1946) general test for trend, unless otherwise noted. All differences called significant, by whatever test, are at $p \leq .05$.

TABLE 4.4

Slopes of P(s) *Curves as a Function of Ss' Information About Their Performances*

Performance			
Start	Rate	Condition	Slope of $P(s)$ curve
High	High	1	-2.64
	Low	2	-3.23
Low	High	5	-4.77
	Low	6	-5.00

(After Diggory, Riley, and Blumenfeld, 1960, p. 48.)

a function of rate and level of the performance curves. All differences among slopes are significant, and since the initial levels do not differ, it should come as no surprise that the average levels of the $P(s)$ curves are also significantly different.

Thus, by manipulating the information we gave S about his performance, we found that the closer the average performance to the goal, the higher the average $P(s)$; the rate, or change of rate, in the performance curve also produced corresponding changes in the rate of change in $P(s)$. The rapid *initial* rise of the negatively accelerated performance curves (Conditions 3 and 7) was accompanied by a rise in $P(s)$. When the curve rose to within one point of the performance goal and stayed there (Condition 3), the $P(s)$ average generally continued its rise, though after trial 6 the course is somewhat erratic. When the final level of performance is 11 points below the goal (Condition 7), the $P(s)$ trend reversed and after trial 5 it steadily declined. With the positively accelerated performance curves it appears that the initial sequence of no improvement is so discouraging that the subsequent increasingly rapid rise in performance does no more than retard the rate of decrease in estimated $P(s)$; it certainly does nothing to make it increase. The next experiment, also done by Riley, was designed to show that the nearness and clarity of the deadline is important in determining the $P(s)$ trends.

Vague and Clear Deadlines

Riley used two types of performance curves in this experiment: (*1*) the negatively accelerated curve shown in Condition 3 of

Fig. 4.4, and (2) the curve of constant increment (one unit per trial) shown in Condition 2, Fig. 4.4. Both of these curves can be extended beyond ten trials without crossing the goal line: the negatively accelerated curve indefinitely so, and the constant rate curve to 18 trials. Sixteen Ss with "high motivation" (Hi Mot) instructions were started out on each curve. Their "testing" appointments had been scheduled for one hour, and they were told at the outset that E was uncertain about the number of trials there would be time for. However, he promised each S at least ten trials and said he would check his watch after the tenth trial and then decide how many more trials S would get. Fig. 4.5 shows the average $P(s)$ estimates over trials 0–9 while the deadline was vague. At trial 10, the deadline was announced to one quarter of the Ss as one trial away; another quarter of the group was promised two more trials; another quarter, four more trials; and another quarter, eight more trials. This accounts for the eight sets of data points in the right-hand section of Fig. 4.5. The announcement of the position of the deadline was made *after* S had completed trial 10 but *before* he knew his score for that trial; thus the estimate of $P(s)$ for trial 10 belongs to the clear deadline condition. This is the point in the experiment at which sudden revelation of nearness of the deadline might be expected to be effective, so we analyzed the changes in the estimates of $P(s)$ between trials 9 and 10. These mean changes, associated with their respective distances from the announced deadline, are as follows:

Number of trials after trial 10. . . .	1	2	4	8
Mean change of $P(s)$ trials 9–10. . .	-5.25	-3.00	0.00	$+1.13$

Obviously, the correlation between distance from the deadline and change in $P(s)$ between trials 9 and 10 is high. The effect of nearness of the deadline on the trend of the $P(s)$ estimates after trial 10 is shown even more clearly by the course of the curves in the right-hand half of Fig. 4.5. As every successive trial brings Ss nearer to the deadline, their mean estimated $P(s)$ declined at a rate corresponding roughly to the nearness of the deadline. The exception to this rule occurs with the steadily rising curve when Ss were allowed eight additional trials, and the exception itself is no doubt due to the continued steady approach to the goal.

In the first experiment there was no clear decrement in $P(s)$ when Ss were given a negatively accelerated performance curve which leveled off only one point below the goal level, but in the experiment

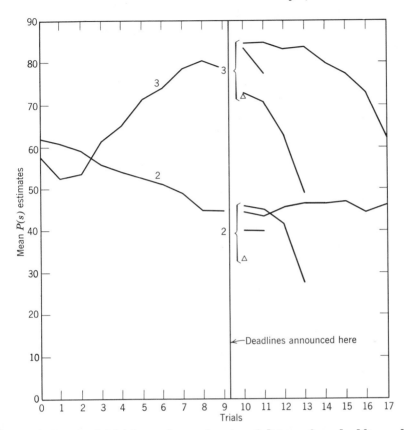

Fig. **4.5** Estimated $P(s)$ by trials as a function of distance from dead-line and type of performance curve (2 and 3, Fig. 4.4). Every point for trials 0–9 is the mean of 16 Ss; after trial 9, every point is the mean of four Ss. (After Diggory, Riley, and Blumenfeld, 1960.)

just reported it appears that using the same curve for a longer number of trials ultimately leads to a large reduction in estimated $P(s)$. Thus, we can conclude tentatively that the failure to find the decrement in $P(s)$ in the first experiment was due, at least in part, to the fact that in some sense S did not have enough information in the ten trials.

Value of Being Successful (Motivation)

At Riley's urging we turned next to the problem of varying motivation. Since, in the two experiments just described, we had reason to believe that the motivation of all the Ss was as high as we could plausibly and safely make it, we arranged another set of instructions to reduce it. In the low motivation (Lo Mot) instructions, we simply told prospective Ss that we were engaged in experiments on the acquisition of skill in complex performances, and we chose half of our Ss from students who volunteered in their classrooms in response to this appeal. In other classrooms we made the announcement appropriate to the Hi Mot condition and recruited the rest of our Ss from those who volunteered to take the "test." We also decided to explore the limits of our ability to manipulate the *level* of the performance curves; we made up five curves, all identical in form to those shown in Conditions 3 and 7 of Fig. 4.4, but differing in starting level. The starting levels chosen were 5, 9, 12, 17, and 21 cards correctly sorted, with the announced goal (or "passing score") of 40. We had four Hi Mot and four Lo Mot Ss for each performance (40 Ss in all). We observed that the mean $P(s)$ level over all trials was consistently higher for Ss in the Hi Mot conditions than in the Lo Mot conditions, but the difference steadily decreased with increasing nearness of the performance curve to the goal. Since this effect was of considerable interest the entire experiment was repeated by Ruth Blumenfeld exactly as Riley had done it first. Blumenfeld's replication was made eight months after Riley's, with a different group of Ss.

The data from the two experiments were combined for presentation here because there were no significant differences between them. Thus we have a total of eight Ss in each of the ten conditions defined by the two levels of motivation and the five levels of reported performance. The effect of level of performance curve on $P(s)$ estimates is shown in Fig. 4.6: a clean separation of the average $P(s)$ trends. Each curve differs significantly from those adjacent to it, both in mean level and in best fitting linear slope.

The effect of level of motivation is shown in Fig. 4.7 which presents the averages at each trial of the Hi Mot and Lo Mot Ss separately, without regard to level of performance curve. The Hi Mots have consistently higher average $P(s)$ estimates at every trial, but otherwise the *forms* of the $P(s)$ trends are identical.

The effect that made us repeat the experiment is illustrated in Fig. 4.8. It appears that, with the two sets of data combined, there is no tendency for a gradual reduction in the size of the difference between Hi Mot and Lo Mot, but rather that, at some point between the average performances represented by the highest and the second highest performance curves, the difference simply disappears. There is the possibility that within that interval there is a gradual reduction of the difference, but we have no data on this point. We were im-

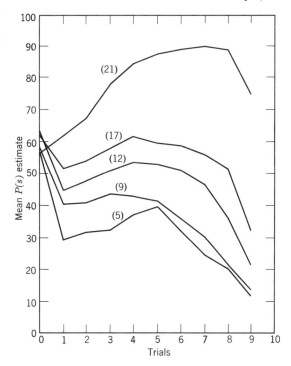

Fig. 4.6 Estimated $P(s)$ by trials as a function of distance between reported performance curve and goal. The reported performance curves had the form shown in panels 3 and 7 of Fig. 4.4; the numbers in parentheses indicate their starting levels. Each point is the mean of 16 Ss. (After Diggory, Riley, and Blumenfeld, 1960.)

pressed by the similarity of outcomes obtained when two different Es, one male and one female, repeated the same procedure on Ss who were exclusively male. There is every reason to believe that differences in the sex of E should in some cases make a difference to the way S responds (particularly if S is male) to a situation where his abilities are on trial. Apparently this is not one of those situations.

Interrupted Series of P(s) Estimates

Next, we wanted to find out whether the $P(s)$ trends as a function of variations in motivation, clarity of deadline, and nearness of performance to the goal would have the same form as those we had found so far if we sampled $P(s)$ at only a few trials instead of at every trial. This is important because, if our Ss were responding as much or more to their own *previous sequence* of $P(s)$ estimates than they were to the experimental conditions, then our experiments did not come sufficiently close to representing reality. In real life a person may undertake to reach a goal by a long series of different operations (corresponding to the trials in our situation), but he need not necessarily estimate his $P(s)$ after every attempt. Indeed, the occasions for such estimates may be less numerous than the actual attempts, and they may be spaced quite randomly through time. Nevertheless S's momentary estimate of $P(s)$ should vary with his view of his history of performance to date and with the nearness and clarity of the deadline against which he is working. We thought we could get at this issue by putting Ss through the same procedures as in our earlier experiments, but having them state $P(s)$ estimates only at the beginning (trial 0), middle (trial 5), and end (trial 9) of the sequence. Thirty-two male college students, half of them Hi Mots and

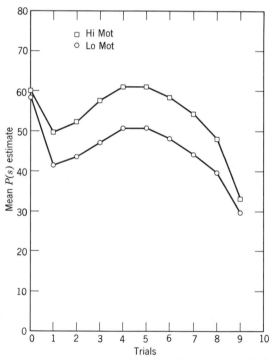

Fig. 4.7   Estimated $P(s)$ by trials as a function of motivation. Each point is the mean of 40 Ss.

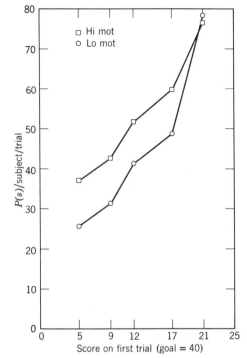

Fig. 4.8 Estimated $P(s)/S/$ trial as a function of motivation and level of reported performance curve. Each point is the mean of eight Ss $\times$ 10 trials. (After Diggory, Riley, and Blumenfeld, 1960.)

half Lo Mots, were assigned in sets of eight to each of four conditions defined by vague or clear deadlines and high or low performance curves (curves from Conditions 3 and 7, Fig. 4.4). In Fig. 4.9, panel A shows the effects of motivation, panel B the effects of clarity of deadline, and panel C the effect of nearness of performance to the goal. Both clarity of deadline and distance from the goal had significant effects on both the means and the slopes of the three-point $P(s)$ curves.

The broken curves in Fig. 4.9 are drawn from previously reported experiments under conditions comparable with those of the present experiment. They are presented to facilitate comparison of the estimates of $P(s)$ made at all trials with those made only at trials 0, 5, and 9. There is one respect in which the condition of vagueness of deadline is not strictly comparable with that of the previous experiment. In the earlier experiment, all the Ss were recruited for a

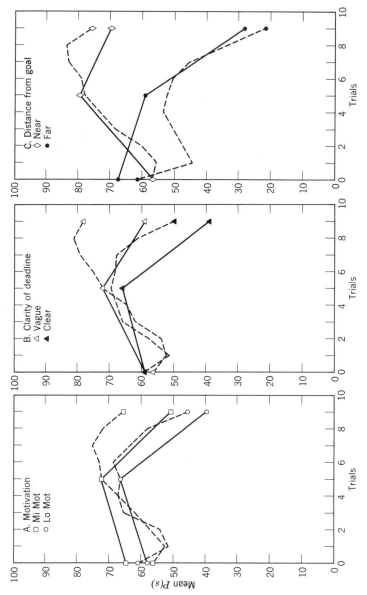

Fig. 4.9 Comparison of completely sampled and incompletely sampled $P(s)$ estimates as a function of motivation, clarity of deadline, and level of reported performance curve. Solid lines connect mean $P(s)$ points (16 Ss each) for incompletely sampled data (trials 0, 5, and 9); broken lines show completely sampled data from comparable conditions in other experiments. (After Diggory, Riley, and Blumenfeld, 1960.)

hour session, whereas in the present experiment half-hour sessions were scheduled. Thus, in the previous experiment S could realistically expect an extended number of trials, but in the present experiment he could hope for only one or two trials after the tenth, because it was obvious, by the time trial 10 had been completed, that little time was left for additional attempts. Nevertheless, the differences between the partially sampled and the completely sampled $P(s)$ curves are very small and are maximal only at trial 9, where the difference in procedure would be expected to have its greatest effect. There are no significant differences in means or slopes between trials 0, 5, and 9 of the present experiment and those of the earlier experiments.

In the present experiment the motivational variable had no significant main effect, probably because of the small number of Ss. The differences due to motivation are in the same direction and of about the same magnitude as those previously found. The motivational variable was not completely without effect, however, because the difference between motivation conditions is significant when the deadline is vague though not when it is clear.

From these results we concluded that, at least within the limits of our procedures, estimates of $P(s)$ are more dependent upon motivation, nearness to the deadline, and distance from the goal than they are upon each other. If serial effects occur, they are for most purposes not important enough to cause concern. This finding is of some technical interest because it provides opportunity to use "blank" trials for getting other types of data; for example, LA data, if circumstances require that they not be collected simultaneously with $P(s)$ statements. Generally we have not taken advantage of the availability of "blank" trials. We have collected $P(s)$, LA, and self-evaluation estimates for every trial of a series, and we have also noted S's choice of other options presented to him at every trial.

So far we had paid no systematic attention to individual differences in the way our Ss set their $P(s)$ estimates. Though we were continuously aware that such differences occurred, we were satisfied only that they were not great enough to obscure the effects of our experimental variables. However, because of our interest in self-evaluation, individual differences are of great importance; therefore, we decided to begin studying them systematically.

Variability in Reported Performance Curves

With the help of Bena Ostroff, we began to concern ourselves seriously with differences in response to the negatively accelerated performance curve which leveled off at one point below the goal (Fig. 4.4, Condition 3). Some Ss to whom this curve was presented kept their $P(s)$ estimates very high throughout the series, *contrary* to the general trend of lowering them as the deadline approached. We thought that some of them might have done this because they expected some irregularity in their performance—an upward deviation of only one unit would spell success. In fact, some Ss said that they regarded their reported performance curves as trend lines around which they expected some variation to occur. If this explanation is valid, then Ss in the same conditions who did lower their $P(s)$ estimates either expected no fluctuations at all, or thought they would be negative. If S views his performance curve as a trend line, then a highly regular curve allows him a more accurate prediction of its future course than would an irregular one. This puts our procedures in the context of the "expanded judgment" situation studied by Irwin and his students (Irwin, Smith, and Mayfield, 1956; Irwin and Smith, 1956, 1957). They showed that a naive S's confidence in his judgment that two means differ, or that one mean differs from zero, varies inversely with the standard deviation of the presented data. If their results are applicable to our situation, then it follows that the more smooth and regular the progress of performance, the more confidently S will predict his own failure; however, on empirical grounds, we expected Ss with fluctuating performance curves, in spite of the relative difficulty of predicting the course of their improvement, to make a constant error in the direction of anticipating success rather than failure. Note our own findings with regard to the motivation variable, the general tendency to keep LA above performance (Lewin, Dembo, Festinger, and Sears, 1944), and the fact that Festinger, discussing judgments in social comparison processes, found it necessary to explain differences between judgments of ability and judgments of opinion by invoking the notion of an "upward push" with respect to abilities (Festinger, 1954).

We introduced variability in two types of curves: (1) a negatively accelerated curve like those in Conditions 3 and 7 of Fig. 4.4 and (2) a curve like those of Conditions 1 and 5, Fig. 4.4, which rose at the constant rate of two units per trial. Both curves started at 19 points and ended at 37 points (3 units below the goal level of 40) for the high performance conditions, and ten points lower for the low performance conditions. The regular, smooth curves are shown by the broken lines in the upper four panels (1, 2, 3, 4) of Fig. 4.10. The irregular curves, shown in panels 5–20 of Fig. 4.10, were constructed by drawing an envelope, ±1 or ±2 units in amplitude, around each smooth curve and selecting points within the envelope,

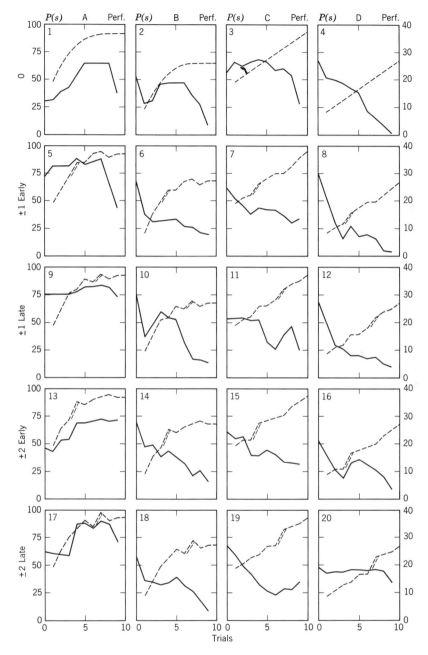

Fig. 4.10 Estimated $P(s)$ by trials as a function of form, level, and irregularity of reported performance curves. The broken lines are performance curves to be read on the scales at the right. The solid lines show mean estimated $P(s)$ for four Ss in each condition, to be read on the scales at the left. The numbers 0, ±1, and ±2 at the left indicate the amount of variability in the reported performance curves. "Early" and "late" refer to the position of the "maximal jump" in performance, which is also shown by the doubling of the broken lines. (After Diggory and Ostroff, 1962.)

subject to the following restrictions: (a) the irregular curves should generally rise, (b) they should have as few reversals as possible, and (c) they should have the same overall means as the corresponding smooth curves. This produced three levels of irregularity: zero, ±1, and ±2. Furthermore, in each of the irregular curves we introduced what we called "maximum jump," a rise in one trial from the lower bound to the upper bound of the envelope. The position of the "maximum jump" was either relatively early (between trials 3 and 4) or late (between trials 6 and 7). The purpose of this variation was to see whether such a discontinuity would have more than a transitory local effect on $P(s)$ estimates. Four male college student Ss in the Lo Mot group were assigned to each of the 20 conditions shown in Fig. 4.10.

This figure also shows the mean trends of $P(s)$ for each of the conditions (solid lines). For the entire set of data, the slope of the best fitting straight line is significantly different from zero and is negative. Furthermore, the mean $P(s)$ and slopes for the high performance conditions are significantly greater than for low performance, confirming our earlier results. These and other features of the curves are reported in Table 4.5. Since there were no significant differences between the ±1 and the ±2 irregular performance conditions, these are combined into a single irregular performance condition for further analyses. The differences in position of the "maximum jump" produced only local perturbations and no overall differences in the means or slopes of the $P(s)$ trends, so they will not be discussed further.

TABLE 4.5

Characteristics of P(s) *Curves as a Function of Experimentally Controlled Characteristics of Performance Curves*

	Conditions (cf. Fig. 4.10)				
Characteristics	A	B	C	D	P
Overall mean performance	32.6	22.6	28.0	18.0	—
Mean initial $P(s)$	58.2	64.1	59.1	65.2	>0.05*
Mean $P(s)/S/$trial	69.1	41.9	45.4	32.9	<0.01#
$P(s)$ slope	−1.48	−3.98	−3.16	−4.76	<0.01#
Mean final $P(s)$	59.7	13.0	30.5	12.2	<0.01*

For each mean, $n = 20$. (After Diggory and Ostroff, 1962.)
* Analysis of variance.
# Kruskal-Wallis one-way nonparametric analysis.

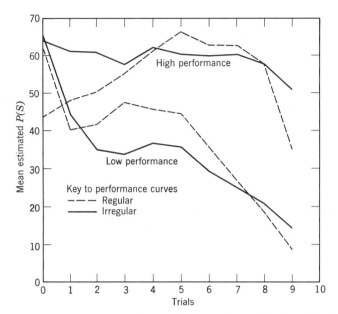

Fig. 4.11 Estimated $P(s)$ by trials as a function of irregularity and level of reported performance curves. The curves labeled high performance are averages of the $P(s)$ curves in Columns A and C of Fig. 4.10; Low performance data are from columns B and D of Fig. 4.10. Each point is the mean of eight Ss in the "regular" curves, 32 Ss in the "irregular" curves. (After Diggory and Ostroff, 1962.)

Fig. 4.11 shows that introducing irregularity into the performance curves retarded the decrease in $P(s)$ estimates in the later trials. As Table 4.6 shows, the final mean estimates are generally higher for the irregular performance curves than for regular ones. The slopes of the best fitting straight lines are significantly more negative in the last five trials for the regular performance conditions than for the irregular ones. Furthermore, 100% of the Ss in the regular conditions showed a greater decrease in the second half of their $P(s)$ estimates than in the first half, but this is true of only 59.5% (38/64) of the Ss in the combined irregular conditions. Thus it appears that a history of variability in performance retarded the decline in $P(s)$ estimates as the deadline approached.

Certain difficulties presented in the analysis of these data led to an interesting finding related to individual differences in estimating $P(s)$. The difficulty was that, although there were no significant

TABLE 4.6

Slopes of P(s) *Curves, Trials 5-9, and Final* P(s) *Estimates for Regular and Irregular Performance Curves*

	Conditions (cf. Fig. 4.10)						
	A		B		C		D

Performance Curve Type	Slope	Final mean	Slope	Final mean	Slope	Final mean	Slope	Final mean
Regular	−5.40	40.0	−9.38	10.5	−8.02	29.8	−8.38	18.8
Irregular	−3.86	64.6	−6.53	13.7	−1.08	30.7	−4.11	24.3

For the regular curves each condition has $n = 5$; for the irregular curves $n = 16$. (After Diggory and Ostroff, 1962.)

ences in initial $P(s)$ level as a function of performance curve type (that is, among columns A, B, C, and D of Fig. 4.10 and Table 4.5) there were significant differences among conditions *within* those columns. Note especially that in column A of Fig. 4.10, the initial mean $P(s)$ for the smooth performance curve is markedly below that for any of the irregular curves. This is a case where randomization of Ss over conditions failed to control for initial level of the dependent variable. This made straightforward interpretation of the results difficult, so we decided to see if the trends in $P(s)$ showed any systematic differences depending on whether S's initial estimate was above or below the median for his experimental condition. Fig. 4.12 presents the results of this analysis for the irregular conditions. In all four sets of conditions (A, B, C, and D), the $P(s)$ curves with the higher initial level fall significantly more rapidly than those with the lower initial level. This is not because initial $P(s)$ estimates were so low that they had no room to go lower, since one of the low-starting curves (A) has a generally positive slope (2.31) with plenty of room to fall even faster than the corresponding high-starting curve (slope = −0.75); the low-starting curve in part C (slope = −1.35) has plenty of room to fall at the same rate as the high-starting curve (slope = −4.02); and in conditions B and D (low average performance level, the high-starting curves end significantly below the low-starting curves.

Now if, as we have supposed, and hope yet to prove, estimated $P(s)$ is related to S's conception of his power to achieve the goal

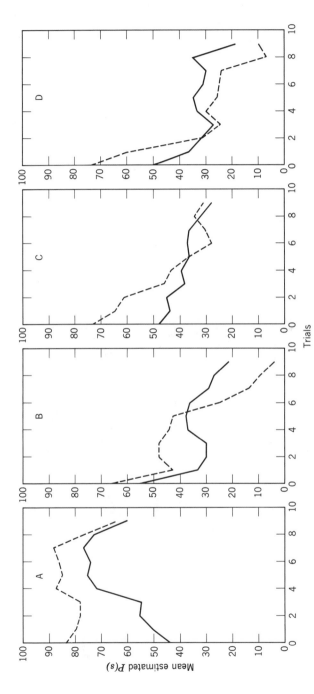

Fig. 4.12 Estimated $P(s)$ by trials as a function of level of initial estimate. These data refer only to the irregular performance conditions (Fig. 4.10). The broken lines connect the mean $P(s)$ estimates for 16 Ss whose initial estimates were above the median of their group; solid lines are for 16 Ss whose initial estimates were below the group median. (After Diggory and Ostroff, 1962.)

157

he is trying to reach, and thus is ultimately related to his estimate of his own value as an instrument for attaining such goals, then this finding (as pure a case of serendipity as we can present) relates to assertions that people with high self-esteem—our Ss with high initial $P(s)$—tend to withdraw more from situations which threaten their self-esteem than do people whose self-esteem is low to begin with (cf. Rosenzweig and Mason, 1934; Rosenzweig, 1943; Alper, 1946a, 1952; Eriksen, 1952; and Cohen, 1956). Thus, as the evidence of impending failure accumulates, the more rapid decline of $P(s)$ from the higher initial level reflects a more rapid gain in S's tendency to withdraw from the situation if he were permitted to do so. By the same token, Ss with initially low $P(s)$ estimates would have a weaker tendency to withdraw from the situation, especially in the later trials in our Conditions B and D (Fig. 4.12).[5]

$P(s)$ Estimates from Children

Having come this far in our understanding of some of the conditions that determine changes in estimated $P(s)$, we next turned to the question whether physically disabled individuals would set $P(s)$ differently when they were working on a motor task directly or indirectly related to their physical handicap than they would on a "mental" task where their handicap was presumably less involved. Sylvia Farnham-Diggory then had a fellowship from Children's Seashore House, a hospital for physically disabled children in Atlantic City, N.J.[6] Under the terms of the fellowship, the young patients at the hospital could be used as Ss in experiments. This gave us the opportunity both to compare disabled with intact individuals, and to compare children with the adult Ss in our other experiments. We also decided to study whether success or failure in one task would affect the $P(s)$ trends not only for that task, but also for a subsequent task in which performance curves were identical for all Ss.

[5] We gratefully acknowledge the various ways in which the University of Pennsylvania supported the work so far described. The present author had a summer research grant from the University's Committee on the Advancement of Research. The salaries of Mr. Riley and Dr. Blumenfeld were on the budget of the Department of Psychology. Miss Ostroff was supported on a special research scholarship budget of the University Scholarship Office.

[6] This fellowship, made possible by a grant from the Ford Foundation, was administered by Dr. George Moed, then Research Director at Children's Seashore House. Our thanks to Dr. Moed; to Dr. Harvey Vandergrift, Medical Director; and to Byron Wight, Dr. Moed's assistant, for their support and encouragement of these studies with children.

Farnham-Diggory's technique for getting $P(s)$ estimates from children has already been described above. The conditions of her first experiment were defined by the order in which S worked at two kinds of tasks (motor-mental or mental-motor) and whether or not they were permitted to succeed or fail. Ten disabled children and five "intact" children were Ss in each of these four conditions. Ss were told that each of the ten trials on each task would last for one minute, though actually E disregarded time and stopped each trial when S had made a predetermined score. Each S was told that at least once within the ten trials he should try to complete at least 20 performance units correctly. The performance information was controlled and presented to the children exactly as described earlier with college students. The disabled and intact children were matched in distribution of age (6 to 10 years) and IQ (Ammons Picture Vocabulary Test), and the proportions of the two sexes did not differ in the two groups. The intact children were from schools in a suburb of Philadelphia.

In the *motor task*, S attempted to string 20 large wooden beads on a heavy cord (none of the disabled children were affected in the arms or hands) and the string was emptied after each trial.

In the *mental task* (Otis Alpha Test, Form A, Grades 1–4) S tried to correctly identify 20 pictures that "don't belong." This is a standard concept formation task. For example, given four objects— shoes, boots, overshoes, and a baby carriage—the baby carriage obviously "doesn't belong" in the set of foot coverings. S started with row 1 of the Otis booklet. His "score" was his number of correct identifications which E announced at the end of each trial. The S was never told exactly which answers were wrong and which were correct, so for each trial he began again at row 1. Thus, he became familiar with some rows, and in later trials he was able to proceed faster and progress further into the set of problems.

The design of the experiment and the results are shown in Table 4.7 and in Fig. 4.13. The portion of the table enclosed in heavy lines contains the overall mean $P(s)$ estimates corresponding to the curves in Fig. 4.13. The rest of the table shows means for various combinations of conditions.

On the first task, the overall mean $P(s)$ in success is higher than in failure; and the slope of the combined $P(s)$ curves in success is positive, but it is negative in failure. Therefore we concluded that these young children were responding consistently to the same features of the situation even though the instructions they got and their mode of responding were not identical to those we used with college students.

TABLE 4.7
Overall Mean P(s) Estimates (per subject per trial) Given by
Intact and Disabled Children as a Function of Success or
Failure in the First Task and Task Type and Task Order

	Disabled (n = 10)		Intact (n = 5)		Combined	
	Task 1	Task 2	Task 1	Task 2	Task 1	Task 2
	Motor (A1)	Mental (A2)	Motor (A1)	Mental (A2)	(n = 15)	
	69.9	55.5	74.3	55.3	71.3	55.4
Success,	Mental (B1)	Motor (B2)	Mental (B1)	Motor (B2)		
Task 1	77.3	72.7	79.5	70.8	78.0	72.1
	Motor (C1)	Mental (C2)	Motor (C1)	Mental (C2)		
Failure,	70.1	68.8	63.3	65.6	67.8	67.7
Task 1	Mental (D1)	Motor (D2)	Mental (D1)	Motor (D2)		
	74.4	64.9	58.1	55.2	69.0	61.7

Combined	(n = 20)		(n = 10)		(n = 30)	
Success	73.6	64.1	76.9	63.0	74.7	63.7
Failure	72.2	66.8	60.7	60.4	68.4	64.7
Motor	70.0	68.8	68.8	63.0	69.6	66.9
Mental	75.8	62.1	68.8	60.4	73.5	61.5

General	(n = 40)		(n = 20)			
means	72.9	65.4	68.7	61.7		

The section inside the heavy lines gives the design of the experiment and the means
for each condition. The number of Ss (n) for each group of means is shown in
parentheses. The codes A1, B1, . . . D2 refer to the corresponding panels of Fig.
4.13. (Data collected by S. Farnham-Diggory.)

The $P(s)$ curves from the disabled children are closely similar
in form to those from the intact children. They are markedly similar
in overall level in the success conditions (panels AI and BI of Fig.
4.13). In the failure conditions, however, (panels C1 and D1 of Fig.
4.13) the overall mean $P(s)$ is higher for the disabled children than
for the intact ones. Thus, there is a significant difference between the
means of all intact children and all disabled children.

In the first task there are no significant differences in overall mean
$P(s)$ as a function of type of task (mental or motor).

In the second task, during which all Ss received identical failing
performance curves, all the $P(s)$ curves are what we have come to
regard as typical of failure conditions. There are no significant main
effects of disability, or of previous success and failure, on the overall
mean $P(s)$ estimates (see Fig. 4.13, panels A2, B2, C2, D2; and Table
4.7). The significant difference between the overall $P(s)$ values for
motor (66.9) and mental (61.5) tasks is due entirely to the fact that

both groups of children set higher $P(s)$ estimates for the motor task after success on the mental task (panel B2) than they did on the mental task after success on the motor task (panel A2). The only significant difference in overall mean $P(s)$ between intact and disabled groups is shown in panel D2: $P(s)$ estimates during motor task after failure on mental task are higher for disabled (64.9) than for intact (55.2).

Nevertheless, both task type and previous success or failure operated together to produce the effect (shown in Fig. 4.14 and in the first four means in the extreme right-hand column of Table 4.5) that, when the second task is a mental one, the mean $P(s)$ associated with it is significantly *higher after failure* on the previous motor task (67.7) than it is following *success* on the previous motor task (55.4). Mean $P(s)$ for the second task, when it is a motor task, is significantly lower after failure on the previous mental task (61.7) than it is after success on the previous mental task (72.1). What is happening here?

If failure of success on one task generalizes to subsequent tasks, then $P(s)$ estimates should generally be lower after failure than after success. However, generalization in this sense occurred only during failure on a motor task when success or failure was previously incurred on a mental task. The difference in mean $P(s)$ during failure on a mental task as a function of previous success and failure on a motor task is in the opposite direction to that predicted by the generalization hypothesis. It suggests compensation of some sort, so we are faced with the opportunity to discover something about the conditions which determine whether generalization or compensation will occur.

Normal human Ss will often work harder, and often produce more, after a poor (or failing) performance and relax their efforts after a good (or successful) performance (Atkinson et al., 1956, 1960; Leshner, 1961; Olson, 1958). But there is also some evidence (e.g., Diggory, Klein, and Cohen, 1964; Farber, 1944; Lewin, 1941), discussed more fully below, that increased effort after failure occurs only if S views the subsequent task as a "second chance" to restore his self-esteem or self-confidence, or to get what he failed to get by his previous unsatisfactory performance. In addition, the general finding in the LA literature, that S raises his LA after success, leads to the prediction that success itself may lead to increased self-stressing as the individual pits himself against increasingly difficult goals. This is not the same as saying that lowering the LA after failure leads to the prediction that less self-stressing will occur after failure. S may set a lower LA *and* work harder to achieve it because his experience

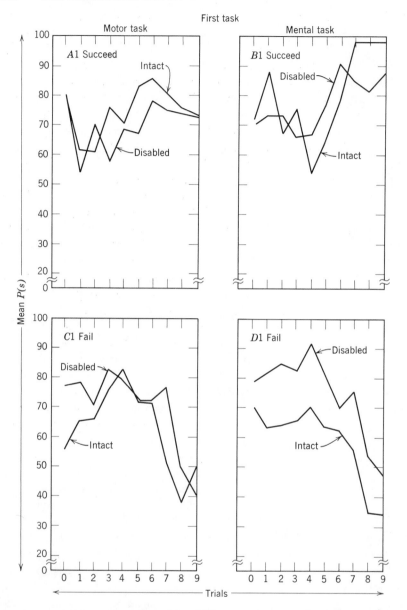

Fig. 4.13 $P(s)$ by trials estimated by children on two successive tasks as a function of disability, task order, and success or failure. Each point for the disabled group is the mean of ten Ss; each point for the intact group is the mean of five Ss. (Data collected by S. Farnham-Diggory.)

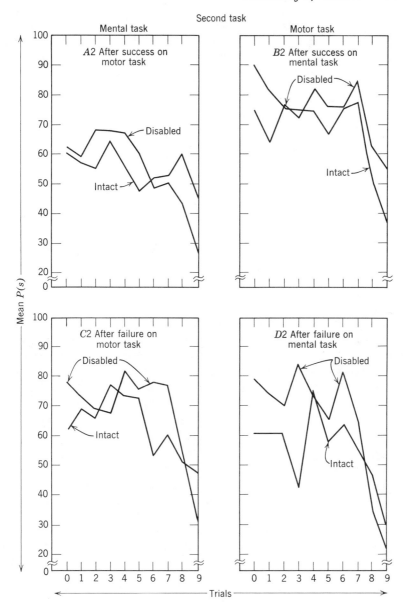

Fig. 4.13 (*Continued*)

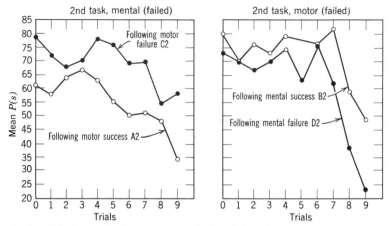

Fig. 4.14 P(s) by trials from intact and disabled children during the second task as a function of outcome and type of first task. Each point is the mean of 15 Ss. (Data collected by S. Farnham-Diggory.)

of failure shows him that he underestimated the difficulty of the task. We expect that relaxation of effort, even to the point of abandoning the task though continuing to manipulate the materials (the hopeless fumbling noted by Hoppe in 1931), would occur after failure if the experience has proved to S *that he has not the ability to perform the task at hand.* Thus, the LA literature leads to the prediction that both success and failure may lead either to generalization or to compensation, depending on how the experiences are interpreted by S. Generalization of LA level from one task to another has been found to be a function of the degree of objective similarity in the operations required by the two tasks (Frank, 1935a; Stotland et al., 1957, 1958) and has been predicted as a function of the conditions that determine cosatiation or mutual substitute value between tasks (Henle, 1944; Lewin, 1935; Lissner, 1933; Mahler, 1933).

By the time we had analyzed the first experiment on children we also had evidence that generalization might be a function of the relative value which S assigned to the ability which was being tested.[7] We followed this lead in designing the second experiment which Farnham-Diggory carried out with normal (intact) children matched in age and IQ distributions with those from the first experiment. We assumed that the momentary value of the ability under test could

[7] Diggory and Magaziner (1959), discussed in Chapter 5.

be varied by manipulating the value of the outcome of the task, as well as by the demonstrating to S that he had or didn't have the power to produce the required output. We used the same tasks as in the previous experiment, the task order was counterbalanced in the same manner, and the same success and failure curves were used. The value of the outcome promised for a successful performance was manipulated in the manner described earlier in this chapter. The intact children from the first experiment served as a control (no-prize) condition. Thus there were three prize levels (high, low, and none), success and failure, and two task orders.

Table 4.8 shows the design of the experiment and the overall mean $P(s)$ estimates for each condition, plus means for various combinations of conditions. Fig. 4.15 compares the combined $P(s)$ trends on the first task for the children in the high- and low-prize conditions, with those in the no-prize conditions from the previous experiment. The effects of success and failure on $P(s)$ trends in the first task are

TABLE 4.8

Mean P(s) per Subject per Trial as Estimated by Children in the Indicated Conditions

	High Prize (n = 5)		Low prize (n = 5)		No Prize (n = 5)		Combined (n = 15)	
Outcome of Task 1	Task 1	Task 2	Task 1	Task 2	Task 1	Task 2	Task 1	Task 2
Success	Motor 91.6	Mental 89.8	Motor 89.3	Mental 65.9	Motor 74.3	Mental 55.3	Motor 85.7	Mental 70.3
	Mental 84.5	Motor 68.0	Mental 74.1	Motor 58.9	Mental 79.5	Motor 70.8	Mental 79.4	Motor 65.9
Failure	Motor 68.5	Mental 63.9	Motor 55.9	Mental 48.5	Motor 63.3	Mental 65.6	Motor 62.6	Mental 59.3
	Mental 70.1	Motor 66.8	Mental 69.2	Motor 55.1	Mental 58.1	Motor 55.2	Mental 65.8	Motor 59.0
Combined	(n = 10)		(n = 10)		(n = 10)		(n = 30)	
Success	88.0	78.9	81.7	62.4	76.9	63.0	82.2	68.1
Failure	68.3	65.1	62.5	51.8	60.7	60.4	64.2	59.1
Motor	80.0	76.8	72.6	57.2	68.8	60.4	73.8	64.8
Mental	77.3	67.1	71.6	57.0	68.8	63.0	72.6	62.4
General means	(n = 20)		(n = 20)		(n = 20)		(n = 60)	
	78.7	71.9	72.1	57.1	68.7	60.2	73.2	63.6

(Data Collected by S. Farnham-Diggory.)

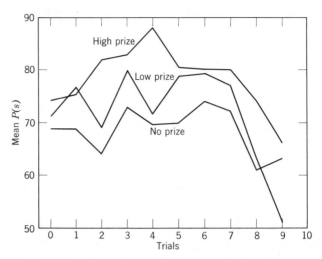

Fig. **4.15** Mean $P(s)$ on first task as a function of prize level. Each point is the mean of ten normal Ss. (Data collected by S. Farnham-Diggory.)

similar to those found in the previous experiment: the higher the value of the prize the higher the mean $P(s)$ level. However, the differences between prize and no-prize conditions are significant only during success on the motor task and failure on the mental task.

Generally, during the second task, mean $P(s)$ is lower after failure (59.1) than after success (68.1), and it is lower in the combined low-prize and no-prize conditions (58.7) than in the high-prize condition (71.9). The difference between low prize and no prize does not, however, persist into the second task, nor is there a main effect of task type. There is an effect of task type in combination with previous success or failure and the presence of a prize. In the no-prize group, the $P(s)$ level is higher for a mental task *after* failure on a motor task than it is after success on the motor task. This situation is *reversed* in both the low-prize and high-prize groups, as Fig. 4.16 shows, but the $P(s)$ level of the no-prize group for a motor task is lower after failure on a mental task than it is after success on the mental task. There are no differences as a function of previous success or failure, during the second *motor* task in either the high-prize or low-prize groups. Table 4.9 summarizes the *differences* between overall $P(s)$ means in the second task following success and failure as a function of prize condition and type of previous task. Since all performance curves reported to Ss were identical during the second task,

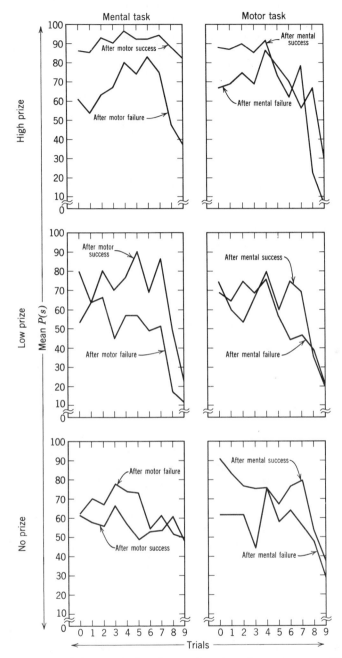

Fig. 4.16 Mean $P(s)$ on second task as a function of experience on first task: type, prize value, and outcome. Each point is the mean of five normal Ss. (Data collected by S. Farnham-Diggory.)

TABLE 4.9

Differences, Mean P(s) /S/*Trial During Second Task, Between Groups Which Succeeded on the First Task and Groups Which Failed on the First Task* (*Success mean* minus *Failure mean*), *By Prize Level and Type of First Task*

	Prize Offered During First Task		
Type of First Task	High	Low	None
Motor	25.9	17.4	−10.3
Mental	1.2	3.8	15.6
Combined	13.8	10.6	2.6

Note: The larger the absolute value of the difference, the more promounced the direct effects of previous success and failure on $P(s)$ during the second task. (For each entry, $n = 10$) (Data collected by S. Farnham-Diggory.)

ences between the mean $P(s)$ values can reasonably be attributed to the variables operating during the first task. It is clear from the table that previous failure on a motor task had a profoundly depressing effect (relative to that of previous success) on $P(s)$ levels for a second mental task, an effect which decreased as the value of the prize decreased, and reversed when there was no prize. When the first task was a mental one, this relative depression of the $P(s)$ by previous failure was generally smaller and decreased as the value of the prize increased.

This seemed to leave us nowhere to turn at the moment except to explore the cognitive view which the children had of these tasks. Which task do they say they like? Which is harder? Which would they like to do again? Would their answers to these questions throw any light on the mysterious, persistent, and systematic effects of task type?

The major methodological difficulty with the two previous experiments was that the second task was not constant for all groups. Thus, although we have presented the second task $P(s)$ data primarily in terms of first task influences, we actually have no way of knowing the extent to which the difference in the quality of the second task may have influenced the $P(s)$ estimates.

A further problem was the unknown value of succeeding on the second task when no prize was offered.

Still more problems had been raised by the lack of information about Ss' preferences for the tasks and their perceptions of relative difficulty and of similarity between the motor and mental tasks. Any or all of these variables may have affected the results of our previous experiments (cf. Le Ny, 1961; Heath, 1959; and Marks, 1951). Thus, in the next experiment all Ss performed three tasks: the mental and the motor tasks used in the previous experiments and task MM, a *combination* of the mental and motor task, made by cutting out the Otis pictures and pasting them on large cubical wooden beads, and instructing S to string 20 "don't belong" pictures in at least one 1-minute trial. Since this procedure added a task and some questioning of each S, we shortened the stint for each task to five trials, so that the total length of time a child was involved in the experiment was about the same as that for the previous experiments.

In order to control for task effects, and for the order of success and failure, Ss were randomly assigned to four experimental treatments as shown in Table 4.10. The age and IQ distributions for these children were comparable with those of the Ss in the previous experiments. All Ss were tested at their public school in the Philadelphia suburbs.

For the MM task, a covered tray was prepared, sectionally divided into rows. Each row corresponded to one of the concepts of the Otis test, except that there were several beads for each "belong" and "don't belong" picture. The blocks with the same pictures on them were placed side by side to let S see immediately how many pictures that "don't belong" were in any given row. As S worked at stringing the "don't belong" beads, E slid the cover back to expose one new

TABLE 4.10
Design of Three Task Experiment

Group No.	N	Task 1	Task 2	Task 3
1	16	Af	Bs	ABf
2	16	Bs	Af	ABf
3	16	As	Bf	ABf
4	16	Bf	As	ABf

(f = failure; s = success)

row at a time. *E* had a table of the cumulated number of "don't belong" beads in successive rows. Thus, she could stop *S* after he had finished a given row and know exactly how many beads he had strung correctly. After each trial, the tray was replenished, *S*'s string was emptied, and *S* started again at row 1. Thus, *S* became familiar with the early rows and actually progressed faster so that on subsequent trials he worked on rows not previously exposed. The scores Ss were allowed in the various conditions on each trial are shown in Table 4.11.

After the first trial of task MM, but *before they knew their scores* for the trial, Ss were asked to make the following choices:

1) Similarity: The game I am playing now is *most like* (*a*) the bead game, (*b*) the picture game.
2) Preference: The game I *liked best* was (*a*) the picture game, (*b*) the bead game.
3) Difficulty: The *hardest* game was (*a*) the bead game, (b) the picture game.
4) Try Again: The game I would *most like to try again* is (*a*) the game I won, (*b*) the game I lost.

Ss then proceeded through the remaining 4 trials of task MM, making *P*(*s*) estimates before each trial.

To vary the presence or absence of a prize, four $1.00 items from a local science museum were shown to half of the Ss, prior to the start of task MM, and each was asked to select the item he wanted to try to win. Prizes were not mentioned to the other half of the Ss (the no-prize group). The Ss in the prize group were told that they had been selected to try for prizes on the basis of chance and that no personal favoritism was implied. ("Because the children have been so nice in

TABLE 4.11
Performance Scores Allowed on Each Trial in the Three Task Experiment

	Trials				
Tasks	1	2	3	4	5
Mental and Motor Tasks					
Success	10	13	16	18	21
Failure	11	13	15	16	17
MM Task (failure only)	10	12	14	15	16

TABLE 4.12
*Numbers of Ss in Prize and No-Prize Groups Who Nominated
Motor and Mental Tasks in Their Similarity, Preference,
Difficulty, and "Try Again" Statements*

Statements	Prize		No Prize		Combined Prize and No Prize	
	Mental	Motor	Mental	Motor	Mental	Motor
"Similar" to						
Task MM	12	20	9	23	21	43[a]
"Preferred"	10	22	9	23	19	45[b]
"Difficult"	20	12	21	11	41[c]	23
"Try Again"	17	15	14	18	31	33

[a] .67 of the group. Departure of this proportion from .50 is significant at $p < .01$.
[b] .70 of the group, significant at the .01 level.
[c] .64 of the group, significant at the .05 level.
(Data Collected by S. Farnham-Diggory.)

helping us out, we've decided to let some of them try for prizes on the last game. We didn't have enough prizes to go around, so we had to say, 'Eeney, meeney, miney, moe,' and you were a 'moe', so you get to try for a prize.")

From Table 4.12, it is apparent that both groups considered task MM most similar to the motor task, preferred the motor task, and considered the mental task difficult. They were about equally divided in their statements about whether to try the mental or the motor task again. These data suggested that the associations between the statements ought to be examined. The results of this analysis are shown in Table 4.13, where the data from the prize and no-prize groups are combined because there were no significant differences between them. The only significant association is the one between preference and difficulty statements: Ss generally preferred the task they called "easy."

The mean $P(s)$ levels during task MM were significantly affected by the presence or absence of the prize. The overall mean for the prize group (74.8) is significantly above that of the no-prize group (62.5). Is the $P(s)$ for the third task affected by different previous histories? The answer is "Yes" in the no-prize group, "No" for the prize group. As Table 4.14 shows, the $P(s)$ level for the MM task

TABLE 4.13

Associations Among Similarity, Preference, and Difficulty Statements for Combined Prize and No-Prize Groups

		"Similar" to MM				
		Mental	Motor	Totals	Chi-square	P
	Mental	13	28	41		
"Difficult"	Motor	8	15	23		
	Totals	21	43	64	0.06	.80
		"Similar" to MM				
		Mental	Motor	Totals		
	Mental	4	15	19		
"Preferred"	Motor	17	28	45		
	Totals	21	43	64	1.60	.20
		"Preferred"				
		Mental	Motor	Totals		
	Mental	6	35	41		
"Difficult"	Motor	13	10	23		
	Totals	19	45	64	12.30	.001

(Each of the Chi-squares has 1 degree of freedom.) (Data collected by S. Farnham-Diggory.)

in the no-prize group corresponds to whether success or failure had been experienced on the previous mental task. However, this effect did not appear in the prize group.

Since the majority of Ss in both the prize and no-prize groups said that task MM was most like the motor task, and they also preferred the motor task, then neither *stated similarity* nor *preference* could have mediated the effects of previous task history on $P(s)$ during the MM task. However, the majority of Ss thought the mental

TABLE 4.14

Mean P(s)/S/Trial During MM Task by Indicated Conditions

Previous Tasks and Outcomes	No Prize	Prize
Succeed Motor and Fail Mental	60.6	74.7
Fail Motor and Succeed Mental	66.2	74.8

Each mean summarizes 80 observations: 16 Ss × 5 trials. (Data collected by S. Farnham-Diggory.)

TABLE 4.15
Mean P(s)/S/Trial During MM Task by Indicated Conditions

Previous Outcomes and *Ss'* Designation of Tasks	No Prize	Prize
"Easy" Success and "Hard" Failure	58.6[a]	76.4
"Easy" Failure and "Hard" Success	68.6[b]	72.6

[a,b] Difference significant, $p < .01$.
These are the means for the curves shown in Fig. 4.17, which gives
the number of *Ss* for each mean. (Data collected by S. Farnham-
Diggory.)

task was most difficult, so we considered the possibility that the factor
of *perceived difficulty* was instrumental in the mental task outcome
generalization shown by the no-prize group. To test this, both groups
were dichotomized on the basis of their difficulty judgments, and the
question was asked: does the direction of generalization now follow
the outcome (success or failure) of the easy or of the hard task?

Table 4.15 shows that the lines of generalization follow the outcome of the "hard" task in the no-prize group, and of the "easy" task
in the prize group, despite the fact that there were no differences
between the groups in frequency of "easy" and "hard" judgments. This
phenomenon is illustrated in Fig. 4.17, which also shows that Ss in
the prize group responded somewhat rigidly and unrealistically to
score information: compared to the no-prize Ss, they did not lower
their $P(s)$ level as the deadline approached.

A comparison of Fig. 4.17 and Fig. 4.16 suggests that the factor
of perceived difficulty may have been responsible for the different
task effects on the prize and no-prize groups in the previous experiment. When the first task was the motor one, it may have been perceived by Ss as "easy." When the first task was the mental one, they
may have perceived it as "hard." According to the present data, outcome generalization from an "easy" task will be dominant in a group
which is working for a prize, but outcome generalization from a "hard"
task will be dominant in a no-prize group. Apparently the effect will
appear whether the prize is offered for the first or second tasks, although a complete test of this has not been made.

In order to explore as far as she could with her data the question
of what these results mean for the self-evaluative mechanisms of

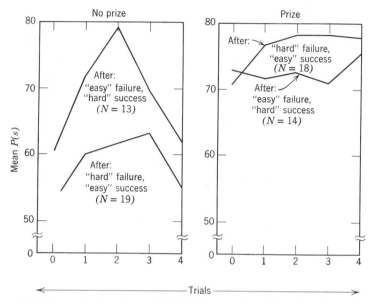

Fig. 4.17   Mean $P(s)$ during third (MM) task as a function of presence of prize, outcomes of two previous tasks, and Ss' judgments of the difficulty of the previous tasks. (Data collected by S. Farnham-Diggory.)

young children, Farnham-Diggory studied the relation of the previously mentioned variables to the age and IQ of her Ss.

"It is clear that the aroused needs of the individual will have a part in determining what similarities exist for him" (Henle, 1944). Preston, et al. (1952) and Bardon (1956), among others, have demonstrated that motivation affects perceived similarity between tasks.

Cartwright (1942) reported that Ss preferred tasks on which they had succeeded. Rosenzweig (1933) and Gewirtz (1959) found evidence that brighter Ss preferred failed tasks and wished to try them again. These experimenters did not empirically separate failure and perceived task difficulty. Gebhard (1948, 1949) showed that among adult females, success increased the attractiveness of a task especially when Ss had been told that success was uncommon, but that failure on a reportedly often-failed task did not decrease, and sometimes increased, its attractiveness. Here, peer comparison, rather than personal experience, operationally defined task difficulty. Feather (1959) reported that male children stated that they wished to try a difficult task, but actually selected the easier task. He did not vary age, IQ, or task outcome.

In the third of Farnham-Diggory's experiments, Ss who said that task MM was similar to the motor task were significantly younger (8.37 years) than those who said it was similar to the mental task (9.11 years). Contrary to Henle's supposition, none of the motivational correlates (success, relative ease of task, S's preference for the task, his wish to try it again, or the chance of winning a prize) were significantly associated with similarity judgments. Instead, the data suggested that, in an ambiguous task situation, younger Ss may be influenced more by concrete similarity elements (motor task) and less by abstract similarity elements (mental task).

A significant majority ($^{45}/_{64}$) of the Ss preferred the motor task, which $^{41}/_{64}$ said was easier. There was a significant relation between perceived ease and preference, regardless of age or IQ ($^{48}/_{64}$ Ss preferred the "easy" task). Contrary to Rosenzweig's findings, Ss were fairly evenly divided between preference for the succeeded and failed tasks, and Ss who preferred the succeeded task were significantly older (9.14 years) than those who preferred the failed task (8.19 years).

However, in line with Rosenzweig's findings, Ss who wished to try again the failed task were both older and more intelligent than Ss who wished to try again the task on which they had succeeded (mean age 8.99, 8.27 years; mean IQ 108.3, 99.7, respectively). However, age and IQ were not significantly associated with wanting to try the "hard" task again. The opportunity to try something difficult again is apparently not the same thing as the opportunity to recoup past failures, as far as age and IQ correlates are concerned. However, a significant majority of Ss ($^{21}/_{32}$) in the no-prize group wished to try the difficult task again, regardless of age or IQ. Possibly, when a prize is at issue, the incentive value of repeating a difficult achievement diminishes by comparison. As further evidence for this, Ss in the prize group who wished to try the motor task again had a significantly higher IQ (108.4) than Ss in the same group who wanted to try the mental task again (98.4). There was no significant association between the preference and "try again" judgments.

A majority of Ss ($^{41}/_{64}$) in both groups thought the mental task was harder, regardless of its outcome, and regardless of the fact that the score sequences were the same as those for the motor task. The quality of a task, not merely the score obtained, appeared to be an important variable in the experience of difficulty. However, Ss who said the successful task was harder were significantly younger (8.11 years) than Ss who said the failed task was harder (8.99 years), in both the prize and the no-prize groups. The direct association between difficulty and failure may develop in later childhood. Younger children may need to feel that success is difficult, and hence praiseworthy; older children may have learned to explain or excuse failure by reference to difficulty.

These results suggest that task outcome, task difficulty, and the intellectual (abstract) properties of the task should be empirically separated, and may be responded to differently by children of different age and IQ levels, under different motivational conditions.

Among children who were successful in the second experiment the correlation between age and initial $P(s)$ estimate is significantly negative ($-.33$). Among those who failed the correlation is positive (.23) and significantly different from the negative correlation. The expectancies of very young children appear to be more directly linked to their actual performance: if they are failing, they expect to fail; if they are succeeding, they expect to succeed. As a child ages, however, he appears to develop more complex "compensatory" expectancies—such that success may lead to caution and failure may induce hopefulness. This suggests the "negative recency" effect described by Stevenson and Weir (1961) as being so characteristic of children in this age range. These "compensatory" expectancies may also explain the failure of older children to extinguish more quickly than younger children when reinforcement stops (Kass, 1962). If it were purely a matter of cognizing the reality of the reinforcements, then older children should recognize the change more quickly, but they do not. This suggests a parallel with the finding of James and Rotter (1958) that college student Ss extinguished less rapidly when they were told that their rewards were contingent on their skill in discovering the temporal pattern of correct choices than when they thought reinforcements were controlled randomly by the machine and hence outside their ability to control or predict, although the average number of reinforcements was identical for both groups.

The extent to which task quality, availability of prize, and disability affected the correlations of age and IQ with $P(s)$ level were analyzed for the initial (trial 0) $P(s)$ estimates only. This initial $P(s)$ estimate was unaffected by performance information, and was thus our purest measure of the strength of the above relations.

The correlations between $P(s)_0$ and IQ for Ss in all the experiments who had the mental task first is positive (.14) and the correlation for those who had the motor task first is significantly negative ($-.44$) and significantly different from the positive coefficient. This suggests that if a relatively dull child (below median IQ) is presented with a "mental" task, he doesn't expect to be very good at it—which is reasonable—but if you present him with a simple non-mental task

TABLE 4.16

Correlations (Pearson r) of Age and IQ with $P(s)_0$ *Before First Task by Prize Conditions*

Prize Conditions	Age—$P(s)_0$		IQ—$P(s)_0$	
	r	n	r	n
None	.23[a]	10	−.63[b]	10
Low	−.27	10	.48[c]	10
High	−.37	10	−.01	10
Combined High and Low	−.32[d]	20	—	—

[a,d] Difference significant at .05 level.
[b] Significant at .01 level.
[c] Significant at .05 level.
[d] Significant at .05 level.
(Data collected by S. Farnham-Diggory.)

he expects to be *very* good at *that*.[8] On the other hand, a relatively bright child (above median IQ), expects to do well on a complex mental task, but not quite so well on a simple, rather trivial motor task. This suggests that children in this age range (6–11 years) may be quite realistically differentiated about their abilities; and that a mechanism may, by this time, have been established such that self-esteem will assuredly come from something, if not from the exercise of one ability, then from the exercise of another.

The introduction of a prize appears to reverse the direction of the association between age and $P(s)_0$ from positive to negative. With no prize offered, older Ss are more confident than younger Ss, but with a prize at stake the older Ss are more cautious (cf. Table 4.16).

When a child is working on a task with no prize there is a significant negative correlation between IQ and $P(s)_0$. The brighter the child, the more cautiously he estimates his chances of success. When, however, a child is forced to work for a non-preferred goal (low-prize condition) the previously mentioned relation between IQ and $P(s)_0$ is reversed; the brighter the child, the more he appears to assume that something trivial is easy to get. When a child is permitted to work for

---

[8] The expectations involved in stating $P(s)_0$ for the first task did not depend on a comparison of the two tasks because the nature of the second task was not revealed to S until he had finished the first one.

the more desired prize, however, any relationship between IQ and $P(s)_0$ is obliterated.

In the intact group ($N = 20$) there is a correlation of —.63 (significant) between IQ and $P(s)_0$; the brighter the intact S, the more cautiously he estimates his chances of success. No such relationship between mental ability and expectancy appears among the disabled children ($r = -.07$, $N = 40$). The difference between the two coefficients is significant. Physical disability thus appears to eliminate a negative relationship between intelligence and expectancy—as if IQ had ceased to operate as a mediating variable in the self-estimation of power among physically damaged children.

The extent to which S's chronological and mental age mediate this estimation of power appears to depend upon the nature of the independent variable. The effect of the outcome of a task on $P(s)$ level appears to be relatively independent of IQ, but not of age—younger Ss may react quite differently from older ones, regardless of intelligence. The nature of the task, however, appears to interact with IQ, but not with age—brighter Ss may estimate $P(s)$ in one way for one kind of task and in another way for a different kind of task, regardless of how old they are. The effect of payoffs on estimated $P(s)$, however, appears to be mediated by both age and IQ.

This sort of thing has been largely overlooked in the literature on subjective probability and may partially account for the variability that makes model construction so difficult. In our view the relation of these mediating variables to $P(s)$ differences signifies the probable dependence of self-evaluative mechanisms on developmental factors. The way in which a child's self-evaluation is influenced by what he is doing may depend on his intellectual development; the way in which his self-evaluation depends on *how well* he is doing may depend on how old he is; the way in which his self-evaluation is influenced by *what he is working for* may be affected in quite different ways by both his mental ability and his chronological age.

LA versus P(s) as a Criterion of Discouragement or Encouragement

In our discussion of LA and $P(s)$ we argued that LA may be a valid index of S's feelings of success or failure in a situation in which he is free to change his goal from one trial to the next; but if the goal he is trying to achieve is established and maintained by agencies over which he has no control, his estimate of $P(s)$ is the preferred criterion of his feelings of success or failure. Henry Morlock performed an experiment (Diggory and Morlock, 1964) which

TABLE 4.17
Ten-trial Means of LA and Estimated P(s) by Experimental Conditions

		Hi Mot		Low Mot	
		High Performance	Low Performance	High Performance	Low Performance
Neg.	LA	35.8	29.5	37.3	30.9
	$P(s)$	63.2	47.3	71.6	42.8
Pos.	LA	35.9	23.6	29.9	19.8
	$P(s)$	45.4	15.6	47.7	27.1
Zero	LA	33.7	29.0	32.6	23.6
	$P(s)$	48.9	24.3	62.3	26.9

The plan of the table corresponds to that of Fig. 4.18. Neg., Pos., and Zero refer, respectively, to the acceleration characteristics of the three types of performance curves used. $N = 4$ per cell. (After Diggory and Morlock, 1964.)

showed that *S*'s LA may increase as long as his performance curve rises, even though he is becoming increasingly discouraged about achieving the fixed goal toward which he is working. Fig. 4.18 shows the design of this experiment and the mean $P(s)$ and LA trends for each condition. The corresponding overall means for $P(s)$ and LA are shown in Table 4.17. There were 24 Hi Mot and 24 Lo Mot *S*s randomly assigned, four to each of the six conditions defined by the three types and two levels of the performance curves.

Though analysis of variance of the initial LAs (trial 0) showed no significant differences, $^{14}/_{24}$ Hi Mot *S*s set first LAs of 40 or higher, i.e., at the level of the fixed performance goal, and only $^{6}/_{24}$ Lo Mots did so. These proportions are significantly different by chi-square test. The mean $P(s)$ at trial 0 for the Hi Mots (52.8) is significantly below that of the Lo Mots (63.8).

Overall $P(s)$ trends as a function of the three independent variables are shown in the three upper panels of Fig. 4.19 and the corresponding means over all trials are given in Table 4.17. Hi Mots have significantly lower overall mean $P(s)$ than Lo Mots, in contradiction to the findings of four previously reported experiments (Figs. 4.7, 4.9, and 4.17). But the fact that overall mean $P(s)$ is significantly higher for high than for low performance curves, and is significantly

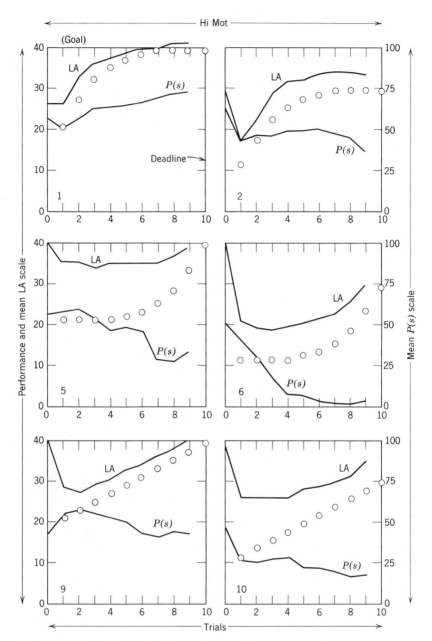

Fig. 4.18 Mean LA and $P(s)$ trends as a function of motivation and characteristics of performance curves (circles). Each point is the mean of four Ss.
(After Diggory and Morlock, 1964.)

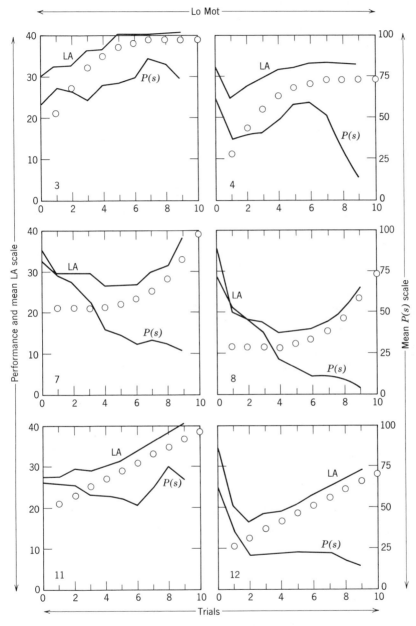

Fig. 4.18 (*Continued*)

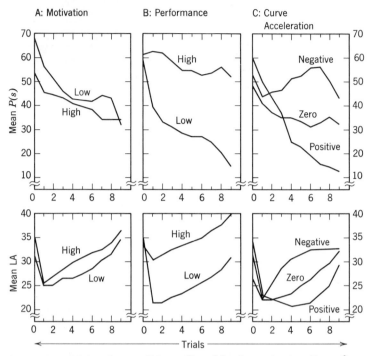

Fig. 4.19   Mean $P(s)$ and mean LA as affected by A: motivation; B: performance level; C: shape of reported performance curves. In A and B each point is the mean of 24 Ss; C has 16 Ss per point. (After Diggory and Morlock, 1964.)

affected by type of performance curve agrees with previous findings. The effect of the Hi versus Lo Mot conditions on overall mean $P(s)$ level depends on certain features of the reported performance curves as shown by panel A in Fig. 4.20. In that figure the overall $P(s)$ means from Table 4.13 are plotted against the mean level of reported performance which is confounded with curve type and curve level. Fig. 4.20 shows that Lo Mot Ss (in comparison with Hi Mots) have the higher overall $P(s)$ estimates in the two cases where the mean reported performance was nearest the goal, and in the one case where it was farthest from the goal, all three differences are significant. However, where performance levels are at intermediate distances from the goal, the differences in $P(s)$ between Hi Mot and Lo Mot Ss are not significant. It appears that in this set of data, the effect of the motivation conditions on overall mean $P(s)$ was determined more by the mean level of the reported performance curves than by their form.

The overall LA trends as shown in Fig. 4.18 and Fig. 4.19 reflect the shapes of the reported performance curves. In nine of the 12 conditions LA decreased sharply between the initial and second estimates, but thereafter the average trend of successive LAs was steadily upward, except that with positively accelerated performance the decline did not cease until trial 4. The LA mean is higher than the performance mean in every condition (cf. Fig. 4.20B). Hi Mot Ss generally set significantly higher LAs than Lo Mots, as Fig. 4.19 shows, but Fig. 4.20B shows that these differences are a function of the form of the performance curve. In both the high and low negatively accelerated performance conditions Lo Mots have the higher means LAs. The difference is significant only with the high level performance curve. In all other cases, Hi Mot LA is the higher, though the difference is not significant in the case of the high constant rate performance curve. It thus appears that the difference between Hi Mot and Lo Mot Ss in LA is a function of the shape of the performance curve rather than its level.

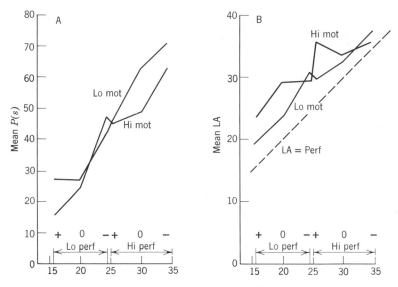

Fig. 4.20 Means (per S per trial) of $P(s)$ and LA as a function of motivation and mean level of reported performance. The ranges of the means for the high and low performance curves are indicated just above the abscissa in each panel. The symbols +, 0, and − refer to the acceleration characteristics of the reported performance curves. Each point is the mean of four Ss × 10 trials. (After Diggory and Morlock, 1964.)

We can consider three aspects of the relations between LA and $P(s)$: (a) initial level, (b) changes over the series of trials, and (c) final level. Over all Ss there is no significant relation between initial LA and $P(s)$ estimates. Chi-square computed from the 2×2 contingency table formed by median splits of both distributions is not significant. A significant Spearman rank-correlation coefficient of $-.67$ was found between the mean initial LA and $P(s)$ levels, with the 12 experimental conditions as the units of observation. Within the six Mi Mot conditions the corresponding coefficient is $-.47$ and within the Lo Mot conditions it is $-.14$, neither of them significant. Thus, the significant negative relation over all 12 conditions does not result from a general tendency to make LA high when $P(s)$ is low (and vice versa). Rather it is due to the effect of the motivation variable which, when it is high, elevates LA and lowers $P(s)$. There is no evidence that initial LA level can be predicted from initial $P(s)$ level, or the reverse, unless the payoff conditions are taken into account.

Over the ten trials, the general $P(s)$ trend is consistently negative while that of LA rises (cf. Fig. 4.18 and Fig. 4.19). Sooner or later the Ss became convinced that they would do better on the next trial than they did on the last, but at the same time they became less hopeful of achieving the fixed goal. Furthermore, performance curve type and level both affect LA and $P(s)$ levels in the same way: LA is high when $P(s)$ is high.

Thus, the *final* LA and $P(s)$ estimates have a significant positive relation over all Ss, by chi-square test. The median LA on the last estimate is 40.5. Ss with LAs above the median have higher mean $P(s)$ estimates (50.8, range 4–100) than Ss with LA below the median (16.5, range 0–80). The rank correlation coefficient between final mean $P(s)$ and LA over all 12 conditions is .97. The corresponding coefficient for the six Hi Mot conditions taken alone is .83, for the Lo Mot conditions it is .96. These coefficients all differ significantly from zero, but not from each other. Thus the experimental treatments changed the relation between $P(s)$ and LA from initially nonsignificant to finally significant and positive.

On the final trial $14\frac{2}{24}$ Hi Mot Ss and $11\frac{1}{24}$ Lo Mots set LAs ≥ 40, the fixed performance goal. This difference is not significant. In the conditions with the high, negatively accelerated performance curves (Conditions 1 and 7, Fig. 4.18), the mean LA for both Hi Mots and Lo Mots is very close to the fixed performance goal from the fifth trial on. In such cases $P(s)$ and LA no longer refer to different goals, so it is of some interest to note that the $P(s)$ trends differ for the two motivation groups: Hi Mots kept increasing $P(s)$ at a moderate

rate throughout the series, but Lo Mots sharply lowered theirs after trial 7.

The finding that Ss in the Hi Mot condition generally set lower mean $P(s)$ estimates than did Lo Mot Ss directly contradicts the results of three earlier experiments and therefore deserves some attention. We cannot do much with it at present because there is nothing in the data or in any records available to us which helps to explain it. The mystery can be settled only by further investigation. Furthermore, the unexpected finding, that the Hi Mot-Lo Mot differences in $P(s)$ are a function of the mean level of reported performance, needs to be verified. The question of how a person's estimate of the likelihood of an event is biased by his desire for it is merely complicated by these data.

$P(s)$ *and n-Ach*

The generally higher level of LA in the Hi Mot than in the Lo Mot condition is analogous to the finding that persons high in achievement motivation (n-Ach) (cf. McClelland, Atkinson, Clark, and Lowell, 1953; McClelland, 1955; Atkinson, 1957) set consistently higher LAs in a learning situation than did Ss low in n-Ach (Kausler and Trapp, 1958). Presumably those high in n-Ach set a higher value on performing as well as they possibly could, so they might correspond to our Hi Mots in that sense. This led to Morlock's next experiment.

We considered what McClelland (1955) and Atkinson (1954) had to say about the origin of individual differences in n-Ach in the amount of "independence training" which parents (especially mothers) give their children. So far, the evidence for this hypothesis is indirect (McClelland and Friedman, 1952; Winterbottom, 1958; McClelland, 1955) but the discussions suggest that among the things that may be learned during (or as a result of) independence training are concepts relating to goal-directed activity. Concepts about the value of the best possible performance in all situations, the individual himself as the responsible agent or cause of the outcomes he seeks, discrimination among ends or means with respect to their value, the various cognitive and motor skills needed to plan and execute a purposive course of action—these appear, on *a priori* grounds, as possible consequences of independence training. They are also consistent with what has been written about the characteristics of people with high n-Ach. McClelland et al. (1953) and Kausler and Trapp (1958) proposed that differences in LA as a function of n-Ach should be minimal when the reality determiners of LA are strong. Now Morlock had just shown that among the reality determiners of LA are the mean level, shape, and general slope of performance curves, and we supposed that another reality determiner might be the presence of a fixed goal. With a fixed goal present, Ss high in n-Ach might aspire to higher standards of performance on each trial, and hence their LAs would be higher than those whose n-Ach is relatively low. If no fixed goal is imposed, the differences in LA as a function of n-Ach should be larger because Ss high in n-Ach presumably bring with them a stronger and clearer valuation of high performance standards than the lows do. In other words, if Ss are free to impose standards of performance on themselves, those with high n-Ach should impose higher ones (and hence, higher LAs) than those with low n-Ach, and this difference should be greater than when S's standard of performance is *given to him* by some agency other than himself. The same argument should apply to the prediction of differences in actual performance on a task; i.e., the predicted differences in LA should be paralleled by differences in real performance. Thus we had to measure n-Ach as a basis for choosing our Ss before the experiment, and during the experiment we had to measure real performance without S's being aware that we were doing so. The latter was measured by means of the hidden kymograph technique described above.

To measure n-Ach we used French's (1955) "Test of Insight" in which S is given a series of descriptions of behavior (e.g., "John is always willing to lend money") and asked to explain each of them. The scoring is based on a content analysis of S's explanations in which "achievement imagery" is defined in accordance with the criteria developed by McClelland et al. (1953) and elaborated by Atkinson and his colleagues (Atkinson, 1958). A large number of college undergraduate men were given mimeographed copies of the "Test of Insight" in their classrooms with the request that they fill them out outside of class and return them to us either directly or through their instructors. Both Morlock and the author independently scored the same small sample of these returns according to French's instructions. Then we reviewed our results, resolved our differences, and Morlock scored the rest. Again we reviewed the scores and resolved all our differences. The final distribution of achievement scores ranged from zero to ten with a median of four. The high and low n-Ach groups were formed by selecting Ss from above and below the median of this distribution. We finally used 17 Ss high in n-Ach (mean achievement imagery, 6.0) and 18 who were low in n-Ach (mean achievement imagery, 3.0). In the experiment all Ss operated under the Lo Mot conditions.

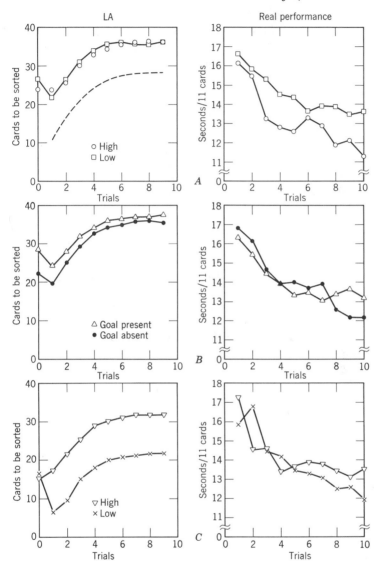

Fig. 4.21   Mean LA and real performance trends as affected by A: *n*-Ach; B: presence of fixed goal; C: level of reported performance curve. The broken line in the upper left-hand panel indicates the shape of the performance curve reported to Ss. The numbers of Ss at each data point are shown in Table 4.18, and the differences are shown in the text.(Data collected by H. C. Morlock, Jr.)

The Ss high and low in n-Ach were assigned randomly to the experimental conditions defined by high and low performance curves and presence or absence of a fixed goal. The performance curves were those shown in Conditions 1 and 2 of Fig. 4.18. The fixed performance goal was 40 cards to be sorted correctly on at least one of ten trials. However, for the conditions with no fixed goal, we left the goal marker off the display panel and told the Ss only that we wanted them to see how many cards they could learn to sort in ten trials. Since it would be nonsense to ask Ss about $P(s)$ when there was no fixed goal, we abandoned it altogether as a dependent variable in this experiment, so LA and actual performance are our only dependent variables. We lost the actual performance data for seven Ss because the kymograph failed during their experimental sessions, but it is unlikely that our outcomes would have been much different even if we had their data.

The results are shown in Fig. 4.21 and the corresponding ten-trial means are shown in Table 4.18. These presentations are limited to "main effects" of the three independent variables, because no interactions were significant. We have included all the Ss in the LA data, even those whose real performance records were lost. We analyzed the LA data without these Ss' records and found nothing different from what we are reporting here.

TABLE 4.18

Means of Level of Aspiration and Real Performance Over Ten Trials

	Level of Aspiration			Real Performance		
	N	Mean	P(diff.)	N	Mean	P(diff.)
n-Ach:						
High	17	31.9	N. S.	12	13.2	.01
Low	18	32.3		16	14.6	
Goal:						
Present	18	33.3	.01	15	14.1	N. S.
Absent	17	30.8		13	13.9	
Performance Curve:						
High	19	36.4	.01	13	14.1	N. S.
Low	16	27.0		15	13.8	

(Data collected by H. C. Morlock, Jr.)

As the results clearly show, LA was not significantly affected by n-Ach, but it was significantly affected by the level of the reported performance curve and by the presence or absence of a fixed goal. The latter result confirms our auxiliary hypothesis, that presence of a fixed goal is a reality determiner of LA. However, compared to shape and level of performance curve, it is a weak determiner: the differences in LA between the goal and no-goal conditions are small, but consistent.

The pattern of significant effects of the independent variables on actual performance is exactly the reverse of their effects on LA; that is, where there is a significant effect on LA, there is none on actual performance, and vice versa. If we did not have the real performance data, we could not have decided whether LA is unrelated to n-Ach or whether we had failed to select groups which differed sufficiently in n-Ach. We cannot conclude the latter because high n-Ach produces consistently better average performance than does low n-Ach on every trial. This agrees with findings by Lowell (1952), French (1955), Wendt (1955), and Atkinson and Reitman (1956). Presence or absence of goal and level of reported performance curve had no significant effects on real performance level.

Since there are no interaction effects in either the LA or the real performance data, the main hypothesis, that differences between high and low n-Ach Ss in both LA and performance would depend on the presence of an explicit goal, was not confirmed. There are only the main effects described above. Comparison of these results with those of previous studies already cited leaves us in a quandary about the conditions under which LA and actual performance will vary in parallel and the conditions under which they will not.

It is possible that we failed to choose Ss who were sufficiently different in n-Ach to produce differences in our LA measures. Some doubt exists on the adequacy of this explanation in view of the large and consistent differences in real performance associated with the n-Ach variable. Perhaps we did not introduce sufficient achievement cues into the situation. This is possible, but achievement cues were present in the instructions about what was necessary to "do a good job," and in the questioning of Ss about their LA before each trial. The most likely explanation is that there was not enough difference between our goal and no-goal conditions in reality determiners of LA. We assumed we could produce the expected differential between high and low n-Ach by removing only one reality determiner of LA from the situation—the fixed goal. This was in fact a reality determiner because with the fixed goal present the mean LAs were higher on every trial than when there was no fixed goal. This finding also means that Ss were not restricting themselves to a single narrow range of LAs; that is, there was *room* for LA differences if the n-Ach variable were effective in producing them. In addition to the presence of the fixed goal, there was another powerful reality determiner of LA—the reported performance curve. Just how powerful a determiner this was can be seen by how closely the LA trends parallel the reported performance curves. (Figs. 4.18, 4.19, and 4.21). We are justified in expecting that variation in Ss' presumed motivation (n-Ach) will affect his LA because several investigators had already reported a positive relation between them, and we ourselves had shown that differences in the outcome value of a performance affected the LA level. Therefore we must continue to search for the conditions under which level of motivation affects LA, but we have nothing more to say about it here.

Several Means to the Same Goal

We are interested in the determiners of an individual's estimate of the "power" he can apply in attempting to gain an objective. So far we have concentrated exclusively on the estimation of $P(s)$ when only one ability or capacity was used, but it is likely that estimates of personal power extend also to cases where more than one ability can be applied in the pursuit of a goal. Each of several abilities may be regarded as an alternate means (or "pathway" in Lewin's sense, Lewin, 1936) for getting to the goal, and if, in the course of several attempts, the person convinces himself that one ability is inadequate to the task in hand he need not be discouraged to the point of abandoning the goal if he has other abilities that he can apply. To make this situation quite concrete, imagine a man who has to get over a high stone wall. He might jump, catch the top, and drag himself over; construct a rope or a makeshift ladder; or pile up earth to make a ramp. If his objective were simply to get over the wall, he should not despair of doing so even if he discovered that jumping would not work because he is too short or because his arms are too weak to pull himself over once he has grasped the top of the wall. He has the other methods to rely on, so the failure of jumping should not lead him to lower his $P(s)$ for getting over the wall. A decisive diminution in $P(s)$ to the point where he quits should occur only after he has proved by actual trials that no available method will work. Generally, we assumed that under certain circumstances $P(s)$ should vary not only with the power of a single ability but as a function of the number of abilities which are available for attempts at achievement.

R. E. Cetlin (1964) addressed himself to an experimental analogue of this problem. His 64 Ss (45 men and 19 women) were members of the staff at a U.S. Army hospital. Fifty-eight of them had attended college-level curricula in liberal arts, occupational therapy, and nursing, and the other six had above-average scores on Army aptitude tests and had taken specialist courses in the Army. Their Army job classifications included medical technicians (neuropsychiatric, social work, psychology, pharmaceutical, and administrative), social work, occupational therapy, and nursing. Their ages ranged from 19 to 45 years. They were divided into four groups of 16 each for the four experimental treatments by a pseudo-random process; that is, after precautions had been taken to assure that the groups would not differ in composition with respect to sex, military rank, and educational level, the assignment to the four groups was strictly random.

Cetlin devised four tasks which differed sufficiently in their obvious requirements so that Ss would believe that each task corresponded to a different ability:

(1) "Judgment in unstructured situations" corresponded to the task in which S had to estimate various time intervals ranging from 17 to 33 seconds.

(2) "Spatial relations" ability was tested by a series of puzzles which required S to construct circles, squares, triangles, hexagons, trapezoids, and parallelograms from pieces cut out of gray cardboard. Each puzzle contained six segments that S was to assemble in the form of a model of the completed figure. The areas of the completed figures ranged from six to 16 square inches.

(3) "Quantitative reasoning" was tested by requiring S to furnish the seventh terms of various number series of which the first six digits were given. Each series was designed to appear as if some order were inherent in it and yet to be ambiguous enough so that S could not be sure of choosing the correct number.

(4) "Verbal facility" was tested by requiring S to find a word, beginning with any one of four specified letters, which would fit a given definition. Definitions of rare words were selected from a dictionary. Each definition was presented to S on a card along with four letters, among which was allegedly the initial letter of the correct word, but the correct initial was in fact never there.

The criteria of correct performance on three of these tasks were sufficiently unclear so that E could declare any performance successful or unsuccessful if he liked. In the puzzle assembly task (number 2, above) correct solutions were possible, but apparently not in less than one minute per puzzle. Since a uniform time limit of 35 seconds per trial was maintained throughout the experiment, no S in fact succeeded on the puzzle task, and all trials on the other tasks were scored as wrong.

Ss were invited to participate in an experiment in which they would be given a series of problems to solve. They were told that they were invited because of their high aptitude scores, and (where appropriate) their college-level training. They were told that most people enjoyed trying their hand at these tasks. The purpose of the experiment was explained as follows: "I am investigating the mental estimates people frequently make while they are trying for a difficult, long-term goal. For example, when you began high school or college you may have estimated your chances of graduation as 75 out of one hundred. You may have received a grade of 'B' in mathematics and then raised your estimate to 90 out of one hundred. Or, you may have flunked English and lowered your estimate to 40 out of one hundred. Here, in this situation, you must successfully complete any six of the 24 tasks you will be given."

To facilitate Ss' accepting this standard as a goal and judging it as moderately difficult to obtain, the instructions continued: "These are difficult tasks, even for college students, and worthy of your utmost concentration. I'm sure you will not solve all of them correctly, nobody has so far, but some previous subjects did solve six of the problems and so achieved the goal."

Though each S was to get 24 problems, not all were to be of the same task (same ability). The plan of the experiment, shown in Table 4.19, was to announce to one group that all their problems would tap the same ability (Group 1); another group would have problems representing two types of abilities (Group 1-1); and the two remaining groups (Groups 3-1 and 1-3) would have four abilities tested. Those with more than one capacity to be tested were told that *any* six successes, whether from a single capacity or not, would achieve the goal. Furthermore, the multiple-capacity groups were told that the different capacities would be tested according to a schedule which was explained to them before they began to work. A copy of this schedule was kept in sight throughout the experiment and Ss were invited to refer to it several times during the series of trials. The schedules were varied so that one group (Group 1-3) spent the first 12 trials on tests of the same capacity; on successive blocks of four trials thereafter they used other capacities. The schedule for Group (3-1) was the reverse of that for Group (1-3). Group (1-1) was

TABLE 4.19
Number of Capacities Available to Each Group at Given Trials

Group	Trials					
	0	5	9	13	17	21
(1–3)	4	4	4	3	2	1
(3–1)	4	3	2	1	1	1
(1–1)	2	2	2	1	1	1
(1)	1	1	1	1	1	1

(After R. E. Cetlin, 1964.)

scheduled to use one capacity for the first 12 trials and the other for the second 12 trials. Group (1) used the same capacity throughout. After all instructions had been given and S had worked a solvable sample problem from each test, each S made an estimate of $P(s)$ on a linear rating scale as in the previous experiments. $P(s)$ was estimated again after every subsequent trial.

The results are shown in Fig. 4.22. Until trial 12, the $P(s)$ estimates for Groups (1–3) and (1–1) are significantly higher and decline at a slower rate than do those for Groups (1) and (3–1). Data are not reported after trial 19 because by then all $P(s)$ estimates had gone to zero and stayed there in subsequent trials. Over trials 13–19, the relative rates of decline in $P(s)$ are reversed; that is, the groups whose decline was slowest in the first 12 trials now have the more rapid decline. Obviously there is a deadline effect operating here, but it is reasonable to suppose that in addition to the "trial deadline" of the previous experiments, there is here an "ability" or "capacity" deadline. Group (1), operating with a single ability, is comparable to the conditions of the previous experiments where only a "trial deadline" was involved. The other groups had to consider not only the exhaustion of their opportunities to get the goal but also the gradual exhaustion of the number of different *ways* (abilities) in which they could try to reach it. Group (3–1) had its magazine of abilities exhausted quickly and the decline in its mean $P(s)$ is practically identical with that of Group (1). But, at the end of trial 12, Group (1–1) still had 50% of its original capacity endowment left to try and Group (1–3) had still 75% of its initial endowment untried. The marked early

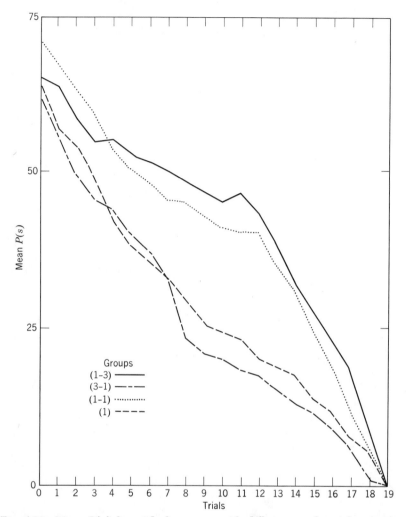

Fig. 4.22   Mean $P(s)$ by trials for groups with different numbers of capacities available. Each point is the mean of 16 Ss. See text and Table 4.19 for explanation of groups. (After R. E. Cetlin, 1964.)

retardation of the decline in $P(s)$ in these latter two groups suggests the operation of a capacity deadline. These data also show that we can hold *number* of past failures constant up to any point in time and still produce large differences in people's expectations of ultimate success by systematically varying the *meaning* of these failures in terms of the number of abilities which have proved to be inadequate.

P(s) and Self-evaluation

We now directly confront the question whose answer will validate or discredit, for our immediate interests, all of our previous work on the determinants of $P(s)$. Can we get empirical evidence that estimated $P(s)$ is related to direct statements of self-evaluation? The answer (it is affirmative) has been supplied by research carried out by I. G. Cetlin (1964) and B. S. Rosen.

For the immediate purpose, it is unnecessary to describe all the details of Cetlin's experiment. A fuller treatment of her results is given in Chapter 5. Her Ss were 60 students in high schools in the Philadelphia suburbs, ranging in age from 14 to 18 years. They were selected from a group of students who had responded to a letter inviting them to express their interest in a "Space Science Program." Cetlin and other psychologists were allegedly serving to provide information about the program and to administer preliminary screening tests to interested students. The information given in the first part of the experimental interview included the following descriptions of positions for which S might try: "Research Scientists," "Instrument Development Engineer," "Specifications Developer," and "Project Coordinator."

These descriptions were designed to create the impression of a hierarchy of jobs with respect to status, responsibility, and importance of the assigned work. Stated starting salaries, coordinated with these descriptions, ranged from $7,500 for the "Research Scientist" down to $4,000 for the "Project Coordinator," and the required "passing scores" on the test allegedly ranged, respectively, from 50 to 19.[9]

The task was presented as a test of Ss' ability to receive, organize, and reproduce complex information. On each trial S listened to a complex rhythm of auditory taps reproduced from a tape playback. S attempted to reproduce the pattern by tapping on a telegraph key, and his responses were recorded on a wax paper kymograph. After each trial, E pretended to evaluate S's recorded performance by comparing it with an impressive looking book of "norms." She then wrote S's "score" for that trial, and his cumulated score over all trials to date, in a table and marked the position of the cumulated score on a graph. The table and graph were visible to S throughout the experiment.

All Ss rated the "Research Scientist" position as the most desirable and said it was the one they wanted to qualify for, so all subsequent discussion of this experiment in this chapter will relate to that position. The Ss were told that the minimum passing score on the preliminary

[9] The information presented in these instructions is presented, with a more detailed description of Isabelle Cetlin's experiment, in Chapter 5.

nary test was 50 and that the maximum number of points that could be earned on any one trial was 6. Therefore the maximum possible score for the entire test was understood to be 60, and the passing score of 50 was relatively high for that range. The Ss were assigned randomly to four groups (15 Ss each corresponding to the predetermined cumulated performance curves shown in Table 4.20.

TABLE 4.20
Sequences of Cumulated Scores on each of Ten Trials

Groups I and IV:	1, 1, 2, 2, 4, 5, 7, 8, 9, 10
Group II:	5, 10, 15, 20, 25, 29, 34, 36, 40, 44
Group III:	5, 11, 17, 23, 28, 34, 39, 44, 49, 55

(After I. G. Cetlin, 1964.)

These curves are presented, as they appeared to the Ss, in Fig. 4.23. The lowest cumulated curve (Groups I and IV) ends after the first three trials in the graphic presentation, because *all Ss in these conditions had quit after the third trial.* Table 4.20 describes what Cetlin would have presented to Groups I and IV on later trials; Fig. 4.23 shows what she actually presented.

Before, each trial, including the first, Ss estimated $P(s)$, relative to passing the test. In addition, before each trial (including the first) these Ss marked another linear rating scale to answer the question: "How would you rate yourself as a candidate for this position?" Along the scale were equally spaced marks corresponding to the ordered descriptions: poor, fair, good, very good, superior. Responses were measured on a scale of 100 units from the "Poor" end of the scale. The $P(s)$ trends are shown in Fig. 4.24A. It is clear that they correspond closely to the level of the performance curves presented to Ss—a familiar story by now. The new thing about *this* story is that the self-evaluation trends (Fig. 4.24B) are closely parallel to those of the $P(s)$ data. The *trends* are parallel. Metrically the $P(s)$ estimates and self-evaluations are incommensurate, so nothing can be made of the relative positions of the two kinds of curves, nor of the correspondence of particular points in them. However, as $P(s)$ varies up or down, in response to the experimental treatments, so does self-evaluation, and we could not wish a prettier demonstration that we can take $P(s)$ as an index of S's evaluation of himself as an instrument for doing some particular thing. But we wanted to know more about this correspondence, so we performed two more experiments which were carried out by B. S. Rosen.

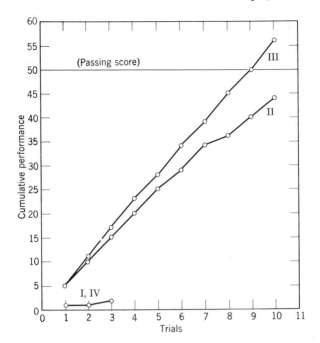

Fig. 4.23 Cumulated performance curves reported to groups I–IV. See text for explanation. (After I. G. Cetlin, 1964.)

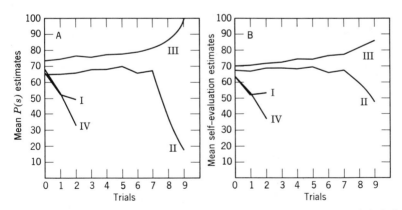

Fig. 4.24 Mean $P(s)$ and self-evaluation for groups I–IV. At each trial (T) the numbers of Ss are as follows: Group I: T_0–T_1, 15; T_2, 11. Group II: T_0–T_8, 15; T_9, 12. Group III: T_0–T_9, 15. Group IV: T_0–T_2, 15, The exception is that in the self-evaluation data for Group I, $n = 14$ at T_0. (After I. G. Cetlin, 1964.)

Rosen's first experiment is an object lesson in what can be learned through failure. Ever since we planned Morlock's second experiment, we had been intrigued by the idea of manipulating the "reality determiners" of LA and $P(s)$. Furthermore, we had learned that our methods for manipulating success and failure were very potent because Ss would often tell us, before the last trial, that they had *already* failed and it was useless to continue. Often we had to readjust the sequence of scores for a "failure condition" simply to keep the Ss from quitting before the end of the series of trials.[10] Clearly we were able to manipulate the reality determiners for the expectation of failure or success. By contrast, many previous Es had induced failure by simply announcing at the end of a test that S had not achieved a passing score, or that his score was lower than that of some designated group. This suggested that if we did *not* report performance information to S throughout the series of trials, but only informed him of his success or failure after the last trial, we should see some differences in the trends of self-evaluation and $P(s)$ in comparison with conditions where S received continuous reports about his progress toward the fixed goal or passing score. Accordingly, we made half of the college student Ss in this experiment go through the task with no performance information at all, while the other half had their performances reported visually and orally after each trial. We also set up a "success" curve and a "failure" curve and assigned half the Ss to each of these conditions. The success and failure curves were determined by the following sequences of numbers of cards allowed to be correctly sorted at each trial (with fixed goal of 40 cards on at least one 25-second trial):

TABLE 4.21

Sequences of Scores for Ten Trials, Success and Failure Conditions

					Trial					
Condition	1	2	3	4	5	6	7	8	9	10
Success	19	25	29	32	34	36	37	40	42	43
Failure	19	25	29	32	34	36	37	38	38	39

[10] Isabelle Cetlin's experiment included a deliberate attempt to make Ss quit; the incomplete data for her Groups I and IV was no accident, as will be explained in Chapter 5.

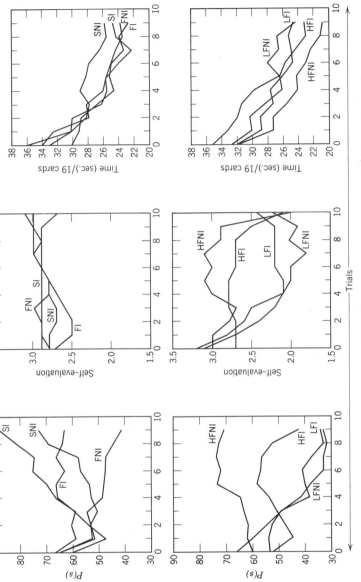

Fig. 4.25 Mean $P(s)$, self-evaluation, and real performance in two experiments. Upper panels are for one experiment, lower panels for the other. See text and Tables 4.21, 4.22, and 4.23 for explanation of the performance curves which defined the conditions. Key: F = failure; S = success; H = high reported mean performance; L = low reported mean performance; I = complete performance information reported to S; NI = no performance information reported to S. (Data collected by B. Rosen.)

The Ss were told that the experiment was one of a series which was "aimed at a better understanding of a very important ability which we call psychomotor coordination." Before each trial, they estimated $P(s)$ and they also answered the question, "How good is your psychomotor coordination?" The question was answered by marking a linear rating scale with equally spaced gradations labeled from left to right: 0, completely inadequate; 1, inadequate; 2, so-so; 3, adequate; 4, completely adequate. Self-evaluation ratings were read to the nearest tenth of one of these divisions—a different scheme than I. G. Cetlin used. Rosen also recorded real performance in terms of time taken on each trial to sort the first 19 cards (the minimum number for all trials and all Ss).

The results are shown graphically in the three upper panels of Fig. 4.25. The overall means for the various conditions are presented in Table 4.18. It is clear that mean $P(s)$ is significantly higher for success conditions (63.2) than for failure conditions (57.0), and it is also higher for Ss who were given full performance information (65.8) than for those who received no such information (54.4). However, there are no significant effects at all on self-evaluation ratings or on actual performance. The graphs of the self-evaluation data (Fig. 4.24, upper middle panel) are not designed to confuse. They show exactly how the data ran—fluctuating unsystematically within a very narrow range near the high end of the scale and running into each other so as to be indistinguishable—and the corresponding means in Table 4.22 show the same thing. This experiment signally failed to reproduce I. G. Cetlin's findings.

Fortunately we listened to the Ss' reasons for not changing their self-evaluation ratings during the series of trials. In sum, they said that nothing had been done to alter their opinion of their psychomotor coordination (whatever that was), that they thought they could use their eyes and hands as well as ever in customary tasks outside the laboratory, and that they might conceivably change their ratings of their ability *only* if they received a lot more information than this one puny little test provided. Furthermore, they weren't seriously engaged with the task—they were not really trying to get any more out of it than the satisfaction of their curiosity or trying to be good fellows and please the attractive young lady experimenter. With these clues it didn't take us long to realize that I. G. Cetlin's Ss were engaged in a task with a serious outcome which they had volunteered to try to win, that her self-evaluation question ("How would you rate yourself as a candidate for this position?") was directly addressed to Ss' goodness *as operators* in a specific, important function, and that

TABLE 4.22
Overall (per trial) Means of P(s), *Self-Evaluation Ratings, and Real Performance, by Conditions*

	N	P(s)	Self-Evaluation	Real Performance (Seconds to sort 19 cards)
First Experiment				
Success—Information	9	67.8	2.9	26.5
Success—No Information	9	58.5	2.9	28.4
Failure—Information	9	63.7	2.8	25.9
Failure—No Information	9	50.2	2.9	26.9
Combined				
All Success Conditions	18	63.2	2.9	27.5
All Failure Conditions	18	57.0	2.9	26.4
All Information Conditions	18	65.8	2.9	26.2
All No Information Conditions	18	54.4	2.9	27.7
Second Experiment				
High Failure—Information	9	51.4	2.7	26.7
High Failure—No Information	9	67.6	2.9	24.5
Low Failure—Information	9	45.1	2.4	26.8
Low Failure—No Information	9	41.8	2.2	29.0
Combined				
All High Failure	18	59.5	2.8	25.6
All Low Failure	18	43.5	2.3	27.9
All Information	18	48.3	2.6	26.8
All No Information	18	54.7	2.6	26.8

(Data collected by B. Rosen.)

B. S. Rosen's Ss had none of these conditions. We fixed all that in Rosen's second experiment.

First, we wanted, without too much elaborate introductory maneuvering, to get college students to volunteer to take our experimental task as a "qualifying test" for an activity they wanted to get into. Therefore, the Ss were recruited from among those who volunteered to take a test to see whether they had at least the *minimum* ability to be acceptable Ss in an experiment on the learning of complex motor skills. When they came to be "tested," they were told that we had to know something about their psychomotor coordination, and that was what we were going to test. To pass the test they had to sort

40 cards correctly on at least one of ten trials. Half of them were assigned to each of the following performance curves:

TABLE 4.23
Sequences of Scores for Ten Trials, Two Failure Conditions

Conditions	\multicolumn{10}{c}{Trials}
	1	2	3	4	5	6	7	8	9	10
High Failure	19	25	30	32	35	36	37	37	37	37
Low Failure	19	19	19	19	20	21	23	26	31	37

These are simply a positively accelerated curve and a negatively accelerated one that start and end at the same points. The designations "High Failure" and "Low Failure" are based on our expectations, derived from previous experiments, that the positively accelerated curve would prove more discouraging to the Ss, that it would make their $P(s)$ estimates go down faster, than the negatively accelerated curve.

We also provided half the Ss with complete performance information after every trial and withheld all such information from the others.

The results are shown in the lower three panels of Fig. 4.25 and in the lower section of Table 4.22. Here we have I. G. Cetlin's finding all over again. The means for the $P(s)$ estimates (Table 4.22) vary over conditions *exactly* as do the means for self-evaluation, and the first two panels in the lower half of Fig. 4.25 show almost as neat a correspondence between the $P(s)$ and self-evaluation trends as in Cetlin's data. Why? Now Rosen's Ss were answering a question about their presumed goodness for a specific enterprise; "How good do you think you would be as a subject in the experiment. . . ?" Furthermore, the mean quality of actual performance varies over conditions exactly as $P(s)$ and self-evaluation do! (Remember that performance is measured in terms of *time* to produce a standard amount, so lower scores mean higher output.) We will take up the performance data in Chapter 5.

It is noteworthy that giving Ss information about their performance (as compared with no information) kept $P(s)$ generally lower when S's average reported performance was relatively high, and kept $P(s)$ generally higher when the reported performance was in fact low. Another way of looking at it must be introduced by another observa-

tion about the psychological situation of the Ss in these last two experiments. We began by thinking that half of the Ss were absolutely
deprived of information about their performance—and we have per-
petuated this bias by labeling the conditions "No Information" in Fig.
4.25 and Table 4.22—but we are fully aware (*now,* by hindsight)
that this is not true. Since S holds the pack of cards to be sorted
face down in one hand, he can be aware after each trial that the
pack of unsorted cards is thinner than on some previous trial. He
can pay attention in a general way to the number of motions he had
made, or he may actually count the cards as he lays them down. Most
of our Ss did not resort to this latter method, at least not consistently,
because it seemed to interfere with their concentrating on identifying
each card as they turned it up and with their search for its proper
place on the table. Nevertheless, it is clear that the $P(s)$ curves (Fig.
4.25) for all groups of "No Information" Ss have the characteristic
forms which indicate what kind of performance curve they were associated with—in fact they are not markedly different *in form* from the
curves produced by the corresponding groups of Ss in the "Information" conditions. Only the average levels of the $P(s)$ (and other)
curves are affected by the relative lack of information Ss had, and
this suggests that they knew very well that they were improving and,
in a vague way, how fast their improvement was, but they could not
be absolutely certain about the form or level of their performance
curves. Therefore, during "Low Failure" the Ss with no information
take a generally pessimistic view of their likelihood of succeeding,
but during "High Failure" they are relatively optimistic and overrate
their chances of success.

SUMMARY

The results presented in this chapter can be summarized
in the following propositions. A person's estimate of his $P(s)$ for a
given undertaking is an index of his evaluation of himself as an instrument for doing whatever he is trying to do. Estimates of $P(s)$ are
higher when rate of improvement is high, when the average distance
between performance and goal is small, when the deadline for the
operation is distant or vaguely located, when the rate of performance
improvement is relatively irregular, and (perhaps) when the goal to
be achieved by the performance is an important one for S.

LA may increase from trial to trial if performance likewise im-
proves, and at the same time S may become increasingly discouraged
about achieving his ultimate goal. Therefore, $P(s)$ is the better index
of S's feelings or anticipations of success or failure.

The greater the number of abilities a person has tested (and found inadequate) in a given number of trials, the lower his $P(s)$ will be.

Finally, from Bonnie Rosen's data, we have the interesting finding that a person's *actual output* is related to his $P(s)$—which suggests an analogy to the familiar goal gradient phenomenon (Lewin, 1935; Miller, 1944). It suggests some other things as well, which will be discussed in Chapter 5, where we consider other behavioral consequences of discouragement or encouragement during the pursuit of our goals.

Chapter 5
SOME CONSEQUENCES
OF CHANGES IN
SELF-EVALUATION

The data presented so far indicate that we can exercise considerable control over whether or not a person anticipates or experiences success or failure. His $P(s)$ estimates rise or fall as a function of the history of his approach to a goal, the number of mutually substitutable abilities he has, the distance and clarity of the deadline, the value he puts on the goal, and the concrete demands of the task. Furthermore, if self-evaluation is construed, not as global appraisal of "the whole self," but as S's evaluation of his power to accomplish a specific objective, then $P(s)$ can be taken as an index of self-evaluation, for the two covary to a marked degree. However, these facts are worthless if we cannot say what they lead to. What practical difference does it make if a person has failed and is therefore discouraged or even despairing; what difference, by contrast, if he has succeeded and is therefore encouraged or heartened, or even hopeful and elated? What does he *do* next?

In this chapter we will give the results of our attempts to answer some of these questions. The results to be presented deal with the level of self-stressing; with "defensive" maneuvers of withdrawal, persistence, and substitution; with the effects of success or failure, in the use of one ability, on self-evaluation of other abilities; with spontaneous changes in fantasies about death; and with changes in evaluations of important goals.

PERSISTENCE AND WITHDRAWAL

Changes in Self-stressing

We have already told, in Chapter 3, how James (1890), Höffding (1891), and Freud (1926) subscribed to the general view that a person's conviction of his own power or helplessness, in the

205

face of demands that he act, would lead him to expect happiness or unhappiness, or would make him confident or anxious, or would make him persist or give up. The phenomenon of quitting or giving up was ascribed by Hoppe (1931) to any of three conditions: (*1*) *S*'s profound or repeated failure in attempts to do what he wanted with the task materials; (*2*) so complete and skillful an achievement of the manipulations involved in the task that the task itself was exhausted of opportunities for further improvement; (*3*) a task which is, from the beginning, so easy to accomplish that no levels of increasing achievement could be defined no matter how often it was repeated. Monotonous routine tasks of the latter type produce "psychic satiation" (Karsten, 1928; Hoppe, 1931) or "boredom" (Viteles, 1932), an experience which may be so crushing that death seems preferable. The attempts of subjects in satiation experiments and of workers on assembly lines to vary the conditions of work, sometimes in ingenious and beneficial ways, sometimes in ways that are disastrous for the quality of the product and may threaten life and limb or expensive equipment, are probably to some extent their attempts to escape boredom.

Lewin (1942) set hope and hopelessness in the broad context of "time perspective." His discussion is based on the reactions of two groups of Jews in Germany to the Nazi threats against them and on Farber's (1944) study of the correlates of suffering among prisoners. Lewin's point about the Jews seems to be that where group consensus defines the goal and the means for the survival of the group rather than that of any particular individuals, then the individuals have a goal and an instrument for attaining it which renders their situation relatively hopeful. Farber found that prisoners who suffered conceived that they were in a bad situation through no fault of their own and they had neither goals for the future nor implements for improving their situation. On the other hand, those who suffered less were making the best of a bad situation for which they accepted responsibility, and they expected to be able to terminate the situation and move on to something better.

Whether the situation is one of total failure, complete achievement, or boredom, success as a future prospect has a probability of zero or nearly zero. The person who has experienced only failure has very likely convinced himself that his abilities are simply inadequate instruments for achieving the goals he attempted to reach, but the person who has exhausted the possibilities of the task has no reason to distrust his abilities; what he suffers from is lack of opportunity to exercise his abilities. Either way, they quit; one abandons the vain pursuit of any success at all, and the other gives up the equally vain pursuit of any additional success.

At the limits suggested by these situations there is, first, the man who has never succeeded in achieving a single goal he has attempted, though he sees other men achieve similar goals every day. He may be in the most profound despair, for his experience tells him that as an instrument for achieving ordinary human aims he is totally inadequate. At the other extreme is the man with a past history, not necessarily of uninterrupted easy successes but of a fair share of successes achieved by various amounts of self-stressing and a sufficient sprinkling of genuine failures to add the spice of anxiety to his striving. If he now stands, with his abilities perfectly adequate and unimpaired, but convinced as far as conviction is possible that there are no more opportunities to pursue the ends for which his abilities are suited, that every path is a blind alley, every door firmly bolted, that all avenues of achievement are closed to him, then are not his abilities analogous in value to that of a pocketful of money when there is nothing to buy? In such an environment he is just as worthless as the man who could achieve nothing in a rich field of opportunities.

Cognitive Defenses

It is indisputable that people withdraw, in some sense, from situations where the probability of success appears to be low. Nor is there any reason to challenge the idea that such withdrawal is somehow connected with a person's desire to prove that he has the right to the most favorable possible adjectives (Lovejoy, 1961). We must be clear about the specific behaviors that are called "withdrawal," about the conditions under which they occur, and the functions they serve. A person's defense of his right to favorable "adjectives" appeared in the literature of the seventeenth century as *self-deception* and *self-justification* (Lovejoy, 1961). By self-deception a person avoids the recognition of facts which might indicate that he has less right to approbation or adjectival value than he would like. Self-justification does not characteristically ignore or deny facts; it reinterprets them and perhaps drags in some that might otherwise be overlooked (Claparede, 1926; Frenkel-Brunswik, 1939; Lovejoy, 1961). In these modes of defense the activity is primarily cognitive: failure to *recognize* facts or the attempt to *reinterpret* them. The defenses of *"repression"* and of *"denial" of certain stimuli* are of this cognitive type (Freud, 1893, 1894, 1915a, 1926, 1940), and a great deal of recent psychological experimentation has concentrated on cognitive defenses: on certain conditional *memory* decrements as "repression," and on certain conditional *recognition* or receptive decrements as "denial."

Psychologists are, or should be, aware by now that the attempt to study the cognitive defenses is no easy matter. It is easy to see many situations in which they might plausibly be operating, but very hard to prove, in most cases, that they are in fact operating. For example, Frenkel-Brunswik (1939) studied "self-deception" in 40 students in the institute of psychology at the University of Vienna whose statements about their own behavior, the principles guiding their conduct, and about the changes they would like to see made in the institute, were compared with ratings and evaluations made of them by four independent judges. If S said that he was generally "sincere" and the judges unanimously declared him "insincere," then S was "distorting into the opposite." If S didn't mention a trait (usually an undesirable one) which all the judges said he had, then S was deceiving himself by "omission." If the judges labeled S as "aggressive," and S said, ". . . will not let myself be intimidated," then S was indulging in "justification." If the judges mentioned S's facetiousness and S said that he is "somewhat playful," then S indulged in "belittling." There was more disagreement between Ss and judges about very generalized behavior dispositions than there was about concrete behavior in specific situations. "The assertion of principles directed toward character traits and social attitudes would seem to be in the nature of a compensation for the actual lack of such traits and attitudes" (Frenkel-Brunswik, 1939, p. 415). An impious critic who accepted the implied theory of self-deception might be tempted to say *"tu quoque"* to the judges on behalf of the Ss. Even without accepting the theory it is evident that studies of this kind have little regarded the *criteria* for deciding that S is sincere, or helpful, or facetious. An interesting little study of "forgetting" of "selfish" choices (Adler, 1941) made the latter point even more sharply. After 37 children had rated several tasks on a five-point scale ranging from "like" through "neutral" to "dislike," Adler gave each S a liked and a disliked task and told him to do one himself and leave the other for his absent partner to do later. Ninety-two per cent of all choices were "selfish" (S left the disliked task for his partner), and 73% of all Ss made *only* selfish choices. The percentages of the three classes of tasks which Ss *did not* recall later were: 44% neutral, 16% of tasks in selfish choices, and only 4% in unselfish choices. To an uncritical devotee of the idea of defensive forgetting, it would appear that these Ss were repressing or ignoring the evidence of their selfishness. However, the group of children, of which the Ss were a sample, and from which the "partners" would have come, rated Ss' selfish choices less highly and the tasks Ss left for the "partners" more highly than the Ss had rated them. Thus, in keeping an activity he likes for himself and assigning one he doesn't like to his partner, S may be taking account of differences between what he and his partner like, in which case he is acting neither selfishly nor altruistically, but *congenially*. Then how close can we come to explaining the fact that these Ss recalled fewer of the tasks that they actually completed than of the tasks that they left for their partners? That is part of another story to which we now turn.

It is a basic premise of Lewin's psychological theory that when a person has the intention to complete a task there is in him a hypothetical "tension" or "quasi-need" to maintain contact with that task in memory or in action, or to resume contact with it after an interruption (Lewin, 1926). If the task is completed the "tension" is discharged, and the need to maintain contact with the task terminates. These propositions were first systematically investigated by having Ss work on several tasks, half of which were interrupted before their completion by the carefully staged "accident" of having E called out of the room to answer the telephone, receive a caller, or to return a set of keys. Later, when Ss were asked to write down a list of the tasks they had worked on, they recalled on the average more of the incomplete (I) tasks than completed (C) ones (Zeigarnik, 1927). Other Ss were presented with both C and I tasks on a later date, including some tasks which had been left incomplete by other people, and they not only resumed operating on I more often than C tasks, but they chose *their own I* tasks to work on (Ovsiankina, 1928). The theory to which these experiments are related explains Alder's (1941) results, discussed above, just as well as Zeigarnik's (1927), though Adler's difference between recalled performed tasks (13%) and unperformed tasks (17%) was very small. But psychologists generally had a hard time replicating the effect.[1] Later research has shown that the effect depends on a very complex set of conditions which even now are not well understood, though Zeigarnik's own article hinted

---

[1] The mixture of success and failures in early attempts to replicate the Zeigarnik effect was so frustrating that some psychologists became "superstitious." Professors F. W. Irwin and M. G. Preston used to tell their graduate students at the University of Pennsylvania about the "M-effect": If your surname began with M, or a later letter in the alphabet, you could replicate the Zeigarnik effect (e.g., Preston); but you couldn't replicate it if your surname began with a letter that came before M (e.g., Irwin). There were other distinguished names involved, but I forget them.

at some of them. Zeigarnik used the ratio of number of I tasks recalled to the number of C tasks recalled (I/C) as the measure of her dependent variable. The Lewinian tension theory accounts only for those ratios which are larger than 1.00. In fact, a bare majority of Zeigarnik's university student Ss had $I/C > 1.00$, and she reported that the average ratio was larger for Ss rated as "ambitious" than for those rated "unambitious," and lower for university students (1.9) than for children 13–14 years old (2.1) (Zeigarnik, 1927). The fine details of Zeigarnik's report were largely overlooked, until later, by psychologists who seized eagerly on the "interrupted task technique" as a means to study "repression." Had not Zeigarnik shown differences in *memory* that were independent of, and perhaps opposite to, what would be predicted simply from amount of exposure to the material?

Most of the experiments on selective recall using the "interrupted task technique" have followed the general outline of Zeigarnik's experiments, but with one crucial difference. The later investigators produced "interruption" of their tasks in such a way that the Ss could only blame *themselves* for having *failed* to complete them, whereas Zeigarnik was careful to have the interruptions blamed on E or on circumstances over which neither E nor S had any control. Thus, in the group of experiments we are about to discuss, "interruption" or "incomplete" means *failure* and "complete" means *success*. And so it follows that we should read "Zeigarnik effect" with tongue in cheek in the following experiments, unless I/C ratios greater than 1.00 occur under conditions where S was not deliberately exposed to failure.

Another feature of experiments on cognitive defenses is the use of instructions to induce, in Ss, some degree of what is variously called "threat," "anxiety," "stress," "ego threat," "self-esteem threat," "ego orientation," or "ego involvement" (Iverson and Reuder, 1956). This variety of labels often obscures the experimenter's intent, but the actual operations used have a distinguishable common thread. At one extreme, the intent is to impress S with the idea that the task is testing *him*, usually in an important area such as his intelligence or degree of "neuroticism," and that the outcome of the test will have consequences of great moment. At the other extreme, the instructions are intended to relax S, to make him think that his performance will be evaluating the *task*, that he is providing normative data, and the outcome of his efforts will have no important consequences for him. "Ego involvement" or "ego orientation" in its various degrees involves testing the *person*, and at the other extreme, "task involvement" or "task orientation" means that the person is testing the *task*. Thus, many researchers in this area would regard our manipulation of high and low motivation conditions as referring, respectively, to "ego involvement" and "task involvement."[2] The term "ego involvement" has also been used by Allport (1943) and by Sherif and Cantril (1947) to refer to the passionate attachment of individuals to a general way of life, group loyalties, or familiar aspects of their culture such as their native language. It is obvious from the context of this usage that evaluations, including self-evaluations, are involved, but their precise connections with experimental studies of self-evaluation are not clear. We now summarize some of the experimental conditions which have been found to emphasize either incomplete (I) or complete (C) tasks in memory.

Since none of these investigators has used Zeigarnik's ratio (I/C) and each of them has made up his own index, it will be less confusing to speak of I and C independently or to use the simple inequalities $I > C$ and $C > I$. Some very impressive data indicate that college students produce the $I > C$ pattern only when the task is being tested (task orientation) and the $C > I$ pattern when the *agent* is being tested (Lewis and Franklin, 1944; Rosenzweig, 1943). In other data the proportion of recalled C did not change with the degree to which Ss were tested, but the proportion of recalled I decreased as this testing became sharper (Eriksen, 1954; Glixman, 1949). Alper insisted that there is no reason for expecting randomly selected Ss to produce systematically different recall for I and C merely as a function of ego orientation, and indeed she found no such differences with college students (Alper, 1946a). Alper thought that differential recall of I and C tasks should depend very strongly on the characteristics of the individual recaller. She referred to Zeigarnik's (1927) finding that $I > C$ increased with Ss' rated "ambition," and that among crippled children it was highest for those with relatively low mental age who had been rated low in "pride" by their teachers (Rosenzweig and Mason, 1934). Alper (1946a, 1952) wrote that people differ in their ability to "tolerate" the evidences of their own failures. If failure tolerence is low, S has a "weak ego" and is likely to feel that he is being tested (i.e., to become ego-involved) only under serious testing conditions with potentially serious outcomes.[3] She reported experi-

[2] Alper (1946b) preferred the word "orientation" to "involvement" in either case because, though E may intend to involve S, it can be demonstrated only that he attempted to orient or point S in a particular direction. The success of this attempt may not be demonstrable.

[3] Using clinical assessments, Alper (1957) later described strong egos as having strong needs for dominance and recognition, rated high in ego strength [sic!] and conative conjunctivity; and rated low on dejection, pessimism, and ego ideal intragression. Weak egos were rated high on dejection, pessimism, and ego ideal intragression; rated low on narcissism, and on needs for recognition, dependence, and counteractive achievement. These terms are defined in Murray (1938).

ments (Alper, 1946a, 1948, 1957) in which $I > C$ was the typical recall pattern for strong egos who were testing the tasks, and for weak egos who were themselves being tested. Conversely, $C > I$ occurred most often among strong egos who were being tested and among weak egos who were testing the tasks. Similar findings were reported by Eriksen (1954). Another set of Alper's (1957) data confuses the picture even more. They are presented in Table 5.1, which shows that the $C > I$ pattern prevails in all conditions, that strong egos generally recall more of *both* I and C tasks than do weak egos, that the patterns of recall of I and C are the same for strong and weak egos under conditions of task orientation, and different under ego orientation. In this experiment Alper also got performance measures for Ss and reported that the shift from task to ego orientation produced a significantly greater performance decrement for the weak egos than for the strong ones. Atkinson (1953) reported that both output and recall of I and C tasks varied as a function of relaxed and "achievement-oriented" instructions. Output increased as a function of achievement pressure whether Ss were high or low in n-Ach, and output did not differ as a function of n-Ach. With increasing achievement pressure the dominant recall pattern, $I > C$, increased in the high n-Ach group and declined in the low n-Ach group. At the highest achievement pressure, the recall pattern was $C > I$ for the low n-Ach group, the only such case in the data. Kausler (1951) reported that ego-involved Ss produced more than non-ego-involved Ss, but the two groups did not differ in their recall of attempted problems which were correct or incorrect.

What can be said about these data? Rosenzweig (1943) maintained that when S is being tested (ego-involved) his ego defenses

TABLE 5.1
Proportions of Tasks Recalled by Conditions

	Task-Oriented		Ego-Oriented	
	I	C	I	C
Strong Ego	.37	.57	.26	.46
Weak Ego	.29	.48	.31	.32

(Arc sin square root percentage transform, after Alper, 1957 p. 154.)

are alerted and he recalls $C > I$; the $I > C$ pattern which occurs when S is not being tested indicates the operation of continuing tensions to complete the tasks, the pure Zeigarnik effect. His earlier finding among crippled children attempting to win a prize, that $C > I$ was the predominant recall pattern for those who were intellectually mature and "proud," was interpreted as indicating that the "proud" Ss were "repressing" their failures (Rosenzweig and Mason, 1934). Alper (1952) pointed out that these data confounded "pride" and mental age and suggested that the Ss with low mental age (also low in pride) may have been less ego-involved because they failed to recognize the seriousness of the ego threat. This of course assumes that the predominant $I > C$ recall pattern of the latter children was a pure Zeigarnik effect. Eriksen (1952), commenting on Alper's (1946a) finding that strong egos recall $I > C$ when they are not being tested and $C > I$ when they are being tested, and the reverse for weak egos, wrote, ". . . weak egos are threatened by the objective, non-threatening, task-oriented conditions, and bolster self-esteem by recalling their successes. However, when the threat becomes objectively more severe, they are overwhelmed by their inadequacy and recall their failures. Strong egos, on the other hand, are less easily threatened and when threat does occur they cope with it by emphasizing their successes rather than being overwhelmed by their inadequacy" (Eriksen, 1952, p. 45). Glixman (1949) suggested that, without regard to ego strength, the forgetting of failures is a more efficacious defense than the remembering of successes, and therefore the former will occur under extreme conditions of threat to self-evaluation. Cohen (1956) suggested that people with high self-evaluation will more often use avoidance as a defense, while those with low self-evaluations favor projection.

Clearly in these interpretations, the emphasis is that relative deficiency in the recall of failures is a cognitive withdrawal from facts that might tend to decrease self-evaluation. What about motor withdrawal? We must be careful to distinguish two kinds of motor phenomena, both of which have been associated with danger situations which threaten life and limb or self-evaluation. The first is actual locomotion away from the danger situation or refusal to approach it, which was discussed by Freud (1926, p. 19) in connection with defensive behavior. The second, also discussed by Freud (1926, p. 55), is simply doing nothing or markedly reducing the intensity of effort. This latter is like the "blind, hopeless fumbling" which Hoppe (1931) noted in his Ss who had experienced a series of failures which they sometimes interpreted as reflecting on their own value. It is also like

B. Rosen's finding that, while their $P(s)$ estimates and self-evaluations were declining, Ss were correspondingly *producing* less (Table 4.22 and Fig. 4.25). One interpretation of this kind of relaxation as defending self-evaluation is suggested by James' (1890) remarks that "with no attempt there can be no failure; with no failure no humiliation;" and that when "disappointment is incessant and the struggle unending," men will always seek the relief of giving up their "pretensions." Why, then, do the Ss continue to work at all? Possibly because there are other motives which cause them to continue to operate, if only in a perfunctory way. In experiments like Rosen's, S has made an informal contract with E, a contract which requires him to wait until E dismisses him. He may also want to please E, as the male college students probably wanted to do with the attractive young female E. Or S may be motivated only by curiosity about what will happen next, and this might include testing his own hypothesis about the purpose of the experiment. For any or all of these reasons he might continue to work simply in order to remain in the situation for the agreed-upon time though he has given up serious pursuit of the primary goal of his activity, or the goal has radically changed. Another possibility is that he has abandoned, as unrealistic, the goal which E wants him to work for and simply pursues his own goals (LAs) without telling E about them. All these interpretations apply to situations in which quitting in the face of actual or anticipated failure is not in S's contract; that is, where he has no opportunity or permission to quit. Thus, they will not apply to experiments like Hoppe's where, as part of his contract, S could at any moment abandon a given task and take up another one. The blind, directionless fumbling with the materials of a presumably hopeless task, which Hoppe noted, might be sheer motor automatism while S is engaged in thinking about which new task to take up or what new strategy to try next on the old one, or this might be the human analogue of those tentative movements, without full commitment, which Tolman (1932) saw in rats and called "vicarious trial-and-error."

On the other hand, there are many experiments in which failure spurs S to greater exertions. There is some evidence that people try their hardest, other things being equal, when the decision between success and failure is most uncertain, that is, when $P(s)$ is approximately .50 (Atkinson, 1957; Atkinson, Bastian, Earl, and Litwin, 1960). The performance of both normal and schizophrenics Ss is likely to improve after failure (Olson, 1958), and the muscle-action potentials (MAP) of normal Ss are likely to be greater after failure than after success (Klein, 1951; Leshner, 1961), especially under "task-oriented" rather than "ego-oriented" instructions (Reuder, 1956). A large literature suggests that MAP is an index of S's energy expenditure, though not necessarily of his effectiveness and efficiency as a producer, since MAP increases with the duration of the task (Davis, 1937; Smith, 1953; Bartoshuk, 1955; Stennett, 1957); as S gets closer to the goal or to the end of the task (Davis, 1937; Malmo, Shagass, and Davis, 1951; Smith, 1953; Bartoshuk, 1955); with the difficulty of the task (Davis, 1938; Shaw and Kline, 1947; Surwillo, 1956); and with S's intelligence (Shaw and Kline, 1947).

Changes in Muscular Self-stressing

We had noted in many of our experiments that when $P(s)$ first began to decline S worked so much harder for a few trials that his increased effort was noticeable to E without special instrumentation, and sometimes S became so energetic that the quality of his performance deteriorated and his errors increased. Putting this together with the observations that $P(s)$, output, and self-evaluation covary, we supposed that failure or expected failure can have two different meanings for S which will determine different kinds of behavior. If failure or its anticipation indicates that the task is harder than S had imagined, or that he had not used the optimal method, then he will work harder or introduce different methods of work, and possibly he will do both. In such a situation we imagine that S still hopes to achieve his goal, or to make a better performance *this* time than *last* time. However, the failure may also mean that S has exhausted his resources, that nothing he can do will improve his performance, in which case he gives up. This is a plausible interpretation of B. Rosen's data, and so Sherwin J. Klein, Malcolm Cohen, and I attempted to see whether MAP would covary with conditions which we knew would affect estimated $P(s)$.

We thought it should happen somewhat like this if S were operating in one of our typical $P(s)$ experiments with a fixed performance goal and deadline. The early stages of decline in $P(s)$ would indicate S's discovery that the task was more difficult than he thought at first, so he should work harder and his MAP should rise, but S can stress himself only up to some limit. If, in spite of the increased effort, $P(s)$ continues to fall (as we could arrange that it inevitably would) then he should "give up" and his performance should degenerate to a mere going-through-the-motions and his MAP should thenceforth decline with $P(s)$. Generally, the hypothesis was that overall MAP level and its rate of change should vary directly with the level of $P(s)$.

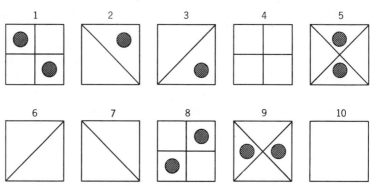

Fig. 5.1   Photograph of the key card for the modified digit symbol tapping task. (After Diggory, Klein, and Cohen, 1964.)

Since we measured MAP from a working muscle we had to attach electrodes to S's arm and this made the card-sorting task impractical because the hand and arm motions in card sorting are too gross and violent for reliable MAP work. We made an adaptation of the "digit-symbol" type of code task. The digits and the corresponding symbols were drawn in ink on a heavy piece of cardboard five inches by eight inches in the arrangement shown in Fig. 5.1. In the original drawing the symbols are one-inch squares. This card stood on the lower frame of the performance display panel about four feet from S's face and approximately at eye level. The E had a pack of 100 three-inch by five-inch cards on each of which appeared one of the symbols without the number. There were ten cards for each symbol and they had been put into a random order by shuffling, though E took great care, for reasons explained below, to show S that he was keeping the cards in a particular order. During the task E placed the cards one at a time in a tray on the left-hand end of a board which was on S's lap while S was in a semi-reclining position on a contoured lounge chair. At the right-hand end of the board (all Ss were right-handed) was a telegraph key on which S tapped out the number corresponding to the symbol on the card which E had just exposed. The Ss were instructed to relax, except for their tapping movements, and various methods of tapping were demonstrated to them. They were told to use a method which would permit the most rapid tapping possible consistent with accurate counting of the taps.

One $E(E_1)$ and the S were together in an electrostatically shielded room and another $E(E_2)$ tended the amplifying and recording apparatus in an adjacent shielded room. The two Es communicated by talking slightly louder than normal, so S heard everything that passed between them.

The E_1 had a stopwatch and he told S that there would be ten trials, each lasting one minute. On each trial S was told to respond to as many cards as he could, with the ultimate aim of responding correctly to 40 cards on at least one trial. Goal and deadline were clearly marked on the performance display panel. From S's telegraph key a thick multi-strand cable led to a hole in the wooden floor of the room—and it ended under the floor, but S didn't know that. This cable, S was told, led to a counter (in the other room) which was programmed to the order of the cards in the pack so it could count the number of cards to which he responded correctly. This number was S's score for each trial. At the end of a trial E_1 asked E_2 for the score which was read off a list of predetermined scores corresponding to the condition to which S had been randomly assigned. The score was repeated to S and a golf tee placed in the appropriate hole in the masonite panel. Before each trial S made $P(s)$ estimates, but, in this case, to preserve S's immobility during the rest period between trials, E_1 marked the linear rating scale at a point designated by S.

Figure 5.2 shows the performance curves used in the various conditions and the $P(s)$ and MAP trends both for work and rest periods.[4] There were no significant differences among the conditions in the initial levels of working and resting MAP, or in $P(s)$ estimates. The *overall* mean $P(s)$ estimates are significantly higher in the high performance conditions (I and III) than in low performance (II and IV). They are also significantly higher when the performance curve is negatively accelerated (I and II) than when it is positively accelerated (III and IV). The overall trend of the $P(s)$ estimates is negative and the slope is significantly different from zero. Since in Condition I $P(s)$ continues to rise, contrary to the trend in the other conditions, this can be called the most "encouraging condition." Thus, generally $P(s)$ estimates become successively lower as the deadline is approached and the rate at which they change depends on both the level and shape of the performance curve, in agreement with the findings reported in Chapter 4.

---

[4] For details about the recording and analysis of MAP data in this experiment, see Diggory, Klein, and Cohen (1964). This experiment was performed in Dr. Klein's laboratory at the Aerospace Crew Equipment Laboratory of the Philadelphia Naval Base, and was supported by Naval Air Engineering Center Foundational Research Project No. 19, a grant to Dr. Klein. Twelve of the 16 Ss were Navy enlisted men. The other four were civilian employees of the Navy.

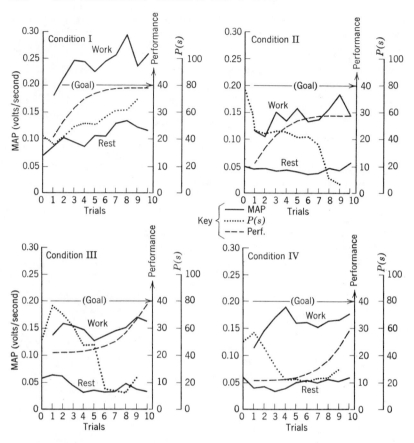

Fig. 5.2 Experimental conditions, showing performance curve presented to Ss in each condition, mean working and resting MAP at each trial, and mean estimated $P(s)$ at each trial. Each data point is the mean of four Ss. (After Diggory, Klein, and Cohen, 1964.)

In the MAP data, the overall slopes for both work and rest are opposite to those of the $P(s)$ data; that is, though $P(s)$ generally decreases as the deadline approaches, MAP rises. The overall slopes of both working and resting MAPs are positive and significantly different from zero. A general rise in MAP with the approach of the end of the task has been reported previously (Davis, 1937; Malmo, Shagass, and Davis, 1951; Smith, 1953; Bartoshuk, 1955), but, since our performance curves were all generally rising toward the performance goal, we may have witnessed a goal gradient phenomenon (cf. Bartoshuk, 1955). However, the goal gradient effect, if such it is, or the effect of the approaching end of the task in *these* data is a function of the average distance from the goal and the way in which the rate of approach to the goal changes. In Condition I, the most "encouraging" condition, the working MAP continued to rise throughout the ten trials. In the other conditions, most of the rise in working MAP occurred during the first three trials and thereafter it stayed on a plateau. Thus, in line with our hypothesis, MAP rose during the early decline in $P(s)$, but *contrary* to the hypothesis it did not drop noticeably during the latter part of the declining $P(s)$ series. So much for the detailed aspects of our hypothesis.

As to the more general aspects of the hypothesis, they seem to be confirmed in that the different types of performance feedback had the same effects on overall MAP as on overall mean $P(s)$. As Fig. 5.3 shows, the MAP was significantly higher for negatively accelerated than for positively accelerated performance curves (part A) and also it was higher for high performance curves than for low ones (part B), during both work and rest.

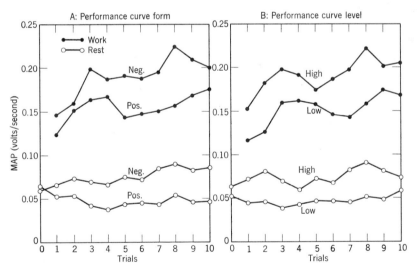

Fig. 5.3   Mean resting and working MAP by trials as a function of performance curves reported to Ss. Part A: effect on MAP of positively and negatively accelerated performance curves (Conditions I and II versus Conditions III and IV, Fig. 5.2). Part B: effect on MAP of average distance of performance curve from the goal (Conditions I and III, high versus Conditions II and IV, low, Fig. 5.2). Each data point is the mean of eight Ss. (After Diggory, Klein, and Cohen, 1964.)

Therefore we have evidence in addition to Bonnie Rosen's data, with another criterion of muscle stressing, that people work harder when $P(s)$ is relatively high than when it is lower. Note that in neither set of data could we have detected this from examining only the initial measures of $P(s)$, output, or MAP. Our interpretation is that the course of S's performance curves in these experiments gradually discouraged them and they became convinced that trying hard in this situation would do no good, so they relaxed. We still need an experiment in which we measure product and MAP simultaneously from the same Ss.

Now Ss' relaxation, while they continue to go through the motions of a hopeless task, may be the only kind of withdrawal available to them in the above experiments. They had no opportunity to quit, but functionally the more discouraged of them did quit.

SUBSTITUTE OR QUIT?

In the discussions of defensive behavior which we have reviewed the assumption seems to be that the various modes of defence are adaptive in some sense, but the intent of this adaptive maneuvering could stand some clarification. Freud's conception was that the ego defended itself by marshaling evidence that it could effectively carry out its functions, by avoiding situations in which evidence to the contrary might arise, or by not registering such evidence at all. In other words, the ego primarily defends itself against being recognized as helpless, or more specifically, against *anxiety* which is the effect generalized from earlier situations in which the individual was helpless or thought he was. In the context of our own thinking about self-evaluation in terms of one's goodness as an instrument for achieving his goals the notion of helplessness equates to powerlessness, low $P(s)$. The feeling of helplessness aroused by irrefutable evidence of failure should vary in intensity or seriousness with the value the individual puts on the particular goal he seeks or on the ability he is using, or both. One obvious type of defense against accepting the implications of a bad performance is for the performer to extricate himself, *as instrument*, from the causal nexus of the event. Thus he may say that a performance was not a real test of his ability at all, for the outcome was manipulated by trickery, or he might say that the evidence so far produced is insufficient to demonstrate his inadequacy, or that the conditions under which he had to operate rendered a good performance impossible for any human being. Maneuvers such as these are, we believe, properly classed as excuses, as the Latin roots of "excuse" (*ex*, out of, from; *causa*, cause) suggest.

There is no reason why such defensive behavior should not be mingled with reality testing. In suggesting excuses a person may be advancing hypotheses about the cause of a poor performance and the extent to which he, as an instrument, was actually involved in the cause. Some of these hypotheses might be confirmed; for example, the assumption that he would perform better if the lighting or temperature were adjusted, or that the outcome of the performance was rigged, or that his deficiency could be cured by practice. Such "defensive behavior" is clearly adaptive and its outcome makes the person wiser about the conditions of his future attempts. However, excuses may involve real self-deception; the person only *says* that he is not involved in the cause of his "failure" in order to keep somebody else from "rubbing it in," though he has no intention of making a real exploration of the causal nexus or his involvement in it. Only if he comes to believe these lies could we say that he is engaging in a form of *self*-deception. Whether or not an excuse is a *true* explanation for an unfortunate outcome cannot be determined from its verbal expression alone, and therefore truth or falsity has no business in the defining criterion for excuses. It is interesting to speculate how many of the other defense mechanisms might be similarly interpreted. We might find that defensive behavior varies with the circumstances in which defense is called for. For example, if a person expects that he might fail if he persists in using a given method to attain his goal, he could reasonably be expected to search for other methods only if there were sufficient time. If time is short, the most adaptive thing might be to simply work harder. On the other hand, we might expect him to seek substitute goals only if they are actually available. In any case, so typically adaptive an organism as man should be creative in his defensive behaviors in accordance with the objective realities of the situation. If he has opportunities to test various hypotheses about how to improve his performance we should expect him to do so before he becomes really hopeless about the prospect of achieving his goal. In our way of thinking, hopeless and helpless come rather close to the same thing, and we think that people really test situations as much as they can before they accept the notion that they are powerless to get what they want.

With these considerations in mind, I. G. Cetlin designed the experiment which was partially described in Chapter 4 (Table 4.20; Figs. 4.23 and 4.24). She used high school students as Ss because at the time she was prepared to collect her data, we had saturated the University of Pennsylvania campus with a large number of students who were aware of the general nature of our experiments—and we didn't care to trust our luck any further. The prospective Ss were asked if they were interested in being tested to see whether they qualified for an attractive career opportunity, and only volunteers served as Ss. The Ss performed the experimental task after having been told that it was the preliminary screening test for the career program. They had complete information about their performance after every section of the "test" and they estimated their $P(s)$ and their goodness as candidates for the job before every section of the test, including the first. Also after each trial they were required to consider several alternative acts (continuing the test without change, having a free practice period, changing the conditions of work, shifting to the attempt to qualify for a different position, and quitting altogether).

With the cooperation and permission of principals in several high schools in the suburbs of Philadelphia, a letter was distributed to male students in the tenth, eleventh, and twelfth grade academic programs. The letter invited their participation in a series of tests to determine whether they were qualified for a fictitious space science program (Appendix C). Enclosed with the letter was a two-page questionnaire (Appendix D). On the first page the student supplied information about his education to date and about his father's formal education. On the second page there were descriptions of four abilities, each with a linear rating scale on which the student was asked to rate himself with respect to the abilities described. The abilities were labeled as ability to think creatively; leadership ability; discriminative ability; and ability for quick, efficient reaction. On a fifth linear rating scale the student was asked to rate himself in a general way, considering all of his abilities, including the four listed above.

Sixty students, 14 to 18 years old, were selected by the following criteria: (1) their returned questionnaire showed that they had rated themselves high on one of the capacities (relative to their ratings of the others), and (2) when they came for the interview they agreed to take the qualifying "test." Fifteen Ss were assigned randomly to each of the four experimental conditions defined by the performance curves shown in Fig. 4.23. Groups I and IV were distinguished by information about the available positions, as explained below.

In the initial part of the interview each student was given the following instructions and job descriptions:

Rank the following positions from 1–4 such that: 1 represents the position you are *most* interested in, 2 represents the position you are *next* interested in, 3 represents the position you are *less* interested in, and 4 represents the position you are *least* interested in.

Research Scientist: The position requires background training in the physical, biological, and social sciences. It includes responsibility for the investigation of problems related to environmental effects, including such areas as endurance, stress, physiological changes, effect on mental functions, etc.

Instrument Development Engineer: This requires background training in the physical sciences, mathematics, and design. It includes responsibility for the design and developmental stages of all space instrumentation projects. Work will be done in cooperation with other basic research projects.

Specifications Developer: This position requires background training in general science and English. It includes responsibility for the development of all specifications for project materials to be developed or procured. Must operate in liaison with project directors, and in accordance with technical requirements and other available literature.

Project Coordinator: This requires background training in the general sciences and English. It includes responsibility for setting up and maintaining systematic files on all on-going projects within and without a research center. Comprehension as well as familiarity with materials is essential so that guidance may be offered regarding any particular investigation.

For the Ss in Group IV the description of "Instrument Development Engineer" was modified to make it less prestigious than "Research Scientist" and more comparable to the other two positions:

Instrument Development Engineer: This requires background training in science and mathematics. It includes a minimum of responsibility for the design and developmental stages of all space instrumentation projects. All work will be done under close supervision of chief research scientists. Work will be in close cooperation with basic research projects.

After S had ranked the four positions, E gave him further information about salary and difficulty of qualifying, as shown in Table 5.2. Note that this information was selected by E to be attached to *any* of the jobs to which S had assigned the indicated rank. For Groups I, II, and III this information was designed to make the first two ranked jobs appear more attractive than those ranked third and fourth in that they offered greater rewards and were more difficult to qualify for. The information given to Group II differed from that given to Groups I and III in that the two lowest ranked jobs for the latter groups were easier to qualify for; i.e., a smaller proportion of available test points was needed. The information given to Group IV was designed to make *all three* of the jobs ranked second, third, and fourth appear decidedly less attractive than the one that was ranked first.

The task on which Ss worked required them to reproduce, by tapping on a telegraph key, complex auditory rhythmic patterns which

TABLE 5.2

Salary Information and Qualifying Scores Linked with Positions as Ranked by S

S's Ranking of Position	Salary	Total Test Score for Minimum Qualification	Maximum Points Available on Each of Ten Parts of Test
Groups I and III			
1	$7500	50	6
2	7000	42	6
3	4200	18	3
4	4000	17	3
Group II			
1	7500	50	6
2	7000	42	7
3	4200	18	10
4	4000	17	10
Group IV			
1	7500	50	6
2	4200	18	3
3	4200	18	3
4	4000	17	3

(After I. G. Cetlin, 1964.)

had been recorded on tape. Each pattern had been recorded at three different speeds so that if S requested a change in the speed of presentation, E could comply. If S asked to have the loudness of the stimuli changed, E could adjust the amplifier gain on the playback equipment. Each part of the "test" began with the presentation of a single rhythmic pattern and ended when S had completed his attempt to reproduce the pattern. When S tapped the telegraph key the individual taps were recorded on a wax paper kymograph, and E immediately pretended to "score" the record by comparing it with an impressive-looking set of "norms." The E then announced the score to S and wrote it down, with his cumulated score to date, on a scoring table which S could look at any time during the experiment. The prearranged cumulated score sequences reported to the different groups of Ss are shown in Table 4.20 and Fig. 4.23.

Since all Ss had their allotted score information available to them throughout the experiment, it was expected that those in Groups I and IV would recognize early in the trial series that it was impossible for them to pass the test. In fact, they could have calculated that success was impossible after trial three. On the other hand, Group

II was expected not to recognize the serious possibility of failing the test until relatively late in the series of trials. In fact, failure was not a mathematical certainty in the Group II sequence until after trial 8. Group III had a success sequence: on the ninth trial they achieved the minimum passing score and on the tenth trial they advanced to within four points of the maximum possible score (60) for the entire test.

The instructions read to Ss were as follows:

We have a number of very short tests available which have been found to be quite useful in indicating potential for successful training in each of the positions we have discussed. We have been attempting to test students out on the position they are most interested in. Would you be interested in taking one? [If S answered, "Yes," the instructions continued.] As you are being considered for (name of position S had ranked first) you will be given a test which is heavily loaded with (name of capacity chosen as the one on which S had rated himself highest). You will recollect that you rated yourself quite highly on this ability. The test includes a series of ten signal patterns which will be presented one at a time from this recorder. Each pattern will be presented following a report of the trial number. As soon as a pattern is administered, you are to duplicate it by tapping this telegraph key. For example, let me hear you duplicate this simple pattern. That was fine. [Sometimes E made suggestions for improving the performance.]

Notice that the pattern you tapped leaves a record which will be used to determine your score by matching it against a standard. To be taken into a training program, for the assignment you are interested in, you will have to obtain a minimum cumulative score of 50 points over ten trials. Thus, in order to succeed you will need to obtain, on the average, five points per trial, where the maximum score possible for any one trial is six points. As was indicated, the other positions we have discussed require different scores and different standards. But, for any given test, you can only be striving for a single position. Please remember this. Your score will be determined by a number of factors, such as the number of signals you pick up, rhythm, spacing, etc. Your score will be reported to you on this form at the end of each of the ten trials so that you will see just how you are progressing.

This testing procedure will vary tremendously from almost all other tests you have taken. Due to the complex and specialized nature of these careers, we want to take into consideration as many personal and situational factors as possible. This means that you will be free to make several choices and requests as we go along. For example, you may feel free to leave at the end of any trial. You do not have to continue with all ten trials. This test is for you and you are the best judge of whether or not you should leave. Remember, nothing will be held against you if you decide to leave. Of course, if you do discontinue, you will not be considered for the position you are interested in. You may request to stop this test so as to consider another position. You may also request certain changes in testing, or ask for a practice interval. You are free to do any of these things, and they will not influence your score in any way.

It is important to keep in mind that regardless of your decision to continue or discontinue with a test, you will have only ten possible trials with which to work. For example, if you decide to stop after trial six in order to consider another position, you will have only four trials with which to reach the required score on the second test. Is this clear?

Now look at these forms on the table in front of you. You are to fill one of them out before we start testing and at the end of each trial you complete. Notice that there are only two sections, B and C, on the first sheet but that the other sheets are identical and include three sections, A, B, and C. Also notice that you are to check only one of the items listed in A, and that sections B and C are to be completed regardless of your decision in A. Are there any questions?

The three sections of the forms referred to in the last paragraph were constructed in the following manner. *Section A* listed several alternatives among which S was instructed to indicate his choice by checking appropriate boxes on the form:

1. I wish to withdraw from this entire testing situation.
2. I wish to discontinue this test in order to try out for a different position. Which one? ——————.
3. I wish to continue with the test in an uninterrupted manner.
4. I wish a practice interval before continuing with the test.
5. I wish to have the volume altered before continuing with the test. Increased? Decreased?
6. I wish to have the rate altered before continuing with the test. Accelerated? Reduced?

Section B was a linear scale with equally spaced gradations 0, 25, 50, 75, and 100 on which S indicated his estimated $P(s)$ in response to the question: "In your opinion, what are your chances out of a hundred for succeeding on this test?" *Section C* was another linear rating scale with equally spaced points designated by the adjectives: poor, fair, good, very good, and superior, on which S was asked to indicate his momentary self-evaluation by marking the scale so as to answer the question, "How would you rate yourself as a candidate for this position?"

After the last trial in which S participated, he was asked to rate his abilities and his "global" self-evaluation on a clean copy of the first rating form which he had returned in response to the introductory letter.

The alternatives offered to S after each trial in Section A of the checklist include various realistic possibilities for adaptive (and perhaps defensive) behavior in this situation. The alternatives fall into two sets. The first two (quit outright, and try for a different position) are "non-persistive," and the others (continue as before, ask for practice, ask for change in stimulus presentation) are "persistive." The kind of persistive choice S made gave some indication of the kind of hypothesis he was testing (perhaps the kind of excuse he would have verbalized) to account for his poor performance. For example, if he chose to go ahead with neither practice nor change in conditions he was either not being defensive at all or he is making use of some defense we couldn't learn about in this procedure. However, if he asked for practice we suspect that it was to test some remediable deficiency in his skill, or some feature of the situation; if he asked to have the conditions of work altered we can be a little more certain about which of the available hypotheses he was testing. If S were to test any hypothesis or seek in any way to improve his performance and thus raise his $P(s)$, the rigged situation quickly showed him that such maneuvers were totally ineffective; that is, nothing he could do, and nothing he could ask E to do for him, could significantly increase the rate at which his scores were cumulating.

We expected at least to see a definite difference between the early failure groups (I and IV) and the late failure or success groups (II and III) with respect to the point in the trial sequence at which modal non-persistent behavior became evident. This expectation was amply justified, because in the early failure groups (I and IV) 28 of the 30 Ss had withdrawn from the test by the end of the sixth trial. The other two stuck it out to the bitter end. In Groups II and III, only three of the 30 Ss withdrew from the test, all of them after the eighth trial, and all of them from the late failure group. All 15 of the Ss in the success group (III) continued for all ten trials, and there were only five requests from them either for a practice session (one request) or for change in conditions of work (four requests). On the other hand, the late failure group (II) produced 14 requests either for changes in conditions of work (7 requests) or for a practice session (7 requests), more than half of these ($\%_{14}$) occurring in trials 7–9. Of the three Ss in the late failure group who finally stopped work on the test, only one asked to try to qualify for another position (not an unrealistic decision because he needed only 18 points to qualify for the best of the remaining positions and he had two trials left on each of which he could make 10 points), and the other two quit outright.

In the two low failure groups there were 31 requests either for practice (19 requests) or change of working conditions (12 requests), and 27 of these 31 requests were made on trials 2 and 3, even though by that time more than half of the Ss ($^{17}\!/_{30}$) had quit. It is quite likely that Ss were using the outcomes of their adaptive attempts on which to base their decision to stay with the test a little longer. Note that, given the opportunity to do something which might increase $P(s)$, the modal response was to seize that opportunity *before* they accepted the evidence that their abilities were inadequate.

What did the early failure Ss do when they quit? Twenty-nine of the 30 *substituted;* that is, they elected to try for another position, and only one withdrew completely. Now presumably the occurrence of substitution should be contingent upon the availability of an attractive substitute, and that was the point in giving different information about the attractiveness of the alternative space science positions to Groups I and IV. If Group I Ss wanted to substitute, they could quit early and still have a respectable $P(s)$ for achieving their second ranked position, which was almost as attractive in terms of prestige and salary as the one they had chosen first, but Group IV Ss had only far less attractive alternatives to turn to than the position for which they had been tested. Thus, it is interesting to see that there are no significant differences in the frequency of persistent responses between Groups I and IV. In fact, the only two Ss in the early failure groups who did not substitute (persisted instead) belonged to Group I, which had the most attractive substitute goal available. Otherwise, there are no differences in the point of the trial sequence at which these Ss gave up their attempt to achieve the first objective.

Cetlin also collected from each S post-experimental ratings of his abilities, including the one under test, and of his "global" self-evaluation. These data are of considerable interest but we defer discussion of them until we have introduced the next topic, to which they are directly relevant.

SPREAD OF EVALUATIVE CHANGES

Wylie concluded her survey of studies on experimentally induced success and failure with the following statement: "It seems that Ss will, under certain conditions, change their self-evaluations after experimentally induced success or failure. These changes are most likely to involve self-ratings on the experimental task itself, or on the characteristic which has been evaluated, and are least likely to involve reports on global self-regard. The latter seems to be affected little if any by a single experimental failure or evaluation. There is some evidence that changes in self-rating upward after success are more frequent than are changes downward after failure" (Wylie, 1961). The non-change in the global ratings she thinks is congruent with self-concept theory: covert evaluation may change even if overt does not; defensive behaviors may occur instead of changes in self-regard; and other characteristics of S may be important conditions for behavior following success or failure. In another place she wrote of the choice of level of aspiration as a defensive maneuver: "A plausible hypothesis would be that self-accepting persons will have small, probably positive, goal-discrepancy scores on the LA task. The prediction for the self-rejecting person is less clear: (1) Perhaps he would protect his self-regard by negative goal-discrepancy scores which he could easily exceed; or (2) perhaps he would show unusually high positive goal-discrepancy scores. The latter might stem from a desire to demonstrate superior ambition, or a need to punish the unworthy self through failure. Or it might simply be one more reflection of the type of generally unrealistic goal-setting which underlies his poor self-regard" (Wylie, 1961, p. 244). Students of "phenomenal self-concept" have quite often charged that the more objective methods of psychological experimentation cannot, or at least do not, deal with the evaluation of *the* self, taken as a "whole." We, in turn, take the position that people sometimes do evaluate themselves more or less highly in some impressionistic, global, or undifferentiated way, and that the devotees of the phenomenal self-concept have signally failed to induce such changes or to explicate their source in specific conditions because their preconceived notions of what *the* self *is* prevent them from adopting flexible ways of thinking and more powerful methods of investigation. We offer in this section some hypotheses and experiments which suggest a way (not necessarily *the* way) out of these difficulties.

If we put together our general impressions of objective failure situations which we have witnessed or experienced, it appears that there are two general classes of reactions. In one case, a single failure seems to crush the individual so that he behaves and talks as though he were not good for anything, in spite of all evidence to the contrary. Other people seem to shrug off failures and quickly take up some other task in which they become equally absorbed. Experiences of success in the achievement of some goal seem to operate in somewhat the same manner, though the effects are the reverse of those found in failure. After success some people are in a state of very high elation;

judging from their words and actions, there is nothing they could not do or would not dare. Others who have succeeded, though they may act quite pleased, have a more sober or moderate reaction, and they quickly take up the pursuit of some other goal. In short, it appears that for some people, or in some conditions, either success or failure will generalize their evaluative effects to many other aspects of a person's goal-striving attitudes, but in other cases this generalization is much more limited if it occurs at all. In 1959 D. Magaziner and the author (Diggory and Magaziner, 1959) published the results of an exploratory experiment designed to test what seemed to us a plausible guess about some of the conditions under which such generalization might or might not occur. We guessed that generalization was more likely to occur when S was engaged in the pursuit of a highly important goal or when he was using what he regarded as a highly important ability in his attempt to achieve a goal. Like all experiments, the design of this one was a compromise between the practical realities of what we could do and what we wanted to do.

First we sent a fairly vague but intriguing letter to all male students in the College of Arts and Sciences at the University of Pennsylvania who had completed three terms of work, had grade averages of "B" or higher with no grades below "C," and who had never had a course in psychology. We used underclassmen in order to trade on their relative ignorance of campus affairs and also to make our appeal plausible in that it was presented early in their college career. The letter invited them to participate in a project from which they might realize some important personal benefits. They signified their willingness to explore the proposition further by returning to us a simple questionnaire which was enclosed with the letter. On the questionnaire there were five linear rating scales, each relating to a so-called ability which was briefly described. On each rating scale S was asked to indicate the percentage of times that he had used that ability successfully when he had the opportunity to use it at all. The names of the abilities were: ability to judge character in others, ability to persuade others, ability to persist in spite of frustration, ability to be pleasant and affable, and ability to plan. A sixth rating scale listed the adjectives poor, fair, average, good, and superior at equal distances along a line and asked the respondent: "Considering all your capacities, including those rated above, what is your overall estimate of yourself as an adequately functioning person?" On the basis of the returned questionnaires we picked out a group of students who had rated one of the five abilities outstandingly higher than all the others, regardless of its absolute level; and another group who had rated one of the five abilities outstandingly lower than all the others. When the students appeared, at our invitation, for an interview, we told them that we were fulfilling a practical function of psychologists, namely that of helping to select new recruits for an organization called the "Career Liaison Group." The function of this group, to which people were admitted by invitation only, was to give selected undergraduate men an opportunity to integrate their academic studies more closely with their vocational careers. To do this, we said, the group arranged periodic meetings with businessmen, members of the professions, scientists, and scholars, and the heavy emphasis was on the use of the latter specialties in business and industry.

If a student said he was interested, he was told that he had to pass five qualifying tests, corresponding to the abilities on which he had rated himself previously. It was emphasized that all these abilities were equally important for success in the "Career Liaison Group" so he would have to pass all the tests. If he agreed to take the tests we declared ourselves ready to give them to him right then and there. If he said he was not interested, he was dismissed with expressions of full acceptance and respect for his decision, but no further comments or explanations were given.

The tests were word-association tests in which S had to respond to each of a series of stimulus words by writing down the first word that he thought of. The S used a blank sheet of paper on which he wrote the numbers from 1 to 20 in a vertical column near the left-hand margin, spacing the numbers in groups of five. He was told that much previous data had permitted us to identify classes of responses which were characteristic of successful members of the "Career Liaison Group" and not of unsuccessful members; and that there were also classes of responses characteristic of unsuccessful members and not of successful ones. These categories of responses had been given scoring weights in accordance with their ability to identify successful members: a score of 5 for a response most clearly identifying successful members and a score of zero for a response most clearly identifying unsuccessful members, with intermediate scores of 4, 3, 2, and 1 assigned in order of the relevance of the response to the identification of successful members or unsuccessful members. Thus, with 20 words on the test the maximum possible score was 100 and the group had decided, with the help of expert advice (allegedly ours), to set the minimum passing score at 80 points—which a candidate had to achieve on *every one* of the five tests. We told S that he would take the test by responding to sets of five stimulus words, one after the other, and that after every set of five words E would score his re-

sponses by referring to the established norms and would write down
S's cumulated score for all portions of the test so far. To lend a little
additional plausibility to the tests in Ss' views, we constructed lists
of words that were obviously related to the ability under test, and
none of the lists had any words in common with the others. For example, the list for "ability to judge character" included the words
trust, earnest, avarice; that for "ability to withstand frustration" included success, barrier, gain; and that for "ability to plan" included
prospect, crucial, and theme.

The S was given three practice words to respond to, and then
the test began. After each five responses E took S's paper and pored
over it and the "scoring norms" and shortly announced S's cumulated
score, in accord with a predetermined *schedule which was the same
for all Ss*, thus: 15, 32, 48, 64. By this means all the Ss experienced
an obvious and profound failure on the very first test. Regardless of
the name of the specific ability tested, half (15) of the Ss experienced
this failure on the test for the ability which they had rated themselves
highest in the set, and the other 15 failed in the test of the ability
which they had rated *lowest* in the set. Then, while E was ostensibly
preparing for the second test, S was asked to rerate himself on the
five abilities and the overall ("global") self-evaluation scale, using a
clean copy of the rating form which he had returned in response to
our initial letter.

We compared the first with the second ratings on all five scales
with respect to the amount and direction of change. The two groups
(high ability failed and low ability failed) did not differ significantly
in their initial mean ratings of any of the capacities. Table 5.3 shows
the distribution of number of capacities in the set of five whose ratings
were decreased in the two groups, and the mean number of capacities
whose ratings were lowered. These means are significantly different
by the median test. Likewise there is a significant difference (median
test) in the amount and direction of change: the mean algebraic sum
of changes in the group that failed on the test of their highest-rated
capacities was —12.9 mm, and the corresponding mean for the other
group was +6.5 mm. The mean changes on the overall self-evaluation
scale were —8.2 mm for the high-capacity failure group and +0.8
mm for the low-capacity failure group.

The results are clear enough, but their interpretation is uncertain.
We had argued that since the Ss had presumably adopted the goal
of joining the "Career Liaison Group" they *needed* to demonstrate
their power in *all the five* abilities because that had been declared
as the sole mode of entrance into the group. We further supposed

TABLE 5.3
Frequency Distributions and Means of Number of Capacities Reduced in Rating from First to Final Rating

	S Failed Test of Capacity on Which he Had Rated Himself:	
Number of Ratings Reduced	Highest	Lowest
5	2	0
4	3	2
3	5	1
2	4	4
1	1	2
0	0	6
Means	3.1	1.4

(After Diggory and Magaziner, 1959.)

that, in such a situation, S would value most highly his highest capacity as the one on which he depended most to help him negotiate the path toward the goal. By the same argument, he would put least value on his lowest rated capacity because he could least depend on it to advance him toward the goal. Thus we presumed that the spread of evaluative effect we noted in one group, and the relative lack of it in the other group, was a function of the value to S of the capacity which had been tested and found wanting. However, Wylie (1961), among others, pointed out that this interpretation is not unique. An alternative explanation is that S, in failing the test of his highest rated ability, suffered a disconfirmation of his expectations and therefore lowered his ratings quite generally on all or most of the other scales in the belief that the disconfirmation resulted from his generally overestimating his power in these particular abilities. Conversely, failure with the lowest rated capacity is not a disconfirmation, but something S might have expected, so there is little reason to change his ratings on any of the scales.

This critique did not discourage our confidence in the hypothesis that the amount of spread of evaluative effects from one ability to others in a set was somehow a function of the *value* which S placed on the tested ability; that is, its importance induced by its instrumental connection with some valued end. Fortunately, the critique itself is open to test by the simple expedient of including a success condition along with our failure condition. The "scale shift" theory and the "value" theory make different predictions about the occurrence of evaluative spread in a success condition. The "scale shift" predictions are that if S succeeds on a test of his highest-rated ability, he has achieved a confirmation of his evaluations and will not revise his ratings on any of the scales; and, if he succeeds on the test of his lowest-rated ability, that is a disconfirmation (a happy one) and he might be moved to revise many of his scale ratings upward. The "value" theory predicts that changes in evaluation of the highest-rated ability will be accompanied by corresponding changes in a relatively large number of the ratings of the untested abilities, and therefore it predicts a spread of evaluative effect in the high-ability success condition where the "scale shift" theory predicts none. Conversely, the "value" theory predicts little if any spread of evaluative change from a low-rated ability, and therefore predicts relatively little change in ratings of untested abilities in a low-ability success condition, where the "scale shift" theory predicts that most of the change will occur.

An experiment that included a success condition, and the additional modification of an "irrelevant" condition, was done with the help of R. Blumenfeld and V. Rudraswamy. The design and main results of this experiment are summarized in Table 5.4. The "fail-relevant" conditions are exact replications, in every detail, of the Magaziner experiment just discussed. The success conditions were introduced by changing the instructions about the passing score on the test and about the total range of the test scores. In the low-success

TABLE 5.4

Mean Number of Four Untested Abilities Reduced in Self-Evaluations

| | Relevant | | | | Irrelevant | | | |
| | High | | Low | | High | | Low | |
	Mean	n	Mean	n	Mean	n	Mean	n
Pass 50/80	1.5	10	2.1	10	1.6	10	2.2	10
Pass 60/100	1.8	13	1.5	13	1.5	13	1.5	13
Fail 80/100	1.9	13	1.6	13	1.8	13	2.1	13

(Data collected by Ruth Blumenfeld, and by the author with the assistance of Mr. V. Rudraswamy.)

condition, Ss were told that the passing score was 60 out of 100 points, so when they were presented with the sequence of cumulated scores (15, 32, 48, 64) they had obviously passed the test, but they had just *barely* passed it. Of the total range of 40 points between minimum pass (60) and the test maximum (100) their final score was only 10% above the minimum pass, and this was obviously a disappointment to the Ss for they *lowered* their estimates of the tested capacity when they thought it was their best of the lot. We did not bother to make a special experiment to find out why the Ss behaved this way—we thought we knew. They had simply set their personal LAs at some point higher than the official minimum pass and the mere fact that they had passed *de jure* was not sufficient to satisfy them. They wanted to pass, if not with *éclat*, at least *respectably*—and they defined *respectably* for themselves. We did not proceed to ask the Ss to make formal statements of their LAs because we did not want to add any more extraneous procedures to those already in force. To do so might have made it plainly obvious to the Ss that the "test" was only incidental to our real interests and we wanted them to continue to believe with all their hearts in the genuineness of what we told them about our activities. We simply accepted our own assumption that we were dealing with LA phenomena in the "success" conditions and added another success condition to increase the likelihood that the conditions of passing would include more of the Ss' LAs. Thus the "high-success" condition was set up by instructing the Ss that the maximum score for each of the 20 responses was four rather than five, and thus the maximum score on the test was 80. The official minimum passing score was 50, and the sequence of cumulated scores was the same as in the other conditions, so that when S saw that his final score was 64 he could have calculated that his score stood at 48% of the total range of 30 points between minimum pass (50) and test maximum (80). The results for change in evaluation of the tested ability (Table 5.5) clearly suggest that the Ss "felt better" about this situation.

The "irrelevant" conditions were exact duplicates of the "relevant" procedures except that the Ss were all told that the first test they took was only a practice test. We said that we had included a full-scale practice test because we thought it only fair not to throw Ss into such a completely unfamiliar test procedure without giving them the experience of what it was like to go through such a procedure with nothing at stake. We also told them that, fortunately, we could do this because the test (of S's highest- or lowest-rated ability, depending on the condition to which he was assigned) had shown that this ability was hardly of any importance for success in the group—it did not distinguish between successful and unsuccessful group members. Furthermore it did not correlate at all with any of the other tests. Its only value was its similarity in procedure to the real tests, a fact which made it an ideal practice test.

In the Magaziner experiment, we assumed that the *spread* of evaluative change we were looking for occurred when a majority of all the five relevant abilities were reduced in evaluation on the second (post-test) ratings. In the present experiment we were a little more meticulous and separated the tested abilities from the untested abilities. Table 5.4 shows that in the relevant-fail condition, there are more untested abilities lowered when the tested ability was initially rated high by S (1.9) than when it was rated low (1.6), and in the high-relevant conditions, there is an increase in the number of untested abilities with reduced ratings as we go from the best pass to the failure condition, a situation which does not appear in any of the other columns of the table. However, none of these differences are significant so we cannot trust the trends that we see here.

What about *amount* of change in the untested abilities? Is it affected by our experimental conditions in the way our hypothesis demands? These data are presented in Table 5.5. In the high-relevant column of that table it appears that the net change in untested abilities was *upward* in the best pass ($^5\%_{80}$) conditions and *downward* in the other conditions, and this relation does not appear in any of the other columns of Table 5.5. The data summarized in Table 5.5 were subjected to an analysis of variance. The hypothesis demands that systematic changes in the untested abilities should be most noticeable in the conditions where the highest rated ability was tested by a relevant test—a test whose outcome would mean that S had actually succeeded or failed in qualifying for membership in the "Career Liaison Group"—and that no such systematic relation to the outcome of the test should be seen in the other conditions. This seems to be the case by inspection, but for the test of significance, this amounts to predicting a significant *triple interaction* in the analysis of variance—the same thing as saying that the amount of change in untested abilities would depend simultaneously on the kind of ability that was tested, on whether the test was relevent, and on the outcome of the test (pass or fail). The interaction is not significant. So we still have no evidence in support of the hypothesis. However, we will not give it up because all the trends we observe in the data are in the right direction. We suspect that it is not the hypothesis that is wrong, but that the experiment is not a good test of it. Variability between Ss,

TABLE 5.5

Mean Change, in Millimeters, in Self-Evaluations of Tested (T) and Untested (U) Abilities

	Relevant		Irrelevant		Totals	
	High	Low	High	Low	Mean	n
Pass 50/80	T − 3.7	+5.2	−1.9	+7.0	+1.65	40
	U + 0.7	−0.7	+0.6	−0.9	−0.08	
Pass 60/100	T − 6.2	+9.5	−3.5	+10.7	+2.61	52
	U − 0.7	−0.8	+2.3	+1.1	+0.52	
Fail 80/100	T − 11.4	+1.3	−2.5	+1.8	−2.69	52
	U − 0.6	−0.3	+2.5	+1.6	+0.81	
Totals (n = 36)	T − 7.38	+5.36	−2.72	+6.47		
	U − 0.81	−0.59	+1.92	+0.74		

Combined Relevant (n = 72)   T − 1.01
                              U − 0.37
Irrelevant   (n = 72)   T + 1.87
                              U + 1.34
Combined:
  High Capacity Test (n = 72)   T − 5.05
                                U + 0.86
  Low Capacity Test (n = 72)   T + 5.91
                                U + 0.07

The ns for the individual conditions are given in Table 5.4.
(Data collected by Ruth Blumenfeld, and by the author with the assistance of Mr. V. Rudraswamy.)

used as our measure of error, was very great, so great that it swamped the effects of the experimental variables on the changes in ratings of untested abilities. It is quite likely that we can reduce this error in future experiments by doing two things. First, make the success conditions dependent not only on *de facto*, official passing scores but also on whether or not S passes in a manner satisfying to him. Examination of the reratings of the high tested abilities in Table 5.5 shows that net change in rating of these abilities was *downward* on the average, indicating that even when S had passed the test he saw no reason to increase his evaluation of the high-rated ability, or even to keep it the same. The general trend for all high-rated *tested* abilities was downward (mean change overall was −5.05 mm.) but the change for the low-rated tested abilities was upward (5.91) and this difference is significant in the analysis of variance. Also, the overall effect of the success-failure variation was significant in change of ratings of tested abilities; that is, in the success conditions, the overall net change is an increase, but it is a decrease in the failure condition.

There is one other analysis of the data which is relevant to our hypothesis: that is to examine the relation between change in the tested abilities (whether the change is an increase or no change on the one hand, and a negative change, on the other) and in the untested abilities. This analysis does not make the picture crystal clear because most of the Ss whose tested abilities were high lowered their ratings of the tested abilities and the reverse occurred even more decisively for those whose tested abilities were rated low to begin with. Thus the distributions are highly skewed, and in half of each of the contingency tables shown in Table 5.6 there is a very small number of cases. For this reason, the significance tests were carried out by Fisher's "exact probability" test for 2×2 contingency tables. When S's highest-rated capacity was subjected to a relevant test there is a barely significant relation ($p = 0.5$, one-tailed test) between direction of change in the ratings of the tested and untested abilities. None of the other relations are significant. Thus, while there is no reason to crow about smashing confirmation of the hypothesis, there is no reason to abandon it.

TABLE 5.6

Associations of Changes in Tested and Untested Capacities

	Relevant						Irrelevant					
	High Tested			Low Tested			High Tested			Low Tested		
	+, 0	−	Total	+, 0	−	Total	+, 0	−	Total	+, 0	−	Total
−	1	16	17	14	6	20	4	9	13	15	5	20
Untested +, 0	7	12	19	14	2	16	8	15	23	13	3	16
Total	8	28	36	28	8	36	12	24	36	28	8	36
	p = .05			p > .20			p > .20			p > .20		

Fisher's exact probability test, one-tailed.
(Data collected by Ruth Blumenfeld, and by the author with the assistance of Mr. V. Rudraswamy.)

Furthermore, Table 5.5 contains refutation of the "scale shift" theory of the spread of evaluative change. According to that theory, in the relevant test conditions, increases of evaluation of the tested ability should be accompanied by increases in evaluation of the untested abilities, and this does not happen in a single case. Furthermore, as just noted, there is effectively zero correlation between direction of change in tested and untested abilities in the low-relevant condition (Table 5.6).

What else can be said about spread of evaluative change from one ability to others? I. G. Cetlin collected some appropriate data which we have not yet examined. In one respect her procedure was like that of the two experiments just discussed. Her Ss indicated their interest in the testing procedure by returning a questionnaire on which they indicated their self-ratings of four abilities (ability to think creatively, leadership, discrimination, and speed and efficiency of reactions). All the Ss she used had rated one of these abilities outstandingly higher than all the others and that was the one on which they were allegedly tested. Furthermore, she used three different failure conditions and a success condition, so her conditions are comparable to the high-relevant pass and fail conditions of the last experiment.

TABLE 5.7
Mean Number (Out of a Possible Three) of Untested Abilities Reduced in Rating, By Experimental Conditions and Whether or Not S Reduced His Rating of the Tested Ability

Severe Early Failure ($n = 30$)	1.24
Mild Late Failure ($n = 15$)	1.47
Success ($n = 15$)	0.80
Ss Lowered Rating of Tested Ability ($n = 44$)	1.60
Ss did not Lower Rating of Tested Ability ($n = 16$)	0.70

(After I. G. Cetlin, 1964.)

Table 5.7 summarized her findings with respect to number of untested abilities which showed reduced scond ratings. There were no significant differences in mean number of untested abilities reduced in rating as a function of her success and failure conditions. However, regardless of experimental condition, lowering of the rating of the tested ability went along with tendency to lower more of the untested abilities than did non-reduction of rating of the tested ability. These results are very much like those of the Blumenfeld-Rudraswamy data just presented. Table 5.8 presents Cetlin's findings on change in evaluation of the tested ability. The frequency and amount of reduction did not

TABLE 5.8

Frequency and Average Amount of Reduction in Ratings of Tested Abilities by Experimental Conditions

	Number of Ss	Mean Change
Severe Early Failure ($n = 30$)	26	-12.38
Mild Late Failure ($n = 15$)	12	-9.25
Success ($N = 15$)	6	1.75

(After I. G. Cetlin, 1964.)

differ significantly between the failure conditions, but both failure groups differed significantly from the success group on both measures.

Doreen Rothman (1963) also collected data relevant to the present issue. Her Ss were 40 high school students from the Philadelphia suburbs, all with "normal" MMPI profiles. Their mean age was 16.66 years (range, from 13–2 to 20–0) and their mean IQ was 99.0 (range 76–127). By permission of the school authorities, each S was interviewed individually in two separate sessions. The first session was devoted to administering personality and IQ tests (where these results were not available in the school counselor's records) and to giving the prospective S a chance to say whether he wanted to participate in the experiment. The instructions about the experiment were as follows: "First I want to tell you about a very interesting experiment I'm going to do. Some people at the University of Pennsylvania are performing some experiments on methods of teaching complex skills. One of these experiments requires the selection of a number of people who will receive basic instructions in the general characteristics of games of strategy such as chess, Go, and other two- and three-dimensional board games. We have found, thus far, that the boys and girls who have participated in the study have enjoyed it very much.

"You have been recommended as a possible participant in this study. Since we want to select those most likely to succeed, it will be necessary to have a preliminary meeting with each candidate in order to determine whether they possess the prerequisite abilities to profit from the instruction methods to be used." If S said he was interested, he was scheduled for a second interview.

In the second interview each S first rated himself on seven 7-point rating scales, each scale corresponding to one of the following abilities: concept formation, two- and three-dimensional perception, planfulness, abstract reasoning-intellectual relationships, adaptability, and numerical ability. Next, all Ss worked on 40 problems from the space relations subtest of the Differential Aptitude Test (DAT). These problems were grouped into eight blocks of five problems each. Each block was timed separately and the times were falsified in order to manipulate experiences of success and failure. For the failure Ss (half the group) only one minute was allowed for each block of five problems, thus giving them time to complete no more than three of the problems, some of which they got wrong. The success group was allowed at least three minutes per block, or at any rate enough time to complete every problem, whether they got it right or not. The Ss were told that in order to qualify for the experiment on games of strategy they had to perform at least as well as the average of their age group. The success Ss were told that this average was 45 of the available cumulated points on the test and the failure group was told that the average was 65. Each S was given a record sheet, on which E wrote his "obtained" score opposite the "maximum possible" score for each block of problems, and a mimeographed copy of a graph which showed the "average" or "passing" score and on which E recorded S's cumulated "score" after each block of problems. After the test, each S again rated himself on the seven abilities listed above. Table 5.9 shows the mean changes in tested and untested abilities. The difference between the relevant and irrelevant conditions was induced by instructing half the Ss that the first test they took was only a practice test, thus: "This task is unlike any you'll get but is designed only to give you practice in taking tests. The way you perform on this test has nothing to do with how you'll perform on the real test." Changes on the *tested* abilities were affected by the experimental con-

TABLE 5.9
Mean Changes in Self-Evaluation of Tested (T) and Untested (U) Abilities: Normal Ss

		Relevant	Irrelevant	Combined
Success	T	−.20	.25	.03
	U	.01	.20	.11
Failure	T	−.40	−.70	−.55
	U	−.95	−1.05	−1.00
Combined	T	−.30	−.23	
	U	−.47	−.43	

For each condition, $n = 10$. (After Rothman, 1963.)

ditions in a complex way. Evaluations were significantly lower after failure than after success but the effect of the relevant condition was to make the changes negative in both cases, only more negative after failure. On the other hand, the effect of the irrelevant condition was to make the changes positive after success and strongly negative after failure, even more negative than in either of the relevant test groups.

There is no opportunity, in this experiment, to study the effect of type of ability *tested* on changes in evaluation of *untested* abilities because the procedure was so arranged that the groups were *equated* for number of Ss tested on each of the seven listed abilities, regardless of their initial self-evaluations of them. Thus, we can only study the effects of success-failure and relevance-irrelevance on changes in the untested abilities. The *interaction* of the effects of success and relevance which appeared with the tested abilities is absent in the data for the untested abilities. Instead, there is a significant effect only of the success-failure variable: the mean change for success is .11 scale units *per ability* and that for failure is −1.00 units.

It is clear that we are far from understanding the mechanism which produces changes in untested abilities as a result of the successful or unsuccessful use of a tested ability. On the other hand, there is no reason to suppose, *a priori*, that such changes are the result of a general revision of S's position on all rating scales for ability: we have one instance where the scale shift theory clearly will not work. Of course it is possible that scale shift and value-induced changes both operate, but under different conditions, and this can be easily checked by providing for the relevant observations in the design of future experiments. Of even greater general interest is the possibility that, by experiments of the type we have presented here, we can discover whether certain clusters of abilities change together in Ss' self-evaluations independently of other clusters. This could be the beginning of an objective description of the rather elusive notion "personality structure," or at least *another* objective dimension for describing it.

So far we have not succeeded in designing an experiment on spread of evaluative change which makes use of the knowledge clearly revealed about changes in self-evaluation by B. Rosen's experiment, described in Chapter 4. We have not been able to assure ourselves that the Ss were evaluating the untested abilities as instruments to some specific end-in-view. B. Rosen's results show clearly that changes in self-evaluation occur in a systematic and predictable manner only when that condition is realized. We tried to impress on the Ss in the Magaziner-Blumenfeld-Rudraswamy experiments that their evaluations were to be made only with respect to the abilities as they related to the goal of getting into the group, and Rothman used analogous instructions, but it was clear from the post-experimental interviews with our Ss that only *some* of them responded in this way. We need a procedure that will make it unreasonable or impossible for most of the Ss to respond in any other way.

This brings us to a part of the data in these spread of evaluation experiments which has been thoroughly misunderstood; that is, changes on "global" overall self-evaluation scales. In addition to the five specific abilities listed on their self-evaluation questionnaire, Diggory and Magaziner (1959) had a sixth scale on which S was to answer the question, "Considering all your abilities, including those rated above, what is your opinion of yourself as an adequately functioning person?" The same question was used in the experiment done by Blumenfeld and Rudraswamy, and Isabelle Cetlin had a scale on which Ss marked their answer to the question, "Considering all your abilities, including those listed above, how would you evaluate yourself?" Questions of this type are of interest to the American "phenomenologists" who study the "self-concept" and distrust objective methods (cf. Wylie, 1961). They believe that nothing important has been accomplished unless a large and statistically significant change, consistent with "self-concept theory," has been found in "global" self-evaluations. Therefore they criticized (in private communications, but see the general critique by Wylie, 1961, of similar experiments) the Diggory and Magaziner experiment because we reported that average changes on the overall self-evaluation scale were in the same direction as changes in the five specific abilities, but did not differ significantly from each other, and neither differed significantly from zero. These critics have overlooked our clear statement of intent on this point. We did *not* intend that differences in the spread of evaluation should show up on the overall self-evaluation scale. In fact, we went out of our way to instruct the Ss to *restrict* their evaluations of the five abilities to the immediate situation. This was our first attempt to grapple with the problem of spread of evaluative effect and we wanted to proceed as cautiously as possible, without creating unknown dangers for our Ss. Perhaps we dreamed too grandly of the possibility that our little stage setting would completely crush the overall self-evaluation of some of our Ss. Nevertheless, we attempted to guard against that possibility and we congratulated ourselves on having devised a tolerably safe procedure exactly because we got no large and significant effects on overall self-evaluation. Table 5.10 shows the Blumenfeld-Rudraswamy data for changes in the overall

TABLE 5.10

Mean Changes on Global Self-Evaluation Scale by Experimental Conditions

| | Relevant | | Irrelevant | | |
	High	Low	High	Low	Combined
Pass (50/80)	+0.60	+5.20	−2.80	+4.30	+1.83
Pass 60/100	+2.54	+1.00	+0.08	+0.08	+0.92
Fail 80/100	+0.31	+4.15	+0.23	−4.08	+0.15
Combined	+1.19	+0.31	−0.67	−0.25	

The *ns* for each condition are shown in Tables 5.4 and 5.5.
(Data collected by Ruth Blumenfeld, and by the author with the assistance of Mr. V. Rudraswamy.)

self-evaluation scale. There are no significant differences associated with any of the main variables or interactions, though there were significant effects of the experimental treatments on both tested and untested specific abilities. None of the mean changes in the global self-evaluation scale are significantly different from zero. However, before we conclude that all such procedures relate only to changes in the specific abilities under consideration, whether or not they are tested, we must look at Isabelle Cetlin's results for changes in the overall self-evaluation scale. They are summarized in Table 5.11. Neither in

TABLE 5.11

Mean Changes, in Millimeters, on Overall Self-Evaluation Scale as a Function of Indicated Conditions

| | Ss Who Lowered Self-Evaluation | | Mean Change Overall Scale |
	n	%	
Severe Early Failure ($n = 30$)	22	73.5	−3.8
Mild Late Failure ($n = 15$)	9	60.0	−3.0
Success ($n = 15$)	4	26.7	+5.4
Persisters ($n = 14$)	7	50.0	+1.0
Substituters and Quitters ($n = 16$)	14	87.5	−7.6

(After I. G. Cetlin, 1964.)

number of Ss reducing their overall self-evaluations nor in the average amount by which it was reduced do the early severe failure groups differ significantly from the late moderate failure group. The early severe failure group differs significantly from the success group, which had a fairly large increase in overall self-evaluation. The mild late failure group does not differ significantly from the success group in either respect. We cannot tell whether this difference between Isabelle Cetlin's findings and those of the other two experiments is due to something associated with differences in the ages of her high school Ss and the college student Ss, or perhaps due to some subtle feature of the experimental set-up she used. Perhaps the way she introduced the "goal" (qualifying for a career in space science) made it more credible or more important to her Ss than the "Career Liaison Group" was to the college students. This is all we have to say about this important problem of how a single success or failure is likely to affect the spread of changes in self-evaluation to few or many of the evaluators' other capacities.

CHANGES IN DEATH-IMAGERY

In much of the literature dealing with suicide and attitudes toward death there is reference to discouragement, hope, depression, elation, self-negations, or self-assertion. Generally, the positive aspects of feelings about one's self are associated with avoidance of the idea of death, or with a low tendency to commit suicide, while the reverse is true for the negative aspects of attitudes toward one's self. This literature is discussed more fully in Chapter 8. Right here we are going to discuss some *experimental* results relating to attitudes toward death. These experiments were completed by D. Rothman in 1960 and 1963.

In one sense it is ludicrous to talk about doing *experiments* in this area for exactly the behavior which should serve as the dependent variable (i.e., suicide, or covert destructive tendencies, or carelessness about the prospect of potentially lethal dangers) is what we want to prevent. It is not that we are concerned with the commonplace of research in disasters: you can only interview the survivors. We want to have *nothing but* survivors, so we have to proceed by the utmost indirection. To put it quite simply, leaving *action* aside, could we observe that thinking about death increased after failure and decreased after success? A paper by Eron and Ritter (1951) suggested that we might be able to detect such changes in death-imagery by examining stories people wrote about the pictures in the Thematic Apperception Test.

The first experiment was merely an exploration of whether there was anything in the idea worth pursuing. A letter was sent to a group of undergraduate students in psychology courses, describing an experiment we were doing. This experiment, it was alleged, was investigating the efficacy of various teaching methods in the communication of complex skills in handling concepts and specifically the concepts involved the fundamental principles behind games of strategy like chess and Go. The students were told that others who had participated in the experiment had enjoyed it and all of them had learned something useful about thinking in complex situations. Twenty Ss (18 women and 2 men) were used in the experimental group and another seven women served as the control group. The experimental Ss were assigned randomly to success and failure treatments which have already been described (pp. 240–241). They performed the experimental task, the problems of the space relations section of the DAT, singly or in small groups. When group sessions were used, all the Ss present were in either the success or the failure condition because the procedures did not admit of applying the success and failure conditions simultaneously to different Ss. At the beginning of the testing session the Ss evaluated seven of their own abilities on separate seven-point linear rating scales; then they took the test on which they either succeeded or failed in attempting to qualify for inclusion in the game experiment; and then they made new ratings of their abilities.

As soon as the Ss were assembled, the E told them that she would like to have them write eight brief stories about some pictures. This she was asking as a favor to a friend of hers, another graduate student, who also needed Ss but couldn't get any.[5] The purpose of this explanation was to reduce the likelihood that the Ss would suspect a connection between the test procedure and the story writing. After the "test" procedure and after the Ss had rerated their abilities on the seven scales, E told them that her friend wanted two stories, so they proceeded to write *different* stories in response to the same TAT pictures. The TAT pictures used were selected so that some of them were likely to elicit death-imagery and others were less likely to do so. The standard designations of these pictures, in the order of their presentation

---

[5] This was a plausible ruse at that time. It was late in the spring term, and undergraduate students were well aware of the anguish felt by many staff members and graduate students of the Psychology Department because of the dearth of human Ss. A year's work had nearly exhausted the supply of naive, unused Ss, and the students were disinclined to spend time on anything but preparing for examinations.

to our Ss are: 1, 20, 3 BM, 13 MF, 7 BM, 8 BM, 14, and 15. The procedure for scoring death-imagery was simply to count the number of words or phrases that could be recognized as related to death. No attempt was made to distinguish suicidal from murder imagery, nor to distinguish among causes of death, nor to adopt the notion that the protagonist in the story was a projection of the author. Thus, we have emphasized our interest in undifferentiated occurrence of death-related ideas by referring to total death-imagery (TDI). The results of the exploratory experiment are shown in Table 5.12.

The first two sections of the table show that both changes in self-evaluation and changes in death-imagery were significantly related to the experimental treatments of success and failure. After success, death-imagery either decreased or remained at the same level for the majority of Ss, while self-evaluation either increased or remained the same. The reverse of these relations occurred after failure. Death-imagery in the control group, which wrote the TAT stories without the intervening test or success or failure procedures, also tended to decline, with about the same frequency and amount as in

TABLE 5.12

Associations Among Success—Failure, Changes in Self-Evaluation, and Changes in Death-Imagery, College Students

A. Changes in Self-Evaluation	Success	Failure	Totals
Up or None	6	1	7
Down	2	11	13
Totals	8	12	20
B. Outcome of Test:	Changes in Death-Imagery		
	Down or None	Up	Totals
Success	6	2	8
Failure	3	9	12
Totals	9	11	20
C. Changes in Self-Evaluation:	Changes in Death-Imagery		
	Down or None	Up	Totals
Up or None	7	0	7
Down	4	11	13
Totals	9	11	20

For all associations, $p < .05$, Fisher's exact probability test. (Data collected by Doreen Rothman.)

the success group. Therefore, relative to the controls, the main effect of the experiment lies in the reactions of the failure group. Part C of Table 5.12 shows that changes in death-imagery and self-evaluation were even more closely related to each other than either of them were to the success-failure variable.

In her Ph.D. dissertation, Rothman (1963) verified these relations in a group of normal high school students and also in two groups of the same age and present level of intelligence who were psychologically abnormal. The comparison of the normal and abnormal data is made in Chapter 7. Here we consider only the normal data, which are summarized in Table 5.13. The experimental procedure for inducing success and failure and for making the test appear either relevant or irrelevant has already been described. Essentially it was the same as that of the pilot experiment on death-imagery. Table 5.13 shows that success produced a small decrease and failure a large increase in TDI only in the relevant conditions; that is, when the test was *real*. But in the irrelevant conditions, when Ss had taken only an otherwise meaningless practice test, there was a sizable decrease in death-imagery for both success and failure groups, with no significant difference between them. We have no complete theoretical interpretation to offer for these results other than that implied in our reasons for doing the experiments in the first place. It appears that, under some conditions, failure to achieve a goal by the use of his own ability will lead a person to reduce his evaluation of that ability (and others) and to think more about death. We certainly are in no position to argue, as perhaps we could with the old ideomotor theory of action, that we are closer to predicting the likelihood that a person who has failed will take overt action with respect to his death or that of others.

TABLE 5.13

Mean Changes in Total Death-Imagery by Experimental Conditions, High School Students

	Relevant	Irrelevant
Success	−0.80	−1.70
Failure	+2.00	−1.05

Success–failure difference is significant in relevant condition, but not in irrelevant condition.

For each condition, $n = 10$. (After Rothman, 1963.)

We are still bound by the necessity to explore the possibility of such connections with the utmost circumspection and indirection of method.

Simply counting the number of death-related words in the Ss' stories obscures the flavor of the stories themselves, so we will quote some of them here. As her first story about picture 15 one S wrote, "This is a ghost rising out of his grave in the cemetery. He was sentenced to death as the result of a murder he committed. He went to hell. Now he is returning to haunt the people responsible for his fate and end. He has grown mean and ugly as a result of living in hell." After a success experience the same S wrote (in response to the same picture), "These are a series of buildings in an abstract painting. The man or painter sees himself as master of the world and begins to stretch his arms to envelop the entire universe." These two stories clearly show a change in mood and a marked decrease in death-imagery.

Another S, who had a failure experience, showed no change in *amount* of death-imagery, but the content of her two stories suggests an increase in its directedness and salience. On the first presentation of card 15 she wrote: "This is an old man who, because of waning health, has had to stop working and give up all his hobbies. Consequently, he has taken up going to funerals to fill his time. Here he is attending the burial of one of his old friends. He will leave soon to go home where he will tell his wife that it was a very dignified, but sparsely attended funeral." After failure, she wrote: "The man is in a graveyard which is on top of a very high mountain. He is very unhappy because he has become cynical. Presently he is standing on the very edge of a cliff which descends very sharply to a deep ravine. He is thinking about jumping in order to end it all but he won't because he's afraid he won't kill himself."

P(S) AND ATTRACTIVENESS OF GOALS

Marvin Rosen (1960) undertook to explore the question of how S's persistence in attempting to reach what he said was an attractive goal would be affected by his $P(s)$ and the attractiveness (valence = Va) of the goal. He also looked to see what kinds of changes in evaluation of the goal would occur if S was informed that his $P(s)$ was high or low. What would S do about his evaluation of an initially unattractive goal if he were suddenly told that such a goal were easily available to him, and conversely how would he change his evaluation of an initially attractive goal if it were suddenly revealed that he was not likely to be able to achieve it? First, high school students from the Philadelphia suburbs were given a list of about 50 occupations which required college, professional, or graduate training. They were also given a linear rating scale with the letters A, B, C, D, and E designating equally spaced index marks from one end of the line to the other. The letter A designated the most attractive end of the scale and S chose the occupation on the list which he thought was most attractive and wrote the letter A next to it. Then he chose the occupation which he thought least attractive and wrote the letter E next to it. Next, he was told to choose the occupation which, in his opinion, was equidistant from A and E in attractiveness; he labeled this one C. The occupation to be labeled B was midway in attractiveness between A and C; and the one called D was midway in attractiveness between C and E.

Then all Ss took the entire Differential Aptitude Test (DAT) after they had volunteered for a "free vocational aptitude testing program." They were led to expect that the test would decide whether or not they were qualified for certain kinds of occupations. They were promised that they would receive various kinds of information about their qualifications and vocational opportunities in subsequent meetings. Before these informational meetings E had assigned the Ss to six treatment groups which were to get systematically varied instructions. The Ss were given information about only *one* occupation: half of them (the high valence condition) about the one they had rated at A on the attractiveness scale, and the other half (the low valence condition) about the one they had rated at C. The moderately attractive (C) occupation was chosen for the low valence condition, rather than occupations D or E, in order to increase the likelihood that these Ss would have some minimal tendency to *approach* this occupational goal rather than a tendency to *avoid* it.

This information was presented to each S in a specially prepared booklet which also contained his test results (falsified) and information on employment opportunities. In the explanation, S's alleged abilities and the available opportunities to enter the occupation described were combined to give an estimated probability of S's actually entering the occupation; that is, a $P(s)$ estimate made by the "experts." Three such ratings were used: .91, .51, and .11, for the high, fifty-fifty, and low $P(s)$ treatments, respectively. The layout of Table 5.14 gives the design of the experiment.

After they had a chance to digest the information about the occupation each S was asked to "complete his records" by doing the following: (*1*) Make a second estimate of the attractiveness of the occupation under consideration by marking the linear rating scale *at any point;* (*2*) Write a short paragraph describing his evaluation of the adequacy of the test results as an indication of his true capacities, his feelings about the results, and any extenuating circumstances which might account for a poor performance; (*3*) In response to a series of questions, estimate the relative ease or difficulty of his entering and succeeding in the occupation under discussion; (*4*) List the favorable and unfavorable characteristics of the five occupations he mentioned in the initial valence ratings; and (*5*) Check one of the three alternatives (high, fifty-fifty, or low) to indicate his perception of the likelihood of his entering and succeeding in the discussed occupation.

Next, the Ss were told about a fictitious "Special Acceleration Program" which was to be established in cooperation with certain high schools and universities. Qualified students were to be given a chance to attain their vocational goals in a shorter time than would be ordinarily possible. This was to be accomplished by means of accelerated classes, extra assignments, summer sessions, and other "forced draft" methods. Different programs were to be tailored to the specific types of vocation for which the students were being trained. On the basis of the tests already taken, a preliminary screening had been done and certain students would be given the chance to compete for the program by taking a long series of tests. In fact, the first test of the set for the accelerated program was ready and would be given *right now.*

The test then administered was a four-minute digit-symbol exercise. The Ss were asked to mark the symbol they were working on when E called out, "Time," at one-minute intervals.

Next, the Ss were told that the rest of the qualifying tests were to be given on a Saturday during the Easter vacation and would last all day. Those who were interested were asked to sign up. Those who were not interested were asked to say so. They were all cautioned about wasting their time and perhaps depriving someone else of a chance to take the tests. This choice is later referred to as return for further testing (RFT). In another choice, the Ss were asked whether they would like to speak individually with a psychologist about the information they had just received; that is, their aptitude for the experimental occupation. This conference would confirm what they had already been told, but more specific details would be provided. This choice is called return for further information (RFI).

Performance and Choices for Action

Table 5.14 summarizes the results of the two choices: whether or not to return for further testing, whether or not to return for further information, and performance on the digit-symbol test (the first section of the qualifying test). Generally, the higher the $P(s)$ *and* the higher the valence the greater the proportion of Ss who chose to return for further testing. It looks as though having a high probability of getting an attractive goal is most likely to enlist Ss in trying to get it. The proportion of Ss who wanted more testing is significantly higher in the high than in the low valence condition, and the decrease in this proportion as a function of $P(s)$ is also significant. Though a significantly higher proportion of Ss wanted more information (78%) than wanted more testing (65%), there are no differences in proportions choosing to return for further information resulting from any of the experimental treatments. This may be comparable to I. G.

TABLE 5.14
Numbers and Percentages of Ss Who Chose to Return for Further Testing (RFT) and for Further Information (RFI) and Their Mean Performances on a "Preliminary Qualifying Test"

		Announced $P(s)$							
		.91		.51		.11		Combined	
Va		n	%	n	%	n	%	n	%
	RFT	22	86	23	83	24	70	69	79
High	RFI	21	71	23	91	23	87	67	79
	Test	22	129.6	23	135.2	24	131.8	69	132.2
	RFT	22	68	25	52	23	35	70	51
Low	RFI	21	76	25	68	22	68	68	71
	Test	22	134.9	25	141.7	23	138.8	70	138.5
	RFT	44	77	48	67	47	53	139	65
Combined	RFI	42	74	48	79	45	68	135	78
	Test	44	132.3	48	138.6	47	135.3	139	135.7

Valence (Va) of occupations is defined by Ss' ratings; $P(s)$ was announced by E. (After M. Rosen, 1960.)

Cetlin's finding that even among Ss who dropped out (either withdrew completely or substituted another goal) they all *first* asked for either a practice period or some change in conditions of work, and the proportion of Ss requesting such a change was the same among the persisters as among the non-persisters. The present data are comparable with Cetlin's if we assume that her Ss were making "persistive" choices in order to test hypotheses about how to improve their performance—or whether it could be improved under any conditions; that is, it is likely that her Ss were seeking information, and if so, there are two sets of data which show that the search for information is unrelated to Ss' decision whether to keep striving or not.

Performance on the digit-symbol test was analyzed over the four one-minute sections of the test by Alexander's (1946) trend test. The general finding is that Ss in the 50–50 $P(s)$ group produced significantly more correct solutions than those in the High or Low $P(s)$ groups. The latter groups did not differ significantly in output. Output on the digit-symbol test was not affected significantly by any of the other experimental variables. Certainly it did not parallel the proportions of choices of further testing. There is also the fact that Ss who chose to return for further information produced significantly more than those who did not so choose.

Cognitive Changes

Rosen was also interested in observing cognitive changes both in valence and in $P(s)$, and in another aspect of Ss' descriptions of the experimental variables which, following Festinger (1957), he called "cognitive overlap." The data relating to changes in perceived $P(s)$ are shown in Table 5.15. The upper section of the table shows the relation between S's own rating of the likelihood of his entering and succeeding in the given occupation and the likelihood presented to him in the information distributed by E. The high and low valence groups show significantly different patterns in this relation. To emphasize these differences, the modal numbers of Ss in the rows and columns have been enclosed in connected boxes. In the high valence group there is a significant positive relation between the *announced* $P(s)$ and S's *estimated* $P(s)$ as shown by the fact that the modes in the three columns for the high valence group are all on the main diagonal; that is, 64% of the high valence Ss estimated $P(s)$ at the same level as that given by the experimental instructions, and only 51% of the low valence Ss did so. Put another way, only 36% of the high valence Ss shifted $P(s)$, and 49% of the low valence Ss did so. This difference must have been due largely to Ss' perceptions of the influ-

TABLE 5.15
Frequency Distributions of P(s) *Assigned by Ss as a Function of* P(s) *Announced by* E *and Valance* (Va) *Assigned by* S; *and Mean Opportunity Ratings by* Ss

| P(s) Assigned by Ss | Va Assigned by Ss | P(s) Announced by E | | | |
		.91	.51	.11	Totals
High	High	15	5	2	22
	Low	9	6	7	22
50–50	High	7	16	9	32
	Low	12	18	12	42
Low	High	0	2	13	15
	Low	1	1	9	11
Totals	High	22	23	24	69
	Low	22	25	23	70
Means of Ss' Opportunity Ratings:	High	5.61	4.74	4.65	4.93
	Low	5.18	4.92	4.83	4.99
	Combined	5.40	4.84	4.75	—

Numbers in boxes are the modes of the high and low Va groups. (After M. Rosen, 1960.)

ence of their *abilities* on $P(s)$ for, as the last three rows in Table 5.15 indicate, their judgments of the *opportunity* (in terms of available jobs) do not correspond to the $P(s)$ estimates. Only those with the highest assigned $P(s)$ (.91) saw the opportunities as significantly better than the other groups. There is no general effect of differences in valence and no interaction between valence and opportunity level. The high $P(s)$-high valence group, however, does not differ significantly in its mean opportunity rating (5.61) from the high $P(s)$-low valence group (5.18). The overall difference between the combined high $P(s)$ (.91) groups and the combined low $P(s)$ (.11) groups is nearly significant at the .05 level: the required value of t is 1.9864; the obtained value is 1.90, with 91 degrees of freedom.

The assessment of changes in valence of the experimental occupation was carried out in two ways, summarized in Tables 5.16 and 5.17. Table 5.16 shows the results of allowing the Ss to revise the position of the experimental occupation on the original rating scale of attractiveness. On their revision the Ss were allowed to put the occupation at *any point* along the scale. A position was counted as *changed* only if S's revision was at least one scale-division distant from its original position, a conservative estimation of change; that is, a highly valenced experimental occupation, originally rated at A (the top of the scale) would be judged as changed in valence only if it fell at B, or lower, in the second rating. This puts limitations on the interpretation of these data because Ss in the high valence group had no room to change upward—all their changes are necessarily downward—while those in the low valence group had room to move in either direction. It is interesting to note that $51/69$ high valence Ss did not change their ratings (by this criterion) but that only $14/70$ low valence Ss failed to change. Within the high valence group there was a greater frequency of downward change as $P(s)$ decreased and the mean *amount* of decline was greater as $P(s)$ decreased; both relations are significant. The effect of $P(s)$ on valence can be seen even more clearly in the low valence group, where there was greater opportunity for movement. Twenty out of 22 Ss in the high $P(s)$ low valence condition revised their ratings upward. In spite of the negative

TABLE 5.16
Numbers of Ss who Changed Rated Valence (Va) of Experimental Occupation and Average Amounts and Directions of Change on a Sixteen-Point Scale, as a Function of P(s) Announced by E and Va Initially Assigned by S

Initial Va Assigned by S	Change in Va	$P(s)$ Announced by E			
		.91 ($n = 22$)	.51 ($n = 23$)	.11 ($n = 24$)	Totals ($n = 69$)
High					
	Up	0	0	0	0
	None	20	19	12	51
	Down	2	4	12	18
	Mean Change	−0.1	−0.8	−1.8	−0.92
Low		($n = 22$)	($n = 25$)	($n = 23$)	($n = 70$)
	Up	20	12	5	37
	Same	0	9	5	14
	Down	2	4	13	19
	Mean Change	+3.9	+2.0	−2.0	+1.28

(After M. Rosen, 1960.)

effect of the two Ss who revised their ratings downward, the net mean increase of 3.9 units is almost one quarter of the total scale—that is, to the next highest grade, from C to B. In the low valence group this tendency to raise valence decreases with decreasing $P(s)$ and the tendency to lower valence increases with increasing $P(s)$ in almost exactly the same proportions of Ss as in the high valence group. All these relations are statistically significant.

These changes in the rated valence of the experimental occupation were not accompanied by any large systematic changes in the cognitive attributes assigned to the various occupations. The data on Rosen's other measure of valence are summarized in Table 5.17. This measure involved analyzing the pre- and post-experimental descriptions of the favorable and unfavorable characteristics of the experimental occupations as written by the Ss. The number of *unfavorable* characteristics (F) was subtracted from the number of *favorable* ones (U) for each S to yield an index (F − U) which could be positive only if more favorable than unfavorable characteristics were mentioned. This index was computed for both the pre- and post-experimental descriptions and the difference between the two indices was taken. Only its sign has been noted in preparing Table 5.17; that

TABLE 5.17
Numbers of Ss Who Made the Indicated Changes in Relative Frequency of Assigning Favorable and Unfavorable Characteristics (F − U) to Experimental Occupations as a Function of Initial Valence (Va) Assigned by S and P(s) Announced by E

Initial Va Assigned by S	Change in (F − U)	P(s) Announced by E			
		.91	.51	.11	Totals
High	Up	11	5	11	27
	None	3	7	3	13
	Down	8	11	10	29
Totals		22	23	24	69
Low	Up	6	11	4	21
	None	10	7	7	24
	Down	6	7	12	25
Totals		22	25	23	70

(After M. Rosen, 1960.)

is, the index is said to increase if $(F - U)$ is larger on the second writing than it was on the first. No change means that the two indices were identical, and a negative change means that $(F - U)$ was smaller on the second writing than on the first. No account was taken of changes in the content of the various kinds of characteristics, nor do the data admit of analysis in terms of which characteristics the Ss thought most important. The data shown in Table 5.17 yield no significant effects of any kind. Indeed, the only trend that can be pointed to is the tendency for a higher proportion of decreases to occur in both high and low valence groups as $P(s)$ gets lower, but even this trend is not absolutely consistent, and it is a weak one. We are still far from understanding the connection between the cognitive assigned characteristics of an object and its rated level of attractiveness, but no doubt there is a connection.

The possibility of such a connection is shown in the final analysis of Rosen's data to be reported here, Table 5.18. The measure of "cognitive overlap" used here is an attempt to realize one of the

TABLE 5.18
Numbers of Ss Who Changed "Cognitive Overlap" of Experimental Occupation with Other Occupations as a Function of Initial Valence (Va) Assigned by S and P(s) Announced by E for Experimental Occupations

Initial Va Assigned by S	Change in "Cognitive Overlap"	$P(s)$ Announced by E			Totals
		.91	.51	.11	
High	Up	4	10	11	25
	None	7	7	6	20
	Down	11	6	7	24
Totals		22	23	24	69
Low	Up	12	4	3	19
	None	5	11	11	27
	Down	5	10	9	24
Totals		22	25	23	70
Combined	Up	16	14	14	44
	None	12	18	17	47
	Down	16	16	16	48
Totals		44	48	47	139

(After M. Rosen, 1960.)

nisms suggested by Festinger (1957) for reducing "cognitive dissonance." To put it briefly, Festinger asserts that among the large number of cognitive elements or "knowledges" that an individual has or
may get, some may be inconsistent or incompatible with others and
this is the condition of "dissonance." Dissonance is psychologically
uncomfortable, according to Festinger, and if it occurs or is likely
to occur then the individual may either engage in cognitive revision
of the dissonant elements in an attempt to reduce the dissonance *or*
he may systematically avoid getting into situations which will produce
dissonance. The likelihood that he will do either of these things increases with the degree of dissonance, which is a function of the relative importance of the conflicting "knowledges" to the individual.
Rosen supposed that his high valence-low $P(s)$ and the low $P(s)$-
high valence conditions, would produce relatively high dissonance,
and so he examined changes in $P(s)$, in belief in the proffered information, in valence, and in "cognitive overlap" as being likely to indicate attempts at dissonance reduction. In the first three of these
variables there was little to support the cognitive dissonance theory.
Now, what about "cognitive overlap?"

Rosen defined this as the degree to which S failed to discriminate
the features of the experimental occupation from those of the other
occupations. He measured it by counting, in both the first and second
occupational descriptions, the number of times that S assigned a feature of the experimental occupation to one of the four other occupations on his initial valence rating scale. Then he looked to see whether
this number increased or decreased between the first and second descriptions. The dissonance reduction theory says that relative failure
to discriminate the features of several items previously graded according to preference will tend to reduce dissonance, since everything will
then be seen as pretty much like everything else. Thus, in the high
valence-low $P(s)$ and the low valence-high $P(s)$ groups, there should
be more cognitive overlap than elsewhere. Furthermore, since the tendency to reduce dissonance is likely to occur only with important issues, this tendency should be more evident in the high valence than
in the low valence group. The first clause of this requirement is met
according to the analysis of Table 5.19, but the second one is not;
that is, there is more increase in cognitive overlap in the highly dissonant conditions *when the valence is high,* but when the valence is
low there is a sizable *increase* in cognitive overlap for high $P(s)$,
and an almost equally proportioned *decrease* when $P(s)$ is 50–50 or
low. It appears, then, that cognitive changes are reported by Ss as
a function of both valence and $P(s)$ for vocational objectives, but

so far we do not have the theory which will account for the changes which do occur. We cannot say for certain under what conditions such changes will take place, nor what their function is.

SUMMARY

To our demonstration that $P(s)$ can be systematically manipulated by changing the type of performance information given to S, and by altering his perception of the importance of the outcome to which his task is instrumental, we first added the demonstration that under certain conditions there is a marked parallel between the course taken by $P(s)$ in successive trials and that taken by S's evaluation of himself as a striver for that particular goal. In this chapter we have further added the fact that people will not stress themselves in task performances when $P(s)$ is low as much as they do when it is high. This can be detected either in S's actual output or in the MAP from his working muscles. Thus, there is a relation between S's perception of his power to achieve something he wants, his estimate of his power as an instrument of achievement, and the extent to which he will spend his energy in pursuit of a goal.

We have also found reason to believe that, if S changes his estimate of his value as an instrument as the result of his use of a single ability, this change in evaluation will be accompanied by corresponding changes in other abilities provided that: (a) the effort expended on the "test" could actually result in getting him to the goal, and that (b) the ability tested was initially highly valued by S. Furthermore, changes in self-evaluation resulting from failure are likely to be accompanied by an increase in spontaneous thinking about death. It is not clear whether success produces corresponding decreases in death-imagery, because control groups seem to decrease their death-imagery about as much as successful people do.

These data go to the point that changes in self-evaluation of single specific abilities may, under appropriate conditions, have more far-reaching effects on *general* self-evaluation than many writers on the subject have so far admitted. We are not disputing the proposition that despair and general self-denigration are characteristic of people who have been crushed, or whose worlds are out of joint. Our question is, under what conditions does such crushing occur, or worlds become bleak, empty, or absurd, and we point to our own experiments with their relevant, if only tentative, answers to these questions as evidence that we need not abandon objective methods of investigation to get our answers.

Chapter 6
THE SOCIAL CONTEXT

Ever since Mead (1934) and Cooley (1922) discussed social influences in the formation of self-related ideas and attitudes, the notion that self is defined, and that self-evaluation takes place, exclusively in social interactions has approached the solidity of holy dogma among social scientists. Among contemporary social psychologists there is a misinterpretation of Festinger's theory of social comparison processes (Festinger, 1954) so that such statements as, "We know that self-evaluation occurs exclusively in social terms," are likely to occur in critiques of innovative thinking in this area. It is not the purpose here to argue at length against that oversimplified notion, but a few points can be made briefly. Self-evaluation can and does occur in private, without social comparisons, as the data from the previously discussed experiments in this book clearly show. Furthermore, Festinger is misunderstood if he is made the modern representative or leading thinker of such a view. His theory of social comparison processes is explicitly *conditional* on this point. Social comparisons are likely to be used as a basis for self-evaluation when more objective criteria are lacking. The fact that Festinger (1954) emphasized intragroup phenomena merely reflected his interest in self-evaluations *in social contexts;* he was not interested in a *general theory* of self-evaluation.

Followers of Freud and borrowers of his ideas have also insisted on the notion of the ubiquity and unique importance of interpersonal relations in self-evaluation. Freud's (1914) notion of the ego ideal, derived from the teachings of parents, parent-surrogates, and a host of other admired or authoritative persons, as the standard by which the ego measured its accomplishments and shortcomings clearly implies a social origin for self-evaluation. However, Freud was never very explicit about the details of the process of evaluation, nor about the terms in which evaluations occurred. From his vague references to the ego's "accomplishments" it can only be inferred that its success in preventing untimely or inexpedient irruptions of actions aimed at gratifying socially forbidden impulses is one of these accomplishments. He also clearly regarded the artist's mastering fantasies and diverting energy to the socially acceptable and useful communication of fantasy as an achievement (Freud, 1908, 1911). Generally, a relatively strong ego, capable of mastering instinctive impulses in accord with the reality and pleasure principles is an achievement of no mean proportions, but exactly what is a strong ego and what are to be accounted among its achievements are points still moot even among the psychoanalysts themselves. Only recently, with the development of latter-day "ego psychology" are they beginning to consider some of the aspects of ability and purposive activity which psychologists have been interested in, independently of psychoanalysis, at least since the days of the Functionalist school, and probably as early as William James (cf. James, 1890; Woodworth, 1918; White, 1959, 1963). There is still plenty of room for speculations which deviate from received doctrine, especially when the doctrine is based so little on fact.

There can be little doubt that the social organization of the community into which an individual is born is decisive for the number and types of goals among which he may choose as he matures. There seems also to be little doubt that no society of which we have any record, certainly no society which depends upon specialization of function to keep it going, has ever been completely successful in pouring every individual into some unbreakable mold. We cannot afford to be led astray by stereotyped descriptions of *modal* personalities in various societies which we hardly understand at all. Many ethnographer's reports speak of "deviants" and what is done about them by the group. Indeed, innovation of any kind would have been impossible during the history of the race without the appearance of individuals who were, in some sense, deviants from the social norms of their day (cf. Barnett, 1953). It is probably safe to say that such creatively deviant individuals were driven by an inner necessity to solve some problem by means which, so far as they knew, had occurred only to them, or they might have been, like Galileo, simply so open to evidence, so assiduous in seeking it out that they were literally forced by external, nonsocial (nay, even antisocial) necessity to revise their views of life and the world. Galileo's life is evidence that this urge to deviate is not always realized in a climate of careless, permissive toleration; often, as it was in his case, innovation is persisted in in spite of the most awful sanctions that society can threaten an individual with (De Santillana, 1955). And even when the probability of the extremest possible sanction rapidly approaches 1.00, some deviants persist either secretly like Roger Bacon, who never was caught out in heresy, or openly like Giorano Bruno, who was caught and killed by the anti-deviants of his day (Singer, 1923).

It is a commonplace, when such cases are in evidence, to observe that not only were these people strangely "driven" but that their evaluations were different from those of the usual member of their societies. Their evaluations of the means-ends chains were obviously different, sometimes to the point of inverting the generally received order; their self-evaluations were probably different too, at least to the extent that they regarded themselves as adequate instruments for carrying out their hitherto unheard-of schemes. This is not intended to say that their mechanisms of valuing were different in kind from those of Everyman, but only that the content of what they valued was different. Derived from evidence which was also available to everybody with eyes to see it,[1] their evaluations were largely independent of those prescribed by established social norms, but, to judge from the tremendous impact of their ideas on subsequent generations, their evaluations were closely relevant to reality. Looking back, we now evaluate many deviants highly, and their detractors or opponents, though at our best we try to understand them sympathetically, we generally value negatively. Indeed, many people are now suggesting that we might be better off if there were more of these useful deviants around. If there were more of them they would be more likely to discover exactly what ails our world and suggest ways to fix it, though the process of fixing it might cause considerable dislocation and inconvenience (if that is not too mild a term) to the interests of individuals who have no quarrel with the *status quo*. There is a considerable and increasing research effort aimed at discovering the personal characteristics of so-called "creative" individuals. Then, it is hoped that the conditions for their generation will be discovered so that they can be fostered and encouraged to accomplish their "creative" best for the benefit of us all (Crutchfield, 1963; Gardner, 1964; Guilford, 1950, 1959; MacKinnon, 1962).

Another point in favor of the possibility of self-evaluation independently of social norms can be made out in the literature on "role-taking" behavior (Sargent, 1951). If a role is a set of expected and prohibited behaviors for holders of particular social positions or statuses, then roles, as described, are certainly not often straitjacket prescriptions which prevent innovation completely. More often they seem to state in a general way the functions that are to be carried out,

---

[1] Galileo pleaded with his adversaries to look through his telescope at the little model of the Copernican solar system—Jupiter and its moons—but they steadfastly refused.

the bad side effects that are to be avoided, the domain to which the expected activities shall apply, and the rest, the details of method, timing, planning, and execution are left up to the individual. Indeed, it is characteristic of high-status roles that they leave relatively great areas of activity open to the free choice of the individual incumbent, while roles of low status are much more detailed and limiting of the individual in their lists of prescriptions and prohibitions. Furthermore, people with high status act with greater independence of group norms than do people with lower status (Feshbach, 1956; Hollander, 1958; Kelley and Shapiro, 1954).

It is possible that modern social scientists who insist on the complete social determination of all self-evaluation are simply defining value by describing its lowest common denominator in a particular society—that is, the modal evaluations approved in the population at large. For instance, what is one to make of the assertion that an "achievement-oriented" culture now exists in the United States, and the associated implication that some societies are less "achievement-oriented?" Does it mean that there are some human beings to whom considerations of purposive action and achievement cannot be applied? Or is it only the savant's underhanded way of sneaking a value referent into a discourse where value referents are officially taboo? In the mouths of many, the assertion that a culture is "achievement-oriented" is an accusation of malefaction, not a statement of fact. Theories of self-evaluation like that sketched in this book are suspect to these people. They might hold, they say, for an "achievement-oriented" society but not for a more "reasonable," humane, less "demanding" society. Haven't our savants fallen into the old cultural relativity trap by refusing to accept that some kind of purposive activity (both appetitive and aversive) and with it, *de facto* achievements or non-achievements, successes and failures, competent (good) and incompetent (not so good, or downright bad) people exist by *any* society's standards? Isn't it easier to see that what differentiates most markedly among the classes of men we call societies is the content or type of the goals they pursue, not the question of whether they have any goals at all? We may not approve of the goals some other men have, or we may not believe they are important enough for us, or we may not believe they are after goals that are "real" in our sense, but that does not get rid of the fact that they are real goals in the sense that they determine behavior by constituting the quiescence (terminating) conditions of more or less long sequences of persistent, organized activity. If such things be, then to say that evaluations are typically different in different societies is to say that some people value "achievement" and others do not. To give a word a merely narrow domain of application is not necessarily the same as defining it precisely. The terms "achievement," "ability," "power," and "probability of success," related to the verifiable processes of purposive activity can be defined with the utmost generality, not merely as pejorative labels for certain features of a particular social organization which is not very widespread spatially and is hardly noticeable on the dimension of time.

The experiments to be discussed in this chapter relate to several topics which are important in current social psychology: (1) the effect of witnessing another person's success or failure on one's own estimated $P(s)$; (2) the effect of different levels of self-evaluation on the extent to which an individual's behavior is affected by actual or implied group pressures—the problem of conformity; and (3) the role of self-evaluation in the choice of associates for an enterprise in which the chooser can evaluate both himself and his potential associates with respect to the ability which must be used in the enterprise. Our argument above must not be construed as indicating that we believe that social factors are ineffective in determining self-evaluations. Rather, we recognize the potential importance of such factors, but we also recognize that self-evaluations, which are independent of any extant social norm, may affect group formation and behavior in groups. It is possible that the influence of social norms and self-evaluations is *mutual*, that cause moves in both directions between them. Our plea is therefore not to disregard social factors in the consideration of self-evaluations, but to get the whole nest of problems out of the realm of dogma and into the realm of questions of fact.

ESTIMATED P(S) DEPENDENT ON OTHERS' SUCCESS

The two experiments under this heading relate to the confusing area of "identification." It is confusing simply because workers in this field cannot agree on basic definitions of terms. Present investigators of these problems trace their intellectual ancestry to Freud, who used "identification" with several different referents. Apparently, he first used "identification" to refer to a person's *playing a significant fragment of a conventional role,* illustrated by the " . . . case of a patient who tore off her dress with one hand (as the man) while she pressed it to her body with the other (as the woman) . . ." (Freud, 1909b). And, similarly, a person with a humorous attitude toward others ". . . is adopting toward the other the attitude of an adult towards a child, recognizing and smiling at the triviality of the interests and sufferings which seem to the child so big. Thus the humorist acquires a superiority by assuming the role of a grown-up, identifying himself to some extent with the father while he reduces the other people to the position of children" (Freud, 1928b, p. 218). This *identification with the father* points to the most famous of Freud's referents for "identification," and one for which he attempted to formulate an explanatory psychological mechanism. However, the explanation does not extend to the important initial component of this referent, namely an infant boy's *feeling of affection* toward his father which is unmixed with rivalry, pre-Oedipal, and pre-ambivalent, and which is itself called identification (Freud, 1921b, 1923, 1925). The Oedipal stage of psychosexual development, during which the boy recognizes that he and his father are competitors for his mother as a love object, is terminated by the almost literal *incorporation* of the parents into the boy's ego, so that his own ego, or part of it, is *identified* with important aspects of both parents (Freud, 1914, 1921b, 1923, 1925, 1928). This incorporation includes the father's powers, so the son can enjoy them at least in fantasy (Freud, 1909b), but it also includes the father's actual or threatened use of these powers to bar the son from usurping certain of the father's prerogatives, especially that of taking the mother as a sexual object (Freud, 1914, 1920, 1921b). This incorporation forms in the ego a "precipitate" which is the core of the ego ideal (Freud, 1914) or superego (Freud, 1923). "Its relation to the ego is not exhausted by the precept: 'You *ought to be* such an such (like your father)'; it also comprises the prohibition: 'You *must not be* such and such (like your father); that is, you may not do all that he does; many things are his prerogative' . . ." (Freud, 1923, p. 44). To the parental core of the superego are later added the influences of other powerful and authoritative people representing education, religion, and political power. Thus, when an individual adopts a humorous attitude toward *himself*, it is his superego taking its original role of parent toward its own ego as child (Freud, 1928b). "Identification" also referred to *affectionate ties among members of groups* (e.g., military or religious groups) which result either from a common love of their leader (Freud, 1921b) or from working together to achieve common ends (Freud, 1921b, 1932), and these influences can make even coerced and exploited classes "identify" with their rulers (Freud, 1927, pp. 22–23).

Both identification with the father, and with other people who share a commom aim, relate to ongoing, or intended, or wished-for appetitive action. Part of the identification with the father arises from the child's wish to have father's powers in order to usurp his prerogatives with the mother. In identification with other people the desire to attain an end, or to maintain one's current position, is equally emphasized. In the latter case Freud did not explicitly mention the usurpation or development of needed or wished-for instrumental powers, but they are there by implication, nonetheless. In fact, his discussion of combinations of weaker individuals to counter the actions of naturally more powerful individuals suggests strongly the mutual lending and borrowing of capacities for a specific purpose (1921b). This comparison points up at once a *similarity* in the acquisition or development of the capacities needed to increase $P(s)$ in some purposive activity, and a *difference* in the goal structure itself. Specifically, in the father-child relation there is but a single object (the mother), so father and son are engaged in a two-person, zero-sum game, to use modern parlance; that is, one of them has to lose. In the group situation, presumably *cooperation* is effective just because, whatever the individuals are after, there is enough for everybody, or at least enough for all the cooperators, so in this kind of game, each cooperator can win at least enough to satisfy him for the moment. Whether the realities of the situation define it as one of cooperation or of competition, the *powers* of the individual as an achiever (or helper-in-achievement) of some goal are clearly in question. This feature of whatever it is we mean by identification appears, with more or less emphasis, in several modern proposals about the concept.

We introduce our experiments with a brief resumé of some recent discussions which link identification closely to purposive activity (Sears 1957; Kagan, 1958b). This will eliminate the bulk of the literature which purports to deal with identification because most writers have taken cognitive-affective similarities between parents and children as the criterion of identification (e.g., Beier and Ratzeburg, 1953; Cava and Raush, 1952; Lazowick, 1955; Payne and Mussen, 1956; Stoke, 1950) though some have urged that a theory of identification should account for differences, as well as similarities, between S and his model (M) (Stoke, 1950). Typically the criterion of identification has been taken as similarities between S's own responses to questionnaires and responses which S *attributes* to his parents (e.g. Beier and Ratzeburg, 1953; Cava and Raush, 1952)[2] or to the parents' own responses to the same questions (e.g., Lazowick, 1955; Payne and Mussen, 1956). The criterion of similarity was accepted by Sanford (1955)

---

[2] Child (1954) pointed out that this method cannot distinguish between *introjection* and *projection*, both of which might arise from the child's desire to resemble his parents.

though he urged that many behaviors called "identification" could be explained by "development," "learning," or "empathy," for example, and that "identification" properly applies only to a narrow range of (mostly unconscious) imitations which are likely to occur during "crises of selfhood" in which S's self-esteem, his physical integrity, or his life itself, are threatened. Thus, "resisting" patients may "identify" with their therapists, or "insecure" children with their parents, by unrealistically, maladaptively trying to be exactly like their *M*s. Such behavior is a rigid, stereotyped, mechanical caricature of *M*'s, rarely an appropriate means to any end in *S*'s long-range interest, but it may be important to S that this similarity is recognized by *M* or by another person.

Sears (1957) described identification as *acting like another person* (one's parents, at first) with respect to: *qualities* (mannerisms, motives, and temperament), *roles* (duties, attitudes, and actions characteristic of particular statuses), and *demands* (standards of conduct imposed on self and others). An infant's mother typically responds to his *de facto* dependence by affectionate nurture and this response develops a secondary *dependency drive* in the infant. However, the mother's gratification of the infant is not perfectly consistent and so, as the child develops, he takes to producing by himself those acts by which his mother has customarily gratified him because, said Sears (1957), at the outset the child cannot distinguish himself from other persons or his acts from theirs. Since the child's own acts bring him gratification (reward or reinforcement) he develops a stable *habit* of imitating and another secondary *"motivational system"* for which the terminating condition (goal) is acting like the mother in *any* way. It is unfortunate that Sears did not apply this description, nor the hypotheses he drew from it, to observations of concrete behavior. No doubt such application would quickly reveal several flaws in the argument; the theory clearly relates to observations about purposive action.

Kagan (1958b) discussed four classes of behaviors which might be thought to have some connection with identification because S resembles *M* ($S \uparrow M$) in all of them.[3] In *imitation learning* $S \uparrow M$ in gestures, dress, speech, etc., because he has been rewarded for "matched dependent" behavior or "copying" (Miller and Dollard, 1941); or because S rewards himself by producing $S \uparrow M$ "to reproduce

---

[3] If we let ($S \uparrow M$) stand for S *resembles, M,* and ($S \downarrow M$) stand for S *does not resemble M,* then we have a handy notation which avoids ambiguities latent in other obvious notations: "r," for *"resembles"* might also suggest *"responds to,"* and "d" for "is *different* from" might suggest *"dislikes."*

bits of the beloved and longed-for person" (Mowrer, 1950, p. 615). In *prohibition learning* S adopts prohibitions from parents or their substitutes, perhaps because he fears rejection and loss of love if he doesn't (Kagan, 1958a; Knight, 1940; Mowrer, 1950; Sanford, 1955; Sears, Maccoby, and Levin, 1957). In *identification with the aggressor* (A. Freud, 1936) S ↑ M who is threatening or aggressive because of S's anxiety over aggression or domination by M. In *vicarious affective experience* S ↑ M affectively because of an event that has happened to M; for example, when children are elated or depressed at the success or failure of a parent, or *vice versa*.

Whatever our view of identification in general, some instances of it may result from "motivation to command or experience the desired goal states of a model . . ." (Kagan, 1958b, p. 298). As we have already seen, this notion accords well with what Freud said about identification of son with father and of group members with one another. Kagan suggested that there are two major goals which S may want to achieve along with M: mastery over the environment, and love and affection.

"Identification is defined as an acquired, cognitive response within a person (S). The content of this response is that some of the attributes, motives, characteristics, and affective states of a model (M) are part of S's psychological organization. The major implication of this definition is that the S may react to events occurring to M as if they occurred to him" (Kagan, 1958b, p. 298). Kagan further specifies that identification is not necessarily available to consciousness nor easily verbalized; that it may vary in strength, not only between Ss, but from time to time within the same S; and that one S may have many different Ms. The conditions which Kagan assumed to be required for the process of identification are: (1) that S perceives that M commands goals which S desires; (2) S wants to be like M to increase the likelihood of his commanding the same goals; (3) identification is reinforced whenever S is told that he is similar to M; (4) the maintenance of identification requires that S perceive similarities between himself and M and that S experience some of the "desired, affective goal states of M" (Kagan, 1958b, p. 300).

These phenomena, imitating the purposive *acts* of another person, adopting the same *goals*, or imitating *both* ends and means, are important because they relate to behavioral development. And we must pursue the origins of self-evaluations-as-instrument into childhood, indeed into infancy, if we can push that far down the age range. In the present book we deal with this problem only incidentally rather than systematically, and in the two experiments to be described next, carried out by Floyd Shupp and Robert Cutick, we grappled as much with the problem of technique as with that of developing theory.

In planning Shupp's experiment we took our lead from Kagan (1958b) since he introduced notions that were most consonant with our own. First, we were alerted by Kagan's notion that "identification" involves S's desire for a goal which he sees another person enjoying. In Kagan's discussion it is left open whether the goal-seeking occurs in a two-person, zero-sum game situation or whether two or more people can enjoy the goal state simultaneously. We thought it would be easier, with techniques already familiar to us, to explore the latter situation. We were also intrigued by Kagan's assertion that S may desire to be like M to increase the likelihood of his enjoying the same goals and that "identification" (perhaps this desire itself) is reinforced whenever S is "told" that he is like M. Now it is exactly on this issue of the "likeness" of S and M that writers on identification are least clear and where the empirical data are weakest. They are unclear and weak because, with the exception of Miller and Dollard's (1941) experiments on "copying," they never specify clearly *exactly in what respects* there should be likeness between S and M, they do not set up outcome contingencies to control the relative importance to S of various modes of likeness, and they usually have no way of determining in advance whether S for any reason regards this or that specific likeness between M and himself as more or less important. We thought we could do a little better than that. Specifically, if S wants to be like M (or is pleased to learn that he *is* like M) because this increases the likelihood that he will get the goals that M can get, then it seems that S should value most, and react most strongly to, his likeness to M *in those abilities which are relevant to acquiring the goal of the moment.* Kagan's discussion implies that if S does not want a particular goal then even if he sees M get it and enjoy it, he should be relatively indifferent to his actual, or prospective, possession of the abilities by which M got the goal.

How would we know whether or not S was indifferent regarding an actual or potential likeness to M? Here again, we took our clue from Kagan. It seemed to us that his view of the hallmark of identification that distinguishes it from all other instances of S's being or wanting to be like M lies in what he called "the major implication" of his definition of identification: "that the S may react to events occurring to M as if they occurred to him" (Kagan, 1958b, p. 298).

The previous discussion suggests that identifications of the sort referred to may terminate if S discovers that M does not have the power to achieve the goals S wans, or when S chooses different goals than M, or when S has so thoroughly explored his own capacities that he has developed his own standards and techniques for goal accomplishment. Identification should occur more frequently in Ss whose confidence in their abilities is relatively low, so that their self-evaluation is either low or uncertainly based. Different aspects of S's goals and means techniques may be derived from different Ms. Furthermore, S may not be aware of the similarity between his and M's behavior even if, in some sense, identification with M has occurred. As Kagan pointed out, not all similarities in the behavior of two people need imply that they are identified. Such similarities may result, even without identification, if two people are affected by the same determining conditions, or because one of them can *force* the other to do as he does. To translate Kagan's criterion into an experiment, we supposed that S's estimate of his own $P(s)$ for a given goal might be raised if he sees another person succeed and lowered if the other fails, and that this effect ought to depend on S's observation of M's power to move toward the goal, and on S's similarity to M in those characteristics that are relevant to getting the goal.

Shupp's experiment had a limited objective: to test whether the criterion, responding to another's fate at though it were one's own, is available in any practical sense; that is, could we get people to make statements about their own expected fate under conditions where we could tell whether or not it was influenced by the fate of another person.

Accordingly, in our situation three people watched each other working to achieve the same goal. Because the goal was available to all of them independently, they could not be said to be competing for it. We took no special precautions to note or prevent the spontaneous rise of competition in the sense that one would derive greater satisfaction if he succeeded where others failed, or if he succeeded first. However, there is little evidence that such competitive attitudes, if they occurred, had much effect on the outcomes. We also arranged that S would be likely to see that, in the rate at which his performance approached the goal, he resembled one person (M) and not the other $(\text{non-}M)$. Half the Ss saw M succeed; the other half saw him fail. Non-Ms always failed.

The Ss, 64 white male undergraduates at the University of Pennsylvania, were assigned randomly to the eight experimental conditions defined by two kinds of Ms ($M1$ and $M2$), two orders in which M and non-M worked (M first vs. non-M first) and the two fates of M (success vs. failure). All Ss (and Ms and non-Ms) worked on the card-sorting task used in our first $P(s)$ experiments (see Chapter 4) under low motivation instructions. A performance display panel eight feet long was mounted on a wall of the laboratory room so that it was directly in front of S when he sat down at the table to sort cards. The panel was divided vertically into three equal areas, each labeled with the name of one of the three undergraduates present, and each area was marked like a graph to show trials, performance level, performance goal, and deadline.

When S reported for his session in the experiment he was introduced to two other undergraduates who were also said to be Ss. The E said we were saving time by having three Ss present at once, and we could give each a rest period after his first five trials while the others were working. Actually the other two students were E's paid confederates who had been trained and fully informed about all parts of the experiment. Hereafter, they are referred to as M1 or M2 if their performance curves were similar to S's. The confederate whose performance curve differed from S's is called non-M. The confederates were all psychology majors, either juniors or seniors. The real Ss were all lowerclassmen, not psychology majors, and they knew the confederates only casually, if at all. After the introductions, E explained the card-sorting task, using low motivation instructions (see Chapter 4, pp. 131–133, 145–146), and the layout of the performance display panel and its use. He then continued, "Since we have only one set of cards, and one stopwatch, we can run only one person at a time. But in order to offset boredom, and other possible effects of just waiting, we will divide the task into two sets of five trials each, with a rest period between them, while the others are working. Of course you will be able to see each other work. We will decide on the order in which you work by drawing straws. Long straw goes first, short straw goes last." The straw drawing was "rigged" so that S was always the last to start. Thus, when S began to work he had before him the performance curves of the two confederates over the first five trials. As his own performance curve was inserted into the panel, peg by peg, he could see that his was quite like one (M's) and very different from the second (non-M's). This was our sole similarity manipulation. No verbal assertion was ever made about similarities among the three students.

The performance curves were controlled, as usual, by E's stopping each trial when a predetermined number of cards had been sorted, without regard to the real elapsed time. This method involved some risk that while S was not actively working he would notice the time discrepancies and get suspicious. We attempted to reduce this risk by training the confederates until they were very facile card-sorters and could pace themselves so as to sort the predetermined number of cards in a time period that was relatively constant over trials. Furthermore, the confederates were so familiar with the design of the experiment that *E* had only to tell *S* (in their hearing) that he was "subject number so-and-so" in order for each confederate to know what performance curve he was supposed to produce.

It was impossible, even by training the confederates, to match true times from trial to trial. *S* might amuse himself during his rest period by doing a little timing on his own account. So, if *S* had a watch, *E* went into an act representing a harassed, overworked graduate student, trying to please a slave-driving professor; said he had forgotten his own watch—and borrowed *S*'s on the spot and thereafter kept it where *S* could not see it. As another means of allaying any suspicions *S* might develop, the performance curves used were slightly irregular in form, and though *S*'s performance curve was clearly more like *M*'s than non-*M*'s, the two were not absolutely identical. The performance curves for *M1* and *M2* and *S* are shown in Fig. 6.1. If *S*'s performance curve resembled that of *M1*, then non-*M*'s curve was the *failure* curve for *M2*, and *vice versa*.

Before the first of the trio began sorting cards, each was given a packet of blank *P(s)* rating scales and their use was explained.

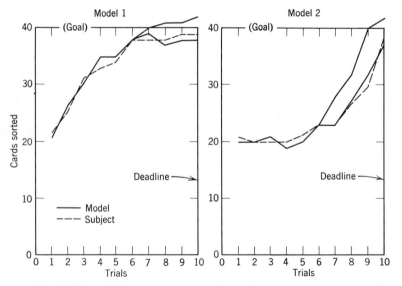

Fig. 6.1 Rigged performance curves used in Shupp's experiment to induce *S* ↑ *M* for two curve-types and *M*'s success or failure. See text for explanation.

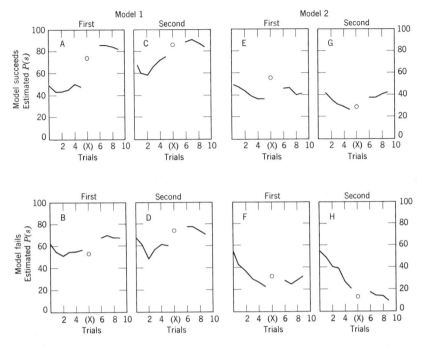

Fig. 6.2 Course of Ss' mean estimated $P(s)$ by conditions in Shupp's experiment. Each data point is the mean of eight Ss.

Each of the students estimated $P(s)$ for himself before the first trial and for every trial thereafter, but only while he was working. All estimates referred only to the rater's expectation that *he* would succeed and were kept strictly private. Though their ratings were meaningless, the confederates went through the motions of making them, as part of the stage setting. After S had completed his first five trials, the confederate who had started first completed his second five and it was evident to all whether he had succeeded or failed. Thereupon S and the other confederate each made an additional $P(s)$ estimate *for himself*, labeled "trial X." Thus, changes in S's estimated $P(s)$ between trial 5 and "trial X" indicate the effect on S of the success or failure of the first M (or non-M); changes between "trial X" and trial 6 indicate the effect of the fate of the second M (or non-M).

The results, and the design of the experiment are summarized in Fig. 6.2. It is clear that when M succeeded *first*, there was a significant increase in S's mean $P(s)$ between trials 5 and X. If M succeeded *second*, the net change was smaller, but the significantly larger

TABLE 6.1

Mean changes in P(s) *Between Indicated Trials*

	Change Between Trials:	
	5 and X	X and 6
Model succeeds		
First	22.1	1.3
Second	5.8	7.8
Model fails		
First	2.5	4.8
Second	4.3	2.3

Note, all signs are positive; $n = 8$ for each mean.
(Data collected by Floyd Shupp.)

portion of it occurred between trials X and 6. The overall mean changes are summarized in Table 6.1.

Since all these mean changes are positive, the expectation that M's failure would lead to lowering of S's $P(s)$ is not confirmed. Over all conditions, the mean gain in $P(s)$ after M's success (15.0) is significantly greater than that following M's failure (2.4) or the failure of non-M (4.1). Though the gain was smaller when M failed than if non-M failed, the difference is not significant. Thus it appears that S's $P(s)$ estimates were affected only by M's *success* in reaching the goal they are both seeking. Ss seemed to detach their fate from, perhaps never attached it to, that of failing Ms even if M and S were very similar in the way their performances approached the goal. However this may be interpreted, it does not fit the simple assumption that S, assuming regularity in the world, picks out people who resemble him and uses their fate to predict his own. The use of another's fate to predict one's own is probably complicated by the desire to succeed.

Sometimes a person may not actually have evidence that he possesses the same power as another person to gain a goal which they are both after; indeed, the evidence may be that he does not have it. In either case, he presumably desires it. So he may not be affected by failures who resemble him, no matter what their early promise, but instead shifts his allegiance to another person, who may be unlike him and a failure in the bargain, but whose performance gives such evidence of power that S's hope of success continues or is revived.

Some such explanation may account for S's responses to non-Ms with positively accelerated performance curves (non-$M2$). Regardless of the fate of M, or whether it occurred first or second, Ss in all conditions raised their $P(s)$ estimates, on the average, by 10.4 to 14.3 points as soon as non-$M2$ had completed his last trial; on the other hand, the mean changes when non-$M1$'s fate was known ranged from —9.0 to 1.3. Table 6.2 is designed to show that this effect is independent of the order of M and non-M and of the fate of M, and thus depends only on the form of the $M1$ and $M2$ performance curves. The difference between the two conditions is significant below the .01 level by the median test. The positively accelerated curve of non-$M2$ showed just what S needed—power to make rapid improvements in his performance in the last few trials; while the curve of non-$M1$ showed nothing S needed, but rather something he probably did not want—a steady decline in the rate of improvement ending in a dead level several units below the goal.

Thus, changes in $P(s)$ show that Ss responded to a successful, but not to a failing M. This indicates that S did not use M's fate simply to predict his own. Furthermore, when non-$M2$ demonstrated power to approach the goal rapidly in the later trials, S raised $P(s)$; but if non-M showed no such power, S's $P(s)$ declined. This suggests wishful, or fearful, responses on S's part which are independent of perceived similarity between himself and another person with respect to rate of approach to the goal.

Our interest in this experiment lies mainly in its relevance to the kind of evidence one uses in evaluating his ability as an instrument for achieving goals he desires. From the data it appears that there are some conditions in which one's estimated $P(s)$ depends on his observations of other people's attempts to achieve the same goal. We should be able to specify these conditions more fully by experiments to answer the following questions. What variations in age, race, sex,

TABLE 6.2
Mean Change in S's P(s) *Estimates in Response to:*

	Non-$M1$	Non-$M2$		Non-$M1$	Non-$M2$
A. When M goes			B. When M		
First	−1.2	12.5	Succeeds	−3.9	11.0
Second	−6.3	12.4	Fails	−3.6	13.8

(Data collected by Floyd Shupp.)

social status, or physical condition will make a person accept another as M? Is it necessary that such variations all be open to objective inspection, or can they be mediated merely by the verbal assertion of similarity, as Kagan (1958b) suggested? Can we make different Ms acceptable or unacceptable merely by changing the goal S is working for, a notion also derivable from Kagan's notions (Kagan, 1958b)? Will acceptance of a person as M in one situation generalize to accepting him as M under other conditions? Can we get evidence that S seeks to increase the resemblance between himself and M, and if so, in what respects and under what conditons? To what extent can we test Kagan's assertion that identification should decrease as S becomes more independent in the choice of goals and of means for attaining them? In this connection, we offer the hypothesis that low self-evaluation, or lack of a clear basis for high self-evaluation, will be most likely to produce identification, especially when attempts at mastery occur. Thus, the importance of identification should be greatest in childhood, and thereafter should decrease with advancing age. With age held constant, identification should be a more important process for people whose self-evaluation is low. This latter hypothesis was tested by Robert Cutick (1962).

Cutick used the same criterion of identification that Shupp had borrowed from Kagan, but he noted that not all theories accept the view on which this criterion is based. Identification may be a case of incidental learning (Bandura and Huston, 1961; Stotland and Hillmer, 1962), a special case of generalization of perceived similarity in which S believes he shares both good and bad attributes of M because they are *contiguous in* M (Stotland and Hillmer, 1962). Some of these authors had earlier emphasized *selective* generalization of perceived similarity which S employed instrumentally to acquire only desired traits and thereby improved his self-evaluation (Stotland, Zander, and Natsoulas, 1961; Burnstein, Stotland, and Zander, 1961).

So there is some disagreement with the notion that identification is used instrumentally to improve S's evaluation of his goal-getting powers and thus to increase his self-evaluation. This body of opinion is not well supported by data and it is clearly at variance with Shupp's data, which indicate selectivity in the direction of increasing $P(s)$.

One important determiner of identification, according to Kagan's (1958b) views, is the general level of self-evaluation that S brings with him to the situation. A number of considerations suggest that Ss low in general self-evaluation will identify more readily than those whose self-evaluation is high. If S is generally confident of his ability to achieve his goals he should be less likely to identify with successful

Ms; but Ss lacking in self-confidence should more readily seize on the evidence of their similarity to successful Ms because they lack their own independent evidence that they are competent to achieve the goals they want. Furthermore, if there is anything to the notion that identification serves to reduce threats, then the greater the threat, the more likely we are to see identification. If we assume that people whose self-evaluation is already low would be aroused to avoid prospective failures more than those whose self-evaluation is high, then this is simply another way of saying what has already been said about the greater likelihood of identification among those with low self-evaluation. Finally, Kagan asserted that identification is less likely among those who have achieved a measure of independence in their views of themselves as adequate instruments for goal attainment, and this may be related to their having relatively stable or "impenetrable" "self-concept" (Engel, 1959; Stotland and Cottrell, 1962; Stotland, Thorley, Thomas, Cohen, and Zander, 1957). From these assertions Cutick (1962) argued that he would get more evidence of identification from a group of people who came to the experiment with relatively low self-evaluations; and that he would also get more, according to Kagan, from Ss who were *informed* that $S \uparrow M$; and, following Shupp's results, that in any case there would be more evidence of identification with successful Ms.

His first problem was to find a way of measuring initial general self-evaluation so that he could select Ss who were low and others who were high on this measure. After carefully examining several extant "instruments" for measuring "global" self-evaluation, or self-acceptance, or positive self-concept, we decided that none of them was quite suitable because they involved tortuous assumptions and interpretations in their scoring, or they did not specify the conditions which S was to assume in giving his answers. Therefore we constructed a self-evaluation questionnaire in accordance with our view that people evaluate themselves as goal-achieving instruments, using the same general format developed by Magaziner and Isabelle Cetlin for their studies of the spread of evaluative effect (cf. Appendix D). Cutick's questionnaire is reproduced in Appendix E. The first seven items refer to specific abilities and the eighth is intended as a "global" or summary scale.

This questionnaire was filled out by all students who volunteered to participate in Cutick's experiment before they were accepted as Ss. The features of this scale which are especially important from our viewpoint are that (1) each of the items, except the eighth, asks about a specific class of purposive activity, (2) the classes of purposive acts

are such that any person should have experienced them relatively frequently, (3) the classes are not defined with respect to specific means
of accomplishment, and (4) S's mode of response, indicating the proportion of times he thinks he acted satisfactorily, is neither unrealistically restricted to the "Yes," "No," or "Uncertain" categories so often
used, nor are the questions so indeterminate as to ask "Do you ever
do . . . ?" As will be seen from Cutick's data and from our uses of
this questionnaire in other contexts (cf. Chapters 7 and 8), there is
some reason to believe that it is a sufficiently *valid* measure of self-
evaluation for our purposes. Another attractive feature of the questionnaire is that it is easily alterable for special purposes. Classes of
purposive activity can be added or removed from the list, and the
response can be made by S with a pencil, or he can respond orally
or by moving a mechanical pointer on a scale.

Cutick recruited his Ss, all men, from first-year English and introductory psychology classes at the University of Pennsylvania and
Brooklyn College. He said that he was part of a research team working
for the fictitious "National Institute for Higher Education." The team
was investigating a battery of tests, developed by psychologists,
which could accurately predict success in graduate school; and the
immediate problem was to get normative data from students in large
Eastern colleges and universities. Each man in the class was then
given a booklet. The first page of the booklet asked for "Preliminary
Information" to "aid in proper classification of . . . test results:"
name, campus address and telephone number, school and class, major
field, fraternity affiliation, occupational choice, and marital status. At
the top of the next page appeared the following instructions: "Describe yourself as an individual, focusing on your most important and
typical personal traits, habits, and beliefs. Include both those which
you regard as favorable and those with which you are dissatisfied."
The remainder of the page was blank and the students wrote their
paragraphs there. The page for the self-descriptive paragraph was followed by the self-evaluation questionnaire just described.

During the recruiting speech, E explained that the biographical
and personal information was necessary for proper classification and
therefore the students should be as candid as possible in supplying
it. He assured them that the results of the tests would be kept confidential and would affect neither their current standing as students
nor as potential applicants for graduate school, and that they would
be given their test results immediately after they finished the test.
They were told that the task was interesting and involved no physical
pain, and that they would each be paid one dollar for approximately

25 minutes of their time. The *E* also said that he had found it efficient and time-saving to have two people take the test together, if possible, so some of them could expect to have another student working along with them. As in Shupp's procedure, the other "test takers" were *E*'s paid confederates. There were eight of them, fully informed about the nature of the experiment and trained in their roles, and each was assigned randomly several times to each of the experimental conditions to reduce the likelihood that *M*'s personal characteristics would get confounded with the experimental conditions. Care was taken to see that *S*s and *M*s were not well acquainted with each other, and after they were introduced at the beginning of the experimental session their interaction was strictly determined by *E*'s and *M*'s role-playing as prescribed by the experimental plan.

The sum of each *S*'s self-ratings on the eight scales of the self-evaluation questionnaire was used as his score, and the frequency distribution of these scores was tabulated for the 163 initial respondents. The distribution was divided into thirds and ultimately 50 *S*s were selected from the lower third (the low self-evaluation group) and 50 from the upper third (the high self-evaluation group). The students from these two groups were assigned randomly, at the rate of ten from each group, to our experimental conditions, and one control condition.

In the control condition there was no *M* present. With this exception, and the absence of critical references by *E* to the likeness or dissimilarity of *S* and *M*, the control and experimental conditions were identical. After *S* arrived at the laboratory room, the *M* appeared and the two "volunteers" were introduced. After they were seated, *E read* instructions—"to insure standard testing procedures:"

As indicated in the booklet you were given, we are in the process of collecting norms for one of a large battery of tests used to determine admissions to graduate school. It has already been used to good advantage by many schools—professional, as well as graduate schools of arts and sciences.

Even though the test is short and relatively easy to give, it requires skill in a number of mental functions necessary for success in graduate school. You'll be able to appreciate this more when you see it and actually work at it.

We'd like you to do the very best you can. If you apply your abilities in the best way you can, your performance will give you a good idea of where you stand in relation to other groups, such as medical students, engineers, etc. We'll give you your score right after the test so you can see just how well you've done.

At this point E suggested that they might want to know how they compared with other volunteers. Then he continued:

So much for the preliminaries.

The test is a card-sorting task in which you are required to correctly sort 35 cards into the appropriate ten piles, according to the designs on each card. You'll have ten trials to do this. Each trial is 25 seconds long, and your score for each trial will be the number of cards you've sorted correctly within that time limit. If either of you satisfy this success criterion within the ten-trial deadline, you'll all be finished. In order to let you know how you're progressing from trial to trial, we'll plot your scores after each trial on this pegboard graph. In this way you'll be able to see how well you are doing and how many trials you have left.

The test demands not only concentration, but manual dexterity, visual-motor coordination, memory and learning as well. In order to reduce the effects of fatigue and boredom, one of you will go first for five trials, and then will rest while the other fellow does his first five trials. Then the first fellow will finish his last five trials, and so on. Is that clear?

Just one more thing before we start the test itself. Immediately before every trial I'm going to ask you what you think your chances are of correctly sorting 35 cards within 25 seconds on any one of your remaining trials. You'll do that by marking this scale as follows.

The E showed S and M a sample of the $P(s)$ scale described in Chapter 4 and told them how to use it. Throughout, the instructions were modified from plural to singular address for Ss in the control condition.

The actual procedure was like that of any other $P(s)$ experiment, and like Shupp's experiment, except that only one M was present. The rigged performance curves allotted to S and M are shown in Fig. 6.3. All Ss had identical performance curves, and they differed slightly from the M's curves. However, the M's curves were all identical over the first five trials. Over the last five trials they differed, as Fig. 6.3 shows, to define M's succeeding and failing. The breaks in the curves indicate that after M worked for five trials he and S changed places and S did his first five trials.

Another experimental variable—the allegation of similarity or dissimilarity between S and M—was introduced between trials 5 and 6. Both M and S were instructed to estimate $P(s)$ for the sixth trial only just before beginning that trial, after the rest period. Thus, S could see M's final fate (pass or fail) before he estimated his own $P(s)$ for the sixth trial. Also, after M's fate was known, but before S had recorded his own $P(s)$ prior to the sixth trial, E remarked to both the men that he generally tried to schedule for a single ses-

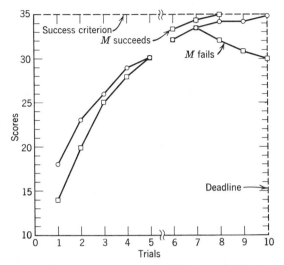

Fig. 6.3   Rigged performance curves reported for Ss and Ms in Cutick's (1962) experiment.

sion two students who were alike in background, interests, and attitudes, as judged from what they said about themselves in their preliminary questionnaires. Doing this, he said, enabled him to fill up the cells in the normative table at an even rate. He then told half the Ss (the S↑M group) that he had been eminently successful in doing this in their case; but to the other half (the S↑M group) he said that due to a last-minute substitution (the M's) he had been unable to do so; in fact it was notable how *different* the two of them were. In these remarks E never mentioned similarity or dissimilarity in skills, abilities, or capacities, because he was attempting to make a rigorous test of the notion that identification might take place even if similarity were asserted on dimensions not relevant to the task.

Thus there were eight treatment conditions comprised of two levels of each of the three dependent variables: S↑M versus S↓M; Ss high versus low in self-evaluation; and M succeeded versus M failed. There were two control groups, one for each level of self-evaluation, who took the test with no M present. In the interval between trials five and six, the control Ss were instructed to rest for two or three minutes, corresponding to the time it took in the experimental groups for S and M to exchange seats and for E to deliver the similarity-dissimilarity information.

TABLE 6.3

Selected Characteristics of P(s) Trends from Experimental and Control Groups in Cutick's (1962) Experiment

	High S-E		Low S-E		Combined (n = 20)	
	$S \uparrow M$	$S \downarrow M$	$S \uparrow M$	$S \downarrow M$	$S \uparrow M$	$S \downarrow M$
Overall	62.2	70.2	54.5	63.8	58.4	67.0
0–4	45.4	60.0	41.4	49.3	43.4	54.7
5–9	78.9	80.4	67.6	78.3	73.3	79.4
M Succeeded 4	60.9	71.2	40.5	64.8	50.7	68.0
5	67.0	71.0	55.0	65.4	61.0	68.2
(5) − (4)	+6.1	−0.2	+14.5	+0.6	+10.3	+0.2
(5–9) − (4)	+18.0	+9.2	+27.1	+13.5	+22.6	+11.4
Overall	70.4	70.4	64.4	68.8	67.4	69.6
0–4	61.3	61.5	53.9	63.8	57.6	62.7
5–9	79.6	79.3	74.9	73.8	77.3	76.6
M Failed 4	73.8	67.0	65.6	70.0	69.7	68.5
5	75.1	71.1	69.0	64.3	72.1	67.7
(5) − (4)	+1.3	+4.1	+3.4	−5.7	+2.4	−0.8
(5–9) − (4)	+5.8	+12.3	+9.3	+3.8	+7.6	+8.1
Overall	77.5		61.5			
0–4	70.1		51.2			
5–9	84.9		71.9			
Control 4	78.8		60.9			
5	80.0		62.0			
(5) − (4)	+1.2		+1.1			
(5–9) − (4)	+6.1		+11.0			

	High S-E		Low S-E	
Combined (n = 20)	$S \uparrow M$	$S \downarrow M$	$S \uparrow M$	$S \downarrow M$
Overall	76.3	70.3	60.0	66.3
0–4	53.4	60.8	47.7	56.6
5–9	76.3	79.9	71.3	76.1
4	67.4	69.1	53.1	67.4
5	71.1	71.1	62.0	64.9
(5) − (4)	+3.7	+2.0	+8.9	−2.5
(5–9) − (4)	+8.9	+10.8	+18.2	+8.7

TABLE 6.3 (*Continued*)

Experimental (n = 40)	All High S-E	All Low S-E
Overall	73.3	63.2
0–4	57.1	52.2
5–9	78.1	73.7
4	68.3	60.3
5	71.1	63.5
(5) − (4)	+2.8	+3.2
(5–9) − (4)	+9.8	+13.4

(n = 10, except when otherwise noted)

Selected characteristics of the $P(s)$ trends are shown in Table 6.3 for all the treatments, conditions, and various combinations of them. The table also summarizes the design of the experiment. First it should be noted that the high S-E Ss, both in experimental and control conditions, have significantly higher overall mean $P(s)$ estimates than low S-E Ss in corresponding conditions and, as Fig. 6.4 shows, this difference is consistent over trials. This is evidence for the validity of the self-evaluation questionnaire, if only in the sense that Ss selected on the basis of their different responses on that questionnaire also show systematic differences in the way they respond to a standard experimental procedure. However, the evidence goes beyond that, for it shows a relation between *pre-measured* self-evaluation with respect to a number of specific abilities and S's expectation that another ability is powerful enough to succeed in a particular undertaking. In interpreting the experiment we may presume that the Ss considered as high or low in self-evaluation really do differ in that way.

The curves in Fig. 6.4 also show another interesting difference between the high S-E Ss and their low S-E counterparts. Among the high S-E experimental Ss overall mean $P(s)$ (73.3) is significantly lower than for the high S-E controls (77.5)—and this is so on every trial. Among the low S-E Ss the reverse relation holds between experimental (63.2) and control (61.5), though to be sure the difference is smaller and exceptions occur (trials 0, 4, and 6, Fig. 6.4)—and the difference is not significant. We cannot say why it should be that people with high general self-evaluation should set lower $P(s)$ estimates just because another person works in the same room on the same test. This cannot be due to similarity or success considerations because it shows up during the first five trials when no such differences had been introduced. Nor can it be due to actual publicity of the $P(s)$ estimates because both S and M kept them private throughout the experiment; and E paid them no attention, except to be sure that S made them when he was supposed to. We cannot say, before it is verified in other data, whether this is a genuine finding. If it is, we need still other data before we understand the conditions that produce it.

Since, between the recording of his fifth and sixth $P(s)$ estimates, S saw M succeed or fail and heard that he and M were alike or dissimilar, we looked at changes between the fifth and sixth $P(s)$ estimates as one of the dependent variables. It is possible, however, that changes occurring after trial five as a function of our experimental treatments would be delayed to some later trial or would show up only as differences in trends in the second halves of the $P(s)$ curves. Consequently there are two other dependent variables: (1) the difference between $P(s)$ before trial five and the *average* $P(s)$ over the last five trials, and (2) differences in trends (slopes) during the last five trials. A major problem in analyzing these data arises from the fact that mean $P(s)$ levels before trial 5 differ widely over the various conditions, so if that trial is taken as the reference point for figuring

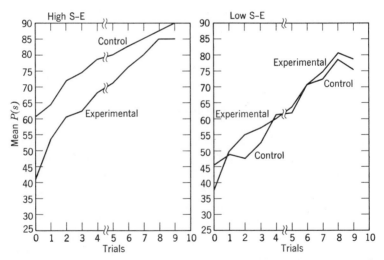

Fig. 6.4 Comparison of mean $P(s)$ trends of Ss high and low in initial self-evaluation when M was present (experimental) and when no M was present (control). Each data point in the control conditions is the mean of 10 Ss; in the experimental conditions, each point is the mean of 40 Ss. (After Cutick, 1962.)

changes, not all groups start from the same base line. This was accounted for by analyzing the data by covariance analysis, with variations in fifth $P(s)$ level held constant statistically. This was done for the change from fifth to sixth $P(s)$ and for change between fifth $P(s)$ and mean $P(s)$ over the last five trials.

By this analysis, the gain between fifth and sixth $P(s)$ means was significantly greater when $S \uparrow M$ (+6.3) than when $S \downarrow M$ (−0.3), and this is the only difference that was significant by the analysis. The gains between the fifth $P(s)$ and the average $P(s)$ over the last five trials were in the expected direction (13.6 for $S \uparrow M$, and 9.8 for $S \downarrow M$), but the difference was not significant. These data are given in Table 6.3 and summarized graphically in Fig. 6.5.

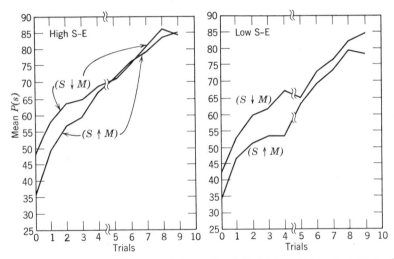

Fig. 6.5 Comparison of mean $P(s)$ trends of Ss high and low in initial self-evaluation when $S \uparrow M$ and when $S \downarrow M$, experimental groups only. Each data point is the mean of 20 Ss. (After Cutick, 1962.)

Changes between fifth $P(s)$ and mean $P(s)$ for the last five trials were also significantly greater when M succeeded (17.0) than when he failed (7.9), and they were greater for Ss *low* in self-evaluation (13.4) than for those whose self-evaluation was high (9.8). The success-failure comparison is shown graphically in Fig. 6.6, and the comparison of low and high S-E in Fig. 6.4.

These outcomes, though they are in the predicted direction, do not go far enough to support our hypothesis. We expected that generally there would be little or no change in $P(s)$ in any condition if M failed, *and* that relatively large positive changes would occur if M

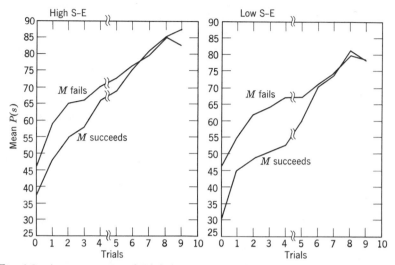

Fig. 6.6   Average course of $P(s)$ for experimental groups high and low in initial self-evaluation, when M failed and when M succeeded. Each data point is the mean of 20 Ss. (After Cutick, 1962.)

succeeded, *and* that the positive changes would be significantly largest in the Ss with low self-evaluation. In the language of analysis of variance this is asking for a significant "triple interaction" of $S \uparrow M \times M$'s fate $\times$ Ss' self-evaluation. As Fig. 6.7 shows, the obtained form of the interaction in both dependent variables is just what we predicted, but alas it is not significant. Generally, it is the Ss with low self-evaluation whose $P(s)$ changes are most responsive to the similarity and fate of the model, but the experiment certainly offers no resounding statistical support for that view.

On the other hand, the experiment offers no reason to abandon the hypothesis. Together with the non-chance findings that we did obtain, the fact that all relevant differences were of the kind we had predicted leaves us believing still in the hypothesis and willing to put the blame on the experiment (which didn't do what we wanted it to) or on ourselves as experimenters. From a purely technical viewpoint, the experiment had two disadvantages.

The first of these disadvantages is the enormous variability among the Ss in all conditions with respect to the various measures of change in $P(s)$. In attempting to prove that the means are different by a conventional statistical criterion, we put this inter-subject variability in the logical position of *error*—and error it surely is, but it may not all be random error. The distributions of change scores for the high and low S-E group differ in that the lows have more *large* changes in both directions than do the highs. In the lows the changes between fifth and sixth $P(s)$ estimates range from 42 to −32 *on a 100-point scale;* among the highs the range is from 18 to −21. This suggests that perhaps in both groups there were included some Ss whose scores on the self-evaluation scale did not reflect their self-evaluation as it might be revealed by their choice of goals, or their behavior in the face of difficulty or criticism. Some of them might not have had a very firm idea about their various abilities, and others simply did not want to say what they really thought. We have criticized the questionnaires used by the "self-concept" students on exactly these grounds and we have no desire to argue that our questionnaire is immune to these defects. Suppose, for whatever reason, that there are both

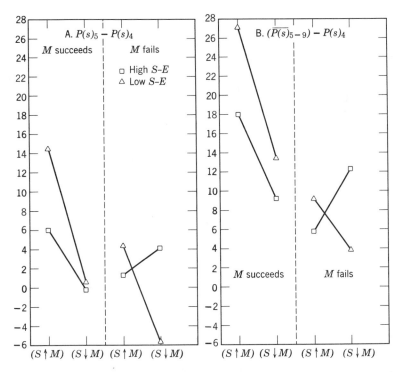

Fig. 6.7 Changes in mean $P(s)$ estimates between indicated points in the sequence of trials, experimental conditions only. A: Change from $P(s)_4$ to $P(s)_5$. B: Change from $P(s)_4$ to mean $P(s)$ over the last five trials (5–9). Each data point is the mean of 10 Ss. (After Cutick, 1962.)

false highs and false lows in our different self-evaluation groups, and suppose further that these falsely classified people could not avoid behaving objectively in terms of their real value as goal-achieving instruments. On these assumptions, then, their presence should inflate the variability in our dependent variables, and the way to deflate it is to get rid of the false highs and false lows. Just how to do this we are not sure. Perhaps some kind of screening interview would help, or perhaps we should take preliminary tests of their reactions to objective tests of some of their real abilities. Perhaps we could extend this preliminary testing to a program of shaping them to evaluate in accordance with objective criteria. Whatever can be done, we have not yet done it.

The other deficiency of the experiment is that the motivational pressure on the Ss was relatively low. On the one hand we told them that what they were doing was relevant to goals that were important for some people, but we never bothered to find out whether these goals were important to our Ss. Furthermore, the instructions included both ego-involving and non-ego-involving elements which may have tended to mutually cancel each other's effects. S was urged to do well on the test, but if he actually tried to do well it was just because he was a good fellow and tried to please the E. What pressure was on him to exert himself when he was told (a) that the test would have no effect on *his* chances of getting into graduate school (supposing he wanted to go there) and (b) that *he* was helping to establish the standards by which his peer group would presumably be judged in its performance on the test? There is every reason to believe that if the motivational pressure was stronger and clearer, the effects we looked for (and found) would be even more pronounced, even to the point of overriding sizeable random errors. We can certainly make the motivational pressures stronger than we made them in this experiment.

To sum up, whether or not it is agreed that the phenomena we have been studying in these two experiments throw any light on the concept of identification, the experiments have told us something about the conditions under which a person will use the evidence of another's success or failure to influence his own. Both experiments indicate that the S will *raise* his $P(s)$ to a greater extent after witnessing the success of M whom he resembles. Together, the two experiments seem to indicate that it makes no difference whether S sees objectively that he is like M with respect to the way his performance approaches the goal they are both after, or whether S is merely told that he resembles M in ways that are not necessarily relevant to this particular attempt at goal achievement. Shupp's experiment suggests that S will shift his identification if he sees that a person, initially a non-M, displays the power which S lacks to approach the goal rapidly late in the series of trials. But this is only one among possible interpretations of Shupp's data. There are no data known to us which prove that this interpretation is the correct one. We offer it here merely because it is consistent with our general notions about identification as it might relate to abilities.

Cutick's experiment produced the finding that Ss whose average pre-experimental self-evaluation was determined to be high set consistently higher $P(s)$ estimates throughout the experiment than did those whose pre-measured self-evaluation was low. Furthermore, the highs set consistently lower $P(s)$ estimates when M was present than did the high control group with M absent. The lows actually didn't differ significantly from their control group, but the *obtained* difference was in the opposite direction; that is, the experimental lows set higher average $P(s)$ estimates than did the low control group. The experiment *did not* demonstrate, by conventional statistical criteria, the hypothesis that Ss with low initial self-evaluation would change their $P(s)$ estimates in response to the fate and similarity of M more than the highs would, but all obtained differences favored the hypothesis, so at least there is no reason to reject it. The hypothesis is analogous to a familiar one in social psychology to the effect that people who have power or high status in a group will feel free, or be accorded by the group the freedom, to deviate from the group norms of opinion or conduct; that is, they will be allowed or will allow themselves to behave more independently of the group than will those who are not powerful or are held in less esteem or accorded lower status. Put the other way around, those without power or who are not approved of are likely to be more dependent in their behavior and that, in the field of identification, is what Kagan's (1958b) hypothesis and our attempts to realize it in experiments, comes to.[4] An experiment by Stanley Fagen (1963) beautifully illustrates this kind of dependence among people who have a low opinion of themselves with respect to a relevant ability, and relative independence among those who think more highly of themselves.

CONFORMITY AND SELF-EVALUATION

Fagen defined conformity in terms of differences in the number of wrong answers a person would give to standard sets of problems which he worked on in two conditions: (a) alone, and serving as his own judge of the correctness of his solutions, and (b) where

[4] Cf. Kagan's (1958b) statement that the tendency to make identifications should decrease as S becomes more independent as an agent.

he could hear the answers given by three other people, all of whom gave *wrong* answers (Fagen, 1963). He wanted to see how these error rates would be affected by what S believed about his own ability, and about the abilities of the other people. He also studied the way in which the manner that a person evaluated his own ability influenced the assumptions he made about the abilities of the others.

The Ss were 151 male university undergraduates, mostly lowerclassmen, without previous courses in psychology. They volunteered to participate in a "pilot project on spatial relations ability being conducted through the auspices of the United States Public Health Service." Fagen actually used an additional 24 Ss, but 18 of them were excluded from the data analysis because after the experiment they expressed disbelief or suspicion about some parts of the procedure, and six of them simply couldn't (or wouldn't) do the problems when they were working alone in the experiment proper. For his initial recruiting appeal, Fagen presented a brief sketch of the alleged objectives of the research program in various classrooms. The students were told that first they would have to take a 20-minute spatial relations test, and that they would be asked to return later for a one-hour session of additional testing. In the first testing session, the students took either Form AA or Form BB of the Revised Minnesota Paper Form Board Test, under standard, honest conditions. Then they were told that the second testing session would require them to use their spatial relations ability under various conditons. At the end of the second session, it was promised, they would get a preliminary evaluation of their ability, based on all previous test results. Other information indicated that the research was educational, self-enlightening, and of national importance, and there was really nothing to be afraid of or anxious about. Students then filled out a questionnaire to provide information about how many terms they had been in college, how many credits they had earned, subjects in which they had had at least one course, and whether (and under what circumstances) they had ever taken a spatial relations test before. Also each S answered the question, "If you had to rate yourself on this ability, how would you do so?" by marking a linear rating scale at any point he chose. The scale had the following descriptions under equally spaced division marks, from left to right: extremely poor, very poor, somewhat poor, fair, good, very good, excellent.

The experiment proper took place in a large laboratory room in which there were four soundproof booths, each occupied by one S. Ss were requested to report for the experiment in groups of four, but the arrangements were such that only a single S could be used, and he would still have the impression that each of the other booths was occupied. If the single S arrived a little early he was ushered into his booth, told to relax, read the preliminary instructions, and just wait until the other Ss showed up. A few minutes later E pretended to usher other people into the adjacent booths and slammed the doors hard enough for S to hear them. During subsequent parts of the experimental session S actually heard, through his earphones, three other voices (in addition to E's) of people who seemed to be carrying out E's instructions. In no case did S hear the voices of other real Ss, even when such were present. Every S heard a series of reports which had been recorded on tape by four of Fagen's fellow graduate students who had very different voices, and accentuated their differences during the recording session.

Each booth was equipped with a small desk and a chair, earphones, and a four-switch response box. The four switches were numbered (1–4) and the box had a red jewel light to serve as a signal. On the *inside* of each compartment door there hung a white cardboard sign: "Compartment 4," so when Ss were asked to report in order, each S waited until the "others" had done so because every S thought he was number 4. In order to make the verbal reporting plausible, there was a microphone mounted on the top of each switch box, and S was advised to lean close when he spoke into it, but the microphone was inoperative.

When S entered his booth he found on the desk an elaborately prepared booklet which contained the test problems he was to work on, various kinds of information and instructions, and forms for recording his answers and for making various ratings of himself and the "others." These are explained in detail at the appropriate places.

The test problems were adapted from the originals in Forms AA and BB of the Revised Minnesota Paper Form Board Test by changing the order of the alternatives and eliminating the most obviously incorrect alternative to reduce the number of alternatives from five to four. Half of the problems S worked on were actually the same as those he saw on the initial test; the others were from the alternate form which he had not seen. They were all selected from the more difficult section of the test (numbers 37–64, inclusive). The problems were organized into five sets corresponding to the five successive treatment conditions of the experimental session, and the sets were roughly equated for difficulty.

The five treatment conditions were as follows.

Isolation 1. S worked on ten problems without hearing any voice but E's.

Social Context Unappraised. S worked on 13 problems, and before he "announced" his response aloud to *E* he had to wait until he heard the voices of the other three "Ss" reporting their choices. For ten of these problems, all three voices reported wrong answers, for two of them all three voices gave the correct answer, and for one of them only one of the voices gave the correct answer. This is called the "unappraised" series because *S* had no information about the tested abilities of the other three "Ss."

Isolation 2. An exact repeat of the Isolation 1 conditions with a new set of ten problems.

Social Context Appraised. Before this series of problems *S* was told to open a sealed envelope stapled to a page of his test booklet and read the information on the enclosed form. The form identified each of the other three Ss by compartment number and gave his purported percentile standing from the results of the initial honest test. These purported scores were chosen so that *S* would get the impression (if he computed it) that the mean standings of the others were as shown in Table 6.4. The scores actually reported for the other three Ss ranged from 6 points above to eight points below the indicated means. This procedure actually divided the Ss into eight treatment conditions during this social context period. The numbers of subjects, who were randomly assigned, in those conditions are shown in parentheses in Table 6.4. Otherwise, the procedure in this sequence was exactly the same as in Social Context Unappraised.

TABLE 6.4

Information Given to S about Abilities of the Other Alleged "Subjects"

	If *S* was told that his own score was	
	High (71st percentile)	Low (31st percentile)
Then, the mean percentile of the standings attributed to the other three *S*s was one of these:	91 (9)	91 (8)
	71 (10)	51 (8)
	51 (10)	31 (7)
	11 (10)	11 (8)

(After Fagen, 1963.)

Isolation 3. Identical with the previous isolation sections.

This design uses each *S* as his own control through the sequence of conditions and the alternation of the isolation with the social context series permits us to see whether or not we should worry about counterbalancing orders. The orders were not counterbalanced, each S went through the series in the order given above, and there was no evidence that this made any important difference in the outcomes of the experiment. Of course this is not to say that putting the Appraised Social Context first would have had no effect on the behavior in the Unappraised Social Context. It probably would have a profound effect unless the Ss completely forgot what they were told about the abilities of the others, but we were not interested in that question. The only thing we have to worry about is whether failure to counterbalance produced difficulties in interpreting the results and there is no evidence that it did. In fact one of the charms of this experiment is the remarkable clarity of the effects of the various experimental manipulations.

On the basis of their performance on the real initial test, a percentile score, based on the published norms, was assigned to each student. Subjects were selected who scored either at the sixtieth percentile or higher, *or* at the fifty-third percentile or lower. The rest were excluded—simply never called for the experiment—in order to get a clear separation between groups whose real ability was either high or low. The median percentile scores were 81 for the high group and 35 for the low group. Prior to the first isolation series, S opened a sealed envelope stapled to page 2 of his booklet. The enclosed form bore the S's name and read as follows:

"Your performance on the previously administered test of spatial relations ability places you at the _____ percentile of all those who were tested earlier. This means that you have done _____ and that your ability level appears to be _____. Further testing will enable us to evaluate this ability more precisely." The blanks were filled as follows: The percentile score given was either 71 or 31, and corresponding descriptions were entered in the other blanks, either "quite well" and "high," *or* "rather poorly" and "low," respectively. Half of the Ss with really high scores were *told* they were high, and half were told they were low, and similarly for the Ss whose scores were really low. Thus, at the outset the Ss were classified into four groups according to combinations of their real tested ability and the (true or false) information they were given about that ability. This enables us to see the effect on conformity measures both of Ss real ability and what he was *told* about his ability. In addition to the Ss treated as described above, there was a control group of seven Ss who performed the first three sets of experimental problems as though they were in an isolation condition and without being given any information about their own ability.

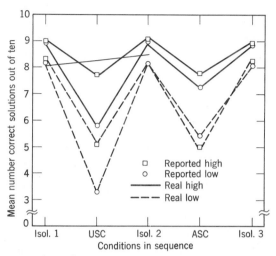

Fig. 6.8   Mean number of correct solutions out of ten problems for Ss passing through five experimental conditions. Each data point is the mean of 40 Ss in both of the "real high" groups; 32 Ss in both of the "real low" groups; 7 Ss in the control group (plain solid line, first three conditions only). (After Fagen, 1963.)

The mean accuracy scores as a function of actual ability and of alleged ability are plotted in Fig. 6.8 for the five sequential treatments. None of the mean differences among the three isolation series is significant, but the means for both of the social context series are significantly lower than those of the isolation series, for every group of Ss. Furthermore, Ss with truly high ability conform less than do those with truly low ability, when they are grouped without regard to what they were *told* about their ability. Also, at least in the Unappraised Social Context, those who were *told* they had high ability conformed less than those who were told they had low ability, when Ss were grouped without regard to their real ability. Thus, hearing three other Ss give wrong answers definitely influenced the listener to give wrong answers too, regardless of his real ability or what he was told about his ability. However, the increase in wrong answers in this situation was most pronounced among those whose ability is really low or who were told that it is low, and this tendency to make errors depended on what Ss heard the others say, because it was "turned off" when Ss were returned to isolation, and because the control group made no more errors on the problems in the first two isolation conditions.

The finding that differences in the amount of real ability and "information" about ability *both* affect the tendency to conform raises the question about how the Ss got the information about their real ability and how it might have mediated their varying amount of re-sistances to conformity. Note that in both social contexts any real highs who were told they were low are second in the group order with respect to accuracy scores; that is, they are exceeded in resistance to conformity only by the real highs who were told they were high. This must mean that the fact of their being good in this particular ability somehow mediated their conformity behavior in spite of *E's* false statement that they were low. The statement obviously had its effect but it did not offset the effect of *S's* real ability. Possibly some concept that S has about his ability, or some attitude of independently judging the accuracy of his choices, is the influence which produces this phenomenon.

Fagen also obtained ratings of Ss' confidence, self-evaluation, and evaluation of the others. After each problem, each S made a *certainty estimate* in accordance with the printed instructions: "Indicate by marking the exact point on this scale, what you believe to be the certainty (i.e., probability) of your having solved the above problem correctly." These scales were linear rating scales numbered and labeled, beginning at the left-hand end, as follows: 0.00—"Absolutely certain that I was incorrect"; .25—"Chances are ¼ that I was correct"; .50—"Chances are ¾ that I was correct"; .75—"Chances are ¾ that I was correct;" 1.00—"Absolutely certain I was correct." Between these suc-cessive numbered marks there were additional, equally spaced but un-numbered graduation marks corresponding to intervals of .05 on the scale between 0.00 and 1.00.

The mean certainty estimates per problem are shown for the four groups of Ss in the Isolation 1 conditions in Table 6.5. The differences in certainty between real highs and real lows *and* between reported highs and reported lows are significant, but the corresponding differ-ences in accuracy were not. Thus, there was no correspondence be-tween judged certainty of being right and actually being right in Isola-tion 1. However, the significant differences in certainty estimates in Isolation 1 follow exactly the same pattern as the differences in accu-racy scores in the Unappraised Social Context series—the Ss who were less confident of being right were also the ones who allowed their judgments to follow the (wrong) judgments of the others.

Table 6.5 also shows mean self-evaluations (S-E) made by Ss at the end of the Isolation 1 and the Unappraised Social Context se-ries. These were made on linear rating scales with the following instructions: "Indicate . . . , by marking the exact point on this scale, what you believe to be the level of your ability to solve spatial rela-tions problems:" The scale had seven equally spaced marks labeled

TABLE 6.5

Mean of Certainty, Accuracy, Response Latency, and Self-Evaluation for Selected Conditions

		Certainty	Accuracy				Response Latency	Number of Judgments Heard	Self-Evaluation, After:	
Ability	n	I_1	I_1 USC	I_2 ASC	I_3		I_1	USC	I_1	USC
Real High										
Reported High	40	91.4	9.03 7.70	8.95 7.72	8.80		17.98	1.50	84.12	80.56
Reported Low	40	78.6	8.88 5.73	8.83 7.28	8.78		19.98	1.57	61.94	62.21
Real Low										
Reported High	32	80.1	8.19 4.94	8.12 4.96	8.37		21.03	1.88	74.16	64.81
Reported Low	32	70.1	8.00 3.28	8.16 5.37	8.03		22.39	1.98	45.15	43.25

I = an Isolation condition; USC = Unappraised Social Context; ASC = Appraised Social Context. (After Fagen, 1963.)

from left to right: extremely poor, very poor, poor, fair, good, very good, and excellent. It was scored by measuring the distance of S's mark in millimeters from the left-hand end. The mean self-evaluations of the four groups in Isolation 1 correspond exactly to their mean certainty scores, and the pattern of significant differences is the same. In the Unappraised Social Context the pattern of significant differences is repeated, and the order of the means is the same as in Isolation 1. Between Isolation 1 and Unappraised Social Context, only one group made a significant *change:* Ss with really low ability which was *reported* high, significantly lowered their self-evaluations. In both sets of self-evaluations, regardless of the *changes* that occurred between Isolation 1 and Unappraised Social Context, the mean level varied both with Ss' real abilities and with what they were told about them. Thus, the level of self-evaluation did not result from a social comparison explicitly introduced in this experiment.

In this experiment the Ss could behave in such a way as to indicate whether or not they were making use of the available social comparisons in the two social context series, unappraised and appraised. They could record their answers before they had heard any judgments from the "others," or they could wait until they had heard various

numbers of judgments from the "others." This is confounded by the
fact that the *latency* of response for the low ability Ss is longer than
for the highs, even in the Isolation 1 series, as Table 6.5 shows, but
there is evidence to indicate that deliberately waiting to hear the
other's judgments is part of the difference in latency in both of the
social context series. In the Appraised Social Context, latency, and
therefore the number of others' judgments listened to, declined both
as a function of the information that others' abilities are below S's
abilities and as a function of S's tendency to rate his ability above
others. Indeed, this tendency is related to the objective difficulty of
the problems. With easy problems, the false lows selected their answers rapidly and conformed only slightly more than true highs, but,
compared to the false highs, the false lows behaved much more independently. However, for the more difficult problems the false lows
did not answer until they heard the others' judgments, and then they
attached more weight to those judgments than did the false highs.
In other words, false lows conformed less on the easy problems than
false highs because of their lower attentiveness to others' judgments,
and they conformed more on the difficult problems because of their
greater acceptance of others' judgments.

The relation, as reported by the Ss, between others' ability and
their own is an important correlate of conformity behavior. This relation, even in the Unappraised Social Context series, was affected both
by S's real ability and by what he was told about it, as Table 6.6
shows. In this table, the terms "below" and "above" refer to Ss who

TABLE 6.6
*Number of Ss, After Unappraised Social Context, Who Re-
ported the Indicated Relation of Others' Ability to Their Own
Ability*

	Relation of Others' to Own Ability			
	n	Below	Equal	Above
Real High	78	40	27	11
Reported High	39	29	8	2
Reported Low	39	11	19	9
Real Low	63	10	23	30
Reported High	32	8	18	6
Reported Low	31	2	5	24

(After Fagen, 1963).

estimated the average ability of the others as at least one scale division different from their own in the indicated direction. "Equal" means that ratings of others' abilities differed by less than one scale unit from Ss' ratings of their own ability. These conventions are the same in all future discussions of this relation. Therefore, the above data indicate that the social comparisons available in this experiment were affected by what S was told or assumed about his own ability, independently and in advance of any specific social comparison offered in the experiment. Furthermore, these social comparisons, made without any information at all about the abilities of the other students, were associated with Ss' tendency to follow the lead of the voices of the "others" as indicated by the decline in accuracy score from the Isolation 1 series to the Unappraised Social Context series, as Table 6.7 shows. Clearly, resistance to conformity was greatest when S believed the "others" were below him in the relevant capacity, and least when he thought they were above him. This conclusion is even more dramatically supported by data from the Appraised Social Context series. Here, we restrict the comparison to the "true" highs and lows; i.e., Ss whose ability *as reported* to them was consistent with

TABLE 6.7

Decline in Accuracy (Isolation 1 to Unappraised Social Context) as a Function of Rated Relation of Others' Ability to Own Ability

Decline in Accuracy Score	Others' Ability in Relation to Own Ability		
	Below	Equal	Above
0	14	1	0
1	16	2	0
2	12	8	0
3	6	21	2
4	2	14	7
>4	0	4	37
Totals	50	50	41
Means	1.14	3.14	5.44

Chi-square = 144.5; d.f. = 10; p < .00005; C = .71
Body of Table shows frequency in each category. (After Fagen, 1963.)

TABLE 6.8
Frequencies of Ratings of Others' Ability in Relation to Own Ability (After Appraised Social Context) as a Function of Information About Own and Others' Ability

| | | | S Rated Others' Ability in Relation to Own Ability As: | | |
| | | | | | |
S's Real Ability		*n*	Below	Equal	Above
High					
Reported at Percentile: 71					
Others Reported at Percentile:	91	9	2	4	3
	71	10	3	6	1
	51	10	10	0	0
	11	10	10	0	0
Totals		39	25	10	4
Low					
Reported at Percentile: 31					
Others Reported at Percentile:	91	8	0	0	8
	51	8	0	3	5
	31	7	2	4	1
	11	8	7	1	0
Totals		31	9	8	14

For HH and LL groups only. (After Fagen, 1963.)

their real ability. The relations between others' and own ability derived from the estimates of these Ss are shown in Table 6.8 as a function of the information they were given about the mean ability of the three "others." Clearly, the information had a profound effect on their reports of the relation between others' ability and their own. Furthermore, this information also had a decisive effect on their conformity behavior as shown in Fig. 6.9. The information that others were below them in ability led to a decrease in errors between the Unappraised and the Appraised Social Context series, and generally, the information that others' ability was higher led to an increase in errors. Reports that others' ability was equal to S's own led the high ability Ss to increase their errors significantly, but the lows made essentially no change, though they had "room" to do so. When low ability Ss were told that the "others" were better than they were by 20 percentile points, their errors increased by almost 2.5 out of ten problems, while those of the high ability Ss with qualitatively the same

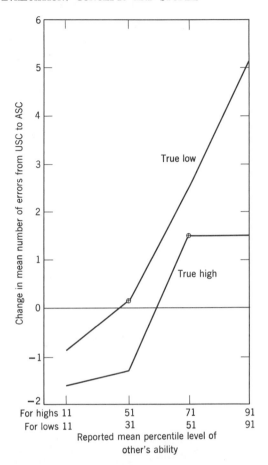

Fig. 6.9   Mean change in errors between USC and ASC as a function of Ss ability and mean percentile of others' ability announced by E. The symbol ⊕ denotes the groups in which E announced the same percentile of ability for S as for others. Each data point is the mean of eight Ss in the true low group, 10 Ss in the true high group. (After Fagen, 1963.)

information did not increase at all. After the Appraised Social Context series, none of the 39 "true high" Ss who made the estimates (one made no estimate) estimated their own ability *as low as* "fair," and only two of the 31 "true low" Ss who made estimates (one did not) estimated their abilities as high as the lowest estimate given by the highs.

We must next consider the changes that Fagen observed in certainty, self-evaluation, evaluation of others, and latency of responding during the successive treatment conditions. These will be presented chiefly for the four initially differentiated groups: the real highs, reported high; the real highs, reported low; the real lows, reported high; and the real lows, reported low.

As Fig. 6.10 shows, the general level of certainty is a function, as was actual performance (Fig. 6.8), of Ss' real abilities and what they were told about them, except that the low-highs and the high-lows are not significantly different. The three upper curves are quite similar in form, and if summed they would indicate that when Ss entered the Unappraised Social Context from the Isolation 1 condition their certainty estimates went down, rose again in Isolation 2, fell again in the Appraised Social Context, and rose once more in Isolation 3. Exposure to the judgments of others lowered Ss' confidence that their own answers were correct, but only for Ss with truly high ability (regardless of what they were told about it) or for those who were told they had high ability (though it was really low). Those who were correctly informed that their ability was low *increased* their certainty ratings between Isolation 1 and Unappraised Social Context, and *lowered* them again when they went into Isolation 2. The differences, in both these trends, between the low-low group and the others are significant ($p = .02$). From Isolation 2 to Appraised Social Context, certainty decreased significantly for the three upper groups (high-high, high-low, and low-high), but not for the low-lows. The increase

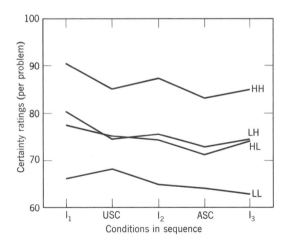

Fig. 6.10   Mean certainty ratings (per problem) by conditions in sequence. HH (n = 40)—real high, reported high; HL (n = 40)—real high, reported low; LH (n = 32); real low, reported high. LL (n = 32)—real low, reported low. (After Fagen, 1963.)

in confidence between Appraised Social Context and Isolation 3 is significant for the high-high and high-low groups, but not for the other two—low-high and low-low.

The overall levels of self-evaluation (Fig. 6.11) differentiated the four groups even better than did the certainty ratings. The wide separation of the low-high and the high-low groups on this measure indicates that under the conditions of this experiment the Ss' statements of how good their abilities were depended more closely on what they had been *told* about those abilities that did either their actual performance or their average confidence in their performance. Clearly, the real level of their ability had an influence on self-evaluation also (even when *E*'s information was directly contrary to their real ability), otherwise the low-highs would not have such distinctly lower self-evaluations than the high-highs, and the self-evaluations of the high-lows would not be so much greater than those of the low-lows.

The decrease in self-evaluation between Isolation 1 and Unappraised Social Context is significant for all groups, and thereafter general similarities cease. The course of the average changes in self-evaluation for the high-high group is closely parallel to the trend of their certainty ratings (compare Figs. 6.10 and 6.11), and all of their changes in self-evaluation are significant. The same parallel between

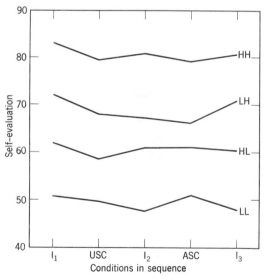

Fig. 6.11   Mean self-evaluations of ability by conditions in sequence. Symbols and *ns* are the same as for Fig. 6.10. (After Fagen, 1963.)

changes in self-evaluation and certainty holds (almost) for the low-high group, the exception being the non-significant decline in self-evaluation between Unappraised Social Context and Isolation 2. The self-evaluation and certainty trends of the high-low group are never parallel after the initial decrease between Isolation 1 and Unappraised Social Context. In the low-low group the trends of self-evaluation and certainty would be parallel only if we reversed one of the graphs—split at the middle and exchanged right and left halves. The reader has our complete assurance that this has not in fact been done by accident in preparing the graphs. So we see, as we go from high-high to low-low, a progressive detachment of trends in self-evaluation from those of certainty, two measures that might be expected to vary together. That they do vary together for the high-high group and not for the low-lows is a matter worth pondering, especially in view of the previous observation that both the certainty and self-evaluation trends differentiate the two groups. Is it possible that the Ss whose truly low ability was confirmed by E's statements have a relative dearth of cues on which to base independent judgments of their own accuracy. If so, then the relative absence of firm standards for evaluating their own behavior—a condition cited by Festinger as predisposing to dependence on social standards of evaluation—also occurs in them. Indeed, their behavior is consistent with the hypothesis that they are dependent on the group consensus, and, by contrast, the behavior of the high-highs suggests that though they are *influenced* by the opportunity to make social comparisons, they are not dependent on them. Specifically, moving the low-lows from isolation to a social context, where they hear three other people give wrong answers to the problems they are working on, led them to increase their stated certainty of giving right answers even though their average number of right answers decreased from nearly eight to just over three! At the same time they significantly lowered their estimate (as did the other groups) of their ability—as though they admitted the independence of their objective self-evaluation and their feelings of certainty, in agreement with the obvious fact that the latter depended on other people's opinion. Brandt (1958) has shown that being good at something carries with it a knowledge of the criteria for judging excellence of performance, so that the better performers were more able than the poor ones at ranking others accurately with respect to their abilities.

Then what about the evaluation of others in the present experiment, and its relations to self-evaluations? Here we are limited to considering the only two conditions, the social contexts, in which evaluations of others were made. During Unappraised Social Context the Ss had no information about the abilities of the "others," but they did have it at the beginning of the Appraised Social Context. Table 6.6 clearly indicates that the relation between self-evaluation and evaluation of others depended on Ss' real and alleged level of ability. During Unappraised Social Context this relation did not vary significantly with information about the "others." Therefore, the interpretation of what happened in Appraised Social Context can be relatively straightforward. Fig. 6.12 shows the change between Unappraised and Appraised Social Contexts in the mean relation of self- and other-evaluations. The differences among the four groups are significant in both conditions, and there is a remarkable constancy in the size of the differences among the four groups. All of them showed a stronger tendency to rate themselves higher in relation to others in the Appraised Social Context, but the change is *only in this relation* because for the four original groups the overall decrease in the evaluation of others between Unappraised and Appraised Social Contexts is not significant. *Self-evaluation* rose significantly between Unappraised and Appraised Social Context but only for the low-low and the high-low groups; changes for the high-high and the low-high groups and the change over all Ss are *not significant*. However, there were highly significant changes in evaluation of others as a function of information about the others' abilities, as Table 6.9 shows.

Latency data are shown in Fig. 6.13. It is necessary to discuss the isolation conditions separately from the social context conditions.

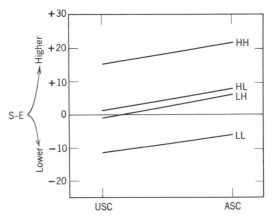

Fig. 6.12 Self-evaluation in relation to Ss' evaluation of others in USC and ASC. For symbols and *ns*, see Fig. 6.10. (After Fagen, 1963.)

TABLE 6.9

Frequencies of Changes in Evaluations of Others' Ability Between Unappraised Social Context and Appraised Social Context (ASC) as a Function of Ss' Real and Reported Ability, and Ability of Others Announced in ASC

Ss' Ability Reported as:	Alleged Ability of Others (Percentile)	High				Low			
		Up	Same	Down	Total	Up	Same	Down	Total
High	91	10	0	0	10	8	0	0	8
(Percentile 71)	71	3	5	2	10	6	1	1	8
	51	1	2	7	10	1	0	7	8
	11	0	2	8	10	0	0	8	8
	Totals	14	9	17	40	15	1	16	32
Low	91	10	0	0	10	8	0	0	8
(Percentile 31)	51	2	4	4	10	4	1	3	8
	31	1	0	9	10	2	1	5	8
	11	1	0	8	9	0	0	8	8
	Totals	14	4	21	39	14	2	16	32

N.B. The lines within the tables show where the distributions were split to make 2×2 contingency tables for testing significance of association between others' alleged ability and change in Ss' ratings of others. All the above associations are significant ($p < .01$) by Fisher's "exact probability" test (hypergeometrical distribution), extended tables to $n = 60$ in Diem (1962). (After Fagen, 1963.)

In the isolation conditions latency was measured as seconds elapsed between the starting signal for a problem and S's pushing a response switch; but in the social context conditions latency was measured by how many of the "others" had announced their solutions before S pushed his response switch. Over the three isolation conditions, latency differentiates significantly among the four groups, but not in the social context conditions. In the isolation conditions, latency shows a significant overall increase for the high-high group and no significant changes in the other groups. However, the reversed trends in the low-low and the high-high groups are significantly different. During the two social context conditions, there are no significant differences among the four groups, and no significant changes between the two

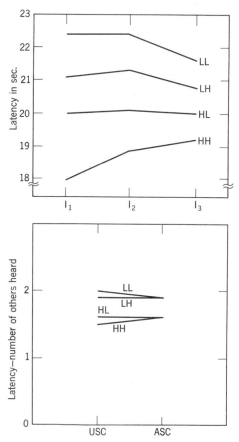

Fig. 6.13 Two measures of response latency by indicated conditions. For symbols and *ns*, see Fig. 6.10. (After Fagen, 1963.)

conditions. Clearly, over the four ability-evaluation groups, latency was perfectly inversely related to self-evaluation, certainty, and error score, but its changes from Isolation 1 to Isolation 3 are not related in this simple way to changes in the other three variables. For example, the high-high group had a significant increase in latency, corresponding to its decrease in certainty, *without* an increase in its error rate. On the other hand, the low-lows had a *decrease* in both latency and certainty and no increase in error rate. It appears as if the high-highs' two certainty-reducing experiences in the social contexts had genuinely lowered their confidence and made them more cautious about giving hasty answers (hence progressively increasing latencies) without affecting the soundness of their judgment—guaranteed by their genuinely high ability. However, the low-lows, dependent, as we have argued, on the opinions of other people to validate their judgments, went through two certainty-*increasing* experiences (the social contexts) without detecting that their confidence in the "others'" judgments was misplaced and decreased their latency without increasing their error scores over the three isolation series; their certainty was lower in Isolation 3 than in Isolation 1 simply because the only prop of their confidence was removed.

It is clear from this experiment that people whose ability was either really high or alleged to be high were less dependent on "others'" judgments about the correctness of their offered solutions to problems than were those whose ability was either really low or reported as low. This independence is reflected in the fact that the highs waited less time and listened to fewer judgments by "others" before giving their answers, and also by the fact that the increase in errors, as a function of reported relations between their own and "others'" ability, was far less for the highs than for the lows. The fact that the real level of a person's ability affected his dependence on the judgments of others suggests that previous use of his abilities has affected his knowledge of that specific ability or his general attitude toward himself as an instrument for solving problems. Whether or not this supposed mediating variable was installed exclusively by social comparisons, S brings it with him to a specific problem-solving situation where it operates whether or not social comparisons are available there, and, when the basis of social comparisons is clarified, this mediating self-evaluation variable is not swamped by their effects, but interacts with them.

Next we consider the effects of an individual's information about his own ability and the ability of others on the kinds of people he chooses for partners or associates in situations where he must cooperate with another person to get to a goal.

EVALUATION OF ABILITIES AND CHOICE OF PARTNERS

The experiments to be described in this section were begun with the collaboration of David Cohen and John Whitmyre (Whitmyre, Diggory, and Cohen, 1961).[5]

They have in common that information was given to S about:

[5] All, but the original pilot experiment (Whitmyre, Diggory, and Cohen, 1961), were supported by a grant to the present author from the American Philosophical Society (see the Society's *Yearbook*, 1962, pp. 278–279).

(*a*) his own ability, (*b*) the abilities of potential partners, (*c*) the values of prizes which S and his partner might win in competition with other pairs, and (*d*) the rules for dividing the prize between winning partners. As a standard preliminary procedure, each S ranked all the other people in the group as to how much S would like "to do things with them"; that is, to have them as close companions in leisure-time activities.

We presumed that if the rankings for "liking" were to mean anything about Ss' actual preferences, we would have to use fairly large groups of Ss who associated with each other both at work and in their living quarters for most of their waking life during the period of the experiment, and that this association should have been in existence for at least a year prior to the experiment. Of available groups which met these criteria, student nurses were easiest to get in touch with, and so we used several groups of students at nursing schools within a fifty-mile radius of Philadelphia. Resident members of college fraternities, or members of military units might have served as well, but the military were not easily accessible, and during the working part of the day fraternity members do not associate as closely as do student nurses. Furthermore, at least in the schools we entered, the student nurses are organized into class groups which are rarely less than 20 or more than 35 in number, group sizes which were just right for our purposes. After the relevant authorities had given us permission to do the experiment, we met the students, by groups, in two sessions. In the first session each girl was given a mimeographed, alphabetized list of the names of her classmates, including her own. She crossed out her own name (for identification and to make sure she didn't include herself in the rankings) and then she ranked all of her classmates, assigning 1 to the "most liked" and the final number to the "least liked." During the interval (usually a week) before the second session, we examined each S's rankings and selected the names of five girls at roughly equal rank intervals over the whole range. For example, in the very first of these experiments (Whitmyre, Diggory, and Cohen, 1961) each S ranked 23 classmates, so the names chosen were those to which ranks 1, 6, 12, 18, and 23 were assigned—not likely to be the same set of names for any two Ss.

Also during the first session, after the ranking papers were collected, we tested the "auditory discrimination" ability of the Ss by having them take the pitch, loudness, and timbre sub-tests of the Seashore Measures of Musical Talent, Series B. Series B involves the more difficult discriminations so we used it because we wanted, not an accurate test, but a procedure in which the Ss would not be able to estimate accurately how many items they had got right. Moreover, the standard procedure for the Seashore test keeps S so busy that he would have a hard time keeping track of his correct answers even if he wanted to. It was important to convince each S that her level of "auditory discrimination" ability was, as we told her privately in the second session, either high (90 points out of 100), medium (50 points out of 100), or low (10 points out of 100). The Ss also had to realize that their classmates had taken the same test so that they could evaluate the information we gave them about the scores attributed to their potential partners.

Before the second session E prepared several identical three-inch by five-inch cards, individually designed for each S. At the top of each card was S's name and her fictitious score on the test. Below this in a vertical list were the names of the five girls chosen, as described above, from S's own liking rankings. There was no attempt made to remind S of how she had ranked these five. Opposite each of the names was an alleged score for the test of auditory discrimination. These scores covered an 80-point range (from 10 to 90) in five equal steps. As assigned to the five names on the card, these scores were *in exactly the reverse order* of the liking rankings. The actual order of the names and scores on the card was scrambled so that neither of these orders would be immediately apparent to casual inspection.

In the second session E first explained the fictitious 100-point scoring scale for the "test." Then he distributed one card to each S in a sealed envelope identified by her name written on the front. The E then explained that up to now our procedures had been preliminary to some intensive experiments on the use of auditory discrimination ability under various conditions. In order to motivate the Ss to do their best these experiments were going to be run as *competitions,* and so far as possible each S would have as a partner a person she nominated, or at least the most highly preferred nominee which the schedule, and the preferences of the other girls, would allow. In fact, said E, there will be several competitions, each with a different prize. Each girl then opened her envelope, digested the information on the card, and ranked the five names in the order in which she thought she preferred them *as partners* in a competition with other pairs where the prize would be merely that *the names of the members of the winning pair would be prominently displayed on the school bulletin board.* We have persisted in referring to this "reward" among ourselves as "fame"—as good and succinct a label as any. The cards were then collected and an identical blank set was distributed, and this time the girls were told that the prize in the competition would be *one dollar,* to be *shared equally* by the members of the winning pair. After the second rankings were completed and the cards collected, a new (identical) set of cards was distributed and the girls ranked their potential partners for a competition where they might get equal shares of a $10.00 prize. Yet a fourth ranking was made with the announcement that there would be a competition for a $100.00 prize.

We sought to make these prizes believable to the Ss by telling them that we were not using our own money but the resources of a wealthy foundation where the administrators were intensely interested in our research and had more money available than they knew what to do with.[6] When all the rankings had been collected E at once told the group that the experiment was over, we had all the data we wanted, there would be no competitions and no prizes. He then explained in detail exactly what we were studying and finally announced that, though no prizes were available, the group would be given a sum of money to do with as they pleased. These "consolation" awards were never offered without the prior consent and understanding of the supervisor or director in charge of the class. Our first group and several subsequent ones used the money to give parties. Another large group (which we dealt with in several class sections) gratefully informed us that we had saved their class yearbook project from foundering for lack of funds. The average per capita disbursement in all these experiments was in the neighborhood of $2.50.

It is clear from our procedure that the Ss were faced with the problem (if they saw it that way) of whether to make their *partner* rankings agree with the rankings of *liking* or of *ability.* They might do neither, but they could not do both, for we had deliberately put the liking and ability rankings in strict opposition. This, we thought, would be the severest test of the proposition that people choose as their associates and collaborators those who are most like them in ability. We wanted to avoid as far as possible the difficulties of interpretation that would arise if we gave the Ss a chance to nominate partners who were both able and well liked. Then we had to find a single-numbered index of whether the partner rankings were in agreement with the liking rankings, with the ability rankings, or with neither. We chose Kendall's (1948) statistic, S (the numerator of his rank correlation coefficient "tau"). When five items are ranked by two

[6] After our preliminary experiment, for which the money was provided out of research funds of the Psychology Department at the University of Pennsylvania, the statement that we had prize money from a research foundation came true in the form of the aforementioned grant from the American Philosophical Society.

criteria, as they were by our Ss, the value of S can range between 10 and —10, and we have always computed it so that 10 means that the partner ranking agrees with the liking ranking, and —10 means that the partner ranking agrees with the ability ranking.

It should also be clear from our procedure that we have used a mixed type of design. When we compare the effects of varying information about S's own ability, the Ss in the different self-score groups are always different people, but when we compare across prize conditions, the same Ss appear in every prize condition. This latter situation makes the changes we observed all the more remarkable because each S served as her own control over the prize conditions and any changes she made as a function of announced prize were presumably made against whatever tendency she had to appear consistent.

The results of the first experiment are shown in Fig. 6.14, panel A. When the prize was "fame" (getting one's name on the school bulletin board) all Ss, regardless of their own self-scores, ranked potential partners in close accord with the liking ranking, but when money was the prize, the Ss with the higher self-scores shifted their partner rankings in the direction of making them agree with the ability ranking; this shift was proportional both to S's own self-score level and to the value of the prize. Clearly, the greater the potential reward, the more "selfish" the choices of the high ability Ss: they abandoned their friends (who are relatively powerless but who might be helped by S's own considerable abilities) and chose able people whom they liked less.[7]

Panel B of Fig. 6.14 shows the results of the first experiment *combined* with those of 21 additional Ss. Obviously the replication did nothing to change our conclusions based on the first experiment alone.

Fig. 6.15 presents the results of three additional experiments. The three curves near the bottom of the graph are from Ss who ranked potential partners when only the scores *and not the names* of the potential partners were listed on their cards. Thus, when the Ss knew only about the abilities of the potential partners and nothing about who they were (so information about liking was excluded), all of them, regardless of self-score and prize value, made their partner rankings correspond closely to the ability ranking. It is noteworthy that at every prize level the low self-score group had the least close correspondence between partner and ability rankings, and as the value

---

[7] We have no reason to say that the lowest girls in the liking rankings were actively *disliked* (regarded aversively) by the rankers. The parsimonious interpretation is that they were *less* liked than those with higher rankings, but how much less we have not tried to discover.

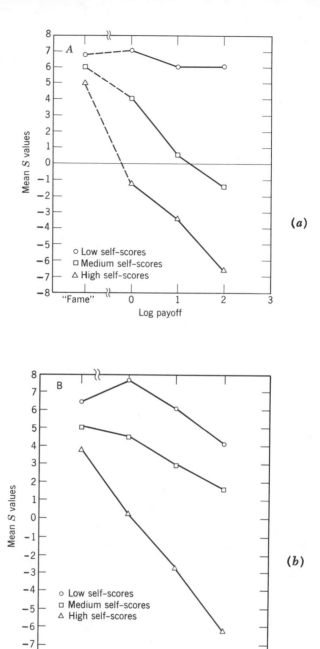

(a)

(b)

Fig. 6.14 Partner choice index (S) as a function of prize-value and self-score with a single prize to be shared equally by the winning pair. A: First experiment (Whitmyre, Diggory, and Cohen, 1961), *n* = 8 at each data point. B. Replication by same authors, *n* = 15 at each data point. Negative S means partners ranked by ability; positive S means partners ranked by liking.

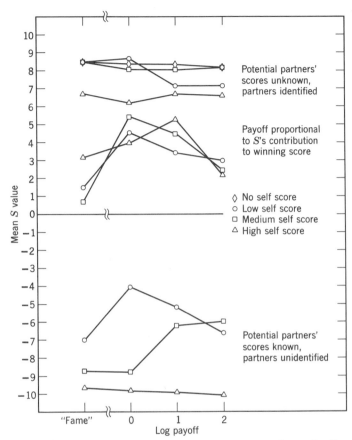

Fig. 6.15   Partner choice index (S) as a function of prize-value and self-score as a function of indicated experimental conditions. In the four curves at the top and the three at the bottom a single prize at each level was to be shared equally by the winning pair. At each data point *n* = 12 in the upper four curves; *n* = 17 in the three middle curves, a combination of identical experiments on two distinct groups; *n* = 8 in the three curves at the bottom. (Data collected by Whitmyre, Cohen, and Diggory.)

of the prize increased, the medium ability group moved away from a near-perfect correspondence of partner and ability rankings. This suggests that the Ss who thought their ability was low and, when the prize was high, those who thought they had moderate ability, tended to *avoid* associating with the most able partners available. This interpretation is reinforced by the results shown in the four upper curves of Fig. 6.15. Here are the results of Ss (including a group who had no information even about their *own* scores) who were told only the *names* of the potential partners *and not their scores*. There are no significant differences at all among the self-score groups either as a function of self-score or the value of the prize—they all made the partner ranks correspond closely to the liking rankings and the separation noted in the bottom set of curves is absent. None of the groups avoided people they liked. This makes it more likely that in the other experiments the Ss who thought they had high ability were seeking to enhance their own prize-winning power by alliance with others of high ability, while the low self-score Ss avoided such alliances.

The three closely coinciding curves in the middle of Fig. 6.15 are from a group of Ss for whom the pay-off conditions were altered, as compared with the other experiments. In this case, each S was told that the prize would be divided between the winning partners on the basis of the proportion which each contributed to their total score. Thus, the prize would be shared equally only if the partners made equal contributions to the winning total. Otherwise, though this was not explicitly emphasized to the Ss, it was likely that the abler Ss would walk off with the lion's share of the prize and the less able ones would have the smaller portion. In these conditions there were no significant differences among the groups as a function of prize or self-score. The position of the three curves on the graph relative to the other two sets of data indicates that all Ss ranked their partners in a way that deviated more from the pure liking ranking than was the case where they knew only the liking ranking, and at the same time they avoided choosing completely in accordance with the ability ranking. From an objective viewpoint, though the Ss had no way of knowing it, this is the most equitable distribution of talent choice that could be made. It nearly equates the probability of winning over all pairs, and it preserves the advantages of possessing high ability in that the high self-score Ss stand to win more than the others. The low self-score Ss stand to win *something* so under these conditions they do not avoid high ability partners any more than the high self-score Ss do.

Fig. 6.16 shows the results of yet another variation in the pay-off conditions. This time there was to be a prize for every pair of partners. The amount of the maximum prize ("fame," $1.00, $10.00, and $100.00) awarded to each pair would be determined by the proportion which their total score represented of the highest total obtained. For example, if the highest total for any pair was 100 points, any number of pairs who tied at that total would each receive the maximum

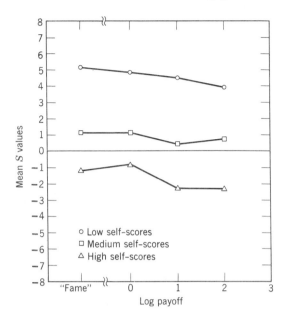

Fig. 6.16   Partner choice index (S) as a function of prize-value and self-score under non-competitive conditions. Every pair could win a prize at every level, prize to be shared equally by the partners. At each data point *n* = 8. (Data collected by Whitmyre, Diggory, and Cohen.)

prize—to be shared equally by the partners—but if one pair got only 25 points, they would share equally in ¼ of the maximum prize. Under these conditions there is a significant segregation by self-score groups, but not by prize value. The partner rankings of the high self-score group are closer to ability rankings and those of the low and medium self-score groups are closer to liking rankings.

In the next experiment we varied liking for partner, S's alleged ability, and partner's alleged ability each at three levels: high, medium, and low. Thus we had a 3 × 3 × 3 or 27-condition experimental design. This time, after preliminary procedures identical with those described above, we gave the Ss no *choice* of partners in the second session. Instead, we announced to each S her own score on the test and the name and score of the partner we had assigned to her—*fait accompli*. The Ss then had to choose the one of a series of competitions they would be willing to enter. It was carefully explained that these competitions were graded in difficulty and this grading was reflected in the values of the prizes to be awarded—from $1.00, $10.00, and so on by increments of ten to $100.00. The written instructions were:

> You and your partner will be invited to enter a contest in which you will compete with other pairs of nursing students from this school and other schools in the area. In the contest you will have to solve problems which require the use of the auditory abilities for which you have been tested, and for which you know your score and your partner's score. The members of the winning pair will share equally the prize of a sum of money.
>
> The amount you win, and the difficulty of winning it, will depend on what you bid for. You may win either exactly the amount you bid for, or nothing. Indicate your bid by marking X in one of the boxes below. In making your bid, remember: the higher the prize, the more difficult the task. Also remember there are 11 prize categories and you will compete only with those whose bid is the same as yours. Do not concern yourself now with the possibility that your partner may bid differently than you. If your bids are different, you will have a conference later in which you can come to agreement. The bid you make now should be entirely your own.

Analysis of variance of the dollar values of the prizes bid for by the Ss in the various conditions revealed significant effects only of the main variables of self-score and partner score. The mean dollar values as a function of the main variables are shown in Table 6.10. Fig. 6.17 shows how mean dollar value of bids changed as a function of self-score and partner score. Liking for the partner had no significant effect on value of prize bid for and self-score and partner score seemed to summate to determine the value of the bids (cf. Fig. 6.17). Thus, to our previous observations, the present experiment adds

TABLE 6.10

Average Dollar Values of Prizes Bid For by Ss as a Function of Levels of Three Variables

	Level			
Variable	High	Medium	Low	p
Self-score	$62.00	47.00	32.00	< .01
Partner's score	58.00	46.00	37.00	< .01
Liking for partner	46.00	49.00	47.00	> .20

Significance test was analysis of variance, F-test.
(Data collected by Diggory, Whitmyre, and Cohen.)

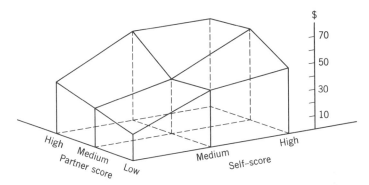

Fig. 6.17   Mean dollar values of prizes bid for as a function of self-score and partner's score when partner was assigned by *E* rather than chosen by *S*. At each data point *n* = 10. (Data collected by Diggory, Whitmyre, and Cohen.)

that *S*'s perception of the total power of himself and his associates determines the difficulty (and, because we rigged it that way, the value) of the task he will aspire to. When *S* cannot choose in such a way as to affect that total power (that is, when a partner has been *assigned* to him), then the extent to which he likes the partner has nothing to do with his aspirations.

Having digested the previous results we decided to investigate a somewhat freer situation, one in which the ability of the potential partners and *S*'s liking for them was varied independently in the choices presented to *S*. Bernard Liberman's position as a part-time teacher at a synagogue Hebrew school gave us the opportunity to study this problem in a group of children ranging in age from seven to sixteen years, and spread over the five grades of the school. Generally, Liberman's procedure was identical with that of the other partner-choice experiments, with exceptions indicated below.

The first change in Liberman's procedure stemmed from our suspicion that money prizes might not have the same effectiveness with children, especially with the younger ones, as with adults. Therefore, in the pre-preliminary procedure all the children were given lists of toys, games, equipment, and sums of money which they might possibly desire. They were instructed to rank the items in order of their preferences for them. The list and accompanying instructions were presented on a mimeographed form as shown in Appendix F.

As might be expected, the rankings obtained from this list were quite varied, but one interesting fact emerged. The younger *S*s consistently ranked the $10.00 cash higher than the $5.00 cash, but they also consistently ranked several other things higher than either amount of cash. The rank order of preference given to the cash increased steadily with increasing age of the Ss until, among the oldest students, the $10.00 cash was ranked as most preferred on the average. Parenthetically, it seems as if this increasing preference for money is correlated with the increasing freedom and opportunity to use money without adult restraint as children grow older. No doubt their increasing experience in the use of money also plays a part here. However that may be, the heterogeneity of the rankings of the various items on the list warned us that we should use a procedure which allowed each S considerable freedom in nominating his own prize in the experiment proper. Accordingly, we had two prize conditions, high and low. For the low prize condition, we simply promised that the names of the winners of the competition would be posted on the bulletin board at the school—the "fame" treatment of the previous experiments. For the high prize condition each S was given a list of ten items from the upper ranks of the original list and was told that if he and his partner won, he could choose as a prize anything he wanted from that list. Actually, no such prizes were distributed, but instead a substantial amount of cash was put at the disposal of the school director who used it for a "treat" for all the children.

The presentation of information about the names and test scores of potential partners also differed from the procedure of the previous experiments. We wanted to present to each S the names of four possible partners, two of them high and two of them low in the liking rankings, and two high and two low in ability, independent of liking. We decided not to use either those ranked highest or lowest in liking, because they might be too decidedly liked or disliked, so that, for example, if we chose the classmates ranked first and second in liking they might not be sufficiently similar in liking when they were presented as different in ability. Accordingly, for the highly liked potential partners, we chose the second and third ranked pupils from each S's list and for half the Ss their alleged order in ability was counterbalanced; that is, half of the Ss were told that their second-ranked classmate (in liking) had a low score on the test, and the other half were told he had a high score, and conversely for the third-ranked classmate. For the low-liked people we avoided the nth rank by choosing the classmates ranked $n - 1$ and $n - 2$, and counterbalancing their alleged abilities as for the highly liked classmates. The four names and alleged ability scores of the potential partners were presented to S on two separate sheets of paper—one for the low prize condition and one for the high prize condition. The order of the names and scores was scrambled to obscure the orders we had imposed, and Ss were simply told about the proposed experimental competitions and the prize conditions and then were asked to rank the four people listed in the order in which they preferred them as partners.

In Fig. 6.18, the mean ranks assigned by Ss to the potential partners are given in terms of parners' characteristics, S's own score, and grade in school. The mean rank assigned to potential partners who are both able and liked decreases in the high self-score group with increasing age, and the mean rank assigned to relatively disliked unable partners increases. The reverse holds for the low self-score group. But in the groups where there is a conflict apparent between how much the potential partner is liked and how able he is, that is in the HL and LH groups, there is more variability as a function of Ss' age, and the trends are roughly the same in the two groups though relatively less in the Ss whose own scores are low. From grades 1 to 4 there is a sharp increase in the mean rank assigned to the high ability classmate who is relatively disliked, and a corresponding

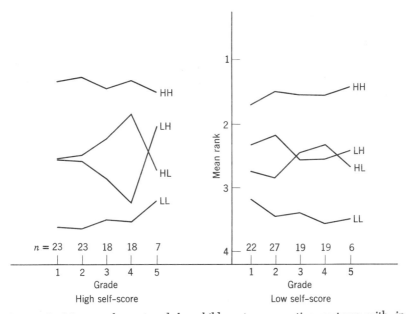

Fig. 6.18 Mean ranks assigned by children to prospective partners with indicated characteristics, by Ss' grade and self-score. H and L stand, respectively for "high" and "low"; the first letter relates to partner's ability, the second to his liking rank. (Dated collected by B. Liberman.)

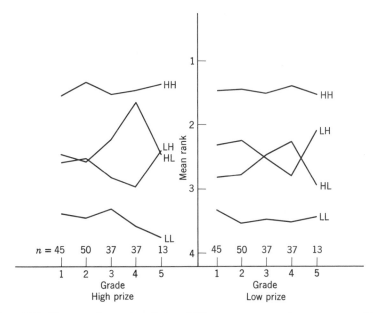

Fig. 6.19 Mean ranks assigned by children to prospective partners with indicated characteristics, by Ss' grade and by prize value. See Fig. 6.18 for interpretation of H and L. (Data collected by B. Liberman.)

decrease in the rank assigned to the low ability partner who is strongly liked, and between the fourth and fifth grades there is a sharp reversal of this relation. So, over the first four grades, on the average, the highest rankings for partner preferences went to the most able available classmates, but the older children gave the highest rankings to those whom they most liked.[8]

Fig. 6.19 shows that these relations are duplicated when the results are divided according to prize conditions, though here more credence should be accorded to the differences because, between prize conditions, each S is his own control.

Further examination of the data from the rankings where liking for the classmate and his ability are in conflict gives the following interesting result as a function of Ss' own alleged ability and value

[8] Note that the age-grade correlation in this situation is different from that found in the typical public school—the children are older, on the average, grade for grade in the Hebrew school, and the grades are less homogeneous with respect to age of the pupils. These facts result from the students' later (and more heterogenous) start in the study of Hebrew and from their being assigned to grades strictly on the basis of their facility in that language.

of the prize. In order to explain it clearly, it will help to bear in mind the following arbitrary symbolization for the conditions:

TABLE 6.11
Key to Letter Designations of Conditions in Partner Choice Experiment with Children

		Partner's Score	
		High	Low
Ss' ranked liking for partner	High	A	B
	Low	C	D

Now if S ranks C higher than B he is choosing on the basis of ability rather than liking and we arbitrarily code the order $(C > B)$ as plud $(+)$. If the reverse ranking occurs $(C < B)$ then S chooses on the basis of liking rather than ability and we code the difference minus $(-)$. Next, remembering that between the prize conditions each S is his own control, we take the difference between the two differences, so that if S ranks by ability when the prize is high and by liking when the prize is low, we call the second difference positive. The size of the difference will then tell us about the tendency to regard ability rather liking in ranking potential partners, as a function of the value of the prize. Table 6.12 shows that among

TABLE 6.12
Mean Partner-Rank Differences $(C - B)$ by Self-Score, Prize Level, and Grade

	High Self-Score			Low Self-Score		
Grade	High Prize	Low Prize	Diff. (L − H)	High Prize	Low Prize	Diff. (L − H)
1	− .52	+ .48	+1.00	+ .27	+ .50	+ .23
2	− .35	+ .18	+0.53	+ .41	+ .89	+ .48
3	− .83	+ .23	+1.06	− .36	+ .16	+ .52
4	−1.56	−1.22	+0.34	− .52	+ .16	+ .68
5	+ .29	+1.00	+0.71	− .17	+ .86	+1.03

For interpretation of $(C - B)$ see Table 6.11.
(Data collected by B. Liberman.)

the Ss of low ability the tendency to favor ability over liking as a basis for choosing partners, as prize grows in value, increases among the Ss of low ability monotonically as a function of grade (age), but the fluctuations among the Ss of high ability are irregular and unsystematic.

Between the Ss with high self-scores and those with low self-scores, combined without regard to grade or prize value, there are no significant differences in the mean ranks assigned to the four potential partners. However, *within* the low self-score group the mean ranks assigned to the various potential partners are related to the prize and age variables differently than they are within the high self-score group. The relevant means and the rank orders of potential partners based on those means are shown in Table 6.13. From the rank orders given in that table it can be determined that over all grades there is an invariant pattern of average ordering by low self-score Ss in the low prize condition. They assign the first two ranks to the best liked potential partners and discriminate them as ranks 1 and 2 on the basis of ability; they assign the last two ranks to the best liked potential partners and discriminate them as ranks 3 and 4 on the basis of ability. We may call this the low-self-score-low-prize pattern. The only different pattern of ordering appears almost universally in all grades (grade 5 only, *excepted*) among the high self-score Ss in the high prize condition. This high-self-score-high-prize pattern assigns the first ranks to the two potential partners with high ability and distinguishes them as ranks 1 and 2 on the basis of liking; it assigns the last two ranks to potential partners with low ability and distinguishes between ranks 3 and 4 on the basis of liking. It is easy to ascertain that the presence of one of these patterns is a function of value of prize, level of S's own alleged ability, and S's age (grade). In grades 1 and 2 only the high-self-score-high-prize Ss show the pattern of mean ranks which we named for them. All other groups, regardless of self-score or value of prize offered, show the low-self-score-low-prize pattern. In grades 3 and 4 only the low-self-score-low-prize Ss show the pattern named for them, and all other groups show the characteristic pattern of the high-self-score-high-prize conditions. In any condition, the HH potential partner is ranked first on the average and the LL potential is ranked last. The changes in patterns shown in Table 6.13, therefore, are due to changes in the average rank position given to the two potential partners whose level of liking and level of alleged ability do not agree: the one who is liked but said to lack ability (HL) and the one who is relatively less liked but said to be very able (LH). The changes in rank order of these

TABLE 6-13

Mean Ranks Assigned to Potential Partners by Ss in Various Conditions

Grade	Liking	Partner Score	High Self-Score High Prize	High Self-Score Low Prize	Low Self-Score High Prize	Low Self-Score Low Prize
1	High	High	1.43	1.26	1.68	1.73
		Low	2.78	2.35	2.41	2.32
	Low	High	2.26	2.83	2.68	2.82
		Low	3.52	3.57	3.23	3.14
2	High	High	1.23	1.35	1.44	1.56
		Low	2.74	2.43	2.33	2.07
	Low	High	2.39	2.61	2.74	2.96
		Low	3.65	3.61	3.48	3.41
3	High	High	1.44	1.50	1.58	1.53
		Low	3.00	2.56	2.68	2.47
	Low	High	2.17	2.33	2.32	2.63
		Low	3.39	3.61	3.42	3.37
4	High	High	1.39	1.22	1.53	1.58
		Low	3.28	3.22	2.68	2.37
	Low	High	1.72	2.00	2.16	2.53
		Low	3.56	3.50	3.63	3.53
5	High	High	1.57	1.43	1.17	1.67
		Low	2.14	2.00	2.67	2.17
	Low	High	2.43	3.00	2.50	2.83
		Low	3.86	3.57	3.67	3.33

(Data collected by B. Liberman.)

two potential partners are shown graphically in Fig. 6.20. These graphs correspond to the verbal descriptions given above and are presented here for visualization.

The figure shows that the average rank orders of the LH and HL potential partners are reversed between the high-prize-high-self-score and the low-prize-low-self-score Ss. The LH potential partner has a significantly higher overall mean rank in the high-prize-high-self-score group than in the low-prize-low-self-score group, and the reverse is true (also a significant difference) for the LH partner. From the point of view of significance tests, the progression of change in

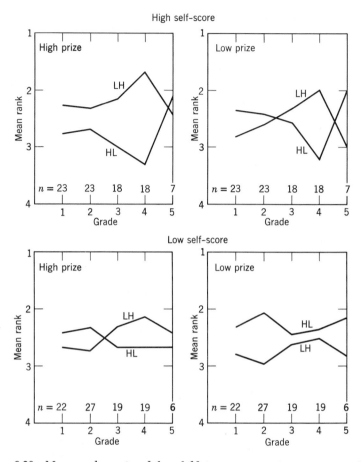

Fig. 6.20   Mean ranks assigned by children to prospective partners with conflicting ability and liking characteristics, by Ss' grade, self-score and by prize-value. See Fig. 6.18 for interpretation of H and L. (Data collected by Liberman.)

the LH and HL mean ranks from grade 1 to grade 4 is elusive. Only in the high-self-score-low-prize group can we prove that the mean rank of LH is significantly higher in grade 4 than in grades 1 and 2, and the mean rank of HL is lower in grade 4 than in grades 1 and 2. The similar progression that appears for the high self-score Ss under the high prize condition is not supported by tests of significance, nor can we pool the data with those of the high-self-score-low-prize condition, because they are the same Ss. This means that their self-score is constant, and the progression is probably a real one.

Its generality is obscured here by the fact that even the youngest children with high self-scores in the high prize condition give relatively high ranks to the LH potential partner. The overall effect of prize on preference for the LH partner is significant—he is ranked significantly higher in the combined high prize conditions than in the combined low prize conditions, and the reverse is true for the HL potential partner.

Another way to look at the graphs in Fig. 6.20 is in terms of the average rank distance between the disliked but able (LH) partner and the liked but unable (HL) partner. This is ordinarily a risky test to attempt with ranking data because it lays us open to relying upon mere artifacts. Specifically, if the number of things ranked is very large (at least larger than the number we have used here) and we attempt to prove that there is a significant difference between two adjacent ranks, we run afoul of the fact that the ranks are not independent. If one object has been assigned a high rank then some other object must *necessarily* have a lower rank, and if we are *averaging* ranks, we cannot always tell exactly *which* of the other objects was affected. In the data at hand, the two ends of the average ranking scale the HH and LL potential partners are assigned average ranks that are practically invariant over all conditions, so differences between the HL and the LH potential partners are the only ranks that vary significantly even between groups. And if we look at the differences in their average ranks within groups of Ss we can estimate the extent to which the Ss discriminate them. Thus, combining all Ss without regard to grade, it appears that in the high prize condition the low self-score Ss don't discriminate between LH (mean rank, 2.47) and HL (mean rank, 2.49), and in the low prize condition the high self-score Ss don't discriminate (mean rank for LH, 2.53; for HL, 2.52), that is, there are no significant differences between the mean ranks within each pair.[9] However, in the low prize condition the low self-score Ss give a significantly higher mean rank to the HL potential partner (2.29) than to the LH potential partner (2.78). In the high prize condition, the high self-score Ss give a higher mean rank to the LH potential partner (2.19) than to the HL potential partner (2.87).

This is consistent with our findings with the student nurses: that low ability Ss favored similarly endowed partners regardless of the value of the prize; and high ability Ss favored similarly endowed partners, even if they did not like them, when the value of the prize

[9] All these significance tests were made by the Kolmogorov-Smirnov one-sample test with significance level at p = .05 (cf. Siegel, 1956).

was high; when the prize is low, they are just as likely to stick with their friends as the low ability Ss are. To that finding the present experiment adds that low ability Ss, when the stakes are high, are not immune to choosing partners for ability rather than for general liking, but that this tendency appears to increase with age. At least it increases with age in our data from grades 1 to 4. The general pattern of our results seems to suggest that low ability Ss, though they were not immune to the lure of prizes to be gained in cooperation with partners, and though they recognized that choosing able partners would increase their probability of winning, were nevertheless more reluctant than high ability Ss to choose a disliked, able partner when the stakes were worth it. Regardless of the chooser's ability, if the potential partner is both liked and able he is given first consideration, but if he is both disliked and unable he is universally given last place.

The behavior of the fifth grade Ss is an enigma and we can only speculate on why they behaved so differently from the fourth graders. The fifth graders are a special problem because they clearly reversed the age trends in the high self-score conditions, but not in the low self-score conditions. It may be fortunate that we got such results. Otherwise, we might have failed to comment on other conditions than those we have studied which might contribute to the consistent preference for well liked partners, which characterizes their rankings in three of the four conditions. The fourth and fifth graders did not differ significantly in mean age, so we cannot attribute their differences to factors associated with age, such as adolescent idealism, loyalty, antagonism to authority figures, etc. One group is no more likely to be "adolescent" than the other in these respects, but the fifth graders had one property that sharply differentiated them from the other grades—the size of their group and the length of time they had been together. There are only 13 of them altogether, and that is all that there were in the whole class—we used them all. This is the smallest group we have ever used and it is possible that this group is abnormally cohesive, or that it is divided sharply into cliques, that to them a friend is a friend, no matter what the circumstances. We can do no more here than point out that the phenomena we have focused on will not be understood thoroughly until they have been studied under systematically varied conditions of group life, such as cohesiveness, the presence of coalitions, etc.

Chapter 7
A GLANCE AT PSYCHOPATHOLOGY

One does not have to read very extensively in the literature on psychopathology before he comes across references to disturbances in self-awareness and self-evaluation. Nor need one talk to many patients, whatever their diagnoses, before he becomes aware that the kinds of remarks they make about themselves are outside the "normal" range of self-evaluative statements.

EXPERIMENTS ON SCHIZOPHRENIC PATIENTS

We will not attempt to review the literature on psychopathology extensively. For all of its bulk, relatively little of it depends on experimental results or even suggests experiments which might be done. One hundred years ago psychiatrists were suggesting in their case studies that some of their patients might be diagnosed on the basis of disturbances in self-awareness, and a good deal of this literature was reviewed by Hirt (1909, 1910) and by James (1890) in his chapter on Consciousness of Self. The preoccupation of Morton Prince and his collaborators with multiple personality (Prince, 1905, 1920) led to many speculations about the basis of self-awareness. Freud (1916–18) stated categorically that any man who verbally degrades and berates himself, as the typical melancholiac does, is sick even if that is the only thing which differentiates him from other men. In the same article Freud asserted that schizophrenics (paraphrenics in his nomenclature) suffered from overweening megalomania, that they withdraw all cathexes on to "the ego" without setting up even fantasied objects there. This lack of a reality handle by which a schizophrenic could be grasped was the reason why these patients could not be treated by psychoanalysis. This consideration also led Freud to emphasize the importance of learning more about the ego as prerequisite to developing methods of treatment for schizophrenics (Freud, 1916–18, 1920).

Bellak's (1958) recent editorial survey of the literature on schizo-

327

phrenia led him to conclude that these patients suffer, among other things, from a deficiency in "coping" behavior. By "coping behavior," psychologists usually refer to planning, scheduling, insight, and foresight, the marshalling of abilities and information for the pursuit of goals, and the actual striving itself—exactly the domain of behavior we have been considering in this book. Rodnick and Garmezy (1957) advanced a developmental hypothesis about schizophrenia which differentiates their coping behavior from that of normals as a function of the content of the situations in which they are acting. Schizophrenics are said to be systematically deficient, relative to normals, when threatening social situations or stimuli representing them are involved, but the differences between the patients and the normals are reduced and sometimes absent when non-social goals are involved. Cavanaugh (1958) found that schizophrenic patients did not do as well as normals on a concept learning task when neither group was rewarded for correct answers, but the patient's performance was indistinguishable from that of the normals when both groups were rewarded for correct answers by a momentary cessation of loud "white noise" sounded through earphones. Olson (1958) compared the performances of schizophrenics and normals after they had either succeeded or failed on a similar task. In the normals the experience of success produced, if anything, a slight decrease in performance between the first and second tasks, and failure produced a large and significant increase. The reverse was true for the schizophrenics: failure produced no significant change between their first and second performances, but success produced a large increase. Thus, as Olson put it, success is a better motivator for schizophrenics than it is for normals.

Possibly continued experimentation of this type will lead ultimately to a precise description of just what it means to say that schizophrenics are deficient in coping behavior. Clinical observations also contain suggestive hints: for example, the observation by Goldfarb (1958) that there is a sizable proportion of autistic children (possibly young schizophrenics) who do not respond to cues which tell a normal child that he has finished some process or activity sequence. In one case the child's mother was in a quandary about whether to help him by telling him that he had had enough to eat! According to the usual criteria it seemed pretty clear that the child himself was genuinely confused about it. The empty plate, the time he had spent emptying it, the food in his stomach, and his repeated swallowing and chewing motions "meant nothing" to him in this context. Other children with a similar diagnosis seemed not to be sure that they had completed a puzzle even when all the pieces were in place. There is a variety of plausible explanations for such behavior. For example, a person may persist because he can't recognize completion, or because he can't think of anything different to begin, or because he can't imagine raising his LA to create a new transaction with the same materials. Whatever the explanation, whatever proves to be the best way to describe the defect in detail, it appears that the life space of some schizophrenic patients is relatively undifferentiated through time, lacking the nodal points, the terminations of old strivings and the beginnings of new ones, which are so characteristic of "normal" behavior. Only continued detailed observation, preferably in experimental situations, can clarify this picture for us. Such observation, no matter how extensive, can only reveal the *status quo* differences and similarities between the patients and the normals; it could not, by itself, yield a theory of the origin of schizophrenic pathology. A theory of origins will depend heavily on experimentation and observation aimed specifically at the *general* process of psychological development, but a good descriptive differentiation would put the developmentalist's problem within definite limits, suggest what to look for, and what not to bother with. It would give him narrower, more precise focus.

There seems every reason to believe that normal purposive behavior involves the conceptual processes of generalization and abstraction. Even with human beings there is no need to assume that such processes are necessarily conscious or depend in a rigid way on the organism's ability to describe his problem and his related behavior in words. It is a truism in studies of concept formation that Ss may make completely correct assignments of new instances[1] to categories and be unable to give an adequate verbal description of the class characteristics which define the membership of some instances and the exclusion of others. Given concrete instances he can assign them correctly but he cannot tell us in words how he does it and he probably cannot teach anyone else to do it except by example. In Tolman's (1932) description of purposive behavior the notion of "means-end capacities" rests on observations of the behavior of rats, in part on Krechevsky's (1932) notion of hypothesis testing in rats. In Maier's (1929) early experiments on "reasoning," rats combined two hitherto unrelated experiences to get from one place to another by a route they formerly never used, when the usual route was blocked. Needless

---

[1] Writers on concepts usually refer to an individual member of a category as an *instance* of the class or concept. For example, *a* tiger is an *instance* of the concepts animal, carnivore, cat, and tiger.

to say, this observation was independent of the rat's verbal report about his thinking. The infrahuman primates obviously behave in a conceptual way (Hebb and Thompson, 1954), even to the point where an observer can decide that chimpanzees behave deceptively—appearing to be engaged in one kind of behavior while actually planning another. In chimpanzees, the "deception" is designed to lure the victim of aggression within effective range, or to permit the aggressor to approach close enough. Piaget's (1952, 1954) observations on the development of concepts in human children extend well below the age of language use and strongly suggest that the purposive activities of very young children include concept-like behavior. Our own experiments with children (Chapter 4) suggest the interpretation that involves concepts of value, likelihood of success, and power, even though we could not expect children to give a coherent verbal account of any of these notions. They *act as though* they had such concepts, and that is enough.

Indeed the very notion of purposive behavior seems to imply concept-like behavior which can be described apart from detailed knowledge or speculation about the precise central mediating processes involved. Therefore, when we ask about the behavior of schizophrenics or other pathological cases in situations where purposive behavior is required, we are necessarily involved in confronting the question about the patient's degree of "contact with reality."

Can Schizophrenics Be Motivated?

Armin Loeb and the present author undertook to explore the general nature of the concepts which schizophrenic patients have about their own ability relative to that of others (Diggory and Loeb, 1962).

Discussions with schizophrenic patients and reading of case reports suggests that they suffer (among other things) from a sense of failure, inadequacy, and lack of hope that they could better their condition by their own efforts even if they had the opportunity. In other words, they suffer from low self-esteem, which may account for their well-known lack of initiative. Of course, with hospitalized patients, this attitude may be due, in part, to lack of encouragement and dearth of opportunities in their environment. Accordingly, in this experiment we (1) manipulated the evidence we gave the Ss about their abilities, and (2) provided them with opportunities to act on the implications of that evidence. Because of our ignorance of the consequences to the patient of a strong increment in his motivation, and of the relation of motivation to other aspects of his condition, we deliberately designed a low-pressure experiment. The whole situation was embedded in a play or recreational context, the abilities allegedly tested were of limited utility, and the opportunities for future action were restricted to the present and expected future hospital environment of the patients. Nevertheless, there was considerable interest among those who participated, and *E* was frequently approached, long after the data were collected, by patients who wanted to know about the future activities.

The experiment was designed to test the hypothesis that, in schizophrenic patients, evidence about the power of their abilities would affect their initiative to use their abilities. As evidence of motivation and initiative, we asked them to volunteer for activities more or less closely related to the abilities which had been tested. The variety of these activities provided an opportunity to explore the generality of motivational arousal. In order to discover whether the patients responded appropriately to evidence of different levels of ability, we also asked them to vote for other patients (whose abilities they knew about) for the same tasks as those for which they had offered themselves as volunteers. We compared patients from different wards, differing in their average degree of pathology, in order to see whether level of illness affected either volunteering or voting.

The Ss were male chronic schizophrenics, without known organic impairment, from three continuous treatment wards at a VA hospital.[2] All were privileged, but the three wards differed roughly in the degree of morbidity of their patient populations. Ss met in groups of three—one member from each ward. Thirty-two three-man groups were run, each in a single session lasting about a half hour. Of these, 24 groups (72 Ss) are included in the analysis. The other eight groups were eliminated for the following reasons: one because one S claimed he couldn't read, one because E handed out the wrong tasks, and six because the "medium" and "low" ability Ss' performances were inconsistent with E's intent. Because they came from different wards. Ss in each group knew each other only casually, if at all.

In each session, Ss were introduced and seated at separate desks. E explained that he was a psychologist who had been asked by the Recreation Service to invent some new games so the patients would not get tired of playing Bingo all the time; they were now going to

[2] The Ss in this experiment were patients at the VA Hospital, Coatesville, Pa. The experiment was done while Dr. Loeb was a social psychology trainee there. We are grateful to the administrative officers of the hospital, and especially to our friend and colleague, Dr. David Cohen, Chief of Psychological Services, for the opportunity to do this research.

play the games developed so far. Rules and scoring procedures were carefully explained and each S scored his own performances (which was done with consistently high accuracy). The scores were announced aloud and E recorded them under each S's name on a blackboard. Each S completed four tasks.

Each task had a variant for "easy," "medium," and "hard" difficulty levels. The correct *answers* for each variant were identical but, without Ss' knowledge, the difficulty of *finding* the answers varied. For any given S, all four tasks were either "easy," "medium," or "hard." Thus, when scores on all four tasks were reported, one S was consistently superior to the other two, one was consistently lower, and the third consistently mediocre. The results justified the assumption that Ss interpreted these differences in terms of their own abilities. In half the groups all Ss worked on mental tasks; the remainder did motor tasks. Task type produced no differences on any of the dependent variables. We used only those groups in which the intended order of performance occurred on all four tasks.

The mental tasks were three-minute word games, each a list of twenty words of a particular category: fruits, animals, vegetables, and birds. The problem was to fill in the missing letters for each word. Every S had the same words, in the same order, but the number of blanks required to complete each word differed. There was only one possible correct answer for each word and the score on each game was the total number of words correctly completed. Table 7.1 gives an example of each of the mental games.

For the motor tasks, S received two identical copies of each and was instructed to turn the first one face down as soon as he had finished it and go on immediately to the second. The first motor game

TABLE 7.1
Examples of Mental Tasks

	Tasks			
Category	Easy	Medium	Hard	Answer
Fruit	b_n_na	_ _n_na	_ _n_ _a	banana
Animals	ch_pm_ _k	c_ _pm_ _k	c_ _pm_ _ _	chipmunk
Vegetables	l_tt_ce	l_t_ _e	_ _t_ _e	lettuce
Birds	can_r_	c_n_r_	c_ _ _r_	canary

(After Diggory and Loeb, 1962.)

required drawing a line through the numbers 1 to 50 consecutively, with the numbers, more or less difficult to locate, scattered in irregular arrays on a sheet of paper, eight and one-half by eleven inches. The score on the first game was the number of consecutive integers correctly connected. In the second motor game S had to connect successive letters of the alphabet which were irregularly scattered, and his score was the number of consecutive letters connected. In the third game, S had to trace a line through a series of gaps without touching either side of the gap. The gaps varied in width: narrowest in the hard task, widest in the easy. Score was the number of gaps successfully traced through. The fourth motor task required mirror tracing between the borders of a twenty-sectioned design without touching either side. The space between the borders was widest for the easy condition, narrowest for the hard. Score was the number of sections correctly traced through. The time allowed for each motor game was two minutes.

After the four games were completed, and while the scores were still on the blackboard, S answered ten questions, each on a three-inch by five-inch card:

1. His guess, anywhere between 0 and 100, of how many different English words he could write in three minutes (he was not, actually, expected to write them).

2. His willingness to volunteer to compete with other groups in the same games just played.

3. His vote for one of the three men, including himself, to compete with other groups in the games just played.

4. His willingness to volunteer to compete with other groups on the same kinds of games, but *harder* ones.

5. His vote for one of the three men, including himself, to compete with other groups on the same kinds of games, but *harder* ones.

6. After E explained how to play one of the motor games to those who just played the mental games, and *vice versa*, S stated his willingness to volunteer to play the *new* game with other groups.

7. His vote for one of the three men, including himself, to compete with other groups in the *new game*.

8. After E said that some men did much worse on the games than anyone present (a statement designed to alleviate the anxiety of those who had performed relatively poorly), S expressed his willingness to try and teach them to play the games.

9. His enjoyment of the games played.

10. His willingness to meet again with the same group to play some other games.

The question is whether "ability," as indicated by repeated "success" relative to others, differentially affected attitudes toward the self (volunteering) and toward others (voting for them). The principal results are shown in Table 7.2. Frequency of volunteering to compete with others in the *same games* was high in all ability conditions and did not differ significantly as a function of manipulated ability. However, differential ability did affect volunteering for *harder* games of the same kind: the "high ability" Ss did this significantly more often than the "low ability" Ss. There were no differences in volunteering for a *different kind* of game as a function of ability level. The incidence of volunteering to teach others is also unrelated to ability level, probably because the "others" were said to have done worse than any

TABLE 7.2
Frequencies of Volunteering and Rating by Expected Task Type and Induced Ability Level

A. Frequency of Volunteering by Type of Task Expected

Induced Ability Level	Same		Same but Harder		Different		Teach Others	
	Yes	No	Yes	No	Yes	No	Yes	No
High	16	8	15	9	14	10	12	12
Medium	14	10	11	13	16	8	15	9
Low	13	11	8	16	14	10	14	9

Not signif. χ^2(Hi vs. Lo) = 5.26, Not signif. Not signif.
df = 1, p < .05

B. Frequency of Votes Received by Type of Task Expected

Induced Ability Level	Same		Same but Harder		Different	
	1 or 2 Votes	None	1 or 2 Votes	None	1 or 2 Votes	None
High	20	4	21	3	15	9
Medium	10	14	12	12	12	12
Low	8	16	6	18	9	15

$\chi^2 = 12.7$, d.f. = 2, $\chi^2 = 19.2$, d.f. = 2,   Not signif.
p < .01   p < .001

(After Diggory and Loeb, 1962.)

of the Ss. To summarize the results on volunteering: the majority of Ss (an average of about 59%) regardless of their own supposed ability, volunteered to compete with others in the same games, to compete with others in different games, and to teach less able people to play the games better. Manipulated ability level made a difference in the incidence of volunteering only when (*a*) there was a challenge; i.e., when the expected task was harder than the one already done, and (*b*) one in which Ss' abilities have already been tested to some extent. The Ss with high ability volunteered for all tasks with about the same frequency, so in the "same-but-harder" tasks it was the refusal of the low ability Ss to volunteer which produced the association with ability level.

Voting for another man in the group to compete with others on the same game, or in a game of the *same type, but harder,* was directly related to demonstrated "ability." Voting for others to compete in different games varied in the same direction, but not significantly. Ss did not vote for each other as teachers. The pattern of voting generally varied directly with the "ability" of the person voted for, regardless of whether or not the expected task would be more challenging. Since Ss were explicitly permitted to vote for themselves (a kind of volunteering), it is appropriate to mention that incidence of self-voting, though low throughout, paralleled incidence of volunteering, but the trends were not significant.

Mean level of expectation, indicated by S's estimate (between 0 and 100) of how many different words he could write in three minutes, was significantly affected by the induced ability levels. The means were 58 for high ability, 45 for medium, and 25 for low ($F = 5.81$, p. $< .001$).

When asked if they enjoyed the games, Ss' responses were mostly affirmative: $^{23}\!/_{24}$ for high ability, $^{22}\!/_{24}$ for medium, and $^{20}\!/_{24}$ for low. The proportions of affirmative responses were lower when it came to the question of meeting with the same group to play other games: $^{12}\!/_{24}$ for high ability, $^{16}\!/_{24}$ for medium, and $^{15}\!/_{24}$ for low ability. Neither stated enjoyment nor desire to join the group again were significantly associated with induced ability level.

The choice of Ss from three different wards permitted a rough estimate of the effect of degree of morbidity on volunteering, voting, and level of expectation because the wards were ordered in the average "sickness" of their patients. This ordering was not perfect, because assignment of a patient to a particular ward was determined not only by how sick he was but also by other factors, such as the location of available beds. Since there is probably considerable overlap in morbidity among the three wards, the data on the effects of morbidity have a lot of error in them, and the effects are probably minimal.

There is no evidence from volunteering, voting, or level of expectation that presumed morbidity level and manipulated ability level interacted. Furthermore, Ss from the allegedly poorer wards gave no consistent evidence of an ordering of adjustment. Therefore, Table 7.3 shows the data on volunteering and voting without regard to ability level and with the two more "poorly adjusted" groups combined for comparison with the "better" group. The notable effect is that Ss from the better ward volunteered to compete in some tasks, and in same-but-harder tasks, in higher proportions than those from the "poorer" wards, but morbidity is not significantly associated with volunteering for different tasks, nor is voting significantly affected on any issue by the ward of origin of the patient voted for.

TABLE 7.3
Volunteering and Voting by Adjustment of Patients in Different Wards

A. Volunteering for tasks:

Patient Adjustment	Same		Same but Harder		Different	
	Yes	No	Yes	No	Yes	No
Better	19	5	15	9	17	7
Worse	24	24	19	29	27	12
	$\chi^2 = 4.80$, d.f. $= 1$, $p < .05$		$\chi^2 = 3.43$ (need $\chi^2 = 3.84$ at $p = .05$)		Not signif.	

B. Voting for others to work on tasks:

Patient Adjustment	Same		Same but Harder		Different	
	1 or 2	None	1 or 2	None	1 or 2	None
Better	12	12	14	10	12	12
Worse	26	22	25	23	25	23
	Not signif.		Not signif.		Not signif.	

(After Diggory and Loeb, 1962.)

We decided that these patients did not suffer from a *generalized* deficiency either with respect to recognizing the "demonstrated fact" of their superiority or inferiority to others in certain abilities, or in their tendency to act rationally in accordance with those "facts," except that the sicker they were, the less tendency they showed to volunteer for a job even when they had more of the required ability than any other patient present at the time.

P(s), LA, and Actual Performance of Schizophrenics

Next we turned our attention to other details of schizophrenics' responses to goal-seeking situations. We repeated, with a group of schizophrenic patients at the same hospital, several of the experimental manipulations we used with normals Ss as described in Chapter 4.

With only E present, each S performed two card-sorting tasks in succession. Five suits were sorted in the first task and five different suits in the second task. S sorted from a pack of 35 cards (7 of each suit) which he held face down in one hand. Each task consisted of seven 20-second trials and, in order to eliminate variations in difficulty over Ss on any one trial, E gave S a new, prearranged pack for each trial. The order of cards in these packs differed for every trial, but on any one trial the order was the same for all Ss.

S was told that he should try to sort 20 cards correctly on at least one of the seven trials, and that each trial was 30 seconds long. S sat facing a panel of perforated masonite which was arranged to look like a graph (see Fig. 4.1). A horizontal string stretched across the graph at score level 30 indicated the score S was going to try to equal or exceed. A vertical string after trial 7 marked the deadline.

To control the performance curves reported to Ss each trial was stopped, not when a fixed time had elapsed, but when S had correctly sorted a predetermined number of cards. There was no evidence that any of the Ss suspected this deception. S's score for each trial was announced to him aloud and then recorded for him by E's placing a colored golf tee in the appropriate hole in the masonite panel.

The three dependent variables were measured as follows. For actual performance (AP), E recorded the true elapsed time for each trial, which was later used to compute the number of seconds per card sorted. All trials can be compared on this measure. Before each trial S marked a 100-point linear rating scale to show his estimate of the "chances in a hundred" that he would reach the goal at least once within the remaining trials—the P(s) estimate. LA was S's statement, before each trial, of the score he would try to make on that trial.

Male chronic schizophrenic patients, all from the hospital's "best" ward, were randomly assigned to four conditions defined by the

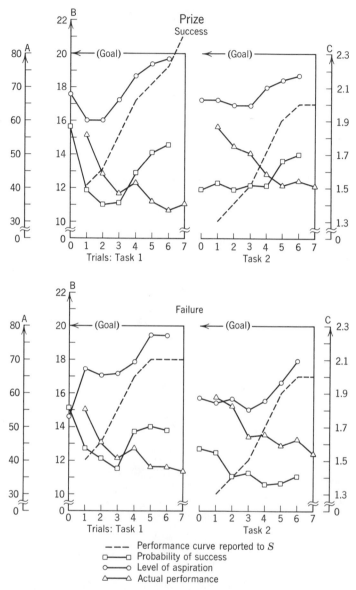

Fig. 7.1 Experimental conditions and associated means of estimated $P(s)$ (Scale A), LA (Scale B), and actual performance (AP) (Scale C), for hospitalized schizophrenic patients. Each data point is the mean of 15 Ss. (Data collected by Armin Loeb.)

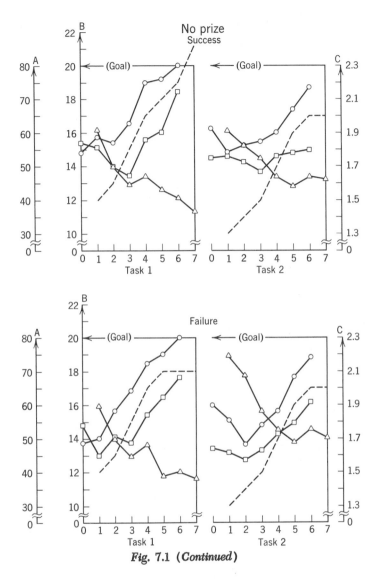

Fig. 7.1 (*Continued*)

combinations of the success-failure and prize-no prize variables. The design of the experiment is shown in Fig. 7.1 and in Table 7.4. On the first task, half the Ss failed and half succeeded. This required two different performance curves: one continuously rising and showing a clearly successful performance on the last trial. The other curve was identical with the first over the first five trials, but remained at a failing plateau over trials 6 and 7. For half the Ss (the prize condition) a crisp new one-dollar bill was displayed near the performance display panel throughout the first task. Successful Ss were allowed to take it and keep it.[3] Unsuccessful Ss watched it disappear into E's pocket. Nothing was said about a prize to the other Ss, and all of the no-prize Ss were run before mention of a prize was made to anybody.

After a brief rest of about two minutes, S performed the second task, "just to see how well he could do," with no expectation of any kind of reward. All Ss had identical, failing performance curves in the second task (different from the failure curves of the first task). Thus, in the second task, we can look for the effects of the success-failure and the prize-no prize variables under conditions where feedback from S's present performance is constant, and only previous experiences differed.

To find out whether Ss would report various feelings which reflected the influence of the independent variables of the experiment we asked the following questions at the end of task 1: Did you like the task you just finished? How do you feel right now? How many different words do you think you could write down in three minutes, any number between 1 and 100? These questions were repeated after task 2, and then two additional questions were asked: Which task did you like better, the first one or the second one? Would you like to come back again to participate in another experiment?

The results are shown in Fig. 7.1. Note that the success and failure conditions are distinguished by the different performance curves reported to Ss in task 1. In task 2 all reported performance curves are alike. Since, in task 1, the rigged performance curves reported to Ss were the same only over the first five trials, the analyses of the effects of the independent variables on $P(s)$ and LA were done two ways: (1) only through the first five trials, and (2) over all trials. The results of both analyses were the same.

Fig. 7.2 summarized the trends of LA, $P(s)$, and actual performance in both tasks as a function of success-failure and prize-no prize conditions in the first task. The overall means per S per trial are summarized in Table 7.4. In the first task, only the prize-no prize conditions affected the dependent variables significantly: Ss working for a prize worked faster, and stated higher LA and lower $P(s)$ than did those not working for a prize. There were no significant differences

[3] We wish to thank Dr. Robert R. Bush, then Chairman of the Department of Psychology, University of Pennsylvania, for providing the prize money from departmental research funds.

due to the success-failure variable because the difference between success and failure did not occur until the last two trials. There was no significant interaction between the prize and success variables.

The effects of the prize variable persisted into the second task, where no prize was offered. In addition, there were marked effects due to the previous experience of success or failure: for the previously successful group, LA was higher, $P(s)$ was higher, and actual performance was better (faster) than for the previously unsuccessful group. Note that the legitimate comparisons are between conditions on each task separately. Comparisons of task 1 and task 2 are risky because the two tasks were not strictly equated for difficulty. Task 2 seemed slightly harder.

An interesting fact emerges from the covariation of the dependent variables as a function of the experimental conditions. When the effect of the value of a successful performance is considered (differences between the prize and no-prize groups) the *better* performance and higher LA in the prize conditions is associated with lower $P(s)$ in both tasks, but, when the effects of success and failure are considered for the second task only, the *worse* performances and lower LA are associated with the lower $P(s)$. In general terms, this finding amounts to saying that the relations among $P(s)$, LA, and actual performance depended on the conditions used to induce differences in these variables.

Responses to the questions about feelings are summarized in Table 7.5. There is little of interest in these data. In comparison with those who succeeded on task 1, a smaller proportion of those who failed gave positive descriptions of their feelings ("All right," "Pretty good," etc.), but the difference is not significant. Ss who had succeeded in winning a prize guessed that they could write *fewer* words in three minutes than did any other group of Ss. Furthermore, after failing the second task, the prize-winning Ss significantly reduced the number of words they thought they could write in three minutes. This is noteworthy only because no other group of Ss did likewise. S's guess about how many different words he can write in a given period of time is a kind of LA statement. In our first experiment with psychotic patients, responses to this question varied significantly, and *directly*, with evidence that S had previously received about the rank of his abilities in a three-man group. The evidence of ability was of a different kind, but just as objective as that presented in the present experiment. There are detailed differences in the psychological situations presented in this experiment and the previous one. They may suggest where to look for the explanation of this minor reverse effect. Without

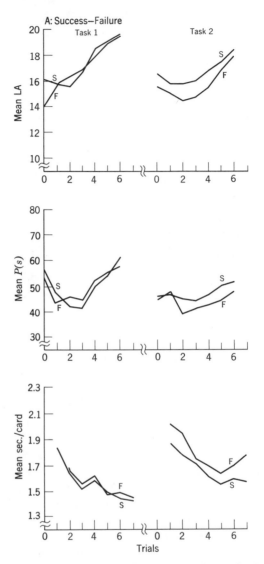

Fig. 7.2   Mean trends of LA, $P(s)$, and AP among hospitalized schizophrenic patients as a function of conditions during task 1: success—failure (Part A); prize–no prize (Part B). Each data point is the mean of 30 Ss. (Data collected by Armin Loeb.)

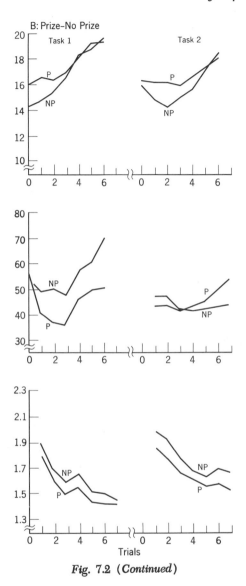

Fig. 7.2 (*Continued*)

any evidence it is fatuous to pursue the matter, so we will drop it here.

Now what do we conclude about schizophrenics from these data?

Regardless of comparisons with normal Ss, it is clear that the patients responded systematically to the presence or absence of a prize

TABLE 7.4

Means, per Subject per Trial, of Actual Performance (AP), Level of Aspiration (LA), and Estimated Probability of Success (P(s)), as a function of Experimental Conditions

	Prize		No Prize		Prize and No Prize Combined ($n = 30$)	
	Task 1	Task 2	Task 1	Task 2	Task 1	Task 2
Success						
AP (sec./card)	1.51	1.63	1.62	1.70	1.57	1.67
LA	17.7	17.4	17.0	16.1	17.4	16.8
$P(s)$	44.9	42.5	56.8	52.0	50.9	47.3
Failure						
AP (sec./card)	1.55	1.68	1.61	1.85	1.58	1.77
LA	17.4	15.8	16.7	15.8	17.1	15.8
$P(s)$	46.0	36.8	54.9	49.7	50.5	43.3
Success and Failure Combined ($n = 30$)						
AP (sec./card)	1.53	1.66	1.62	1.78		
LA	17.6	16.6	16.9	16.0		
$P(s)$	45.5	39.7	55.9	50.9		

$n = 15$ for each condition, 5 trials for task 1, 7 trials for task 2. For explanation of significant outcomes, see text.

(Data collected by Armin Loeb.)

and to the experiences of success or failure; that is, their *average levels* of $P(s)$, LA, and AP were responsive to aspects of reality which were manipulated in the experiment. However, these aspects of reality generally had no effect on their statements about their feelings after each task (Table 7.5). If we compare the psychotics with normal Ss from previous experiments where the same variables were manipulated, we find striking similarities, with a single difference. As we noted previously, the effect of the prize variable was to make LA low when $P(s)$ was high, and vice versa, a relation which Morlock found with college students (Figs. 4.18–4.20; Table 4.17).[4] Normal Ss also show lower LA and lower $P(s)$ when reported performance is low; that is, when

[4] Morlock's finding stood alone among our results until we got the present data from psychotic patients. Normal college students most often had higher $P(s)$ when the goal was important (Figs. 4.7 and 4.9) and so did normal children (Fig. 4.15).

it looks most likely that S will fail (Figs. 4.4, 4.6, 4.9, 4.11, 4.19, 4.24, and 5.2). The experiments with normal children showed that the effects of prize and success variables on $P(s)$ estimates in a subsequent task are the same as those shown by the patients in the present experiment (Table 4.8).

None of our findings contradicts Olson's (1958) report, that failure improved the subsequent performance of both schizophrenics and normals, because his Ss confronted different goals than ours. In response to the statement that they were not doing well, Olson's subjects could work harder and so improve their output. Our Ss, trying to reach a fixed performance goal, found that no matter how hard they worked, they could not succeed, so they probably got convinced that

TABLE 7.5

Summary of Responses by Fifteen Ss in each Experimental Condition after Completion of Task 1 and Task 2

	Prize		No Prize	
	Task 1	Task 2	Task 1	Task 2
A. Success on Task 1				
Number who liked task just finished	15	14	15	15
Number giving positive description of feelings	10	7	10	10
Mean number of words Ss thought they could write in three minutes	23.2*	18.0*	35.0	32.5
Number who preferred task 1 to task 2	—	12	—	14
Number who would like to return for another experiment	—	14	—	11
B. Failure on Task 1				
Number who liked task just finished	13	13	14	13
Number giving positive description of feelings	7	6	5	9
Mean number of words Ss thought they could write in three minutes	33.8	35.5	31.0	32.0
Number who preferred task 1 to task 2	—	13	—	11
Number who would like to return for another experiment	—	11	—	11

* These two means are significantly different (p < .05, t-test); they also differ significantly from all the other means in the table.
(Data collected by Armin Loeb.)

their ability was simply inadequate for the task. Faced with such discouragement, they simply do not try as hard on subsequent tasks.

Schizophrenics Ignore Deadlines

The only difference we can observe is that, generally, normal Ss successively lower their $P(s)$ estimates as the deadline gets nearer, but the schizophrenics in this experiment did not. Note, in Fig. 7.1 and Fig. 7.2, that the $P(s)$ curves of the schizophrenics continued to rise throughout the series of trials. The single exception to this is in the second task following failure to win the prize (Fig. 7.1). This might be interpreted as a special case of schizophrenic "lack of contact with reality," but if these Ss were generally and indiscriminately out of contact with reality, how could the other features of our data be so regular and systematic?

Of course we want to know why the patients did not lower their $P(s)$ estimates as they got closer to the deadline, as normal Ss usually do, but nobody offered us any explanations and we couldn't think of any, so, while we waited for the lightning to strike, we decided to see whether the phenomenon was reproducible. We repeated the experiment which was designed to prove that the position and clarity of the deadline affected the decline in $P(s)$ estimates in normal Ss (Fig. 4.5). As done with normal Ss, the experiment involved telling only some of the Ss, at the beginning, exactly where the deadline was; that is, they were told how many trials they would have (ten, for example) and there was a deadline marker on the performance display panel. The rest of the Ss were told at the beginning that they would have *at least* ten trials. They may have more, but E was not sure about how many more. The E promised to check his watch at the end of the tenth trial and to allow as many additional trials as time permitted. At the outset, there was no deadline marker for these Ss. The graph showed only room for a large number of trials—and the performance goal. When S completed the tenth trial, but before his score was announced and before he made his next $P(s)$ estimate, E told him that he would have eight, four, two, or one more trials, and an appropriate deadline marker was placed on the graph. Then we announced his score for the last trial that he completed, he made his next $P(s)$ estimate, and the procedure continued until the promised additional trials were finished. We persuaded Stanley Fagen, who was then a trainee at the Coatesville Veterans Administration Hospital, to repeat this experiment on patients at the hospital. Fagen's Ss came from exactly the same wards that Loeb and I had previously invaded, but they were not the same people we used. Thus, Loeb's patients closely resembled Fagen's, on the average, in age, length of hospitalization, diagnosis, morbidity, and ability and willingness to cooperate in the experiment.

The whole story of Fagen's results is briefly told by Fig. 7.3. Panel C, at the lower left of the figure shows the results from normal Ss (cf. Fig. 4.5). The vertical line marked X shows where the deadline always was for the clear deadline condition, and where it was ultimately clarified for Ss in the initially vague deadline condition. The curves to the left of that vertical marker, $P(s)$ estimates zero through nine, are for two groups of Ss who gave $P(s)$ estimates under conditions where the deadline was clear and where it was vague. They were trying to sort at least forty cards correctly in 25 seconds and the performance curve reported to them was the one shown in Fig. 4.4, condition 3. It rose very rapidly at the outset and decreased its rate of rise until, at trial seven, it reached a dead level one unit below the performance goal. Over the first five trials, the $P(s)$ curves for the clear and vague deadline conditions are quite similar, but in the last five trials, when the deadline is vague, $P(s)$ keeps rising, though when the deadline is clear it drops sharply. The four curves (really, three curves and one point) to the right of the vertical marker show the trends of $P(s)$ estimates for groups of four Ss to whom the position of the deadline was first revealed after the tenth trial. They are distinguished by the lengths of the curves: one, two, four, and eight points. Obviously, when the deadline was clear from the beginning, these normal Ss lowered their $P(s)$ estimates as the deadline neared, and when the deadline was vague at the outset, this reduction appeared only after is was made clear, and as a function of its distance.

Panel A of Fig. 7.3 shows the results of Fagen's identical procedure with a group of schizophrenic Ss, one-third of whom were given a clear deadline of ten trials from the beginning. The others were given an unclear deadline at the beginning, and after the tenth trial half of them were told they would have one more trial and the rest were promised eight more trials. Clearly, the effect of the deadline on the schizophrenics' $P(s)$ estimates is quite different from that on the normals'. Furthermore, in the schizophrenics' data, every downward turn is caused by a *single* S, but the *majority* of normal Ss showed these downward trends: that is, lowering $P(s)$ estimates as the deadline nears is *unusual* among schizophrenics and quite *common* among normals.

Panel B of Fig. 7.3 shows the same effect for a group of schizophrenic patients which Fagen ran under the same conditions which

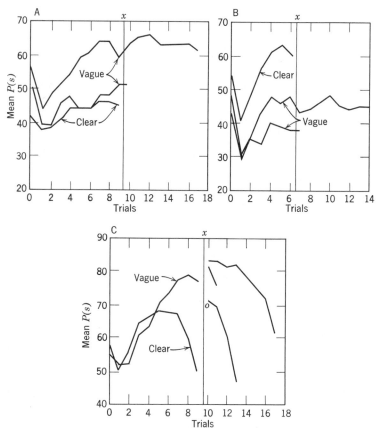

Fig. 7.3   Mean $P(s)$ trends for schizophrenic and normal Ss in card-sorting tasks with fixed performance goal and variable deadline. Part A: Three groups of schizophrenics (8 per group), goal was 40 cards correctly sorted on at least one 60-second trial, minimum trials allowed—10. Part B: Three groups of schizophrenics (8 per group), goal was 20 cards correctly sorted on at least one 30-second trial, minimum trials allowed—7. Part C: Normal Ss with goal of 40 cards correctly sorted in at least one 25-second trial. Each data point is the mean of 12 Ss in "clear" condition with deadline set at 10 trials from the beginning; 16 Ss in "vague" condition with deadline at the beginning said to be "more than 10 trials"; deadline after tenth trial announced as 1, 2, 4, or 8 more trials (4 Ss each). In each section the vertical line marked X shows when the deadline was made clear to the groups for which it was previously vague. (Data on the schizophrenic patients collected by Stanley A. Fagen; data on normals selected from experiments previously reported in Figs. 4.5 and 4.6.)

Loeb used in the previous experiment: seven trials rather than ten, a goal of twenty cards correctly sorted, and trials said to last 30 seconds. The conclusion is inescapable that, at least under the conditions of these experiments, schizophrenics do not lower their $P(s)$ estimates as normals do in response to a near approach to the deadline—the situation which we had noticed, without expecting it, in our previous data.

So we have a reproducible phenomenon that differentiates schizophrenic patients from normal people, and we don't know how to explain it. However, we can eliminate some possible explanations. In the first experiment reported in this chapter, another group of patients, with much the same characteristics as those we used in the other two experiments, responded quite reasonably to managed evidence that they were superior to other patients in the ability to perform certain tasks. The best ones *volunteered* more often than the others to participate in activities where the tested abilities would be used, and the others most often nominated the "best" man to take part in these activities. So we cannot say that these patients completely lack the concept of what it means to have better or worse ability than somebody else. Furthermore, there is the finding in Loeb's second experiment that schizophrenic patients change the overall average levels of LA and $P(s)$ as a function of the presence or absence of a prize, and of previous success or failure, in just the same way that normals do. Thus we cannot say that schizophrenics are totally devoid of the concept of what goals of different value imply, or that they fail completely to respond to the implications of their own success or failure. Therefore, we can no longer accept the glittering generality that schizophrenics are "out of contact with reality." Our data, and those of other investigators, show that they are in contact with some aspects of reality—at least as firmly as normals are. The question is, why this *particular* difference between the patients and the normals? Some people think of the reported defect in schizophrenics' ability to estimate time. Certainly, responding to a deadline requires some kind of time concept, but *what* kind? We must be careful here, too, to avoid over-generalizing and suggesting easy answers which do not relate to the specific problem. Our results recalled the observation that some schizophrenics (children, at least) have difficulty in terminating acts because the normal cues for termination do not work for them (Goldfarb, 1958). We have already noted that this observation itself is in need of explanation, so we could hardly advance it as an explanation of our latest findings. However, it is the one instance known to us in the literature on schizophrenia which bears even a slight analogy to our data on schizophrenics' apparent disregard of deadlines.

Let us speculate a little on this without prejudice to the facts. Suppose that schizophrenics are less sensitive than normals to cues which indicate that a drive (e.g., hunger) has been reduced or an act completed because its goal was achieved. How extensive might be the effects of such a condition on a person's behavior? Let us make one more supposition consistent with Goldfarb's description: that people suffering from such a defect *can* respond correctly when other people tell them the act is completed, or command them to stop. Let us assume that, though they cannot dependably recognize terminations for themselves, they can recognize and remember those that are signaled by other people. If such a defect existed, and was recognized by the patient as a difference between himself and other people, then from that defect alone we might perhaps account for the apathy, narrowness of interest, fixity of preoccupation with on-going tasks, lack of initiative in changing activities, and dependence on others, all of which are characteristic of many chronic, hospitalized schizophrenic patients. It is clear that this list, extensive though it is, neither defines schizophrenia nor reveals its origin, but the list, and the way it was derived, suggests a fruitful line of experimental research which might lead to a better understanding of schizophrenia.

Self-Evaluation and Death-Imagery

Rothman also obtained some interesting data on the differential reactions of schizophrenics and normals to success and failure experiences (Rothman, 1963). Part of her data that applies to normal Ss has already been discussed (Tables 5.9, 5.12, and 5.13). She was interested in three phenomena as consequences of the experience of success and failure: changes in self-evaluation on tested abilities, changes in self-evaluation of untested abilities, and changes in death-imagery. Her procedure, described more fully in Chapter 5 (pp. 62–67), consisted in telling the prospective Ss that she was selecting Ss for an experiment where they would learn the general principles of games of strategy (e.g., chess and Go) and, if they were interested, she was prepared to test them to find out whether they had the minimum ability to serve as Ss. She wanted to compare the responses of normals, schizophrenics, and neurotics, so she began with the hardest group to locate and test: young hospitalized schizophrenic patients between the ages of 13 and 19 years.[5] Then she went to high schools in

---

[5] Dr. Rothman obtained these Ss at State Hospitals in Allentown and Norristown, Pennsylvania, and at Trenton, New Jersey.

the Philadelphia suburbs to get the normal and "neurotic" Ss who could be matched for age and present functioning intelligence level with the already constituted schizophrenic group.

For inclusion in the schizophrenic group a S was required to have been hospitalized at least three weeks before the preliminary session of the procedure with an uncontested diagnosis of schizophrenia and a psychotic profile on the Minnesota Multiphasic Personality Inventory (MMPI). The normal Ss were students in high school who were functioning adequately, with their scores on all MMPI scales (except the masculinity-femininity—Mf—scale) less than 70, and who were considered by the school guidance counselor to have no outstanding emotional or academic problems. The "neurotic" group represents a wish rather than a reality. Rothman thought that she would be able to find, in the student populations of the large high schools she surveyed, a sufficient number of people with neurotic MMPI profiles and considered to have adjustment problems in the opinion of the guidance counselors. However, in 800 records which she made, she found only 15 students whose MMPI profiles fit the criteria of "neuroticism" developed by Miller (1951) from extensive empirical data. Of course, Miller's Ss were adults, and there is no reason to expect that Rothman's younger group should have a high proportion of what he called "neurotics," especially if we hold the view that a full-blown neurosis is more likely to be recognizable in mature individuals. Be that as it may, the facts as stated created a difficulty and we decided to include the group of student Ss with adjustment problems and abnormal MMPI profiles, even though the profiles were clearly not what Miller called "neurotic." In fact, it is clear from Fig. 7.4, that these students, though they were not hospitalized, had average MMPI profiles which are distinctly like those of the hospitalized schizophrenic group. Both these groups clearly differ from the normals on this criterion. It should be borne in mind then, that "neurotic" here is only a convenient label for non-hospitalized Ss with behavioral and tested "abnormalities" as described above.

For the death-imagery data *only*, Rothman used five Ss from each diagnostic category as controls, and another 40 Ss from each diagnostic category were randomly assigned to four experimental treatments. Half the Ss succeeded and half failed on the first (and only) qualifying test they took, and half of each success and failure group took the "test" under the impression that their score on it would really help, along with the other tests, to decide whether or not they would be accepted as Ss in the main experiment (relevant test conditions). The other half of both the success and failure groups took

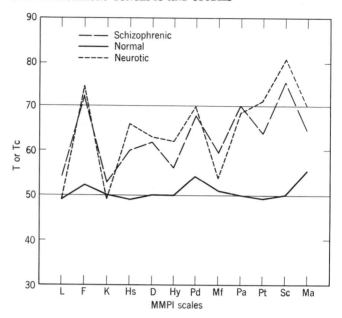

Fig. 7.4   Mean MMPI profiles for three diagnostic groups. Each group has 45 Ss, and appropriate K-corrections were made for each S. (After Rothman, 1963.)

the first "test" under the impression that it was only a practice test, that it would not help to decide whether or not they could enter the main experiment (irrelevant test conditions). The design of the experiment and the mean outcomes for the different variables are shown in Table 7.6.

With respect to changes in self-evaluation of the *tested* ability, from before the test to after it, the effect of success and failure produced a significant difference in the amount and direction of change *only* in the irrelevant condition, as Fig. 7.5 shows. In that condition, regardless of the Ss' diagnostic category, success and failure operated as expected: success produced an increase in the rating of the tested ability and failure lowered it. In the relevant condition, the normals and "neurotics" did not change their evaluations of the tested ability as a function of success or failure, but the schizophrenics did—in the direction opposite to that expected; they increased the evaluation of the tested ability after failure and lowered it after success! It is difficult to account for these findings on the basis of anything we know at present. In the relevant condition the normals seemed to behave as expected. The slight lowering of their tested ability in the relevant

TABLE 7.6

Mean Changes, Pre-Experimental to Post-Experimental, in Self-Evaluation of Tested Abilities (SE_t), Un-tested Abilities (SE_u), and in Total Death-Imagery (TDI)

| Diagnosis | Variable | Control | Experimental | | | | Totals (Experimental only) |
| | | | Success | | Failure | | |
			Relevant	Irrelevant	Relevant	Irrelevant	
Schizophrenic	SE_t	—	−.75 (4)	.10 (2)	.40 (1)	−.30 (3)	−.14
	SE_u	—	−.19 (3)	.40 (1)	−.33 (4)	−.02 (2)	−.04
	TDI	−.40	−1.30 (2)	−.10 (1)	−2.80 (4)	−2.10 (3)	−1.58
Normal	SE_t	—	−.20 (2)	.25 (1)	−.40 (3)	−.70 (4)	−.26
	SE_u	—	.01 (2)	.20 (1)	−.95 (3)	−1.05 (4)	−.43
	TDI	−3.04	−.80 (2)	−1.70 (4)	2.00 (1)	−1.60 (3)	−.60
"Neurotic"	SE_t	—	−.10 (3)	1.05 (1)	−.05 (2)	−1.30 (4)	−.10
	SE_u	—	.12 (1)	.04 (2)	−.46 (3)	−.76 (4)	−.27
	TDI	−1.06	−3.04 (4)	−1.60 (2)	−1.40 (1)	−1.70 (3)	−2.00
All Ss	SE_t	—	−.35	.47	−.02	−.77	
	SE_u	—	−.02	.21	−.58	−.61	
	TDI	−2.70	−1.83	−1.13	.73	−1.80	

$n = 10$ for each experimental mean; $n = 5$ for each control mean. (After Rothman, 1963.)

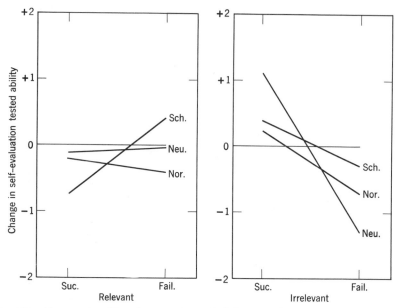

Fig. 7.5   Changes in self-evaluation of tested ability as a function of experimental conditions in three diagnostic groups. Each data point is the mean of 10 Ss. (Drawn from data presented by Rothman, 1963.)

success condition is consistent with the data from college students (Table 5.5) a feature that can easily be explained by the fact that though S succeeded according to the official criteria, the amount by which he exceeded the minimum pass criterion may not have been enough to achieve his LA.

Changes in evaluation of the five *untested* abilities are summarized in Figs. 7.6 and 7.7. Fig. 7.6 illustrates a significant interaction of success-failure and diagnosis; that is, the number of untested abilities changed, and the direction of the change was a function of the diagnostic category S was in and whether he had succeeded or failed on the test. Success or failure apparently made no difference to the schizophrenics; made the biggest difference to the normals, though failure was more effective in reducing their evaluations than success was in raising them; and the pattern of the "neurotics" is similar to that of the normals though somewhat less in amplitude. The *amount* of change, per ability, in the untested abilities follows a similar pattern, as Fig. 7.7 shows, but with respect to amount of change there is also a significant main effect of diagnosis. The overall average

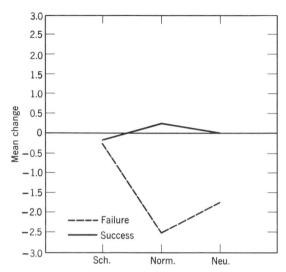

Fig. 7.6 Joint effects of success-failure and diagnostic category on mean number of untested abilities changed in self-evaluation. Each data point is the mean of 20 Ss. (After Rothman, 1963.)

amount of change per untested ability orders the groups: schizophrenic < "neurotic" < normal. This order can be inferred from Fig. 7.7 and the relevant means are in the Totals column at the right-hand edge of Table 7.6. The reader should be cautioned again not to interpret these changes in untested abilities as bearing on the hypothesis, discussed in Chapter 5, that this kind of change is a function of the initial level of the tested ability. In Rothman's experiment, the tested abilities were selected so that, on the average, the three diagnostic groups were equal in their initial evaluations of the abilities actually tested. The present data show only that self-evaluations of untested abilities change also as a function of S's mental health; and as a result of his success and failure, provided that he is not diagnosed as schizophrenic. The relevance or irrelevance of the test which S took made no difference in the subsequent changes in self-evaluation of the untested abilities. So, apart from the fact that relevance-irrelevance of the test had the effect previously noted on changes in self-evaluation of the tested abilities, we would have precious little evidence that relevance was an important variable were it not for the important role it played in changes in total death-imagery (TDI).

Changes in total death-imagery are presented graphically in Fig. 7.8. Panel A shows a significant relevance × diagnosis interaction: all

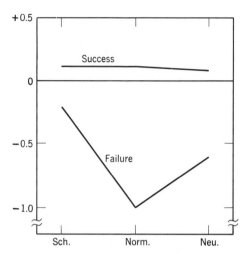

Fig. 7.7 Joint effects of success-failure and diagnostic category on average amount of change (per ability) in untested abilities. Each data point is the mean of 20 Ss. (After Rothman, 1963.)

diagnostic groups reduced death-imagery by about the same amount after an irrelevant test (whether or not it was successful), but after a relevant test the normal Ss increased their death-imagery slightly, while the schizophrenics and "neurotics" reduced theirs even more than they did in the irrelevant condition. Panel B of Fig. 7.8 diagrams the significant triple interaction in which success-failure plays a role in addition to diagnosis and relevance-irrelevance. The point is that, in the relevant test condition, success and failure produced distinctly different patterns of change in death-imagery among the three diagnostic categories. The normals increased their death-imagery after failure and reduced it after success. The schizophrenics and neurotics reduced death-imagery after either success or failure, but the order of the amounts of reduction is different in the two cases—the "neurotics" reduced death-imagery less after failure than after success, and the schizophrenics did the reverse. Following an irrelevant (practice) test both normal and neurotic Ss reduced death-imagery by the same amount, regardless of whether or not they got a "passing" score on the practice test. The schizophrenics, however, though they reduced TDI after either success or failure in the irrelevant condition, were affected by success and failure in a manner opposite to that of the schizophrenics in the relevant test condition; that is, in the irrelevant condition, the schizophrenic Ss showed less decline in death-imagery after success than they did after failure.

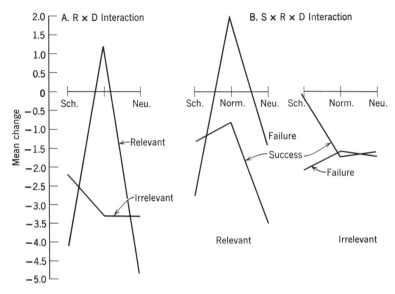

Fig. 7.8 Significant interaction effects on changes in total death-imagery (TDI). A. The joint effects of test relevance and diagnostic category. Each data point is the mean of 20 Ss. B. The joint effects of success-failure, test relevance, and diagnostic category. Each data point is the mean of 10 Ss. (After Rothman, 1963.)

In attempting to summarize the outcomes of this experiment it is best to consider, for each of the diagnostic groups, the rank order of the mean changes in self-evaluation of tested abilities, untested abilities, and death-imagery. These are the numbers shown in parentheses in the body of Table 7.6. In the normal data there is a perfect correspondence in the order of mean changes over experimental conditions for tested and untested abilities, and a close negative correspondence of change in death-imagery with changes in tested and untested abilities. That this latter correspondence should be negative follows from our previous findings that death-imagery increases after failure (when self-evaluations of abilities are reduced) and decreases after success. In the schizophrenic group the change in self-evaluation of the tested abilities is negatively related, over experimental conditions, to both changes in self-evaluation of untested abilities and to changes in TDI, the latter two being positively related. In the neurotic group there is a still different pattern—a negligible correspondence between changes in self-evaluations of tested and untested abilities and a relatively close positive correspondence between changes in TDI and changes in evaluation of the tested ability. Thus, the pattern of change in TDI is quite different among the three groups. The normals increased TDI when, objectively, their outlook was bad, and lowered it when the outlook was good. The other groups generally lowered TDI no matter what happened. This may be defensive, or a symptom of some kind of defensive readiness, and there are some who will doubtless interpret it that way, though in fact there is no explanation of these outcomes.

AN EXPERIMENT ON DEPRESSIVE PATIENTS

The relation, among normal Ss, between spontaneous increase in death-imagery (thoughts about death) and reduced self-evaluation of abilities (Tables 5.12 and 7.6) is paralleled in psychiatric descriptions of "depression" (Strecker et al., 1940; Bibring, 1953; White, 1956; Kraines, 1957, Busse, 1959). The defining characteristic of "depression," and therefore an invariant item in descriptions of it, is the gloomy affect or "mood" which the patient may describe as moderately sad, or "blue," or with the more emphatic terms of hopelessness, helplessness, or despair. Facial expressions, non-verbal vocalizations (groans, moans, and sighs), gestures, and posture, often accord with the verbal descriptions of "feelings," and some cases of depression can be recognized from these without the patients' saying anything at all (cf. Strecker et al., 1940). Frequently, though not invariably, the affective symptoms are accompanied by disinclination to eat, weight loss, decreased vigor of motor activity, feeling of tiredness which is unrelieved by unusually long periods of sleep, unresponsiveness to opportunities for purposive activity which have usually aroused the patient in the past, slowing down of conscious mental processes, decline in sexual activity, fears of fatal or crippling diseases regardless of the objective basis of such fears, intractable insomnia, self-derogation, whether specifically moral or otherwise; delusions of loss of body organs or functions; and a general, sometimes terrifying, impression that sensed objects, including one's own body, are no longer "real." It has long been observed that people who are depressed in the manner described often recover without having been subjected to physical, chemical, or psychological treatments, and without obvious improvement in their living or working conditions. After a "normal" interval, varying from a few days to several years, some of them may have another depressed episode, though many seem to have only one such spell in their lifetime. In still other patients some of the "abnormal" episodes may be exactly the opposite of depression, with respect to affect and all other symptoms, and these are labeled as various degrees of *mania*. For some individuals, the recovery from a manic spell is permanent, but others may have additional manic periods at varying intervals. Sometimes, there is an alternation of depressed and manic attacks, with or without intervening "normal" periods, and patients have been known to go from relatively severe depression to extreme mania within a few hours (cf. Beers, 1931). This tendency to alternation, though by no means demonstrated to be the *modal* phenomenon associated with mania or depression, was the basis for Kraepelin's (1899) theory that mania and depression are features of the same disease process: manic-depressive insanity. The theory includes one of the earliest formal "models" of psychological interest, the assumption being that alternations of mood, even in normal people, can be mapped by some mathematically describable cyclic process, a notion that has most recently been formulated by insisting that the *ideal* process follows a *sine wave* (Kraines, 1957). This preoccupation has had little effect beyond that of cementing "manic-depressive insanity" and "cycloid psychosis" into the literature of abnormal psychology, and Kraepelin and other proponents of his view were careful to cite many cases which cannot by any stretch of the imagination be regarded as cyclic.

The quest for an adequate description of the etiology or causation of depression and mania has led to an equally confusing state of affairs. Though psychoanalysts, particularly the "ego psychologists," have departed in various ways from Freud's description of the "psychic apparatus" they have generally retained the features of his broad outline of the different causations of depressed affect in bereavement and "melancholia" (Freud, 1916–18). They have insisted on various psychogenic interpretations in which self-esteem is threatened in a "narcissistically significant" way by demonstrated or imagined incapacity to achieve narcissistic gratifications (Bibring, 1953) or by a deviation in the development of secondary narcissism which makes individuals, who may be otherwise very effective in achieving all kinds of goals, especially vulnerable in their self-esteem to withdrawal of love by their love objects (Jacobson, 1953). The psychoanalytic discussions of depression give very little space to the fact that the symptoms of depression may appear among the consequences of insult to the brain by cellular degenerations of unknown origin: e.g., Pick's disease (White, 1956; Busse, 1959); infections, especially syphilitic ones (Strecker et al., 1940; White, 1956); neoplasms, benign or malignant (Strecker et al., 1940; White, 1956; Busse, 1959); arteriosclerotic atrophy; or the presence of various toxic agents. On the other hand, the more conventional or eclectic writers (e.g., Strecker et al., 1940; White, 1956; Busse, 1959) place considerable emphasis on evidence which suggests that depressions may have an organic basis, perhaps a subtle one, even in cases where no gross brain damage can be demonstrated or suspected. This evidence includes the demonstration that depressive episodes are more likely in children whose parents have also suffered from depressions and the very high incidence of depressive episodes in *both* members of monozygotic twins (Kallman, 1954); the association of depressive episodes with "pyknic" ("endomorphic") body type (Kretschmer, 1925; Sheldon and Stevens, 1942); and the high incidence of gratuitous onsets which, though refractory to most therapeutic procedures, eventuate in "spontaneous recoveries" (Kraines, 1957). Kraines (1957) used these facts to argue that depressions are all basically of "physiogenic" origin. He then maintained that, since their symptoms are chiefly psychological or psychosomatic, the locus of the physiological disturbance must be in the brain, especially in those parts which are somehow involved in the functions of sleeping and waking, eating, emotion, and general mental "alertness"—hence in the diencephalon in which he includes the thalamus, hypothalamus, the "limbic system," the "reticular formation," and the rhinencephalon (Kraines, 1957, Appendix I, pp. 487–519). In this view, depression and mania occur as the result of functional fluctuations in these cerebral structures and the role of psychogenic factors is limited to choice of symptoms, "mild precipitating effects," or explanations by patients (rationalizations) as to why they are depressed or elated and what they are disturbed about.

From the evidential point of view both of these extreme positions have flaws. The flaws in the psychoanalytic position lie in its failure to deal with many of the phenomena associated with depression and, more profoundly, in the refractoriness of its theoretical formulations to attack by any experimental evidence. The flaw in Kraines "physiogenic" theory is that there is simply not enough detailed evidence to accept or reject it. Over all ranges of opinion about the causation of depression there is considerable agreement that along with the gloomy affect there appear specific fears about the loss of capacity, whether the loss is real or only imaginary, and also frequent self-derogatory statements which are variously interpreted as indicating "unworthiness," "uselessness," "powerlessness," "helplessness," "guiltiness," "sinfulness," and lowering of "self-evaluation" or "self-esteem." It is on these presumed associations which we wish to focus because of their obvious relevance to our interest in self-evaluation-as-an-instrument.

It is generally accepted that severe and intractable depressions are much less common in young people than in older ones. When depressions do appear in the young they are likely to be of short duration and to clear up rather easily with the administration of antidepressant drugs, psychotherapy, or change of activity (Faretra, 1960). The increase in frequency of depression with age, apart from the increased likelihood of cerebral damage, is associated with real decline in abilities (Strecker et al., 1940; Kraines, 1957; Busse, 1959; White, 1956), a feature which, along with the persistence of desire to achieve the customary goals, has been noted as universally occurring in cases of depression (Bibring, 1953), even in those cases where the chief failure lies in winning or retaining the regard of a "love object" (Jacobson, 1953; White, 1956). In groups of people over 60 years of age the incidence of reported depressive episodes was as high as 48 per cent among the retired or unemployed, regardless of their financial security; among those who were gainfully employed, or engaged in some other absorbing creative activity, only about 25 per cent reported depressive episodes (Busse, 1959). Those who had interesting purposes to pursue were mostly continuing to engage in activities which had been a significant feature of their lives prior to retirement. Furthermore, the depressions reported by these older people were remarkably free of symptoms of guilt (Busse, 1959), though guilt is very frequently reported in the depressive episodes of young or middle-aged adults (Strecker et al., 1940; Jacobson, 1953; White, 1956; Busse, 1959). "Instead, . . . , the depression is primarily related to the loss of self-esteem which is directly related to the aged individual's inability to supply his needs and drives or to defend himself against threats to his security" (Busse, 1959, p. 391). These data should not be interpreted as indicating that purposive activity has the major role in preventing or reducing depressive episodes because, as Busse (1959) pointed out, the ability to continue purposive activity and freedom from depression may both be produced by some unknown causative factors. Nevertheless it is clear that we might profitably study the ways in which depressed individuals would differ from those not depressed with respect to $P(s)$, LA, and actual performance. Though we could hardly expect a single experiment to throw much light on the mechanism of depression, we might obtain data that would validate the usefulness of our procedures and the meaning of some of our dependent variables.

Loeb arranged to have the design and procedures of our second experiment with schizophrenic subjects (Fig. 7.1 and Table 7.4) built into the intake procedure, as a "test," at an outpatient clinic which dealt exclusively with depression.[6] The patients who came to this

[6] A clinic for the study of depression headed by Aaron T. Beck, M.D., through a grant from the National Institute of Mental Health. Patients came either to the Hospital of the University of Pennsylvania or to the Philadelphia General Hospital. Dr. Beck's interest in and encouragement of this study were invaluable. Mr. Robert Tuthill, a member of Dr. Beck's staff, collected the data under Dr. Loeb's supervision.

clinic were selected as Ss if they met *both* of the following criteria:
(*1*) scores on Beck's (1961) Depression Inventory, at least 22 for
"severely depressed" Ss, or from 0 to 13 for "lightly depressed" Ss;
(*2*) independent blind ratings by a psychiatrist on a seven-point scale,
0 to 3 for "lightly depressed" Ss, or 4 to 7 for "severely depressed"
Ss. The mean age of the Ss was 31.0 years, and the experimental
groups did not differ in age, nor in proportions of Negro and white
Ss (63 per cent white, 37 per cent Negro). The design of the experiment is shown, along with the results, in Fig. 7.9 and Table 7.7.

Figure 7.9 shows that mean LA was consistently above the reported performance curve on every trial for all groups. Mean $P(s)$
showed no consistent tendency to decline as the deadline approached,
though there is a slight decline between the last two trials of task
2 in three of the four conditions. Mean actual performance (AP) generally showed consistent improvement throughout task 1, though it
mostly got worse over the last four trials of task 2. The effects of
success and failure in task 1 and of degree of depression on LA, $P(s)$,
and actual performance are shown in Fig. 7.10. Alexander's (1946)
general trend test was used to analyze the data on $P(s)$, LA, and
actual performance.

During task 1 the success-failure manipulation produced no significant difference in LA, nor should it have, because the difference
between the performance curves for success and failure occurred only
on the last two trials. During task 2 the LA of previously successful
Ss was consistently higher at every trial than that of Ss who had previously failed and the difference between the overall means (see Table
7.7) is significant, though the absolute difference is small.

During task 1 the mean $P(s)$ of Ss assigned to the failure group
was significantly (and unaccountably) higher than that of the Ss assigned to the success group. During task 2, the overall mean $P(s)$
was significantly higher for Ss who had succeeded than for those who
had failed on task 1.

Success and failure made no difference in the level of AP on
either task. Mean AP, with all Ss and conditions combined, was
significantly worse during task 2 than during task 1.

As Fig. 7.10 and Table 7.7 show, degree of depression had no
effect on either LA or AP during either task. However, severely depressed Ss made $P(s)$ estimates that were significantly lower, by a
larger amount, than those of the lightly depressed Ss on evey trial
of both tasks. It is especially noteworthy that this difference appears
on trial 0 in both tasks though there are no corresponding differences

in LA at trial 0 or any other trial. This recalls our previous argument that $P(s)$ is better than LA as an index of encouragement or discouragement when S is approaching a fixed goal stepwise (Figs. 4.18–4.20 and Table 4.17), and our demonstration that $P(s)$ can be an index of self-evaluation of the ability under test (Figs. 4.23–4.25 and Tables 4.20–4.23. On this basis, the $P(s)$ curves of Fig. 7.10 indicate that the severely depressed Ss were influenced as much as the lightly depressed Ss by the characteristics of the reported performance curves, for the curves of the two groups do not differ much in *form*. But the severely depressed Ss were always less convinced of their power, as instruments, for achieving the fixed goal since their $P(s)$ curve is at least 10 units lower than that of the lightly depressed Ss at every trial. The same relation holds for Ss' retrospective evaluation of their own performances (Table 7.8).

Close examination of the seven-trial means in Table 7.7 suggests that the data might contain some interactions which are hard to detect in Fig. 7.9. The statistical analyses supported this impression in the following ways. First, during task 1 among lightly depressed Ss, those assigned to the failure group had a significantly higher mean $P(s)$ estimate (77.0) than did those assigned to the success group (62.9). The corresponding difference among the severely depressed Ss was in the opposite direction, but it was too small to be significant. Thus, the previously mentioned unaccountably higher $P(s)$ among Ss assigned to fail on task 1 is due to the influence of a single experimental group, though, to be sure, this makes it no more understandable. There is no evidence of such an interaction in $P(s)$ estimates during task 2.

The other interaction effects both occurred in task 2. One is that the severely depressed Ss who succeeded on task 1 had significantly higher mean LA statements than those who had failed task 1. The corresponding difference between the two lightly depressed groups was in the same direction but it was not significant. Perhaps, after all, it is presumptuous to call this an "interaction." However, a genuine interaction seems to appear in the data on actual performance during task 2, with the severely depressed Ss who succeeded on task 1 performing significantly better than those who had failed. A significant difference occurred, in the *opposite direction*, for the lightly depressed Ss. Since actual performance was worse in task 2 than in task 1 for all groups, we cannot clearly argue about the differential incentive value of success and failure as a function of degree of depression. Considering the relative magnitudes of the deterioration in performance,

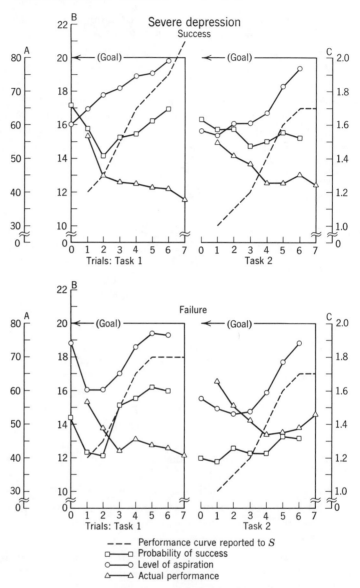

Fig. 7.9 Experimental conditions and associated means of estimated $P(s)$, (scale A), LA (scale B), and AP (scale C), for severely and lightly depressed psychiatric outpatients. Each data point is the mean of 10 Ss. (Data collected by Robert Tuthill.)

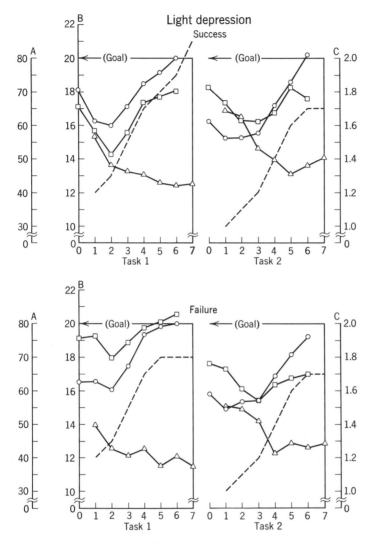

Fig. 7.9 (*Continued*).

it appears that severely depressed Ss who had succeeded were better off than those who had failed, and that the lightly depressed Ss who had failed were better off than those who had succeeded.

During the experiment S's mood was sampled by having him rate his feelings of (*a*) nervousness, (*b*) sadness, and (*c*) anger on linear rating scales numbered in equal intervals from 1 (meaning *extremely*

TABLE 7.7

Means, Per S, Per Trial, of Actual Performance (AP), P(s), and LA by Indicated Conditions

	Depression				Combined Severe and Light	
	Severe		Light			
	Task 1	Task 2	Task 1	Task 2	Task 1	Task 2
Success						
AP (sec./card)	1.28	1.33	1.31	1.45	1.30	1.39
LA	18.2	16.8	17.9	17.0	18.1	16.9
P(s)	59.5	57.7	62.9	66.5	61.3	62.1
Failure						
AP (sec./card)	1.31	1.39	1.24	1.34	1.27	1.37
LA	18.0	16.1	18.0	16.5	18.0	16.3
P(s)	53.0	42.5	77.0	63.4	65.0	53.0
Combined Success and Failure						
AP (sec./card)	1.30	1.36	1.27	1.40		
LA	18.1	16.5	18.0	16.8		
P(s)	56.3	50.1	70.0	65.0		

(Data collected by Robert Tuthill.)

nervous, sad, or angry) to 11 (meaning *extremely* calm, or happy, or not angry at all), with 6 as the midpoint of the scale. The E said to S, "First I would like to ask you a few questions about how you're feeling now. As you know we feel differently at different times for many reasons. The person himself can usually best tell how he feels. So I'm going to ask you how nervous or calm, how sad or happy, and how angry you are feeling. Please answer as to how you are feeling right now, not how you feel at other times." When E presented the rating scales, in the order given above, he always set the scale pointer at 6 and S moved it to indicate his mood.

After task 1, S rated how well he had performed on the same eleven-point scale with 1 meaning "extremely poorly" and 11 meaning "extremely well." Then S again rated his nervousness, sadness, and anger, in that order, and finally, S rated how enjoyable he thought the task was: 1 meant "extremely unenjoyable" and 11 meant "extremely enjoyable." These five ratings were made again after task 2, and finally S answered the question: "If you were given three minutes right now how many different words do you think you could write?"

Fig. 7.11 indicates that the severely depressed Ss rated themselves on all three occasions as more nervous, sadder, and angrier than did the lightly depressed Ss. The difference is not significant for the ratings of nervousness. In no case was there a significant change between successive ratings, so the severely depressed Ss were simply consistently more sad *and* angry than the lightly depressed Ss.

As Table 7.8 shows, ratings of quality of performance were lower after task 2 than after task 1, but the difference is significantly only when the Ss had succeeded on task 1. Also, after task 1, the lightly depressed Ss gave significantly higher ratings to their own performances, regardless of whether they succeeded or failed, than did the severely depressed Ss. No other differences are significant.

There were no significant differences in rated enjoyment of the tasks.

The mean differences in LA for a task not yet performed, the number of words S said he could write in three minutes, cannot be compared with the results obtained on this measure in the first two experiments reported in this chapter. In the first two experiments, Ss responded with any number between 0 and 100, but in this experiment he was allowed to mention *any* number. Actually there were only two Ss who gave responses higher than 100, and Table 7.8 shows where they were and the effects of their extreme responding. Among the means for "words" in Table 7.8 the numbers in parentheses are the means with the extreme responders included. Analyses of variance, with and without the extreme responders, show that none of the differences on this measure are significant.

In this experiment the experiences of success or failure produced corresponding changes in LA, $P(s)$, and on change in rating of quality of own performance between task 1 and task 2. Success versus failure had no effects on ratings of nervousness, sadness, or anger; on rated enjoyment of the tasks; or on LA for an untried task. On the other hand, degree of depression by itself was not associated with differences in LA, AP, nervousness, or enjoyment of the tasks; but it was associated with differences in $P(s)$; rated quality of own performance (on task 1 only); and ratings of S's own sadness and anger. There is also evidence that the effects of the success-failure variable were different in the severely depressed than in the lightly depressed Ss. Though $P(s)$ is an index of self-evaluation, and it is lowest among severely depressed Ss, this hardly qualifies a new insight into depression. Even the momentary lifting of sadness among the severely depressed Ss who succeeded on task 1 (Fig. 7.11) is only a random event. The change is not significant: five Ss increased their ratings,

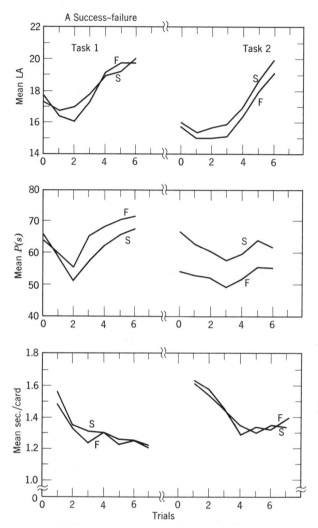

Fig. 7.10 Mean trends of LA, $P(s)$, and AP, among psychiatric outpatients as a function of: success-failure on task 1 (part A); degree of patients' depression (part B). Each data point is the mean of 20 Ss. (Data collected by Robert Tuthill.)

one lowered his, and four made no change. About the only thing this experiment has shown us is a tendency for $P(s)$ to correspond to S's mood, specifically his ratings of his own sadness and anger. But we certainly do not know whether the low estimate of one's own power, $P(s)$ produced the sadness, whether the influence was the

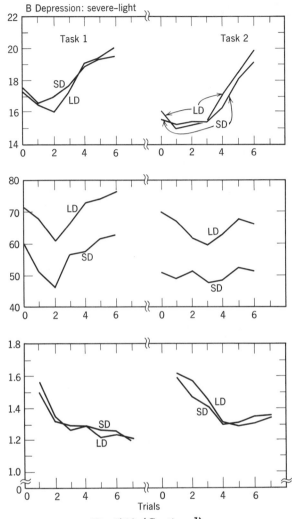

Fig. 7.10 (*Continued*).

other way around, or whether both were determined by other factors yet unknown.

SELF-EVALUATION IN "SUICIDAL" PATIENTS

Throughout the literature on abnormal psychology there is a high likelihood that discussions of psychosis and neurosis, depression, suicide, and lowered "self-esteem," will occur together (e.g.,

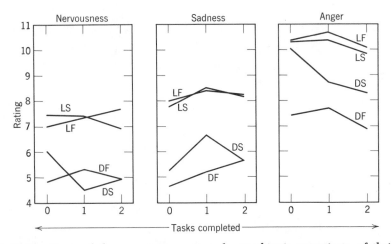

Fig. 7.11   Means of three successive ratings, by psychiatric outpatients, of their nervousness, sadness, and anger, by experimental conditions of success (S) or failure (F) and patients' deep (D) or light (L) depression. Each data point is the mean of 10 Ss. (Data collected by Robert Tuthill.)

Hirt, 1909; Freud, 1916–18). Though suicides do occur among psychiatric patients, there is increasing evidence that suicide and the standard psychopathologic conditions are not closely linked. Though the incidence of depressive illness in both members of monozygotic twins may be as high as 90 per cent, the incidence of suicide in both has been reported as low as 5 per cent, even when both were depressed (Kallman and Anastasio, 1947). Dahlgren (1945) found that various estimates of the incidence of psychotics among completed suicides averaged 25 per cent, and the estimates by subsequent investigators have an upper limit in the neighborhood of 30 per cent.[7] The observations by Sylvia Farnham-Diggory on some relations between suicide and self-evaluation are included in this chapter only because the subjects were all psychotic patients in a mental hospital. As our fuller discussion in the next chapter will indicate, we hold no brief for the popular folklore that suicides are *ipso facto* mentally ill.

Farnham-Diggory (1964) collected her data on the relation be-

[7] Of 114 American military men who had attempted suicide, 28 per cent were diagnosed as psychotic (Fisch, 1954); of 114 actual suicides in Seattle, public records showed that 29 per cent had been diagnosed as psychotic prior to their deaths (Dorpat and Ripley, 1960); 28 per cent of 155 people who attempted suicide in Massachusetts were diagnosed as psychotic (Sifneos, Gore, and Sifneos, 1956); and of 200 consecutive people admitted to a general hospital in England for attempted suicide, 24 per cent were discharged to mental hospitals (Batchelor and Napier, 1953).

TABLE 7.8

Mean Ratings of Evaluation of Own Performance, Enjoyment of Task, and Mean Number of Words S Thought He Could Write in Three Minutes

	Succeed Task 1		Fail Task 1		Combined Success and Failure	
After:	Task 1	Task 2	Task 1	Task 2	Task 1	Task 2
Severe Depression						
Performance	7.15	4.70	5.25	5.15	6.20	4.93
Enjoyment	8.35	7.15	7.05	7.35	7.70	7.25
Words	—	47.5	—	37.3	—	42.4
		(30.5)				(34.9)
Light Depression						
Performance	8.45	5.05	7.75	7.40	8.10	6.23
Enjoyment	8.85	8.10	9.30	8.75	9.08	8.43
Words	—	26.0	—	65.4	—	45.7
				(44.9)		(34.1)
Combined Deep and Light Depression						
Performance	7.80	4.88	6.50	6.28		
Enjoyment	8.60	7.63	8.18	8.05		
Words	—	36.8	—	51.4		
		(28.2)		(40.8)		

(Data collected by Robert Tuthill.)

tween suicide and self-evaluation by interviewing 96 male patients hospitalized with diagnoses of acute psychosis.[8] From evidence in the patients' hospital records she identified 21 "overt suicidals," who had made actual attempts to kill themselves and had scars or reliable testimony to prove it; 22 "covert suicidals," who had talked about suicide, not necessarily in a threatening way, and for whom no actual attempts were recorded; and 53 "non-suicidals," whose records contained no suggestion that they had ever been considered suicidal by anyone. The patients gave information about their name, date of birth, years of schooling, religion, marital status, and number of children, information which agreed almost perfectly with data from independent sources. The three groups did not differ significantly in the following characteristics: diagnosis (85 per cent schizophrenic); number of

[8] At Eastern Pennsylvania Psychiatric Institute, in Philadelphia.

hospitalizations, including the current one (mean = 2.3); length of current hospitalization to time of interview (mean = 4.5 months); drugs (60 per cent on tranquilizers); Ammons Picture-Vocabulary IQ (mean = 95.0); years of formal schooling (median = 11.7); number of siblings (median = 2); birth order of patient (median = second); age in years (median = 28); race (20 per cent non-white); marital status (67 per cent single; 20 per cent married; 13 per cent widowed, separated, or divorced); number of children (28 per cent had one or more); patient's usual occupational level (57 per cent skilled or better); father's occupation (65 per cent skilled or better); or religion (42 per cent Catholic, 44 per cent Protestant, 14 per cent Jewish).

During the interview each patient responded to two sets of questions. The first set of questions was designed and previously used by the present author to obtain a relative measure of "subjective life expectancy"(SLE) from normal Ss. On this questionnaire (Appendix G), S was asked to describe briefly what he expected to be doing in each of several future time periods: e.g., tomorrow, next week, one month from now, six months from now, . . . , and so on, up to ninety years from now. The "six months" item was not used in the original work with normal Ss; it was added here because the six-month interval seemed important to the patients in connection with their expectations of leaving the hospital. The respondents were asked to answer briefly with a word, a phrase, or a short sentence; long answers were discouraged, and did not occur often. These questions have been presented in either written or oral form, and the respondents have answered in either of these ways. The patients in the present study responded orally to oral questions—as a natural part of an interview.

The rationale of this procedure is the expectation that, as a person describes his activities in futures that are increasingly remote, he will sooner or later have to consider a future so distant that he will recognize a high probability that he will be dead by that time, and he will say so. We used this technique to avoid the high likelihood of stereotyped responses if we had asked, "How many more years do you expect to live?" or "At what age do you expect to die?" Our questions leave it up to the respondent to say *that* he is going to die, and when. As we explain more fully in Chapter 8, the question *that* a person is going to die is not, in this context, a meaningless one.

The second series of questions which the patients were asked in the present study were the questions of Cutick's (1962) self-evaluation (SE) questionnaire (cf. Chapter 6 and Appendix E), modified for oral administration and responding (see Appendix H). Each question asked the respondent to say "what per cent of the time" he successfully achieved a described objective. When, as occasionally happened, a patient did not understand "per cent of the time," the interviewer said: "Just give me a number, from 0 to 100, that shows how you feel about your ability. Zero would be 'never,' and 100 would be 'all the time.' You can pick any number you want, big or little, just so it's closest to how you feel." This seemed to settle the difficulty permanently.

The following comparisons of the responses of the patients and groups of normal Ss to these two sets of questions are presented only for general interest. The reader is cautioned not to make too much of these comparisons because the "normal" and "psychotic" groups are distinguished by other things than the mere presence or absence of psychosis and being in or out of a mental hospital. For example, though Table 7.9 shows that the psychotics had a significantly lower overall subjective life expectancy than the normals, the meaning of this difference is obscured by the fact that the normals were brighter than the patients and also came from more privileged socio-economic-cultural backgrounds. Note that within the psychotic group there is no significant difference in subjective life expectancy between the combined suicidals and the non-suicidals (Table 7.9).

Fig. 7.12 shows the significant difference *in overall level* of self-evaluation—lower for the psychotics than for the normals. But the

TABLE 7.9

Mean Subjective Life Expectancies (SLE) by Age for Psychotic Males, Suicidal and Non-Suicidal, and for Normal Males

Real Age in Years	Suicidal Psychotics		Non-Suicidal Psychotics		All Psychotics		Normals	
	SLE	n	SLE	n	SLE	n	SLE	n
18–24	91.8	15	83.7	22	87.0	37	91.8	55
25–34	87.0	13	93.5	18	90.8	31	98.4	13
35–44	83.5	6	89.0	8	86.6	14	100.0	6
45–65	92.4	9	75.4	5	86.3	14	97.1	26
Overall Mean SLE	89.3	43	87.0	53	88.0[a]	96	94.5[b]	100
Mean Real Age	32.6		29.0		30.6		29.8	

[a,b] Difference significant; t = 2.42, p < .05.
(After Farnham-Diggory, 1964.)

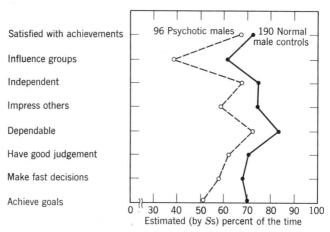

Fig. 7.12 Mean self-evaluation profiles of hospitalized male psychotics and normal male college students. (After Farnham-Diggory, 1964.)

normals in this case include the college students whom Cutick tested to select Ss for his experiment (cf. Chapter 6), who are both brighter and younger than the psychotic patients. However, it is interesting to note that, in spite of the confounding of intelligence with mental health in this comparison, the *shapes* of the two profiles are strikingly similar and differ only in their general level.

The important and legitimate comparisons to be made in these data are between suicidals and non-suicidals *within* the group of patients. The overall mean self-evaluation of the non-suicidals (62.2) was significantly higher than that of the covert suicidals (53.1), but the mean of the overt suicidals (59.2) doesn't differ significantly from either of the other two means. Testing the differences in self-evaluation between the *combined* overt and covert suicidals and the non-suicidals, *item by item,* revealed only two significant differences, in both of which the suicidals were lower than the non-suicidals: ability to influence groups (suicidals, 30.0; non-suicidals, 45.0) and the "omnibus scale," ability to achieve important goals (suicidals, 44.1; non-suicidals, 56.8). The self-evaluation profiles for the three psychotic groups are shown in Fig. 7.13.

There were no significant differences between the overt and covert suicidals in any comparisons, so for subsequent discussion they are combined into a single suicidal group and compared with the non-suicidals. First it was established, by arranging the data for the

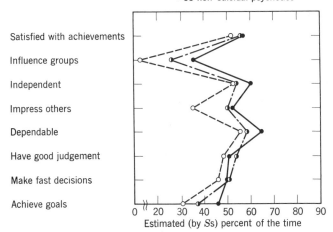

o 22 Covert suicidal psychotics

o 22 Overt suicidal psychotics

• 53 non-suicidal psychotics

Fig. 7.13 Mean self-evaluation profiles of hospitalized male psychotics separated according to their "suicidal" histories: talked about suicide (covert), attempted suicide (overt), neither talk nor attempts (non-suicidal). (After Farnham-Diggory, 1964.)

entire psychotic group as shown in Table 7.10, that subjective life expectancy and self-evaluation had a significant positive association. Then the protocols from the subjective life expectancy questions were examined for content of responses, and three categories emerged:

TABLE 7.10
Relation of Self-Evaluation and Subjective Life Expectancy in 96 Male Psychotic Patients

| Self-Evaluation (Median = 61.3) | Subjective Life Expectancy (Median = 88.0) | | Totals |
	Above Median	Not Above	
Above Median	28	19	47
Not Above	18	31	49
Totals	46	50	96

Chi-square = 5.01, d.f. = 1, p < .05.

(After Farnham-Diggory, 1964.)

TABLE 7.11

Relations of Self-Evaluation and Work-Plus/Work-Only Expectancies in Suicidal and Non-Suicidal Psychotics

Self-Evaluation (Median = 61.3)	Suicidal (n = 43)		Non-Suicidal (n = 53)	
	Work +	Work O	Work +	Work O
Above Median	14	6	20	7
Not Above	4	19	16	10
Totals	18	25	36	17
Mean Self-Evaluation	67.8	47.0	63.4	60.5

For *totals:* Chi-square = 6.54, d.f. = 1, p < .01.
Association of Work +/O responses with Self-Evaluation (Fisher's exact probability test): Suicidal group, p < .01; Non-Suicidal group, p > .20.
(After Farnham-Diggory, 1964.)

(1) *Planless;* e.g., "I don't know," "I haven't any idea," or "Nothing"; (2) *Work Only,* in which the *only* planful activity mentioned is occupational; e.g., "Job," "Working," or "Making a living"; and (3) *Work-Plus,* in which, in addition to work, some reference was made to establishing a home, having children, or to recreational activities. The median number of planless responses was two, and the suicidals and

TABLE 7.12

Relations of Subjective Life Expectancy and Work-Plus/Work-Only Expectancies in Suicidal and Non-Suicidal Psychotics

Subjective Life Expectancy (Median = 88.0 years)	Suicidal (n = 43)		Non-Suicidal (n = 53)	
	Work +	Work O	Work +	Work O
Above Median	12	10	16	9
Not Above	6	15	20	8
Totals	18	25	36	17

For *totals:* Chi-square = 6.80, d.f. = 1, p < .01.
For entire table (8 cells): Chi-square = 9.1, d.f. = 3, p. < .05.
(After Farnham-Diggory, 1964.)

non-suicidals did not differ significantly in this respect. However, as the Totals row in Table 7.11 shows, there were significantly more work-only responders among the suicidals than among the non-suicidals. Furthermore, also from Table 7.11, the association between work-plus responses and higher self-evaluations is significant in the suicidal group, but not in the non-suicidal group. The association of work-plus responses with subjective life expectancy was not significant for the psychotic group as a whole, nor was it significant within the suicidal or non-suicidal groups taken separately, but the distributions of work-plus responses as a function of subjective life expectancy were significantly different in the two groups, as Table 7.12 indicates.

Since there appeared to be associations of self-evaluation with a patient's having talked about suicide or having attempted it, with his subjective life expectancy, and with his tendency to describe his future in terms of work only, Farnham-Diggory sought to show the relation between the *joint occurrence* or non-occurrence of (*1*) being suicidal, (*2*) having a subjective life expectancy below the group median, and (*3*) emitting work-only responses. All of these characteristics, as described, she called *negative* and their opposites she called *positive*, and thus generated the plus and minus signs used in Table 7.13. The mean self-evaluation of the group with three negative signs (i.e., the group which is suicidal, has short subjective life expectancies, and work-only responses) is significantly lower than that of any of the other groups. Among the other three groups, with 0, 1, or 2 negative signs, the differences in self-evaluation are not significant, but there is a consistent ordering of mean self-evaluation within the subgroups of the two middle categories (1 or 2 negative signs). Farnham-Diggory suggested that if subjective life expectancy is relatively long, and work-plus responses occur, a history of suicidal thoughts or acts need not associate with low self-evaluation (mean = 67.2). On the other hand, when subjective life expectancy is relatively short and the future is described as work only, the *absence* of suicidal thoughts and acts does not guarantee a high self-evaluation (mean = 57.6).

Among these patients, then, there was an association between their level of self-evaluation and a history of talking about, or attempting, suicide (Fig. 7.13). Previous attempts to demonstrate such an association have not been successful (e.g., Farberow, 1950), but the complexities of our data strongly suggests two additional considerations which must be mentioned briefly here. The first of these arises from observation that the covert suicidals, who had only *talked* about suicide, had the lowest average self-evaluation of the three psychotic

TABLE 7.13

Mean Self-Evaluation as a Function of Joint Suicidal History, Subjective Life Expectancy (SLE), and Work-Plus/Work-Only Expectancies

Number of Negative Characteristics	Suicide[a]	SLE[b]	Work[c]	Self-Evaluation Mean	n	Summary
None	+	+	+	66.0	16	
One	−	+	+	67.2	12 ⎫	
	+	+	−	63.1	9 ⎬	63.0
	+	−	+	60.5	20 ⎭	($n = 41$)
Two	−	−	+	67.0	6 ⎫	
	−	+	−	59.2	10 ⎬	60.6
	+	−	−	57.6	8 ⎭	($n = 24$)
Three	−	−	−	40.3	15	

[a] Plus means non-suicidal history.
[b] Plus means above median (88.0 years) for all psychotics.
[c] Plus means description of future includes more than work.
(After Farnham-Diggory, 1964.)

groups, and the overt suicidals, who had made at least one actual "attempt," had an average self-evaluation which was closer to that of the non-suicidals. From the conventional viewpoint it appears paradoxical that those who have apparently been more "serious" about taking their own lives should evaluate themselves more highly. The suggestion that a suicide attempt has a "cathartic" effect (Farberow, 1950; Rosen, Hales, and Simon, 1954) on individual functioning may be relevant to this problem, but we cannot accept it as an explanation until we have a more objective notion of what "catharsis" means and how it might influence self-evaluations. Another strategy involves considering the *intent* of suicidal acts. To deal only with the firmness of the individual's intent to cause his own death (e.g., Shneidman, 1963, 1964), or to regard *all* suicidal behaviors as containing a more or less muted "cry for help" (Farberow and Shneidman, 1961) is to apply tunnel vision to the field of intent. It leaves out the question whether a suicidal act, "successful" or "unsuccessful," was essentially appetitive or aversive, and if this question is not raised we are not likely to learn what *any* act was directed *toward* or *away from*. For example, Stengel (1962) pointed out that suicide attempts have appeal characteristics and he urged that more attention be turned to the reactions of suicide attempters to the generally helpful reactions of others. We need not press this idea much further to suggest that the elicitation of such attentive helpfulness from others was precisely the *aim* of some apparent suicide attempts. Such "suicide attempts" would then be judged successful, not from the point of view of suicide (which was never aimed at), but because by his act the attempter realized his aim of controlling other people. In our view, it is reasonable that self-evaluations should increase in such a case, either because of the increase in narcissistic inputs or because of the agent's demonstrated power to manipulate others.

The second general point to be made arises from consideration of the fact that the presence or absence of a suicidal history was not the strongest determiner of the level of self-evaluation in these patients. A much more potent determiner was S's description of his future either as relatively long and with opportunities for a relatively large variety of activities *or* as shorter and constrained to a narrower set of activities (Table 7.12). Only when a history of suicidal thoughts or acts was associated with the latter of these future time perspectives did the very lowest self-evaluations appear. The fact that suicidal history sometimes coincides with the highest self-evaluations requires that we carefully consider our research strategy in this area. For example, in the present study no attempt was made to control for the *recency*, frequency, and objective seriousness of suicidal attempts and thoughts. A person may have spoken of, or attempted, suicide a long time ago and in the interim his situation has changed for the better so that he now has a higher self-evaluation—and may have no active preoccupation with suicide; only his history tells us that he once did.

SUMMARY

The experiments presented in this chapter seem to indicate that psychotic Ss, diagnosed as schizophrenics, are not impervious to the influence of variables which affect the directed behavior of normal Ss, or their self-evaluations. This is not to say that normals and schizophrenics are identical in all respects. Schizphrenics do not show the normals' response to deadlines when they are estimating $P(s)$, their self-evaluations of specific abilities change differently than those of normals, and so does their total death-imagery. Indeed, under the conditions of Rothman's experiment, the changes in self-evaluation by the schizophrenics suggest that they are afraid of the implications of their success, a result which at first blush looks contradictory to the results of the first of Loeb's experiments. There is a difference, however, Loeb and I were careful to limit the tasks, for which the schizophrenics Ss were invited to volunteer, to the kinds of hospital activities with which they were already familiar. The announced further interaction with other groups of *patients* implied that we were not urging them out of the hospital. Rothman's proffered goal, on the other hand, was stranger to the patients, appeared more serious, and may have suggested implications about getting better which they were not prepared to face. It is a plausible hypothesis that the normality of the behavior of hospitalized schizophrenics in the face of evidence about the goodness of their abilities is limited by the seriousness of the tasks they might be expected to undertake, and the degree of independence they might be expected to assume if their abilities prove to be "good." The less serious the tasks proffered, and the less independence demanded of them, the more "normal" their responses will be. But serious tasks, and the expectation of a "normal" amount of independence might frighten them into dependent self-derogation or downright refusal to participate in tests of their abilities. Recently discharged schizophrenic patients pose exactly such problems for psychologists and psychiatrists who are trying to rehabilitate them and integrate them to some extent into the workaday community. This notion needs a more direct test than we have given it so far. It may be true, and if it is, it might explain Rothman's results.

Our brief look at the specific condition of "depression" revealed only that severely depressed patients had lower $P(s)$ estimates than those who were lightly depressed. The presence of depression had nothing to do with the mean level of LA or actual performance. The depressed patients also reported themselves as sadder and less free from anger than did the lightly depressed ones. Further experiments of this kind with depressive Ss should be designed to throw light on the conditions under which a person aspires normally in relation to his performance on each trial, works just as hard as anyone else, and still believes that his efforts will ultimately be fruitless. Observations of this kind may ultimately yield an objective means for determining the ways in which "subjective" moods affect behavior, and are in turn affected by the outcomes of purposive striving.

The finding that a history of suicidal thoughts or actions was associated with the lowest self-evaluations only among Ss who described their futures in terms of "work only" indicates that the investigation of personal "time perspectives" (cf. Lewin, 1941) would be a useful aid in the study of self-evaluation and suicide. In an objective sense, the ultimate realistic limit of a future time perspective is one's own death, and so we consider attitudes toward death and suicide in Chapter 8.

Chapter 8
DEATH AND SELF-EVALUATION[1]

FEAR OF DEATH

The Death of Others: Bereavement

Much of the previous discussion can be summarized in the proposition that to a large extent our self-evaluations depend on estimates of our $P(s)$ in purposive undertakings, estimates which, in normal children and adults, are strongly affected by the nearness and remoteness of deadlines and the clarity with which the deadlines are defined. Even if we were to imagine a human being devoted to the achievement of a single end—a thing in itself impossible—we should have to admit another impossibility to imagine that he has infinite time in which to accomplish his purpose. For all men are mortal, and death, however, poetically we conceive it, terminates all our strivings and experiences of which we have any knowledge. Death is the ultimate deadline, a certainty for each living person *in that it will* surely happen, but nebulous for most of us as to the *how* and the *when* of it. Among events that can happen to human beings, death is one of the most *personal*. It is a unique event, exactly as unique as the personality it terminates. Among the vicissitudes of a single individual death is unique in another sense: it is the one event which has not yet occurred to any of us from which we can gain no profit in learning or knowledge because it cannot serve as the occasion for our considering various alternative actions; no one can say of death, "If that happens to me, I will then do . . ."

The question of attitudes about death has been a matter of concern and puzzlement to a great many writers. On one hand there is probably no tradition more ancient than that of the "fear of death." The expectation that men will accept any other alternative than death has been used by soldiers, legislators, jurists, priests, and criminals

---

[1] This chapter is an expanded version of a paper, "Death and Self-Esteem," presented at the American Psychological Association Convention, St. Louis, August 30, 1962.

in their efforts to regulate the behavior of others. However, the assumption, that men in all circumstances will avoid dying or being killed, has often been proved wrong. Soldiers have faced death without retreating, and some have sought to damage their enemies with the almost certain expectation that they themselves would be killed in the process; legal death penalties, even when enforced, have not reduced crime (Schuessler, 1952); heretics have impudently failed to recant, or have rejoiced in becoming martyrs for their faith; and the victims of criminals have resisted them. Some people have risked, and some have lost, their lives in attempts to rescue others. There are many hazardous workaday occupations which do not lack for workers, though it is well known that others have already died doing such work. Furthermore, some people kill themselves. All of these observations suggest that, though death itself may be feared, there may be something to the notion of "a fate worse than death."

In view of this possibility it is somewhat strange to come across a variety of assertions that the idea of one's own death is, from the very nature of consciousness, a psychological impossibility. "Our own death is indeed unimaginable, and whenever we make the attempt to imagine it we can conceive that we really survive as spectators- . . . at bottom no one believes in his own death, or . . . in the unconscious every one of us is convinced of his own immortality" (Freud, 1915b, pp. 304–305). Consciousness cannot "realize absolute unconsciousness, its own annihilation"; we cannot, when awake, experience what it is like to be asleep; and this impossibility, arising from the alleged nature of consciousness itself, is connected with our "immortal yearning for immortality" (Unamuno, 1912, p. 38; cf. also Malinowsky, 1925). Since being dead is, by definition, the impossibility of experiencing anything at all, then I cannot experience my own death (Bridgman, 1938; Kellersohn, 1938). These sentiments, far from being of merely antiquary interest, are used currently, though perhaps in a misunderstood form, to explain the behavior of people who are confronted with another's death or with the prospect of their own (e.g., Schilder and Wechsler, 1934; Orlansky, 1947; Wahl, 1957; Shneidman, 1963). Gorer (1956) has said that, by comparison with the openness with which death was presented and discussed in the nineteenth century, we in the twentieth century have, by elaborate concealment and circumlocutions, put death in the category of pornography. Mead (1949) thought that the concealment of death results from the fact that, like divorce, it is sorrowful. Feifel (1963) described the barriers of professional reticence that physicians erected against his attempts to discuss attitudes toward death with seriously or terminally ill patients. However, not all physicians were so reluctant, so Feifel managed to interview 60 patients and found, to the discomfiture of the concealers, that 82 per cent of them wanted to know the likelihood of their dying. Furthermore, most of them were not disturbed by the discussion. They wanted to know, either because they felt they had an absolute right to know about the end of their own lives, or they discovered in the discussion that death was not so frightening after all, or they could take the remaining time to put their affairs in order. On the other hand, "69 to 90 per cent of physicians, depending on the specific study," said that patients ought not to be told that they would probably die of their present diseases.

It seems likely that the present reticence and concealment about death in our society does not necessarily reflect a common desire on the part of the society's members. Where then does it come from? We cannot say for sure, but we can eliminate some of the possibilities. First, as to the allegation that the experience of, conception of, imagination of, or belief in, one's own death is a psychological impossibility, there is no sense in quarreling with the assertion that it is impossible to experience a given condition, if the essence of the condition is the impossibility of experiencing anything. In this sense the experience of one's own death, like division by zero in algebra, doesn't happen because it is simply not defined. However, to press the mathematical analogy further, the calculus permits us to say something meaningful about the limit of a function whose denominator approaches zero as a limit. Now, to emerge from the analogy, we note that experience, narrowly considered, in the only way that Bridgman (1938) or Kellersohn (1938) could have reasonably intended to use the term, is distinguished from the other conscious conditions of conceptions, imagination, and belief. By a process something like that of successive approximation I can imagine that I can come, as I know others have, to the condition in which bodily movement and every physiological process ceases, there is a total lack of all experience, and no possibility or even no desire that these processes will ever occur again. I can imagine that the body will decay and dessicate though I cannot predict whether it will ultimately become a fossil or mingle inextricably with the earth. In imagining all this, I make what I call "myself" an instance of the concept of death as I understand it. Someone can doubtless devise a criterion against which it would appear that I do not surely *believe* in my own death. And others could argue that I "really" fear death and don't want to die. Henceforth, let there be no talk of the psychological impossibility of a man's conceiving or imagining his own death; I have just done that. Investigations by

Anthony (1940) and Nagy (1948) suggest that our concepts of death, like other concepts, develop as a function of age (experience) and intelligence, and the implications of this idea should be followed up more systematically.

Some people seem eager to talk about death, but are afraid to do so lest they offend the sensibilities of others. Others, perhaps, would talk about it if they knew how, if they had the words. Perhaps the prevalent euphemisms which substitute for plain and direct language are taken by some as an indication that there is a genuine taboo here, something which can be mentioned only in appropriate ritual phrases, if at all. On the other hand, we must not forget that the experts who view with alarm what they call our "concealment" of death have not specified exactly how much we should talk about it, and to what purpose. Death is a fact, and facts which are not relevant to on-going human purposes are shunted aside. It may be true, from one point of view, that, "All the time you live you steal it from death; it is at her charge. The continual work of your life is to contrive death; you are in death, during the time you continue in life: for, you are after death, when you are no longer living. Or if you had rather have it so, you are dead after life: but during life, you are still dying: and death doth more rudely touch the dying than the dead, and more lively and essentially" (Montaigne, 1603). Montaigne also noted that some men ignore the possibility of death during the pursuit of their plans and projects, and some of them are more fearful of death's interruption of these activities than they are of death itself. We may be dying while we live, but we are also living, and that means to detect and solve problems, to develop plans, plots, schemes, and purposes, and to carry them as near to completion as possible. In the midst of a death propaganda campaign more massive than most people now living have ever imagined, people were not traumatized; life went on. This occurred in Europe at the close of the "middle ages."

The earliest Christian writings, partly to emphasize the Church's commitment to the life hereafter and partly to combat the "sin of pride," contained many references to death and exhortations to think about it, but these circulated mostly among people who had already renounced the world. From about the thirteenth century, the exhortation to keep death always in mind was directed in an ever-swelling flood to the masses until, in the fifteenth century, "an everlasting call of *memento mori* resounds through life" (Huizinga, 1924, p. 138). In the preaching of the mendicant orders and in popular woodcuts this theme was presented. Both media were limited to crude effects, so they dwelt persistently on the perishing nature of all earthly things: the departed glory of the great achievers of the past, the decay of human beauty, and the death dance, with death dragging along men of all ages and conditions of life. There was also special emphasis on the *agony* of death in the popular legend that Lazarus, after his resurrection, spent the rest of his days in terror at the thought that he would have to die again, and in the two traditional literary forms, "The Art of Dying," and "The Last Four Things of Man." This gigantic propaganda campaign, whether intentionally or not, clearly tended to a mockery of all values which are uniquely human: striving and achievement, delight in affectionate social ties and in human beauty. But, like many other propagandists before and since, these people went too far. They reduced death, even in its most starkly disgusting forms, to the merely trite and banal. People looked at the images, heard the sermons, saw the piles of exhumed bones, read the crude verses—and life went on. In Huizinga's (1924) description, the churchyard of the Innocents at Paris was filled with images of all kinds intended to invoke the horror of death. It was the most preferred place of burial for the people of 20 parishes, so the dead were ex- humed soon after burial and their gravestones sold, to make room for the newly dead. The exhumed bones were piled in charnel houses along the cloister that enclosed the ground on three sides. There were representations of the death dance, the legendary three living and three dead men, and later, in the fifteenth century, a large statue of Death (now in the Louvre). "Day after day crowds of people walked under the cloisters looking at the figures and reading the simple verses, which reminded them of the approaching end. In spite of the incessant burials and exhumations going on there, it was a public lounge and a rendezvous. Shops were established before the charnel houses and prostitutes strolled under the cloisters. A female recluse was immured on one of the sides of the church. Friars came to preach and processions were drawn up there. A procession of children only (12,500 strong, thinks the Burgher of Paris) assembled there, with tapers in their hands, to carry an Innocent to Notre Dame and back to the churchyard. Even feasts were given there" (Huizinga, 1924, p. 149).

This persistent application to purposive activity without conscious regard for the present indicators of death and its possibilities also seems to occur among men who engage in hazardous occupations. Few mines have been dug, or great structures erected, or voyages and explorations completed, without involving, as a matter of course, the deaths of some of the men involved. Yet while men are working at these things, their preoccupation is not with the hazards as hazards, but as barriers to getting the job done. The thought that a man might die if "something goes wrong" occurs to him only intermittently. The possibility of lethal accidents is most clearly considered at length during the planning of the operation, and is ultimately represented only in the various safety devices, special tools, and special methods of work. During the operation itself, the concentration is not on the possibility of death, but on doing the job right. In this sense, we might say that death is ignored because it is simply not in the life space of these people. The notion that the penalty for murder is death appears to be absent from the life space of many murderers at the time of their crime. Investigations into the ineffectiveness of the death penalty as a deterrent to murder revealed, among other things, that some murderers were so busy with other things during the events preceding the murder that they simply did not think of the death penalty, and others were interacting with their victims in such an extremely emotional way that the consequences of their murderous act were not considered (Schuessler, 1952). All this suggests that arguments pro and con about an individual's fear of death are futile if it has not been ascertained whether or not the possibility of death is in his life space.

Perhaps the fact that death is not talked about very much means that it is only a matter of indifference. This possibility was formally raised and explored in experiments where the Ss' autonomic ("emotional") responses to words relating to death were seen to be significantly higher than their responses to words in other categories. So, the authors concluded, death is not a matter of indifference (Alexander and Adlerstein, 1960; Alexander, Colley, and Adlerstein, 1957; Meissner, 1958). Of course death is not a matter of indifference. It is bad; it is feared. Precisely what about it is bad and feared, and under what conditions? Psychologists and psychiatrists are most likely to write about the fear of death. Anthropologists speak also of fear of the dead. Let us keep these two fears distinct from each other. Then we will first consider fear of the dead because that relates to the death of others, the first intimation that we have of the possibility of our own death.

We do not have to read many ethnographers' descriptions of "primitive" or "preliterate" peoples before we realized the emptiness of the phrase "the primitive mind." With respect to attitudes toward death there is no one primitive mind. There are at least several groups of primitive minds, and scanning their attitudes toward death will give us a greater range of the human possibilities in this connection than will all the literature that relates only to our own society. Let us begin with the specific aversion for corpses. A corpse, depending on the way death was incurred, may directly present features which are extremely negative in the strictly hedonic sense—that is, disgusting. No doubt a great deal of aversion to corpses is determined by their negative hedonic value, but that is not the whole story. Mohammedans are said to show extreme fear of corpses and of anything associated with them, even the water in which they were washed (Lane-Poole, 1911); some Australian aborigines crush the skull and break the legs of a corpse so that the dead cannot follow the living (R. Benedict, 1934). However, in other Australian tribes families carry the corpses of deceased members around with them for three or four years, opening the bundle at intervals to see how decomposition is progressing (and at these times taking occasion to keep hair, hands, or bones of the corpse as mementos or amulets), and finally they bury the bundle or stuff it into a hollow tree only when nothing remains but the bones (Fison and Howitt, 1880). The Parsis of India have still more differentiated attitudes. Relatives of the dead person sit next to the corpse for a certain time to provide a bridge for the escape of the soul, even though they believe that because all corpses are avidly sought by the corpse demon, they are unclean and those who have touched a corpse must be ceremonially purified. They believe that the death of a bad person is a triumph of good, so such corpses are not unclean; while the death of a good person is a triumph of evil, so his corpse is unclean (Soderdelon, 1911).

In most cases, fear of corpses is rationalized by the notion that death is a contaminant, and without proper precautions those who handle the corpse or approach too near it are also in mortal danger. Thus it appears that fear of a corpse may often be basically a fear of one's own dying. Even apart from any clear indication that the notion of contamination from corpses plays a role, the aversion to dead persons and their effects may suggest other more specific kinds of fear; for example, the fear that those who mourn excessively are being invited by the ghost of the dead person to go along with him—noted among the Pueblo Indians (R. Benedict, 1934) and among the Bagobo in Malaya (L. W. Benedict, 1916). Ceremonies aimed at preventing ghosts from making reprisals against the living, either for frustrations incurred before the death or for impious neglect after it, have been noted among the ancient Babylonians (Langdon, 1911), Chinese (Walshe, 1911), and Japanese (Lloyd, 1911); in modern India both among Hindus (Hillebrandt, 1911) and the non-Aryan tribes (Crooke, 1911); and among the Hopi (Eggan, 1948) and

Apache (Opler, 1938) Indians of the southwestern United States. On the other hand, there is a positive aspect in some ceremonies in which the ghosts are invited to continue their beneficial participation in the life of the family or that of the larger community; for example, the frequent uses of corpses or parts of them in rainmaking ceremonies (Frazer, 1941), the ancient Roman ceremonies which were more elaborate and frequent in connection with those who had been more powerful and influential for the common good while they were alive (Showerman, 1911), and the Hopi's invoking the spirits of their dead to produce rain and good crops (Eggan, 1948).

The most violent public displays of mourning and propitiation of the dead are sometimes quite closely correlated with the characteristics of the individual at the time of his decease. Among the Apaches, the greatest fear is shown toward those whose deaths were "untimely," who died in full possession of their strength, and while they were still engaged in the formal competitions and mutual frustrations required of adults (Opler, 1938). There is far less fear of those whose deaths occurred in old age, "timely," like ripe fruit, or of the very young who had died while they had "no experience." Similarly, in ancient China, elaborate propitiatory ceremonies were held only for those dead who had powerful and influential status, not for people who died past the age of 70 nor for infants and unmarried persons (Walshe, 1911). In some cases the precautionary ceremonies were omitted because the survivors believed that the ghost, too, would die after a short time; e.g., some non-Aryan tribes in India (Crooke, 1911), and among the Apaches in the case of deaths of infants (Opler, 1938).

The Abipones feared that the sight of a dead or dying person would make the fighting men of the tribe afraid of risking their lives in battle, so they often hastened the death of persons they thought were already dying, and got rid of corpses with great speed (Dobrizhoffer, 1922).

In some cultural patterns the announcement of the death or impending death of a powerful, wealthy person, or of a king or leader, was reasonable grounds for other people to fear for their own lives. In ancient Japan (Lloyd, 1911), in ancient Mesopotamia and Egypt, and in several African tribes as late as the nineteenth century (Wallis, 1939), servants (including wives) were required to be killed or to commit suicide so they could be buried with their masters.

Thus, in a variety of ways, the death of another person may be a threat to the well-being or continued existence of his survivors, a threat which, whether based on reality or delusion, can occasion real fear. There is another negatively valued aspect of the death of others which is revealed in mourning at bereavement. For the bereaved, "the world has become poor and empty" (Freud, 1916–18), but empty of what? Two kinds of values are lost with the death of a loved one: hedonic values, reflected in the direct contribution of the beloved to beauty in our lives, and conative-achievement values, reflected in the number of our purposive activities which are pointless without the continued existence of the loved one (cf. Lindemann, 1944). Bereaved people feel restless and look for something to do, but they often cannot initiate anything, everything they think of undertaking is soon regarded as pointless and abandoned if they begin it at all, and they often carry out routine maintenance functions in an apathetic way (Becker, 1933; White, 1956). They may spend an inordinate amount of time examining the extent to which they have been guilty of failing to do things, or not having done things properly, in the interest of the person who is now dead (White, 1956). The fact that the beloved is dead makes it impossible for them to make amends for any real faults or omissions, and thus the difficulty of escaping the guilt is increased. This frustration of the survivors' purposes by the death of the beloved is nowhere better illustrated than among the Arapesh, described by Margaret Mead (1949). The future bride of an Arapesh boy is selected by his parents when both future bride and groom are still young children. Thenceforth the little girl lives in the home of the boy's parents and, as the Arapesh say, he "grows her," providing all maintenance functions until they reach the age of about 17, at which time the marriage is quietly consummated and the young couple establish their own household. If the girl should die before the marriage is consummated, this would not only frustrate future activities in her interest, but also it renders the activities of more than half the boy's lifetime pointless. The relation of dependency, in a material sense, which is determined by the structure of marriage and the traditional position of women in many cultures other than our own makes women particularly vulnerable to loss of financial security and status when their husbands die, in addition to the loss of the possibility of performing those purposive acts which were relevant only while the husband lived. Needless to say, bereavement extends beyond the partners of conjugal love to include the death of friends, business partners, and professional colleagues. Alfred Lunt's funeral oration for Robert E. Sherwood in 1955 speaks of the loss of the functions which he performed in a unique way and the inability of his surviving friends to perform certain of their functions in their usual way after he was dead. In many a memorial minute of university faculties, departed colleagues are spoken of in the same vein. Statements of loss are not always insincere, *pro forma* accommodations to custom. Often enough they are as true as any human language can be. Similar statements of a sense of "loss" have been made on the occasion of the deaths of political leaders (cf. Johanssen, 1946; Orlansky, 1947).

One's Own Death

Though it may be plausible, from what has been said so far, to infer that the death of others is feared, or negatively valued, to the extent that it thwarts important purposive activities of the living, it is still not clear what a person might fear about his own death. It is possible, of course, to consider the hypothesis that we fear the same thing about our own death as we fear in the death of others—the loss of the very possibility of exercising our capacities in purposive achievement or for hedonic enjoyment. We cannot hope to offer definitive proof that this is so, but there is some evidence that accords with it, and which suggests at the same time that the final statement of any such hypothesis cannot be a simple one.

First of all, let us consider the real extent and meaning of the alleged fact that people avoid discussions about death. Certainly it is true that some do. They will abruptly warn others not to mention the subject in their presence, or they will leave the room if they cannot stop the discussion, but there is no evidence that this is true of the majority of individuals. Several investigations have found that Ss will spontaneously talk or write about death even when they are not specifically required to do so (e.g., Means, 1936; Rothman, 1963). Feifel (1963) reported that many of the seriously ill patients he interviewed were glad that he had talked about death to them, and a majority of them expressed the desire to have their physicians tell them about the likelihood of their dying. It has been my experience, with few exceptions, that people who are engaged in conversation about death end by expressing surprise that what they thought would be a gruesome and depressing experience was a highly interesting intellectual problem. No investigators, of whom I have knowledge, expressed any difficulty in getting their Ss to talk about death at the interviewer's request (Bromberg and Schilder, 1933, 1936; Schilder, 1936; Schilder and Wechsler, 1934; Middleton, 1936; Anthony, 1940; Nagy, 1948). Resistance to talking about death appears to come less from the individuals concerned than it does from people in positions of authority who feel moved to steer public discussion away from the topic.

Means (1936) scaled 349 items that were reported as feared by 1,000 college women. The various aspects of death were not all near the top of the list where they would be if they were most feared.

Snakes, cancer, death of loved ones, and death by burning had the first four ranks. Death by drowning was 12; slow death, 17; death by murder, 19; death by suffocation, 21; painful death, 29; death by starvation, 49; corpses, 76; suicide, 93; dying people, 97; asphyxiation, 116; cemeteries, 184; sudden death, 189; skeletons, 201; and hearses, 232. This list suggests that there are some things more feared than death, or at least more feared than certain kinds of death. Can there be a fate worse than death? It seems that there can, at least in some psychological situations. Religious convictions about the hereafter may facilitate death, as it appeared to do for the throngs of early Christian martyrs who wanted to realize their heavenly reward earlier, and a bigger reward at that, by laying down their lives for the faith (Gibbon, 1788). Their numbers became so large, and their provocations of the civil authorities to impose the death penalties became so outrageous, that they led to the development of the present strictures in the Roman Catholic Church against suicide. However, what is a true believer to do when the religious authorities persuade him that he may be forever lost unless he dies now in a prescribed way?

In some parts of Europe, as late as the last century, universal suicide was preached by fervent missionaries who represented it as the only means of escape from the snares of Antichrist, the only assured way of eluding earthly sins and sorrows and securing the eternal joys of heaven. Communities hailed with enthusiasm the gospel of death and hastened to put its precepts into practice. Through northern and northeastern Russia, as a result of such preaching, there were many suicides. As establishment for the reception of religious suicides, a building without doors or windows, was founded in the forest of Vetlouga. Through a hole in the roof aspirants to heaven were lowered into the building, and the hatch was battened down. Men armed with clubs patrolled the outer wall to prevent the escape of those who might change their minds. Here hundreds of persons perished. At first, sounds of devotion issued from the walls; but later these were replaced by entreaties for food, prayers for mercy, and imprecations on the miscreant who had lured the victims to destruction. Subsequently priests, monks, and laymen preached salvation by flame. They seduced children by promises of gay clothes, apples, nuts, and honey in heaven. Adults who hesitated to comply were assured that troops were then on the way to deliver them to Antichrist, and thus rob them of eternal bliss. Thousands of men, women, and children rushed into the flames and were destroyed (Wallis, 1939, p. 281).

In India, suicide was often recommended by Hindus, less often by Jains, when it terminated a religious career so perfect that continuing to live involved the risk of backsliding (Jacobi, 1911). Many ancient Mayas committed suicide when they were depressed, or even only slightly annoyed, in the belief that suicides had a favored place in heaven under the protection of Ixtab, the goddess with the rope around her neck (Wallis, 1939).

SUICIDE

Even apart from special views about what is to be gained or lost in a supposed *post mortem* survival, some suicides appear to be rational, aversive, purposive acts. Most common in this category are cases of suicide under the pressure of intractible physical suffering (Pepper, 1958, p. 515). James gave a somewhat broader perspective on the aversive content in suicide when he wrote: "When possessed by the emotion of fear . . . we are in a negative state of mind; that is, our desire is limited to the mere banishing of something, without regard to what shall take its place. In this state of mind there can unquestionably be genuine thoughts, and genuine acts of suicide. . . . Anything, *anything*, at such times, so as to escape and not to be! But such conditions of suicidal frenzy are pathological in their nature and run dead against everything that is regular in the life of the Self in man" (James, 1890). On the other hand, Pepper distinguished suicide as a "rational choice" from neurotic suicidal impulses leading to suicide attempts: "The avoidance of frustration is a deep-seated natural norm in human behavior, and supplies the dynamics of the integrative action of the personality. A suicidal neurotic impulse represents an increase in frustration, not a decrease. If suicide is attempted it will simply add more conflict, count as an error, and increase the exasperation. Besides, recent study of these acts indicates that they are all blindly and mistakenly trying desperately to reduce the frustrations motivating them. Suicidal attempts are regular appetitive and apprehensive acts seeking satisfaction, but, because of the repressed segments, meeting inexplicable frustrations. In short, an empirical description of a suicidal impulse shows that it is a mistake in terms of the ends the impulse is seeking to satisfy" (Pepper, 1958, p. 515).

James gave a satisfactory general empirical description of aversive behaviors and showed how genuine acts of self-destruction might be among them. However, he proceeded to confuse the situation by characterizing suicidal acts as "frenzy" and "pathological" and "against everything that is regular in the life of the Self in man." Pepper, on the other hand, admitted a category of "rational" suicide, but then he proceeded to discuss "suicidal neurotic" impulses as mistakes, and it is not clear from either of these presentations just what is mistaken and what is rational. Neither of them gave detailed discussions of actual cases of suicide, and we must begin there.

According to Plutarch (d. 120 A.D.), Cato the Younger killed himself rather than be indebted for his life to the "tyrant," Julius Caesar. Cato and a few of his friends and some soldiers had shut themselves up in the walled town of Utica in north Africa, but they had no hope of making a successful resistance against Caesar's advancing legions. Caesar was willing to give Cato honor, preferment, and perpetual safety, if only he would grasp his hand in friendship. The delegate, who had been chosen to convey to Caesar the formal obeisance of the 300 members of the equestrian class remaining in Utica, offered to "kiss the hands and fall at the knees of Caesar" on Cato's behalf. Cato's answer may have given his friends and servants the first hint of his intention, for he said, ". . . As to myself, if I would be preserved by Caesar's favor, I should myself go to him; but I would not be beholden to a tyrant, for his acts of tyranny. For it is but usurpation in him to save, as their rightful lord, the lives of men over whom he has no title to reign." Later, after a good dinner and a spirited discussion, Cato retired to his own quarters to read and after awhile he looked for his sword, which his friends had taken away. He had to ask several times, and finally to make a peremptory demand, before it was produced. In one of these altercations he had struck a servant and injured his own hand. When his friends and his son tearfully sought to dissuade him from suicide he said, "When and how did I become deranged, and out of my senses, that thus no one tries to persuade me by reason, or show me what is better, if I am supposed to be ill-advised? Must I be disarmed, and hindered from using my own reason? And you, young man, why do you not bind your father's hands behind him, that when Caesar comes, he may find me unable to defend myself? To despatch myself I want no sword; I need but hold my breath awhile, or strike my head against the wall." Later, to two friends who had stayed in his room, he said, "And you, do you also think to keep a man of my age alive by force, and to sit here and silently watch me? or do you bring me some reasons to prove that it will not be base and unworthy for Cato, when he can find his safety no other way, to seek it from his enemy? If so, adduce your arguments, and show cause why we should now unlearn what we formerly were taught, in order that rejecting all the convictions in which we lived, we may now by Caesar's help, grow wiser, and be yet more obliged to him than for life only. Not that I have determined aught concerning myself, but I would have it in my power to perform what I shall think fit to resolve; and I shall not fail to take you as my advisers, in holding counsel, as I shall do, with the doctrines which your philosophy teaches; in the mean time, do not trouble yourselves, but go tell my son, that he should not compel his father to do what he cannot persuade him to." Later, when his sword was returned, he looked at it and said, "Now I am master of myself." Then he read some more, and went into a sound sleep for several hours. After midnight he called his physician to bandage the hand he hurt in striking the servant, and he sent another servant to the port to make sure that all of his friends had got safely away by sea. When he was informed that preparations were mostly completed for the departures, Cato sent his servant back to the port again with instructions to inform him immediately if any of the refugees needed anything before they left. Then he slept until the servant returned the second time with the news that all was now quiet in the port. After he dismissed the servant Cato stabbed himself, but it was not a clean stroke because his injured hand made him clumsy. He fell off the bed and the noise brought the rest of the household on the run. He resisted all efforts to help him, tore open the wound, and expired.

Marcus Brutus, one of Julius Caesar's assassins, after being finally defeated in battle by Caesar's son and Mark Antony, asked several of his friends and companions to hold his sword to help him commit suicide. Several refused, and Plutarch did not make it clear whether Brutus succeeded in killing himself with the help of a friend, or whether he did it alone. Plutarch's description of Brutus' final conversation with his companions runs as follows: "Then giving each of them his right hand, with a countenance full of pleasure, he said, that he found an infinite satisfaction in this, that none of his friends had been false to him; that as for fortune, he was angry with that only for his country's sake; as for himself, he thought himself much more happy than they who had overcome, not only as he had been a little time ago, but even now in his present condition; since he was leaving behind him such a reputation of his virtue as none of the conquerors with all their arms and riches should ever be able to acquire, no more than they could hinder posterity from believing and saying, that being unjust and wicked men, they had destroyed the just and the good and usurped a power to which they had no right. After this, having exhorted and entreated all about him to provide for their own safety, he withdrew from them with two or three only of his peculiar friends . . ." (Plutarch, d. 120 A.D.).

C. C. Wertenbaker considered suicide by drowning on the day

after he discovered that he had cancer. As his wife later wrote (Wertenbaker 1957) it was his principle that he had a right to die when and how he wished. However, he postponed his suicide on the grounds that the cancer had not been demonstrated to be inoperable or fatal, and to act as though it were would be to ask his wife to have an unreasonable faith in him. Furthermore, he thought it would be difficult for her to explain the situation to the children, and he also felt "that he owed his manhood a test of pain . . . before he died" (Wertenbaker, 1957, p. 17). Before he died he and his wife returned to New York from France where he underwent an operation which revealed the cancer to be inoperable. Returning to Europe on a ship, he managed, with only the help of his wife, a large abcess in the operation incision which developed and broke on the ship. He underwent increasing need for sedation to endure one crisis after another. In this he was helped by his wife, a French physician, and some friends who supplied the drugs. Between crises he worked on a book about his last days, entitled *Sixty Days in a Lifetime*, learned from his son how to play a *paso doble*, "Sol y Sombra," on the guitar, held long conversation with his wife, wrote to friends, lunched with a few friends, and reviewed his life, of which he said, "I'll settle for it." Finally, when intestinal blockage and liver dysfunction were so complete that he could not retain food, he attempted to take his own life by massive doses of morphine, failed three times; tried to inject an air bubble into a vein, failed; and finally succeeded, by cutting his wrists after a small dosage of morphine, 12 days after the first attempt. That he would take his own life sooner or later was known to his wife who·helped him in every way she could, leaving the decision of when entirely up to him. Both American and French physicians were apprised of this and strongly argued against it. His wife remained adamant, as she had when telling him the complete truth about his condition, which was also opposed by the doctors. Before the cancer developed, Wertenbaker had written these notes which his wife later found: "Problem with death is to recognize the point at which you can die with all your faculties, take a healthy look at the world and people as you go out of it. Let them get you in bed, drug or cut you, and you become sick and afraid and disgusting, and everybody will be glad to get rid of you. It wouldn't be such a problem if you can remember how it was when you were young. You wouldn't give up something for instance to add ten years to your life. All right, don't ask for them now. You wouldn't give up drinking and lovemaking and eating—and why should you have given them up? Nothing is ever lost that has been experienced and it can all be there at the moment of death—if you don't wait too long" (quoted by Wertenbaker, 1957, p. 16).

Each of these men, Cato, Brutus, and Wertenbaker, took his own life to avoid the deterioration of his self-evaluation. In all of their statements it appears that they had reached a point beyond which they could not hope to continue the kinds of purposive achievement which they prized. This disability came from different sources. Cato and Brutus saw the social structure around them changing so as to drastically reduce the probability that the goals they sought would be available, even though their capacities were undamaged. Wertenbaker witnessed his own physical deterioration toward the point where he would no longer be able to engage in any purposive activities regardless of what objective opportunities were presented. At the time of their deaths these men were patently not worthless, but in one way or another each recognized the high probability that he would become worthless—as an instrument for achieving goals which he valued. There can be no doubt that each of these men fully and clearly intended to kill himself. Their planfulness, persistence, and adaptive circumvention of obstacles in their way to that end are sufficient witness to their intentions.

However, the circumstances surrounding some acts of self-destruction, or potential self-destruction, indicate just as clearly that the diagnosis of intention is not always so easy. Here is a good example. One morning in Los Angeles, Sandra, a young woman, saw her husband off to work and sat down and wrote a long note to him. Then she neatly arranged some paper money on a table, and on top of it she placed another brief note which requested that her husband use the money in a certain way. Sometime that morning, either before, during, or after these preparations, she made herself a large, strong drink of whiskey and drank some of it. She also took a sufficiently large dose of fast-acting sleeping pills to render her unconscious, probably enough to kill her eventually. If her husband had returned from work at his usual time he would probably have found her dead and he could have read in her note that she loved him, that he had always been good and kind to her, that he was *too* good for her; and of herself, that she was "garbage," and we throw garbage away. She hated herself; she was nothing, and people who are nothing can do nothing—even when they try to help other people, they make a mess of it. A beautiful case, we would say, of suicide coupled with exceedingly negative self-evaluation, no recollection of a higher self-evaluation in the past, and none hoped for in the future, *but,* just as she was on the point of lapsing into unconsciousness she went to the telephone and called the Suicide Prevention Center. She was barely able to mumble her address before the receptionist at the Center heard her fall to the floor. The police were called and they took her to the hospital. That "suicide" was "prevented" or, at least, postponed. Now usually, the first and only question that is asked in such cases is, "What was her *real* intention?" A proper response to this question, though not the usual one, is to ask, "When?" Clearly we are dealing here with at least two intentions, the one of seeking death while professing her love for her husband and justifying the suicide in terms of her own worthlessness, and the other of calling to be rescued from the results of the first and helped back to life. Unless the very concept of intention itself is empty both of these intentions were as well supported by facts, and were therefore as *real*, as any intentions can be. The whole episode is understandable on the sequence of the intentions: first she intended to die and then she intended to live.

There is a third possibility—that Sandra's intention involved no aim at her death at all; nor did she aim at continuing to live without a drastic change in the conditions of her life. Her intention may have been to manipulate other people, to make them listen, to force them to do what she wanted. On this hypothesis, the whole episode was a stage setting in which she went through the motions of killing herself, and in which the "cry for help" was the meaning of the whole thing—not just the telephone call which resulted in her "rescue." Since this slightly more complicated hypothesis covers the facts as well as does the hypothesis that her intentions changed, we are in no position (without gathering more facts) to know which hypothesis describes the truth *in this case*. Perhaps even if we had all the facts about Sandra's situation we would not know which hypothesis to choose. Maybe we should have asked earlier whether there is reason to believe that either hypothesis could possibly be true in this case or any other. There are several cases on record in which a self-destructive intent was permanently abandoned. Joe, a middle-aged man with inoperable cancer decided to kill himself, but his plans went awry and he was rescued. He was deeply chagrined at this instance of his ineptitude, for he had always valued, with good justification, his ability to handle instruments and apparatus effectively. That, and the uproar raised by his friends and family, made him promise never again to attempt to kill himself. He kept the promise and died of his cancer, though nothing of any great significance changed in his life between his attempted suicide and his final "natural" death.

The other hypothesis, that some "suicide attempts" are falsely labeled because the intent is not to kill but to manipulate others, is supported by an illustrative case described by Shneidman (1963). Judy,[2] a young woman about 30 years old, was worried about her husband's intemperate drinking. Her efforts to persuade him to change his ways seemed ineffective so, to force him to heed her, she threatened to kill herself. This didn't work either, and finally, to demand his attention during one of their conversations, she went into the bathroom, cut one wrist with a razor blade and immediately returned and said, "Look at me, I'm bleeding." She was taken to the hospital, where two stitches were taken to close the cut, and she was allowed to rest there in bed for a few hours. The official diagnosis was "attempted suicide." "Attempted social manipulation" would have been nearer the mark. The circumstances and the timing involved in many self-directed, potentially lethal, gestures, with drugs or gas or wrist-cutting, strongly suggest that the act involved a stage setting along with the expectation that the victim would be rescued, but the expected rescuer arrived later than the "victim" planned, only to discover a victim in sober fact. According to present classification systems there is no category for such cases other than "suicide," though consideration of the discrepancy between the supposed intent and the real outcome might suggest that they are "accidents" which occurred during unusually hazardous attempts to put social pressure on others. I know of at least one other instance of accidental "suicide" in which, however, there was no reason to expect an intent to manipulate others. Horace, an able, apparently well-adjusted, reasonably satisfied young university undergraduate was found by his parents, hanged from a joist in the cellar of his home. He was an eager, curious, exploring boy and fortunately he kept notes about most of his ideas, observations, and projects. His notebooks told the story of his death as a plan gone wrong. "What does it feel like to be hanged?" was the question. To get the answer he fastened a stout noosed rope to a joist in the cellar. Then he stood on a chair and adjusted the rope so the noose would not tighten until he stepped off the chair. He planned to step back on the chair in plenty of time so he would live to record how it felt to be hanged, and perhaps to repeat the experiment many times. Whether he panicked or, being nearly unconscious, suffered a loss of coordination we'll never know. When he was found dead, the chair was overturned on the floor too far away from his feet to have offered him any support.

    [2] This is my fictitious name for her; Shneidman gave her none. I have given fictitious names to all these cases except for Cato, Brutus, and Wertenbaker, whose lives are matters of public record. It will be convenient later on to refer to them by name.

The things we might learn about intent from these illustrative cases can be most conveniently summarized by classifying them in Table 8.1. In the labels for the four cells of the table, "on purpose" means that intended and real outcome agree and "by mistake" means that they do not agree. Six of the cases just described are named in their appropriate category. Only Sandra is missing because we cannot classify her intent. In the light of this table, Sandra reveals a few more problems for the classifiers. If she had become unconscious before she could mumble her address into the telephone we might have called her "dead on purpose"—an unquestioned suicide unless by some lucky accident it were discovered that she had made a telephone connection to the Suicide Prevention Center. The mere finding of the telephone off its cradle might have made us suspect that she wanted help and that suspicion would have made us waver between "dead on purpose" and "dead by mistake." We can be pretty sure that she is alive, but not "by mistake," for that would render inexplicable her calling the Suicide Prevention Center at all. So she is alive "on purpose," but only in view of her latest purposive act—the telephone call. The column in the table for intended outcome headed "not dead" conceals a *mélange* of all the possible appetitive and aversive purposes which might be the objectives of any potentially lethal act which a person who does not want to die could direct at himself. Though Sandra is alive "on purpose" we cannot tell whether, in the midst of succumbing to the drugs she took, she re-evaluated her life situation, discovered that her initial lethal intent was a mistake, abandoned the intent to die, and called for help. On the other hand, is the aim

TABLE 8.1

Classification of Potentially Lethal Acts Directed at Self, by Logically Possible Intended and Real Outcomes

Real Outcome	Intended Outcome: To be	
	Dead	Not Dead
Dead	"Dead on purpose" Cato the Younger Marcus Brutus C. C. Wertenbaker	"Dead by mistake" Horace
Not Dead	"Alive by mistake" Joe	"Alive on purpose" Judy

of her act still in the process of being realized? Will she get whatever it is she wants from other people?

What is the possible role of self-evaluation in a case like Sandra's? Her expressed self-evaluation was strongly negative, and though it was vague and general it seemed to relate *exclusively* to her relations with other people. By contrast, the self-evaluations of Cato, Brutus, and Wertenbaker included more than their interpersonal relations and spilled over into achievements of intellect and physical skill which they did not have to validate by comparison with the opinions of others. We have seen some experimental results relevant to this distinction in Chapter 6. Fagen's experiment (cf., especially, Table 6.5) showed that people whose ability was genuinely high were made slightly less confident by hearing that the opinions of others disagreed with their own, but they showed only a slight tendency to be trapped by the others into giving wrong answers. On the other hand, the Ss with genuinely low ability had their confidence greatly improved by being placed in the social context and had practically no resistance at all to being led by the others into giving a large proportion of wrong answers. From this we argued that people with low ability might be critically (perhaps exclusively) dependent for their confidence, their evaluation of themselves, upon whether or not their acts were validated by agreement with those of others or evoked a positive response from others—this, because they simply have no criteria for evaluating their own acts independently. Other evidence was cited in Chapter 6 to show that Fagen's results are not alone in suggesting this hypothesis. Now if Sandra's self-evaluation depended exclusively on some kind of social validation we might suppose that her suicide attempt was aimed at extracting more satisfying evidence of her worth to others and that therefore it was an attempt to manipulate. Judy's openly declared attempt to manipulate her husband by a superficial "attempted suicide" is clearly an attempt to wield power, to validate herself as an effective instrument. Stengel's (1962) suggestion that the appeal characteristics of attempted suicides may evoke a satisfying response from other people is relevant here. If the evoked response is *satisfying*, then we should be able to detect some material change in the behavior of "significant others," a non-recurrence of suicide attempts, and an increase in the self-evaluation of the "attempters." Farberow (1950) found, in a group of hospitalized mental patients, that those who had threatened (but not attempted) suicide showed more guilt and hostility and less easy accommodation to frustration than did either suicidal attempters or a non-suicidal group of patients. Farnham-Diggory (1964) reported similar outcomes among mental

patients, using Cutick's (1962) self-evaluation scales: the self-evaluation of the attempters was nearly as high as that of the non-suicidal
group, which was significantly higher than that of the group which
had merely threatened suicide. Farberow (1950) noted a trend toward
lower mean self-esteem scores with the presence of a history of threats
of suicide, but since the trend was not significant he suggested that
his self-esteem scale needed refinement.

We have mentioned the possibility that two kinds of values,
hedonic and conative-achievement, are threatened by death. Wallis
(1939) pointed out that many cultural groups have the notion that
the manner in which a man dies is significant for his fate in the hereafter or for the honor in which he will be remembered by his survivors. One aspect of the way of dying is the specific type of damage
to the body which "causes" death. Many people say that dead is dead
and the manner of their dying is of no concern to them. Yet the persistence of notions like "quick and easy," "merciful," or "horrible"
deaths suggested that there might be some consistent preferences
among possible ways of dying and that the preferences, if any, might
be consistent with people's beliefs about the degree of social stigma
attached to the various causes of death. Table 8.2 shows the results
of presenting 17 ways of dying to groups of college students and asking them to rank them, assigning the first rank to the most feared.
The attempt to get an estimate of the extent to which these fear rankings correlated with rankings by social stigma was indirect in order
to avoid the possibility of contamination between criteria and to reduce the burden of the task for the respondents. The method was
to give the list of ways of dying to different student groups each
of which received instructions to rank only by a *single* criterion—fear
or social stigma. While this runs us into the danger of considerably
reducing the precision of our results, we were less concerned about
that than about the aforementioned contamination. There is a significant rank correlation (rho = .86) between the median ranks of
the men's and women's data in Table 8.2. This, together with the
fact that there was only a single item in which the median rank
differed as a function of sex might suggest that sex differences are
negligible. However, the magnitude of the correlation between rankings of fear and the rankings by social stigma was directly related
to the socio-economic status of the fear respondent, and this variation
of the correlation with the respondent's class was more marked among
women than among men. The latter may reflect the fact that women
value their social status relations more than men do, and have their
beliefs and opinions more rigorously determined by social influences

TABLE 8.2

Median Ranks Assigned to Indicate Relative Badness of Various Ways of Dying

| Ways of Dying | Median Ranks | |
	Men (n = 126)	Women (n = 139)
Burning	1.53	1.40
Scalding	3.64	4.25
Mauled by wild animal	5.78	4.36
Suffocation	5.00	6.04
Strangulation	5.25	5.75
Drowning	6.57	6.61
Starvation	5.80	7.69
Disease	8.38	9.50
Falling from a height	9.50	9.32
Sharp instrument	10.33	8.85
Run over by a car	9.91	9.97
Freezing	10.25	8.78
Explosion	11.77	8.85*
Poisoning	9.75	11.16
Electrocution	11.69	12.55
Gunshot	12.75	12.13
General failure due to age	16.11	16.28

* Difference significant at .05 level, Kolmogorov-Smirnov test.

Rank 1 is the worst, rank 17 the least bad.

The composite rank order for all respondents is indicated by the order in which the items are listed.

than men do (Diggory, 1953, 1962b). There is of course no way to tell from these data what the connection is between social stigma and way of dying, why a status-oriented person would value one way of dying differently than a less socially determined person. However, the consistent ordering of the ways of dying is interesting enough itself.

Burning to death is more feared by far than any other form of dying. Is this why heretics and witches were burned? I doubt it, because there is evidence that many of the faithful considered death by fire as a desirable way to die (Gibbon, 1788), or a way to avoid falling into the hands of Antichrist (Wallis, 1939). Is death by fire feared today because of its association with heretics and the exaggerated horrors of the Inquisition? Perhaps so, but only partly so. This form of death seems to have been inflicted on heretics by a French king for the first time in 1017. Why he did it that way is not known. At any rate, Frederick II first wrote a law providing for the burning of heretics, and that law was the precedent from which were derived all subsequent civil laws which supported the Inquisition in its fiery career (Bury, 1913). Possibly the historical association of fire with a noteworthy example of man's inhumanity to man accounts for some of the modern fear of death by fire. More of it may be accounted for by a combination of other factors, such as the expectation that it is extremely painful and, considering its supposed degree of painfulness, it probably lasts too long. Furthermore, fire unpleasantly disfigures the corpse and we have the tradition, reinforced by refinements of the embalmer's art, that we want to look pretty at our last show, even if we can do nothing else. Perhaps it would be as well to present the facts we know and to wait for more data before we venture too far in search of an explanation. There is one other fact that bears on this point. It has been reported by experienced infantrymen that flamethrowers were effective weapons against enemy soldiers encased in bunkers and pillboxes not only because the physical effects of the weapon could reach them, but also because it frightened and panicked them so that they did very little shooting.

We made no attempt to find out *how* our respondents expected to die, but Middleton (1936) has some interesting data on that point. Twenty-one per cent of his 825 college student respondents said that they sometimes thought that they might die of some particular disease because the disease was in the family, or it had a widespread prevalence, or a relative or friend had died of it, or the respondent had a "natural horror" of it, or a desire to die of it. Similar thoughts of death by "accident" were reported by 51 per cent of the respondents, with reasons for these thoughts including respondent's own narrow escape or fright, people he had known who were killed that way, witnessing or seeing pictures of such an accident, or recognizing the opportunity for such accidents in his own life space.[3]

[3] The lists of these imagined events, in order of frequency of mention are: Diseases—cancer, tuberculosis, heart disease, pneumonia, appendicitis, childbirth, spinal meningitis (there had been a severe and well-publicized meningitis epidemic in the state two years before the survey), sleeping sickness (there was an epidemic of sleeping sickness in a large nearby city at the time of the survey), diabetes, influenza, apoplexy, paralysis, diphtheria; Accidents—automobile, railroad, airplane, drowning, falling, burning, shooting, suffocation, asphyxiation (Middleton, 1936).

Though we have little reason to doubt that people do in fact fear and avoid the negative hedonic values associated with death, there is also reason to believe that death, as the absolute termination of self, implies fear of the loss of other values, namely the conative-achievement values. Part of the evidence for this we have already considered in the facts about suicide, especially those cases in which an individual seems to choose death as a way of avoiding an even worse fate. Suicide rates, especially among men, have been observed to rise during periods of general economic depression (*U.S. Vital Statistics*, 1942; Henry and Short, 1954). Suicide rates also change in a remarkable parallel with unemployment rates, especially in men at the ages most likely to be affected by unemployment (MacMahon, Johnson, and Pugh, 1963). The impact of unemployment on the thwarting of the discharged person's purposes and the purposes of members of his family has been well documented (e.g., Elderton, 1931; Hall, 1934; Bakke, 1940; Ginzberg, Ginsburg and Lynn, 1943).

People who expect to die within a short time frequently express concern over tasks they will leave undone, responsibilities they have not discharged, and will exert a great deal of thought and action to doing as much as they can to repair these deficiencies (Fairbanks, 1948; Eissler, 1955; Feifel, 1963). The contents of many suicide notes include not only requests for things that the survivors are to do in the deceased's behalf, but they also indicate a profound negative self-evaluation. There is very little evidence from suicide notes to support the psychoanalytic interpretation of suicide as a death wish directed against another with whom the suicide is identified (Freud, 1916–18; 1928a). Notes which express hostility toward the survivors, as in saying, "I hope you'll be able to live with my death on your conscience," while they do occur, are found in relatively small proportions. The focus of most suicide notes is concern and solicitude for the survivors and sorrow and regret over the suicide's own real or imagined shortcomings (Shneidman and Farberow, 1956; Tuckman, Kleiner, and Lavell, 1959; Cohen, 1961).

With these considerations in mind we (Diggory and Rothman, 1961) tried to find out whether there are any systematic orders among the values which people conceive they will lose by their own death. People of various ages and statuses ranked the following consequences of their own death: (A) I could no longer have any experiences; (B) I am uncertain as to what might happen to me if there is a life after death; (C) I am afraid of what might happen to my body after death; (D) I could no longer care for my dependents; (E) my death would cause grief to my relatives and friends; (F) all my plans and projects would come to an end; (G) the process of dying might be painful. The paired comparisons method was used, and the respondents were to indicate the most distasteful (more feared) item in each pair. In the final determination of rank orders, the most feared (most often chosen) item was given rank *one* and the item least feared (least often chosen) was given rank *seven*. Figure 8.1 shows how the items were scaled for various classes of respondents in terms of the median frequency of assignment to a particular rank. In the classification by marital status, no longer being able to care for dependents (item D) rose steadily in the rankings from single, through engaged, to married, and stayed high in the post-marital statuses of widowed and divorced. This same item is no higher than fourth rank in groups below 40 years of age, but it is in the top rank for groups over forty, probably because the fact of having dependents correlates with age. Also, caring for dependents ranked first for men, but only fifth for women, because the modal adult male *has* dependents while the modal female *is* a dependent. The other "purposive activity" items (A: I could no longer have any experiences, and F: All my plans and projects would come to an end) are always near the top of the scale, seldom more than one rank apart. These facts suggest that people fear death because it eliminates opportunities to pursue goals which are important to their self-esteem. These data also permit us to say something about the fear of negative hedonic values (item C, concern for the body after death, and item G, the supposed painfulness of the process of dying). The fear of pain was always ranked higher than fear of the post mortem fate of the body, a fact which is consistent with our previous observations about hedonic preferences among ways of dying (Table 8.2). The fear of pain during the process of dying (item G) was not in the first rank for the majority of the respondents, being superseded among all respondents by the fears that one's death would cause grief for relatives and friends (item E) and that all plans and projects would come to an end (item F). The rank of the fear of the pain of dying does not differ significantly as a function of age; among the age categories it fluctuates between ranks 2 and 4. It was significantly more feared by women than by men, and by Catholics and Jews than it was by Protestants and adherents of other religions or none at all, and it was more feared by members of upper and lower socio-economic classes than by the middle class. We have no way of explaining these fluctuations in the relative fear of the supposed pain of dying. Our point is that it is not usually the thing *most* feared.

Another way to get at the question of whether and how people

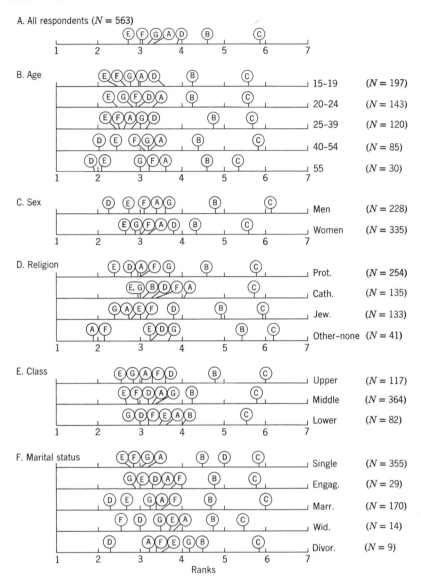

Fig. 8.1 Median-rank scale positions assigned to seven consequences of one's own death by respondents in various categories. The item key is given in the text. (After Diggory and Rothman, 1961.)

relate the idea of their own death to their value as instruments for achieving goals is to ask them, "Under what circumstances, if any, would you be relatively indifferent to the idea of your own death?" Stanley Fagen assisted in the analysis of about 600 responses to this question, which was part of a larger questionnaire dealing with attitudes toward death. Some people simply did not answer the question at all. Others simply said that there were no such circumstances, and others expressed some religious sentiment which was irrelevant to the question. Of those who answered in any way, either by denial, by irrelevancy, or with a direct and relevant response, 57 per cent fell into one of the following categories: (1) loss or decline in capacity from disease, accident, or senility; (2) high achievement so that capacity had reached its limit or desire for further achievement was exhausted; (3) an environment where desirable goals are absent and will probably never exist. These categories seem to be functionally equivalent conditions for the lowering of self-evaluation-as-instrument. It is the same if capacities are inadequate, if no desire exists, or if goals which might be both desired and achieved do not exist. In either case, if an object we desire cannot be had for money or if the object does not exist, money has no value; in the analogous cases, our capacities, and therefore ourselves, have no value either.

THE DEADLINE

We have already presented the importance of deadlines in people's estimates of their own power, and death is a deadline—*the* deadline. What can we say, then, about a possible relation between self-evaluations and estimates of one's own longevity? We have already introduced this notion in Farnham-Diggory's (1964) finding that psychotic patients with relatively high self-evaluations also had a relatively higher "subjective life expectancy" (SLE) (Table 7.10). We will here present some data from normal respondents.

The device we used to assess subjective life expectancy was the series of questions used by Farnham-Diggory (see Chapter 7 and Appendix G). Table 8.3 shows a tabulation of the responses of normal Ss of both sexes, from a variety of socio-economic and educational backgrounds, and ranging in age from 8 to 65 years. We thought that by such a series of questions we could push every person in imagination so far into the future that he would come to a period so remote that he knows, expects, believes, fears, or hopes that he will be dead by then. The table shows that this expectation is justified in about 57 per cent of the cases in hand so far. This refers to category 3. A good many of the responses in category 3 are euphemistic, and

TABLE 8.3

Distributions of Male and Female Respondents by Response Categories on the Subjective Life Expectancy (SLE) Scale

		Response Categories*				
		0	1	2	3	Totals
Male	Number	90	33	20	188	331
	Proportion	.27	.10	.06	.57	1.00
Female	Number	76	20	19	159	274
	Proportion	.27	.09	.06	.57	1.00

* Key to Response Categories:

0: Reference to activity, doing nothing, or ignorance of one's condition, but no mention of death.

1: Hint at the possibility of death, but no clear affirmation.

2: Description of activities in the hereafter, physical death indirectly inferred.

3: Direct affirmation of death, often euphemistic.

some of them are intended to be funny. Some respondents took a wry delight in pushing the literal interpretation of the lead question, "What do you expect to be doing . . . ," into their answers. Thus, the inevitable "pushing up daisies" comes in handy, also "pushing up sod," "decomposing," and "attending my funeral." Others expressed the idea of death, without using the word or its cognates, as: "six feet under," "laying in a grave," "not living," "not here," "won't be around then."

Twenty-seven per cent of the respondents made no mention of death at all in the hypothetical ninety-year span. These are in category 0 of Table 8.3. They say they "do not know" what they will be doing in the distant future, or they say they will be doing "nothing," or having "a peaceful and restful life," or just "sitting" or "waiting" or "relaxing." Some written responses show nothing but blanks after the last mention of a definite activity, others put ditto marks in all the final blanks to indicate the continuation of the last mentioned activity. Some say they have "no plans" for the remoter years, or that their activities then are "beyond my comprehension," or only "the Lord knows" what they will be doing. Some mention traveling to improbable places such as the moon or the other planets, others mention departing on a world cruise 90 years from now.

Categories 0 and 3 are the extreme categories. Together they include 84 per cent of the respondents. The other 16 per cent are included in the two intermediate categories, 1 and 2. Category 1 includes responses in which death is mentioned, but only as a possibility. For example, in the last five questions beginning with "fifty years from now" an eleven-year-old girl says she will be "resting, eating, or dead," and she wrote that in every blank including the last one, "ninety years from now." A twenty-year-old young man said at seventy years from now, "I'm lucky if I live so long," and then added that he would be a "rich old codger" eighty and ninety years from now. Another man, 32 years old, wrote that tomorrow he would be "gardening," next week he would be "working," a month from now he would be "living"—which he dittoes through all the subsequent spaces through fifty years from now; at sixty years from now he wrote merely, "I hope," dittoed it through eighty years from now, and at ninety years from now he wrote, "had enough." In such responses we can identify some period at which the person suggests a momentous change or the likelihood of one, but they refer to death in the most circuitous terms and parallel it or follow it with the possibility of continued activity in this life, so we keep them in a separate category.

Category 2 includes cases where activity is transferred abruptly to the after-life with no direct mention of physical death, or cases in which the respondent ends his sequence of responses by reference to some conventional religious notion without coming right out with the idea of death. In answer to the question about "fifty years from now" a thirty-one-year-old woman wrote, "Reposed—and enjoying (LET'S HOPE) the great beyond, where I am sure the good Lord has taken my first-born (a baby boy 3 days old)." Another woman, 41 years old, writes at forty years from now, "Meeting St. Peter," and then at fifty years from now she adds, "Just memories left," which she dittoed through the rest of the blanks to the end. Another woman, 49 years old, bracketed all the blanks from fifty to ninety years from now and wrote at the bottom of the page, "New Testament, Romans, 5:12 'Therefore being justified by faith, we have peace with God through our Lord Jesus Christ: By whom also we have access by faith into this grace wherein we stand, and rejoice in hope of the glory of God.' I Corinthians 15:12–54, especially 22: 'For as in Adam all die, even so in Christ shall all be made alive'; and 54: 'Death is swallowed up in victory.'" A man, 56 years old, wrote at twenty years from now, "Hope to be happy in retirement," then, beginning with thirty years from now he drew an arrow toward the bottom of the page through all the remaining blanks. Next to the shaft of the arrow he wrote, "Man proposes but God disposes," and at the head of the arrow this footnote, "Predicting future happenings seems like a form of desecration, particularly if you believe as I, in man's predestination." A twenty-one-year-old man, beginning at sixty years from now, repeated in all subsequent blanks, "I expect to be in heaven," and a ten-year-old boy, beginning at eighty years from now wrote simply "in glory."

People who respond as defined in categories 1, 2, and 3 probably are expressing, with various degrees of clarity, a subjective life expectancy (SLE). This is easily computed by adding their real age in years at the time of their answers to the number of years from then at which they indicate, more or less definitely, the end of their life. Many of these SLEs are obviously inaccurate. For example, twenty-six people 20 years old or younger, first mentioned the likelihood of their own death at 90 years from now. Their subjective life expectancies ranged from 97 to 110 years. There are a few even more fantastic: for example, the forty-seven-year-old man who puts his death at 80 years from now and the twenty-six-year-old who puts his at 90. However, the *average* subjective life expectancy declined steadily as the age of the respondents increased, and it is significantly lower for respondents 40 years of age or older than for younger ones. Comparing the course of subjective life expectancy with that of *actuarial* life expectancy shows that both curves decline, but they are not parallel. Up to the age of 30, respondents set their subjective life expectancies up to 47 years higher than their actuarial life expectancies. The only exceptions to this general overestimation by younger people are those of a twenty-year-old whose subjective life expectancy is 8 years less than his actuarial expectancy, and two nine-year-old boys who said they expected their lives to end 27 years before the actuaries would give up on them. Above the age of thirty, there is a higher proportion of respondents whose subjective life expectancies are lower than actuarial life expectancy (though these are small underestimations), and the overestimations (no more than 10 years) are smaller than at the younger ages. All this is true of responses in category 3, the most definite and realistic category. In categories 1 and 2, the same general picture holds, but there are no underestimations, the overestimations are larger at all ages, and the errors grow smaller with increasing age of the respondents. This far we can go with the opinion expressed by Schilder and Wechsler (1934): a child's death is a remote event to him. We can add with considerable confidence that one's own death seems to be a pretty remote event for young adults, too. Only in people of considerably advanced age, with reality closing in on them by many indications, have we found a more or less realistic estimation of the number of years they have left.

Among our respondents, 27 per cent fell in category 0; that is, they ran right off the end of our time scale, 90 years into the future, and never mentioned the idea of their own death in any way. On the face of it they appeared to ignore the possibility of their own death. This "ignoring" is not a function of sex or of age. The age of our category 0 respondents ranged from five to 52 years with a median of 18 years, about one-half year lower than the median for the other categories.

Some of our respondents evaluated themselves on the Cutick scales and also answered the subjective life expectancy questions. Their mean responses on the eight self-evaluation scales and on the total of all scales are shown in Table 8.4. The averages are presented separately for those who were in category 0 or in categories 1, 2, and 3 on the subjective life expectancy scale. Regardless of sex, the older respondents have higher overall mean SLEs than the younger ones, but the obtained differences are not significant, probably because of the small numbers 40 years of age or older. There is reason to suspect that, with more adequate sample size, the difference between older and younger respondents would be significant because the men 18–21 years old have a significantly higher overall mean self-evaluation than both the men and women in the 14–19 age group. This latter difference should be interpreted with caution as indicating the effect of age, because the youngest group were high school students unselected for ability or future educational plans, and the men 18–21 years old were the group of college students which Cutick (1962) sampled for his experiment. Thus the obtained significant differences may reflect ability rather than age differences. The point is presented here only because the *significant* difference obtained is about the same size as the differences between the 14–19 and the ≥40 age groups. The latter differences would, therefore, probably be significant if there were an adequate number of older respondents. Within the groups of men and women high school students there is no significant increase in self-evaluation with yearly differences in age.

A more detailed look at the differences on the individual scales and the shapes of the profiles defined by the eight self-evaluation scales may strengthen the impression that there is some change in self-evaluation as a function of age. The shape of the profile for Cutick's college group is shown in Fig. 7.12. The profiles of the other groups can be drawn from the data given in Table 8.4. Graphic

TABLE 8.4
Mean Self-Evaluations on Cutick's Scales

Scale Number	Women						Men						
	(14–19)			(≥40)			(14–19)			(18–21)*	(≥40)		
	(1,2,3)	(0)	Total	(1,2,3)	(0)	Total	(1,2,3)	(0)	Total		(1,2,3)	(0)	Total
n	128	47	175	22	8	30	130	44	174	162	15	8	23
1	77.0	80.8	78.0	67.8	75.9	70.0	72.2	79.2	74.0	73.2	71.1	69.5	70.5
2	53.2	46.8	51.5	57.6	41.1	53.2	50.1	56.4	51.7	61.7	60.9	56.8	59.4
3	70.6	65.4	69.2	77.8	74.5	76.9	70.5	70.8	70.6	72.3	81.3	88.4	83.8
4	76.0	70.8	74.6	73.8	70.4	72.9	70.6	74.8	71.7	76.0	66.1	70.6	67.7
5	83.2	79.6	82.2	93.3	89.9	92.4	80.2	84.6	81.3	83.6	86.0	88.9	87.0
6	67.6	64.9	66.9	70.4	65.8	69.2	60.5	72.4	63.5	71.4	68.3	68.9	68.5
7	58.6	51.4	56.7	60.3	57.8	59.6	57.8	66.5	60.0	67.4	75.7	71.1	74.1
8	70.7	67.9	69.9	74.7	65.6	72.3	68.2	72.3	69.2	69.1	76.5	75.5	76.1
Average	69.6	66.0	68.6	72.0	67.6	70.8	65.6	73.9	67.7	71.2	73.2	73.7	73.4

* Cutick's (1962) college students. They cannot be separated into SLE categories because they were not given the SLE questionnaire.

The scales are described completely in Appendix E.

412

comparison of all of these profiles would be confusing so a different analysis was made by ranking the means of the eight scales within each group and then computing rank correlation coefficients among the groups. If two profiles are identical in shape then the rank correlation will be 1.00, and the more different two profiles are the smaller the value of the coefficient will be. All the rank correlation coefficients thus available from the data in Table 8.4 are summarized in Table 8.5. Generally these coefficients show that in the younger group the men's and women's profiles are very similar; among the men the profiles differ more as a function of age than they do among the women, and the profiles of the younger women differ most markedly only from those of the older men.

The most remarkable, and puzzling, facts emerge with the attempt to see whether there is any relation between subjective life expectancy and self-evaluation. In these data there are no such relations in categories (1, 2, 3) on the subjective life expectancy scale in which a definite end of life is indicated. When the self-evaluation of respondents in category 0 is compared with that of respondents in the other categories it is apparent that overall mean self-evaluation varies as a function of both sex and subjective life expectancy scale category. The mean self-evaluation of the women in category 0 is lower than that of women in the other subjective life expectancy categories, and exactly the opposite is true for men. Furthermore, if our small numbers of older respondents provide an adequate basis for judging, then this effect increases in magnitude as women get older, but it decreases as men get older. This latter effect is of course not significant. When the age groups are combined and the men and women divided by their position in or out of category 0 there is a significant interaction, as previously described. A preliminary concise description of this result is that the fact of describing a definite end of ones' life, without regard to the accuracy of the "prediction," goes along with lower average self-evaluations among women, and with higher average self-evaluations among men. The women who described no definite end to their lives had lower average self-evaluations on seven of the eight scales. The single exception was scale 1, "When doing things that interest you most, in what per cent of such cases are you fully satisfied with your performance?" On scale 1, the women who put no definite term on their lives evaluated themselves more highly than did the others. Among the younger men (14–19 years old), those who described no end to their lives evaluated themselves more highly than the others did on every scale. In the older group of men (≥40 years old), those who set no terminations had a lower

TABLE 8.5

Intercorrelations (Spearman's ρ) Based on Rankings of Mean Self-Evaluations on Cutick's Eight Scales

	Women						Men						
	(14-19)			(≥40)			(14-19)			(18-21)*	(≥40)		
	(1,2,3)	(0)	Total	(1,2,3)	(0)	Total	(1,2,3)	(0)	Total	(18-21)*	(1,2,3)	(0)	Total
Women (14-19)													
(1,2,3)		.98	1.00	.67	.93	.79	.98	.93	.93	.91	.48	.45	.48
(0)			.98	.55	.86	.69	.95	.88	.95	.86	.38	.35	.38
(Total)				.98	.88	.79	.98	.93	.97	.91	.48	.52	.48
(≥40)													
(1,2,3)					.73	.95	.73	.55	.69	.69	.76	.83	.76
(0)						.81	.95	.86	.88	.93	.55	.52	.55
(Total)							.83	.64	.83	.83	.69	.81	.69
Men (14-19)													
(1,2,3)								.94	1.00	.93	.50	.55	.50
(0)									.91	.91	.31	.31	.31
(Total)										.95	.50	.55	.50
(18-21)*											.36	.47	.38
(≥40)													
(1,2,3)												.93	1.00
(0)													.93

* Cutick's (1962) college students. They cannot be separated into SLE categories because they were not given the SLE questionnaire. N.B. with 8 items ranked, a ρ of .74 is significant at p = .05.

mean self-evaluation than the others on scales 1, 2, 7, and 8; and higher mean self-evaluations on scales 3, 4, 5, and 6. These latter findings give us the suspicion that there is much of interest to be found in pursuing the problem of sex differences in self-evaluation. On the basis of the vague hunch that there might be such differences, we have, with the single exception of Rothman's (1963) experiment (cf. Figs. 7.4–7.8), used only men as Ss in our studies. Sex differences are obviously interesting, and probably of some theoretical importance, but we avoided them in favor of the strategy of exploring the phenomena more thoroughly in men only.

SUMMARY

The anecdotes and data presented in this chapter have been designed to explore the possibility that attitudes toward death are connected somehow with our self-evaluations. What has been done so far is a mere beginning, a partial laying bare of the problem. What fuller inquiry may reveal we could only guess. To the extent that we have seen even a partial outline of the situation, it appears to be this. Death has at least two faces, each confronting us with an aspect of the frustration of our purposive activities, frustration which leads to a lowering of self-evaluation. The death of those we love or depend on frustrates us by destroying the objects or means of some of our most important purposive activities. Our own death will permanently frustrate us by removing the possibility of any purposive activity. On its other face, death is a refuge, the final withdrawal from frustrating prospects where, either because of the deterioration of our capacities or the lack of opportunities to exercise whatever power we have, our purposive acts can no longer coincide with our values.

Chapter 9
RETROSPECT AND PROSPECT

When we undertook to study self-evaluation we faced an enormously complex field of phenomena which has been written about extensively, but not always satisfactorily from the scientific point of view. In fact, some recent writers have said that the *real* problems of self are beyond the reach of laboratory experimentation and statistical analysis. To bring such methods to bear upon genuine human problems is to degrade man. To analyze self is to do violence to it.

However, we have not discovered any sound reason why experiments cannot be done on self and related phenomena. One of the advantages of the experimental method is that experiments are impossible unless the phenomena which they are about are clearly defined to begin with. General definitions are admissible as long as they are clear, and as long as they admit of reduction to the specific details required for experimental operations.

In quest of this clarity we devoted the first three chapters of this book to an attempt to discover what meanings, if any, the words "self," "value," and "self-evaluation" could have in a program of experimental investigation. We sought for the minimum meanings in each case because we wanted to avoid the "rich mud of conceptions" against which Pierce warned all those who would make their ideas clear. It was our faith that if our axioms were meager and restricted we could, by playing our hunches, make knowledge grow gradually but surely into an edifice firmly supported by fact.

The meaning of the word *self*, we decided, is its reference to any situations in which the agent and the object of the act are one and the same organism. To be an agent is simply to exercise any function of which organisms are capable: thinking, loving, caressing, striking, smelling, conceiving, classifying, and evaluating, and a host of others. These functions, exercised under the various conditioning circumstances of the world, are the acts to which the statement refers. To be the object of an act is merely to be that which is thought about, caressed, loved, or evaluated, etc. The implication of this view to which we paid most attention is that any act in which actor and object are the same is a *self*-relevant act, regardless of how trivial or global, how central or peripheral the act and its outcomes may be. This frees us from the worry, which oppresses some to the point of inactivity, that we are not *really* talking about self unless we are talking about what we already know to be the ineffably valuable, inviolably private, unmitigatedly central "core" of an individual's personality. If we adhere to our view, then what we say about self is as "real" as anything that can be said. Whether the aspect of self that we are talking about is more or less valuable or important, and what difference its degree of value and importance makes in the problem under investigation, are questions of fact to be settled by experiment.

Psychologists who are interested in value can hardly do better at the present time, we believe, than adhere to the definitions which have been developed by value theorists who had more than a nodding acquaintance with psychology. The latest of these, and the one which makes the soundest use of the best available psychological experimental data is the one proposed by Stephen Pepper (1958). Pepper's view is that we can discern in the behavior of organisms several natural norms in terms of which objects and activities are selected either to be avoided or to be approached or repeated. The scope of operation of any one of these natural norms defines a selective system which Pepper calls the structure of appetitive and aversive purposive acts. In that selective system, the behavioral product is learning; the criteria in terms of which the natural norms operate are success or failure. Success is good, failure is bad, and together these two are called the "conative-achievement" values.

Self-evaluation, by juxtaposition of the definitions of self and value, means simply that the object being evaluated is a part, aspect, or product, of the very organism which does the evaluating. It is possible then to evaluate a previous evaluation. Roughly, when we change our evaluation of something we change our behavior toward it, even if it is an aspect of ourselves. We may be more resistant to changing self-evaluations than to changing our evaluations of other people or of inanimate objects. That is another question of fact. In any case, a reduced evaluation of an object is signaled by behavior which is more indifferent or more actively avoidant than formerly.[1] In extreme cases, destruction of low-valued objects is the rule. Conversely, increasing evaluation of an object is indicated by behavior which is more strongly appetitive with respect to that object than formerly.

[1] By "object" here is meant anything that can be valued: thing, act, function, idea, person, etc.

In our quest for criteria or bases of self-evaluation we were directed to the conative-achievement values by the fact that many previous writers have emphasized that human beings value themselves on the skill, adroitness, or efficiency with which they accomplish their purposes. Man then might be viewed as a purposive instrument, and might evaluate himself in quite the same terms as he evaluates any other instrument. Many people might object and say that this reduces man to the status of an implement and so degrades him, which is only what they were afraid we would do in the first place. However, if it is mystery and miracles we crave, then here is the mystery and the miracle right under our very noses. What a marvelous engine this is which is inherently no specific instrument but whose usefulness can range from counting bits of atoms to weighing the stars! He can not only solve problems; he can define problems so that they can be solved. Before we decide that man is degraded by our calling him an instrument, we should first decide what kind of an instrument he is.

If man regards himself as an instrument and values himself as such, then he values himself on what we may broadly call his "power" to achieve goals. As the level of aspiration literature shows, a man's approach to goals is not simply a repetitive one of achieving over and over again the goals which he has already achieved. Having accomplished one thing, his next choice usually contains something of novelty; the next thing he tries is more difficult than the thing he just completed. Nevertheless, even after a series of goal-directed attempts most of which were successful, or in which at least improvement was consistently shown, some people will decide that they lack the power to achieve the ultimate goal which they had been approaching stepwise. This makes them stop trying to achieve that goal, and that decision means that they have formulated a prediction, an expectation, an estimate of their probability of success—which is low.

In our initial experiments we set up a situation in which people worked toward more or less valuable goals which were said to be contingent on their achieving a strictly defined performance level within a strictly defined number of attempts. The immediate performance goal and the deadline (the end of their opportunities) were both prominently displayed on the same "graph" on which their "scores"—the alleged results of their successive attempts—were presented to them. The sequences of scores which constituted the "performance curves" presented to the subjects were actually controlled, by various ruses, in order that we could systematically manipulate them as experimental variables. Before every trial the subjects stated their estimated probability of success, $P(s)$; that is, the likelihood that they would attain the fixed performance goal at least once within the remaining trials. We also recorded other aspects of behavior. We used this technique in a variety of settings with subjects ranging in age from six years to about 40 years. In most of our experiments on $P(s)$ the subjects were made to fail, and the $P(s)$ trends generally declined. Hereafter, conditions which produced relatively little decline in $P(s)$ are called "encouraging," and those which produce greater declines in $P(s)$ are "discouraging." Generally the discouraging conditions are low rates of improvement in performance; low average levels of performance, regardless of rate of improvement; smooth predictable performance trends rather than irregular, unpredictable ones; deadlines which are close and clear, rather than distant and vague; and a previous experience of failure, rather than success, on a similar task. When people are told that they can qualify for their desired activity by using one or all of a specified set of abilities, the degree of discouragement at any time depended not on the number of previous failures, but on the number of abilities previously tested and found wanting.

The expectation, that there would be a close functional connection between estimated $P(s)$ for a given task and direct self-evaluations as a performer of that task, was confirmed *provided that* the required self-evaluations related specifically to the task being performed or to the utimate goal for which the person was trying to qualify. We take this to suggest that self-evaluations are highly resistant to change when they relate to general, unspecified fields of functioning, but they are quite easily changed when performance relates to a well-defined goal which must be achieved under clearly specified conditions of work.

However, conditions of work are not absolutely immutable. Even on factory assembly lines, as many a rigid supervisor knows to his despair, the workers are mightily clever at introducing surprising variations in their methods of work without falling below the imposed standards of quality and quantity of production. In that situation, the possibility of changing the *way* a thing is done is probably exploited to avoid boredom. There is another function for which possible changes in conditions of work might be explored; that is, that the job be done at all, and the agent's self-evaluation as an achiever be preserved or increased. One of our experiments presents evidence that people who are obviously failing to qualify for an activity which they chose above several others will not immediately abandon it for an available alternative of almost equal attractiveness *until* they have first tried out at least one alternative method of attempting the first undertaking. We believe that experiments of this type offer some promise of examining the conditions under which various "defenses" against the lowering of self-evaluation will be employed.

In general, the psychological literature on persistence in the face of difficulties has not taken sufficient account of the role played by the existence of available alternatives in determining persistence or the lack of it. For the most part, subjects do not abandon even hopeless tasks unless they have implied or explicit permission to do so. Even then, most of those who quit turn immediately to alternative activities provided by the experimenter, or they leave the laboratory and pursue ends of their own. When, as in one of our experiments, the subjects' contract with the experimenter is that they continue working for a fixed number of trials no matter how nearly certain the prospect of failure becomes, even then the subjects continue to work at the task, *but,* in effect, they have actually quit. The lower their estimated $P(s)$, the less effort they put into the task performance as shown by the action potentials from their working muscles. To superficial observation they were good fellows and did all that the experimenter asked them to do, but covertly, perhaps without knowing it themselves, they abandoned the goal and merely went through the motions. In other experiments we have corresponding observations: the actual number of units produced per second declined in parallel with decreases in estimated $P(s)$ and self-evaluations.

We have also found that if failure to achieve a desired goal is accompanied by a reduction in self-evaluation, then it is also quite likely to be accompanied by spontaneous increases in the number of references to *death* in stories which the subjects tell. In our experiments, at least, there was no evidence that increased self-evaluations following a success were accompanied by a corresponding decrease in the number of death references.

It has often been suggested that suicide, or an accepting or indifferent attitude toward impending death, is related to a low degree of self-evaluation. To this suggestion, and to the results of our experiments, we can add the results of a couple of questionnaire studies. In one of these it appeared that what people fear most as a *consequence* of their own death is their inability to carry out that function which they have chosen or to which they are committed by their status or role in society. For example, being no longer able to care for dependents was more feared by men (who have dependents) than by women (who are dependents); it was more feared by those who were married than by those who were single and not engaged to be married; and it was more feared by the middle-aged than by the younger respondents. In another question we asked approximately 600 people, "Under what conditions, if any, would you be relatively indifferent to the idea of your own death?" Some people did not respond at all to this question. Some gave responses that were not answers; just irrelevant emotionally triggered conventional sentiments about death, the great beyond, and the hereafter. Of those who answered, some said that they would never be *indifferent* to death. This betrays a flaw in our way of asking the question. We could doubtless have obtained more relevant information from some of these people in face-to-face interviews, because, though some of them indicated that they would always *fear* and abhor the idea of their own death, others suggested that there might be conditions under which they would *welcome* death. Of course, neither fearing or welcoming are indifferent, so most of those who denied their indifference wrote nothing more. However, we were able to classify 57 per cent of all the answers, including the denials of indifference, as follows. People said they would be indifferent to the idea of their own death if: (a) they had suffered loss or impairment of their abilities through disease, accident, or senility; (b) they had achieved so much that they could desire no further achievements; (c) they were in an environment in which all opportunities for choosing and pursuing goals were denied to them.

We have also studied the conditions under which change in the evaluation of a single *tested* ability is accompanied by a corresponding change in several other abilities which were not tested. In two experiments on this point the subjects were attempting to qualify for a goal which they had chosen. They were told that five different abilities, all briefly described, and on which they had rated their own power, were all equally important in their being admitted to the chosen activity. When they failed on the test of the one ability which they had rated as their best of the set they subsequently reduced their ratings of over 60 per cent of the abilities in the set of five, and by fairly large distances on the linear rating scales. However, when the tested (and failed) ability was the one of the set they had rated lowest, they reduced the ratings of only 20 per cent of the abilities in the set, and the net amount of change per ability was in the direction of a slight increase in self-evaluation.

If the subject was successful on the test of highest-rated ability, there was little subsequent change in the rating of the tested ability, but there was a fairly substantial increase in the ratings of most of the untested abilities. If the success was incurred on a test of the lowest-rated ability, then there was a large subsequent increase in self-evaluations of the tested ability and practically no change at all in ratings of the untested abilities.

On the average, no such changes occurred if the "test" was given under otherwise identical conditions, but only for practice; that is, the test (and by implication the ability tested) was declared to be irrelevant to whether or not the subject would qualify for the activity he wanted to get into. In the irrelevant test condition, we seem to have stumbled across two extremely different styles of personal reaction to situations in which self-evaluations might be changed. On the one hand there is the person who rather quickly and completely capitulates and reduces the evaluation of many of his abilities when he has been denied the use of an ability he deemed more powerful. How many people have such an attitude? How is this attitude developed? Is it in any sense an adaptive attitude, or is its effect deleterious for the individual in the long run? On the other hand there is the person who appears to have made himself vulnerable in his self-evaluations by declaring that no test is irrelevant. We can ask the same questions about him as about the other. Of both we can inquire what other behavioral characteristics go along with their special evaluative attitudes.

One obvious refinement that should be made in these "generalization" experiments is to control for the type of ability tested, as well as its initial level of evaluation. In three experiments with children, the only ones in which the experimental design permitted this observation, we obtained strong evidence that the level of $P(s)$ depended on previous experiences of success or failure and on the value of the rewards achieved or lost. However, these effects were conditioned by the *quality* of the task (i.e., mental or motor) on which the success or failure was incurred. There is also some evidence that this effect depended upon whether the children regarded a previous task as easy or difficult.

The effect of the importance of the subject's goal on his level of estimated $P(s)$ is equivocal. In three experiments with college students and two experiments with children, average $P(s)$ was much higher when success led to an important goal or to a costly prize than it was when the value of goal or prize was trivial. In another experiment with college students we found an equally convincing difference—in the reverse direction. This should lead us to be cautious in interpreting the relation between $P(s)$ and self-evaluation. Probably the absolute level of a $P(s)$ estimate tells us nothing reliable about how the subject evaluates the capacity in question. It is the trend of the successive $P(s)$ estimates through time, and as a function of the person's experiences in trying to reach the goal, that tells us (under the conditions previously discussed) whether his self-evaluation is changing upward or downward. Another reason for attending to the trend rather than to the level of $P(s)$ as an index of self-evaluation is that the $P(s)$ levels of a group of physically disabled, hospitalized children were consistently higher than those of a group of otherwise comparable normal children, though the normals' $P(s)$ levels were more sensitive to the effects of success and failure. We take this to mean that we were not seeing the effects of disability, but of the kindly, supportive, sheltered, and encouraging atmosphere which the disabled children enjoyed in the hospital.

There is more than that to these findings. Five of our six experiments would lead to the conclusion that the more desirable a thing is the more convinced we are that we will get it by our own efforts. The sixth experiment is consistent with the view that what we most desire is *ipso facto* hard to get. Both of these notions relate to live theoretical issues in the psychology of human motivation so they cannot be lightly brushed aside. Though we have no data at present by which these divergent results might be explained, we have some which may suggest where to look for the explanation. People whose general self-evaluation, or real ability, is high make higher $P(s)$ estimates when they are working alone than when another person who is working on the same task is present. Exactly the reverse is true of people whose general self-evaluation, or real ability, is low. Also, in the experiments with children, the correlations of $P(s)$ level with age and IQ indicate that when no prize is offered, older children are more confident, but when a prize is offered they are more cautious. Without a prize, the *brighter* normal children are less confident, and with the introduction of trivial prizes their confidence increases. With a highly valuable prize at stake, the correlation between $P(s)$ and IQ disappears and all children have a common (high) $P(s)$ level. It was the older and brighter children who wanted to try a failed task again, but neither age nor IQ were correlated with wanting to try the "hard" task again. Perhaps wanting to recoup past failures is not the same as wanting to repeat what proved to be difficult.

It has been said that patients diagnosed as "schizophrenic" suffer, among other things, from various defects which lie specifically in the field of purposive behavior or motivation. In our experiments they appeared to suffer *no defect*, by comparison with normal children and adults, in their ability to recognize the evidence that their abilities are superior or inferior to those of other patients, or in their ability to make rational choices about themselves and other people on the basis of this evidence. These patients' levels of estimated $P(s)$, level of aspiration, and real performance were affected by prizes and by success and failure in pretty much the way our normal subjects' were. However, in one experiment we noticed a striking difference between schizophrenics and normals, a difference which we later confirmed in a second experiment. The difference is that the schizophrenic patients did not lower the $P(s)$ estimates as the deadline approached, which is one of the most striking features of normal behavior. The schizophrenic patients seemed simply to disregard the deadline. We have no explanation for this phenomenon, but we have pointed out that if a person fails, for whatever reason, to recognize the importance of the *ending* of any sequence of process, that failure alone might account for a great many of the bizarre features of the behavior of mental patients. An automobile without brakes could only be driven in a very erratic and unusual fashion. It may be that this analogy is by no means too far-fetched to apply to our understanding of schizophrenia.

It has been said that patients who suffer from "depression" have lost the capacity to be motivated by events or objects around them. Nothing interests them. If someone is kind to them it only deepens their sense of worthlessness and guilt. In extreme cases they suffer from a slowing down of the processes of thought and action. However, our depressed subjects did not differ at all from non-depressed patients in how hard they worked in their average levels of aspiration, nor in their reported degree of "nervousness" or agitation. The depressed patients said they were consistently sadder; they reported a significantly greater tinge of anger in their moods; and their average $P(s)$ levels were 15 to 20 points lower (in a scale of 100) than those of the non-depressed patients. The depressed patients were simply gloomier and more pessimistic than the others. It should be pointed out that these depressd people were by no means hopeless and despairing, for they were outpatients, not confined to a hospital, and they came on their own initiative to the clinic where they served in our experiment.

In a series of detailed interviews with psychotic patients in a hospital it was found that the lowest average general self-evaluations we have ever recorded were made by the patients who (a) were regarded as "suicidal" because they had attempted, threatened, or talked about suicide; and (b) described their own future lives as relatively short and bleakly devoid of anything but "work."

In all of the experiments mentioned so far we have carefully arranged conditions so that the individual subject could automatically see for himself whether his efforts were likely to be successful or not;

that is, the criteria were objective and independent of praise, approval, or gratification of other people. However, these social criteria, the approval or disapproval, praise or reproach, that we get from other people also operate to affect our self-evaluations just as the more objective criteria do. In fact, many students of human behavior might give a reverse emphasis to the statement and say that social criteria are paramount, and the objective criteria *also* exist, but their effects are not very important. Our attitude is simply to take as given the fact that these two classes of evaluative criteria exist and that the extent to which they are used in self-evaluation can be studied. Questions like that of their relative importance, the conditions under which one or the other of them will be used, and the social and individual consequences of their use, are questions of fact. We have focused on just three of the possible questions that might be asked about self-evaluation in a social context. First, under what conditions will a person's estimate of his own $P(s)$ be affected by his witnessing the success or failure of another person's attempts to get the same goal? Second, on the relations between self-evaluation and "conformity," under what conditions does a person's real ability determine the extent to which his behavior is radically influenced by what he sees or hears other people doing? Third, to what extent do a person's evaluations of his own abilities and the abilities of others affect his choice of associates and collaborators? Though we have barely scratched the surface of any one of these sets of phenomena, we have scratched it at a somewhat different angle than other students have done, and I think we can offer some compelling suggestions for further exploration along these lines.

The problem of whether and to what extent a person's estimate of his own $P(s)$ is affected by his witnessing the fate of another's efforts to get a goal which they both want was suggested to us by Kagan (1958b). Kagan embedded this problem in the larger area of "identification." He argued that identification is most likely to occur when two people want to get the same thing. If one of them, the subject (S), is uncertain of his ability to achieve the goal, but sees that another person can get it, then S will take the other person as a model (M). S will imitate those aspects of M's behavior which are relevant to achieving the goal, and perhaps other aspects of M's behavior as well. The fact that both S and M want the goal is already an important point of similarity between them, but Kagan said that *any* perceived or asserted points of similarity should reinforce S's attempt to be like M. We know that identification has taken place, Kagan wrote, when we see one person (S) respond to the fate of another person (M) as though it were his own. We thought that $P(s)$

estimates as we have described and studied them might be sufficiently sensitive indicators of whether or not identification had occurred. Specifically, if S resembles M, then S ought to be encouraged by M's success and raise his own $P(s)$, and he ought to be discouraged by M's failure and lower his own $P(s)$. This of course implies the assumption that both S and M can enjoy the goal; if M gets to it first, there is still the possibility that S can get there too. Thus, we are not talking about a two-person zero-sum game in which if one wins the other automatically loses. The literature on identification includes such situations (e.g., the Freudian Oedipus conflict), but our experiments do not. In our experiments, the possibility of conflictual competition arises only if S or M, or both of them, care who gets to the goal first. Some of our subjects may have cared about this but their feelings were not obtrusive and there is no evidence that such considerations affected our results.

The standard session in our first experiment involved three subjects, all college students who had not met each other before. Two of them (the Ms) were paid confederates of the experimenter and the third (the true S) was ignorant about all details of the experiment. The most striking outcome of this experiment is that the course of S's successive $P(s)$ estimates was totally unaffected by the failure of either M. However, when the M whose performance curve resembled S's succeeded, S responded by an instant elevation of his own $P(s)$ estimates to a high level from which they did not thereafter descend. The evidence of similarity between S and M seemed to be effective, and the Ss seemed to follow the successes and ignore the failures.

In a second experiment on this topic, subjects were chosen only after they had answered a lot of questions about their own characteristics and had filled out a special self-evaluation questionnaire, which we devised according to our own views about self-evaluation. Subjects were selected so that half of them had very high self-evaluative responses, and the other half had very low self-evaluations. When he came to the laboratory, each subject (S) was introduced to another student (M) and the experimenter explained that, according to the personal data they had provided, S and M were very much alike *or* they were as dissimilar as two people could be. This was an attempt to induce differences in S's conception of his similarity to M by *assertion*. According to Kagan, this should have an effect on S's response to M, and it did, especially among the subjects with initially low *general* self-evaluation.

Throughout the experiment, the subjects whose *general* initial level of self-evaluation was high made $P(s)$ estimated that were well above those made by the subjects who came to the experiment with general self-evaluations that were low. This lends support to the contention that there is a connection between our estimate of the power of our abilities and the level of our self-evaluations. All the experimental subjects worked in the presence of a model; no model was present for the control groups. Among the high self-evaluators the mean $P(s)$ levels of all the experimental groups was significantly lower than that of the control group. The corresponding difference among the low self-evaluators was well within the limits of experimental error and therefore not significant statistically, but it was in the opposite direction. Furthermore, the high self-evaluators were, on the average, supremely indifferent to whether the model succeeded or failed. By contrast, the low self-evaluators showed quite decided upward shifts in $P(s)$ level after the model succeeded, and small (statistically nonsignificant) downward shifts after the model failed. Clearly, here are two reactions to the minimal social situation defined by another person's presence: (1) the reaction of humility or caution or deference by which the mere presence of the other makes the high self-evaluators reduce their $P(s)$ estimates, a reaction which is decidedly lacking among the low self-evaluators; and (2) the reaction to the outcome of the other's work, very prominent in the low self-evaluators, and absent among the highs.

In another experiment the subjects were pre-selected, not for high or low self-evaluation, but for high or low actual ability to solve problems which involved the imaginal rearrangement of visual forms. They were set to doing sets of similar problems under the following sequence of conditions. First four subjects were isolated each in a soundproof booth. Communication between subject and experimenter took place by means of microphones and earphones; when the experimenter wished, he could let the subjects listen to each other by means of the same apparatus. The subjects had to report their solutions to each problem to the experimenter by voice and they also had to write down their answers. During work on the first ten experimental problems, the subjects reported to the experimenter but they could not hear each other. In this condition the abler subjects had more correct answers than the less able ones, but the difference between the groups in this respect was not very large. Also, in this condition, the abler subjects recorded far greater self-confidence that they were giving correct answers than the less able ones did. For the second set of ten problems, the subjects were permitted to hear the reports that the other subjects made to the experimenter—or at least they thought they were hearing these reports. What they actually heard was a carefully prepared tape recording of the voices of three young men, *all* of whom gave *wrong* answers. In this circumstance the average number of correct answers from the truly abler subjects decreased slightly and so did their self-confidence; the less able subjects gave very few correct answers (they conformed, or followed the majority) and their self-confidence that they were giving correct answers *increased* enormously. Returned to the isolation condition for a third set of problems, the subjects reverted almost exactly to the behavior they had shown in the first isolation condition.

The experiments just described seem to suggest that, under appropriate conditions, general high or low self-evaluations may play a similar role to that of genuinely high or low ability in determining how a person evaluates his own current or recent efforts. People with high self-evaluation (or ability) make lower estimates of self-confidence or of $P(s)$ when they are confronted with other people than they do when they are working alone. Furthermore, their $P(s)$ estimates are unaffected by what the other does, or the answers they give to problems are only slightly guided by the errors of others. In their private estimates of how well they are doing, or will do, they are affected by the presence of the other in the direction of being more modest, but they are independent of the other's performance and fate either in respect to their own subsequent $P(s)$ estimates, or in their tendency to follow the other's lead in solving problems. To people with genuinely low self-evaluations or with genuinely low ability, the presence and behavior of others are potential snares and bases of delusion. They are not made humbler or more cautious by the presence of the other, and when the other succeeds they believe more strongly that they will succeed. When, as they did with such *éclat*, they follow the others blindly into error, *then* they believe most strongly that their own answers are correct!

Our third "social" question related to the way in which a person's conception of his own abilities might enter into his choice of associates. The experiments were carried out in groups of about 20 to 30 people who had been together in both working and living arrangements for about a year. To meet these minimum conditions, we used groups of student nurses and the experiments were carried out in their classrooms, in two separate sessions. During the first session each subject was provided with a list of the names of all the people in the group, including her own. She ranked all the names (not including her own), assigning rank 1 to the girl she liked most as a friend and companion, and rank n to the girl she liked least. The first session ended after the girls had taken an impressive and elaborately administered test of "auditory discrimination ability." In the second session, each girl was given a card, especially made up for her, on which appeared her own name and "score" on the auditory test. There also appeared the names of five other girls selected to lie at the top, middle, and bottom of her "liking" ranking, with a fourth ranked midway between top and middle and the fifth midway between bottom and middle. With each of these five names was associated a number purporting to be the other girl's score on the auditory test. These numbers were approximately 90, 70, 50, 30, and 10, in a range of 100 points and the numbers were assigned to the names so that there was a perfect inverse correlation between liking and ability rankings. The subject was told to rank the five girls according to her preference for them as partners. A competition was described in which she and her partner would compete against other pairs for prizes. They would have to solve problems which required careful auditory discrimination. One prize we called "fame": it meant simply that the names of the winning pair would be posted on the school bulletin board. The other prizes were one dollar, ten dollars, and one hundred dollars, to be shared by the winning partners according to different schemes which will be described below. In one experiment with children, we had to depart from the scale of money prizes because we found out that although all the children preferred ten dollars more than five dollars, the younger ones preferred certain special pieces of apparatus, toys, or books more than either amount of money. Therefore, with the children we compared a no-prize condition with a condition where we allowed each subject to choose his own prize from a list of the things that had been most highly ranked by the whole group.

For each subject we computed a single number which told us whether her ranking of the five potential partners corresponded to her original liking ranking, to the ranking of their abilities as indicated by their scores on the auditory test, or to neither of these rankings. When the prize was to be shared equally by the two members of the winning pair, the subjects who were told that their own ability was low made partner rankings that corresponded very closely to their liking rankings (that is, automatically, to the inverse of the ability rankings) regardless of the value of the prize. However, subjects who were told that their own ability was high behaved quite differently. At the level of the least valuable prize their partner rankings, too, correspond very closely to liking rankings; as the value of the prize increased, their partner rankings departed more and more in the direction of ranking by ability (that is, automatically, the inverse of the liking rankings), until at the level of the most valuable prize they corresponded almost perfectly with the ability rankings. Thus, at least under these conditions, the abler subjects chose partners with whose cooperation they would be more likely to win the most valuable prizes, even though those partners were the people they liked least in the group.

Were the subjects with low ability only apparently choosing their friends but really always choosing partners who matched their own ability? The design of these experiments will permit no certain answer, but there is a little more to be said about it. In one experiment, all procedures were identical with those just described with the exception that the subjects received only the names (not the ability scores) of their potential partners; with only the liking information available, all subjects' partner rankings corresponded almost perfectly with their liking rankings, regardless of the value of the prize. This effect appeared in another group of subjects who received no scores at all, not even their own. Thus we can conclude that the abler subjects are not simply being mean to their friends when they choose able people whom they do not especially like when a valuable prize is at stake. In still another experiment, we gave the subjects nothing but a list of five scores to which no names were attached. In this condition, regardless of the prize value, the partner rankings of the abler subjects corresponded almost perfectly with the ability rankings—even though they had no way of knowing who these five potential partners were. This was not true of the least able subjects; though their partner rankings were far closer to agreement with ability rankings than they were in any other condition, they were by no means as close to complete agreement as were those of the abler subjects. It appears then that there may be some pressure on the least able people to avoid choosing the most able partners available. At the moment we can only speculate on why this happens, but speculation is deferred until more relevant data are available.

In the experiment with children we broadened the conditions of choice by presenting them with four potential partners to be ranked *as partners;* a well liked child with high ability, a well liked child with low ability, a less well liked child with high ability, and a less well liked child with low ability. The most preferred rank was almost universally given to the well liked, able child, and equally often the least preferred rank went to the less liked, less able child. Our search for experimental effects on the rankings, therefore, concentrated on the two middle rankings; that of the well liked child with low ability and that of the less liked child with high ability. Under which conditions was either of these preferred over the other? Generally, the more able subjects preferred the more able partner, particularly in the prize conditions, and this tendency seemed to be stronger in the older subjects. Unfortunately, the very oldest group of children not only halted this trend, but completely reversed it, and we are left to contemplate only our ignorance and our inability to account for this event. We shall only add it to our mixed bag of puzzlements which await further investigation.

In two other experiments with student nurses, we varied the rules by which the prizes were to be distributed, but the conditions were otherwise identical with the experiments already described. The first variation of rules for sharing the prize was that each member of the winning pair would receive that proportion of the prize which matched the proportion which her own score contributed to the winning total. Under this rule, partner rankings were all alike, regardless of the total value of the prize and of the subject's own ability. The rankings of choice as partners did not correspond perfectly with either the liking ranking nor with the ability ranking, but on the average they came closer to corresponding to the liking ranking; that is, they were not at the point of complete independence of either ranking. This might mean that a less able subject would choose a slightly more able partner than otherwise; after all, they might win and then the partner would receive the lion's share of the prize and the subject would at least get *something*. More interesting is the fact that the most able subjects behaved in such a way as to suggest that this was their strategy too. It is still more interesting to consider that this strategy results in an equitable competition only if everybody chooses it, and then to realize that they did—and without consulting among themselves or having it urged on them by the experimenters!

The other prize-sharing rule was what we called the "marriage model." There was a prize for everybody—not necessarily the best, but something. The subjects were told that the maximum total score by two partners would win them the total amount of the announced prize (e.g., ten dollars), and they would share it equally. Other pairs would receive prizes whose total amounts would be computed by multiplying the maximum prize by the proportion which their total score constituted of the best total score. Partner pairs with identical total scores would receive identical prizes. Under this condition the partner rankings were the same across all prize levels, but they were sharply segregated according to the ability of the subjects. The least able subjects ranked partners closely, though not perfectly, in accord with liking; and the most able subjects ranked closely, though not perfectly, in accord with ability. This is the nearest we have come, in all our experimental choice, to observing subjects' nearly consistent choice of partners in terms of matching their own ability, yet to speak of matching is perhaps to suggest more than we have seen. There was no precise matching, though that would have been possible with the information the subjects were given. Instead, there was some sort of compromise in which matching ability predominated over, but did not exclude, choice by liking. The domination of the ability criterion was strongest in the ablest subjects and weakest in the least able ones.

Our final partner-choice experiment was not really on partner choice at all. In this experiment the choice requirements were reversed from those previously described. Instead of offering the subjects a fixed prize and asking them to choose a partner, we gave them a partner and asked them to choose the prize they thought they could win. The first session of this experiment was the same as that of all the others: the subjects ranked their classmates according to how much they liked them and they all took the auditory discrimination test. In the second session each subject was given her own test score and the name and score of the girl who had been *assigned* as her partner. The previously assigned liking of the partners and the scores attributed to them were each systematically varied over three levels, as were the scores assigned to the subjects themselves. The subjects were given a list of prizes: ten dollars, twenty dollars, and so on by tens to one hundred dollars. They had to "bid" for one of these prizes with the understanding that the greater skill was required to win the more valuable ones. The average value of prizes bid for increased with increasing subject scores and increasing partner scores. Liking for the partner had no effect at all. The subjects seem to have estimated their total team power by a simple combination of their own and their partners' scores, whether an additive or multiplicative combination we do not know, and chose their prizes to match that total power.

With this summary our progress report ends. We have probably raised, directly or implicitly, more questions than we have answered, but we hope this account of our progress will convince others that even more important questions can be raised and that their answers are within our grasp. We do not know the shape of our final knowledge about self-evaluation; we do not know what will turn up next, and that is part of the fun. Our results clearly point to the agonizing questions of the individual's happiness and how that is to be integrated with his social thwartings and responsibilities. When we understand all this better, it may turn out that happiness is not some kind of Nirvana, but a condition in which people have the power and the freedom to gratify themselves and others. An individual's happiness may prove to be the state in which he can justly conceive a high probability that he will achieve the next goal he chooses.

APPENDICES

APPENDIX A

Linear rating scales for obtaining Ss' estimates of their own probabilities of success (P(s)) (see Chapter 4).

1. *For Lo Mot conditions.*

Project No. 372

Trial No. _____   Score _____

What, do you think, are your chances of sorting 40 cards correctly in 25 seconds on at least one of the remaining trials? Mark the scale anywhere to show your estimate.

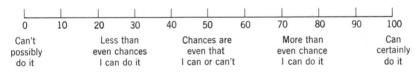

0	10	20	30	40	50	60	70	80	90	100

Can't possibly do it	Less than even chances I can do it	Chances are even that I can or can't	More than even chance I can do it	Can certainly do it

2. *For Hi Mot conditions.*

Project No. 372

Trial No. _____   Score _____

What, do you think, are your chances of having your name placed on the list by scoring 40 or more on this test? Mark the scale anywhere to show your estimate.

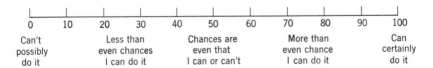

0	10	20	30	40	50	60	70	80	90	100

Can't possibly do it	Less than even chances I can do it	Chances are even that I can or can't	More than even chance I can do it	Can certainly do it

APPENDIX B

Announcement used to recruit college student Ss for the Hi Mot conditions of experiments on probability of success (P(s)) (see Chapter 4).

BASIC SCIENCE ABILITY SURVEY

U. of P. Project 372

The Psychology Department is cooperating in a nationwide survey designed to discover people whose basic abilities would make it worthwhile to give them training in the physical sciences in the event of a national emergency. The funds for this work come from private sources but the results of the study will be made available to Federal and State governments.

It is strongly suspected that many people who might contribute to the advancement of the physical sciences are not planning scientific careers nor even taking any training in these sciences. We are asking for volunteers to take a simple preliminary test. The outcome of the test will determine whether or not a person is eligible to be placed on the roster of those for whom such training might be profitable.

We recognize that if a person has no interest in scientific work he is unlikely to do well in it even if he has the necessary basic abilities. Thus, as a preliminary measure of interest, we are asking only for volunteers for the test.

Even if you should pass the test, your name will not be placed on the list unless you authorize it. Moreover, the list will be reviewed continuously in the future so that those whose interests change can be eliminated. Thus, the list can be kept up to date.

James C. Diggory
Research Supervisor
Eugene J. Riley
Research Specialist

APPENDIX C

Letter used to recruit high school students for preliminary testing for a fictitious Space Science Program. (After I. G. Cetlin, 1964. See Chapter 5.)

Dear Mr.

The Psychology Department of the University of Pennsylvania is cooperating with other colleges throughout the country in order to facilitate the selection and development of our country's scientific manpower. Various research projects have been started and the purpose of this letter is to call your attention to one of the newest of these, the Space Science Program.

In spite of the great demand for highly expert personnel in this critical, fascinating, and "wide open" area, opportunities to be introduced to space science have been limited. Training facilities have been equally limited. The program undertaken by the Psychology Department will permit prospective college students to become acquainted with various career and training possibilities in space science. If you are interested in this information, please complete the enclosed questionnaire and return it to:

> Psychology Department
> Room 106 College Hall
> University of Pennsylvania
> Philadelphia 4, Pennsylvania
> Att: Mrs. R. Cetlin

Arrangements for a personal interview will be made shortly after the forms have been returned. During the interview, we will discuss career and training opportunities in space science. Also, for interested students, we will have a number of "brief" tests available which will determine eligibility for training. All information submitted on the enclosed questionnaire will be kept in strict confidence. We would appreciate your returning it by (date), so that plans for the individual interviews may get underway as soon as possible. Thank you for your cooperation.

> Sincerely,
> (signed)
> Isabelle Cetlin
> Asst., Space Science Project

APPENDIX D

Questionnaire which accompanied the letter shown in Appendix C.

(page 1)

STUDENT QUESTIONNAIRE

(Note: All information submitted will be regarded as *Confidential*)

Name: _____

Date of Birth: _____ Telephone No. _____

Major Course at High School: _____

    Courses in Major Area: _____ Course Marks: _____

                                       _____   _____

                                       _____   _____

                                       _____   _____

                                       _____   _____

    You intend to go to college: Yes   No

    Father's educational background: High School—Completed
                                                       Incompleted
                                    College—   Completed
                                                        Incompleted
                                    Other Training

(page 2)

Self-Evaluation Scale

In each of the following, please indicate the point that best describes you by drawing a vertical line through the scale.

1. *Ability to think creatively.* Considering all the school projects you undertake, in which per cent of the cases do you succeed in making a novel or worthwhile contribution?

2. *Leadership ability.* At school and work situations when you are required to direct the activities of others, in what per cent of the cases can you

436

accomplish this with ease, receiving the cooperation and respect of those directed?

3. *Discriminative ability.* In what per cent of the cases are you sensitive to changes in your environment and in the behaviors and appearances of persons you know?

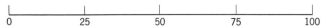

4. *Ability for quick, efficient reaction.* In situations where it is necessary for you to speed up your performance in order to meet a deadline, in what per cent of the cases can you do so without sacrificing the quality of your work?

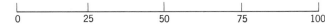

5. *Considering all your abilities, including these listed above, how would you evaluate yourself?*

APPENDIX E

General self-evaluation questionnaire (After Cutick, 1962. See Chapter 6.)

Answer the following questions by placing a check-mark on, or drawing a single line through, the scale at any point.

1. When doing things that interest you most, in what % of such cases are you fully satisfied with your performance?

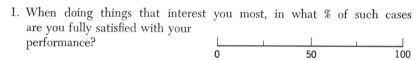

2. When you participate in group activities that call for decisions to be made, in what % of such cases do your ideas and opinions influence the group decision?

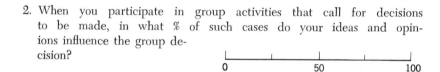

3. When a situation demands that you take initiative and act independently, in what % of such cases can you function effectively and efficiently on your own?

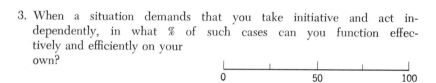

4. When meeting new people for the first time in social, business, or academic settings, in what % of such cases are you able to impress them favorably and form good relations?

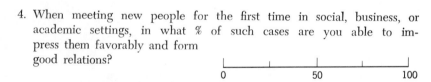

5. When others trust and depend on you to carry out a certain job for them, in what % of such cases do you behave dependably?

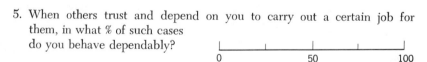

6. When sound judgment is needed about the appropriate actions to be taken in special situations, in what % of such cases do you make sound judgments?

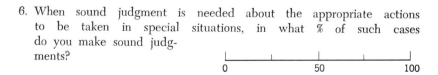

438

7. When you face new situations which require rapid and accurate problem-solving ability, in what % of such cases and your solutions rapid and accurate?

```
|—————————|—————————|—————————|
0                  50                 100
```

8. When you try to reach important goals of any kind and to succeed generally in your everyday activities, in what % of such cases do you attain your goals and function consistently with satisfactory results?

```
|—————————|—————————|—————————|
0                  50                 100
```

See Appendix H for a modification of this questionnaire for use in interviews with hospitalized psychotic patients.

Preference questionnaire used with students aged 7 to 16 years (see Chapter 6.)

One of the teachers in this school is interested in finding out something about the things which boys and girls like.

On this list you will find a number of things which have blank spaces next to them. The *first* thing you are to do is to write in the blanks the one thing which you would most like to have within that category, for example, SPORTS EQUIPMENT *baseball glove;* BOY SCOUT EQUIPMENT *sleeping bag;* BOARD GAMES *Monopoly;* BICYCLE ACCESSORIES *speedometer;* etc.

After you have finished this, read over the entire list and choose from it the thing which you would most like to have. Place a number "1" by your first choice, a number "2" by your second choice and so on, until you have given a number to all of the things on the list.

MODEL KITS _____

ONE YEAR SUBSCRIPTION TO "MAD" MAGAZINE

$5 IN CASH

TELESCOPE (4″ reflector—see the moons of Jupiter!)

CHEMISTRY SET

MICROSCOPE

SPORTS EQUIPMENT _____

BOARD GAMES _____

$10 IN CASH

DOLLS _____

BOOKS _____

ROCKET (Shoots 500 ft. into the air!)

ELECTRIC TRAIN SET

BICYCLE ACCESSORIES _____

TOY KITCHEN

RADIO KIT

BOY SCOUT EQUIPMENT _____

SEWING KIT

ELECTRIC BALL GAME _____

APPENDIX G

Questionnaire Intended to Obtain Estimates of Subjective Life Expectancies (SLE).

Answer each of the following questions briefly with a word, a phrase, or at most with a short sentence.

What do you expect to be doing . . .
Tomorrow? _____
Next week? _____
One month from now? _____
*Six months from now? _____
One year from now? _____
Five years from now? _____
Ten years from now?. _____
Ten years from now? _____
Thirty years from now? _____
Forty years from now? _____
Fifty years from now? _____
Sixty years from now? _____
Seventy years from now? _____
Eighty years from now? _____
Ninety years from now? _____

❋ ❋ ❋ ❋ ❋

These questions have been administered in several ways: (1) respondents read the questions and write their answers; (2) interviewer reads the questions aloud and respondents write their answers on numbered lines (group administration), (3) interviewer reads the questions aloud and writes down the oral response, or records the answers in magnetic tape.

❋ ❋ ❋ ❋ ❋ ❋ ❋ ❋ ❋ ❋

* This item was introduced by S. Farnham-Diggory (1964) for use with hospitalized psychotic respondents (see Chapter 7). It was not used in the work with normal respondents (see Chapter 8).

441

APPENDIX H

Cutick's (1962) Self-Evaluation Questionnaire (see Chapter 6 and Appendix E) as Modified by S. Farnham-Diggory (1964) for oral administration to hospitalized psychotic patients (see Chapter 7.)

1. When doing things that interest you most, what per cent of the time are you satisfied with your performance?

2. When you're part of a group activities, what per cent of the time do your ideas and opinions influence the group?

3. When you have to take the initiative and act independently of others, what per cent of the time can you handle things on your own?

4. When meeting new people for the first time, what per cent of the time are you able to impress them favorably and form good relations?

5. When others trust and depend on you for something, what per cent of the time do you live up to this?

6. When wise, careful judgment is needed about something, what per cent of the time do you make sound judgments?

7. When you face new situations which require fast decisions, what per cent of the time can you make them effectively?

8. When you try to reach important goals of any kind, what per cent of the time do you feel you have really succeeded?

Subject Index

Author Index and References

Pages in this book on which reference is made to any of the following items are indicated by numbers in parentheses at the end of each citation.

Ach, N. *Über den Willensakt und das Temperament.* Leipzig: Quelle & Meyer, 1910. (38)

Adler, D. Evidence for repression and rationalization in the solution of a moral conflict. *Psychol. Bull.,* 1941, **38**, 600–601. (Abstract) (208–209)

Alexander, H. W. A general test for trend. *Psychol. Bull.,* 1946, **43**, 533–577. (142, 253, 360)

Alexander, I. E., & Adlerstein, A. M. Studies in the psychology of death. In H. P. David & J. C. Brengelmann (Eds.) *Perspectives in personality research.* (Published under the auspices of the International Union of Scientific Psychology) New York: Springer, 1960. Pp. 65–92. (386)

Alexander, I. E., Colley, R. S., & Adlerstein, A. M. Is death a matter of indifference? *J. Psychol.,* 1957, **43**, 277–283. (386)

Allport, G. W. *Personality: a psychological interpretation.* New York: Holt, 1937. (19, 54–57)

Allport, G. W. Motivation in personality: a reply to Mr. Bertocci. *Psychol. Rev.,* 1940, **47**, 533–554. (56)

Allport, G. W. The ego in contemporary psychology. *Psychol. Rev.,* 1943, **50**, 451–478. (41, 53, 57–60, 101, 211)

Allport, G. W. Effect: a secondary principle of learning. *Psychol. Rev.,* 1946, **53**, 335–347. (53)

Allport, G. W. *Becoming: basic considerations for a psychology of personality.* New Haven: Yale Univer. Press, 1955. (38, 53–54, 56)

Alper, T. G. Memory for completed and incompleted tasks as a function of personality: an analysis of group data. *J. abnorm. soc. Psychol.,* 1946, **41**, 403–420 (a). (211–213)

Alper, T. G. Task-orientation vs. ego-orientation in learning and retention. *Amer. J. Psychol.,* 1946, **59**, 236–248 (b). (158, 211)

Alper, T. G. Memory for completed and incompleted tasks as a function of personality: correlation between experimental and personality data. *J. Pers.,* 1948, **17**, 104–137. (212)

Alper, T. G. The interrupted task method in studies of selective recall: a re-evaluation of some recent experiments. *Psychol. Rev.,* 1952, **59**, 71–88. (158, 211, 213)

Alper, T. G. Predicting the direction of selective recall: its relation to ego-strength and n-achievement. *J. abnorm. soc. Psychol.*, 1957, **55**, 149–165. (211–212)

Amen, E. W. An experimental study of the self in psychology. *Psychol. Monogr.*, 1926, No. 165, 1–72. (38)

Angyal, A. *Foundations for a science of personality*. New York: Commonwealth Fund, 1941. (108)

Anthony, S. *The child's discovery of death*. London: Kegan Paul, 1940. (384, 390)

Atkinson, J. W. The achievement motive and recall of interrupted and completed tasks. *J. exp. Psychol.*, 1953, **46**, 381–390. (212)

Atkinson, J. W. Explorations using imaginative thought to assess the strength of human motives. In M. R. Jones (Ed.), *Nebraska symposium on motivation*. Lincoln, Neb.: Univer. of Nebraska Press, 1954. Pp. 56–112. (185)

Atkinson, J. W. Motivational determinants of risk-taking behavior. *Psychol. Rev.*, 1957, **64**, 359–372. (123, 185, 214)

Atkinson, J. W. (Ed.) *Motives in fantasy, action, and society*. Princeton, N.J.: Van Nostrand, 1958. (186)

Atkinson, J. W., Bastian, J. R., Earl, R. W., & Litwin, G. H. The achievement motive, goal setting, and probability preference. *J. abnorm. soc. Psychol.*, 1960, **60**, 27–36. (161, 214)

Atkinson, J. W., & Reitman, W. R. Performances as a function of motive strength and expectancy of goal attainment. *J. abnorm. soc. Psychol.*, 1956, **53**, 361–366. (161, 189)

Aveling, F. The standpoint of psychology. *Brit. J. Psychol.*, 1926, **16**, 159–170. (39)

Bain, A. *The emotions and the will*. (3rd ed.) New York: Appleton, 1880. (96)

Bakke, E. W. *Citizens without work*. New Haven: Yale Univer. Press, 1940. (404)

Bandura, A., & Huston, A. Identification as a process of incidental learning. *J. abnorm. soc. Psychol.*, 1961, **63**, 311–318. (276)

Bardon, J. I. *Self-other impressions of mothers and sons as a function of the sons' socio-personal inadequacy*. Ph.D. Dissertation, University of Pennsylvania, Philadelphia, 1956. (175)

Barnett, H. G. *Innovation: the basis of cultural change*. New York: McGraw-Hill, 1953. (261)

Barnett, S. A. "Instinct." *Daedalus*, 1963, **92**, 564–580. (56)

Bartoshuk, A. K. Electromyographic gradients in goal-directed activity. *Canad. J. Psychol.*, 1955, **9**, 21–28. (215, 218)

Batchelor, I. R. C., & Napier, M. B. Broken homes and attempted suicide. *Brit. J. Delinqu.*, 1953, **4**, 99–108. (371)

Beck, A. T., Ward, C. H., Mendelson, M., Mock, J., & Erbaugh, J. An inventory for measuring depression. *Arch. gen. Psychiat.*, 1961, **4**, 561–571. (360)

Becker, H. The sorrow of bereavement. *J. abnorm. soc. Psychol.*, 1933, 27, 391–410. (389)

Beers, C. W. *A mind that found itself.* Garden City, N.Y.: Doubleday, Doran, 1931. (359)

Beier, E. G., & Ratzeburg, F. The parental identifications of male and female college students. *J. abnorm. soc. Psychol.*, 1953, 48, 569–572. (266)

Bellak, L. (Ed.) *Schizophrenia: a review of the syndrome.* New York: Logos, 1958. (327)

Benedict, L. W. A study of Bagobo ceremonial, magic, and myth. *Ann. N.Y. Acad. Sci.*, 1916, vol. 25. (387)

Benedict, R. *Patterns of culture* (1934). Reprinted, New York: New American Library, Mentor Books, 1946. (387)

Bentley, M. The psychological antecedents of phrenology. *Psychol. Monogr.*, 1916, 21 (No. 92), 102–115. (40)

Berkeley, G. *A treatise concerning the principles of human knowledge,* 1710. (5)

Berliner, A. Subjektivität und Objektivität von Sinneseindrücken. *Arch. ges. Psychol.*, 1914, 32, 68–119. (38)

Berlyne, D. E. Novelty and curiosity as determinants of exploratory behavior. *Brit. J. Psychol.*, 1950, 41, 68–80. (56)

Berlyne, D. E. The arousal and satiation of perceptual curiosity in the rat. *J. comp. physiol. Psychol.*, 1955, 48, 238–246. (56)

Berlyne, D. E. Attention to change, conditions inhibition ($S^I R$) and stimulus satiation. *Brit. J. Psychol.*, 1957, 48, 138–140. (56)

Berlyne, D. E. The present status of research in exploratory and related behavior. *J. indiv. Psychol.*, 1958, 14, 121–126. (56)

Bertocci, P. A. A critique of G. W. Allport's theory of motivation. *Psychol. Rev.*, 1940, 47, 501–532. (56)

Bertocci, P. A. The psychological self, the ego, and personality. *Psychol. Rev.*, 1945, 52, 91–99. (59, 102)

Bexton, W. H., Heron, W., & Scott, T. H. Effects of decreased variation in the sensory environment. *Canad. J. Psychol.*, 1954, 8, 70–76. (58)

Bibring, E. The mechanism of depression. In P. Greenacre (Ed.), *Affective disorders: psychoanalytic contributions to their study.* New York: International Univer. Press, 1953. Pp. 13–48. (358–359, 361)

Bills, R. E., Vance, E. L., & McLean, O. S. An index of adjustment and values. *J. consult. Psychol.*, 1951, 15, 257–261. (28)

Bleuler, E. Freudsche Mechanismen in der Symptomatologie von Psychosen. *Psychiat.-Neurol. Wschr.*, 1906, 8, 323–324; 338–339. (31)

Blondel, C. La personnalité. In G. Dumas (Ed.), *Traité de psychologie,* Vol. 2. Paris: Alcan, 1924. Pp. 522–574. (41, 108)

Boring, E. G. *A history of experimental psychology.* (2nd ed.) New York: Appleton-Century-Crofts, 1950. (69)

Brandt, R. M. The accuracy of self-estimate: a measure of self-concept reality. *Genet. Psychol. Monogr.*, 1958, 58, 55–100. (303)

Brentano, F. *Psychologie vom empirischen Standpunkt.* Vol. 1. Leipzig: Duncker & Humblot, 1874. (48)

Breuer, J., & Freud, S. *Studies in hysteria.* Trans. A. A. Brill from German ed., 1895. New York: Nervous and Mental Disease Publishing Co., 1936. (31)

Bridgman, P. W. *The intelligent individual and society.* New York: Macmillan, 1938. (382–383)

Bromberg, W., & Schilder, P. Death and dying: a comparative study of the attitudes and mental reactions toward death and dying. *Psychoanal. Rev.,* 1933, **20,** 133–135. (390)

Bromberg, W., & Schilder, P. The attitude of psychoneurotics toward death. *Psychoanal. Rev.,* 1936, **23,** 1–25. (390)

Brown, T. *Lectures on the philosophy of the human mind* (1820). Boston: Hallowell, 1828. (5, 13)

Brownfain, J. Stability of the self-concept as a dimension of personality. *J. abnorm. soc. Psychol.,* 1952, **47,** 597–606. (28)

Burnstein, E., Stotland, E., & Zander, A. Similarity to a model and self-evaluation. *J. abnorm. soc. Psychol.,* 1961, **62,** 257–264. (276)

Bury, J. B. *A history of freedom of thought.* New York: Holt, 1913. (403)

Busse, E. W. Psychopathology, In J. E. Birren (Ed.), *Handbook of aging and the individual.* Chicago: Univer. of Chicago Press, 1959. Pp. 364–398. (358–359, 361)

Caird, E. *Hegel.* Edinburgh & London: W. Blackwood & Sons, 1883. (14)

Calkins, M. W. The self in recent psychology. *Psychol. Bull.,* 1912, **9,** 25–30. (38–39)

Calkins, M. W. The self in scientific psychology. *Amer. J. Psychol.,* 1915, **26,** 495–524. (39)

Calkins, M. W. The self in recent psychology. *Psychol. Bull.,* 1916, **13,** 20–27. (38–39)

Calkins, M. W. The self in recent psychology. *Psychol. Bull.,* 1919, **16,** 111–119. (38, 40)

Calkins, M. W. Review of Robert MacDougall's *The general problems of psychology: conceptions. Phil. Rev.,* 1923, **32,** 536–543. (40)

Calkins, M. W. The self in recent psychology. *Psychol. Bull.,* 1927, **24,** 205–215. (38–40)

Calvin, A. D., & Holtzman, W. H. Adjustment and the discrepancy between self-concept and inferred self. *J. consult. Psychol.,* 1953, **17,** 39–44. (28)

Cartwright, D. The effect of interruption, completion, and failure upon the attractiveness of activities. *J. exp. Psychol.,* 1942, **31,** 1–16. (174)

Cava, E. L., & Rausch, H. L. Identification and adolescent boys' perception of the father. *J. abnorm. soc. Psychol.,* 1952, **47,** 855–856. (266)

Cavanaugh, D. K. Improvement in the performance of schizophrenics on concept formation tasks as a function of motivational change. *J. abnorm. soc. Psychol.,* 1958, **57,** 8–12. (328)

Cetlin, I. G. *Persistence, defensive behavior and self-evaluation as a function of early and late anticipation of failure.* Ph.D. Dissertation, University of Pennsylvania, Philadelphia, 1964. (195–197, 224, 239–240, 244, 435)

Cetlin, R. E. *Estimated probability of success as a function of number of abilities available for goal achievement.* Ph.D. Dissertation, University of Pennsylvania, Philadelphia, 1964. (191, 193–194)

Chapman, D. W., & Volkmann, J. A social determinant of the level of aspiration. *J. abnorm. soc. Psychol.*, 1939, 34, 225–238. (123)

Chein, I. The awareness of self and the structure of the ego. *Psychol. Rev.*, 1944, 51, 304–314. (58–60, 101–102)

Child, I. L. Personality. *Annu. Rev. Psychol.*, 1954, 5, 149–170. (266)

Claparéde, E. L'auto-justification. *Arch. de Psychol.*, 1926, 20, 265–298. (207)

Clark, B., & Graybiel, A. The break-off phenomenon; a feeling of separation from the earth experienced by pilots at high altitude. *J. aviation Med.*, 1957, 28, 121–126. (58)

Cohen, A. R. Experimental effects of ego-defense preferences in interpersonal relations. *J. abnorm. soc. Psychol.*, 1956, 52, 19–27. (158, 213)

Cohen, J. A study of suicide pacts. *London Times*, Feb. 19, 1961. (404)

Cooley, C. H. Personal competition. *Econ. Stud.*, 1899, 4, 73–173. (43–44)

Cooley, C. H. *Social organization: a study of the larger mind.* New York: Scribner's, 1911. (43–44, 102)

Cooley, C. H. *Human nature and the social order.* (rev. ed.) New York: Scribner's, 1922. (43–44, 102–103, 260)

Cowen, E. L., Heilizer, F., & Axelrod, H. S. Self-concept conflict indicators and learning. *J. abnorm. soc. Psychol.*, 1955, 51, 242–245. (28)

Crooke, W. Death and disposal of the dead: India, not Aryan. In *Hastings encyclopedia of religion and ethics,* Vol. 4. New York: Scribner's, 1911. Pp. 479–484. (387–388)

Crutchfield, R. S. Independent thought in a conformist world. In S. Farber and R. H. L. Wilson (Eds.), *Conflict and creativity.* New York: McGraw-Hill, 1963. (262)

Cutick, R. A. *Self-evaluation of capacities as a function of self-esteem and the characteristics of a model.* Ph.D. Dissertation, University of Pennsylvania, Philadelphia, 1962. (276–277, 281–282, 284–287, 372, 401, 411–412, 414, 438, 442)

Dahlgren, K. G. *On suicide and attempted suicide.* Lund: A.-B. Ph. Lindstedts Univ.-Bokhandel, 1945. (371)

Darwin, C. *The expression of the emotions in man and animals.* London: John Murray, 1872. (46)

Davis, R. C. The relation of certain muscular action potentials to "mental work." *Indiana Univer. Publ. Sci. Ser.*, 1937, No. 5. (215, 218)

Davis, R. C. The relation of muscle action potentials to difficulty and frustration. *J. exp. Psychol.*, 1938, 23, 141–158. (215)

Dembo, T. Der Ärger als dynamisches Problem. (Untersuchungen zur Handlungs-und Affektpsychologie, X. Ed. K. Lewin). *Psychol. Forsch.*, 1931, 15, 1–144. (119)

De Santillana, G. *The crime of Galileo.* Chicago: Univer. of Chicago Press, 1955. (261)

Descartes, R. *Principles of philosophy,* Latin, 1644; French, 1647. Trans. E. S. Haldane from collated French and Latin versions, 1911, corrected, 1931. Cambridge Univer. Press, 1931; New York: Dover (reprint), 1955. (2)

Descartes, R. *Les passions de l'ame* (1650). Paris: J. Vrin, 1955. (3)

Dewey, J. Theory of valuation. In *International encyclopedia of unified science,* Vol. 2, No. 4. Chicago: Univer. of Chicago Press, 1939. (72, 75–78)

Diem, K. (Ed.) *Documenta Geigy: scientific tables,* (6th ed.) Ardsley, N. Y.: Geigy Pharmaceutical Co., 1962. (305)

Diggory, J. C. Responses to experimentally induced failure. *Amer. J. Psychol.,* 1949, **62,** 48–61. (123)

Diggory, J. C. Sex differences in the organization of attitudes. *J. Pers.,* 1953, **22,** 89–100. (402)

Diggory, J. C. Review of Stephen C. Pepper's *The sources of value* (1958). *Amer. J. Psychol.,* 1962, **75,** 696–698 (a). (85)

Diggory, J. C. Sex differences in judging the acceptability of actions. *J. soc. Psychol.,* 1962, **56,** 107–114 (b). (402)

Diggory, J. C. Status, ability, and self-esteem in the process of supervision. In G. Fisk (Ed.), *The frontiers of management psychology.* New York: Harper & Row, 1964. (112)

Diggory, J. C., Klein, S. J., & Cohen, M. M. Muscle-action potentials and estimated probability of success. *J. exp. Psychol.,* 1964, **68,** 449–455. (161, 216, 218–219)

Diggory, J. C., & Loeb, A. Motivation of chronic schizophrenics by information about their abilities in a group situation. *J. abnorm. soc. Psychol.,* 1962, **65,** 48–52. (330, 332, 334, 336)

Diggory, J. C., & Magaziner, D. E. Self-evaluation as a function of instrumentally relevant capacities. *Bull. Assoc. Int. Psychol. appl.,* 1959, **8,** 2–19. (164, 230, 233, 243)

Diggory, J. C., & Morlock, H. C., Jr. Level of aspiration, or probability of success? *J. abnorm. soc. Psychol.,* 1964, **69,** 282–289. (178–183)

Diggory, J. C., & Ostroff, B. Estimated probability of success as a function of variability in performance. *Amer. J. Psychol.,* 1962, **75,** 94–101. (153–157)

Diggory, J. C., Riley, E. J., & Blumenfeld, R. Estimated probability of success for a fixed goal. *Amer. J. Psychol.,* 1960, **73,** 41–55. (141, 143, 145, 147, 149–150)

Diggory, J. C., & Rothman, D. Z. Values destroyed by death. *J. abnorm. soc. Psychol.,* 1961, **63,** 205–210. (404, 406)

Dobrizhoffer, M. An account of the Abipones. Trans. S. Loleridge, 1922. Excerpt reprinted in M. Mean & N. Calas (Eds.), *Primitive heritage.* New York: Random House, 1953. Pp. 534–536. (388)

Dodge, R. The conditions of effective human action. *Psychol. Bull.*, 1918, **15**, 137–147. (40)

Dollard, J., & Miller, N. E. *Personality and psychotherapy: an analysis in terms of learning, thinking and culture.* New York: McGraw-Hill, 1950. (21)

Dorpat, T. L., & Ripley, H. S. A study of suicide in the Seattle area. *Comprehens. Psychiat.*, 1960, **1**, 349–359. (371)

Eaton, H. O. *The Austrian philosophy of values.* Norman, Okla.: Univer. of Oklahoma Press, 1930. (69–73, 75)

Eggan, D. The general problem of Hopi adjustment. In C. Kluckhohn & H. A. Murray (Eds.), *Personality in nature, culture, and society.* New York: Knopf, 1948. Pp. 220–235. (387–388)

Ehrenfels, Christian von. Über Fühlen und Wollen. *Sitzb. Akad. Wiss. (phil.-hist. Klasse)*, Vienna, 1887, **114**, 523–636. (69, 71, 73)

Ehrenfels, Christian von, Von der Wertdefinition zum Motivationsgesetz. *Arch. Systemat. Phil.*, 1896, **2**, 103–122. (72)

Ehrenfels, Christian von. *System der Werttheorie*, 2 vols., Leipzig: Reisland, vol. 1, 1897; vol. 2, 1898. (70–72, 85)

Eissler, K. R. *The psychiatrist and the dying patient.* New York: International Univer. Press, 1955. (404)

Elderton, M. (Ed.) *Case studies of unemployment.* Philadelphia: Univer. of Pennsylvania Press, 1931. (404)

Ellwood, C. A. *Sociology in its psychological aspects.* New York: Appleton, 1912. (40)

Ellwood, C. A. *An introduction to social psychology.* New York: Appleton, 1917. (40)

Engel, M. The stability of the self-concept in adolescence. *J. abnorm. soc. Psychol.*, 1959, **58**, 51–59. (277)

Eriksen, C. W. Defense against ego-threat in memory and perception. *J. abnorm. soc. Psychol.*, 1952, **47**, 230–235. (158, 213)

Eriksen, C. W. Psychological defenses and "ego-strength" in the recall of completed and incompleted tasks. *J. abnorm. soc. Psychol.*, 1954, **49**, 45–50. (211–212)

Erikson, E. H. Growth and crises of the "healthy personality." In C. Kluckhohn, H. A. Murray, & D. M. Schneider (Eds.), *Personality in nature, society, and culture.* (2nd ed.) New York: Knopf, 1953. (86)

Eron, L. D., & Ritter, A. M. A comparison of two methods of administration of the Thematic Apperception Test. *J. consult. Psychol.*, 1951, **15**, 55–61. (245)

Escalona, S. K. The effect of success and failure upon the level of aspiration and behavior in manic-depressive psychoses. *Univer. Iowa Stud. Child Welf.*, 1940, **16** (No. 3), 199–302. (123)

Fagen, S. A. *Conformity and the relations between others' competence and own competence.* Ph.D. Dissertation, University of Pennsylvania, Philadelphia, 1963. (289–290, 292, 294, 296–306)

Fairbanks, R. J. Ministering to the dying. *J. Pastoral Care*, 1948, **2**, 6–14. (404)

Farber, M. L. Imprisonment as a psychological situation. *Univer. Iowa Stud. Child Welf.*, 1944, **20**, 153–228. (161, 206)

Farberow, N. L. Personality patterns of suicidal mental hospital patients. *Genet. Psychol. Monogr.*, 1950, **42**, 3–79. (377–378, 400–401)

Farberow, N. L., & Shneidman, E. S. (Eds.) *The cry for help.* New York: McGraw-Hill, 1961. (378)

Faretra, G. Depression in teen-agers. In *Symposium on depression*. Detroit, Mich.: The Michigan and Wayne County Academies of General Practice, 1960. Pp. 85–96. (360)

Farnham-Diggory, S. Self-evaluation and subjective life expectancy among suicidal and non-suicidal psychotic males. *J. abnorm. soc. Psychol.*, 1964, **69**, 628–634. (371, 373–378, 400, 407, 441–442)

Feather, N. T. Success probability and choice behavior. *J. exp. Psychol.*, 1959, **58**, 257–266. (174)

Fechner, G. T. *Einige Ideen zur Schöpfungs- und Entwicklungsgeschichte der Organismen.* Leipzig: Breitkopf & Härtel, 1873. (22, 28)

Feifel, H. Death. In N. L. Farberow (Ed.), *Taboo topics*. New York: Prentice-Hall, Atherton Press, 1963. Pp. 8–21. (382, 390, 404)

Feshbach, N. *The non-conformity of high status individuals: an experimental investigation.* Ph.D. Dissertation, University of Pennsylvania, Philadelphia, 1956. (263)

Festinger, L. A theoretical interpretation of shifts in level of aspiration. *Psychol. Rev.*, 1942, **49**, 235–250 (a). (123)

Festinger, L. Wish, expectation, and group standards as factors influencing level of aspiration. *J. abnorm. soc. Psychol.*, 1942, **37**, 184–200 (b). (123)

Festinger, L. A theory of social comparison processes. *Hum. Relat.*, 1954, **7**, 117–140. (101, 104–106, 123, 152, 260)

Festinger, L. *A theory of cognitive dissonance.* Stanford, Calif.: Stanford Univer. Press, 1957. (253, 258)

Fisch, M. The suicidal gesture: a study of 114 military patients hospitalized because of abortive suicide attempts. *Amer. J. Psychiat.*, 1954, **111**, 33–36. (371)

Fison, L., & Howitt, A. W. Funeral ceremonies in Australia. Excerpt from *Kamilari and Kurnai* (1880), reprinted in M. Mean & N. Calas (Eds.), *Primitive heritage*. New York: Random House, 1953. Pp. 545–547. (387)

Frank, J. D. Individual differences in certain aspects of the level of aspiration. *Amer. J. Psychol.*, 1935, **47**, 119–128 (a). (122, 164)

Frank, J. D. The influence of the level of performance in one task on the level of aspiration in another. *J. exp. Psychol.*, 1935, **18**, 159–171 (b). (122)

Frank, J. D. Level of aspiration test. In H. A. Murray et al., *Explorations in personality*. New York: Oxford Univer. Press, 1938. Pp. 461–471. (122)

Frazer, J. G. *The golden bough*. (abridged ed.) New York: Macmillan, 1941. (388)

French, E. C. Some characteristics of achievement motivation. *J. exp. Psychol.*, 1955, **50**, 232–236. (186, 189)

Frenkel-Brunswik, E. Mechanisms of self-deception. *J. soc. Psychol.*, 1939, **10**, 409–420. (207–238)

Freud, A. *The ego and the mechanisms of defence*. Trans. C. Baines from *Das Ich und die Abwehrmechanismen* (1936). London: Hogarth, 1937. (268)

Freud, S. Some points in a comparative study of organic and hysterical paralyses. Trans. M. Meyer from *Arch. Neurol.*, 1893, **26**, 29–43. In *Collected papers*, Vol. 1. London: Hogarth, 1925. Pp. 42–58. (23, 207)

Freud, S. The defence neuro-psychoses. Trans. J. Rickman from *Neurol. Zbl.*, 1894, **13**, 362–364, 402–409. In *Collected papers*, Vol. 1. London: Hogarth, 1925. Pp. 59–75. (23, 207)

Freud, S. Project for a scientific psychology (1895). In M. Bonaparte, A. Freud, & E. Kris (Eds.), *The origins of psychoanalysis: letters to Wilhelm Fliess*. New York: Basic Books, 1954. Pp. 347–445. (22–24, 26)

Freud, S. *The interpretation of dreams*. Trans. J. Strachey from *Die Traumdeutung* (1900). New York: Basic Books, 1955. (22–23, 57)

Freud, S. *The psychopathology of everyday life*. Trans. A. A. Brill from *Mschr. Psychiat. Neurol.*, 1901, **10**, 1–32, 95–143. New York: Macmillan, 1914. (First published in book form 1904.) (31)

Freud, S. *Three contributions to the theory of sex*. Trans. A. A. Brill from German ed., 1905. New York: Nervous and Mental Disease Publishing Co., 1910 (a). (31)

Freud, S. *Wit and its relation to the unconscious*. Trans. A. A. Brill from German ed., 1905. New York: Moffat, Yard, 1917 (b). (31)

Freud, S. *Sammlung kleiner Schriften zur Neurosenlehre aus den Jahren 1893–1906*. Leipzig and Vienna: Deuticke, 1906. (31)

Freud, S. The relation of the poet to day-dreaming. Trans. I. F. Grant Duff from *Neue Rev.*, 1908, vol. 1. In *Collected papers*, Vol. 4. London: Hogarth, 1925. Pp. 173–183. (261)

Freud, S. Family romances. Trans. J. Strachey from the note in O. Rank, *Der Mythus von der Geburt des Helden* (1909). In *Collected papers*, Vol. 2. London: Hogarth, 1925. Pp. 74–78 (a). (265)

Freud, S. General remarks on hysterical attacks. Trans. D. Bryan from *Z. Psychother. med. Psychol.*, 1909, **1**, 10–14. In *Collected papers*, Vol. 2. London: Hogarth, 1925. Pp. 100–104 (b). (264)

Freud, S. Formulations regarding the two principles in mental functioning. Trans. M. N. Searle from *Jb. Psychoanal.*, 1911, **3**, 1–8. In *Collected papers*, Vol. 4. London: Hogarth, 1925. Pp. 13–21. (22, 260)

Freud, S. *Totem and taboo.* Trans. A. A. Brill from *Imago*, 1912, **1**, 17–33, 213–227, 301–333; 1913, **2**, 1–21, 357–408. New York: Moffat, Yard, 1918. (27)

Freud, S. On narcissism: an introduction. Trans. C. M. Baines, & J. Riviere from *Jb. Psychoanal.*, 1914, **6**, 1–24. In *Collected papers*, Vol. 4. London: Hogarth, 1925. Pp. 30–59. (27, 30, 99–100, 107, 260, 265)

Freud, S. Instincts and their vicissitudes. Trans. C. M. Baines from Z. *Psychoanal.*, 1915, **3**, 84–100. In *Collected papers*, Vol. 4. London: Hogarth, 1925. Pp. 60–83 (a). (21, 23–24, 26–28, 30, 207)

Freud, S. Thoughts for the times on war and death. Trans. E. C. Mayne from *Imago*, 1915, **4**, 1–21. In *Collected papers*, Vol. 4. London: Hogarth, 1925. Pp. 288–317 (b). (382)

Freud, S. Mourning and melancholia. Trans. J. Riviere from *Int. Z. Artz. Psychoanal.*, 1916–18, **4**, 288–301. In *Collected papers*, Vol. 4. London: Hogarth, 1925. Pp. 152–170. (26, 44, 327, 359, 371, 389, 404)

Freud, S. *A general introduction to psychoanalysis.* Trans. J. Riviere from German ed., 1920. New York: Liveright, 1935 (page references are to Permabooks reprint, 1953). (21–27, 99, 107, 265, 327)

Freud, S. *Beyond the pleasure principle.* Trans. J. Strachey from *Jenseits des Lustprinzips.* (2nd ed.) 1921. New York: Bantam Books (reprint), 1959(a). (21–24, 27–30, 100)

Freud, S. *Group psychology and the analysis of the ego.* Trans. J. Strachey from German ed., 1921. London: Hogarth, 1949 (b). (21, 25–28, 30, 44, 99, 265)

Freud, S. *The ego and the id.* Trans. J. Riviere from *Das Ich und Das Es*, 1923. London: Hogarth, 1927. (21–26, 28, 30–31, 265)

Freud, S. Some psychological consequences of the anatomical distinction between the sexes. Trans. J. Strachey from *Int. Z. Psychoanal.*, 1925, **11**, 401–410. In *Collected papers*, Vol. 5. London: Hogarth, 1956. Pp. 186–197. (25, 265)

Freud, S. *The problem of anxiety.* Trans. H. A. Bunker from *Hemmung, Symptom, und Angst*, 1926. New York: W. W. Norton, 1936. (21–24, 26, 30, 100–101, 205, 207, 213)

Freud, S. *The future of an illusion.* Trans. W. D. Robson-Scott from *Die Zukunft einer Illusion* (1927). London: Hogarth, 1928. (265)

Freud, S. Dostoevsky and parricide. Preface to Fülöp-Miller & Eckstein (Eds.), *Die Urgestalt der Brüder Karamazov* (1928). Trans. D. F. Tait, *The Realist*, 1929, **1**, 18. Reprinted in *Collected papers*, Vol. 5. London: Hogarth, 1957. Pp. 222–242 (a.) (26, 265, 404)

Freud, S. Humor. Trans. J. Riviere from *Imago*, 1928, **14**, 1–6. In *Collected papers*, Vol. 5. London: Hogarth, 1950. Pp. 215–221 (b). (265)

Freud, S. Why war? Open letter to Albert Einstein, September, 1932. Trans. J. Strachey. In *Collected papers*, Vol. 5. London: Hogarth, 1950. Pp. 273–287. (265)

Freud, S. *An outline of psychoanalysis.* Trans. J. Strachey from *Int. Z. Psychoanal.*, 1940, **25**, 5–67. Reprinted, with revisions, New York: W. W. Norton, 1949. (21–24, 26, 30–31, 60, 207)

Fromm, E. *Escape from freedom.* New York: Farrar & Rinehart, 1941. (53, 60)

Fromm, E. *The sane society.* New York: Rinehart, 1955. (53, 60)

Frondizi, R. *The nature of the self: a functional interpretation.* New Haven: Yale Univer. Press, 1953. (53–54, 60)

Gardner, J. W. *Self-renewal: the individual and the innovative society.* New York: Harper & Row, 1964. (262)

Gebhard, M. E. The effect of success and failure upon the attractiveness of activities as a function of experience, expectation and need. *J. exp. Psychol.*, 1948, **38**, 371–388. (174)

Gebhard, M. E. Changes in the attractiveness of activities: the effect of expectation preceding performance. *J. exp. Psychol.*, 1949, **39**, 404–413. (174)

Gewirtz, H. B. Generalization of children's preferences as a function of reinforcement and task similarity. *J. abnorm. soc. Psychol.*, 1959, **58**, 111–117. (174)

Gibbon, E. *The decline and fall of the Roman Empire* (1776–1788). H. H. Milman. (Ed.) New York: J. B. Alden, 1885. 5 vols. (391, 402)

Giese, F. Das Ich als Complex in der Psychologie. *Arch. systemat. Psychol.*, 1914, **32**, 120–162. (39)

Ginzberg, E., Ginsburg, E. L., & Lynn, D. L. *The unemployed.* New York: Harper, 1943. (404)

Glixman, A. F. An analysis of the use of the interruption-technique in experimental studies of "repression." *Psychol. Bull.*, 1948, **45**, 491–506. (213)

Glixman, A. F. Recall of completed and incompleted activities under varying degrees of stress. *J. exp. Psychol.*, 1949, **39**, 281–295. (211)

Goldfarb, W. Pain reactions in a group of institutionalized schizophrenic children. *Amer. J. Orthopsychiat.* 1958, **28**, 777–785. (328, 349)

Goldstein, K. *The organism.* New York: American Book Co., 1939. (38, 53, 101, 108)

Gorer, G. The pornography of death. Reprinted from *Modern Writing* (1956), pp. 56–62, in M. Stein, A. J. Vidich, & D. M. White (Eds.), *Identity and anxiety.* Glencoe, Ill.: Free Press, 1960. Pp. 402–407. (382)

Groddeck, G. *The book of the id.* Trans. by the author from *Das Buch vom Es* (1923). *Nerv. Ment. Dis. Monogr.*, No. 49. New York: Nervous and Mental Disease Publishing Co., 1928. (29)

Guilford, J. P. Creativity. *Amer. Psychologist*, 1950, **5**, 444–454. (262)

464

Guilford, J. P. *Personality*. New York: McGraw-Hill, 1959. (262)

Haigh, G. Defensive behavior in client centered therapy. *J. consult. Psychol.*, 1949, **13**, 181–189. (108)

Hall, O. M. Attitudes and unemployment. *Arch. Psychol.*, 1934, No. 165. (404)

Hallowell, A. I. Behavioral evolution and the emergence of the self. In *Evolution and anthropology: a centennial appraisal*. Washington, D.C.: Anthropological Soc. of Washington, 1959. Pp. 36–60. (59, 101)

Harlow, H. F. Mice, monkeys, men, and motives. *Psychol. Rev.*, 1953, **60**, 23–32. (56)

Harlow, H. F., Harlow, M. K., & Meyer, D. R. Learning motivated by a manipulation drive. *J. exp. Psychol.*, 1950, **40**, 228–234. (56)

Hartley, D. *Observations on man, his frame, his duty, and his expectations*. London: J. Johnson, 1749 (reprint, 1791). (5)

Heath, D. Stimulus similarity and task familiarity as determinants of expectancy generalization. *J. exp. Psychol.*, 1959, **58**, 289–295. (169)

Hebb, D. O. The American revolution. *Amer. Psychologist*, 1950, **15**, 735–745. (58)

Hebb, D. O. and Thompson, W. R. The social significance of animal studies. In G. Lindzey (Ed.), *Handbook of social psychology*, Vol. 1. Cambridge, Mass.: Addison-Wesley, 1954. Pp. 532–561. (330)

Henle, M. The influence of valence on substitution. *J. Psychol.*, 1944, **17**, 11–19. (164, 174)

Henry, A. F., and Short, J. F. *Suicide and homicide: some economic, sociological and psychological aspects of aggression*. Glencoe, Ill: Free Press, 1954. (404)

Herbart, J. F. *Psychologie als Wissenschaft*. Königsberg: A. W. Unser, 1824–1825. 2 vols. (21)

Hilgard, E. R. Human motives and the concept of the self. *Amer. Psychologist*, 1949, **4**, 374–382. (57, 101, 108)

Hillebrandt, A. Death and disposal of the dead: Hindu. In *Hastings encyclopedia of religion and ethics*, Vol. 4. New York: Scribner's, 1911. Pp. 475–479. (387)

Hirt, E. Psychologisches in der psychiatrischen Literatur der letzten Jahre. *Arch. ges. Psychol.*, 1909, **14**, 137–164 (Literaturbericht). (31, 108, 327, 371)

Hirt, E. Psychologisches in der psychiatrischen Literatur der letzten Jahre. *Arch. ges. Psychol.*, 1910, **17**, 139–164 (Literaturbericht). (31–32)

Hobbes, T. *Leviathan*. London: Andrew Crooke, 1651. (5, 34, 327)

Höffding, H. *Outlines of psychology*. Trans. M. E. Lowndes, from first German ed., 1891. London: Macmillan, 1919. (17–21, 27, 44, 48, 55, 60, 98, 205)

Hoffman, A. E. A study of reported behavior changes in counseling. *J. consult. Psychol.*, 1949, **13**, 190–195. (108)

Hollander, E. P. Conformity, status, and idiosyncrasy credit. *Psychol. Rev.*, 1958, **65**, 117–127. (263)

Hoppe, F. Erfolg und Misserfolg. (Untersuchungen zur Handlungs- und Affektpsychologie, IX. Ed. K. Lewin). *Psychol. Forsch.*, 1931, **14**, 1–62. (116, 118–119, 121–122, 164, 206, 213)

Huizinga, J. *The waning of the middle ages.* New York: St. Martin's Press, 1924. Reprinted, New York: Doubleday Anchor Books, 1954. (2, 384–385)

Hull, C. L. Simple trial-and-error learning: a study in psychological theory. *Psychol. Rev.*, 1930, **37**, 241–256. (50)

Hull, C. L. Mind, mechanism, and adaptive behavior. *Psychol. Rev.*, 1937, **44**, 1–32. (50)

Hume, D. *Treatise of human nature* (1793). Ed. L. A. Selby-Bigge. Oxford: Clarendon Press, 1888. (8, 66)

Irwin, F. W. The realism of expectations. *Psychol. Rev.*, 1944, **51**, 120–126. (122)

Irwin, F. W., & Mintzer, M. G. Effect of differences in instruction and motivation upon measures of the level of aspiration. *Amer. J. Psychol.*, 1942, **55**, 400–406. (123)

Irwin, F. W., & Smith, W. A. S. Further tests of theories of decision in an "expanded judgment" situation. *J. exp. Psychol.*, 1956, **52**, 345–348. (152)

Irwin, F. W., & Smith, W. A. S. Value, cost, and information as determiners of decision. *J. exp. Psychol.*, 1957, **54**, 229–232. (152)

Irwin, F. W., Smith, W. A. S., & Mayfield, J. F. Tests of two theories of decision in an "expanded judgment" situation. *J. exp. Psychol.*, 1956, **51**, 261–268. (152)

Iverson, M. A., & Reuder, M. E. Ego-involvement as an experimental variable. *Psychol. Rep.*, 1956, **2**, 147–181 (Monogr. Suppl., 4). (210)

Jacobi, H. Death and disposal of the dead: Jain. In *Hastings encyclopedia of religion and ethics*, Vol. 4. New York: Scribner's, 1911. Pp. 484–485. (391)

Jacobson, E. Contribution to the metapsychology of cyclothymic depression. In P. Greenacre (Ed.), *Affective disorders: psychoanalytic contribution to their study.* New York: International Universities Press, 1953. (359, 361)

James, W. *Principles of psychology.* New York: Holt, 1890. 2 vols. (4, 9, 14–17, 20–21, 27, 32, 41, 46, 48, 60, 97–98, 205, 214, 261, 327, 392)

James, W. H., & Rotter, J. B. Partial and 100% reinforcement under chance and skill conditions. *J. exp. Psychol.*, 1958, **55**, 397–403. (176)

Johanssen, D. E. Reactions to the death of President Roosevelt. *J. abnorm. soc. Psychol.*, 1946, **41**, 218–222. (390)

Jones, E. *The life and work of Sigmund Freud.* New York: Basic Books, 1953. 3 vols. (21)

Josey, C. C. The self in the light of Gestalt psychology. *J. abnorm. soc. Psychol.*, 1935, 30, 47–56. (53)

Jucknat, M. Leistung, Anspruchsniveau und Selbstbewusstsein, (Untersuchungen zur Handlungs- und Affektpsychologie, XX. Ed. K. Lewin). *Psychol. Forsch.*, 1937, 22, 89–179. (122)

Jung, C. G. On the psychology of the unconscious. Trans. R. F. C. Hull from *Über die Psychologie des Unbewussten* (1943) (5th ed. of "Neue Bahnen der Psychologie, 1912). Reprinted in *Two essays on analytical psychology*. New York: Meridian Books, 1953. Pp. 11–130. (34–37)

Jung, C. G. The relations between the ego and the unconscious. Trans. R. F. C. Hull from *Die Beziehungen zwischen dem Ich und dem Unbewussten* (1945) (based on La structure de l'inconscient, 1916). Reprinted in *Two essays on analytical psychology*. New York: Meridian Books, 1953. Pp. 133–253. (34, 36–38)

Jung, C. G. *The undiscovered self*. Trans. R. F. C. Hull from German ed., 1957. Boston: Atlantic Monthly Press, 1958. Reprinted, Mentor Books, 1959. (37)

Kagan, J. Socialization of aggression and the perception of parents in fantasy. *Child Develpm.*, 1958, 29, 311–320 (a). (268)

Kagan, J. The concept of identification. *Psychol. Rev.*, 1958, 65, 296–305 (b). (266–269, 276, 289, 425)

Kallman, F. J. Genetic principles in manic-depressive psychosis. In P. H. Hoch & J. Zubin (Eds.), *Depression*. New York: Grune & Stratton, 1954. Pp. 1–24. (360)

Kallman, F. J., & Anastasio, M. M. Twin studies on the psychopathology of suicide. *J. Nerv. Ment. Dis.*, 1947, 105, 40–55. (371)

Karsten, A. Psychische Sättigung. (Untersuchungen zur Handlungs- und Affektpsychologie, V. Ed. K. Lewin). *Psychol. Forsch.*, 1928, 10, 142–254. (116, 206)

Kass, N. Persistence to extinction as a function of age and schedules of reinforcement. *J. exp. Psychol.*, 1962, 64, 249–252. (176)

Katzaroff, D. Contribution à l'étude de la récognition. *Arch. de Psychol.*, 1911, 11, 2–78. (38)

Kausler, D. H. A study of the relationship between ego-involvement and learning. *J. Psychol.*, 1951, 32, 225–230. (212)

Kausler, D. H., & Trapp, E. P. Achievement motivation and goal-setting behavior on a learning task. *J. exp. Psychol.*, 1958, 55, 575–578. (185)

Kellersohn, M. Attitudes devant la mort. In article, La vie mentale de l'enfance a la viellesse, *Encyclopédie Francaise*, Vol. 8, 1938. (382–383)

Kelley, H. H., & Shapiro, M. M. An experiment on conformity to group norms where conformity is detrimental to group achievement. *Amer. Sociol. Rev.*, 1954, 19, 667–677. (263)

Kendall, M. G. *Rank correlation methods*. London: C. Griffin, 1948. (310)

Klein, S. J. *Muscle action potentials produced in various ways and their relation to quantitative and qualitative measures of ergographic work.* Ph.D. Dissertation, University of Pennsylvania, Philadelphia, 1951. (214)

Knight, R. P. Introjection, projection, and identification. *Psychoanal. Quart.,* 1940, 9, 334–341. (268)

Koffka, K. *Principles of Gestalt psychology.* New York: Harcourt, Brace, 1935. (51–52, 54)

Köhler, W. *The place of value in a world of facts.* New York: Liveright, 1938. (53–54)

Kraepelin, E. *Manic-depressive insanity and paranoia,* 1899. Trans. M. Barclay; ed. G. M. Robertson. Edinburgh: E. & S. Livingstone, 1921. (359)

Kraines, S. H. *Mental depressions and their treatment.* New York: Macmillan, 1957. (358–361)

Krechevsky, I. "Hypotheses" in rats. *Psychol. Rev.,* 1932, 39, 516–532. (329)

Kretschmer, E. *Physique and character.* Trans. W. J. H. Sprott. London: Kegan Paul, 1925. (360)

Laird, J. *A study in realism.* Cambridge: Cambridge Univer. Press, 1920. (39)

Lane-Poole, S. Death and disposal of the dead: Mohammedan. In *Hastings encyclopedia of religion and ethics,* Vol. 4. New York: Scribner's, 1911. Pp. 500–502. (387)

Langdon. S. Death and disposal of the dead: Babylonian. In *Hastings encyclopedia of religion and ethics,* Vol. 4. New York: Scribner's, 1911. Pp. 444–446. (387)

Lazowick, L. M. On the nature of identification. *J. abnorm. soc. Psychol.,* 1955, 51, 175–183. (266)

Lecky, P. *Self-consistency: a theory of personality.* New York: Island Press, 1945. (57)

Le Ny, J.-F. Generalisation et discrimination d'un stimulus verbal dans un apprentissage stochastique chez des enfants. *Année Psychol.,* 1961, 61, 79–96. (169)

Leshner, S. L. Effect of aspiration and achievement on muscular tensions. *J. exp. Psychol.,* 1961, 61, 133–137. (161, 214)

Levy-Bruhl, L. *Les fonctions mentales dans les sociétés inferieurs.* (2nd ed.) Paris: F. Alcan, 1912. (40)

Lewin, K. Untersuchungen zur Handlungs- und Affektpsychologie, I: Vorbemerkungen über die seelischen Kräfte und Energien und über die Struktur der Seele. *Psychol. Forsch.,* 1926, 7, 294–329. (52, 209)

Lewin, K. *A dynamic theory of personality.* New York: McGraw-Hill, 1935. (51–52, 164, 204)

Lewin, K. *Principles of topological psychology.* New York: McGraw-Hill, 1936. (51, 85, 190)

Lewin, K. Time perspective and morale. In G. Watson (Ed.), *Civilian Morale*. New York: Reynal & Hitchcock, 1941. Pp. 48–70. (161, 206, 380)

Lewin, K., Dembo, T., Festinger, L., & Sears, P. S. Level of aspiration. In J. McV. Hunt (Ed.), *Personality and the behavior disorders*, Vol. 1. New York: Ronald Press, 1944. Pp. 333–378. (123–124, 152)

Lewis, H. B., & Franklin, M. An experimental study of the ego in work: II. The significance of task-orientation in work. *J. exp. Psychol.*, 1944, **34**, 195–215. (211)

Lindemann, E. Symptomatology and management of acute grief. *Amer. J. Psychiat.*, 1944, **101**, 141–148. (389)

Lissner, K. Die Entspannung von Bedürfnissen durch Ersatzhandlungen. (Untersuchungen zur Handlungs- und Affektpsychologie, XVIII. Ed. K. Lewin). *Psychol. Forsch.*, 1933, **18**, 218–250. (164)

Litwinski, L. Toward the reinstatement of the concept of the self. *Brit. J. Psychol.*, 1951, **42**, 246–249. (54, 60, 101)

Lloyd, A. Death and disposal of the dead: Japanese. In *Hastings encyclopedia of religion and ethics*, Vol. 4. New York: Scribner's, 1911. Pp. 485–497. (387–388)

Locke, J. *An essay concerning the human understanding* (1690). (Twenty-second ed.) London, 1812 (page references to the later edition). 2 vols. (5, 95)

Lough, J. E. *Analyzing yourself*. New York: Business Training Corps., 1916. (40)

Lovejoy, A. O. "Pride" in eighteenth-century thought. *Med. Lang. Notes*, 1921, **36**, 31–37. Reprinted in A. O. Lovejoy, *Essays in the history of ideas*. New York: Braziller, 1955. (95)

Lovejoy, A. O. Terminal and adjectival values. *J. Philos.*, 1950, **47**, 593–608. (95)

Lovejoy, A. O. *Reflections on human nature*. Baltimore: Johns Hopkins Press, 1961. (95, 102, 110, 207)

Lowell, E. L. The effect of need for achievement on learning and speed of performance. *J. Psychol.*, 1952, **33**, 31–40. (189)

Lundholm, H. Reflections upon the nature of the psychological self. *Psychol. Rev.*, 1940, **47**, 110–126. (53–54)

Lundholm, H. The psychological self in the philosophies of Köhler and Sherrington. *Psychol. Rev.*, 1946, **53**, 119–131. (53)

MacDougall, R. The self and mental phenomena. *Psychol. Rev.*, 1916, **23**, 1–30. (39)

Mach, E. *Beiträge zur Analyse der Empfindungen*. Jena: Gustav Fisher, 1886. (8, 13, 20, 32, 50, 53, 66)

MacKinnon, D. W. The nature and nurture of creative talent. *Amer. Psychologist*, 1962, **17**, 484–495. (262)

MacMahon, B., Johnson, S. & Pugh, T. F. Relation of suicide rates to social conditions: evidence from U.S. vital statistics. *Publ. Hlth Rep.*, 1963, **78**, 285–293. (404)

Mahler, W. Ersatzhandlungen verschiedener Realitätsgrades. (Untersuchungen zur Handlungs-und Affektpsychologie, XV. Ed. K. Lewin). *Psychol. Forsch.*, 1933, 18, 27–89. (164)

Maier, N. R. F. Reasoning in white rats. *Comp. Psychol. Monogr.*, 1929, 6, No. 3, 93 pp. (329)

Maine de Biran, P. *Essai sur les fondements de la psychologie et sur ses rapports avec l'étude de la nature* (ca. 1812). In E. Neville (Ed.), *Oeuvres inédites de Maine de Biran.* Paris: Dezobry, Magdeleine, 1859. (33)

Malinowski, B. *Magic, science, and religion* (1925). Reprinted, New York: Doubleday Anchor Books, 1954. (382)

Malmo, R. B., Shagass, C., & Davis, J. R. Electromyographic studies of muscular tension in psychiatric patients under stress. *J. clin. exp. Psychopathol.*, 1951, 12, 45–66. (215, 218)

Marks, R. W. The effect of probability, desirability, and privilege on the stated expectations of children. *J. Pers.*, 1951, 19, 332–351. (169)

Martin, A. H. An experimental study of the factors and types of voluntary choice. *Arch. Psychol.*, 1922, No. 51, 1–115. (38)

Maslow, A. H. Self-actualizing people: a study of psychological health. In W. Wolff (Ed.), *Symposium Number 1, 1950: Values in personality research.* New York: Grune & Stratton, 1950. Reprinted in C. Moustakas (Ed.), *The self.* New York: Harper, 1956. Pp. 160–194. (38, 53)

McCall, R. J. Invested self-expression: a principle of human motivation. *Psychol. Rev.*, 1963, 70, 289–303. (56, 102, 108)

McClelland, D. C. Some social consequences of achievement motivation. In M. R. Jones (Ed.), *Nebraska symposium on motivation.* Lincoln, Neb.: Univer. of Nebraska Press, 1955. Pp. 41–65. (185)

McClelland, D. C., Atkinson, J. W., Clark, R. A., & Lowell, E. L. *The achievement motive.* New York: Appleton-Century-Crofts, 1953. (123, 185–186)

McClelland, D. C., & Friedman, G. A. A cross-cultural study of the relationship between child-rearing practices and achievement motivation appearing in folk tales. In G. E. Swanson, T. M. Newcomb, & E. L. Hartley (Eds.), *Readings in social psychology.* New York: Holt, 1952. Pp. 243–249. (185)

McDougall, W. *An introduction to social psychology* (1908). (15th ed.) Boston: J. W. Luce, 1923. (43, 53)

McDougall, W. Motives in the light of recent discoveries. *Mind*, 1920, 29, 277–293. (56)

McDougall, W. *Outline of psychology.* New York: Scribner's, 1923. (39)

McDougall, W. *The energies of men.* London: Methuen, 1932. (53)

Mead, G. H. The genesis of the self and social control. *Int. J. Ethics*, 1925, 35, 251–277. (45)

Mead, G. H. *The philosophy of the present.* Chicago: Open Court, 1932. (45–46)

Mead, G. H. *Mind, self, and society from the standpoint of a social behaviorist.* Ed. C. W. Morris, Chicago: Univer. of Chicago Press, 1934. (45–48, 104, 260)

Mead, G. H. *Movements of thought in the 19th century.* Chicago: Univer. of Chicago Press, 1936. (45, 47)

Mead, G. H. *The philosophy of the act.* Chicago: Univer. of Chicago Press, 1938. (45–47)

Mead, M. *Male and female.* New York: Morrow, 1949. (382, 389)

Means, M. H. Fears of one thousand college women. *J. abnorm. soc. Psychol.*, 1936, **31**, 291–311. (390)

Meissner, W. W. Affective responses to psychoanalytic death symbols. *J. abnorm. soc. Psychol.*, 1958, **56**, 295–299. (386)

Mendel, E. Hypochrondrie beim weiblichen Geschlecht. *Dtsche Med. Wschr.*, 1889, No. 11. (32)

Meumann, E. *Intelligenz und Wille.* (2nd ed.) Leipzig: Quelle & Meyer, 1913. (39)

Michotte, A., & Prüm, E. Etude experimentale sur la choix volontaire. *Arch. de Psychol.*, 1911, **10**, 113–120. (38).

Middleton, W. C. Some reactions toward death among college students. *J. abnorm. soc. Psychol.*, 1936, **31**, 165–173. (390, 403)

Mill, J. *Analysis of the phenomena of the human mind* (1829). Reprinted, London: Longmans, Green, Roeder, & Dyer, 1869. (8)

Mill, J. S. *An examination of Sir William Hamilton's philosophy.* London: Longmans, Green, 1865. (9)

Miller, D. R. Responses of psychiatric patients to threat of failure. *J. abnorm. soc. Psychol.*, 1951, **46**, 378–387. (351)

Miller, N. E. Experimental studies of conflict. In J. McV. Hunt (Ed.), *Personality and the behavior disorders,* Vol. 1. New York: Ronald Press, 1944. Pp. 431–465. (204)

Miller, N. E. & Dollard, J. *Social learning and imitation.* New Haven: Yale Univer. Press, 1941. (267, 269)

Montaigne, M. de. *Essays.* Trans. John Florio, 1603. (abridged ed.) New York: Carlton House (no date). (384)

Morgan, C. T. *Physiological psychology.* New York: McGraw-Hill, 1943. (49)

Moustakas, C. (Ed.) *The self: explorations in personal growth.* New York: Harper, 1956. (41)

Mowrer, O. H. *Learning theory and personality dynamics.* New York: Ronald Press, 1950. (268)

Murphy, G. *Personality: a biosocial interpretation of origins and structure.* New York: Harper, 1947. (54–55)

Murphy, G., Murphy, L. B., & Newcomb, T. *Experimental social psychology.* (rev. ed.) New York: Harper, 1937. (54)

Murray, H. A., et al. *Explorations in personality.* New York: Oxford Univer. Press, 1938. (49, 54, 127, 211)

Murray, H. A. The personality and career of Satan. *J. soc. Issues,* 1963, 18, 36–46. (111, 113)

Mursell, J. L. The stimulus-response relation. *Psychol. Rev.,* 1922, 29, 549–553. (40)

Nagy, M. The child's theories concerning death. *J. genet. Psychol.,* 1948, 73, 3–27. (384, 390)

Oesterreich, T. K. *Die Phänomenologie des Ichs.* Leipzig: J. A. Barth, 1910. 2 vols. (38)

Olson, G. W. Failure and the subsequent performance of schizophrenics. *J. abnorm. soc. Psychol.,* 1958, 57, 310–314. (161, 214, 328)

Opler, M. E. Further comparative anthropological data bearing on the solution of a psychological problem. *J. soc. Psychol.,* 1938, 9, 477–483. (388)

Orlansky, H. Reactions to the death of President Roosevelt. *J. soc. Psychol.,* 1947, 26, 235–266. (382, 390)

Ortega y Gasset, J. The pride of the Basques. *Atlantic Monthly,* 1961, 207, 113–116. (114)

Ovsiankina, M. Die Wiederaufnahme unterbrochener Handlungen. (Untersuchungen zur Handlungs- und Affektpsychologie, VI. Ed. K. Lewin). *Psychol. Forsch.,* 1928, 11, 302–379. (209)

Parker, De W. H. *The self and nature.* Cambridge: Harvard Univer. Press, 1917. (41–42)

Payne, D. E., & Mussen, P. H. Parent-child relations and father identification among adolescent boys. *J. abnorm. soc. Psychol.,* 1956, 52, 358–362. (266)

Payne, R. *Hubris: a study of pride.* (Rev. ed. of *The wanton nymph: a study of pride,* 1951). New York: Harper, 1960. (110–111)

Pepper, S. C. *The sources of value.* Berkeley, Calif.: Univer. of California Press, 1958. (49, 78–79, 83, 86–87, 89, 104, 392, 417)

Perry, R. B. *General theory of value.* New York: Longmans, Green, 1926. (78)

Petermann, B. *The Gestalt theory and the problem of configuration.* London: Kegan Paul, 1932. (50–51)

Pfander, A. *Einführung in die Psychologie.* Leipzig: Barth, 1904. (39)

Piaget, J. *The origins of intelligence in children.* New York: International Univer. Press, 1952. (330)

Piaget, J. *The construction of reality in the child.* New York: Basic Books, 1954. (330)

Pierce, C. S. Questions concerning certain faculties claimed for man. *J. Specul. Philos.,* 1868, 2, 103–114. Reprinted in P. R. Wiener (Ed.), *Values in a universe of chance: selected writings of C. S. Pierce.* Garden City, New York: Doubleday Anchor Books, 1958. (Page references are to the reprint.) (10, 12, 43, 96)

Pierce, C. S. How to make our ideas clear. *Pop. Sci. Monthly,* Jan. 1878, 286–302. Reprinted in P. R. Wiener (Ed.), *Values in a universe of chance: selected writings of C. S. Pierce*. Garden City, New York: Doubleday Anchor Books, 1958. (ii)

Pierce, C. S. What pragmatism is. *Monist,* 1905, **15,** 161–181. Reprinted in P. R. Wiener (Ed.), *Values in a universe of chance: selected writings of C. S. Pierce.* Garden City, New York: Doubleday Anchor Books, 1958 (Page references are to the reprint.) (12, 96)

Plutarch (d. 120 A.D.) *Lives.* Trans. John Dryden; ed. A. H. Clough. Life of Cato the Younger, Vol. 4, pp. 192–261; Life of Marcus Brutus, Vol. 5, pp. 186–240. Philadelphia: John D. Morris & Co. (no date). (393–394)

Preston, M. G., & Bayton, J. A. Differential effect of a social variable upon three levels of aspiration. *J. exp. Psychol.,* 1941, **29,** 351–369. (123)

Preston, M. G., Peltz, W., Mudd, E. H., and Froscher, H. B. Impressions of personality as a function of marital conflict. *J. abnorm. soc. Psychol.,* 1952, **47,** 326–336. (174)

Prince, M. *The dissociation of a personality.* New York: Longmans, Green, 1905. (327)

Prince, M. Miss Beauchamp: the psychogenesis of a multiple personality. *J. abnorm. Psychol.,* 1920, **15,** 67–135. Reprinted in A. A. Roback (Ed.), *Clinical and experimental studies in personality.* Cambridge, Mass.: Sci-Art, 1939. Pp. 185–268. (327)

Raimy, V. C. *The self-concept as a factor in counseling and personality organization.* Ph.D. Dissertation, Ohio State University, Columbus, Ohio, 1943. (61)

Raskin, N. J. Development of the "Parallel Studies" project. *J. consult. Psychol.,* 1949, **13,** 154–156. (108)

Reeves, J. W. *Body and mind in western thought.* Baltimore: Penguin Books, 1958. (1)

Reuder, M. E. The effect of ego orientation and problem difficulty on muscle action potentials. *J. exp. Psychol.,* 1956, **51,** 142–148. (215)

Rodnick, E., & Garmezy, N. An experimental approach to the study of motivation in schizophrenia. In M. R. Jones (Ed.), *Nebraska symposium on motivation.* Lincoln, Neb.: Univer. of Nebraska Press, 1957. Pp. 109–184. (328)

Rogers, C. R. A coordinated research in psychotherapy: a non-objective introduction. *J. consult. Psychol.,* 1949, **13,** 149–153. (101, 108)

Rogers, C. R. The concept of the fully functioning person (unpublished MS, 1955). Cited in C. S. Hall & G. Lindzey, *Theories of personality.* New York: Wiley, 1957. Pp. 475–476. (53, 60, 108)

Rosen, A., Hales, W. M., & Simon, W. Classification of "suicidal" patients. *J. consult. Psychol.,* 1954, **18,** 359–365. (378)

Rosen, M. *Valence, expectancy, and dissonance-reduction in the prediction of goal-striving.* Ph.D. Dissertation, University of Pennsylvania, Philadelphia, 1960. (249, 252, 254–257)

Rosenzweig, S. Preferences in the repetition of successful and unsuccessful activities as a function of age and personality. *J. genet. Psychol.,* 1933, **42**, 423–441. (174)

Rosenzweig, S. An experimental study of repression with special reference to need-persistive and ego-defensive reactions to frustration. *J. exp. Psychol.,* 1943, **32**, 64–74. (158, 211, 212)

Rosenzweig, S., & Mason, G. An experimental study of memory in relation to the theory of repression. *Brit. J. Psychol.,* 1934, **24**, 247–265. (158, 211, 213)

Rothman, D. Z. *The effects of success and failure experiences in normal, "neurotic," and schizophrenic populations.* Ph.D. Dissertation, University of Pennsylvania, Philadelphia, 1963. (240–241, 248, 350, 352–357, 390, 415)

Rotter, J. B. Level of aspiration as a method of studying personality. *J. exp. Psychol.,* 1942, **31**, 410–422. (122)

Russell, B. *The analysis of mind.* London: Allen & Unwin, 1933. (48–50)

Russell, E. S. *The directiveness of organic activities.* Cambridge: Cambridge Univer. Press, 1945. (49)

Sanford, R. N. The dynamics of identification. *Psychol. Rev.,* 1955, **62**, 106–118. (266, 268)

Sarbin, T. R. A preface to a psychological study of the self. *Psychol. Rev.,* 1952, **54**, 11–22. (57)

Sargent, S. S. Conceptions of role and ego in contemporary psychology. In J. H. Rohrer & M. Sherif (Eds.), *Social psychology at the crossroads.* New York: Harper, 1951. Pp. 355–370. (262)

Schiller, P. H. Innate motor action as a basis of learning. In C. H. Schiller (Ed.), *Instinctive behavior: the development of a modern concept.* New York: International Univer. Press, 1957. Pp. 264–287. (56)

Schilder, P. The attitude of murderers toward death. *J. abnorm. soc. Psychol.,* 1936, **31**, 348–363. (390)

Schilder, P., & Wechsler, D. The attitudes of children toward death. *J. genet. Psychol.,* 1934, **45**, 406–451. (382, 390, 410)

Schuessler, K. F. The deterrent influence of the death penalty. *Ann. Amer. Acad. Pol. Soc. Sci.,* 1952, vol. 284, pp. 54–62. (382, 386)

Sears, P. S. Level of aspiration in relation to some variables of personality: clinical studies. *J. soc. Psychol.,* 1941, **14**, 311–336. (122)

Sears, R. R. Identification as a form of behavioral development. In D. Harris (Ed.), *The concept of development.* Minneapolis: Univer. of Minnesota Press, 1957. Pp. 149–161. (267)

Sears, R. R., Maccoby, E. E., & Levin, H. *Patterns of child rearing.* Evanston, Ill.: Row, Peterson, 1957. (266, 268)

Seeman, J. The process of nondirective therapy. *J. consult. Psychol.,* 1949, **13**, 157–168. (108)

Semon, R. W. *Die Mneme.* Leipzig: W. Engelmann, 1904. (49)

Semon, R. W. *Die mnemische Empfindungen.* Leipzig: W. Engelmann, 1909. (49)

Seward, J. P. The structure of functional autonomy. *Amer. Psychol.*, 1963, **18**, 703–710. (55–56, 84–85)

Shaw, W. A., & Kline, L. H. A study of muscle action potential during the attempted solution by children of problems of increasing difficulty. *J. exp. Psychol.*, 1947, **37**, 146–158. (215)

Sheerer, E. T. An analysis of the relationship between acceptance of and respect for self and acceptance of and respect for others in ten counseling cases. *J. consult. Psychol.*, 1949, **13**, 169–175. (108)

Sheldon, W. H., & Stevens, S. S. *The varieties of temperament.* New York: Harper, 1942. (360)

Sherif, M., & Cantril, H. *The psychology of ego-involvements.* New York: Wiley, 1947. (211)

Sherrington, C. S. *Man: on his nature.* New York: Macmillan, 1941. (53)

Shneidman, E. S. Orientations toward death: a vital aspect of the study of lives. In R. W. White (Ed.), *The study of lives.* New York: Prentice-Hall, Atherton Press, 1963. Pp. 201–227. (378, 382, 398)

Shneidman, E. S. Suicide, sleep, and death: some possible interrelations among cessation, interruption, and continuation phenomena. *J. consult. Psychol.*, 1964, **28**, 95–106. (378)

Shneidman, E. S., & Farberow, N. L. Clues to suicide. *Publ. Hlth Rep.*, 1956, **71**, 100–114. (404)

Showerman, G. Death and disposal of the dead: Roman. In *Hastings encyclopedia of religion and ethics*, Vol. 4. New York: Scribner's, 1911. Pp. 505–507. (388)

Siegel, S. *Nonparametric statistics for the behavioral sciences.* New York: McGraw-Hill, 1956. (325)

Sifneos, P. E., Gore, C., & Sifneos, A. C. A preliminary psychiatric study of attempted suicide as seen in a general hospital. *Amer. J. Psychiat.*, 1856, **112**, 883–888. (371)

Simmel, M. L. Phantoms in patients with leprosy and in elderly digital amputees. *Amer. J. Psychol.*, 1956, **69**, 529–545. (58)

Singer, E. A., Jr. *Modern thinkers and present problems.* New York: Holt, 1923. (262)

Singer, E. A., Jr. Man and fellow-man. In *Mind as behavior.* Columbus, Ohio: R. G. Adams & Co., 1924. (54, 64)

Smith, A. A. An electromyographic study of tension in interrupted and completed tasks. *J. exp. Psychol.*, 1953, **45**, 32–36. (215, 218)

Snygg, D., & Combs, A. W. *Individual behavior.* New York: Harper, 1949. (53, 61, 107)

Soderdelon, N. Death and disposal of the dead: Parsi. In *Hastings encyclopedia of religion and ethics*, Vol. 4. New York: Scribner's, 1911. Pp. 502–506. (387)

Spearman, C. E. *The nature of intelligence and the principles of cognition.* London: Macmillan, 1923. (39)

Stengel, E. Recent research into suicide and attempted suicide. *Amer. J. Psychiat.*, 1962, **118**, 725–727. (378, 400)

Stennett, R. G. The relationship of performance level to level of arousal. *J. exp. Psychol.*, 1957, **54**, 54–61. (215)

Stern, W. Die Psychologie und der Personalismus. *Z. Psychol.*, 1917, **78**, 1–54. (39)

Stern, W. *Die menschliche Persönlichkeit.* Vol. II of *Person und Sache.* Leipzig: J. A. Barth, 1918–1919. (39)

Stevenson, H. W., & Weir, M. W. Developmental changes in the effects of reinforcement and non-reinforcement of a single response. *Child Develpm.*, 1961, **32**, 1–5. (176)

Stock, D. An investigation into the interrelations between the self-concept and feelings directed toward other persons and groups. *J. consult. Psychol.*, 1949, **13**, 176–180. (108)

Stoke, S. An inquiry into the concept of identification. *J. genet. Psychol.*, 1950, **76**, 163–189. (266)

Stotland, E., & Cottrell, N. Similarity of performance as influenced by interaction, self-esteem, and birth order. *J. abnorm. soc. Psychol.*, 1962, **64**, 183–191. (277)

Stotland, E., & Hillmer, M. Identification, authoritarian defensiveness, and self-esteem. *J. abnorm. soc. Psychol.*, 1962, **64**, 334–342. (276)

Stotland, E., Thorley, S., Thomas, E., Cohen, A. R., & Zander, A. The effects of group expectations and self-esteem upon self-evaluation. *J. abnorm. soc. Psychol.*, 1957, **15**, 55–63. (164, 277)

Stotland, E., & Zander, A. Effects of public and private failure on self-evaluation. *J. abnorm. soc. Psychol.*, 1958, **56**, 223–229. (164)

Stotland, E., Zander, A., & Natsoulas, T. Generalization of interpersonal similarity. *J. abnorm. soc. Psychol.*, 1961, **62**, 250–256. (276)

Strecker, E. A., Ebaugh, F. G., & Kanner, L. *Practical clinical psychiatry.* (5th ed.) Philadelphia: Balkiston, 1940. (358–359, 361)

Surwillo, W. W. Psychological factors in muscle action potentials: EMG gradients. *J. exp. Psychol.*, 1956, **52**, 263–272. (215)

Symonds, P. A. *Dynamic psychology.* New York: Appleton-Century, 1949. (57)

Terman, L. M. Tests of general intelligence. *Psychol. Bull.*, 1918, **15**, 160–167. (40)

Thorndike, E. L. *Educational psychology.* Vol. I. *The original nature of man.* New York: Teachers College, Columbia University, 1920. (43)

Titchener, E. B. A note on consciousness of self. *Amer. J. Psychol.*, 1911, **22**, 540–552. (38)

Tolman, E. C., *Purposive behavior in animals and men.* New York: Appleton-Century, 1932. (49–50, 55, 78, 214, 329)

Tolman, E. C. *Drives toward war.* New York: Appleton-Century, 1942. (78, 85)

Tomkins, S. *Affect, imagery, consciousness.* New York: Springer Publishing Co., 1962. 2 vols. (85)

Tuckman, J., Kleiner, R. J., & Lavell, M. Emotional content of suicide notes. *Amer. J. Psychiat.*, 1959, **116**, 59–63. (404)

Unamuno, M. de. *The tragic sense of life* (1912). Trans. J. E. C. Flitch, 1921. Reprinted, New York: Dover, 1954. (382)

United States Department of Commerce. *Vital statistics of the United States,* 1942. Washington, D.C.: U.S. Government Printing Office, 1943. (404)

Viteles, M. S. *Industrial psychology.* New York: W. W. Norton. 1932. (206)

Wahl, C. W. Suicide as a magical act. In E. S. Shneidman & N. L. Farberow (Eds.), *Clues to suicide.* New York: McGraw-Hill, 1957. Pp. 22–30. (382)

Wallis, W. D. *Religion in primitive society.* New York: Crofts, 1939. (388, 391–392, 401–402)

Walshe, W. G. Death and disposal of the dead: Chinese. In *Hastings encyclopedia of religion and ethics,* Vol. 4. New York: Scribner's, 1911. Pp. 450–454. (387–388)

Warden, C. J. *Animal motivation: experimental studies on the albino rat.* New York: Columbia University Press, 1931.

Watson, J. B. *Psychology from the standpoint of a behaviorist.* Philadelphia: Lippincott, 1919. (10)

Weismann, A. *Essays upon heredity and kindred biological problems.* Oxford: Clarendon Press, 1889. (27, 29)

Weismann, A. *Das Keimplasma.* Jena: Fischer, 1892. (27, 29)

Wendt, H. W. Motivation, affect, and performance. In D. C. McClelland (Ed.), *Studies in motivation.* New York: Appleton-Century-Crofts, 1955. Pp. 448–459. (189)

Wernicke, C. *Grundriss der Psychiatrie.* Leipzig: G. Thieme, 1894–1900. 3 vols. (33)

Wertenbaker, L. T. *Death of a man.* New York: Random House, 1957. (395, 396)

Wheeler, R. H. The synasthesia of a blind subject. *Univer. Oregon Publ.,* 1920, 1, No. 5, 1–61. (39)

Wheeler, R. H. Analyzed versus unanalyzed experience. *Psychol. Rev.,* 1922, 29, 425–446. (39)

White, R. W. *The abnormal personality.* (2nd ed.) New York: Ronald Press, 1956. (358–359, 361, 389)

White, R. W. Motivation reconsidered: the concept of competence. *Psychol. Rev.,* 1959, 66, 297–333. (21, 54, 56, 125, 261)

White, R. W. Ego and reality in psychoanalytic theory. *Psychol. Issues,* 1963, 3 (Monograph 11). (21, 56, 261)

Whitmyre, J. W., Diggory, J. C., & Cohen, D. The effects of personal liking, perceived ability, and value of prize on choice of partners for a competition. *J. abnorm. soc. Psychol.,* 1961, 63, 198–200. (307–308, 312)

Winterbottom, M. R. The relation of need for achievement to learning experiences in independence and mastery. In J. W. Atkinson (Ed.),

Motives in fantasy, action, and society. Princeton, N.J.: D. Van Nostrand, 1958. Pp. 435–478. (185)

Woodworth, R. S. *Dynamic psychology.* New York: Columbia Univer. Press, 1918. (55–56, 261)

Woodworth, R. S. *Dynamics of behavior.* New York: Holt, 1958. (102, 125)

Wundt, W. *Grundzüge der physiologischen Psychologie.* Leipzig: Engelmann, 1879, 2nd ed., 1880. (8, 12, 20, 32)

Wundt, W. *Völkerpsychologie.* Leipzig: Engelmann, 1900. 10 vols. (46)

Wylie, R. C. *The self concept: a critical survey of pertinent research literature.* Lincoln, Nebr.: Univer. of Nebraska Press, 1961. (28, 41, 62–63, 101, 108–109, 229, 233, 243)

Zeigarnik, B. Über das Behalten von erledigten und unerledigten Handlungen. (Untersuchungen zur Handlungs- und Affektpsychologie, II. Ed. K. Lewin). *Psychol. Forsch.*, 1927, 9, 1–85. (209–211)